LATE LATIN WRITERS
AND THEIR GREEK SOURCES

LATE LATIN WRITERS
AND THEIR GREEK SOURCES

PIERRE COURCELLE

Translated by
HARRY E. WEDECK

Harvard University Press

Cambridge, Massachusetts

1969

© Copyright 1969 by the President and Fellows of Harvard College

Distributed in Great Britain by Oxford University Press, London

Translated from *Les Lettres Grecques en Occident de Macrobe à Cassiodore*, second edition, Paris, Editions E. de Boccard, 1948

Library of Congress Catalog Card Number 69–12721

Printed in the United States of America

TO MY WIFE

TRANSLATOR'S PREFACE

The conflict between Paganism and Christianity raged, on the intellectual and spiritual level, throughout the earlier centuries when Hellenism was gradually losing its traditional hold and Christian writers had assumed a dominant, aggressive attitude. Plotinus emerged as the paramount spokesman of Neoplatonism, while his disciple Porphyry produced his thunderous Κατὰ χριστιανῶν as a pagan manifesto, the credo of the opposition. Pagan rites and ceremonials still clung tenaciously to their Hellenic anchorage, but the end, though not imminent, was assured.

In many cases, however, the demarcation between essential Christianity and the teleological and metaphysical views of pagan men of letters and professional philosophers was so subtle that even now there is considerable uncertainty about Boethius' Christianity. Both sides produced what they assumed to be irrefutable evidences of inconsistencies and contradictions, both textually and semantically, in the opposing camp. Variant readings, ambivalent interpretations, misrepresentations in the exposition of sacred texts, furnished material for endless polemics.

This is the challenging field of Professor Courcelle's study. Beginning with the death of Theodosius, he examines Hellenism in its pagan and Christian aspects, from Macrobius down to Cassiodorus' monks busy in the *scriptorium* of Scyllacium. With scrupulous logic, often through a series of triumphant sorites, he traces the sources used by both pagan and Christian scholars. With the support of formidable documentation, he points up obscured analogies, flagrant and frequently unacknowledged borrowings, discrepancies brought to light by textual juxtapositions, which illuminate pagan-Christian literary relations. And when the Greek literary tradition died, toward the end of the sixth century, pagan Hellenism did not disappear entirely. It was absorbed into the Hellenism of the Church Fathers.

It was a formidable task to collate, clarify, and interpret this voluminous literary material. Professor Courcelle has achieved it with unique distinction.

HEW

vii

CONTENTS

PART THREE

THE RENAISSANCE OF HELLENISM UNDER THE OSTROGOTHS

LATE LATIN WRITERS
AND THEIR GREEK SOURCES

Sed ideo cum Platonicis magis agere placuit hanc causam, quia eorum sunt litterae notiores. Nam et Graeci, quorum lingua in gentibus praeeminet, eas magna praedicatione celebrarunt, et Latini permoti earum vel excellentia vel gloria, ipsas libentius didicerunt atque in nostrum eloquium transferendo nobiliores clarioresque fecerunt.

Augustine *De civitate Dei* 8.10

ABBREVIATIONS

ALMA: Archivum Latinitatis medii aevi, Bulletin du Cange
CAG: Commentaria in Aristotelem Graeca
CIL: Corpus inscriptionum Latinarum
CMG: Corpus medicorum Graecorum
CML: Corpus medicorum Latinorum
CSEL: Corpus scriptorum ecclesiasticorum Latinorum
CSHB: Corpus scriptorum historiae Byzantinae
FHG: Fragmenta historicorum Graecorum
Manitius: M. Manitius, *Geschichte der lateinischen Literatur des Mittelalters*
MEFR: Mélanges de l'Ecole française de Rome
MGH: Monumenta Germaniae historica
PG: Migne, *Patrologiae cursus completus, series Graeca*
PL: Migne, *Patrologiae cursus completus, series Latina*
PW: Pauly-Wissowa(-Kroll), *Real-Encyclopädie der classischen Altertums-wissenschaft*
RB: Revue Bénédictine
RBPH: Revue belge de philologie et d'histoire
REA: Revue des études anciennes
REAug: Revue des études augustiniennes
REG: Revue des études grecques
REL: Revue des études latines
RHLR: Revue d'histoire et de littérature religieuses
RHE: Revue d'histoire ecclésiastique
RSR: Recherches de science religieuse
Schanz: M. Schanz, *Geschichte der römischen Litteratur*

INTRODUCTION

A bulky volume on Hellenic literature in the West, from the death of Theodosius to the Justinian reconquest, is matter for surprise. The subject seems unrewarding: the fifth and sixth centuries are an era of decadence, wherein the very concept of culture becomes stripped of content.[1] Is it not hazardous to say that this culture remains or even *becomes* Hellenic? Greek literature is not a late importation in Rome. It permitted Latin literature to blossom out. It produced Cicero, the most consummate example of Greco-Roman culture at its height.[2] It almost succeeded too in taking the place of Latin, which was eclipsed in the second century as a literary language.[3] But from that time on, Greek underwent a very marked recession. Latin was the only official language of the Empire, even in Constantinople, the capital. Beginning with the fourth century, it was the only liturgical language of Western Christendom.[4] Hellenism, infected with paganism,[5] seems to have

---

[1] The excellent book by H. I. Marrou, *Saint Augustin et la fin de la culture antique* (diss. Paris 1938), analyzes this notion of decadence, particularly in pp. 85–104 and 469–504. But the very fact that he chose St. Augustine as a type naturally led him to underestimate the Greek contribution in this culture. Furthermore, the author declares, p. xiii n. 1, that he purposely refrained from studying the Neoplatonic influence on Augustinian thought.

[2] *Ibid.*, p. 40.

[3] Cf. J. Carcopino, *La vie quotidienne à Rome à l'apogée de l'Empire* (Paris 1939) 135. In refutation of Marrou, Carcopino considers that Hellenism began to lose its hold on Rome in Quintilian's day. H. I. Marrou, *Histoire de l'éducation dans l'antiquité* (Paris 1948) 350–355, however, repeats his conclusions, although (nn. 10 and 15) making concessions to Carcopino, Boyancé, and the present writer.

[4] Cf. C. P. Caspari, *Quellen zur Gesch. des Taufsymbols und der Glaubensregel*, vol. 3 (Christiania 1875) 267–466. Excursus 1: Griechen und Griechisch in der römischen Gemeinde in den drei ersten Jahrhunderten ihres Bestehens; F. Cumont, "Pourquoi le latin fut la seule langue liturgique de l'Occident," *Mélanges Paul Frédéricq* (Brussels 1904) 63–66; G. Morin, "Formules liturgiques orientales en Occident aux IVe–Ve siècles," *RB* 40 (1928) 134; G. Bardy, "Formules liturgiques grecques à Rome au IVe siècle," *RSR* 30 (1940) 109–112; Th. Klauser, "Der Uebergang der römischen Kirche von der griechischen zur lateinischen Liturgiesprache," *Miscellanea G. Mercati* 1 (Rome 1946) 467–482.

[5] The pagan sense attaching to the term Hellenism is already noted by St. Jerome *In Epist. ad Galat.* 2.4.27, *PL* 26, 369 B: "Pro Graeco *gentilem* accipere debemus, quia

1

succumbed in the reign of Theodosius, after the fruitless attempts of the Emperors Julian the Apostate and Eugenius. How can one believe in a survival or a renaissance of Greek literature in the fifth and sixth centuries? Despite the fictitious *unanimitas* of the two brother-emperors, the West was separated from the East since 395. The Roman political frame soon disappeared under the shock of the invasions of the barbarians. The Latin language itself deteriorated and was on the point of dying out as a spoken language.[6] To consider only the political conditions, a revival of Greek literature did not appear probable until after Justinian's reconquest, when the Empire regained territory in the West. But it was henceforth a Byzantine Empire.

However, several facts already known incline one to believe that this first view of the spiritual aspect is too summary. The works of Henri Pirenne have shown that, in spite of the Vandal fleets, the normal relations between East and West were not broken off before the Arab invasion in the middle of the seventh century.[7] These relations were political,[8] religious,[9] economic, and artistic[10] in character. The travels of Westerners in the East, and of Orientals in the West—diplomats, refugees, pilgrims, merchants—continued to be frequent in the fifth and sixth centuries.[11] I should like to show that there were also close relations between Greek literature and Latin literature and that the Romans had recourse, in the midst of their decadence, to Hellenic

---

῞Ελλην et Graecum et ethnicum utrumque significat." It is still clearer in the age of Justinian (cf. *Codex Iustinianus* 1.11.10, and Procopius *De Bello Persico* 1.20 and 25 in *CSHB*, p. 104, 14 and p. 131, 10), but it appears also in the time of Iamblichus (cf. W. Koch, "Sur le sens de quelques mots et expressions chez Julien: ὁ Ἑλληνισμός," *RBPH* 7 [1928] 539).

[6] Cf. F. Lot, "A quelle époque a-t-on cessé de parler latin?" *ALMA* 6 (1931) 97–159.

[7] See particularly H. Pirenne, "La fin du commerce des Syriens en Occident," *Mélanges Bidez* 2 (1934) 677–687. I purposely omit the year 476 as a chronological terminus. The deposition of the last emperor, Romulus Augustulus, who possessed no real power, was an event of no consequence.

[8] Cf. A. Gasquet, *Etudes byzantines; l'empire byzantin et la monarchie franque* (Paris 1888); F. Martroye, *L'Occident à l'époque byzantine, Goths et Vandales* (Paris 1904); O. Seeck, *Geschichte des Untergangs der antiken Welt*, vol. 6 (Berlin 1920); E. Stein, *Geschichte des spätrömischen Reiches*, vol. 1 (Vienna 1928); F. Lot, *Les destinées de l'Empire en Occident de 395 à 888* (Paris 1928).

[9] On pagan relations, cf. F. Cumont, *Les religions orientales dans le paganisme romain* (4th ed., Paris 1929). On Christian relations, councils, heresies, schisms, pilgrimages, legends, hagiographies, cf., among others, L. Duchesne, *Histoire ancienne de l'église*, vol. 3 (5th ed. 1920) and *L'église au VIᵉ siècle* (Paris 1925); Dom Leclercq, *Dictionnaire d'archéologie chrétienne*, s.v. Pèlerinages; B. Krusch, "Die Einführung des griechischen Paschalritus im Abendlande," *Neues Archiv* 9 (1883) 99–169; H. Usener, "Legendenaustausch der griechischen und römischen Kirche," *Jahrbücher für protestantische Théologie* 13 (1887) 240–259.

[10] See chap. 5 sec. 3 n. 14.

[11] Cf. D. Gorce, *Les voyages, l'hospitalité et le port des lettres dans le monde chrétien des IVᵉ et Vᵉ siècles* (diss. Paris 1925).

culture, for the very reason that they considered the teaching of the Latin *grammaticus* and the *rhetor* insufficient. The relations between the East and the West are of no interest to me except insofar as they were the subject of literary expression, and I shall exclusively study the influence exercised by writers using the Greek language on the Latin scholars who wrote in the West or for the public in the West. It will be necessary to discover and deter-mine how these writers had a knowledge of Greek books, either directly in the original or through translations or adaptations, and to what extent they themselves knew Greek. But knowledge in this area is so fragmentary that it would be impossible to flatter oneself, without the danger of making hasty generalizations, that one was writing the history of Greek education in the West at this period.[12] On the other hand, a mass of material enables us, unless I am mistaken, to study the survivals of Hellenic thought and culture. Such a study is not without significance, for the Western Middle Ages were to be forced to live on these terms, until the day when Arab translations permitted a resumption with Greek antiquity.

Thus defined, the subject appears sufficiently new. The few scholars who have studied Hellenism in the West restrict themselves to devoting a few pages to this period without showing any interest therein. Their works are obsolete. These include a dissertation of thirty-two pages by Cramer, dated 1848, which is perhaps still the best survey on the problem,[13] a memoir by Renan in his younger days, which he considered unworthy of publication,[14]

---

[12] The aid furnished by epigraphy is meager. In Rome, Trèves, Cordova, such in-scriptions mention a Greek *grammaticus* (Dessau, *Inscr. Lat. Sel.* 7766–7769); epitaphs also mention the Greek studies of infant prodigies (cf. Marrou, MOYCIKOC 'ANHP [diss. Grenoble 1938] 203–205); but the dates are uncertain and it is as a rule a question of in-scriptions older than the period here studied.

[13] F. Cramer, *Dissertationis de Graecis medii aevi studiis pars prior: De Graecis per Occiden-tem studiis inde a primo medio aevo usque ad Carolum Magnum* (Stralsund 1848), 32 pages.

[14] E. Renan, *Histoire de l'étude de la langue grecque dans l'Occident de l'Europe depuis la fin du Ve siècle jusqu'à celle du XIVe siècle* (unpublished manuscript in the Bibliothèque de l'Institut, no. 2208). This monograph received a prize from the Académie des Inscriptions in 1848. On the fact that Renan made light of this work, cf. J. Pommier, *Renan d'après des documents inédits* (Paris 1923) 64. Renan's monograph is for the most part not original. The most interesting part is the introduction, particularly this comment on p. 5: "Greek literature was therefore almost unknown in the Middle Ages as well as in the East. This was not the case with the Greek language." On p. 13 Renan notes that he hesitated be-tween a chronological, geographical, or methodical scheme. On p. 17 he apologizes for having exceeded the bounds of his subject in studying also Hebrew and Arabic in the Middle Ages. It is evident that Renan in his maturity was a severe critic of this beginner's work, in which even the style sometimes leaves much to be desired; for instance, the statement on p. 24: "Rome withdrew her legions, *Greece withdrew her language,* and the Middle Ages began." This study was composed too rapidly, as the postscript indicates: "Emendaturus, si licuisset, eram."

a few pages in the antiquated or too general books by Egger, Gidel, Sandys.[15] The theses by Roger and Marrou, which attempt to define the culture of the decadence, offer valuable suggestions but treat Greek studies only incidentally.[16] Even for the earlier periods I do not know any survey that examines Greek influence on Roman thought or culture in the Empire. Jullien and Gwynn merely defined the contribution of Hellenic elements in Roman education in classical times,[17] and it will be seen that the scholastic tradition of the Greek *grammaticus*, who taught Homer and Menander, extended into the sixth century. Canon Bardy has studied the attitude of the Church toward the pagan schools during the first four centuries. He observed two tendencies, one favorable, the other opposed to Hellenism.[18] But what exactly was the Hellenic cultural level of the Fathers of the Latin Church? What was the extent of the knowledge of a man like Arnobius or Lactantius? Those who have been studied from this viewpoint[19] are very few. A recent article by Bardy is the only one that describes Greek culture in the Christian West in the fourth century.[20] But this article is a setting out of facts already known rather than a piece of critical research on the works themselves. Despite its title, it belongs to the problem of teaching the Greek language rather than to the influence of Hellenic culture.

It is particularly strange that the history of Latin Neoplatonism has not yet been written, although this omission was noted a long time ago.[21] There is merely the repeated statement that the last generations of ancient Rome produced compilations lacking in originality. As though man could remain for two centuries without evolving and taking up a set position on the most

---

[15] E. Egger, *L'hellénisme en France*, vol. 1 (Paris 1869); C. Gidel, "Les études grecques en Europe (IVe siècle–1153)," pp. 1–289 in his *Nouvelles Etudes* (Paris 1878); J. E. Sandys, *A History of Classical Scholarship from the Sixth Century* B.C. *to the End of the Middle Ages* (3rd ed., Cambridge 1921). Still more unsatisfactory is the work of the Abbot A. Tougard, *L'hellénisme dans les écrivains du Moyen Age, du VIIe au XIIe siècle* (Paris 1886), 70 pages. For the late Middle Ages, cf. the interesting views of G. Théry, "Scot Erigène, traducteur de Denys," *ALMA* 6 (1931) 202–213.

[16] Marrou, *Saint Augustin*; M. Roger, *L'enseignement des lettres classiques d'Ausone à Alcuin* (diss. Paris 1905).

[17] E. Jullien, *Les professeurs de littérature dans l'ancienne Rome et leur enseignement depuis l'origine jusqu'à la mort d'Auguste* (diss. Paris 1885), particularly chap. 2, "La civilisation grecque à Rome; les fondateurs de l'enseignement littéraire," and pp. 203–206; A. Gwynn, *Roman Education, from Cicero to Quintilian* (Oxford 1926) 92 and 226–230.

[18] G. Bardy, "L'église et l'enseignement dans les trois premiers siècles," *Revue des sciences religieuses* 12 (1932) 1–28; "L'église et l'enseignement au IVe siècle," *ibid.*, 14 (1934) 525–549 and 15 (1935) 1–27.

[19] Cf. however A. d'Alès, "Tertullien helléniste," *REG* 50 (1939) 329–362.

[20] G. Bardy, "La culture grecque dans l'Occident chrétien au IVe siècle," *RSR* 29 (1939) 5–58.

[21] Cf. E. Norden, *P. Vergilius Maro, Aeneis, Buch VI* (2nd ed., Leipzig 1916) 26 n. 2.

serious problems of his fate! The analysis of the works chosen for such a compilation would be sufficient to explain the tastes, preferences, and beliefs of the compiler. And the first generations of a world turned Christian had at least the originality of having to regularize their attitude to a culture that had developed outside the limits of Christendom or even against it. The excessive contempt for the writers of the early period should not therefore justify such an omission in the history of human thought. The only real difficulty is that Greek Neoplatonism, which explains Latin Neoplatonism, is itself quite unknown. It has been scantily studied in France since the distant time when Victor Cousin, Jules Simon, Vacherot, and a few disciples devoted their attention to it.[22] Even the Greek or Oriental schools and the syllabus of their courses in the fourth, fifth, and sixth centuries are insufficiently known, in spite of the mass of documents available on the subject.[23] Now, certain of these schools, as I shall show, exercised a profound influence even on the West, and whenever a period of political tranquillity inspired the men in the West with the hope of rebuilding their civilization, of reviving their culture, it was toward the East, toward the educational methods of the contemporary Greek commentators that they turned their eyes.

Only three recent books have approached the problem of Latin Neoplatonism and proposed various methods. Theiler's book on the relations between St. Augustine and Porphyry, issued in 1933, claimed that Augustine, contrary to the accredited opinion, knew Plotinus only through Porphyry; Porphyry alone probably initiated him into Neoplatonism. Since the

[22] V. Cousin, "Du commentaire inédit d'Olympiodore, philosophe alexandrin du VIᵉ siècle, sur le *Gorgias* de Platon," *Journal des savants* (1832) 398–410, 449–457, 521–531, 621–630, 670–682, 743–753; "Du commentaire inédit d'Olympiodore sur le *Phédon*," *ibid.* (1834) 321–327, 425–434, 482–491; *Procli opera inedita* (Paris 1864); J. Simon, *Histoire de l'école d'Alexandrie*, vol. 2 (Paris 1845); E. Vacherot, *Histoire critique de l'école d'Alexandrie*, vol. 3 (Paris 1851); A. E. Chaignet, *Proclus le philosophe, commentaire sur le Parménide* (translation), vol. 1 (1900), vol. 2 (1901), vol. 3 (1903), and an edition of Damascius, *Problèmes et solutions touchant les premiers principes*, 3 vols. (Paris 1898).

[23] Cf. F. Schemmel, "Die Hochschule von Konstantinopel im IV. Jahrh.," *Neue Jahrbücher für das klass. Altertumgesch. und deutsche Literatur und für Pädagogik* 22 (1908) 147–168; "Die Hochschule von Athen im IV. und V. Jahrh.," *ibid.*, pp. 494–513; "Die Hochschule von Alexandria im IV. und V. Jahrh.," *ibid.*, 24 (1909) 438–457; *Die Hochschule von Konstantinopel vom V. bis IX. Jahrh.* (Progr. Berlin 1912); "Die Schule von Berytus," *Philologische Wochenschrift* 43 (1923) 236–240; P. Collinet, *Histoire de l'école de droit de Beyreuth* (Paris 1925); J. B. Chabot, "L'école de Nisibe," *Journal asiatique*, 9th series, 8 (1896) 43–93; A. Scher, *L'école de Nisibe* (Bayreuth 1905); E. Duval, *Histoire politique, religieuse et littéraire d'Edesse* (Paris 1892); A. Mueller, "Studentenleben im IV. Jahrh. n. Chr.," *Philologus* 69 (1910) 292–317, a vivid study but scarcely touching on more than the physical organization of education and rapidly passing over the authors and subjects of the curriculum. J. Bidez may still be consulted profitably: "Le philosophe Jamblique et son école," *REG* 32 (1919) 29–40; also O. Schissel, "Kaiser Julians Schulbildung," *Klio* 5 (1929) 326–328.

majority of Porphyry's writings are lost, Theiler, in accordance with the methods of *Quellenforschung*, reconstructs them with the aid of the later Greek Neoplatonists and distinguishes a certain number of doctrinal similarities with a work by Augustine taken as an example.[24] His method and his conclusions were vigorously disputed the following year. Father Henry, in his book *Plotin et l'Occident*, is convinced in fact that it was Plotinus, not Porphyry, who exerted a profound influence on the West and in particular on Augustine. His method, in contradistinction to Theiler's, starts with the principle that the slightest textual parallel, in regard to sources, is infinitely more conclusive than a large number of doctrinal similarities, provided that one knows how to use this fact. He therefore advocates an inquiry that is both philological and literary, and thinks that such an inquiry is sufficient to lay a sure foundation for the history of thought and culture. Two years later, Boemer considered that the study of the language and style of Claudianus Mamertus was the best way to discover the sources of his thought and to shed some rays of light on Latin Neoplatonism and Neopythagoreanism.[25]

My view of the often contradictory conclusions reached by these three writers will appear later on.[26] The doctrinal method seems extremely unreliable, especially for the period with which we are concerned. The ideas discussed there have such a long past behind them, the adherents so readily plagiarize their masters, that doctrinal relations between two authors do not cogently prove a reciprocal influence on each other. The grammatical method is hazardous and would furnish convincing criteria only if the different areas and the diverse periods of later Latinity were better established, if they can ever be so established. Too great a margin is left for personal appraisal, as will be proved by the conflict between Boemer and Hårleman.[27] The philological method is still the most convincing. Only frequent readings and parallel analyses of a Greek text and a Latin text that have never yet been compared will shed light on the Greek sources of Latin Neoplatonism. It is not, in fact, a question of determining to what distant ancestor, whether Aristotle or Plato, these late theories go back, but their immediate source. It is a matter of finding the Greek group or school whence a particular concept, belief, or method was transmitted to the Romans, and in what way it was done. To formulate the proof of such contact, the best way will be to discover, through textual parallels, the borrowing of a Latin work from a Greek

---

[24] W. Theiler, *Porphyrios und Augustin*, Schriften der Königsberger gelehrten Gesellschaft vol. 10, 1 (Halle 1933). The methods of *Quellenforschung* have already been sharply criticized in France by P. Boyancé, *Etudes sur le Songe de Scipion* (diss. Paris 1936) 149 n. 6.

[25] F. Boemer, *Der lateinische Neuplatonismus und Neupythagoreismus und Claudianus Mamertus in Sprache und in Philosophie* (Leipzig 1936), 181 pages.

[26] See below, pp. 171–173.

[27] See p. 241.

work. Often, however, the Greek source is lost and the research becomes purely conjectural. It will then be through regrouping, comparing several Latin texts by different writers, that we shall have to establish their common origin.[28] The most delicate point, in which doubt is often the only proper attitude, is to know whether the Greek text was read in the original or in a lost translation. In this regard, Marius Victorinus was for a long time a very convenient possibility. How many works did his assumed translations make known to the Romans, if one were to believe various scholars![29] I shall attempt to reduce the field of conjectures to a more probable state and shall not claim, through some indiscreet subtlety, to fill in for every document that is lacking. Fundamentally, this problem is of secondary interest. It is of no consequence whether a Greek book exerted an influence in its original text, in a translation, or through a Latin intermediary. What is essential is to determine which books have been influential, what spiritual contacts they have established. Sometimes, apart from the textual contact in the doctrines, even the direct and living contact between the men will be discernible.

Several plans presented themselves. One plan, following Father Henry, would have been to study successively the influence that each Greek writer exerted on the West. But this series of monographs would scarcely have fitted into a synthesis. Similarly, a methodical plan, that would include in succession the various disciplines of the ἐγκύκλιος παιδεία, and the advanced culture, would present the serious inconvenience of offering very unequal developments. For instance, the Greek influence on astrology is evident and well known.[30] On the other hand, in the very nature of things, Greek influence on

---

[28] See pp. 30, 37, 241–245.

[29] According to G. Wissowa, *De Macrobii Saturnaliorum fontibus*, pp. 35–43, Victorinus probably translated Iamblichus' Περὶ θεῶν; according to H. Linke, "Ueber Macrobius' Kommentar zu Ciceros *Somnium Scipionis*," p. 256, several commentaries by Porphyry, particularly on the *Timaeus*; according to F. Bitsch, *De Platonicorum quaestionibus quibusdam Vergilianis*, p. 73, a compilation by Porphyry and a Neoplatonic commentator on Vergil; according to Henry, *Plotin et l'Occident*, p. 95, Plotinus' *Enneads*, in whole or in part; according to Theiler, *Porphyrios und Augustin*, p. 3, Porphyry's commentary on the *Enneads*; P. Monceaux's view that made Marius Victorinus Origen's translator has been abandoned since the demonstration by E. Benz, "M. Victorinus und die Entwicklung der abendländischen Willensmetaphysik," *Forschungen zur Kirchen- und Geistesgeschichte* I (1932) 23ff. The only translation extant is that of Porphyry's *Isagoge*: cf. P. Monceaux, "L'Isagoge latine de Marius Victorinus," *Philologie et linguistique, mélanges offerts à L. Havet* (Paris 1909) pp. 291–310. We know too from Cassiodorus' *Institutiones*, ed. Mynors, p. 128, 16, that Victorinus had translated Aristotle's *Categories* and the *De interpretatione*. Everything else is conjecture, sometimes completely lacking plausibility.

[30] Cf. A. Bouché-Leclercq, *L'astrologie grecque* (Paris 1899); H. de la Ville de Mirmont, "L'astrologie chez les Gallo-Romains," *REA* 4 (1902) 115–141; 5 (1903) 225–293; 8

grammar and rhetoric is necessarily minimal. In addition, it would be a matter of excessively subdividing the study of the great Latin writers who, as Marrou has pointed out in the case of St. Augustine, generally have a veneer of all the disciplines. Chronology and geography too could not furnish very exact classifications, for the dates and the country of origin are uncertain. Also, a country such as Spain would furnish very little material. Only the very evolution of culture has permitted me to distinguish several major phases. Hellenism is still alive, in a particular form whose content will have to be determined, at the death of Theodosius, before the capture of Rome by Alaric. Macrobius and St. Jerome are, so to speak, the two poles and mark what Hellenism then represented in the eyes either of pagan or Christian. In the fifth century a general collapse occurred. The framework of the Empire cracked. The fate of culture is not quite the same in Italy, in Africa, and in Gaul. A transient and fictitious renaissance may be observed around some man of talent or in a province momentarily privileged, while the others are a prey to the barbarians. So the geographical classification in extensive regions asserts itself for this period. Lastly, in the sixth century, Greek literary culture disappeared from Gaul and Africa. On the other hand, in Italy the Ostrogothic domination favored a revival notable in scope, wherein Roman culture was to be entirely renewed following the example of the contemporary Greek schools. Justinian's reconquest and the vagaries of the Ostrogothic war, which ravaged Italy for twenty years, were to ruin this magnificent development. Contrary to all expectation, the Byzantine domination was not to produce a revival of Hellenic culture in that country. But through the obscure, patient labor of the monks a share in this culture was to be preserved until the Carolingian Renaissance.

In this second edition I tried to take advantage of the suggestions of many critics who were kind enough to review the book. I cannot thank them sufficiently for the interest they have shown and the favorable reception they have in general given to a book that is withal so rigorous in form. I am indebted to a number of people for the correction of an oversight, or the addition of a valuable reference. May I venture to admit that basically I did not think I should appreciably modify the theses I maintained. Does the term "renaissance" appear excessive, when applied to the movement that led several Gallo-Roman intellectuals, around the year 470, to renew their interest in the study of Greek literature? I should gladly adopt a less imposing expression if the French language would supply it. I never claimed that this renaissance had as its *cause* the nomination of the Greek Anthemius as Emperor

---

(1906) 128–264; 9 (1907) 69–82 and 155–171; 11 (1909) 301–346; R. Bonnaud, "Notes sur l'astrologie latine au VIᵉ siècle," *RBPH* 10 (1931) 557–577; particularly F. Cumont, *Les religions orientales*, chap. 7, "L'astrologie et la magie."

of the West, but that there was, between one circumstance and another, a *coincidence*, on which his contemporaries congratulated themselves.

The interest that readers have displayed in the subject encourages me to pursue an inquiry that is by no means completed, since every chronological limit is arbitrary. If circumstances permit, I shall some day publish a volume on the period immediately preceding this one, which might be called: *Greek Literature in the West, from Plotinus to St. Ambrose.*

PART ONE

THE MAINSTREAM OF HELLENISM
AT THE DEATH OF THEODOSIUS

Chapter I

PAGAN HELLENISM:
MACROBIUS

A very precise idea may be formed of the state of pagan culture in Roman territory at the time of the death of the Emperor Theodosius and of the position that Hellenism still retained therein.[1] Macrobius' *Saturnalia* reveals in fact the existence of quite a homogeneous pagan environment and acquaints us with the talk of this literate society.[2] Macrobius' commentary on the *Somnium Scipionis* and those of Servius on Vergil complete the general picture. They demonstrate the methods of work that were in vogue, the authors to whom they referred most readily, and the doctrines that had taken hold of men's minds.

1. MACROBIUS AND HIS FRIENDS

Unquestionably, the *Saturnalia* is an imaginative work. The author asserts specifically that he did not feel obliged to observe a rigorous chronology. At the symposium of Vettius Agorius Praetextatus he introduces young Servius, who was not yet fifteen at the fictitious date of the *Saturnalia*.[3] We can therefore suspend judgment whether Macrobius makes us acquainted rather with Praetextatus' generation or with that of Servius. However, most

[1] J. Marouzeau remarked in *REL* 16 (1938) 258: "Books on Macrobius have been very rare during these last years, and it is a text, as we know, that calls for commentaries."

[2] On the antichristian aspect of this group, cf. P. de Labriolle, *La réaction païenne* (Paris 1934) 348–353. On the hope with which the usurpation of Europe inspired them, cf. J. R. Palanque, *Saint Ambroise et l'empire romain* (diss. Paris 1933) 264–286, and H. Graillot, *Le culte de Cybèle* (Paris 1912) 550; F. Cumont, "La polémique de l'Ambrosiaster contre les païens," *RHLR* 8 (1903) 417–440, has sketched an excellent picture of pagan society in Rome around 375 and has emphasized the persistent influence of Julian the Apostate. Labriolle, *La réaction*, pp. 497–498, has shown that the Ambrosiaster, in those *Quaestiones veteris et novi testamenti*, challenged the objections of Porphyry's Κατὰ χριστιανῶν.

[3] Macrobius *Saturnalia* 1.1.5, ed. E. Eyssenhardt (Leipzig 1868) p. 5, 19. For the chronology I adopt the conclusions of H. Georgii, "Zur Bestimmung der Zeit des Servius," *Philologus* 71 (1912) 518–526: Macrobius born in 360, Servius around 370; the fictitious date of the *Saturnalia* shortly before 384, date of composition of the *Saturnalia* around 395; Servius' commentaries between 395 and 410.

of the interlocutors, if not all of them, are historical characters. Several were still alive at the time when Macrobius wrote. Thus, even if he borrows from a literary source the talk that he attributes to them, according to the methods of learned compilations, he has not been able seriously to infringe the laws of probability. His characters do not act in the same lively manner as the interlocutors of Plato's dialogues, but the principal features of their personalities are retained, and Macrobius notes with precision their attitude toward Hellenism.

Vettius Agorius Praetextatus, the host of this literary symposium, enjoyed a particular prestige, because he had reached the highest honors,[4] and especially on account of his knowledge of religion.[5] As a philologist he interpreted Greek and Latin[6] poets and prose writers. From the evidence of Boethius, as a philosopher he also translated Themistius' commentary on the *Analytics*.[7] Pseudo-Augustine's *Categories* is reasonably attributed to him; it too derives its inspiration from Themistius' teaching.[8] He must have maintained close relations with Constantinople to be abreast of the training that Themistius then offered in that city. Perhaps he had even made direct contact and formed bonds of friendship with Themistius, when the latter had come to Gaul and Rome on the occasion of the panegyric to the Emperor Julian.[9]

---

[4] On his political career, see Schanz, vol. 4, 2, p. 139. He was consul designate for 385 at his death. The inscriptions relating to Praetextatus will be found in the collection, ed. Seeck, of Symmachus' *Epistulae, MGH, Auct. ant.*, vol. 6, 1, pp. LXXXIII–LXXXVIII, and two studies on his career by J. Nister, "Vettius Agorius Praetextatus," *Klio* 10 (1910) 462–475, and by M. Herzog, *Trierer Zeitschrift* 12 (1937) 126–128.

[5] *Saturnalia*, 1.24.1, p. 129, 8: "Hic cum Praetextatus fecisset loquendi finem, omnes in eum adfixis vultibus admirationem stupore prodebant; dein laudare hic memoriam, ille doctrinam, cuncti religionem, adfirmantes hunc esse unum arcanae deorum naturae conscium qui solus divina et adsequi animo et eloqui posset ingenio."

[6] His epitaph, *CIL* 6, 1779, declares:

> Tu namque, quidquid lingua utraque est proditum
> cura soforum, *porta quis caeli patet,*
> vel quae periti condidere carmina,
> vel quae solutis vocibus sunt edita,
> meliora reddis quam legendo sumpseras.

[7] Boethius *De interpretatione* (2nd ed., Meiser), p. 289: "Vettius Praetextatus priores postremosque *Analyticos* non vertendo Aristotelem Latino sermoni tradidit, sed transferendo Themistium."

[8] Schanz, vol. 4, 1, p. 140. Cf. Prantl, *Gesch. der Logik* 1 (Leipzig 1855) 670–672, and Pseudo-Augustine *Categ.*, *PL* 32, 1422: "ut Themistio nostrae aetatis erudito philosopho placet"; and, in conclusion, *PL* 32, 1440: "Haec sunt, fili carissime, quae iugi labore adsecuti, cum nobis Themistii nostra memoria egregii philosophi magisterium non deesset, ad utilitatem tuam de Graeco in Latinum convertimus, scilicet ut ex iis quoque bonam frugem studii a nobis profecti suscipias."

[9] This journey took place in 376/377. Cf. Stegemann, *PW* s.v. Themistios, col. 1650. L. Méridier, *Le philosophe Themistius devant l'opinion de ses contemporains* (diss. Rennes 1906), merely studies the position of Themistius with regard to philosophy.

Symmachus, the famous orator who takes part in the symposium, also prides himself on Greek culture. In his old age he devotes himself to the study of Greek literature in order to help his son in his studies.[10] He is able to hear and appreciate the Greek orators who declaim in Rome[11] and the Greek philosophers who teach.[12] He reads and esteems the translators.[13] He readily includes Greek terms in his prose, in imitation of Cicero or Pliny the Younger.[14] But Kroll has shown that these numerous references to Greek history derive from Latin writers.[15] His philosophical culture too seems superficial. Although he names Plato, Aristotle, Pythagoras, Heraclitus, it is quite apparent that he is a man of letters and not a philosopher. His purely literary culture is deeper. He mentions or quotes Homer and Hesiod several times,[16] and even a passage from the *Olynthiacs* of Demosthenes and an *Aphorism* of Hippocrates.[17] Most frequently these data were probably transmitted through the medium of Latin writers, as Kroll has shown, but in one

[10] Symmachus *Epistulae* 4.20.2, ed. O. Seeck, *MGH, Auct. ant.*, vol. 6, 1, p. 104, 35: "Dum filius meus Graecis litteris initiatur, ego me denuo studiis eius velut aequalis adiunxi."

[11] *Ibid.*, 1.15.2, p. 10, 29: "movit λόγος Athenaei hospitis Latiare concilium divisionis arte, inventionum copia, gravitate sensuum, luce verborum." The reference is to the Athenian Palladius. On the Greek orators who had settled in Rome at the close of the fourth century, particularly the famous Hierius to whom Augustine dedicated the *De pulchro et apto*, cf. Schanz, vol. 4, 1, p. 129, and G. Bardy, "La culture grecque," p. 10.

[12] Especially the Athenian Celsus, the son of Archetimos. Cf. Symmachus *Relatio* 5, ed. O. Seeck, p. 284, 23 (a letter addressed to the Emperor Theodosius): "Inter praecipua negotiorum saepe curatum est, ut erudiendis nobilibus philosophi praeceptores ex Attica poscerentur; itaque non nullos etiam auctoritas publica in usum nostrae urbis accivit, domini imperatores. Nunc vestri saeculi bonitas ultro optimatem sapientiae Romanis gymnasiis adrogavit. Siquidem Celsus ortus Archetimo patre, quem memoria litterarum Aristoteli subparem fuisse consentit, iuventuti nostrae magisterium bonarum artium pollicetur ... Nam et Carneadem Cyrenaeum et Poenum Clitomachum Atheniensis curia societate dignata est, itidem ut nostri Zaleucum legum Locrensium conditorem civitate donarunt." Symmachus requests the admission of Celsus into the rank of senators.

[13] Notably Naucellius, who translated a Greek historical work. Cf. Symmachus *Epistulae* 3.11.3, p. 73, 29: "non silebo alterum munus opusculi tui, quo priscam rem publicam cuiusque *gentis* (*corr.* Mommsen) ex libro Graeco in Latinum transtulisti; arma a Samnitibus, insignia ab Tuscis, leges de Lare Lycurgi et Solonis sumpseramus: tuus nobis posthaec addidit labor peregrina monumenta." Cf. Kroll, *PW* s.v. Naucellius. The reference is probably to the *excerpta* of Aristotle's *Politeiai*.

[14] Cf. W. Kroll, *De Q. Aurelii Symmachi studiis Graecis et Latinis*, Breslauer philologische Abhandlungen, vol. 6, 2 (Breslau 1891) 7.

[15] *Ibid.*, pp. 8–11.

[16] *Ibid.*, pp. 12–14.

[17] *Ibid.*, pp. 14 and 16. Cf. Symmachus *Epistulae* 1.23.2, which quotes, without the name of Demosthenes as the author, *Olynthiacs* 3.39, and *Epistulae* 6.45 quoting Hippocrates *Aphorisms* 2.46.

place at least the reference appears to presume the reading, if not of the Homeric text, at any rate of a commentary or a lexicon on this text.[18]

Servius, whom Symmachus in the *Saturnalia* respects very highly for his learning,[19] is familiar with Greek literature, even if this learning is usually at second hand.[20] Gessner has shown that he had a general smattering of Greek philosophy.[21] We shall see by his commentaries on Vergil that his Greek culture is very similar to that of Macrobius and is evidence of the same reading matter.

Symmachus likewise eulogizes two other guests at the banquet: Flavianus and Eustathius.[22] This Virius Nicomachus Flavianus translated Philostratus' *Life of Apollonius of Tyre*, as Sidonius Apollinaris informs us,[23] and edited a collection of the *Dogmata* of the philosophers.[24] With regard to Eustathius, Symmachus assures us in the *Saturnalia* that in him is united the wisdom of Carneades of the New Academy, of Diogenes the Stoic, and of Critolaus the Peripatetic.[25] This statement is of no value in characterizing his philosophy,

[18] Symmachus *Epistulae* 9.110.2, p. 265, 13: "ut plane Homerica appellatione usus περιδέξιον [id est aequimanum] te esse pronuntiem." Cf. Homer *Iliad* 21.163. Kroll, p. 13, is surprised that Symmachus (*Epistulae* 1.47.1, p. 24, 10: "lotos arbor . . . et suada Circae pocula et tricinium semivolucrum puellarum") describes the Sirens as three bird-women, contrary to Homer (*Odyssey* 12.39–54, 158–200), who gives no details. But this was the manner in which Homer was interpreted in an entire series of Roman sarcophagi of the late Empire. Marrou, *MOYCIKOC 'ANHP*, pp. 172–177 and 252–253, and F. Cumont, *Recherches sur le symbolisme funéraire* (Paris 1942) 325–332, have proposed divergent interpretations. See my article, "Quelques symboles funéraires du néo-platonisme latin," *REA* 46 (1944) 73–93.

[19] *Saturnalia* 1.24.8, p. 130, 26: "Priscos, ut mea fert opinio, praeceptores doctrina praestat." Cf. 1.2.15, 1.24.20, 6.6.1.

[20] The comments of Servius bear on the etymologies, dialects, stylistic devices. He also quotes Greek writers. Cf. E. Thomas, *Essai sur Servius et son commentaire sur Virgile* (Paris 1879) 184, and A. Gessner, *Servius und Pseudo-Asconius* (diss. Zürich 1888) 39–42. On the other hand, W. A. Baehrens, "Literarhistorische Beiträge," *Hermes* 52 (1917) 51 n. 1, and *Cornelius Labeo atque eius commen. Vergilianum* (diss. Ghent 1918) 61ff, thinks that Servius does not use any Greek writer in the original and that both Servius and Macrobius depend on the *Quaestiones Vergilianae* by Cornelius Labeo. This theory is very conjectural, for Labeo's works are lost.

[21] Gessner, *Servius und Pseudo-Asconius*, pp. 15–17. On Neoplatonic philosophy in Servius, cf. E. G. Sihler, "Serviana," *American Journal of Philology* 31 (1910) 1–24, and Sister E. O. Wallace, *The Notes on Philosophy in the Commentary of Servius on the Eclogues, the Georgics and the Aeneid of Vergil* (Columbia University 1938); a review by Van de Woestijne, *L'antiquité classique* 10 (1941) 144, notes many serious lacunae. A good monograph on this subject is still lacking.

[22] Macrobius *Saturnalia* 1.5.13.

[23] Text quoted below, chap. 5 sec. 2 n. 120. Cf. Schanz, vol. 4, 1, p. 92.

[24] The existence of this work entitled *De vestigiis* or *De dogmate Philosophorum* is attested by John of Salisbury *Policraticus* 2.26 and 8.11 (*PL* 199, 460 B and 755 A). Cf. Schanz, vol. 4, 1, p. 92.

[25] *Saturnalia* 1.5.14–16.

for Macrobius is here merely plagiarizing Aulus Gellius.[26] With this formula he is only trying to lend prestige to Eustathius' Greek and Latin knowledge. Not only has Eustathius studied all the philosophical sects and chosen the best, but he is superior to these three ancient philosophers, who needed an interpreter in Rome, for he expresses himself with equal facility in Latin and in Greek.[27] Eustathius in fact was Greek by birth, of which he is no little proud. Equipped with his quite extensive Greek culture,[28] he attacks the ignorance of the Latin commentators on Vergil who, for lack of Greek, are unable to understand and expound him.[29] His studies have convinced him that Vergil borrows largely from the Greeks, particularly his philosophy and his astrological knowledge.[30]

The rhetorician Eusebius who was invited to the symposium is also Greek. He is reputed to be the best of the Greek rhetoricians then declaiming at Rome.[31] Lastly, of the three self-invited guests, Evangelus, Dysarius, and Horus,[32] Dysarius is a Greek physician;[33] and Horus, who is introduced as a Cynic philosopher, a disciple of Antisthenes, Crates, and Diogenes,[34] is a former boxer, of Egyptian birth.[35]

Evangelus, on the other hand, is the only one who displays hostility to Hellenism. He considers that the Greeks are fine talkers,[36] inclined to exag-

---

[26] Aulus Gellius *Noctes Atticae* 6.14.8.

[27] *Saturnalia* 1.5.16, p. 22, 19: "At hic noster cum sectas omnes adsecutus, sed probabiliorem secutus sit, omniaque haec inter Graecos genera dicendi solus impleat, inter nos tamen ita sui locuples interpres est, ut nescias qua lingua facilius vel ornatius expleat operam disserendi."

[28] *Ibid.*, 5.18.1, p. 319, 27, and 5.22.15, p. 344, 5. See the texts quoted below, p. 27.

[29] *Ibid.*, 5.19.31, p. 332, 13: "absoluta est, aestimo, et auctoribus idoneis adserta explanatio Vergiliani loci, quem litteratores vestri nec obscurum putant . . . quia nec ubi quaerant suspicantur, quasi Graecae lectionis expertes."

[30] *Ibid.*, 1.24.18, p. 132, 24, and 5.2.2, p. 248, 13.

[31] *Ibid.*, 1.6.2, p. 23, 5: "Eusebium Graia et doctrina et facundia clarum rhetorem subrogavi." Cf. 1.2.7, p. 7, 23: "nam facundum et eruditum virum Eusebium rhetorem inter Graecos praestantem omnibus idem nostra aetate professis, doctrinae Latiaris haud inscium, Praetextatus meum in locum invitari imperavit."

[32] *Ibid.*, 1.7.1–3.

[33] Text cited below, n. 35.

[34] *Saturnalia* 1.7.3, p. 29, 16: "Vir corpore atque animo iuxta validus qui post innumeras inter pugiles palmas ad philosophiae studia migravit, sectamque Antisthenis et Cratetis atque ipsius Diogenis secutus inter Cynicos non incelebris habebatur." Cf. *Saturnalia* 7.7.8, p. 423, 13.

[35] *Ibid.*, 1.7.14, he contrasts his Egyptian religion with the Roman cults. Cf. *Saturnalia* 1.15.3, p. 75, 25 and 31; 7.13.10, p. 446, 10.

[36] *Ibid.*, 7.16.1, p. 458, 9: "Inter haec Evangelus gloriae Graecorum invidens et inludens: Facessant, ait, haec quae inter vos in ostentationem loquacitatis agitantur, quin potius siquid callet sapientia vestra, scire ex vobis volo, ovumne prius exstiterit an gallina?" and 7.9.9, p. 430, 3: "vestri oris nota volubilitas."

geration.[37] He is convinced that Vergil knew nothing about the Greeks,[38] and takes a sly pleasure in setting at loggerheads the two Greeks, Eustathius and Dysarius, who are compared to two crows tearing out each other's eyes.[39] But Macrobius presents him in an unfavorable light as a man of difficult character, jealous of the success of the Greeks,[40] who does not comprehend Vergil's mystical meaning, denigrates Cicero as a philosopher,[41] and even leans toward impiety.[42] It is he who, by means of insidious questions, very often startles the discussion. By this device Macrobius is able to familiarize us with the talk of this cosmopolitan society that is so passionately interested in the slightest literary problems and in the divine mystery.

If Macrobius displays such severity toward Evangelus, it is not because he himself is of Greek birth, as was formerly believed. He is a provincial, and probably came from Africa to pursue a career at Rome.[43] Certain defects in his manner of translating indicate that Greek is not his native tongue.[44] Not that he does not know Greek: he reads it at sight, and his rare mistakes in translation are due to carelessness rather than ignorance.[45] Among the most cultured Romans of his circle, Macrobius cuts a figure of a great Hellenist, as Avianus describes him in his dedication of his *Fabulae*.[46] Macrobius himself

---

[37] *Ibid.*, 1.24.4, p. 129, 22: "Graeci omnia sua in immensum tollunt."

[38] *Ibid.*, 5.2.1, p. 248, 4: "opifici deo a rure Mantuano poetam comparas, quem Graecos rhetoras, quorum fecisti mentionem, nec omnino legisse adseveraverim."

[39] *Ibid.*, 7.5.1, p. 412, 16: "Evangelus exclamavit: nihil tam indignum toleratu quam quod aures nostras Graeca lingua captivas tenet et verborum rotunditati adsentiri cogimur circumventi volubilitate sermonis qui ad extorquendam fidem agit in audientes tyrannum; et quia his loquendi labyrinthis impares nos fatemur, age, Vetti, hortemur Eustathium ut recepta contraria disputatione, quicquid pro vario cibo dici potest velit communicare nobiscum, ut suis telis lingua violenta succumbat et Graecus Graeco eripiat hunc plausum tamquam cornix cornici oculos effodiat."

[40] Text cited above, n. 35. Cf. *Saturnalia* 1.7.2, p. 29, 7, and 7.9.26, p. 432, 30: "Euge Graeculus noster," he says, referring to Dysarius.

[41] *Saturnalia* 1.24.3–4, p. 129, 18.

[42] May he not be suspected of being a Christian? He is prepared to leave, if the discussion is of a secret nature, but Praetextatus proudly answers that the pagans have nothing to hide on the nature of the gods (*Saturnalia* 1.7.4–5). After Praetextatus' speech on solar theology, instead of applauding respectfully, like the other guests, he makes ironical reservations (*Saturnalia* 1.24.2, p. 129, 14): "Equidem, inquit, miror potuisse tantorum potestatem numinum comprehendi." Labriolle, *La réaction païenne*, p. 67, had already wondered whether the impious Aemilianus, described by Apuleius, was not a Christian. The name of Evangelus itself is not an indication, for this name may be pagan as well as Christian. If Macrobius is not more explicit, it is perhaps because he does not dare to make a direct assault on Christianity, which had become a state religion.

[43] Cf. Schanz, vol. 4, 2, p. 191, and Wessner, *PW* s.v. Macrobius, 170ff.

[44] Wissowa, *De Macr. Sat. fontibus*, p. 15.

[45] This is already Wessner's view, *PW* s.v. Macrobius, 171.

[46] Avianus *Fabulae, praef.*, ed. L. Hervieux, *Les fabulistes latins*, vol. 3 (1894) 264: "Quis tecum de oratione, quis de poemate loqueretur, cum in utroque litterarum genere et

has a passion for Hellenism; he is extremely proud of his wide reading in Greek and Latin and assures us that he is writing the *Saturnalia* in order to transmit to his son the culture that he has derived from such reading.[47]

In fact, the *Saturnalia* owes a great deal to the Greek type of philosophical symposium. The law governing this genre authorizes the treatment of all kinds of serious or entertaining problems provided that the guests prove their consummate knowledge. I shall first of all attempt to find out the source of Macrobius' borrowing of his immense Greek learning, then in what school his philosophical and religious thought was formed.

2. MACROBIUS' LITERARY CULTURE

It is commonly conceded that Macrobius' erudition is not derived from a primary source. If he collects the quotations of ancient writers, from the most obscure to the most famous, he nevertheless has only a small number of sources, most of them long known. An entire part of his Greek knowledge stems from the *Noctes Atticae* of Aulus Gellius, so called for the specific reason that the author visited in Greece and studied there.[1] But besides that, Macrobius often follows the literary tradition of symposia.[2] He himself refers to Plato's *Symposium*, which banishes austerity,[3] and to the works of

---

Atticos Graeca eruditione superes, et Latinitate Romanos?" It seems certain that the Theodosius to whom this compliment is addressed is not the Emperor Theodosius but Macrobius. Cf. Schanz, vol. 4, 2, p. 33. Robinson Ellis, the editor of Avianus, even proposes to identify this fabulist with Avienus the interlocutor of the *Saturnalia*, but this second identification is quite uncertain. It will be noted that Avianus proposes to make his collection acceptable to Theodosius by recalling the Greek origin of this form, namely, Aesop and Babrius, and particularly by recalling that Socrates used fables as illustrations.

[47] *Saturnalia* I, *praef.* 2, p. 1, 18: "Sed ago ut ego quoque tibi legerim, et quidquid mihi, vel te iam in luce edito vel antequam nascereris, in diversis seu Graecae seu Romanae linguae voluminibus elaboratum est, id totum sit tibi scientiae supellex." This passage imitates Aulus Gellius *Noctes Atticae, praef.*, ed. Hertz (Leipzig 1871) p. 1, 6: proof that Macrobius does not feel inferior, in regard to Greek culture, to his illustrious predecessor.

[1] Aulus Gellius *Noctes Atticae, praef.* 2 and 4, p. 1. There is a list of Macrobius' borrowings from Aulus Gellius in Wissowa, *De Macr. Sat. fontibus*, p. 3 and n. 1.

[2] On this genre, cf. *PW* s.vv. Symposion and Symposion-literatur and J. Martin, *Symposion, die Gesch. einer literarischen Form*, Studien zur Gesch. und Kultur des Altertums 17, 1–2 (Paderborn 1931), of which pages 280–290 are devoted to Macrobius. Some thirty years before Macrobius, the Emperor Julian had also written a *Symposium* of the Saturnalia, in the form of dialogues between the Caesars. Cf. J. Bidez, *La vie de l'empereur Julien* (Paris 1930) 300.

[3] *Saturnalia* 1.1.3, p. 5, 2: "nam cum apud alios quibus sunt descripta convivia, tum in illo Platonis Symposio non austeriore aliqua de re convivarum sermo, sed Cupidinis varia et lepida descriptio est, in quo quidem Socrates non artioribus, ut solet, nodis urget

Aristotle, Plutarch, and Apuleius, who sanction the use of the amusing point (*scomma*) at the symposia.[4]

There is no basis for judging whether the *Saturnalia* derives from Apuleius' *Quaestiones convivales*, which are lost.[5] With regard to Plato's *Symposium*, Macrobius knows the subject, the principal characters, and the setting, which he imitates.[6] But it is not quite certain that he has read it. It was the custom, in the literary symposia, to define the laws of this genre according to Plato, showing that he recommends a disconnected discussion,[7] and to establish a parallel, in point of morality, between several famous symposia.[8] Even the allusion to Agamemnon's banquet that appears in Plato and in Macrobius admits of the possibility that each drew from a different source. Macrobius could very well have known these two texts of Homer and Plato solely through a much later *Symposium*, similar to that of Athenaeus, who has long discussions on this topic.[9] This conjecture is all the more valid as

---

atque implicat adversarium, sed eludendi magis quam decertandi modo adprehensis dat elabendi prope atque effugiendi locum." Cf. 2.1.2–6.

[4] *Ibid.*, 7.3.24, p. 407, 3: "Quod genus veteres ita ludicrum non putarunt, ut et Aristoteles de ipsis aliqua conscripserit et Plutarchus et vester Apuleius, nec contemnendum sit, quod tot philosophantium curam meruit."

[5] The only positive, but very vague, information that we have on this work is from Sidonius Apollinaris *Epistulae* 9.13.3, ed. Luetjohann, *MGH, Auct. ant.* 8, p. 163, 1: "Quin immo quotiens epulo mensae lautioris hilarabere, religiosis, quod magis adprobo, narrationibus vaca; his proferendis confabulatio frequens, his redicendis sollicitus auditus inserviat; certe, si saluberrimis avocamentis, ut qui adhuc iuvenis, tepidius inflecteris, a Platonico Madaurensi saltim formulas mutuare convivialium quaestionum, quoque reddaris instructior, has solve propositas, has propone solvendas, hisque te studiis, et dum otiaris, exerce." Note, however, a suggestion of Apuleius as Macrobius' source in H. Linke, *Quaestiones de Macrobii Saturnaliorum fontibus* (diss. Breslau 1880) 56.

[6] In Plato, Apollodorus, questioned by a friend about Agathon's symposium, at which he was not present, reports the talk of the guest Aristodemus (*Symposium* 172–173b); in Macrobius *Saturnalia* 1.2, Postumianus, questioned by Decius about the symposium of Praetextatus, at which he was not present, reports the talk of the guest Eusebius. In Plato, 212e, Alcibiades and his friends, who had not been invited, appear unexpectedly. Similarly in Macrobius, *Saturnalia* 1.7, with Evangelus and his friends. But the motif of the uninvited guest was common in the symposia; cf. J. Martin, *Symposion*, p. 64.

[7] Text quoted above, n. 3. Cf. Plutarch *Quaestiones convivales* 1.1.4, p. 614c.

[8] *Saturnalia* 2.1.2–6 (a parallel between the symposium of Praetextatus and Agathon's symposium; Macrobius reproaches Plato for having introduced a female flute-player). Cf. Athenaeus *Dipnosophistae* 188c (a parallel between Xenophon's symposium and that of Menelaus in Homer) and Kaibel's edition, vol. 1 (Leipzig 1887) page XXXII. There is the same accusation of immorality in Athenaeus and Macrobius with regard to the female flute-player.

[9] Cf. Homer *Iliad* 2.408–409; Plato *Symposium* 174b–c; Athenaeus 177c–178a; Macrobius *Saturnalia* 1.7.10. The index in Kaibel's edition of Athenaeus, s.v. Plato, Συμπόσιον, gives an idea of the numerous references to Plato's *Symposium* that Macrobius could find in a later symposium. Cf. also T. W. Allen, "Miscellanea—IX" (Macrobius *Saturnalia* 1.7.10), *Classical Quarterly* 26 (1932) 87, which refers to the *Cypria* by Proclus.

Macrobius happens to borrow from Plutarch a comment on Plato's *Symposium*[10] or from Aulus Gellius a passage from Plato's *Laws*.[11]

Aulus Gellius also supplies Macrobius with a long Greek quotation from Aristotle.[12] We have therefore good reason to question whether Macrobius, despite his assertions, read any work of Aristotle relating to symposia.[13] On the other hand, Linke and Wissowa showed long ago in numerous textual parallels that Book 7 of the *Saturnalia* regularly plagiarizes Plutarch's *Quaestiones convivales*. Both critics even agree in thinking that Macrobius preserves Plutarch's original text, of which the Greek manuscripts offer now only a summary.[14] This view has recently been challenged by Hubert. He has shown that it rests on a postulate according to which Macrobius followed a single source. In fact, every time that his text is longer than Plutarch's, he is either merely expanding Plutarch or introducing some personal addition, for instance a line from Vergil.[15] Hubert's proof that shows Macrobius' relative independence in terms of his model would seem to be conclusive. It is sufficient to add that Macrobius was also able to insert into Plutarch's text a marginal gloss that appears in his own manuscript.[16]

Book 7 derives from still another source that explains the additions inserted in a context stemming from Plutarch that are often side remarks, such as the hypothesis of the four digestions[17] and the quotation from Hippocrates' *De natura hominis*, placed in the mouth of the physician Dysarius, who advocates simple foods as being easier to digest.[18] Most of the questions on physics or medicine discussed by Dysarius derive from a Greek

---

[10] *Saturnalia* 7.1.13: "sic Agathonis convivium, quia Socrates, Phaedros, Pausanias et Erysimachus habuit..." Cf. Plutarch *Quaestiones convivales* 613d: ὡς τὸ Ἀγάθωνος, Σωκράτας, Φαίδρους, Παυσανίας, Ἐρυξιμάχους ...

[11] *Saturnalia* 2.8.4ff. Cf. Aulus Gellius *Noctes Atticae* 15.2.3.

[12] *Saturnalia* 2.8.13. Cf. Aulus Gellius *Noctes Atticae* 19.2.5.

[13] Athenaeus quotes from Aristotle a Συμπόσιον ἢ περὶ μέθης and Νόμοι συμποτικοί. Cf. the index in Kaibel's edition. Macrobius *Saturnalia* 7.6.15 quotes Aristotle's *De ebrietate* from Plutarch *Quaestiones convivales* 650a. He quotes (*Saturnalia* 7.13.19) some Aristotelian *Problemata* from Plutarch *Quaestiones convivales* 627a–b.

[14] Linke, *Quaestiones de Macr. Sat. fontibus*, pp. 46–51; Wissowa, *De Macr. Sat. fontibus*, p. 3.

[15] K. Hubert, "Zur indirekten Ueberlieferung der Tischgespräche Plutarchs," *Hermes* 73 (1938) 307–317.

[16] This is the case, for instance, with the line from Homer, *Odyssey* 4.222, that Macrobius quotes, *Saturnalia* 7.1.18, whereas Plutarch 614b only alluded to it.

[17] *Saturnalia* 7.4.14–25. This discussion is introduced with the words, "quod ut omnibus liqueat, paulo altius mihi causa repetenda est," which proclaim the new source.

[18] *Ibid.*, 7.5.19, p. 415, 31. This quotation was in all probability classic among the Neoplatonists, for it reappears in Hermias *In Phaedrum* 270c, ed. Couvreur, p. 245, 18. On medicine in Macrobius, cf. M. Neuburger, "La medicina in Macrobio e Theodoreto," *Rivista storica d. Scienze mediche e naturali* (1923) 241–257.

compilation inspired by Galen's teaching[19] and very like the compilation attributed to Alexander of Aphrodisias.[20]

Still another symposium has been noted as a probable source for Macrobius. This is Athenaeus' *Dipnosophistae*. The editor Kaibel thought that he observed a relationship in the subject and the setting of these two works and noted some textual similarities. In his opinion, they were sufficient to demonstrate that Macrobius had read Athenaeus, granting the hypothesis that we possess not more than an abridged edition of Athenaeus.[21] This hypothesis of an abridged edition must, at first sight, appear dubious, for it recalls too closely the hypothesis, refuted by Hubert, of the abridged edition of Plutarch. But in addition Wissowa had already shown that Macrobius did not lean on Athenaeus, and he maintained his viewpoint even after Kaibel's statement.[22] To him, Macrobius and Athenaeus went back to a common source: the Λέξις τραγική and the Λέξις κωμική of Didymus Chalcenterus, which Macrobius probably knew through a Latin commentator on Vergil. In fact, the parallel passages all appear in Eustathius' exposition of Vergil's Greek sources.

I shall not repeat Wissowa's line of argument. He is correct, I believe, in thinking of Didymus' works as the sources for Macrobius. Is it necessary to assume a Latin commentator on Vergil as an intermediate source? This hypothesis seems at first sight improbable, for the Greek Eustathius, the spokesman for Macrobius, takes care to specify that, contrary to the preceding exposition that put Vergil on a parallel with Homer, Apollonius of Rhodes, and Pindar,[23] his discussion is entirely new to Latin readers. He casts contumely on the Latin commentators, particularly Cornutus and Valerius Probus, for their ignorance.[24] Despite these fine declarations, Macrobius could very well have used a Latin work whose author, imbued with Greek science, denigrated his predecessors. The parallels that follow force us

[19] On the four digestions, cf. Galen *De differentiis febrium*, ed. C. G. Kühn, vol. 7, pp. 381–382.

[20] Pseudo-Alexander Ἰατρικὰ ἀπορήματα καὶ φυσικὰ προβλήματα, ed. J. L. Ideler, *Physici et Medici Graeci Minores* I (Berlin 1841) 3–80. For Macrobius' references to Pseudo-Alexander, cf. Linke, *Quaestiones de Macr. Sat. fontibus*, pp. 52–53.

[21] Athenaeus *Dipnosophistarum libri XV*, ed. G. Kaibel (Leipzig 1887) XXXI–XXXVII; Martin (*Symposion*, pp. 283–286) also notes a certain number of similarities between Athenaeus and Macrobius without taking any issue on the question of their dependence.

[22] Wissowa, *De Macr. Sat. fontibus*, pp. 45–55 (reprinted in *Nachrichten der Gött. Gesellschaft der Wissenschaften*, phil.-hist. Klasse [1913] 325).

[23] Linke (*Quaestiones de Macr. Sat. fontibus*, pp. 42–43) suggests as a source for this extended treatment in *Saturnalia* 5.2–17 the Latin grammarian Asconius Pedianus.

[24] *Saturnalia* 5.18.1, p. 319, 27: "Sed de his hactenus, quorum plura omnibus, aliqua non nullis Romanorum nota sunt. Ad illa venio quae de Graecarum litterarum penetralibus eruta nullis cognita sunt nisi qui Graecam doctrinam diligenter hauserunt." Cf., against the Latin grammarians, 5.18.3, 5.19.2 (Annaeus Cornutus), 5.19.31, 5.21.2, 5.22.7, 5.22.9 (Valerius Probus), 5.22.12.

to admit, for all Wissowa's view that Pseudo-Servius follows Macrobius, that Serenus Sammonicus is the source of all this extended treatment:

I. Macrobius *Sat.* 5.18.2–12, p. 320, 25 *In Georg.* 1.9:
illud antiquo poeta teste monstrabo hunc morem loquendi pervagatum fuisse, ut Acheloum pro quavis aqua dicerent.

(Quotations from Aristophanes and Ephorus)

p. 322, 5: tamen ultra progrediemur. Didymus enim grammaticorum omnium facile eruditissimus, posita causa quam superius Ephorus dixit, alteram quoque adiecit his verbis: ἄμεινον δὲ ἐκεῖνο λέγειν ὅτι διὰ τὸ πάντων τῶν ποταμῶν πρεσβύτατον εἶναι Ἀχελῶον ἀπονέμοντας αὐτῷ τοὺς ἀνθρώπους πάντα ἁπλῶς τὰ νάματα τῷ ἐκείνου ὀνόματι προσαγορεύειν.

Pseudo-Servius *In Georg.* 1.9, ed. Thilo, vol. 3, p. 132, 17:

Sed hic Acheloum non praeter rationem dixit: nam sicut Orpheus docet, et Aristophanes comicus et Ephorus historicus tradunt, Ἀχελῶον generaliter *propter antiquitatem fluminis* omnem aquam veteres vocabant.

II. Macrobius *Sat.* 5.19.3–4, p. 325, 23 *In Aen.* 4.699:
Cornutus . . . ignoravit Euripidis nobilissimam fabulam Alcestim; in hac enim fabula *in scaenam Orcus inducitur gladium* gestans *quo crinem abscidat Alcestidis* et sic loquitur.

Pseudo-Servius *In Aen.* 4.694, ed. Thilo, vol. 1, p. 582, 13:
alii dicunt Euripidem *Orcum in scenam inducere, gladium* ferentem *quo crinem Alcesti abscidat* et Euripidem hoc a Phrynicho, antiquo tragico, mutuatum.

III. Macrobius *Sat.* 5.20, p. 333 (on Gargara):
Significatio nominis et loci duplex est; nam et cacumen montis Idae et oppidum sub eodem monte hoc nomine vocantur.

(Quotations from Homer, Epicharmus, Ephorus, Phileas, Aratus)

p. 334, 10: Cur tamen Gargara posuerit ut locum *frugum feracem* requiramus.

(Quotations from Homer, Alcaeus, Aristomenes, Aristophanes)

Gargara, ut videtis, manifeste *posuit pro multitudine.*

p. 335, 12: *est ergo* secundum haec *sensus* horum versuum talis: *cum ea sit anni temperies ut hiems serena sit, solstitium* vero

Pseudo-Servius *In Georg.* 1.102, ed. Thilo, vol. 3, p. 157, 13:
Sane Gargara multi auctores Graeci, sicut Serenus Sammonicus tradit, altitudinem Idae montis et per hoc abusive omnes summitates montium Gargara appellant; esse etiam Gargara civitatem in provincia Moesia Asiae, quam constat naturaliter uliginosam et ob hoc *frugum feracem* in tantum, ut multi poetae Graeci Gargara abusive *pro cuiusvis rei multitudine* vel copia *posuerint. Ergo* potest et hic *sensus esse,* ut sit: *cum ea sit anni temperies, ut hiemps serena sit et solstitium* umidum, *fructus optime provenire; haec autem adeo esse agris necessaria, ut sine his ne illi* quidem *fecundissimi Moesiae agri*

imbricum, *fructus optime proveniunt; haec autem adeo agris necessaria sunt, ut sine his nec illi* natura *fecundissimi Mysiae agri responsuri sint opinioni fertilitatis, quae de his habetur.*

responsuri sint opinioni fertilitatis, quae de his habetur.

IV. Macrobius *Sat.* 5.22.3–4, p. 341, 17 *In Aen.* 11.532:

Opin inquit comitem et sociam *Dianae*; sed audite unde Vergilius *hoc nomen* acceperit qui, ut dixi, quod epitheton *ipsius* deae legerat *sociae eius imposuit.* Alexander Aetolus, *poeta egregius, in libro qui inscribitur Musae refert* quanto studio populus *Ephesius dedicato templo* Dianae curaverit praemiis propositis ut qui tunc erant *poetae* ingeniosissimi in deam carmina diversa componerent.

Pseudo-Servius *In Aen.* 11.532, ed. Thilo, vol. 2, p. 542, 14:

Sane *hoc nomen* (Ops) *ipsius Dianae* fuisse, ab *Ephesiis dedicato templo* ei *impositum*, Alexander Aetolus *poeta in libro qui inscribitur Musae refert: quod* hoc loco peritissimus antiquitatis *poeta sociae eius imposuit.*

The first parallel shows that Macrobius and Pseudo-Servius are independent of each other. Their common source quoted successively Orpheus, Aristophanes, Ephorus, Didymus. Macrobius has omitted the quotation from Orpheus. Pseudo-Servius has omitted the name of Didymus while preserving his thought, which he wrongly attributes to the three older sources. This conclusion is confirmed by the second parallel, in which Pseudo-Servius alone has preserved the reference to Phrynichus.

The third parallel clearly indicates that the direct source of Pseudo-Servius is not Macrobius, but Serenus Sammonicus. Wissowa gives no proof for his view that the statement "sicut Serenus Sammonicus tradit" is an interpolation, for the manuscript tradition is unanimous.[25] It may be added that several borrowings by Macrobius from the same source have no parallel in Pseudo-Servius.[26] Inversely, Pseudo-Servius borrows at least once more specifically from Serenus Sammonicus, who, here also, quotes Greek writers, while Macrobius makes no allusion to this passage.[27] Macrobius and Pseudo-Servius therefore both refer directly back to Serenus Sammonicus, who transmitted to them both the science and the principles of Didymus Chalcenterus. Everything leads one to believe that Macrobius acquired through the same channel his knowledge of the symbolical value of bronze

---

[25] Wissowa, *De Macr. Sat. fontibus,* p. 55.

[26] For example, on the Aetoli-Hernici (*Aen.* 7.684), *Saturnalia* 5.18.13–21; on Palicus (*Aen.* 9.585), *Saturnalia* 5.19.15–31.

[27] Pseudo-Servius *In Georg.* 1.30, ed. Thilo, vol. 3, p. 139, 12. On Thule: "multa praeterea de hac insula feruntur, sicut apud Graecos Ctesias et Diogenes, apud Latinos Sammonicus dicit."

instruments in ancient drama,[28] and even of the names of the Greek vases. Despite the extensive textual parallels between Athenaeus and Macrobius, Macrobius is more complete and there are several discrepancies between them. The hypothesis postulated by Kaibel of a more complete edition of Athenaeus, of which we have merely an abridgment, does not quite explain these discrepancies.[29] On the contrary, it is not surprising to find Athenaeus and Macrobius plagiarizing from a common source. Athenaeus slightly abridged and copied an alphabetical lexicon of the names of Greek vases, reproducing the order from the letter α to the letter ω. Macrobius, most probably following Sammonicus, retained only the comments relating to the names of vases that appear in Vergil, such as κάνθαρος, καρχήσιον, κυμβία, σκύφος. But he transcribes them in a more complete form, sometimes adopting, where Didymus proposed various explanations, an explanation differing from that adopted by Athenaeus.[30]

Is Sammonicus' book from which Macrobius borrows all this Greek erudition a commentary on Vergil? There is no reason to suppose so. In Book 3 of the *Saturnalia* Macrobius refers to some work by Sammonicus that discussed questions relating to symposia and that condemned greediness.[31] In another passage, he refers explicitly to Book 5 of Sammonicus' *Res reconditae*.[32] I believe that the entire erudite exposition in Book 5 of the *Saturnalia* (chapters 18–22) stems from the same source. Macrobius in fact presents it constantly under the name of *res reconditae*. Vergil's borrowings from the Greeks are concealed, he declares, both because Vergil dissimulates

[28] *Saturnalia* 5.19.6–14, pp. 326–328. The sentence on p. 327, 26, "longum fiat si velim percensere quam multis in locis Graecorum vetustissimi aeris sonos tamquam rem validissimam adhibere soliti sunt," shows that Macrobius possesses an endless repertoire of Greek quotations and that he culls from them.

[29] Cf. Wissowa, *De Macr. Sat. fontibus*, pp. 49–51, in contradiction to Kaibel in his edition, p. xxxv.

[30] Of Kaibel's line of argument in favor of Macrobius' having read Athenaeus there remain only very tenuous clues: the analogy between the cantankerous character of Evangelus in Macrobius and of Cynulcus in Athenaeus (p. xxxiv) and the parallel text on the fictitious age of the characters in the Platonic dialogues (p. xxxiii), intended to defend Plato against the reproaches of Herodicus Crateteus, Πρὸς τὸν Φιλοσωκράτην. But here too Macrobius is fuller than Athenaeus, for the sentence in *Saturnalia* 1.1.5, p. 5, 24, "inclitum dialogum Socrates habita cum Timaeo disputatione consumit, quos constat eodem saeculo non fuisse," has no equivalent in Athenaeus 11.505f. I do not think it is more correct to see, with R. Hirzel, *Der Dialog* 2 (Leipzig 1895) 357–358, a polemic directed by Macrobius against Athenaeus, even if their points of view are really in opposition.

[31] *Saturnalia* 3.16.8, p. 207, 17: "Haec Sammonicus, qui turpitudinem convivii principis sui laudando notat"; Wissowa, "Analecta Macrobiana," *Hermes* 16 (1881) 503–505, acknowledges that Sammonicus is the source of *Saturnalia* 3.13–17.

[32] *Saturnalia* 3.9.6, p. 188, 4: "Nam repperi in libro quinto *Rerum reconditarum* Sammonici Sereni utrumque carmen."

and because the books from which he borrows are quite unknown.[33] The rare items of information that we have on Sammonicus coincide quite well with the model that Macrobius here follows. This was a compiler who had collected a library of 62,000 volumes.[34] He seemed also to Sidonius Apollinaris to be one of the Latin writers who resorted most frequently to Greek.[35] His books were particularly appreciated by Geta, who was obsessed by a lexicographical mania to the point of wanting all the courses in a single banquet to begin with the same letter.[36] Such a writer was quite well equipped to transmit to Macrobius the science of Didymus' lexica. Perhaps it was even Didymus' Συμποσιακὰ σύμμικτα that he used,[37] and not the lexica of the vocabulary of tragedy or comedy, as Wissowa thinks. Macrobius was probably led to plagiarize Didymus on account of the very genre of the learned symposium.

Macrobius therefore had through his intermediate Latin sources a sufficiently thorough knowledge of Greek philological science as it had been established at Alexandria by the works of Didymus at the close of the first century B.C. If he is only the plagiarist of a compiler, there is no less the possibility of discovering Vergil's connection with Greek tragedy. He is equally capable, when not satisfied with the Latin collections, of reading the Greek compilers, such as Plutarch, who preceded him in the symposium genre or who studied problems of physics.

3. MACROBIUS' RELIGIOUS PHILOSOPHY

But Macrobius does not confine himself to the study of philological or

---

[33] *Ibid.*, 1.24.18; Eustathius had promised to show that Vergil followed the Greeks "modo artifici dissimulatione, modo professa imitatione." To this distinction correspond the two treatments, the first on the evident imitations (*Saturnalia* 5.2–17), the second (*Saturnalia* 5.18–22) on the unacknowledged borrowings. On the notion of Vergilian borrowings from very obscure Greek texts, cf. the text quoted above, n. 24, and *Saturnalia* 5.22.15, p. 344, 5: "penitissima Graecorum doctrina"; 5.18.4, p. 320, 19: "nos id altius scrutati"; 5.19.16, p. 328, 13: "de Graecorum penitissimis litteris."

[34] Iulius Capitolinus, "Gordianus," *Script. hist. Aug.* 20.18.2, ed. E. Hohl (Leipzig 1927) p. 42, 18.

[35] Sidonius Apollinaris *Carm.* 14, *praef.* (= *Epist. ad Polemium* 3) ed. Luetjohann, *MGH, Auct. ant.* 8 (Berlin 1887) 233, 7. Sidonius bases his authority on Varro, Sammonicus, and Censorinus in the use of Greek expressions.

[36] Aelius Spartianus, "Antoninus Geta," *Script. hist. Aug.* 14.5.6, ed. E. Hohl, vol. 1, p. 198, 9: "Sereni Sammonici libros familiarissimos habuit, quos ille ad Antoninum scripsit: habebat etiam istam consuetudinem, ut convivia et maxime prandia per singulas litteras iuberet scientibus servis, velut in quo erat anser, apruna, anas, item pullus, perdix, pavus, porcellus, piscis, perna et quae in eam litteram genera edulium caderent, et item fasianus, farrata, ficus et talia."

[37] Cf. *PW* s.v. Didymos, 470, 31.

scientific literature. He has the same lively interest in Greek philosophy and religion. He puts into Praetextatus' mouth discussions that the latter could actually have held. Praetextatus was, as we have seen, a translator and admirer of Themistius. Now, in the *Saturnalia*, he defines philosophy as Aristotle's Greek commentators defined it:

Macrobius *Sat.* 1.24.21, p. 133, 15:
His dictis et universo coetui complacitis, Praetextatus cum in se conversa omnium ora vidisset: *philosophia*, inquit, quod unicum est munus deorum et *disciplina disciplinarum*, honoranda est anteloquio, unde meminerit Eustathius primum sibi locum ad disserendum omni alia professione cedente concessum.

Ammonius *In Isag. Porph.*, ed. Busse, *CAG*, vol. 4, 3, p. 6, 25:
"Εστι δὲ καὶ ἄλλος τῆς φιλοσοφίας ὁρισμὸς Ἀριστοτέλους ἐκ τῆς ὑπεροχῆς αὐτῆς ἧς ἔχει πρὸς τὰς ἄλλας ἐπιστήμας καὶ τέχνας, λέγων· φιλοσοφία ἐστὶ τέχνη τεχνῶν καὶ ἐπιστήμη ἐπιστημῶν.

The philosopher Eustathius also belongs among those commentators on Aristotle who, in the prologue to the commentary on Porphyry's *Isagoge*, reserved the last place for medicine, as being the least noble part of philosophy:

Macrobius *Sat.* 7.15.14, p. 456, 5:
Ad haec Eustathius paulo commotior: "non minus te, inquit, Disari, philosophis quam medicis inserebam, sed modo videris mihi rem consensu generis humani decantatam et creditam oblivioni dare, *philosophiam artem esse artium et disciplinam disciplinarum*, et nunc in ipsam invehitur parricidali ausu medicina, cum philosophia illic se habeatur augustior ubi de rationali parte, id est de incorporeis, disputat, et illic inclinetur ubi de physica, quod est de divinis corporibus vel caeli, vel siderum, tractat; medicina autem phisicae partis extrema faex est, cui ratio est cum testeis terrenisque corporibus, sed quid rationem nominavi, *cum magis apud ipsam regnet coniectura quam ratio?* quae ergo conicit de carne lutulenta, audet inequitare philosophiae de incorporeis et vere divinis certa ratione tractanti."

Ammonius *In Isag.*, p. 7, 7:
Οἱ δὲ τῆς ἰατρικῆς (λόγοι) πταίουσιν, ὡς ὁ λέγων· "τὰ ἐναντία τῶν ἐναντίων ἰάματα," διὰ τὸ μὴ περὶ τὸ ὡσαύτως ἔχον ἀεὶ καταγίνεσθαι· πρῶτον μὲν γὰρ οὐδὲ πάντων τῶν νοσημάτων ἰάματά ἐστι· τί γάρ, ἐὰν ἡ νόσος ὀλεθρία ᾖ; ἄλλως τε ἔστιν ὅτε, οὐ τὰ ἐναντία προσάγουσιν, ἀλλὰ τὰ ὅμοια, ὡς ἐπὶ τῶν κατὰ συμβεβηκός. πολλάκις γὰρ ὕδωρ ἐπιχεόμενον ἠτονηκυίαν ἤδη θερμότητα ἀνεκαλέσατο.

The later commentator Ammonius of Alexandria invites us to believe that Macrobius probably found this information in one of the earlier commentators on Porphyry's *Isagoge*, perhaps in that Themistius, the professor at Constantinople, who was in Praetextatus' opinion the master of philosophy.

Themistius is not a Neoplatonic philosopher. Yet Eustathius shows in one passage what this philosophical sect is that he has chosen and that Macrobius calls the best.[1] In fact, once, on a rare occasion, he has an advantage over Vergil, on the theory of chance. Vergil, despite Homer, grants omnipotence to $Tύχη$, while $Tύχη$, according to the philosophers, is powerless by itself and is restricted to executing the decisions of Providence.[2] This theory is the Neoplatonic theory, which we shall discover again even in Boethius. Macrobius may owe it to Plotinus.[3]

It is likewise from Neoplatonists that Praetextatus borrows his religious doctrine. The long speech on the names of the divinities and their identification with the sun that Macrobius has him deliver (*Sat.* 1.17–23) certainly derives from a Greek theologian who claimed, by the allegorical method, to justify the various epithets of the gods and to prove their fundamental unity. A considerable number of hypotheses have been proposed on the source of this exposition, and the discovery of this source is of the highest interest, for Praetextatus' funerary inscription reveals that he combined the highest political and religious offices. He was initiated into all kinds of mysteries, and in particular as *pontifex solis*.[4] In all probability Macrobius has chosen him purposely as the spokesman of the solar theology that was characteristic of the cultured pagans at Rome at the close of the fourth century. One can realize how great the interest is in knowing what literary works influenced their thought and inspired this last apology of paganism.

According to Wissowa, Macrobius here plagiarized the $Περὶ θεῶν$ of Iamblichus and the Latin writer Cornelius Labeo, but he probably knew them only through Marius Victorinus, who was in all likelihood the author of this contamination.[5] Taube challenges these views and considers that Macrobius

---

[1] Text quoted above, sec. 1 n. 27.

[2] *Saturnalia* 5.16.8, p. 313, 5: "Contra Vergilius non solum novit et meminit, sed omnipotentiam quoque eidem tribuit, quam et philosophi qui eam nominant nihil sua vi posse, sed *decreti* sive providentiae ministram esse voluerunt." It will be noted that Macrobius *In Somn. Scip.* 1.19.27, p. 552, 16, uses in a quotation from Plotinus the expression "decreti necessitas," a quotation that Praetextatus uses for his own purpose, *Saturnalia* 1.17.3, p. 88, 17.

[3] Plotinus *Enneads* 3.3.5, ed. E. Bréhier, vol. 3, p. 55, 14: "$Ἐν δὲ ἐκ πάντων καὶ πρόνοια μία· εἰμαρμένη δὲ ἀπὸ τοῦ χείρονος ἀρξαμένη, τὸ δὲ ὑπεράνω πρόνοια μόνον$. It will be noted that Hierocles' $Περὶ προνοίας$, composed shortly after 412, develops analogous ideas. On Boethius, cf. pp. 305–306 and 311–312.

[4] Cf. Schanz, vol. 4, 1, p. 139, and *CIL* 6, 1779. On the origins of the allegorical method in pagan theology, cf. Cumont, *Recherches sur le symbolisme funéraire*, pp. 3–10.

[5] Wissowa, *De Macr. Sat. fontibus*, pp. 35–43.

follows Porphyry's Περὶ ἀγαλμάτων through the medium of the Περὶ ἀγαλμάτων of Iamblichus and that of Fonteius.[6] Niggetiet reverts to Wissowa's theory and admits as a source Iamblichus' treatise, but he thinks that Cornelius Labeo is Macrobius' direct source.[7] It is futile to dwell on the opinion of Niggetiet, who was satisfied with deducing his theory from the fact that, in his view, Labeo is slightly later than Iamblichus and could have read his books. The hypothesis of the intermediate source, whether it was Labeo or Victorinus, scarcely deserves any greater credence.[8] The technique of the German *Quellenforschung* was in this instance followed because, half a century ago, it saw in Macrobius nothing but a plagiarist. The theory was that Macrobius strung together, end to end, two or three writers, and was incapable of himself handling the contamination between Greek and Latin elements. This concept has now become obsolete, since the labors of Mras, Hubert, and Father Henry agree in recognizing in Macrobius a certain originality in the use of his sources. There remains Iamblichus and Porphyry. The weakness of Wissowa's arguments in support of Iamblichus has been exposed by Traube: the use of Orphic verses, and the allusions to the religion of the Egyptians or the Assyrians constitute no proof whatever that Porphyry could not be the source. A small fragment of Proclus, quoted by Wissowa in support of his theory, proves only that, in the commentary on the *Timaeus*, Porphyry identified Asclepius with the moon and not with the sun, but Porphyry very frequently contradicts himself in one work after another. The similarities between Praetextatus' speech and the speech of Julian the Apostate on the sun reveal a common doctrine, but not a textual dependence. Lastly, Iamblichus' Περὶ θεῶν, on the evidence of Proclus and Damascius, seems to have been a theological *summa*, and not only a study of the names of the gods. These criticisms are just; only the positive part of Traube's demonstration is quite inconsistent and does not prove conclusively, as Boertzler has well observed,[9] that the Περὶ ἀγαλμάτων fits as a better source of Macrobius. Bidez, who assembled the extant fragments of this work of Porphyry and noted all the analogies with Macrobius, is very hesitant about asserting that one is the source of the other.[10] A parallel between Macrobius and Servius, which seems never to have been noted, permits us, however, to specify the work of Porphyry that Macrobius followed:

[6] L. Traube, *Varia libamenta critica* (diss. Munich 1883) 23–37.

[7] G. Niggetiet, *De Cornelio Labeone* (diss. Münster 1908) 44.

[8] Wessner, *PW* s.v. Macrobius, 196, is already much more cautious with regard to Labeo. Most of the speculations on his lost works are quite conjectural. Naturally, the notion cannot be dismissed that Macrobius could have been acquainted with such a treatise by Porphyry through a Latin intermediary, particularly the Περὶ θείων ὀνομάτων, as already suggested by Labriolle, *La réaction païenne*, p. 300 n. 1.

[9] F. Boertzler, *Porphyrius' Schrift von den Götterbildern* (diss. Erlangen 1903) 49–54.

[10] Bidez, *Vie de Porphyre*, p. 150. The most striking similarities are those on Kronos

Macrobius *Sat.* 1.18.8, p. 105, 20:
In sacris enim haec religiosi arcani observatio tenetur, ut *Sol*, cum *in supero*, id est in diurno hemisphaerio est, Apollo vocitetur; cum *in infero*, id est nocturno, Dionysus qui est *Liber Pater* habeatur.

Sat. 1.17.9, p. 89, 25:
alii cognominatum *Apollinem* putant ὡς ἀπολλύντα τὰ ζῶα, exanimat enim et perimit animantes cum *pestem* intemperie caloris immittit . . . *Hinc est quod* arcu et sagittis Apollinis simulacra decorantur, ut per sagittas intellegatur vis emissa radiorum: αὐτὰρ ἔπειτ' αὐτοῖσι βέλος ἐχεπευκὲς ἐφιεὶς βάλλ' [*Il.* 1.51]. *Idem auctor* est et publicae sospitatis, quam creditur sol animantibus praestare temperie.[11]

Sat. 1.17.70, p. 103, 30:
Addita est Gorgonea vestis, quod Minerva quam huius praesidem accipimus solis virtus sit, sicut et Porphyrius testatur Minervam esse virtutem solis quae humanis mentibus prudentiam subministrat; nam ideo haec dea Iovis capite prognata memoratur, id est de summa aetheris parte edita, unde origo solis est.[12]

Servius *In Buc.* 5.66, ed. Thilo, vol. 3, p. 61, 22:
En quattuor aras ecce duas tibi Daphni, duas altaria Phoebo . . . Cur duo altaria Apollini se positurum dicat, cum constet supernos deos impari gaudere numero, infernos vero pari, ut VIII, 75 *numero deus impari gaudet*, quod etiam pontificales indicant libri. Sed constat secundum Porphyrii librum, quem *Solem* appellavit, triplicem esse Apollinis potestatem, et eundem esse *Solem apud superos, Liberum Patrem* in terris, Apollinem *apud inferos*; unde etiam tria insignia circa eius simulacrum videmus, lyram quae nobis caelestis harmoniae imaginem monstrat; grypem quae eum etiam terrenum numen ostendit; sagittas quibus infernus deus et noxius indicatur, unde etiam *Apollo* dictus est ἀπὸ τοῦ ἀπολλύειν; *hinc est quod* et Homerus *eundem* tam *pestilentiae* dicit quam salutis *auctorem*.

Servius *In Aen.* 4.201, ed. Thilo, vol. 1, p. 500, 4:
Est autem (ignis) in templo Iovis qui aether est, et Minervae, quae supra aetherem est; unde de patris capite procreata esse dicitur.

(*Saturnalia* 1.22.8 and Porph. *apud* Bidez, p. 16*, 10), on Dionysus (*Saturnalia* 1.18.12–14 and Bidez, p. 13*, 21), on Artemis (*Saturnalia* 1.15.20 and Bidez, p. 14*, 14), on Asclepius (*Saturnalia* 1.20.2 and Bidez, p. 13*, 14), on the bull Mneuis of Heliopolis (*Saturnalia* 1.21.20 and Bidez, p. 23*, 1). In this treatment of the sun Macrobius often quotes Apollodorus, who was the principal source not only of the Περὶ ἀγαλμάτων but also of Porphyrian mythology in general. Cf. C. Reinhardt, *De Graecorum theologia capita duo* (diss. Berlin 1910) 83ff.

11 Cf. also Macrobius *Saturnalia* 1.16.44; Servius *In Georg.* 1.5, ed. Thilo, vol. 3, p. 130, 24; Lactantius Placidus *In Stat. Theb.*, ed. R. Jahnke, p. 247, 9; *Comm. Bern. in Lucan.* 5.74; Arnobius 3.33, ed. Reifferscheid, *CSEL*, vol. 4, p. 183, 28. Boertzler, *Porphyrius' Schrift von den Götterbildern*, p. 50, already associated this text of Arnobius with Porphyry's *Sol.* He noted, p. 47, the interest of the Servian scholium. So also did Bitsch, *De Platonicorum quaestionibus quibusdam Vergilianis*, p. 65; Baehrens, "Literarhistorische Beiträge," 39–56; M. Schedler, *Die Philosophie des Macrobius*, p. 98. But nobody seems to have noticed the exact parallel with Macrobius.

12 Cf. Augustine *De civitate Dei* 4.10, *PL* 41, 120: "Aut si aetheris partem superiorem Minervam temere dicunt, et hac occasione fingere poetas quod de Iovis capite nata sit, cur non ergo ipsa potius deorum regina deputatur, quod sit Iove superior?"

The source common to Macrobius and to his friend Servius (who is also one of the interlocutors in the *Saturnalia*), is specified by Servius. This was Porphyry's treatise on the sun. This work is otherwise unknown, but I believe that it is identical with the Περὶ ὀνομάτων mentioned by Suidas in his list of works by Porphyry, starting with the philosophical books.[13] Bidez justifiably refused to identify this treatise on the *names of the divinities* with the Περὶ ἀγαλμάτων, emphasizing the fact that the two titles indicate two different subjects.[14] On the other hand, Macrobius' treatment shows that this treatise on the sun, which is his source, is just a commentary on the names of the gods, intended to prove that all those names refer to the sun.

Porphyry's influence on Macrobius' religious thought is confirmed by the study of the *Commentary on Scipio's Dream*. Much has been written on the sources of this commentary, but for a long time the same dubious method was followed as for the *Saturnalia*. An attempt was made to attribute the entire work to a single source that, according to Borghorst, was probably a lost commentary by Iamblichus on the *Timaeus*,[15] and, according to Linke and Bitsch, a lost commentary by Marius Victorinus on the *Somnium Scipionis*, which embraced Porphyry's commentary on the *Timaeus* and a commentary on Vergil.[16] This method, pushed to extremes, results in this absurdity, that the same Latin author was also, according to Linke, the source of a part of the *Saturnalia*, from the fact that the style is the same.[17] As though Macrobius' entire work had consisted in substituting his name for that of the author whom he was plagiarizing and as though it was not natural that two works of one and the same Macrobius should be written in the same style! The recent labors of Mras and Father Henry, who work independently of each other, have rightly dismissed these aberrations. To them, Macrobius, if he is a compiler, is not a plagiarist. He does not transcribe one source only, but his work indicates the extent of his reading.[18] Father Henry even ventures to write that, from the way in which he uses his sources, "this commentator

---

[13] Cf. Bidez, *Vie de Porphyre*, p. 52*. Reinhardt, *De Graecorum theologia*, p. 104, had already thought of this treatise as a source, but did not base his conjecture on the parallel that I have just indicated.

[14] Bidez, *Vie de Porphyre*, p. 149 n. 5. Boertzler, *Porphyrius' Schrift von den Götterbildern*, p. 57 n. 1, was more hesitant. The hypothesis of G. Heuten, "Le 'Soleil' de Porphyre," *Mélanges F. Cumont* 1 (Brussels 1936) 253–259, which identifies this treatise with the *Philosophie des oracles*, seems equally improbable.

[15] G. Borghorst, *De Anatolii fontibus* (diss. Berlin 1905) 38–44.

[16] H. Linke, "Ueber Macrobius' Kommentar," pp. 240–256. Bitsch, *De Platonicorum quaestionibus quibusdam Vergilianis*, pp. 21–52, returns to this theory, but finds difficulties therein and finally is forced to admit, p. 52, that Macrobius followed several commentators on Vergil.

[17] Linke (see preceding note) 254–255.

[18] K. Mras, "Macrobius' Kommentar zu Ciceros *Somnium*, ein Beitrag zur Geistesgeschichte des V. Jahrh. n. Chr.," *Sitzungsberichte der preuss. Akad. der Wissensch.*, phil.-

gives the impression of a thinker and a writer."[19] It would, however, be improper to speak of a philosophy of Macrobius, as Schedler[20] does, for this philosophy has nothing personal in it. Unquestionably, Macrobius, even if there had been before him Latin commentators on the *Somnium Scipionis*, appears not to follow them;[21] but in relation to the Greek Neoplatonists his philosophy contains nothing original.

It is a long recognized fact that the commentary on the *Somnium Scipionis* is for Macrobius merely an excuse to expound his Neoplatonic theories. To realize this, it is sufficient to analyze, as Mras has done, the explicit views that Macrobius entertains on Plato and the Platonists.[22] In Macrobius' opinion Neoplatonism is the doctrine of truth. Indifferent to anachronisms, he interprets the most famous writers, Cicero and Vergil, in terms of this doctrine and offers them as his surety.

Father Henry has already studied in detail Macrobius' borrowings from Plotinus, and shows that he certainly read the *Enneads*, even if his quotations are occasionally very free. It is from Plotinus that Macrobius borrows his theories on the rotation of the heavens, moved by the Soul of the universe,[23] and on the stars that are signs, and not causes, of events.[24] He links together an exposition by Plotinus on the difference between man and animals[25] and an exposition on the flux of the elements that are inexhaustible.[26] The borrowing even seems to go further, as Mras noted, with the comparison

---

hist. Klasse, 6 (1933) 232–286, and Father Henry, "Plotin et l'Occident," pp. 146–192. Henry appears not to have had Mras' work before him until his own book was already prepared, for he mentions Mras only on p. 149 n. 1.

[19] Henry, *Plotin et l'Occident*, p. 192.

[20] M. Schedler, *Die Philosophie des Macrobius*. Schedler's point of view is defensible only if Macrobius is considered operative in the Middle Ages, which did not know his Neoplatonic sources.

[21] The only reference that he makes and one that obliges us not to reject entirely the idea of an earlier commentary on the *Somnium Scipionis*, which he would have known, is *In Somn. Scip.* 1.7.1, p. 503, 7: "Hic *quidam* mirantur quid sibi velit ista dubitatio: *si effugeris*, quasi potuerit divina anima et olim caelo reddita atque hic maxime scientiam futuri professa nescire, possitne nepos suus an non possit evadere."

[22] Mras, "Macrobius' Kommentar," pp. 233–235.

[23] *In Somn.* 1.17.8–11 and *Enneads* 2.2.1.1–49. Cf. Henry, *Plotin et l'Occident*, p. 182.

[24] *In Somn.* 1.19.27, *Saturnalia* 1.17.3, and *Enneads* 2.3. Cf. Henry, *Plotin et l'Occident*, p. 187, and, on the problems raised by the parallel text of Lydus, Henry, "Une traduction grecque d'un texte de Macrobe dans le *Περὶ μηνῶν* de Lydus," *REL* 11 (1933) 164–171, and M. G. Nicolau, "A propos d'un texte parallèle de Macrobe et de Lydus," *REL* 11 (1933) 318–321. Nicolau's position, according to which Lydus translated from Macrobius the quotations from Plotinus, but not the quotations from Ptolemy, seems to me flagrantly indefensible.

[25] *In Somn.* 2.12.7–10 and *Enneads* 1.1.1–7. Cf. Henry, *Plotin et l'Occident*, p. 150.

[26] *In Somn.* 2.12.14–15 and *Enneads* 2.1.1–3. Cf. Henry, *Plotin et l'Occident*, p. 151.

between the immortality of the soul and that of the universe.[27] Similarly, Plotinus' theory of the emanation of the soul and the body when the νοῦς leaves is linked by Macrobius to another treatise of the *Enneads* that contained an exposition of the tripartition of the soul into λογικόν, αἰσθητικόν, φυτικόν.[28]

Macrobius therefore carefully read the *Enneads*, to which his friend Servius[29] also refers occasionally, but it would be a mistake to consider him a disciple of Plotinus exclusively. We have the proof that, mentally, he made no distinction between Plotinus' teaching and that of Porphyry. It is unanimously admitted, even by Father Henry, that Macrobius quotes in the name of Plotinus a long passage from Porphyry's *Sententiae*, which are actually nothing but a summary of the master's doctrine. It is from this manual by Porphyry, and not directly from the *Enneads*, that Macrobius borrows his theory on the virtues.[30] Sometimes, too, the reference to Plotinus is doubtful. It has been maintained that, on the question of metempsychosis, Macrobius supported Plotinus against Porphyry, who, on Augustine's evidence, no longer believed that the human soul could be reincarnated in the bodies of animals.[31] But actually Porphyry's thought varied. Augustine's testimony is based on the *De regressu animae*, but in another work, probably the Περὶ Στυγός, Porphyry accepted Plotinus' theory of metempsychosis into the bodies of animals.[32] We should therefore hesitate in judging whether Macrobius here follows Plotinus or Porphyry.

A study of the sources of the *Commentary on the Somnium Scipionis* indicates that the real master of Macrobius' thought is not Plotinus, but Porphyry.

[27] *In Somn.* 2.13.7 and *Enneads* 2.1.4. Cf. Mras, "Macrobius' Kommentar," p. 275.

[28] *In Somn.* 1.14.5–7 and *Enneads* 5.2.1.1–22 and 3.4.2.3. This last reference is not furnished by Henry, *Plotin et l'Occident*, p. 189.

[29] Servius *In Aen.* 9.182, ed. Thilo, vol. 2, p. 325, 25. Cf. Henry, *Plotin et l'Occident*, pp. 194–196.

[30] *In Somn.* 1.8.3–12 and Porphyry *Sententiae* 32.1–7. Cf. Henry, *Plotin et l'Occident*, pp. 154–162, who should have indicated that this discovery goes back at least to Schedler, *Die Philosophie des Macrobius*, p. 88, a work whose existence seems to be unknown to Henry, for he does not list it in his bibliography or his index. On the theory of the virtues, cf. O. Schissel von Fleschenberg, *Marinos von Neapolis und die neuplatonischen Tugendgrade*, Texte und Forschungen zur byzantinisch-neugriechischen Philologie, vol. 8 (Athens 1928), 124 pages.

[31] *In Somn.* 1.9.5, p. 510, 21: "novi corporis ambit habitaculum, non humani tantum modo, sed ferini quoque." Cf. *De civitate Dei* 10.30, *PL* 41, 310, text quoted chap. 4 sec. 2 n. 133, and Mras, "Macrobius' Kommentar," p. 253.

[32] Porphyry, in Stobaeus *Eclogae* 1.41.60, ed. Meineke, vol. 1, p. 332. It is an indication that Macrobius follows in this passage not the *De regressu animae* but another treatise. There is a presumption in support of the Περὶ Στυγός included in *excerpta, Ecl.* 1.41.50–54. Schedler, *Die Philosophie des Macrobius*, p. 67 n. 2, was wrong in believing, on Augustine's word, that there was a divergence here between Porphyry and Macrobius. On Macrobius' use of the Περὶ Στυγός, cf. below, p. 40.

Macrobius read a number of his works and was constantly inspired by them. He is indebted to him for the method and the content of his commentary and follows his theories on the soul and his astronomical theories.

It was natural that the *Somnium Scipionis* should suggest to Macrobius, imbued as he was with Greek culture, Plato's *Republic*. He begins therefore with a brief parallel between the two Republics, wherein he notes in succession the differences and the similarities, according to the methods of classical rhetoric and of the Latin commentators.[33] But it is in accordance with the Greek commentators that he treats two of the usual points of their prolegomena: the purpose (σκοπός) and the plan (τάξις) of the work, before passing on to the exegesis proper.[34] He borrows the material of his long introduction from Porphyry's commentary on the *Republic*, of which Proclus has preserved several extracts. Mras has already noted that Macrobius follows this commentary when he excuses Plato, who was accused by Colotes the Epicurean, with regard to the myth of Er the Pamphilian, of having disguised the truth under the form of a fable.[35] It should be added that the treatment of the comparative purpose and plan of the *Phaedo*, the *Gorgias*, and the *Republic* derives from the same source.[36] So with the treatment on the necessity, to speak properly of the invisible νοῦς, of comparing it with the visible sun.[37] Later, Macrobius still has frequent recourse to Porphyry's commentary on the *Republic*, for instance when he defends the gods from

[33] *In Somn.* 1.1.1–3. Cf. 1.5.1, p. 479, 27: "quae differentia, quae similitudo habeatur expressimus." Cf. Favonius Eulogius *In Somn. Scip.*, ed. A. Holder (Leipzig 1901) p. 1, 5. Perhaps we have to assume a common Latin source.

[34] Macrobius *In Somn.*, p. 466, 10 mens operis; 13 proposito; 478, 6 ipsam eiusdem somnii mentem ipsumque propositum, quem Graeci σκοπόν vocant, antequam verba inspiciantur, temptemus aperire; p. 467, 14 ordinem. On the prolegomena of the Greek commentators, cf. Rabe, *Prolegomenon Sylloge* (Leipzig 1931) VI–VII, and in this book pp. 286–288.

[35] Macrobius *In Somn.* 1.2 (p. 470, 12 *fabulosa*); Favonius Eulogius *In Somn.*, p. 1, 13 (p. 1, 8 *fabulosa*), and Proclus *In Rem publicam*, ed. Kroll, vol. 2 (Leipzig 1899) 105–108, mentioning Porphyry by name, p. 106, 16. Cf. Mras, "Macrobius' Kommentar."

[36] Macrobius *In Somn.* 1.1.6–7 and Proclus *In Rem publicam*, vol. 1, p. 168, 11.

[37] Macrobius *In Somn.* 1.2.14–16 and Proclus *In Rem publicam*, vol. 1, pp. 274–276. Cf. in particular:

Macrobius, p. 471, 19:	Proclus, p. 276, 23:
Sic Plato cum de τἀγαθῷ loqui esset animatus, dicere quid sit non ausus est, hoc solum de eo sciens quod sciri quale sit ab homine non possit, solum vero ei simillimum de visibilibus *solem* repperit.	Ἵνα μὴ παραδράμωμεν τὴν διὰ τῆς ἀναλογίας διδασκαλίαν, σκόπει πῶς φησιν τῷ μὲν ἀγαθῷ τὸν ἥλιον ἀναλογεῖν.

The passage 1.2.19–21 on Numenius' dream must stem from the same source but has no parallel in Proclus.

the reproach of sending deceptive portents [38] or when he makes the kingdom of Pluto begin with the Milky Way.[39]

Thus, for the first part of his commentary Macrobius constantly refers to the corresponding commentary by Porphyry on the *Republic*. But into this pattern he inserts a number of additional interpretations borrowed from other works by Porphyry. Once, he explicitly quotes his *Quaestiones Homericae*, with reference to the two gates through which the souls descend to earth and rise to heaven, and he translates textually a few lines from Porphyry.[40] Servius too knows at least indirectly the *Quaestiones Homericae*,[41]

[38] With regard to the dream in *Iliad* 2.8–34, where Zeus entices Agamemnon with the hope of victory, cf. *In Somn.* 1.7.4–6 and Proclus *In Rem publicam*, vol. 1, pp. 115ff. I see no decisive reason for thinking, as Mras does, "Macrobius' Kommentar," p. 251, that Proclus is here following not Porphyry's commentary on the *Republic* but his *Quaestiones Homericae*. It was Plato himself who referred to the Homeric passage in question.

[39] *In Somn.* 1.12.3, p. 519, 21:

Hinc et Pythagoras putat a *lacteo circulo* deorsum incipere Ditis imperium, quia animae inde lapsae videntur iam a superis recessisse; ideo primam nascentibus offerri ait *lactis alimoniam*, quia primus eis motus a lacteo incipit in corpora terrena labentibus.

Proclus *In Rem publicam*, vol. 2, p. 129, 25:

Καὶ γὰρ τὸν Πυθαγόραν δι᾽ ἀπορρήτων Ἅιδην τὸν γαλαξίαν καὶ τόπον ψυχῶν ἀποκαλεῖν, ὡς ἐκεῖ συνωθουμένων· διὸ παρά τισιν ἔθνεσιν γάλα σπένδεσθαι τοῖς θεοῖς, τοῖς τῶν ψυχῶν καθάρταις καὶ τῶν πεσουσῶν εἰς γένεσιν εἶναι γάλα τὴν πρώτην τροφήν.

Proclus places these theories under the authority of Numenius. Porphyry's *Commentary on the Republic* must be the intermediary, rather than the *De regressu animae*, as Cumont thought, "Comment Plotin détourna Porphyre du suicide," *REG* 32 (1919) 119 n. 4 and 120.

[40] *In Somn.* 1.3.17–18, p. 477, 10, referring to *Odyssey* 19.560; against Schrader, ed. Porphyry's *Quaestiones*, p. 352, Mras, "Macrobius' Kommentar," p. 238 and n. 3, thinks that the reference is to the *Quaestiones* and not to the Περὶ τῆς Ὁμήρου φιλοσοφίας. But he concludes somewhat impulsively that the classification of the dreams by Macrobius *In Somn.* 1.3.2–4 derives also from this. Schedler, *Die Philosophie des Macrobius*, p. 85 n. 6, associates this classification with Porphyry's commentary on the *Timaeus*; but the terminology of Chalcidius *In Timaeum* 254 is quite different. I am inclined to believe rather that the source is the commentary on the *Republic*, for Macrobius connects this treatment, p. 476, 28, with the episode of Agamemnon's dream (he even translates freely *Iliad* 2.80–82), on which cf. n. 38. Cf. Artemidorus *Onirocriticon libri V*, ed. R. Hercher (1864) 1.2, which is certainly not Macrobius' direct source, and Servius *In Aen.* 6.284: "Qui de somniis scripserunt dicunt quo tempore folia de arboribus cadunt, vana esse somnia . . . vana autem ideo, quia ab inferis; nam vera mittunt superi. Homerus: καὶ γάρ τ᾽ ὄναρ ἐκ Διός ἐστιν [*Iliad* 1.63]." This Servian text and the text quoted in n. 42 do not exclude the possibility that Porphyry discussed dreams both in his *Commentary on the Republic* and in his *Quaestiones Homericae*.

[41] Servius *In Aen.* 5.735, p. 645, 1: "Secundum philosophos elysium est insulae fortunatae, quas ait Sallustius inclitas esse Homeri carminibus, quarum descriptionem Porphyrius commentator dicit esse sublatam." Schrader, ed. Porphyry's *Quaestiones*, p. 353, considers this passage corrupt and does not think that it stems from the *Quaestiones Homericae* but from the Περὶ Στυγός.

and makes very precise reference to the passage on the two gates of heaven, which was certainly well known.[42]

Only the Pythagorean considerations on the properties of number, which constitute chapters 5 and 6, seem to derive, not from Iamblichus' commentary on the *Timaeus*, as Borghorst thinks,[43] nor from Porphyry's commentary on the *Timaeus*, as Mras believes, with less probability,[44] but rather from a Latin commentator. To speak frankly, it is difficult to decide with complete certainty, for these elementary theories, whose remote source was probably Posidonius, passed into the Greek and Latin teaching handbooks. Fries and Praechter, however, thought they discerned two traditions, the tradition of Theon of Smyrna and Chalcidius, which went back to Posidonius through Adrastus as intermediary, and the tradition of Aulus Gellius, Macrobius, Censorinus, Favonius Eulogius, and Martianus Capella, which went back to Posidonius through Varro[45] as intermediary. But even with this hypothesis, which seems to me the most tenable, the Greek quotation and the commentary on the *Golden Verses*[47] of Pythagoras are borrowed by Macrobius from Porphyry's *Life of Pythagoras*,[46] which Mras had previously noted somewhat

---

[42] Macrobius *In Somn.* 1.3.17, p. 477, 11:

Si quis quaerere velit cur porta ex ebore falsis et e cornu veris sit deputata, instruetur auctore Porphyrio qui in commentariis suis haec in eundem locum dicit ab Homero sub eadem divisione descriptum.

Servius *In Aen.* 6.893, p. 122, 21:

Sunt geminae somni portae, pro somniorum. Est autem in hoc loco Homerum secutus ... Physiologia vero hoc habet: per portam corneam oculi significantur, qui et cornei sunt coloris et duriores ceteris membris ... per eburneam vero portam os significatur a dentibus. Et scimus quia quae loquimur falsa esse possunt, ea vero quae videmus sine dubio vera sunt ... et qui de somniis scripserunt dicunt ea quae secundum fortunam et personae possibilitatem videntur habere effectum.

It will be observed that Macrobius connects this Homeric passage also with the passage from Vergil, from which he quotes (p. 474, 10) *Aen.* 6.897. *Fabula* 228 of the first of the *mythographi Vaticani*, ed. Bode, *Script. Rer. Myth.* (Cellis 1834) p. 70, merely plagiarizes Servius. On the theory of the two gates of heaven, cf. Cumont, *Recherches sur le symbolisme funéraire*, p. 201 n. 1.

[43] Borghorst, *De Anatolii fontibus*, p. 43.

[44] Mras, "Macrobius' Kommentar," pp. 238–250.

[45] C. Fries, "De M. Varrone a Favonio Eulogio Expresso," *Rheinisches Museum* 58 (1903) 115–125, and K. Praechter, "Eine Stelle Varros zur Zahlentheorie," *Hermes* 46 (1911) 407–413.

[46] Porphyry *Vita Pyth.* 20, ed. A. Westermann, p. 91, 42:

Διόπερ ἔν τι τῶν παρ᾽ αὐτοῖς ἐν τοῖς μαθήμασι ἀπορρήτων προχειρισάμενοι, γλαφυρὸν ἄλλως τε καὶ πρὸς πολλὰ διατεῖνον φυσικὰ συντελέσματα, τὴν

Macrobius *In Somn.* 1.6.41, p. 493, 2:

Quaternarium quidem Pythagorei quem τετρακτύν vocant adeo quasi ad perfectionem animae pertinentem inter *arcana* venerantur, ut *ex eo* et *iuris iurandi* religionem sibi fecerint: οὐ μὰ τὸν ἁμετέρᾳ

uncertainly as the source of several other passages in Macrobius on the harmony of the spheres.[47]

Macrobius then develops at great length his beliefs in the soul and in suicide. Cumont thinks that this theory of suicide is borrowed from Porphyry's *De regressu animae*.[48] Father Henry feels, on the other hand, that Macrobius takes it directly from the *Enneads*.[49] In my opinion, Father Henry has successfully demonstrated that the passage from Eunapius cited by Cumont does not prove the existence of a special commentary by Porphyry on Plotinus' treatise *On Suicide*.[50] Macrobius had in front of him the text of Plotinus on suicide; but in the treatment itself, which is drawn from Plotinus, he intrudes personal comments that stem from another source.[51] A textual parallel with the *De civitate Dei* confirms, I believe without any possible doubt, Cumont's hypothesis according to which Macrobius followed the *De regressu animae* and interpreted Plotinus' text in the light of the Porphyrian theories:

Macrobius *In Somn. Scip.* 1.13.15, p. 526, 16:

Hanc quoque superioribus adicit (Plotinus) rationem non sponte pereundi. Cum constet, inquit, remunerationem animis illic esse tribuendam pro modo perfectionis ad quam in hac vita una quaeque pervenit, non est praecipitandus vitae finis cum adhuc proficiendi esse possit accessio. Nec frustra hoc dictum est. Nam in arcanis De Animae Reditu disputationibus fertur *in hac vita* delinquentes similes esse super aequale solum cadenti-

$\lambda\epsilon\gamma o\mu\acute{\epsilon}\nu\eta\nu$ $\tau\epsilon\tau\rho\alpha\kappa\tau\acute{\nu}\nu$, $\delta\iota'$ $\alpha\mathring{\upsilon}\tau\hat{\eta}s$ $\mathring{\epsilon}\pi\acute{\omega}\mu$-$\nu\upsilon o\nu$ $\mathring{\omega}s$ $\theta\epsilon\acute{o}\nu$ $\tau\iota\nu\alpha$ $\tau\mathring{o}\nu$ $\Pi\upsilon\theta\alpha\gamma\acute{o}\rho\alpha\nu$, $\mathring{\epsilon}\pi\iota\phi\theta\epsilon\gamma\gamma\acute{o}\mu\epsilon\nu o\iota$ $\pi\acute{\alpha}\nu\tau\epsilon s$ $\mathring{\epsilon}\pi\grave{\iota}$ $\pi\hat{\alpha}\sigma\iota$ $\tauο\hat{\iota}s$ $\mathring{\upsilon}\pi'$ $\alpha\mathring{\upsilon}\tau\hat{\omega}\nu$ $\beta\epsilon\beta\alpha\iota o\upsilon\mu\acute{\epsilon}\nu o\iota s$: $o\mathring{\upsilon}$ $\mu\grave{\alpha}$ $\tau\mathring{o}\nu$ $\mathring{\alpha}\mu\epsilon\tau\acute{\epsilon}\rho\alpha$ $\psi\upsilon\chi\hat{\alpha}$ $\pi\alpha\rho\alpha\delta\acute{o}\nu\tau\alpha$ $\tau\epsilon\tau\rho\alpha\kappa\tau\acute{\nu}\nu$.

Augustine *De civ. Dei* 10.29.1, *PL* 41, 307, addressing Porphyry:

Itaque videtis utcumque, etsi de longinquo, etsi acie caligante, patriam in qua manendum est, sed viam qua eundum est non tenetis. Confiteris tamen gratiam, quandoquidem ad Deum per virtutem intellegentiae pervenire paucis dicis esse concessum. Non enim dicis: Paucis placuit, vel: Pauci voluerunt, sed cum dicis esse *concessum*, procul dubio Dei gratiam, non hominis sufficientiam confiteris. *Uteris* etiam hoc verbo apertius,

$\psi\upsilon\chi\hat{\alpha}$ $\pi\alpha\rho\alpha\delta\acute{o}\nu\tau\alpha$ $\tau\epsilon\tau\rho\alpha\kappa\tau\acute{\nu}\nu$ *per qui nostrae animae numerum dedit ipse quaternum.*

Extended treatment of this interpretation will be found in Hierocles' commentary on the *Golden Verses*, ed. Muellach, *Fragm. philos. Graec.*, vol. 1, pp. 462ff. This commentary is slightly posterior to Macrobius.

[47] Mras, "Macrobius' Kommentar," pp. 264 and 268.

[48] Cumont, "Comment Plotin détourna Porphyre du suicide," pp. 113–120.

[49] Henry, *Plotin et l'Occident*, pp. 173–180.

[50] *Ibid.*, p. 167, opposing Cumont, "Comment Plotin détourna Porphyre du suicide," p. 113, shows that the passage from Eunapius refers to the $\Pi\epsilon\rho\grave{\iota}$ $\epsilon\mathring{\upsilon}\delta\alpha\iota\mu o\nu\acute{\iota}\alpha s$ and not to the $\Pi\epsilon\rho\grave{\iota}$ $\mathring{\epsilon}\xi\alpha\gamma\omega\gamma\hat{\eta}s$.

[51] Henry, *Plotin et l'Occident*, p. 179. The statements are as follows: 1.3.9, "Ergo etsi ante fuit"; 1.13.10, "Et re vera ideo sic extortae animae"; 1.13.12, "Hinc illud est doctissimi vatis"; 1.13.15, "Nam in arcanis de animae reditu disputationibus."

bus, quibus denuo sine difficultate praesto sit surgere; animas vero ex hac vita cum delictorum sordibus recedentes aequandas his qui in abruptum ex alto praecipitique delapsi sint, unde numquam facultas sit resurgendi. Ideo ergo *utendum concessis vitae spatiis ut sit perfectae purgationis* maior facultas.

ubi Platonis sententiam sequens nec ipse dubitas *in hac vita* hominem nullo modo ad *perfectionem* sapientiae pervenire, secundum intellectum tamen viventibus omne quod deest providentia Dei et gratia post hanc vitam posse compleri.

De civ. Dei 30, *PL* 41, 311:

Si enim quod *perfecte* mundantur (animae) hoc efficit, ut omnium obliviscantur malorum . . . profecto erit . . . immunditiae causa summa mundatio . . . Vidit hoc Porphyrius *purgatamque* animam ob hoc reverti dixit ad Patrem, ne aliquando iam malorum polluta contagione teneatur.

Macrobius' design is quite different from Augustine's. The former uses Porphyry to condemn suicide, while the latter uses him to prove Grace. But they refer to the same page of Porphyry's *De regressu animae*, according to which the prolongation of our life in this world (*in hac vita*) is a gift of God (*concessum*), intended to allow us to achieve perfect purification (*perfecta purgatio*).[52]

Cumont, therefore, was quite justified in stressing the Porphyrian tone of Macrobius' thought, even while he quoted Plotinus: while Plotinus was satisfied with noting that the soul of a suicide retains something corporeal, Macrobius, following Porphyry, postulates that this soul remains settled in the corpse and around the tomb.[53] He intentionally omits Plotinus' expression that permits the suicide of a philosopher in certain exceptional circumstances, for he follows Porphyry's doctrine that condemns suicide in every case.[54] There is another point. I am not at all convinced by Father Henry that Macrobius read in Plato himself sections of the *Phaedo* relating to suicide. Despite the parallels established by Father Henry,[55] I think that Macrobius here follows a commentator on the *Phaedo*. Probably the difficulty resulting from the apparent contradiction between these two affirmations: *the philosopher must seek death*, yet *suicide is forbidden*, derives directly from the *Phaedo*.[56] But it was the commentator who would have distinguished the two kinds of

[52] Did Macrobius read this work by Porphyry in the translation by Marius Victorinus, as Augustine did? The title *De reditu animae* inclines one to believe that he did not, for Augustine calls it *De regressu animae*.

[53] Texts quoted by Cumont, "Comment Plotin détourna Porphyre du suicide," p. 115 n. 2. It should not be forgotten that the statement "et re vera" is a personal insertion on Macrobius' part from Porphyry; cf. Henry, *Plotin et l'Occident*, p. 177.

[54] Cumont, "Comment Plotin détourna Porphyre du suicide," p. 115.

[55] Henry, *Plotin et l'Occident*, pp. 170–172.

[56] *Phaedo* 67e and 80e on the philosophy μελέτη θανάτου; cf. on suicide:

death. Physical death is a fact of nature. Spiritual death is a fact of virtue. The latter must be sought, while the former must be left to divine discretion. Father Henry contends that Porphyry's *Sentence* quoted by Cumont is not Macrobius' direct source, because the symmetry is not the same in both.[57] But Cumont never made any such claim. He quotes this *Sentence* merely to give an idea of Porphyry's doctrine and thinks that actually Macrobius borrows this quotation of the *Phaedo*, not from the *Sententiae*, but either from Porphyry's commentary on the *Phaedo* or rather from the *De regressu animae*.[58] The very expression "physical death" that recurs constantly in this chapter of Macrobius, in contradistinction to "spiritual death," is Porphyrian[59] and does not appear in these pages of the *Phaedo*. For to Plato, as Cumont well says, "virtue that frees from passion does not bring an anticipated death, but is only a preparation for death."[60] Hence Macrobius certainly quotes the *Phaedo* in line with an interpretation by Porphyry, and the context leads us to think of the *De regressu animae*. Now a parallel between Augustine and Claudianus Mamertus will confirm that, in fact, in the *De regressu animae*, Porphyry commented at great length on those sections of the *Phaedo* and even quoted extensive textual extracts therefrom.[61] Father Henry could not believe that Macrobius did not have before him the text of the *Phaedo* itself. In my judgment, he did have right before him entire sections of the *Phaedo*, but quoted in the *De regressu animae* and furnished with the Porphyrian commentary. It would not be surprising if the disagreement between Father Henry and Cumont on the subject of the quotation from Plotinus' treatise *On Suicide* is explained in the same way. Cumont insists on the Porphyrian tone, Father Henry on the Plotinian literalness of the quotation from Plotinus taken by Macrobius. The fact is probably that the *De regressu animae* contained, following the excerpts from the *Phaedo*,

---

Phaedo 61d:

Πῶς τοῦτο λέγεις, ὦ Σώκρατες, τὸ μὴ θεμιτὸν εἶναι ἑαυτὸν βιάζεσθαι, ἐθέλειν δ' ἂν τῷ ἀποθνῄσκοντι τὸν φιλόσοφον ἕπεσθαι;

67e: οἱ ὀρθῶς φιλοσοφοῦντες ἀποθνῄσκειν μελετῶσιν.

Macrobius *In Somn.* 1.13.5, p. 524, 9:
Haec secta et praeceptio Platonis est qui in *Phaedone* definit homini non esse sua sponte moriendum. Sed in eodem tamen dialogo idem dicit mortem philosophantibus adpetendam et ipsam meditationem esse moriendi. Haec ergo sibi contraria videntur, sed non ita est.

These similarities should have been noted by Henry, *Plotin et l'Occident*, p. 170.

[57] Henry, *Plotin et l'Occident*, p. 173.

[58] Cumont, "Comment Plotin détourna Porphyre du suicide," p. 115 n. 1 and p. 116.

[59] Porphyry *Sententiae* 8: φύσις λύει σῶμα ἐκ ψυχῆς. Cf. *In Somn.* 1.13, p. 524, 19 natura; 21 naturae; 29 natura; 30 naturam; 525, 29 naturalem; 530, 6 naturalis; 10 natura. It will be observed that this expression, which is not Plotinian, reappears in Macrobius' text even in the passages where he quotes Plotinus.

[60] Cumont, "Comment Plotin détourna Porphyre du suicide," p. 114.

[61] See my demonstration, below, pp. 242ff.

extracts from Plotinus' treatise *On Suicide* and commented on them. It is certain that Macrobius' doctrine on the soul is primarily Porphyrian, and it will be observed that Servius too interprets the episode of the descent of Aeneas into Hades in the light of the theories in the *De regressu animae*.[62]

Must we then believe with Cumont that Macrobius' earlier chapters on the soul also came from the *De regressu animae*? Yet Macrobius himself seems to indicate different sources.[63] The naturalistic interpretation of the infernal myths, which Macrobius asserts to be prior to Neoplatonism, is an interpretation that Porphyry in the Περὶ Στυγός declares as being from Apollodorus:

Porphyry Περὶ Στυγός, *apud* Stobaeus *Ecl.* 1.41.50, ed. Meineke, vol. 1, p. 307, 51:
Τοῦ δὲ Ἀπολλοδώρου ἐν τῷ εἰκοστῷ περὶ τῶν θεῶν συγγράμματι, ὅ ἐστι περὶ τοῦ ᾅδου, τάδε περὶ τῆς Στυγὸς λεγόμενα εὕρομεν . . . ἐκ γὰρ τοιούτων ὁρμημένοι πιθανῶς καὶ τοὺς ἐν ᾅδου νομιζομένους ποταμοὺς κατωνομάκασιν· Ἀχέροντα μὲν διὰ τὰ ἄχη . . . Στύγα δὲ . . . ἀπὸ τοῦ στυγνάζειν τοῖς πένθεσι καὶ στύγεσθαι τὰ ἐν ᾅδου . . . Κωκυτὸν δὲ ποταμὸν ἀνέπλασαν ἀπὸ τοῦ κωκύειν, ὅς ἐστι Στυγὸς καὶ στυγνάσεως ἀπορρώξ· τοιούτου δέ ἐστι γένους καὶ ὁ Πυριφλεγέθων· εἴρηται γὰρ ἀπὸ τοῦ πυρὶ φλέγεσθαι τοὺς τελευτῶντας.

Macrobius *In Somn.* 1.10.9, p. 513, 25:
Antequam studium philosophiae circa naturae inquisitionem ad tantum vigoris adolesceret, qui per diversas gentes auctores constituendis sacris caerimoniarum fuerunt, aliud esse inferos negaverunt quam ipsa corpora . . . (p. 514, 8): pari interpretatione Phlegethontem ardores irarum et cupiditatis putarunt, Acherontem quicquid fecisse dixisseve usque ad tristitiam humanae varietatis more nos paenitet, Cocytum quicquid homines in luctum lacrimasque compellit, Stygem quicquid inter se humanos animos in gurgitem mergit odiorum.[64]

In the second part of the same exposition, Macrobius passes from Apollo-

---

[62] Servius *In Aen.* 6.136, ed. Thilo, vol. 2, p. 30, 9: "sub imagine fabularum docet rectissimam vitam, per quam animabus ad superos datur *regressus*." *In Aen.* 6.137, p. 30, 26: "*de reditu* autem *animae* hoc est: novimus Pythagoram Samium vitam humanam divisisse in modum Y litterae, scilicet quod prima aetas incerta sit, quippe quae adhuc se nec vitiis nec virtutibus dedit . . . ergo per ramum virtutes dicit esse sectandas, qui est Y litterae imitatio: quem ideo in silvis dicit latere, quia re vera in huius vitae confusione et maiore parte vitiorum virtus et integritas latet" (on Y as a Neopythagorean symbol, cf. below, chap. 2 sec. 2 n. 63). *In Aen.* 6.128, p. 28, 5: "quod autem dicit: 'patet atri ianua Ditis, Sed revocare gradum superasque evadere ad auras, Hoc opus, hic labor est,' aut poetice dictum est aut secundum philosophorum altam scientiam; qui deprehenderunt bene viventium animas ad superiores circulos, id est ad originem suam *redire*." Macrobius also connected the Porphyrian theory of suicide with the Neoplatonic commentary on Vergil on the subject of the death of Deiphobus. Cf. *In Somn.* 1.13.12, p. 526, 4, and Servius *In Aen.* 6.545, p. 77, 20.

[63] *In Somn.* 1.13.5, p. 524, 15: "nec hoc nunc repeto, quod superius dictum est duas esse mortes, unam animae, animalis alteram," with reference to 1.11.1, p. 516, 1.

[64] Cf. Servius *In Aen.* 6.1.32, p. 28, 24: "Cocytus . . . dictus ἀπὸ τοῦ κωκύειν, id est lugere: nam Homerus [*Odyssey* 10.514] sic posuit . . ." *In Aen.* 6.134, p. 29, 20: "Styx maerorem significat, unde ἀπὸ τοῦ στυγεροῦ, id est tristitia, Styx dicta est."

dorus' interpretation to the various Neoplatonic interpretations[65] and adopts the one that conceives the soul as descending into the Lower Regions through nine circles.[66] This is the same interpretation that Favonius Eulogius and Servius apply to the verse in the *Aeneid* on the ninefold Styx.[67] Also, contrary to Cumont, who without serious reason refers the entire exposition to the *De regressu animae*, I believe that the borrowings from the *De regressu animae* are restricted to Macrobius' theories on the return of the soul (1.13); but for the descent of the soul into the Lower Regions (1.10–12) Macrobius is inspired by the Περὶ Στυγός. He connects the two treatises with the aid of details borrowed from still other works by Porphyry: the *De antro nympharum*,[68] the commentaries on the *Republic*,[69] the *Timaeus*,[70] the *Phaedo*.[71]

---

[65] *In Somn.* 1.11.1, p. 515, 28: "dicendum est quid his postea veri sollicitior inquisitor philosophiae cultus adiecerit."

[66] *Ibid.*, 1.11.4, p. 516, 22: "Inferos autem Platonici non in corporibus esse, id est non a corporibus incipere dixerunt, sed certam mundi partem Ditis sedem, id est inferos, vocaverunt." Cumont, *Les religions orientales*, p. 301 n. 28, makes a fine analysis of the origin of the three types of Platonic interpretations and shows that Macrobius joins forces with Numenius, whom he must have known through Porphyry and who must be the mediate source of his entire interpretation. Cf. also Cumont's *Recherches sur le symbolisme funéraire*, p. 41.

[67] Favonius Eulogius *In Somn.*, p. 13, 32:

Ex quo mihi videtur Maro doctissimus Romanorum dixisse illud [*Aen.* 6.439]: *Novies Stix interfusa coërcet.* Terra enim nona est, ad quam Stix illa protenditur: mystice ac Platonica dictum esse sapientia non ignores. Nam poetica libertate inserit fontanae animae a caelo usque in terras esse decursum. Nam sub pedibus summi patris, qui dissaepit (hinc dicitur πηγαία), Stix posita per omnes circulos fluit, imponens singulis velut in curru aurigam, id est vitae substantiam, ex qua cuncta viventia originem sortiuntur, et eidem soluta redduntur; manatque illa[s] per cunctos volentes commisceri, quod ex natura sunt hiulci; interiectu sui vigoris separat, et, quod ipse mire Vergilius loquitur, *coërcet*, ut sui generis momenta conservent. Inter caelum et terram novem intervalla ipse consideres licet.

Servius *In Aen.* 6.439, p. 66, 25:

Novies Styx interfusa quia qui altius de mundi ratione quaesiverunt, dicunt intra novem hos mundi circulos inclusas esse virtutes, in quibus et iracundiae sunt et cupiditates, de quibus tristitia nascitur, id est Styx, unde dicit novem esse circulos Stygis, quae inferos cingit, id est terram, ut diximus supra [6.127]: nam dicunt alias esse purgatiores extra hos circulos potestates.

In Aen. 6.127, p. 27, 19:

ergo hanc terram in qua vivimus inferos esse voluerunt, quia est omnium circulorum infima, planetarum scilicet septem Saturni, Iovis, Martis, Solis, Veneris, Mercurii, Lunae et duorum magnorum. Hinc est quod habemus [6.439]: *et novies Styx interfusa coërcet*: nam novem circulis cingitur terra.

[68] Macrobius *In Somn.* 1.12.1–2, ending on p. 519, 19 with the words, "et hoc est quod Homeri divina prudentia in antri Itachesii descriptione significat," referring to Porphyry *De antro nympharum* 28, ed. Hercher, p. 96, 16. Cf. Mras, "Macrobius' Kommentar," p. 255, who notes, p. 264, yet another textual parallel between Macrobius *In Somn.* 1.21.24–26 and Porphyry *De antro nympharum* 22.

For notes 69, 70, and 71, see next page.

These chapters on the soul, then, do not follow the *De regressu animae* exclusively. They seem rather like a mosaic whose Porphyrian motif is the cement. The only passage, apart from chapter 13, that may perhaps refer to the *De regressu animae*, appears in the following chapter. Macrobius, before leaving his source on the soul in order to pass on to the astronomical theories, is anxious to list the definitions of the soul as suggested by the various philosophers.[72] This dry nomenclature might well be derived from the *De regressu animae*, where Claudianus Mamertus found likewise, as we shall see, a catalogue of definitions of the soul, intended to prove its incorporeal character.[73]

[69] Texts quoted in n. 39.

[70] Macrobius *In Somn.* 1.12.14 and Proclus *In Timaeum*, ed. Diehl, vol. 3, p. 355, 13. Cf. Mras, "Macrobius' Kommentar," p. 256. Other texts relating to the qualities that the soul, on becoming incorporated in the body, acquires in succession are quoted by Cumont, "La théologie solaire du paganisme romain," *Mémoires présentés . . . à l'Acad. des Inscr. et Belles-Lettres* 12, 2 (1913) 464 n. 1.

[71] Olympiodorus *In Phaedon* 62b, ed. Norvin (Leipzig 1913) p. 84, 21:

"Ὅτι τούτοις χρώμενοι τοῖς κανόσι ῥᾳδίως διελέγξομεν, ὡς οὔτε τἀγαθόν ἐστιν ἡ φρουρά, ὡς τινες, οὔτε ἡ ἡδονή, ὡς Νουμήνιος, οὔτε ὁ δημιουργός, ὡς Πατέριος, ἀλλ' ὡς Ξενοκράτης, Τιτανική ἐστιν καὶ εἰς Διόνυσον ἀποκρυφοῦται. Οὕτω δὲ καὶ Πορφύριος προυπενόησεν ἐν τῷ ὑπομνήματι.

"Ὅτι οὔσης διττῆς δημιουργίας, ἢ ἀμερίστου ἢ μεμερισμένης, ταύτης μὲν προεστάναι φησὶ τὸν Διόνυσον, διὸ μερίζεσθαι.

p. 85, 22 . . . διὸ καὶ ἀμέριστος ἅμα καὶ μεριστός . . . Διὰ τί λέγονται οἱ Τιτᾶνες ἐπιβουλεύειν τῷ Διονύσῳ;

Macrobius *In Somn.* 1.12.7, p. 520, 20:

Anima ergo cum trahitur ad corpus, in hac prima sui productione silvestrem tumultum id est ὕλην influentem sibi incipit experiri. Et hoc est quod Plato notavit in *Phaedone* animam in corpus trahi nova ebrietate trepidantem, volens novum potum materialis adluvionis intellegi quo delibuta et gravata deducitur. Arcani huius indicium est et Crater Liberi patris ille sidereus in regione quae inter Cancrum est et Leonem locatus . . .

1.12.12, p. 521, 21: ipsum autem Liberum patrem Orphaici νοῦν ὑλικόν suspicantur intellegi, qui ab illo individuo natus in singulos ipse dividitur, ideo in illorum sacris traditur Titanio furore in membra discerptus et frustis sepultis rursus unus et integer emersisse quia νοῦς quem diximus mentem vocari, ex individuo praebendo se dividendum et rursus ex diviso ad individuum revertendo et mundi implet officia et naturae suae arcana non deserit.

[72] *In Somnium* 1.14.19, p. 531, 17: "non abs re est ut haec de anima disputatio in fine sententias omnium qui de anima videntur pronuntiasse contineat. Plato dixit animam essentiam se moventem, Xenocrates numerum se moventem, Aristoteles ἐντελέχειαν, Pythagoras et Philolaus harmoniam . . . obtinuit tamen non minus de incorporalitate eius quam de immortalitate sententia. Nunc videamus quae sint haec duo nomina quorum pariter meminit (Cicero) cum dicit: *quae sidera et stellas vocatis . . .*"

[73] Cf. below, at chap. 5 sec. 2 n. 63. Mras, "Macrobius' Kommentar," p. 259, could

At the end of his book, Macrobius returns again to the soul, with regard to a passage in the *Phaedo* translated by Cicero. According to this, the soul is αὐτοκίνητον;[74] but the academic tone is quite different from the mystical tone of the chapters that have just been studied. Macrobius defends this maxim against Aristotle, who considers the soul immobile by nature, as if it merely transmitted the motion that it receives from the first mover. He does not hesitate to reproduce the Neoplatonic argument.[75] Schedler has already shown that the formulas attributed to Aristotle are a late schema of the Aristotelian theories. He suggests as the source Porphyry's Περὶ ψυχῆς πρὸς Βόηθον, which treated precisely this subject, but he considers that the few fragments preserved by Eusebius are far from conclusive.[76] Mras, on the contrary, believes that these fragments confirm Schedler's hypothesis.[77] In point of fact, at least one of these fragments is the basis of a textual paraphrase by Macrobius.[78] Macrobius thus certainly preserves here the substance of the lost book by Porphyry. We know that he possessed most of Porphyry's books on the soul and that he had steeped his mind in them.

---

not determine the source of this catalogue. The numerous references to the doxographers that Schedler notes, *Die Philosophie des Macrobius*, pp. 36–39, give no solution to the precise question of the direct source.

[74] *In Somnium* 2.13–16.

[75] *Ibid.*, 2.15.2, p. 625, 10: "neque vero tam immemor mei aut ita male animatus sum, ut ex ingenio meo vel Aristoteli resistam vel adsim Platoni, sed ut quisque magnorum virorum qui se Platonicos dici gloriabantur aut singula aut bina defensa ad ostentationem suorum operum reliquerunt, conlecta haec in unum continuae defensionis corpus coacervavi adiecto siquid post illos aut sentire fas erat aut audere in intellectum licebat." Cf. p. 636, 22: "dicit *aliquis.*" Macrobius thus acknowledges that he has several Neoplatonic sources for this exposition. Apart from Porphyry, Mras, "Macrobius' Kommentar," p. 277, is right in connecting *In Somnium* 2.16.23 with Plotinus *Enneads* 3.8.10.

[76] Schedler, *Die Philosophie des Macrobius*, pp. 54 n. 1, 64 n. 3, 65 n. 1.

[77] Mras, "Macrobius' Kommentar," pp. 276–278.

[78] Porphyry Περὶ ψυχῆς, *apud* Eusebius *Praep. evang.* 15.11, PG 21, 1336 B:

Τὸ δὲ βαρύτητι ἀπεικάζειν τὴν ψυχὴν ἢ ποιότησι μονοειδέσι καὶ ἀκινήτοις σωματικαῖς, καθ᾽ ἃς ἢ κινεῖται ἢ ποιόν ἐστι τὸ ὑποκείμενον, ἐκπεπτωκότος ἦν . . . καὶ οὐδαμῶς καθεωρακότος, ὡς παρουσίᾳ μὲν τῆς ψυχῆς ζωτικὸν γέγονε τὸ τοῦ ζῴου σῶμα, ὡς πυρὸς παρουσίᾳ θερμὸν τὸ παρακείμενον ὕδωρ, ψυχρὸν ὂν καθ᾽ ἑαυτό . . . Ἀλλ᾽ οὔτε ἡ θερμότης τοῦ ὕδατος ἡ θερμότης ἦν τοῦ πυρός, οὔτε τὸ πῦρ . . . Ὡσαύτως οὐδὲ ἡ τοῦ σώματος ἐμψυχία, ἥτις ἔοικε τῇ βαρύτητι καὶ τῇ περὶ σῶμα ποιότητι, ἡ ψυχὴ ἡ ἐν

Macrobius *In Somn.* 2.15.6, p. 626, 1:

Plato enim cum dicit animam ex se moveri, id est cum αὐτοκίνητον vocat, non vult eam inter ea numerari quae ex se quidem videntur moveri, sed a causa quae intra se latet moventur ut moventur *animalia* auctore quidem alio, sed occulto, nam *ab anima* moventur . . . Sed Plato ita animam dicit ex se moveri, ut non aliam causam vel extrinsecus accidentem vel interius latentem huius motus dicat auctorem. Hoc quem ad modum accipiendum sit instruemus. *Ignem calidum* vocamus, *sed* et ferrum *calidum dicimus* . . . *Horum tamen singula de diversis diversa significant.* Aliter enim de igne, aliter de ferro calidi nomen accipi-

The rest of Macrobius' commentary deals particularly with astronomical problems, but his principal source is still one of Porphyry's works: this is the commentary on the *Timaeus*. He expressly acknowledges that he borrows from it his exposition on the distances that separate the planets from each other and the position that the sun occupies among them.[79] Following Porphyry, Macrobius makes the mistake of attributing to Archimedes the origin of the geocentric system that reckons the sun as fourth in the series of seven planets, and he rejects this system in the name of Plato, while granting the sun a position much closer to the earth, immediately above the moon.[80] It is futile to emphasize all that Macrobius owes to this commentary. Frequently he adopts the very form of a commentary on the *Timaeus*, when translating a long extract that he then paraphrases. The influence of the commentary on the *Timaeus* is so evident that Linke's old theory made it Macrobius' sole source. Mras reduced this influence to more correct proportions. Probably it has still to be reduced, for such a treatment, which Mras considers to have stemmed from this commentary, surely has the same source as the solar theology of the *Saturnalia*.[81] It is no less true that Macrobius' astronomy proceeds from the *Timaeus* commented on by Porphyry. The only scientific work that he appears to have read personally is Ptolemy's *Harmonica*, unless he quotes it from the commentary that Porphyry had written on this subject.[82]

τῷ σώματι καταταχθεῖσα, δι' ἣν καὶ πνοῆς τινος ζωτικῆς μετέσχε τὸ σῶμα ... ἐπὶ δὲ τῷ λέγοντι αὐτοκίνητον οὐσίαν οὐκ ἄν τις, φησίν, αἰσχυνθείη.

mus, quia ignis per se calet, non ab alio fit calidus, contra ferrum non nisi ex alio calescit ... *Sic* et stare et moveri tam de his dicitur, quae ab se vel stant vel moventur, quam de illis quae vel sistuntur vel agitantur ab alio ... *Ab se ergo movetur anima* ... Anima ergo ita per se movetur ut ignis per se calet.

[79] *In Somnium* 2.3.13–15, ending with the words, p. 584, 25: "Hanc Platonicorum persuasionem Porphyrius libris inseruit quibus Timaei obscuritatibus nonnihil lucis infudit," repeating an explanation previously made, 1.20.9–13, where Eratosthenes, Posidonius, and the Egyptians were quoted, and 1.21.27, where Plato was quoted. Cf. Mras, "Macrobius' Kommentar," p. 261.

[80] Cf. Cumont, "La théologie solaire," p. 471 and n. 3.

[81] Cf. *In Somnium* 2.10.9–10, p. 607, 13, and *Saturnalia* 1.8.6, p. 39, 2, and 1.22.8, p. 124, 8. Cf. Mras, "Macrobius' Kommentar," pp. 269–270; this parallel, however, had previously been noted by Linke.

[82] *In Somnium* 1.19.20–26, p. 551, 1: "Causam si quis forte altius quaerat unde divinis malivolentia ut stella malefica esse dicatur, sicut de Martis et Saturni stellis existimatur, aut cur notabilior benignitas Iovis et Veneris inter genethliacos habeatur cum sit divinorum una natura, in medium proferam rationem apud unum omnino, quod sciam, lectam; nam Ptolomaeus in libris tribus quos *De harmonia* composuit patefecit causam quam breviter explicabo: certi, inquit, sunt numeri ..." It is impossible to verify this quotation, as it was borrowed from the lost ending of chap. 3.16 of Ptolemy's *Harmonica*.

It should be added, in order to form a comprehensive idea of Macrobius' Hellenic culture, that he is also interested in Greek and Latin comparative grammar. His *De differentiis et societatibus Graeci Latinique verbi* connects the teaching of Apollonius Dyscolus' ʹΡηματικόν with that of the Περὶ τῆς παρὰ ʹΡωμαίοις ἀναλογίας by Claudius Didymus.[83] His curiosity thus extends equally to the fields of grammar and of philology, and he takes pride in displaying his treasures before his Latin compatriots. In this respect, he was certainly a pioneer in the field of grammar and was to be followed a century later by Priscian.[84] On the other hand, Greek philological erudition was destined to disappear with paganism, for literary culture properly so called had no value in the eyes of Christians. Philology was not to survive except insofar as it was indispensable for exegesis on sacred texts.

Quite different was the fate of Neoplatonic philosophy. Macrobius is its most brilliant representative and shows the influence that it exerted on the minds of his generation. He read Plotinus, but the real master of his thought was Porphyry. He thinks through him. He reproduces his works, not through indolence as a compiler, but with the respect of an initiate. He can see no more effective way of commenting on Cicero than by applying to him Porphyry's commentary on Plato's *Republic*. When this commentary is not adequate enough to resolve the problems of a scientific nature that the *Somnium Scipionis* may pose, Macrobius resorts to Porphyry's commentary on the *Timaeus*. But above all his essential doctrine on the nature of the soul, and the mystery of human destiny is inspired by Porphyry's basic treatises. The Περὶ ψυχῆς defends against the Aristotelians the autonomy of the soul, which acts on its own motion. The Περὶ Στυγός reveals the secrets of its origin and the course of its fall into the body. The *De regressu animae* brings hope and indicates the means of returning to celestial bliss. The treatise *On the Sun* is the supreme revelation of the divine attributes that are the basis of pagan theodicy. Macrobius long studied these treatises that bear on the most profound subjects. Through his reading he assimilated Porphyry's cosmology, philosophy, and beliefs. But when the opportunity presents itself, he knows too where to draw additional information. The *Sententiae*, the *Homeric Questions*, the *Life of Pythagoras*, the *Cave of the Nymphs*, the commentary on the *Phaedo*, and possibly the commentary on Ptolemy's *Harmonica* allow him to lend precision to Porphyry's doctrine, even on points of detail, and to construct a sort of philosophical system. In fact, he makes light of Porphyry's

---

Porphyry's commentary, in its present state, does not go beyond *Harmonica* 2.7. Cf. I. Duering's edition (Göteberg 1932).

[83] Cf. Schanz, vol. 4, 2, p. 195, and Wessner, *PW* s.v. Macrobius, 197–198, repeating the conclusions of G. Uhlig, "Zu Apollonios Dyscolos," *Rheinisches Museum* 19 (1864) 41–48, qualified by G. F. C. Schoemann, *Commenta Macrobiana* (diss. Greifswald 1871).

[84] Cf. below, pp. 325ff.

evolution and renegations. He does not consider him as a recent philosopher. In his judgment the Porphyrian doctrine is the Truth, revealed and eternal, to which he attempts to subject his Latin culture. The *Somnium Scipionis* and Vergil's poems are interpreted in the light of the Porphyrian theories. In Macrobius' circle itself, Servius shows by his commentary on Vergil that he knows Porphyry's treatises *On the Sun, On the Styx, On the Return of the Soul,* and his *Homeric Questions.*

We touch upon an extremely complex problem, one that can be resolved only when the sources of Servius' commentary become the subject of a special, meticulous investigation. The best work that exists on this question, by Bitsch, is very confused and starts out with the conclusions that were discarded by Linke, according to which Macrobius plagiarized a single Latin source. However, the existence of Neoplatonic *Vergilian Questions,* composed on the model of Porphyry's *Homeric Questions,* and particularly numerous on Book 6 of the *Aeneid,* seems certain.[85] Must this be considered the common source for Macrobius and Servius? But it is impossible to believe that Macrobius did not read most of Porphyry's treatises directly from the text. Can it be said that Servius, like Macrobius, uses Porphyry at first hand? The idea is very improbable, for he merely compiles several Latin commentaries, one of which is this *Quaestiones Vergilianae.* There remains the hypothesis that Macrobius himself is the author of this *Quaestiones Vergilianae* from which Servius has drawn. When Macrobius refers to Vergil, he probably consulted some personal work, perhaps unpublished notes that his friend Servius might have consulted. The fact that Macrobius and Servius both use the same treatises by Porphyry, one directly, the other through a Latin intermediary, would thus be explained with even more exactitude than through the influence of the same environment.

Literary erudition and the study of the Greek philosophers furnished this last pagan generation, which did not dare make a frontal attack on Christianity triumphant, with arguments in support of the traditional mythology and the means of infusing new life into it. Solar theology, revived by Porphyry's treatise, even tempted Christians. Some of them, Leo the Great assures us, worshiped the rising sun on the very steps of St. Peter's in Rome, in the very middle of the fifth century.[86] The promises of immortality must have

---

[85] Cf. F. Bitsch, *De Platonicorum quaestionibus quibusdam Vergilianis,* pp. 8ff, and E. Norden, *P. Vergilius Maro Aeneis Buch VI* (2nd ed., Leipzig 1916) p. 26 n. 2.

[86] Leo the Great *Sermo* 27.14 *in Nativ. Domini* 7, PL 54, 218 C: "De talibus institutis etiam illa generatur impietas, ut sol in inchoatione diurnae lucis exsurgens a quibusdam insipientioribus de locis eminentioribus adoretur; quod non nulli etiam Christiani adeo se religiose facere putant, ut priusquam ad beati Petri apostoli basilicam quae uni Deo vivo et vero est dedicata, perveniant, superatis gradibus quibus ad suggestum areae superioris ascenditur, converso corpore ad nascentem se solem reflectant et curvatis cervicibus in honorem se splendidi orbis inclinent." Cf. *Sermo* 22.6 *in Nativ. Domini* 2, PL 54, 198.

affected many souls in quest of salvation. The attraction that these theories exercised on consciences is measured by the violence of St. Jerome's attacks on them. The death of the pontiff Praetextatus, consul designate, appears to him as the vengeance of the God of the Christians. No, asserts St. Jerome, Praetextatus is not in heaven, in the Milky Way, the paradise of the intellectuals, as his widow engraved on his tombstone.[87] He lies in the darkness of Tartarus;[88] for this rogue saw in religion nothing but a political device.[89] But the Neoplatonic passion with which his widow, the priestess of Ceres and Hecate, believes in the promises of eternity, wrings a cry of admiration from Jerome. He gives this faith as an example to his spiritual daughter Paula whom the death of her child had plunged into despair.[90]

[87] Jerome *Epist. ad Marcellam de exitu Leae* 23.3, *PL* 22, 426: "O quanta rerum mutatio! Ille, quem ante paucos dies dignitatum omnium culmina praecedebant, qui quasi de subiectis hostibus triumpharet, Capitolinas ascendit arces, quem plausu quodam et tripudio populus Romanus excepit, ad cuius interitum urbs universa commota est, nunc desolatus et nudus, *non in lacteo palatio, ut uxor mentitur infelix*, sed in sordentibus tenebris continetur." I see an allusion here to the inscription *CIL* 6, 1779, particularly to the lines quoted above, sec. 1 n. 6. On this theory of the Milky Way in Macrobius and Favonius Eulogius, cf. Cumont, *Les religions orientales*, p. 301 n. 29, and *Recherches sur le symbolisme funéraire*, p. 193 n. 1. For Martianus Capella, cf. below, at chap. 4 sec. 4 n. 75.

[88] Jerome *Epist. ad Marcellam* 23.2, *PL* 22, 426: "designatum consulem de suis socculis detrahentem esse doceamur in Tartaro."

[89] Jerome *Contra Ioann. Hieros.* 8, *PL* 23, 361 C: "Miserabilis Praetextatus, qui designatus consul est mortuus, homo sacrilegus et idolorum cultor, solebat ludens beato papae Damaso dicere: Facite me Romanae urbis episcopum et ero protinus Christianus."

[90] Jerome *Epist. ad Paulam super obitu Blaesillae* 39.3, *PL* 22, 469: "Erubesce, ethnicae comparatione superaris. Melior diaboli ancilla quam mea est. Illa infidelem maritum *translatum fingit in caelum*, tu mecum tuam filiam commorantem aut non credis aut non vis." Cf. *CIL* 6, 1779, especially line 23, "sorte mortis eximens," and the end:

> his nunc ademptis maesta coniunx maceror
> felix, maritum si superstitem mihi
> divi dedissent, sed tamen felix, tua
> quia sum fuique postque mortem ero.

Chapter 2

CHRISTIAN HELLENISM: ST. JEROME

In opposition to traditional Hellenism as represented by Macrobius, St. Jerome is the defender of a new Hellenism that developed in the shadow of the cross, and with which he made direct contact in the East. He is above all a translator and an exegete of the Holy Scriptures, a scholar who has been praised in successive centuries for his threefold culture: Hebraic, Greek, and Latin.[1]

I. JEROME AND THE GREEK LANGUAGE

Latin was his maternal tongue, since he was born at Stridon in Dalmatia. At an early age he came to Rome, where he attended the lectures of the famous *grammaticus* Donatus.[2] In all probability he also took courses with a Greek *grammaticus*, as the custom was,[3] in the elements of the Greek language. He himself alludes to the methods of this rudimentary instruction.[4] Following the course of liberal studies at Rome, he must then have received from the *rhetor* a veneer of classical Greek literature in order to be introduced to the art of oratory.[5] Despite several journeys, it was only in 373, at Antioch, that

[1] See *Sancta veterum testimonia de Hieronymo et eius scriptis*, Migne, *PL* 22, 213–232, and Schanz, vol. 4, 1, pp. 496–497. On St. Jerome's knowledge of the Greek language, several pages may be found in G. Bardy, "La culture grecque," pp. 31–35.

[2] Jerome *Adversus Rufinum* 1.16 (*PL* 23, 428 C).

[3] Cf. Marrou, *Saint Augustin et la fin de la culture antique*, p. 27.

[4] *In Ieremiam* 5.26 (*PL* 24, 838 D): "Sicut apud nos Graecum alphabetum usque ad novissimam litteram per ordinem legitur, hoc est: *Alpha, Betha* et cetera usque ad ω; rursumque propter memoriam parvulorum solemus lectionis ordinem invertere, et primis extrema miscere, ut dicamus: Alpha Ω, Betha Psi, sic et apud Hebraeos primum est Aleph."

[5] *Epist.* 48.13 *ad Pammachium* (*PL* 22, 502): "Legimus, eruditissimi viri, in scholis pariter; et Aristotelea illa vel de Gorgiae fontibus manantia, simul didicimus, plura esse videlicet genera dicendi: et inter cetera, aliud esse γυμναστικῶς scribere, aliud δογματι-κῶς." Cf. *Adv. Rufinum* 1.30 (*PL* 23, 441 C): "Miraris si ego litteras Latinas non sum oblitus, cum tu Graecas sine magistro didiceris? Septem modos conclusionum dialectica me elementa docuerunt: quid significet ἀξίωμα, quod nos *pronuntiatum* possumus dicere;

48

he made contacts with the countries where Greek was the native tongue.[6] He was probably gifted in languages but did not yet speak Greek fluently six years later, when he wrote, not without irony, to the priest Marcus, who was trying to make him leave the Chalcis desert: "Plane times ne eloquentissimus homo in Syro sermone vel Graeco Ecclesias circumeam, populos seducam, schisma conficiam."[7] It was apparently at Antioch that he was initiated into Aristotelian dialectic and read, in the traditional order, Porphyry's *Isagoge*, the *Categories*, the *De interpretatione*, the *Analytics*, the *Topics*, as well as Alexander of Aphrodisias' commentaries.[8] In particular, he attended the lectures on the Scriptures by Apollinaris of Laodicea.[9] After learning Hebrew in the Chalcis desert, he resumed the study of the Greek Fathers. In 381 he was Gregory of Nazianzus' pupil at Constantinople[10] and also associated with

---

quo modo absque verbo et nomine nulla sententia fit, soritarum gradus, pseudomeni argutias, sophismatum fraudes. Iurare possum me, postquam egressus de schola sum, haec numquam omnino legisse." The reference to *PL* vol. 23 will always be given in the 1865 edition, the pagination of which differs from the 1845 edition. My references for this chapter will denote Migne's *Patrologia* and not the Viennese *Corpus*, which is very belated in issuing Jerome's work. The reader, I hope, will take my homogeneous references in good part. The numbering of the *Letters* is the same in the *Corpus* and the *Patrologia*.

[6] Cf. Rufinus *Apol. in Hieron.* 2.9 (*PL* 21, 590 D): "Antequam converteretur, mecum pariter et litteras Graecas et linguam penitus ignorabat." Rufinus is attempting to prove that Jerome studied Porphyry after his *Dream*.

[7] *Epist.* 17.3 *ad Marcum* (*PL* 22, 360).

[8] *Epist.* 50.1 *ad Domnionem* (*PL* 22, 513): "Hunc Dialecticum urbis vestrae, et Plautinae familiae columen, non legisse quidem κατηγορίας Aristotelis, nòn περὶ ἑρμηνείας, non ἀναλυτικά, non saltem Ciceronis τόπους, sed per imperitorum circulos muliercularumque συμπόσια syllogismos ἀσυλλογίστους texere, et quasi sophismata nostra callida argumentatione dissolvere . . . Frustra ergo Alexandri verti commentarios, nequidquam me doctus magister per εἰσαγωγήν Porphyrii introduxit ad Logicam: et ut humana contemnam, sine causa Gregorium Nazianzenum et Didymum in Scripturis sanctis catechistas habui; nihil mihi profuit Hebraeorum eruditio." Jerome boasts of his culture in order to defend his *Adversus Iovinianum* against the criticism of an illiterate person. It was really in Greek territory that he acquired this culture, for he adds: "Nec mirum si me absentem iam diu et absque usu Latinae linguae, semigraeculum barbarumque homo latinissimus et facundissimus superet." On Jerome's professor of Greek at Antioch, cf. Gruetzmacher, *Hieronymus*, vol. 1, p. 125 and n. 5. Gruetzmacher, however, p. 124, thinks that Jerome studied Porphyry's and Alexander's logic at Rome and not at Antioch, in Latin translations. Bardy, "La culture grecque," p. 32, repeats this view. Porphyry's *Isagoge* had been well translated by Marius Victorinus, but there is nothing to prove that the Commentaries of Alexander of Aphrodisias were ever translated into Latin.

[9] *Epist.* 74.3 *ad Pammachium et Oceanum* (*PL* 22, 745): "Dum essem iuvenis, miro discendi ferebar ardore nec iuxta quorundam praesumptionem, ipse me docui. Apollinarium Laodicenum audivi Antiochiae frequenter, et colui; et cum me in sanctis Scripturis erudiret, numquam illius contentiosum super sensu dogma suscepi." I see no positive reason for stating categorically, as Cavallera does, *Saint Jérôme*, 1, 2, p. 19, that Jerome was not acquainted with Apollinarius until his second stay in Antioch.

[10] To the text quoted in note 8 above add *Epist.* 52.8 *ad Nepotianum* (*PL* 22, 534):

Gregory of Nyssa.[11] After a three-year stay in Rome, from 382 to 385, where Pope Damasus commissioned him to revise the text of the Bible, he returned to Antioch by way of Cyprus, where he received the illustrious Epiphanius;[12] then he proceeded to Jerusalem, then to Egypt, where he visited the monasteries.[13] Passing through Alexandria, he stayed a month, to attend Didymus' lectures.[14] In 389 he returned to Jerusalem and settled permanently in Bethlehem. At the monastery that he had just founded Jerome pursued both his active and his contemplative life. He collected a library, expounded the classical writers to the children intrusted to him,[15] and preached in Latin and Greek.[16] Above all, he read and wrote.[17] The purpose of his life, he said, was

---

"Praeceptor quondam meus Gregorius Nazianzenus, rogatus a me ut exponeret, quid sibi vellet in Luca sabbatum δευτερόπρωτον id est secundo-primum [Luke 6.1], eleganter lusit: docebo te, inquiens, super hac re in Ecclesia"; *De viris inlustribus* 117 (*PL* 23, 747 B): "praeceptor meus quo Scripturas explanante didici"; *In Isaiam* 3.6.1 (*PL* 24, 91 D): "De hac visione ante annos circiter triginta, cum essem Constantinopoli et apud virum eloquentissimum Gregorium Nazianzenum, tunc eiusdem urbis episcopum, sanctarum Scripturarum studiis erudirer, scio me brevem dictasse subitumque tractatum"; *In Epist. ad Ephes.* 3.5.32 (*PL* 26, 535 D): "Gregorius Nazianzenus, vir valde eloquens et in Scripturis apprime eruditus, cum de hoc mecum tractaret loco, solebat dicere ..."

[11] *De vir. inl.* 128 (*PL* 23, 754 A): "Gregorius Nyssenus episcopus, frater Basilii Caesariensis, ante paucos annos, mihi et Gregorio Nazianzeno *contra Eunomium* legit libros."

[12] *Adv. Rufinum* 3.22 (*PL* 23, 495 A): "malui per Maleas et Cycladas Cyprum pergere, ubi susceptus a venerabili episcopo Epiphanio." Cf. below, sec. 2 n. 215 and p. 123.

[13] *Adv. Rufinum* 3.22 (*PL* 23, 495 A): "lustravi monasteria Nitriae."

[14] *Epist.* 84.3 *ad Pammachium et Oceanum* (*PL* 22, 745 A): "Perrexi tamen Alexandriam, audivi Didymum: in multis ei gratias ago. Quod nescivi didici; quod sciebam, illo docente, non perdidi." *In Hoseam, praef.* (*PL* 24, 819 A): "Unde ante annos circiter viginti duos, cum ... essem Alexandriae, vidi Didymum et eum frequenter audivi, virum sui temporis eruditissimum, rogavique eum ut quod Origenes non fecerat compleret et scriberet in Hoseae commentarios." Cf. *PL* 22, 513 and 25, 440 B, and Rufinus *Apol. in Hieron.* 2.12 (*PL* 21, 594 D): "Ceterum iste qui in tota vita non totos triginta dies Alexandriae, ubi erat Didymus, commoratus est, per totos paene libellos suos longe lateque se iactat Didymi Videntis esse discipulum, et καθηγητήν, id est praeceptorem, in Scripturis sanctis habuisse Didymum."

[15] Cf. Rufinus *Apol. in Hieron.* 2.8 (*PL* 21, 592 A): "Sed quid immoror tam diu in re quae luce est clarior? Cum ad haec omnia quae supra diximus, etiam illud addatur, ubi cesset omne commentum, quod in monasterio positus in Bethleem ante non multo adhuc tempore, partes grammaticas exsecutus sit et Maronem suum Comicosque ac Lyricos et historicos auctores, traditis sibi ad discendum Dei timorem puerulis exponebat; scilicet et ut praeceptor fieret Auctorum gentilium quos si legisset tantum modo, Christum se negaturum iuraverat."

[16] Cf. Dom Germain Morin, *Etudes, textes, découvertes*, vol. 1 (Paris 1913) 249, on the *Hom. in Ps.* 143, which begins: "Propter eos qui ignorant Latinam linguam, licet multa de evangelio dixerimus, tamen debemus et de psalterio quaedam dicere, ut aliis saturatis alii ieiuni non redeant." Dom Morin wondered whether these Latin homilies of Jerome's that we possess and that teem with Hellenisms had not been delivered in Greek. While reply-

to transmit to the Latin world the erudition of the Hebrews and the Greeks.[18]

This rapid summary of St. Jerome's life suggests that there were two stages in his spiritual development. It was his ecclesiastical vocation that led him to seek Greek-speaking countries. Before his departure for Antioch, Jerome had absorbed only the Latin culture that was traditional since Cicero's days, that is, a Greco-Roman culture. On the other hand, he acquired his clerical culture in Greek-speaking countries and drew it straight from the sources. A study of Jerome's works will let us verify this spiritual viewpoint.

The Greek language became so familiar to Jerome that he borrowed from it a large number of words for which he found it difficult to give a Latin equivalent. Most frequently they are adverbs or adverbial expressions used to explain some particular figure of speech or to characterize the tone of a Scriptural passage.[19] They are also Greek substantives that denote the princi-

ing to this question in the negative, he considered that Jerome certainly delivered some homilies in Greek.

[17] Cf. Sulpicius Severus *Dial.* 1.9: "Totus semper in lectione, totus in libris est, non die neque nocte requiescit; aut legit aliquid semper aut scribit."

[18] *In Ieremiam* 3, *praef.* (PL 25, 757 B): "non est passus diabolus me optata quiete contentum, Scripturarum sanctarum explanationi insistere et hominibus linguae meae Hebraeorum Graecorumque eruditionem tradere."

[19] The principal adverbs that I have noted are: αἰνιγματωδῶς (PL 25, 1293 D), ἀνθρωποπάθως (PL 24: 35 B, 771 C, 800 D, 849 D, 898 B; 25: 541 A, 1421 B, 1546 D), γυμναστικῶς (22, 502), διασυρτικῶς (25, 1351 A), διεστραμμένως (23, 518 A), δογματικῶς (22, 502), εἰρωνικῶς (25: 1279 C, 1374 C, 1505 C), ἐμφατικῶς (24: 161 B, 308 D, 339 C, 740 B, 850 A) and ἐμφατικώτερον (25: 313 A, 1138 C, 1322 A; 22: 572), ἐρωτηματικῶς (24, 738 C), καταχρηστικῶς (24, 451 A; 26, 748 A), μεταφορικῶς (24: 50 C, 143 B, 253 C, 339 A, 341 B, 366 A, 486 C; 25: 233 C, 240 D, 576 B, 1141 A, 1235 C, 1236 C, 1491 C, 1498 D; 26, 503 D), μεταφραστικῶς (25, 246 B), μετωνυμικῶς (24: 25 B, 136 B, 443 B, 653 B; 25: 957 A, 1088 C), ὁμωνύμως (25: 508 B, 944 B; 26: 314 B, 523 D, *Anecd. Mareds.* 3, 1, p. 48, 13), παραφραστικῶς (22: 576, 1030; 24, 326 D; 25: 338 D, 457 A, 551 B, 1261 C, 1268 D, 1502 D), σεμνοτέρως (24, 458 D), συνεκδοχικῶς (24: 59 C, 777 A; 25: 923 C, 1131 C), συνωνύμως (25, 118 C), τροπικῶς (22, 630; 24: 613 B, 684 C; 25: 220 B, 248 B, 1372 A), τροπολογικῶς (25: 216 A, 1076 A), τυπικῶς (25: 907 B, 915 C, 955 A), ὑπερβολικῶς (23, 547 C; 24: 157 D, 351 D; 25: 1079 B, 1363 C), ὑποκοριστικῶς (25, 465 C). The adverbial expressions regularly employed by Jerome are: ἀπὸ κοινοῦ (24: 174 B, 431 A, 570 A, 809 D; 25: 38 B, 571 C, 822 B, 1158 D, 1343 D, 1421 C, 1475 A, 1547 D; 26: 37 A, 465 A, 530 D), *iuxta* ἀναγωγήν (24: 199 D, 239 D, 265 B, 271 A, 344 D, 535 C, 691 D; 25: 61 D, 71 C, 106 D, 249 A, 417 A, 957 C, 1133 B, 1476 A; 26, 209 A) or *secundum* ἀναγωγήν (23, 1142 B; 24: 275 B, 860 B; 25: 553 C, 899 C, 917 B, 1232 B, 1242 D, 1252 A, 1408 D, 1419 B, 1494 B; 26: 63 B, 531 A), *sub* ἀνακεφαλαιώσει (23: 252 A, 1172 C), *cum* ἐμφάσει (24, 399 A), κατ' ἀκρίβειαν (25, 496 A), καθ' ὑπόθεσιν (26, 319 D), κατὰ ἀντίφρασιν (22, 605; 24, 199 A; 25: 1075 D, 1161 B; 26, 200 A), κατὰ λέξιν (25, 837 B), κατὰ συνεκδοχήν (26, 689 B), *per* ὑπέρβατον (25, 1263 B; 26: 318 B, 336 A, 832 A), *per* ὑπερβολήν (24, 711 C). A. Souter, "Greek and Hebrew Words in Jerome's Commentary on St. Matthew's Gospel," *Harvard Theological Review* (1935) 1–4, noted that in certain manuscripts these words still have a horizontal line that Jerome placed over foreign words.

pal rhetorical figures of speech.[20] In necessary cases Jerome gives their Latin equivalent[21] or even takes the trouble, when addressing his monks, to explain the figure in detail, following the grammarians' method.[22] He also readily uses Greek words in his letters, in Ciceronian style, or even entire sentences when he addresses a cultured person such as Pammachius or Domnio,[23] or when he delivers a homily to the monks of Bethlehem who ought to have at least a taste of this language.[24] The frequent insertion of Greek expressions into Latin prose is even one of the principal criteria that helped Dom Morin to identify these hitherto unknown homilies. Lastly, Jerome uses Greek to define philosophical concepts that Latin does not express clearly.[25]

Frequently he observes that a particular Greek text is clearer than his Latin translation.[26] The Latin language, he declares, is sometimes incapable of translating a text with the proper phraseology.[27] He does not hesitate to

[20] Among others: ἀποσιώπησις (24, 709 A), ἐπίτασις (22, 662; 23, 539 B; 24, 190 C), πλεονασμός (25, 564 B; 26, 823 B), προσωποποιΐα (24, 202 A; 25, 1157 A; 26, 525 B), σύλληψις (26, 211 B), ὕστερον πρότερον (26, 832 A).

[21] Cf. *PL* 25, 122 D, "Variis autem similitudinibus, quas Graeci *parabolas* vocant, praenuntiatur subversio urbis Ierusalem," and 25, 289 C: "Nos pro *No, Alexandriam* posuimus per anticipationem, quae Graece πρόληψις appellatur, iuxta illud Vergilianum: 'Laviniaque venit littora'; non quo eo tempore quando venit Aeneas in Latium, Lavinia dicerentur, sed quae postea Lavinia nuncupata sunt, ut manifestior locus fieret lectoris intellegentiae."

[22] *Anecd. Mareds.* 3, 2, p. 200, 20: "Hoc schema Graece dicitur συνεκδοχή, quod dicunt grammatici ἀπὸ μέρους τὸ πᾶν.

[23] Cf. *Epist. ad Pammachium* 49.2 (*PL* 22, 511): "ἀπολογετικόν ipsius operis tibi προσεφώνησα"; *Epist. ad Donnionem* 50.3 (*PL* 22, 514): "cui ego ἀπελογισάμην ut potui"; *Epist. ad Vigilantium* 61.3 (*PL* 22, 604): "alioqui proferrem πᾶσαν τὴν ἀριστείαν σοῦ καὶ τροπαιοφορίαν"; *Epist. ad Damasum* 36.1 (*PL* 22, 453): "ταῦτά σοι ἐσχεδίασα." Cf. Bickel's comments, *Diatribe in Senecae phil. fragm.*, pp. 115–116, on the Greek words changed in Vallarsi's text.

[24] Dom Morin, *Etudes, textes, découvertes*, pp. 250 and 264.

[25] *Dialogus contra Pelagianos* 1.8 (*PL* 23, 524 C): "Aliud namque est *esse posse*, quod Graece dicitur τῇ δυνάμει, aliud est *esse*, quod ipsi appellant τῇ ἐνεργείᾳ." Cf. *Epist. ad Paulinum* 53.3 (*PL* 22, 542): "Mollis cera et ad formandum facilis, etiam si artificis et plastae cessent manus, tamen τῇ δυνάμει totum est, quidquid esse potest."

[26] Cf. *PL* 22, 383: "significantius in Graeco legitur"; 22, 731: "quas significantius Graeci προπαθείας vocant, nos ut verbum vertamus e verbo *antepassiones* possumus dicere"; 22, 1175: "Symmachus significantius transtulit ὁλόκληροι quod magis ad sensum quam ad verbum transferre possumus *universi*"; 23, 529 D: "instar sagittarii ad propositum et ad signum iacula dirigere, quem [*al.*: quod] significantius Graeci σκοπόν nominant"; 23,1093 A: "Hoc est enim quod ait: *Et Deus quaeret eum qui persecutionem patitur*, quod Graece melius dicitur: καὶ ὁ Θεὸς ζητήσει τὸν διωκόμενον"; 24, 581 C: "et transgressionem quae significantius Graece dicitur ἀπόστασις."

[27] *Adv. Iovinianum* 1.13 (*PL* 23, 242 B): "Proprietatem Graecam Latinus sermo non explicat: quibus enim verbis quis possit edicere: Πρὸς τὸ εὔσχημον καὶ εὐπρόσεδρον τῷ Κυρίῳ ἀπερισπάστως? Unde et in Latinis codicibus, ob translationis difficultatem, hoc penitus non invenitur."

indicate mistakes on the part of the translator, whether he has taken one word for another[28] or whether he has not perceived the ambiguity of a Greek word.[29] When one or the other meaning is admissible, Jerome studies them both.[30]

We are informed about the art of translating according to St. Jerome chiefly through one of his letters to Pammachius.[31] He here defends himself vigorously against the attacks of Rufinus, who accused him of having purposely falsified the meaning of Epiphanius of Salamis' letter to John of Jerusalem. Jerome makes the point that he dictated this translation very hurriedly for the personal use of Eusebius of Cremona, who knew no Greek: it was not intended for the public. He adds that this translation, though far from literal, is no less faithful to the text. He clamorously invokes the principles of translation laid down by Cicero and Horace. Without concern for word-for-word transliteration, the meaning must be expressed: "Ego enim non solum fateor, sed libera voce profiteor, me in interpretatione Graecorum,

---

[28] *Epist. ad Principiam* 65.14 (PL 22, 633): "nos transtulimus *domibus eburneis*; quia in Graeco scriptum est ἀπὸ βαρέων ἐλεφαντίνων quidam Latini ob verbi ambiguitatem *a gravibus* interpretati sunt, cum βάρις verbum sit ἐπιχώριον Palaestinae; et usque hodie domus ex omni parte conclusae et in modum aedificatae turrium ac moenium publicorum βάρεις appellentur"; *In Ieremiam* 6.31.2 (PL 24, 872 A): "Ridicule Latini codices in hoc loco ambiguitate verbi Graeci pro *calido, lupinos* interpretati sunt: Graecum enim θερμόν utrumque significat."

[29] *Epist. ad Marcellam* 34.5 (PL 22, 450) with reference to a mistake made by St. Hilary (*Tract. in Ps.* 127.4–5), who was misled by his translator Heliodorus the priest: "sed Latini de Graeci verbi ambiguitate decepti καρποὺς *fructus* magis quam *manus* interpretati sint, cum καρποί manus quoque dicantur"; *Epist. ad Amandum* 55.1 (PL 22, 461): "κακία enim quam Latinus vertit in *malitiam*, apud Graecos duo significat, et malitiam et adflictionem, quam κάκωσιν Graeci dicunt, et hic magis pro *malitia* transferri debuit *adflictio*." The reference is to Matthew 6.34: "sufficit diei malitia sua" (cf. *In Ecclesiasten*, PL 23, 1074 B: "*Sufficit diei malitia sua*, quam Graeci significantius κακουχίαν vocant"); *Epist. ad Oceanum* 69.5 (PL 22, 658): "Mulierem autem, id est γυναῖκα, iuxta Graeci sermonis ambiguitatem in his omnibus testimoniis *uxorem* potius intellego." Cf. *Adversus Iovinianum* 1.26 (PL 23, 256 D): "*Numquid non habemus potestatem mulieres vel uxores circumducendi* (quia γυνή apud Graecos utrumque significat)"; *Epist. ad Cyprianum* 140.14 (PL 22, 1176): "*Corripiemur*. Pro quo in Graeco scriptum est παιδευθησόμεθα, quod verbum ambiguum est et tam correptionem quam eruditionem doctrinamque significat."

[30] *In Isaiam* 7.21.11 (PL 24, 264 B): "Quodque nos diximus *clamat* vel *vocat*, id est καλεῖ, secundum Hebraei et Graeci sermonis ambiguitatem dici potest *clama* vel *voca*"; *In Isaiam* 14.52.8 (PL 24, 501 A–B): "Ὥρα autem, id est *hora* iuxta Septuaginta et ambiguitatem sermonis Graeci aut *tempus* significat, aut *pulchritudinem* . . . potest ὥρα secundum Graecae linguae latitudinem *cura* dici et *sollicitudo*."

[31] *Epist. ad Pammachium* 57, *de optimo genere interpretandi* (PL 22, 568–579). On this question Godofredus Hoberg may be profitably consulted: *De s. Hieronymi ratione interpretandi* (diss. Münster 1886), particularly part 1, "Quae s. Hieronymus de ratione interpretandi ab ipso in translatis bibliis observata, conscripserit." Also see G. Bardy, *Recherches sur l'histoire du texte et des versions latines du "De principiis" d'Origène* (diss. Lille 1923) 158–168.

absque Scripturis sanctis, ubi et verborum ordo mysterium est, non verbum e verbo, sed sensum exprimere de sensu."[32] Jerome refers to the principles that he had previously enunciated in the preface to his translation of Eusebius' *Chronicle*: every language has its own genius; to wish to translate the peculiarities of the Greek language, "hyperbatorum anfractus, dissimilitudines casuum, varietates figurarum," is as futile as wanting to translate Homer into Latin, word for word.[33] Evagrius of Antioch and St. Hilary translated in accordance with the same principles that Jerome used.[34]

A reservation is made, as has been noted, for the translation of the Scriptures, "where the very word order is a mystery" and where the translator must be very faithful. Jerome himself very frequently prides himself on having faithfully reproduced the Greek text of the New Testament.[35] Not that he praises, even for the sacred texts, a literal translation. In the letter to Sunnia and Fretela, where only sacred texts are in question, Jerome postulates the principle: "hanc esse regulam boni interpretis, ut ἰδιώματα linguae alterius, suae linguae exprimat proprietate."[36] He refers, as in his letter to Pammachius, to Cicero's translations, to the adaptations by Plautus, Terence, and Caecilius, and he blames the κακοζηλία of translators who are too literal.[37] The translators of the Septuagint, the Evangelists, and the Apostles translated and quoted the Hebrew text with a certain freedom.[38] Why not imitate them and stress the meaning rather than the words? The rather broad Septuagint version is received by the Church in preference to the more slavish rendering by Aquila.[39] Let us follow the example of these Greek translators, since the Latin language offers no fewer resources for the translator than the Greek language.[40] Jerome does not hesitate, from the moment that they have

[32] *Epist. ad Pammachium* 57.5 (*PL* 22, 571).

[33] *Ibid.*, 57.5 (*PL* 22, 572) quoting *Chron., praef.* (*PL* 27, 35 A); cf. *Epist.* 70.2 (*PL* 22, 665): "Nec mirum si apud Latinos metrum non servet ad verbum expressa translatio, cum Homerus eadem lingua versus in prosam vix cohaereat."

[34] *Epist.* 57.5 (*PL* 22, 572).

[35] *Epist. ad Lucinium* 71.5 (*PL* 22, 671): "Novum Testamentum Graecae reddidi auctoritati"; *De vir. inl.* 135 (*PL* 23, 758 B): "Novum Testamentum Graecae fidei reddidi."

[36] *Epist. ad Sunniam et Fretelam* 106.3 (*PL* 22, 839).

[37] Cf. *PL* 22, 571 and 839. Jerome *Epist.* 106.17 (*PL* 22, 843) gives as an example of κακοζηλία the translation of πᾶς τίς by *omnis quis*. Note that Quintilian *Inst. Or.* 8.3.56ff takes κακόζηλον in quite a different sense.

[38] *Epist. ad Pammachium* 57.7–11 (*PL* 22, 572–578).

[39] *Ibid.*, 57.7–11 (*PL* 22, 577): "Aquila autem proselytus et contentiosus interpres, qui non solum verba, sed etymologias quoque verborum transferre conatus est, iure proicitur a nobis." On the particular character of each of the Greek translators of the Scriptures, cf. *Chron., praef.* (*PL* 27, 35 B).

[40] *Epist.* 106.3 (*PL* 22, 839): "Nec ex eo quis Latinam linguam angustissimam putet, quod non possit verbum de verbo transferre, cum etiam Graeci pleraque nostra circuitu transferant et verba Hebraica non interpretationis fide, sed linguae suae proprietatibus nitantur exprimere." Only certain Hebrew words such as *Hallelujah, Amen*, etc. are un-

understood the Greek text, to retain the translation of his Latin predecessors: *magnificate* for δοξάσατε, while noting that *glorificate* would be more exact.[41] We know besides that this carefulness in the revision of the sacred text in the Greek manuscripts was dictated to Jerome through his anxiety to impress in the least unfavorable way the faithful who were accustomed to the old Latin translations.[42] But he does not hesitate to modify the old version whenever it is too literal and displays bad Latinity. He is taxed with rendering in Psalm 49: κατὰ τοῦ ἀδελφοῦ σου κατελάλεις: *adversus fratrem tuum loquebaris*, because the exact equivalent of the Greek verb is *detrahere*. Jerome answers Sunnia and Fretela that it would not have been Latin to translate: *adversus fratrem tuum detrahebas*. Must one then write: *de fratre tuo detrahebas?* But then κατὰ was not rendered. Literal translation is an impossible and futile undertaking.[43] Good Latin usage often requires the addition of a personal pronoun[44] or its omission, if it is expletive.[45] It is unimportant to him to retain the etymology of the Greek word in order to translate syllable by syllable, or to add to or exclude a word. The essential factor is to preserve the meaning of the text and to respect the language into which it is translated: "Eadem igitur interpretandi sequenda est regula, quam saepe diximus, ut ubi non sit damnum in sensu linguae, in quam transferimus, εὐφωνία et proprietas

---

translatable in one language or the other. Cf. *Anecd. Mareds.* 3, 2, p. 210, 21, "Proprietatem Hebraici Graecus et Latinus exprimere non potest," and *Epist. ad Marcellam* 26 (*PL* 22, 430–431). Jerome, however, acknowledges, *In Epist. ad Ephes.* 1.1.4 (*PL* 26, 466 B) an inferiority of Latin in relation to Greek: "Unde et nos propter paupertatem linguae et rerum novitatem, et sicut quidam ait, quod sit Graecorum et sermo latior et lingua felicior, conabimur non tam verbum transferre de verbo, quod impossibile est, quam vim verbi quodam explicare circuitu"; and *Epist. ad Theophilum* 114.3 (*PL* 22, 935): "facundiam Graecam Latinae linguae volui paupertate pensare."

[41] *Epist.* 106.12 (*PL* 22, 842). Sometimes, too, an approximate translation is the only possibility. Thus Jerome translates Ps. 128.1: "*Posuerunt Ierusalem in pomorum custodiam*; quod Graece εἰς ὀπωροφυλάκιον dicitur, nec aliter potest verti quam a nobis translatum est. Significat autem speculam quam custodes satorum et pomorum habere consueverunt: ut de amplissima urbe parvum tuguriolum vix remanserit" (*Epist.* 106.51, *PL* 22, 856).

[42] Cf. Schanz, vol. 4, 1, p. 452, and Jerome *Epist.* 106.12 (*PL* 22, 842): "et nos emendantes olim Psalterium, ubicumque sensus idem est, veterum interpretum consuetudinem mutare noluimus ne nimia novitate lectoris studium terreremus"; and *Praef. in IV Evangelia* (*PL* 29, 528 A): "Quae ne multum a lectionis Latinae consuetudine discreparent, ita calamo temperavimus, ut his tantum quae sensum videbantur mutare correctis, reliqua manere pateremur ut fuerant."

[43] *Epist.* 106.30 (*PL* 22, 847).

[44] *Ibid.*, 48 (*PL* 22, 854): "Terribili, et *ei* qui aufert spiritum Principum," and 50 (*PL* 22, 855): "Et propitius fiet peccatis eorum, et non disperdet *eos*."

[45] *Ibid.*, 54 (*PL* 22, 856): "Beatus vir, cuius est auxilium abs te," and not "cui est auxilium *eius* abs te," and 62 (*PL* 22, 858): "Oculi mei ad fideles terrae, ut sedeant mecum," and not "ut consederent *ipsi* mecum."

conservetur." It is better, in rendering the Greek εὐδόκησας, to translate *benedixisti, Domine, terram tuam*, rather than *complacuit tibi, Domine, terra tua*.[46] By "euphony," Jerome does not in any sense mean harmony, but what sounds Latin. Thus it is impossible to translate literally *in medio ventris mei*, in order to render the Hebrew and the Greek text. Latin euphony requires *in medio cordis mei*.[47] Jerome scorns the literal translation that, as practiced, leads to barbarism: "ἐξουδένωσας . . . we have interpreted as *despexisti* and *pro nihilo duxisti*. But perhaps you do not think that ἐξουδένωσας can be translated as *despexisti*, but, according to the most learned interpreter of those days, as *annihilasti* or *nullificasti*, or by any other absurd word that can be found among the unlettered."[48] The rhythm too of the text to be translated must be preserved and Jerome ridicules the reproaches that Rufinus had cast against his translation of Epiphanius' letter. He had translated the first sentence: "ἔδει ἡμᾶς, ἀγαπητέ, μὴ τῇ οἰήσει τῶν κλήρων φέρεσθαι: oportebat nos, dilectissime, clericatus honore non abuti in superbiam." Was it necessary to render literally: "oportebat nos, dilecte, non aestimatione clericorum ferri"? Jerome has nothing but contempt for such inelegance. He makes Pammachius the judge and sends him the Greek text and his Latin translation for comparison.[49]

It can be seen, even in the matter of the Scriptures, where the most scrupulous faithfulness to the text is imperative, that Jerome has not ceased his struggle against the literalism of the contemporary translators.[50] He is probably far from being as daring as Cicero, his model, as the comparative study by Cuendet has shown.[51] He translates Greek verses into prose.[52] He is much more exact, shunning paraphrase.[53] He often omits rendering

---

[46] *Ibid.*, 55 (*PL* 22, 857). Cf. *Hom. in Ps.* 84, quoted by Dom Morin, *Etudes, textes, découvertes*, p. 276: "*Benedixisti, Domine, terram tuam. Melius dicitur in Graeco*: εὐδόκησας, Κύριε, *hoc est: Bene placuit tibi, Domine.*"

[47] *Epist.* 106.23 (*PL* 22, 844). On εὐφωνία and κακοφωνία, see the rest of the letter and particularly 26 (846), 29 (847), 59 (858).

[48] *Ibid.*, 57 (*PL* 22, 857). Cf. 67 (862): "*Et inritaverunt ascendentes in mare, mare Rubrum.* Pro quo in Graeco invenisse vos dicitis καὶ παρεπίκραναν, *et putatis verbum e verbo debere transferri* et amaricaverunt. *Sed haec interpretatio adnulationi consimilis est, sive adnihilationi.*"

[49] *Epist.* 57.12–13 (*PL* 22, 578–579). We also learn, *Epist.* 57.2 (*PL* 22, 569) that Jerome was criticized "pro honorabili dixisse *carissimum* et maligna interpretatione, quod nefas dictu sit αἰδεσιμώτατον Πάππαν noluisse transferre." This complaint against Jerome is still made in our time by Maurice Villain, "Rufin d'Aquilée, la querelle autour d'Origène," *RSR* 27 (1937) 12–13. Jerome's translation may be found in *PL* 22, 517–527.

[50] I am therefore not in entire agreement with Franz Blatt, "Remarques sur l'histoire des traductions latines," *Classica et mediaevalia* 1 (1938) 217–220. He distinguishes in Jerome literalism and liberalism according to the character of his translations.

[51] Georges Cuendet, "Cicéron et s. Jérôme traducteurs," *REL* 11 (1933) 380–400.

[52] *Ibid.*, p. 384.

[53] *Ibid.*, pp. 385–386.

Greek participles.[54] Sometimes he copies Greek compounds[55] and admits into the language ecclesiastical Hellenisms recently imported.[56] But Cuendet must recognize that most of the Hellenisms in the Vulgate, especially the Hellenisms in syntax, come from the old Latin translations.[57] Jerome admits them because he is forced to be conservative, but as far as he is concerned he avoids rather than seeks them. Goelzer had already shown in his researches on the language of St. Jerome his concern for Ciceronian purity.[58] He drew up a list of Jerome's borrowings from the Greek vocabulary and the hybrid expressions that Jerome formed through derivation from the Greek.[59] But he notes how careful Jerome is in the use of neologisms. Those that he ventures were already consecrated by usage in the technical vocabularies or are ecclesiastical Hellenisms.[60] Still, he does not use them without fear and without relying on the authority of Cicero's example.[61] Similarly, the Hellenistic syntax that Goelzer noted in Jerome is no novelty in Latin: the use of the accusative of respect,[62] of the infinitive of purpose,[63] of *quia* after *verba sentiendi et declarandi*,[64] of the expressions *id ipsum*[65] and *ut quid*.[66]

    Daring in another direction is Jerome's language of the homilies, discovered by Dom Morin, where the Hellenistic syntax is extremely marked. The author here regularly uses the Greek proleptic device.[67] He uses the indicative for the principal clause of an unreal condition.[68] Some-

---

[54] *Ibid.*, p. 390.

[55] *Ibid.*, p. 397.

[56] *Ibid.*, p. 398.

[57] *Ibid.*, p. 387.

[58] Henri Goelzer, *Etude lexicographique et grammaticale de la latinité de s. Jérôme* (Paris 1884) 32.

[59] *Ibid.*, chap. 5: "Mots grecs."

[60] *Ibid.*, p. 22 and n. 1.

[61] *In Galat.* 1.1.11 (*PL* 26, 323 B): "Si itaque hi qui disertos saeculi legere consueverunt, coeperint nobis de novitate et vilitate sermonis inludere, mittamus eos ad Ciceronis libros, qui de quaestionibus philosophiae praenotantur: et videant quanta ibi necessitate compulsus sit tanta verborum portenta proferre, quam numquam Latini hominis auris audivit: et hoc cum de Graeco, quae lingua vicina est, transferret in nostram." Even in his *Tract. in Ps.* (*Anecd. Mareds.* 3, 2, p. 138, 34) he notes, with reference to an ecclesiastical Hellenism: "*Oecumene* enim melius Graece dicitur quam Latine."

[62] Goelzer, *Etude lexicographique*, p. 311.

[63] *Ibid.*, p. 370.

[64] *Ibid.*, p. 383.

[65] *Ibid.*, p. 407.

[66] *Ibid.*, p. 431.

[67] Morin, *Anecd. Mareds.* 3, 2, p. 33, 14: "fecisti eas, ut ambularent"; p. 64, 17: "legimus decem tribus, quoniam reliquerunt Deum"; p. 68, 21: "animadvertite Scripturam, quid significat"; p. 392, 13: "putabat illum, quod esset hortulanus." Many other examples will be found in his index under "hellénismes."

[68] *Ibid.*, p. 44, 10: "Si esset nunc iudex, peccatores, non erigebantur"; p. 168, 8: "Non enim habebat fumum, nisi ignis esset." See the index under "Condicionalis enuntiatio."

times he even uses a genitive absolute,[69] puts the verb of a neuter plural subject in the singular,[70] uses the preposition *ab*[71] or the verb *mirari*[72] with the genitive, and transposes into Latin the Greek construction ἀρνεῖσθαι μή.[73] Must we conclude that Jerome delivered these homilies in Greek and that we have to deal with a literal rendering? Dom Morin propounded the question and answered it in the negative.[74] It would then be necessary to admit that the language spoken by Jerome, a Bethlehem monk who had for years on end been living in Greek-speaking territory, addressing a public that was half Greek, half Latin, had been thoroughly Hellenized. There is nothing to indicate this in his commentaries, which nevertheless are contemporary with the homilies but are directed chiefly to the Roman public. There is nothing comparable even in his translations, because these are written works.[75] It is therefore principally the search for Ciceronian precision, the desire to conserve, even in translations, the purity of the Latin language, that are strikingly evident in Jerome. We must believe that the development of his Greek culture and the reading of the ecclesiastical writers had not obliterated in him the Latin culture and the pagan studies of his youth.

2. JEROME AND GREEK PAGAN CULTURE

Does that mean that his Greek studies were inferior to his Latin studies? This is the thesis maintained by Luebeck, in an old but quite searching work. In his view, Jerome's Greek studies were superficial. Jerome is unfamiliar with the prose writers, still more with the Greek poets, and he never knew their language very well.[1]

If Luebeck is not in error, we must concede that Jerome wanted to conceal this semi-ignorance of Greek culture. He gladly recalls, in his old age, his

---

[69] Morin, *Etudes, textes, découvertes*, vol. 1, p. 250 n. 2: "videntibus quingentis viris . . . et *omnium apostolorum* ascendisti"; the blending of the ablative and the genitive absolute gives the impression of a real *lapsus*.

[70] *Ibid.*, p. 250: "Quae interpretati sumus de ecclesia *potest* intellegi."

[71] *Ibid.*, and *Anecd. Mareds.* 3, 2, p. 198, 19: "a *quorundam* vocatur dominus."

[72] *Anecd. Mareds.* 3, 3, p. 83, 20: "mirantur philosophorum ac poetarum dicentium."

[73] *Ibid.*, 3, 2, p. 2, 24: "qui negat se peccatum non fecisse."

[74] Morin, *Etudes, textes, découvertes*, vol. 1, pp. 249ff.

[75] Gruetzmacher, *Hieronymus*, vol. 1, p. 182, followed by Hoppe, "Griechisches bei Rufin," *Glotta* 26 (1937) 133, believed he had discovered a refinement of Jerome's style as a translator, because he thought that Jerome's translation of Origen's homilies on Isaiah, the style of which is not so good, was the first to appear. But if we admit with Schanz, vol. 4, 1, p. 458, for nonstylistic criteria, that this translation is posterior to 392, this theory breaks down.

[1] Aemilius Luebeck, *Hieronymus quos noverit scriptores et ex quibus hauserit* (Leipzig 1872) 6–7.

extensive reading.[2] He makes comparisons in Greek literature. Vergil is the Latin Homer.[3] Josephus is the Greek Livy.[4] David is the Christian Simonides, Pindar, and Alcaeus.[5] Theophilus of Alexandria is their Plato and their Demosthenes.[6] Isidore is their Hippocrates.[7] Jerome also delights in honoring his enemies, ironically, with the most famous names in Greek literature. Jovinianus is an Epicurus.[8] Rufinus is an Aristippus.[9] Vigilantius and Rufinus display in their criticisms the intellectual perceptiveness of Chrysippus.[10] Rufinus, who censures Jerome's works, is also pompously termed the Aristarchus[11] or the Theophrastus of our time.[12] Jerome accuses an ignorant monk of thinking himself superior to Cicero, Aristotle, Plato, Aristarchus, Chalcenterus, and Didymus of Alexandria, all of them together.[13] Thus he appears to show the extent of his own culture, but is there something in this attitude other than a witty comment?

What is slightly disconcerting is that Jerome does not conceal the fact that he has read several Greek works in translation. He knows in particular Cicero's translations: Plato's *Protagoras*, Xenophon's *Oeconomicus*, the two speeches of Demosthenes and Aeschines delivered against each other.[14] He even quotes the preface, entitled *De optimo genere oratorum*, that Cicero placed

---

[2] *Tract. in Ps.* 15 (*Anecd. Mareds.* 3, 3, p. 22, 13): "*Insuper et usque ad noctem erudierunt me renes mei . . .* ἰδίωμα Scripturarum est. Nam quantum in memoria mea est, nec apud philosophorum quempiam, nec apud rhetorum, nec apud ipsos quidem medicos qui naturae corporum scientiam repromittunt, umquam legisse me novi *renes* pro intellectibus et profunda cogitatione positos."

[3] *Epist.* 121.10 (*PL* 22, 1030) and *In Michaeam* 2.7 (*PL* 25, 1220 C).

[4] *Epist.* 22.35 (*PL* 22, 421).

[5] *Epist.* 53.7 (*PL* 22, 547).

[6] *Epist.* 99.2 (*PL* 22, 813).

[7] *Contra Ioannem Hieros.* 39 (*PL* 23, 408 D).

[8] *Adv. Iovin.* 1.1 (*PL* 23, 221 A).

[9] *Adv. Rufin.* 3.30 (*PL* 23, 502 A). The same comparison with Epicurus and Aristippus in *Epist.* 33.5 (*PL* 22, 448).

[10] *Epist.* 61.3 (*PL* 22, 604) and *Adv. Rufin.* 1.30 (*PL* 23, 442 B).

[11] *Adv. Rufin.* 1.17 (*PL* 23, 429 A); cf. *Epist.* 57.12 (*PL* 22, 578).

[12] *Adv. Rufin.* 2.8 (*PL* 23, 450 B).

[13] *Epist.* 50.2 *ad Domnionem* (*PL* 22, 513): "Inventus est homo absque praeceptore perfectus, πνευματοφόρος καὶ αὐτοδίδακτος, qui eloquentia Tullium, argumentis Aristotelem, prudentia Platonem, eruditione Aristarchum, multitudine librorum Chalcenterum, Didymum scientia Scripturarum omnesque sui temporis vincat Tractatores." Cf. *Epist.* 33.1 *ad Paulam* (*PL* 22, 447); of Didymus Chalcenterus Jerome seems to know nothing, except his reputation for productivity.

[14] These translations are mentioned together in *Epist.* 57.5 and 106.3 (*PL* 22, 571 and 839), *Adv. Rufin.* 2.25 (*PL* 23, 470 B; cf. 381 C), *Praef. in Pentateuchum* (*PL* 28, 151 A): "Nisi forte putandus est Tullius *Oeconomicum* Xenophontis et Platonis *Protagoram* et Demosthenis *Pro Ctesiphonte* adflatus rhetorico spiritu transtulisse." Cf. *Praef. in Chron.* (*PL* 27, 33 A): "Unde et noster Tullius Platonis integros libros interpretatus est: et cum Aratum iam Romanum hexametris versibus edidisset, in Xenophontis *Oeconomico* lusit."

at the beginning of these two orations.[15] He knows that in translating the *Oeconomicus* Cicero rendered οἰκονομία by *dispensatio universae domus*[16] and severely criticizes Cicero's style in this translation.[17] He knows still other translations: the *Timaeus* by Cicero,[18] the translations of Aratus' *Phaenomena* by Cicero, Germanicus Caesar, Avienus.[19] Lastly, he read Sextus Pythagoreus in the translation that Rufinus had made and erroneously attributed to Pope Sixtus.[20] Does that mean that Jerome usually read the Greek authors in Latin translations? Which of them did he use knowledgeably and in the original text? Only a detailed analysis of his works can inform us.

Jerome frequently mentions but rarely quotes the Greek poets. Homer is a name that often recurs in his writings, especially in his letters.[21] Once he refers to a line in Homer on the wisdom of the aged Nestor,[22] but in a discussion on old age taken, without any possible doubt, from Cicero's *De*

---

[15] *Epist.* 57.5 (*PL* 22, 571).

[16] *Epist.* 121.6 (*PL* 22, 1018).

[17] *Praef. in Chron.* (*PL* 27, 34 A): "In quo opere ita saepe aureum illud flumen eloquentiae scabris quibusdam et turbulentis obicibus retardatur, ut qui interpretata nesciunt, a Cicerone dicta non credant."

[18] *In Isaiam* 12.40 (*PL* 24, 409 D): "Denique *Timaeum* de mundi harmonia astrorumque cursu et numeris disputantem, ipse qui interpretatus est Tullius, se non intellegere confitetur"; and *In Amos* 2.5 (*PL* 25, 1038 A): "Obscurissimus Platonis *Timaeus* liber est, qui ne Ciceronis quidem aureo ore fit planior." The *Timaeus* is again named in *Adv. Rufin.* 3.40 (*PL* 23, 509 A).

[19] *In Epist. ad Tit.* 1 (*PL* 26, 572 B); cf. *Praef. in Chron.* (*PL* 27, 33 A) quoted above, n. 14.

[20] *Epist. ad Ctesiphontem* 133.3 (*PL* 22, 1152): "librum Xysti Pythagorei, hominis absque Christo atque Ethnici, immutato nomine, Sixti Martyris et Romanae ecclesiae episcopi praenotavit, in quo iuxta dogma Pythagoricorum, qui hominem exaequant Deo et de eius dicunt esse substantia, multa de perfectione dicuntur"; and *In Ieremiam* 4.22 (*PL* 24, 817 A): "Miserabilis Grunnius . . . Sexti Pythagorei hominis gentilissimi unum librum interpretatus est in Latinum; divisitque eum in duo volumina et sub nomine sancti Martyris Xysti, urbis Romanae episcopi, ausus est edere: in quibus nulla Christi, nulla Spiritus sancti, nulla Dei Patris, nulla Patriarcharum, Prophetarum et Apostolorum fit mentio, et hunc librum solita temeritate et insania *Annulum* nominavit, qui per multas provincias legitur, et maxime ab his qui ἀπάθειαν et impeccantiam praedicant." Jerome twice quotes the same maxim taken from this book, the first time from Rufinus' text (*Adv. Iovin.* 1.49 = *PL* 23, 293 C): "Unde et Xystus in sententiis: Adulter est, inquit, in suam uxorem amator ardentior"; the second time from memory (*In Ezechielem* 6.18 = *PL* 25, 173 C): "Pulchre in Xysti Pythagorici sententiolis dicitur: Adulter est uxoris propriae amator ardentior." This is sententia 222 in Sextus, in *Maxima Bibliotheca Veterum Patrum*, vol. 3 (Lyon 1677), p. 337 E.

[21] *Epist. ad Paulinum* 58.5, *ad Nepotianum* 52.3, *ad Algasiam* 121, *quaest.* 10 (*PL* 22: 583, 529, 1030). Cf. *In Amos* 1.1 (*PL* 25, 993 B).

[22] *Epist. ad Nepotianum* 52.3 (*PL* 22, 529): "Certe Homerus refert quod de lingua Nestoris iam vetuli et paene decrepiti *dulcior melle oratio* fluxerit." Cf. *Iliad* 1.249: τοῦ καὶ ἀπὸ γλώσσης μέλιτος γλυκίων ῥέεν αὐδή.

senectute.[23] Similarly, he quotes another verse from Homer, on the Chimera, but in the form of the Latin translation made by Lucretius.[24] On another occasion he quotes in Greek a line from the *Iliad*,[25] but it is an apothegm in verse: "Whatsoever word thou speakest, such shalt thou hear," which does not necessarily imply a direct knowledge of Homer, for it is often quoted by the ancients.[26] Perhaps in his youth Jerome read only these centos from Homer in Latin prose, of which he speaks disdainfully.[27]

Jerome names Hesiod[28] once and quotes him once in Latin without naming him.[29] But he appears to borrow this quotation from Clement of Alexandria, who also applied it to the Scriptures.[30] With regard to Simonides,[31] Pindar,[32] Alcaeus,[33] Stesichorus,[34] and Sophocles,[35] Jerome, it appears, knows them

---

[23] Cicero *De senectute* 10.31: "Etenim, ut ait Homerus: Ex eius lingua *melle dulcior fluebat oratio.*"

[24] *Iliad* 6.181: πρόσθε λέων, ὄπιθεν δὲ δράκων, μέσση δὲ χίμαιρα. Quoted in Hesiod *Theogony* 5.323 and translated by Lucretius 5.905 and Jerome *Epist. ad Rusticum* 125.18 (PL 22, 1083): "Prima leo, postrema draco, media ipsa chimaera."

[25] *Adv. Rufinum* 3.42 (PL 23, 510 C): "Si . . . homo sapientissimus magis philosophorum ac poetarum sententiis delectaris, lege illud Homericum: ὁπποῖόν κ᾽ εἴπῃσθα ἔπος, τοῖόν κ᾽ ἐπακούσαις [= *Iliad* 20.250]."

[26] Cf. Plutarch *Adv. Coloten* 26 (ed. Duebner [Paris 1877] vol. 4, p. 1372), Diogenes Laertius *Vita phil.* 9.11 (ed. Cobet [Paris 1878] p. 245, 38), Clement of Alexandria *Stromateis* 1.3 (PG 8, 712 B), and Gregory of Nazianzus *Epist.* 190 (PG 38, 312 A).

[27] *Epist. ad Paulinum* 53.7 (PL 22, 544): "Quasi non legerimus Homerocentonas." Cf. the texts quoted above, sec. 1 n. 33.

[28] *Epist. ad Nepotianum* 52.3 (PL 22, 529).

[29] *In Isaiam* 2.3 (PL 24, 64 A): "Graeci poetae laudabilis illa et admiranda sententia est: Primum esse beatum qui per se sapiat, secundum qui sapientem audiat; qui autem utroque careat, hunc inutilem esse tam sibi quam omnibus." Cf. Hesiod *Works and Days* 293–297:

> Οὗτος μὲν πανάριστος, ὃς αὐτὸς πάντα νοήσῃ,
> [φρασσάμενος τά κ᾽ ἔπειτα καὶ ἐς τέλος ᾖσιν ἀμείνω]
> ἐσθλὸς δ᾽ αὖ κἀκεῖνος, ὃς εὖ εἰπόντι πίθηται·
> ὃς δέ κε μήτ᾽ αὐτὸς νοέῃ μήτ᾽ ἄλλου ἀκούων
> ἐν θυμῷ βάλληται, ὁ δ᾽ αὖτ᾽ ἀχρήϊος ἀνήρ.

[30] Clement of Alexandria *Paedagogus* 3.8 (PG 8, 614 B). Diogenes Laertius *Vita phil.* 1.21 (ed. Cobet, p. 165, 8) also refers to these lines of Hesiod.

[31] *Epist. ad Paulinum* 53.8 (PL 22, 547), *ad Nepotianum* 52.3 (PL 22, 529).

[32] *Epist. ad Paulinum* 53.8 (PL 22, 547), *In Amos* 1.1 (PL 25, 993 B), *Chron., praef.* (PL 27, 36 A).

[33] *Epist. ad Paulinum* 53.8 (PL 22, 547).

[34] *Epist. ad Nepotianum* 52.3 (PL 22, 529) and *ad Augustinum* 102.1 (PL 22, 830): "hortaris me ut παλινῳδίαν super quodam Apostoli capitulo canam et imiter Stesichorum inter vituperationem et laudes Helenae fluctuantem, ut qui detrahendo oculos perdiderat laudando recepit." Perhaps Jerome met with this anecdote in Irenaeus *Adversus haereses* 1.23.2 (PG 7, 672 A): "(Helena) quapropter et Stesichorum per carmina maledicentem eam, orbatum oculis (dicunt): post deinde paenitentem et scribentem eas, quae

only by reputation. In the case of Aratus,[36] Epimenides,[37] and Menander,[38] he only quotes and comments on the verses quoted in the New Testament. He discusses the authenticity of the verse by Epimenides that was probably used later by Callimachus, but all the data of this philological problem come to him from the Greek commentators on the Scriptures.[39]

Jerome also quotes Euripides and Aristophanes. But he has certainly read the verse that he quotes from Euripides' *Andromache* in Plutarch's *De praeceptis coniugalibus*, from which he borrows an entire discussion on women.[40] Another reference to Euripides is derived from Porphyry's *De abstinentia*,

---

vocantur, palinodias, in quibus hymnizavit eam, rursus vidisse." Tertullian *De anima* 34 (*PL* 2, 709 A) repeats this item, but without the word *palinodia*. Cf. below, n. 80.

[35] He mentions him twice: *Epist. ad Nepotianum* 52.3 (*PL* 22, 529) and *In Danielem* 11 (*PL* 25, 558 C), but the first mention comes from Cicero *De senectute* 22, and the second one from Jerome's *Chronicle*, Olympiad 75–78 (*PL* 27, 447).

[36] Aratus *Phaenom.* 5: τοῦ γὰρ καὶ γένος ἐσμέν, translated as "ipsius enim et genus sumus" = Act. Apost. 17.28. Cf. Jerome *Epist. ad Magnum* 70.2 (*PL* 22, 665), *In Ep. ad Tit.* 1 (*PL* 26, 572 B), *In Ep. ad Galat.* 2.4 (*PL* 26, 389 D). Cf. *In Ep. ad Ephes.* 3.5 (*PL* 26, 525 B). On the translations of Aratus known to Jerome, see above, n. 19.

[37] Epimenides (cf. Titus 1.12): Κρῆτες ἀεὶ ψεῦσται, κακὰ θηρία, γαστέρες ἀργαί, translated as "Cretenses semper mendaces, malae bestiae, ventres pigri." Cf. Jerome *Epist. ad Magnum* 70.2 (*PL* 22, 665), *In Epist. ad Tit.* 1.1 (*PL* 26, 571 A), *In Epist. ad Galat.* 1.3 and 2.4 (*PL* 26, 347 A and 389 C: "Hic versus heroicus Epimenidis poetae est, cuius et Plato et ceteri scriptores recordantur"). Cf. *Epist. ad Paulam* 33.1 (*PL* 22, 347) and *In Epist. ad Ephes.* 3.5 (*PL* 26, 525 B).

[38] Menander *Thais* frag. 2 (= I Cor. 15.13): φθείρουσιν ἤθη χρηστὰ ὁμιλίαι κακαί, translated "Corrumpunt mores bonos confabulationes pessimae." Cf. Jerome *Epist. ad Magnum* 70.2 and *ad Demetriadem* 130.18 (*PL* 22, 665 and 1121); *In Matth.* 1.7 (*PL* 26, 48 C); *In Epist. ad Galat.* 2.4 (*PL* 26, 389 D). He translates: "Corrumpunt mores bonos conloquia mala"; *In Epist. ad Tit.* 1.1 (*PL* 26, 572 B). See also *Epist. ad Pammachium* 57.5 (*PL* 22, 571) and *In Epist. ad Ephes.* 3.5 (*PL* 26, 525 B). In the *Epist. ad Nepotianum* 52.8 (*PL* 22, 535), it is probably a Latin work to which Jerome refers: "Unus quidam poeta nominatus homo, perlitteratus, cuius sunt illa conloquia poetarum ac philosophorum, cum facit Euripidem et Menandrum inter se, et alio loco Socratem atque Epicurum disserentes, quorum aetates non annis, sed saeculis scimus esse disiunctas, quantos is plausus et clamores movet?"

[39] Cf. Clement of Alexandria *Cohortatio ad Gentes* (*PG* 8, 116 B), Origen *Adv. Celsum* 3.43 (*PG* 11, 976 B), John Chrysostom *In Epist. ad Titum, hom.* 3 (*PG* 62, 677). Jerome quotes Callimachus *Hymn* 1.8: "Cretenses semper mendaces: qui et sepulchrum eius (Iovis) sacrilega mente fabricati sunt," *In Epist. ad Titum* 1.1 (*PL* 26, 573–574); cf. *Epist. ad Magnum* 70.2 (*PL* 22, 665).

[40] Euripides *Andromache* 930 (Hermione speaks): κακῶν γυναικῶν εἴσοδοί μ' ἀπώλεσαν. Cf. Jerome *Adv. Iovin.* 1.48 (*PL* 23, 292 A), "Totae Euripidis tragoediae in mulieres maledicta sunt. Unde et Hermione loquitur: Malarum me mulierum decepere consilia," and Plutarch *Praec. coniug.* 40, ed. Duebner, *Moralia*, vol. 1, p. 170. On the entire discussion in favor of chastity, directed against women, see below, pp. 71–72.

which supplied Jerome with another series of discussions.[41] Lastly, it was probably from a lexicon that Jerome borrowed two references, one from Euripides' *Medea* to explain the word ἀμβλάκημα;[42] the other from Aristophanes' *Clouds* to explain the exact meaning of the word περιφρόνησις.[43]

There is therefore no justification in asserting that Jerome had any direct and personal contact with the Greek poets. Similarly for the orators. He readily lists the most famous ones: Lysias, Hyperides, Pericles, Demosthenes.[44] Elsewhere he mentions Demosthenes and Aeschines, Lysias and Isocrates;[45] in still other contexts, Demosthenes and Polemon.[46] He knows the names but appears to be ignorant of their works. The only allusion to Lysias' writings refers actually to Plato's *Phaedrus*.[47] With regard to Isocrates, of

---

[41] *Adv. Iovin.* 2.14 (*PL* 23, 317 B): "Euripides in Creta Iovis prophetas non solum carnibus, sed et coctis cibis abstinuisse refert." Cf. Porphyry *De abstinentia* 4.19 (ed. Hercher [Paris 1858] p. 82, 49): μικροῦ με παρῆλθε καὶ τὸ Εὐριπίδειον παραθέσθαι, ὃς τοὺς ἐν Κρήτῃ τοῦ Διὸς προφήτας ἀπέχεσθαί φησι διὰ τούτων . . . τάς τ᾽ ὠμοφάγους δαῖτας τελέσας. On Porphyry, Jerome's source for the entire discussion on abstinence, see below, p. 72.

[42] *In Danielem* 6.4 (*PL* 25, 524 A): "Pro suspicione Theodotio et Aquila ἀμβλάκημα interpretati sunt. Cumque ab Hebraeo quaererem quid significaret, respondit vim verbi sonare δέλεαρ, quam nos *inlecebram* sive σφάλμα, hoc est *errorem* dicere possumus. Porro Euripides in *Medea* ἀμπλακίας per π et non per β, ἁμαρτίας, id est *peccata* appellat." Cf. Euripides *Medea* 116: τί δέ σοι παῖδες πατρὸς ἀμπλακίας μετέχουσι;

[43] *In Epist. ad Titum* 2.15 (*PL* 26, 590 B): "Περιφρόνησις autem illud sonat, sicut Stoici tamen adserunt, qui distinguunt inter verba subtiliter, cum qui confidens sibi, se alio esse meliorem, despicit eum quem inferiorem putat, et super, id est plus sapiens, humiliorem existimat dignum esse contemptu. Tale quid intumescens superbiae vanitate, et caelum ipsum solemque despiciens apud Graecos quidam dixisse deluditur: ᾿Αεροβατῶ καὶ περιφρονῶ τὸν ἥλιον, quod nos Latine possumus dicere: *Scando per aerem, et pluris me novi esse quam solem*"; *In Isaiam* 15.54 (*PL* 24, 524 D): "Porro sapphirus, qui ponitur in fundamentis, caeli habet similitudinem, et supra nos aeris: qui talis est, ut possit illud Aristophanicum dicere cum Socrate: ᾿Αεροβατῶ καὶ περιφρονῶ τὸν ἥλιον, quod nos in Latinum sermonem vertere possumus: *Scando aerem solemque despicio*." The line quoted is *Clouds* 225. Cf. Suidas *Lexicon* (ed. Bekker, Berlin 1854): ᾿Αεροβατεῖν· εἰς τὸν ἀέρα περιπατεῖν, τῷ ἀέρι ἐπιβαίνειν· ὁ Σωκράτης ἔφη· ᾿Αεροβατῶ καὶ περιφρονῶ τὸν ἥλιον. Jerome likewise seems to refer to the use of a Greek lexicon when he says, *In Epist. ad Titum* 2.12 (*PL* 26, 587 A): "Saepe mecum considerans quid sibi vellet verbum περιούσιον, et a sapientibus saeculi huius interrogans si forte alicubi legissent, numquam invenire potui qui mihi quid significaret, exponeret. Quam ob rem compulsus sum ad vetus instrumentum recurrere, under arbitrabar et Apostolum sumpsisse quod dixerat"; and *In Isaiam* 9.28.5 (*PL* 24, 329 C): "ἔμετον δυσαλίας . . . quod verbum ubi apud Graecos lectum sit, invenire non potui, nisi forte novae rei novum finxerit nomen."

[44] *In Amos* 1.1 (*PL* 25, 993 B); cf. *Epist. ad Paulinum* 58.5 (*PL* 22, 583).

[45] *Adv. Rufin.* 1.16 (*PL* 23, 428 A).

[46] *In Epist. ad Galat., praef. lib.* 3 (*PL* 26, 400 C).

[47] See below at n. 80.

whose life he is informed in Cicero's *De senectute*,[48] he quotes only a trite maxim, without naming the author.[49] He considers Demosthenes as the model of eloquence along with Cicero,[50] and he knows that Demosthenes' masterpiece is the *Philippics*.[51] But he evidently knows only the two opposing orations of Demosthenes and Aeschines *For Ctesiphon* and *Against Ctesiphon* that he read in Cicero's translation.[52] The only quotation that he uses from these two orators is a famous remark by Aeschines, which he borrows either from Plutarch or from the Latin writers.[53]

If Jerome's work nowhere indicates a direct knowledge of the Greek poets and orators, the reason may be that both poets and orators were scarcely useful in the exposition of the Scriptures. But is his knowledge of the Greek philosophers greater? He affects the most profound scorn for them, especially in his sermons to the monks of Bethlehem, where his eloquence is given free rein. Socrates, Plato, Aristotle promised to reveal the road to heaven, but they do not keep their promises.[54] Sophistry has discovered the art of lying;[55] hence the heretics are disciples of Plato or Aristotle.[56] Jerome ridicules the

---

[48] *Epist. ad Nepotianum* 52.3 (*PL* 22, 529) = Cicero *De senectute* 5.13.

[49] *In Isaiam* 11.40 (*PL* 24, 402 D): "Quod et egregius apud Graecos scribit orator, speciem corporis aut tempore deficere aut languore consumi." Cf. Isocrates *Ad Demonicum* 6 (ed. Mathieu, vol. I, p. 124): κάλλος μὲν γὰρ ἢ χρόνος ἀνήλωσεν ἢ νόσος ἐμάρανεν.

[50] *Epist. ad Demetriadem* 130.6 (*PL* 22, 1110): "contortae Demosthenis vibrataeque sententiae" (cf. Quintilian *Institutio oratoria* 10.4.55), ad *Pammachium et Oceanum* 84.6 (*PL* 22, 748): "fervens Demosthenis oratio," ad *Sabinianum* 147.5 (*PL* 22, 1199): "torrens fluvius Demosthenis." Cf. ad *Pammachium* 48.13 (*PL* 22, 502).

[51] *Epist. ad Pammachium* 57.13 (*PL* 22, 589): "Optoque, si fieri potest et si adversarii siverint, commentarios potius Scripturarum, quam Demosthenis et Tullii *Philippicas* tibi scribere." Cf. *Adv. Iovin.* 1.48 (*PL* 23, 292 A): "Philippum regem Macedonum, contra quem Demosthenis *Philippicae* tonant."

[52] See the references above, n. 14. The passage *PL* 22, 571 proves that Jerome read these two speeches after the *De optimo genere oratorum*, which served as a preface to them in the Ciceronian translation, which is no longer extant.

[53] *Epist. ad Paulinum* 53.2 (*PL* 22, 541): "Unde et Aeschines, cum Rhodi exsularet et legeretur illa Demosthenis oratio, mirantibus cunctis atque laudantibus suspirans ait: 'Quid, si ipsam audissetis bestiam, sua verba resonantem?'" Cf. Plutarch *Oratorum vitae* 6.10 (ed. Duebner, *Moralia*, vol. 2, p. 1024): Οὐκ ἄν, ἔφη, ἐθαυμάζετε, Ῥόδιοι, εἰ πρὸς ταῦτα Δημοσθένους λέγοντος ἠκούσατε; Cicero *De oratore* 3.56.213: "Quanto, inquit, magis admiraremini, si audissetis ipsum," Pliny the Younger *Epist.* 2.3.10: τί δέ, εἰ αὐτοῦ τοῦ θηρίου ἠκούσατε;

[54] *Anecd. Mareds.* 3, 2, p. 177, 8: "Promisit Socrates, promisit Plato, promisit Aristoteles."

[55] *Ibid.*, p. 215, 13: "invenerunt enim philosophi sua deceptione et propria arte, quo modo in eodem sermone et vera quis discat et mentiatur," and 3, 3, p. 34, 3: "*Calix* vero *aureus* dogmata philosophorum et eloquentia oratorum. Quis enim non inductus a philosophis? Quis enim ab oratoribus mundi istius non seductus?"

[56] *Ibid.*, 3, 2, p. 63, 25: "Omnes vero haeretici Aristotelici et Platonici sunt." Cf. p. 272, 10.

martyrs of philosophy: Zeno, Cleombrotes, Cato.[57] He even denounces the "foul dogmas" of Plato, Aristotle, Zeno, and Epicurus.[58] Yet he prides himself on his thorough knowledge of their works. He claims to have read them *all*.[59] Rhetorical exaggeration is evident. If we are to believe two passages in his letters, he had read at least in his youth the *Consolations* of the principal Greek philosophers: Anaxagoras, Crantor, Plato, Diogenes, Clitomachus, Carneades, Posidonius.[60] He also probably studied the works of Pythagoras, Plato, and Empedocles.[61] As this statement was criticized by his enemy Rufinus, he felt constrained to be precise: "De dogmatibus eorum, non de libris locutus sum, quae potui in Cicerone, Bruto ac Seneca discere."[62] He admits that he knew Pythagoras' doctrine only through the Latin writers, through Iamblichus' commentary on the Χρυσᾶ παραγγέλματα, through Aristotle and Plato, and lastly through Origen's Περὶ ἀρχῶν.[63] It is good to

---

[57] *Epist. ad Marcellam* 39.3 (*PL* 22, 468): "Tales stulta philosophia habeat martyres, habeat Zenonem, Cleombrotum vel Catonem."

[58] *In Marcum* (*Anecd. Mareds.* 3, 2, p. 359, 12): "Voluit Plato, voluit Aristoteles, voluit Zeno Stoicorum princeps, voluit et Epicurus voluptatis adsertor *dogmata* sua *sordida* sermonibus quasi candidis candidare."

[59] *Hom. in Ioannem* (*Anecd. Mareds.* 3, 2, p. 338, 32): "Legimus et litteras saeculares, legimus Platonem, legimus *ceteros* philosophos. Piscator noster invenit quod philosophus non invenit." Cf. *Adv. Rufin.* 3.29 (*PL* 23, 500 D): "Si esset locus, possem tibi vel Lucretii opiniones iuxta Epicurum, vel Aristotelis iuxta Peripateticos, vel Platonis atque Zenonis secundum Academicos et Stoicos dicere."

[60] *Epist. ad Heliod.* 60.5 (*PL* 22, 592): "Quid agimus, anima? . . . Ubi illud ab infantia studium litterarum et Anaxagorae ac Telamonis semper laudata sententia: *Sciebam me genuisse mortalem?* Legimus Crantorem, cuius volumen ad confovendum dolorem suum secutus est Cicero; Platonis, Diogenis, Clitomachi, Carneadis, Posidonii ad sedandos luctus opuscula percurrimus, qui diversis aetatibus, diversorum luctum vel libris vel epistulis minuere sunt conati, ut etiam si nostrum areret ingenium, de illorum posset fontibus inrigari. Proponunt innumerabiles viros, et maxime Periclem et Xenophontem Socraticum, quorum alter amissis duobus filiis coronatus in contione disseruit, alter cum sacrificans filium in bello audisset occisum, deposuisse coronam dicitur et eandem capiti reposuisse, postquam fortiter in acie dimicantem repperit concidisse. Quid memorem Romanos duces . . . quorum orbitates in *Consolationis* libro explicavit, ne videar potius aliena quam nostra quaesisse."

[61] *Epist. ad Pammachium et Oceanum* 84.6 (*PL* 22, 748): "Sed fac me errasse in adulescentia et philosophorum, id est gentilium studiis eruditum, in principio fidei dogmata ignorasse Christiana, et hoc putasse in Apostolis quod in Pythagora et Platone et Empedocle legeram: cur parvuli in Christo atque lactentis errorem sequimini?" Cf. *Adv. Iovin.* 2.6 (*PL* 23, 305 A): "et probabo non Empedoclis et Pythagorae nos dogma sectari, qui propter μετεμψύχωσιν omne quod movetur et vivit edendum non putant, et eiusdem criminis reos arbitrantur, qui abietem quercumque succiderint, cuius parricidae sunt et venefici."

[62] *Adv. Rufin.* 3.39 (*PL* 23, 507 A).

[63] *Ibid.*, 3.39–40 (*PL* 23, 507–509). On Jerome's Pythagorean sources, cf. *Epist. ad Pammachium* 48.19 (*PL* 22, 509): "An forsitan Pythagoram et Architam Tarentinum et Publium Scipionem in sexto *De republica* de impari numero disputantes?" Cf. Cicero *De*

remember this admission and it allows us to give the first passage the same credit as this one. He knows all the Greek philosophers who have written *Consolations* only from Cicero's *De consolatione*. This work is now lost, but all these writers are quoted equally in the *Tusculans*, as well as the heroic words attributed to Anaxagoras.[64]

Actually, Jerome's knowledge of certain philosophers is manifestly very cursory. Of Heraclitus he knows only his name and epithet,[65] and that through Eusebius' *Chronicle*. From the *Tusculans* he takes the little that he knows of the Epicurean theories against Providence and the survival of the soul,[66] and from Cicero's *De fato* he draws his clarifications on the Stoic theory of contingency.[67] Does he know Plato at least? On his biography, he must

---

republica 6.17.19. On a remark by Archytas, cf. *Epist. ad Salvinam* 79.9 (*PL* 22, 731; cf. 25, 953 C); Cicero *De republica* 1.59 and *Tusc.* 4.36, and Iamblichus *Vita Pyth.* 197. On Υ, a Pythagorean symbol, cf. *PL* 22, 645 and 873; Lactantius *Inst.* 6.3 and the texts quoted by A. Brinkmann, "Ein Denkmal des Neupythagoreismus," *Rheinisches Museum* 66 (1911) 616–625, and Cumont, *Recherches sur le symbolisme funéraire*, pp. 423 and 509. It was also through Origen and in connection with the dispute that he aroused that Jerome knew certain doctrines of Zeno and Pythagoras. Cf. *In Ieremiam* 4, praef. (*PL* 24, 794 D): "cum subito haeresis Pythagorae et Zenonis ἀπαθείας et ἀναμαρτησίας, id est *impassibilitatis* et *impeccantiae*, quae olim in Origene et dudum in discipulis eius Grunnio Evagrioque Pontico et Ioviniano iugulata est, coepit reviviscere." On Zeno and Pythagoras, cf. *PL* 25, 115 A.

[64] *Tusc.* 3.6.12 (Crantor), 1.43.103–104 (Plato and Diogenes; cf. 3.23.56), 3.22.54 (Clitomachus and Carneades: "Legimus librum Clitomachi quem ille eversa Carthagine misit consolandi causa ad captivos cives suos . . . in eo est disputatio scripta Carneadis"), 2.25.61 (Posidonius), 3.24.58 (Telamon and Anaxagoras: "Atque hoc idem et Telamo ille declarat: *Ego cum genui . . .* et Anaxagoras: *Sciebam me genuisse mortalem*"; cf. 3.13.28 and 14.29). To the same source probably belongs this preceding passage from Jerome (22, 591): "Immortalem animam et post dissolutionem corporis subsistentem, quod Pythagoras somniavit, Democritus non credidit, in consolationem damnationis suae Socrates disputavit in carcere, Indus, Persa, Gothus, Aegyptius philosophantur." The restoration in the Hilberg edition, vol. 1, p. 454, 11 (*Epist.* 53.7), *Clitomacho* for *stomacho* seems to me very doubtful.

[65] Σκοτεινός = Tenebrosus. Cf. *PL* 27, 443, 451 and 23, 222 A, 442 B.

[66] *In Ecclesiasten* 9 (*PL* 23, 1138 C): "Et haec, inquit, aliquis loquatur Epicurus et Aristippus et Cyrenaici, et ceterae pecudes philosophorum"; *In Isaiam* 7.22.12 (*PL* 24, 272 C): "dicens illud Epicuri: Post mortem nihil est et mors ipsa nihil est"; *Tract. in Ps.* (*Anecd. Mareds.* 3, 3, p. 83, 4): "O vos qui putatis ad Dominum non pertinere mortalia, qui cum Epicuro ab humanis rebus Dei curam dicitis separatam"; cf. *Tusc.*, passim, particularly 3.13.28.

[67] Cicero *De fato* 7.13, ed. Yon, p. 7:

At hoc, Chrysippe, minime vis, maximeque tibi de hoc ipso cum Diodoro certamen est. Ille enim *id solum fieri posse dicit, quod aut sit verum aut futurum sit verum, et quicquid futurum sit, id dicit fieri necesse esse, et quicquid non sit futurum, id negat fieri*

Jerome *Dial. adv. Pelagianos* 1.9 (*PL* 23, 525 A):

Inter Diodorum et Chrysippum valentissimos dialecticos Περὶ δυνατοῦ ista contentio est. Diodorus *id solum posse fieri dicit, quod aut sit verum, aut verum futurum sit. Et quidquid futurum sit, id fieri necesse*

have consulted Latin sources.[68] But Jerome specifies that he has really read Plato.[69] He assumes that it is possible for his contemporaries to read him,[70] while noting that most of them are not even familiar with his name.[71] Plato's name is to him a symbol, and he affects ironical scorn with regard to it. In the final analysis, Plato and his disciples will be found to be stupid.[72] The great mistake on the part of Plato and Pythagoras is to say that souls fell from heaven.[73] A knowledge of Plato is an insufficient recommendation for the episcopate.[74] What have Plato and St. Peter in common?[75]

Such irony is easy, but did Jerome read Plato textually? If he read the *Protagoras*, which he mentions several times but quotes nowhere, it is in Cicero's translation;[76] so, in all probability, with the *Timaeus*.[77] If Rufinus is to be believed, Jerome possessed nevertheless the Greek text of one of these

---

posse. Tu et quae non sint futura, posse fieri dicis, ut frangi hanc gemmam, *etiamsi id numquam futurum sit.*	*esse, quidquid* autem *non sit futurum, id fieri non posse.* Chrysippus vero *et quae non sunt futura posse fieri dicit: ut frangi* hoc margaritum, *etiamsi id numquam futurum sit.*

The borrowing from Cicero is certain. It may be observed that Jerome appears to be trying to conceal it and to make people believe that he has read some Greek treatise.

[68] On the choice of the Academy, cf. *Adv. Iovin.* 2.9 (*PL* 23, 311 C); on Plato's travels, *Epist. ad Paulinum* 53.1 (*PL* 22, 540) and *Adv. Rufin.* 3.40 (*PL* 23, 509 A); on his age at his death, *Epist. ad Nepotianum* 52.3 (*PL* 22, 529), evidently derived from Cicero *De senectute* 13.

[69] *Adv. Rufin.* 3.40 (*PL* 23, 509 B): "ut si dicam, quae in Socrate legi dogmata, putavi vera; non quod Socrates libros ullos scripserit, sed quae legi apud Platonem et alios Socraticos, illum habuisse."

[70] *Epist. ad Pammachium* 48.13 (*PL* 22, 502): "Legite Platonem, legite Theophrastum . . . quid in illis apertum est, quid simplex?"

[71] *In Epist. ad Galat.* 3, *praef.* (*PL* 26, 401 B): "Quotusquisque nunc Aristotelem legit? Quanti Platonis vel libros novere, vel nomen? Vix in angulis otiosi eos senes recolunt," and *Tract. in Ps.* (*Anecd. Mareds.* 3, 2, p. 104, 1): "Plato scripsit in scriptura; sed non scripsit in populis, sed paucis. Vix intellegunt tres homines."

[72] *Epist. ad Heliod.* 14.11 (*PL* 22, 354): "Tunc ignitus Iuppiter adducetur et cum suis stultus Plato discipulis."

[73] *Epist. ad Hedibiam* 120.10 (*PL* 22, 998): "ne iuxta Pythagoram et Platonem et discipulos eorum, qui sub nomine Christiano introducunt dogma gentilium, dicamus animas lapsas de caelo esse: et pro diversitate meritorum, in his vel in illis corporibus poenas antiquorum luere peccatorum," and *ad Marcellinum et Anapsychiam* 126.1 (*PL* 22, 1085): "Utrum lapsa de caelo sit, ut Pythagoras philosophus, omnesque Platonici et Origenes putant." It is always Origen and Rufinus who are envisaged through Plato.

[74] *Adv. Luciferianos* 11 (*PL* 23, 174 B): "Re vera de Platonis et Aristophanis sinu in episcopum adleguntur" (with reference to the Arian bishops).

[75] *Adv. Pelagianos* 1.14 (*PL* 23, 529 A): "Quid Platoni et Petro?"

[76] See the references above, n. 14.

[77] See the references above, n. 18.

two dialogues,[78] more probably, in my opinion, the *Timaeus*, since he compares the obscurity of this dialogue in Plato's text and in the Ciceronian translation. Jerome alludes to the skill of the *Hippias Minor*,[79] to Lysias' speech, to Socrates' recantations, and to the gardens of Adonis that Plato speaks about in the *Phaedrus*, but these are literary allusions that do not necessarily presuppose a personal knowledge of the text.[80] In fact, Jerome has only a cursory notion of Plato's philosophical theories. Of the *Phaedo*, he knows only the school maxim that philosophy is meditation on death.[81] Of the *Republic*, he knows only that Plato advocates communal treatment of women,[82] and repeats with many others[83] the famous maxim that, for the

[78] Rufinus *Apol.* 2.8 (*PL* 21, 591 D): "Mihi quoque ipsi aliquando cum de Bethlehem Ierosolymam venisset et codicem secum detulisset, in quo erat unus dialogus Ciceronis et idem ipse Graecus Platonis quod dederit ipsum codicem et aliquamdiu fuerit apud me, nullo genere negare potest."

[79] *Epist. ad Heliod.* 60.13 (*PL* 22, 597): "Unde et apud Graecos philosophus ille laudatur, qui omne quo uteretur, usque ad pallium et annulum, manu sua factum gloriatus est." Cf. *Hippias Minor* 368b. Notes that Socrates' praise of Hippias is ironical.

[80] *Adv. Iovin.* 1.49 (*PL* 23, 293 B): "Tota amoris insectatio apud Platonem exposita est et omnia eius incommoda Lysias explicat, quod non iudicio, sed furore ducatur: et maxime *uxorum* pulchritudini gravissimus custos accubet." Cf. *Phaedrus* 231ff; but it is evident that Jerome did not have the text of Plato before him, for this speech by Lysias treats not of conjugal love but of the love of young boys. This passage in Jerome is besides part of a discussion whose sources will be studied below, p. 72. On Socrates' recantations, in the style of Stesichorus, cf. *Phaedrus* 243a; Isocrates *Encomium of Helen* 64; and Jerome, text quoted above, n. 34, but I have shown that Irenaeus was perhaps the intermediary. On the garden of Adonis, cf. *Phaedrus* 276b–d and Jerome *In Isaiam* 18.65.2 (*PL* 24, 632 A): "Fertur sapientissimi apud Graecos merito celebrata et laudata sententia, qui omnes saeculi voluptates et pompam mundi atque luxuriam celeriter transeuntem, hortos Adonidis vocat," but the *fertur*, the praise bestowed on Plato, and the ecclesiastical expressions seem to indicate that Plato is not the immediate source. Lastly, the use of the word λογοδαίδαλοι (*Epist.* 57.7, *PL* 22, 574) goes back to Plato *Phaedrus* 266e, but probably through Cicero as intermediary, *Orator* 12.39.

[81] *In Hoseam* 1.1 (*PL* 25, 823 D): "Phaedonem ex cuius nomine Platonis liber est"; *Epist. ad Heliod.* 60.14 (*PL* 22, 598): "Platonis sententia est: omnem sapientium vitam meditationem esse mortis," and *ad Principiam* 127.6 (*PL* 22, 1091): "laudans illud Platonicum, qui philosophiam meditationem mortis esse dixit"; *Adv. Rufin.* 3.40 (*PL* 23, 509 A): "Philosophiam meditationem esse mortis et multa alia quae Plato in libris suis et maxime in *Phaedone Timaeo*que prosequitur"; Plato had merely said (*Phaedo* 67e): οἱ ὀρθῶς φιλοσοφοῦντες ἀποθνῄσκειν μελετῶσιν" and (*Phaedo* 80e): ἦ οὐ τοῦτ' ἂν εἴη μελέτη θανάτου; The formula *Philosophia meditatio mortis*, which we shall find again as late as Cassiodorus, already appears in Clement of Alexandria *Stromateis* 5.11 (*PG* 9, 102 B) and Cicero *Tusc.* 1.30.74: "Tota enim philosophorum vita, ut ait idem (Plato), commentatio mortis est."

[82] *Epist. ad Oceanum* 69.3 (*PL* 22, 656) and *Adv. Iovin.* 2.7 (*PL* 23, 309 A). Cf. Lactantius *Inst.* 3.21 (*PL* 6, 418 A), from which Jerome was able to draw for this discussion, derived from Plato *Republic* 5.457c–461e.

[83] Cf. Cicero *Ad Quintum fratrem* 1.1.29: "Plato tum denique fore beatas respublicas putavit, si aut docti ac sapientes homines eas regere coepissent, aut qui regerent, omne

welfare of the state, kings should be philosophers or philosophers should be rulers.[84] He also makes a brief allusion to a passage in the *Laws*.[85] In conclusion, he knows of the division of the soul into three parts but, for all his insistence that he read it in Plato, he certainly refers to some Christian commentator on Ezekiel,[86] just as a commentator on Matthew instructed him in

---

suum studium in doctrina ac sapientia conlocassent"; Lactantius *Inst.* 3.21 (*PL* 6, 418 A): "at idem (Plato) dixit beatas civitates futuras fuisse, si aut philosophi regnarent aut reges philosopharentur." This commonplace will be found as late as Boethius. Cf. below, chap. 6 (introduction) n. 13.

[84] *In Ionam* 4 (*PL* 25, 1143 A): "Unde et Plato dicit: Felices fore respublicas, si aut philosophi regnent, aut reges philosophentur." This quotation is in no sense textual; cf. Plato *Republic* 5.18, p. 473d.

[85] *In Matth.* 1.10.10 (*PL* 26, 63 A): "Et Plato praecepit duas corporis summitates non esse velandas, nec adsuefieri debere mollitiei capitis et pedum; cum haec enim habuerint firmitatem, cetera robustiora sunt." Cf. Plato *De legibus* 12.2, p. 942d: τὴν τῆς κεφαλῆς καὶ ποδῶν δύναμιν μὴ διαφθείρειν τῇ τῶν ἀλλοτρίων σκεπασμάτων περικαλυφῇ.

[86] Plato *Republic* 4.15, p. 444b. Comparison of the two following texts in Jerome is suggestive:

In Matth. 2.13.33 (*PL* 26, 91 B):

Legimus in Platone, et philosophorum dogma vulgatum est, tres esse in humana anima passiones, τὸ λογικόν quod nos possumus interpretari *rationabile*, τὸ θυμικόν quod dicamus *plenum irae* vel *irascibile*, τὸ ἐπιθυμητικόν quod appellamus *concupiscibile*: et putat ille philosophus rationabile nostrum in cerebro, iram in felle, desiderium in iecore commorari.

In Ezechielem 1.1 (*PL* 25, 22 A) (with reference to the four creatures of Scripture):

Plerique iuxta Platonem rationabile animae et irascitivum et concupiscitivum, quod ille λογικόν et θυμικόν et ἐπιθυμητικόν vocat, ad hominem et leonem ac vitulum referunt: rationem et cognitionem et mentem et consilium, eandemque virtutem atque sapientiam in cerebri arce ponentes; feritatem vero et iracundiam atque violentiam in leone, quae consistat in felle. Porro libidinem, luxuriam et omnium voluptatum cupidinem in iecore, id est in vitulo qui terrae operibus haereat. Quartamque ponunt quae super haec et extra haec tria est, quam Graeci vocant συντήρησιν quae scintilla conscientiae in Cain quoque pectore, postquam eiectus est de paradiso, non exstinguitur, et qua victi voluptatibus vel furore ipsaque interdum rationis decepti similitudine, nos peccare sentimus, quam proprie aquilae deputant . . . quam in Scripturis interdum vocari legimus Spiritum.

Tertullian *De anima* 16 (*PL* 2, 673 A) also knows this classification by Plato, but he uses the terms *rationale, indignativum, concupiscentivum*. On the other hand Origen *In Ezech. hom.* 1.16 (*PG* 13, 681 B) and Gregory of Nazianzus *Significatio in Ezech.* (*PG* 36, 665 A), commenting on the same passage in Ezechiel as Jerome does, agree with him on all points, except that the former calls βοηθοῦσα δύναμις or *fortitudo*, and the latter συνείδησις, the faculty of the soul that Jerome designates as συντήρησις.

the theory of the *Timaeus* that places the soul in the brain.[87] The only time that Jerome reproduces an extensive textual quotation from Plato, to show that he has approved falsehood, a method dear to Origen's adherents, he borrows this quotation from the sixth book of Origen's *Stromateis*.[88] Thus, although he has a general idea of Plato's works, it is not at all certain that he has read them. Or, if he has, it was very rapidly, and with the help, for a text as difficult as the *Timaeus*, of the Ciceronian translation. In Plato, it is the contemporary Neoplatonism that Jerome condemns. He charges Plato with being the distant ancestor of Origen, but he scarcely borrows his philosophy.

With regard to Aristotle, while readily mentioning his name, especially in his listings,[89] Jerome labels him with the same scorn. His syllogisms are thorny bushes.[90] What have Aristotle and St. Paul in common?[91] Very few people

---

[87] *In Matth.* 2.15.19 (*PL* 26, 109 A): "Ergo animae principale non secundum Platonem in cerebro, sed iuxta Christum in corde est," and *Epist. ad Fabiolam* 64.1 (*PL* 22, 608): "Quaeritur ubi sit animae principale. Plato in cerebro, Christus monstrat in corde" (followed by three quotations from Matthew). Cf. Plato *Timaeus* 69dff. The theory that makes the heart the seat of the ἡγεμονικόν is of Stoic origin and must have been transmitted to Jerome by Origen; cf. Origen *In Ioan.* 2.29 (*PG* 14, 177 C and n. 25).

[88] *Adv. Rufin.* 1.18 (*PL* 23, 431 A) = Plato *Republic* 3.8, p. 389b; a comparison of the two texts shows with what Ciceronian elegance, although sometimes lacking accuracy, Jerome can translate Plato:

Ἀλλὰ μὴν καὶ ἀλήθειάν γε περὶ πολλοῦ ποιητέον· εἰ γὰρ ὀρθῶς ἐλέγομεν ἄρτι, καὶ τῷ ὄντι θεοῖσι μὲν ἄχρηστον ψεῦδος, ἀνθρώποις δὲ χρήσιμον, ὡς ἐν φαρμάκου εἴδει, δῆλον ὅτι τό γε τοιοῦτον ἰατροῖς δοτέον, ἰδιώταις δὲ οὐχ ἁπτέον.—Δῆλον, ἔφη. —Τοῖς ἄρχουσι δὴ τῆς πόλεως, εἴπερ τισὶν ἄλλοις, προσήκει ψεύδεσθαι ἢ πολεμίων ἢ πολιτῶν ἕνεκα, ἐπ' ὠφελείᾳ τῆς πόλεως· τοῖς δὲ ἄλλοις πᾶσιν οὐχ ἁπτέον τοῦ τοιούτου.	Nominavi librum, in quo hoc scriptum legerim, id est sextum *Stromateon* Origenis, in quo Platonis sententiae nostrum dogma componens, ita loquitur: Plato in tertio *De republica* libro: Veritas quoque *sectanda* magnopere est. Si enim, ut paulo ante rectissime dicebamus, *Deo indecens* et inutile mendacium est, hominibus *quandoque* utile (ut utantur eo quasi *condimento* atque medicamine); nulli dubium est quin huiusmodi licentia medicis danda sit, et ab *imprudentibus* removenda. — Vera, inquit, adseris. —Ergo principes urbium, si quibus et aliis hoc conceditur, oportet aliquando mentiri, vel contra hostes, vel pro patria et civibus. Ab aliis vero qui uti mendacio nesciunt, *auferendum est omne mendacium*.

[89] *Epist. ad Pammachium* 48.13 (*PL* 22, 502): "Legite Platonem, Theophrastum, Xenophontem, Aristotelem et reliquos qui de Socratis fonte manantes diversis cucurrere rivulis." Cf. *ad Domnionem* 50.1 (*PL* 22, 513); *Adv. Rufin.* 3.29 (*PL* 23, 500 D); *In Amos* 1.1 (*PL* 25, 993 B): "In ore philosophorum semper Socrates et Plato, Xenophon et Theophrastus, Zeno et Aristoteles, Stoici versantur et Peripatetici."

[90] *In Epist. ad Titum* 3 (*PL* 26, 596 A): "Dialectici, quorum Aristoteles princeps est, solent argumentationum retia tendere et vagam rhetoricae libertatem in syllogismorum *spineta* concludere"; *In Nahum* 3 (*PL* 25, 1269 C): "Aristotelis et Chrysippi *spineta*";

nowadays read him.[92] His dialectic particularly serves the Arians.[93] It will hardly serve on Judgment Day.[94] But the only detail of his life that Jerome mentions is taken from Quintilian.[95] He is totally ignorant of Aristotle's metaphysical works. To him, as to his contemporaries, Aristotle is above all a logician and a naturalist. He assuredly read Aristotle's treatises that were part of the course of dialectic studies, at least through the commentaries of Alexander of Aphrodisias.[96] We shall see later what he knows of Aristotle as a naturalist, always associated, for Jerome, with Theophrastus.[97] Of Theophrastus himself, whom he names several times among the pagan philosophers,[98] he barely quotes more than one maxim from the *De amicitia*, which he knows through Cicero.[99]

However, the chapters in the polemic *Adversus Iovinianum* wherein Jerome disparages marriage in contrast to chastity testify to his having read the pagan

---

Adv. Helvidium 2 (PL 23, 194 A): "Non dialecticorum tendiculas, nec Aristotelis *spineta* conquirimus."

[91] *Dial. adv. Pelagianos* 1.14 (PL 23, 529 A): "Quid Aristoteli et Paulo?"

[92] *In Epist. ad Galat.* 3, *praef.* (PL 26, 401 B): "Quotusquisque nunc Aristotelem legit?"

[93] *Adv. Luciferianos* 11 (PL 23, 174 C): "Ariana haeresis . . . argumentationum rivos de Aristotelis fontibus mutuatur."

[94] *Epist. ad Heliod.* 14.14 (PL 22, 354): "Aristotelis argumenta non proderunt."

[95] Quint. *Inst. or.* 1.1.23:   *Epist. ad Laetam* 107.4 (PL 22, 871):

An *Philippus* Macedonum rex Alexandro *filio* suo prima *litterarum* elementa *tradi* ab *Aristotele*, summo eius aetatis philosopho, voluisset, aut ille suscepisset hoc officium, si non studiorum *initia* perfectissimo quoque tractari, pertinere ad summam credidisset.	Nec puto erubescet vir doctus id facere in propinqua vel in nobili virgine, quod *Aristoteles* fecit in *Philippi filio*, ut ipse librariorum utilitate *initia traderet litterarum*. Non sunt contemnenda quasi parva, sine quibus magna constare non possunt.

[96] See the texts quoted above, sec. 1 n. 8, for comparison with *Adv. Rufin.* 1.20 (PL 23, 433 A): "Revolve Aristotelem et Alexandrum Aristotelis volumina disserentem; et quanta ambiguorum sit copia, eorum lectione cognosces."

[97] See below, n. 208.

[98] See the texts quoted above, n. 89.

[99] *In Michaeam* 2.7 (PL 25, 1219 B): "Scripsit Theophrastus tria de amicitia volumina, omni eam praeferens charitati, et tamen raram in rebus humanis esse contestatus est"; *In Hoseam* 3, *praef.* (PL 25, 905 A): "quamquam et amor recipiat errorem pulchrumque sit illud Θεοφράστου, quod Tullius magis ad sensum quam ad verbum interpretatus est: τυφλὸν τὸ φιλοῦν περὶ τὸ φιλούμενον, id est *amantium caeca iudicia sunt*"; *Adv. Ioann. Hieros.* 3 (PL 23, 373 B): "Scribunt saeculi litterae, amantium caeca esse iudicia." The passage from Cicero to which Jerome refers is lost. A similar idea is expressed in his *De amicitia* 85: "cum iudicaris, diligere oportet, non cum dilexeris, iudicare"; cf. Plutarch *De fraterno amore* 8 (ed. Duebner, *Moralia*, vol. 1, p. 584): τοὺς μὲν ἀλλοτρίους, ὡς ἔλεγε Θεόφραστος, οὐ φιλοῦντα δεῖ κρίνειν, ἀλλὰ κρίναντα φιλεῖν. This aphorism goes back to Plato *Laws* 5.4, p. 731e: τυφλοῦται γὰρ περὶ τὸ φιλούμενον ὁ φιλῶν. Cf. Plutarch *Quaest. Platon.* (ed. Duebner, *Moralia*, vol. 2, p. 1223): τυφλοῦται γὰρ τὸ φιλοῦν περὶ τὸ φιλούμενον. Cf. G. Heylbut, *De Theophrasti libris Περὶ φιλίας* (diss. Bonn 1876).

moralists. He has a long textual quotation from Theophrastus and bases his entire discussion on the authority of Aristotle, Plutarch, and Seneca: "scripserunt Aristoteles et Plutarchus et noster Seneca de matrimonio libros ex quibus et superiora nonnulla sunt et ista quae subicimus."[100] These chapters (1.41–49) have been studied by Bock, who investigated the source. Bock concluded that the sole source was Tertullian's lost *De nuptiarum angustiis*.[101] This theory, based on the erroneous interpretation of a parallel between Jerome and the *De nuptiis* by Hugh of Saint Victor, has been easily refuted by Grossgerge, then by Bickel.[102] The latter has shown in a brilliant analysis that the direct sources were, apart from Seneca's *De matrimonio*, Plutarch's Γαμικὰ παραγγέλματα and a lost treatise by Porphyry possibly called Περὶ ἁγνοῦ βίου. Jerome borrowed from Porphyry his quotations from Aristotle and Theophrastus and his entire discussion on chastity among the pagans. He was satisfied with inserting a few comments derived from his personal reading: a quotation from Xenophon and one from Sextus Pythagoreus.[103]

The fact is that Jerome takes a lively interest in the history of religions and in the pagan controversy against Christianity. Porphyry in particular held his attention. He used the *Isagoge* in his youth, in the course of his dialectic studies,[104] but Porphyry's religious treatises attracted him still more. He borrows from them at great length, concealing his source, because he fears that his enemies may accuse him of indulgence to paganism. In the treatise *Adversus Rufinum*, in order to prove that he knows Pythagoras, Jerome quotes a number of Pythagorean apothegms. He even takes care to quote the first one in Greek and to translate it:

Φυγαδευτέον πάσῃ μηχανῇ καὶ περικοπτέον πυρὶ καὶ σιδήρῳ καὶ μηχαναῖς παντοίαις, ἀπὸ μὲν σώματος νόσον, ἀπὸ δὲ ψυχῆς ἀμαθίαν, κοιλίας δὲ πολυτέλειαν, πόλεως δὲ στάσιν, οἴκου δὲ διχοφροσύνην, ὁμοῦ δὲ πάντων ἀμετρίαν, quod in Latinum ita possumus vertere: Fuganda sunt omnibus modis et abscindenda languor a corpore, imperitia ab animo, luxuria a ventre, a civitate seditio, a domo discordia et in commune a cunctis rebus intemperantia.[105]

This Greek fragment is taken word for word from the *Life of Pythagoras*

---

[100] *Adv. Iovin.* 1.49 (PL 13, 293 A).

[101] F. Bock, "Aristoteles, Theophrastus, Seneca de matrimonio," *Leipziger Studien zur class. Philol.* 19 (1899) 3–71.

[102] G. Grossgerge, *De Senecae et Theophrasti libris de matrimonio* (diss. Königsberg 1911) 8–15; Bickel, *Diatribe*, vol. I, pp. 18, 116, 213; chap. 5, pp. 129–220, is entitled "De Porphyrio περὶ ἁγνείας scriptore."

[103] Bickel, *Diatribe*, pp. 325 and 357.

[104] See above, p. 49.

[105] *Adv. Rufin.* 3.39 (PL 23, 507 B).

by Porphyry,[106] just like all the rest of the chapter.[107] The chapters relating to abstinence among the various nations that appear in the treatise *Adversus Iovinianum* are also entirely plagiarized from another work by Porphyry, the *De abstinentia*, which Jerome is at pains not to mention. He begins by collecting in one chapter all that he could gather together in each book of the *De abstinentia* on the various customs of nations, in particular on their food.[108] Then he passes on to the end of Porphyry's Book 1 and most frequently reproduces word for word the substance of each chapter.[109] He does not trouble himself about accuracy. The opinion that Porphyry attributed to the Epicureans is put by Jerome into the mouth of Epicurus himself. Furthermore, he distorts at his discretion Porphyry's thought, shamelessly giving it a Christian tone:

De abstin. 1.52, p. 20, 52:

Εἰ δὲ μὴ πρὸς τὴν Μίλωνος ῥώμην τὰ ἄψυχα συμβάλλεται οὐδὲ ὅλως πρὸς ἐπίτασιν ἰσχύος, οὐδὲ γὰρ ῥώμης οὐδὲ ἐπιτάσεως ἰσχύος χρεία τῷ φιλοσόφῳ, εἰ μέλλοι θεωρίᾳ καὶ μὴ πράξεσι καὶ ἀκολασίαις προσέχειν. Οὐδὲν δὲ θαυμαστὸν τοὺς πολλοὺς οἴεσθαι εἰς ὑγίειαν συντελεῖν τὴν κρεηφαγίαν· τῶν γὰρ αὐτῶν ἦν καὶ τὰς ἀπολαύσεις οἴεσθαι ὑγιεία, εἶναι τηρητικὰς καὶ τὰ ἀφροδίσια, ὧν ὤνησε μὲν οὐδένα τινά, ἀγαπητὸν δὲ εἰ μὴ ἔβλαψεν.

Adv. Iovin. 2.11 (*PL* 23, 314 C):

Si autem Milonis illius Crotoniatae vires olera non ministrant, quae nascuntur et aluntur ex carnibus, quid necesse est viro sapienti et philosopho *Christi* tantam habere fortitudinem, quae athletis et militibus necessaria est, quam cum habuerit, ad vitia provocetur? Illi arbitrentur carnes sanitati congruas, qui volunt abuti libidine, et in coenum demersi voluptatum, ad coitum semper exaestuant. *Christiano sanitas absque viribus nimiis necessaria est.*

---

[106] Porphyry, *Vita Pythag.* 22, ed. Westermann (Paris 1878) p. 92, 17–23. This passage appears to have been translated by Macrobius also, probably at the end of Book 2 of the *Saturnalia*, now in fragments only; for John of Salisbury *Policraticus* 8.15 (*PL* 199, 775 D) quotes it in the form: "Fugienda sunt, inquit Macrobius, omnibus modis et abscidenda *igne et ferro totoque artificio separanda* languor a corpore, imperitia ab animo, luxuria a ventre, a civitate seditio, a domo discordia, et in commune a cunctis rebus intemperantia."

[107] Cf. *Adv. Rufin.* 3.39 (*PL* 23, 507 C–508 A) and Porphyry *Vita Pythag.* 33, 40, 41, 42. It is the Pythagorean maxims of paragraphs 41–42, translated by Jerome, that appear in Seneca's apocryphal *De moribus*, compiled before the year 567, possibly by Martin of Bracara. B. Hauréau, "Notice sur le numéro 16590 des manuscrits latins de la B.N.," *Notices et extraits des manuscrits de la B.N.* 33, 1, pp. 227–233, had not been able to discover from what Greek or Latin Father the compiler of the *De moribus* had borrowed these quotations from Porphyry. Cf. *PL* 72, 32 C and Manitius, *Geschichte*, vol. 1, p. 112.

[108] *Adv. Iovin.* 2.7 (*PL* 23, 307–310) = Porphyry *De abstinentia*, ed. Hercher, Paris 1858. The exact references to the various passages in Porphyry will be found in the critical edition annotated by Bickel, *Diatribe*, pp. 395–420. Jerome's translation *suspendunt*, p. 403, 7 ed. Bickel, although Porphyry has κατακρημνίζουσι, does not prove, as Luebeck claimed, *Hieronymus quos noverit scriptores*, p. 7 n. 1, that Jerome was unfamiliar with Greek. His copy of the *De abstinentia* perhaps read κατακρημνῶσι. It would at any rate be only a case of a careless reading, not a mistake in translation.

[109] *Adv. Iovin.* 2.11–12 (*PL* 23, 314–315) = Porphyry *De abstinentia* 1.47–53.

To the entire discussion taken from Book 1, Jerome adds another taken from Book 4, which he analyzes almost entirely with the support of many authorities brought forward by Porphyry. Among these are: Dicaearchus, Theophrastus, Chaeremon, Josephus, Neanthes of Cyzicus, Asclepiades of Cyprus, Eubulus, Bardesanes, Euripides, Xenocrates.[110] It is even probable that the end of Jerome's chapter, with the examples from Orpheus, Pythagoras, Socrates, Antisthenes, Diogenes, and the quotation from Satyrus[111] are all derived from the last part of Porphyry's Book 14, now lost. Thus, thanks to Porphyry, who is not mentioned, Jerome makes a display of second-hand erudition. His own contribution is confined to a few lines on Persian frugality, for which he is indebted to Xenophon's *Cyropedia*,[112] and to a statement that Philo wrote a book on the customs of the Essenes.[113] He has not even taken the trouble to verify the statement by Porphyry, who wrongly claims that he read in Josephus that the Essenes abstained from meat and wine.[114] The only reference that he appears to have consulted is Chaeremon's work on the life of Egyptian priests.[115] We have therefore to do with a quite flagrant instance of plagiarism. We must assume that Jerome was not in the least afraid that the *De abstinentia* was already known in the West. Otherwise, Iovinianus and his friends would not have failed to make an outcry against the scandal, declaring that their enemy borrowed from the impious Porphyry the arguments that he hurled against them.

While maintaining silence about his source when using Porphyry's *Life of Pythagoras* or the *De abstinentia*, Jerome claimed that he knew quite well Porphyry's Κατὰ χριστιανῶν and mentioned it very frequently.[116] His *Commentary on Daniel*, in particular, includes a very detailed discussion of Porphyry's Book 12.[117] Furthermore, it seems that Jerome promises a total refutation of Porphyry's works, a plan that he never fulfilled.[118] He therefore

---

[110] *Adv. Iovin.* 2.13–14 (*PL* 23, 316–317) = Porphyry *De abstinentia* 4.2–22, ed. Hercher, pp. 68–85.

[111] *Ibid.*, *PL* 23, 317 C–319 A.

[112] *Ibid.*, *PL* 23, 316 A. See below, n. 163.

[113] *PL* 23, 317 A. Jerome does not mention this book in the information in the *De vir. inl.*, chap. 11, which he devotes to Philo.

[114] *PL* 23, 317 A and n. 1.

[115] Cf. Bickel, *Diatribe*, p. 86.

[116] These passages have been collected by Adolf von Harnack, "Porphyrius *Gegen die Christen* 15 Bücher, Zeugnisse, Fragmente und Referate," *Abhandlungen der kön. preussischen Akademie*, phil.-hist. Klasse, 1 (Berlin 1916) 3–115.

[117] Jean Lataix, "Le commentaire de s. Jérôme sur Daniel," *RHLR* 2 (1897) 164–173, was even able to study in detail the *Opinions of Porphyry* from this commentary.

[118] *In Epist. ad Galat.* 1.2.11ff (*PL* 26, 341 D): "Sed et adversum Porphyrium in alio, si Christus iusserit, opere pugnabimus: nunc reliqua prosequamur." This work would have been along the lines of those of the Ambrosiaster, written some twelve years earlier. Cf. above, chap. 1 n. 2.

realizes the danger of Porphyry's works, reserving for him his most violent epithets. He calls him rascal,[119] impious,[120] blasphemer,[121] calumniator,[122] sycophant,[123] mad dog,[124] poisonous serpent.[125] But had Jerome read him? It may be questioned, for Porphyry had been condemned to perdition by Constantine.[126] Most probably Jerome makes several textual quotations from this treatise, but the arguments that he raises against Porphyry's arguments are borrowed, on his own admission,[127] from the three refutations by Methodius of Olympus, Eusebius of Caesarea, Apollinaris of Laodicea, as well as certain chapters in Origen and John Chrysostom.[128] Lataix, who studied Jerome's refutation of Porphyry, even thinks he can conjecture that Jerome follows Eusebius principally.[129] Thus the numerous historians mentioned by Jerome in the preface to his *Commentary on Daniel* were available to him only through the refutations against Porphyry. Hence there is no evidence that he read Callinicus Sutorius, Diodorus Siculus, Jerome of Cardia, Polybius, Posidonius, Claudius Theo, and Andronicus Alipius.[130] In fact, Jerome asserts in the course of his commentary that he finds in Porphyry his quotations from Callinicus Sutorius,[131] Polybius, and Diodorus Siculus.[132]

[119] *PL* 26, 310 C.

[120] *PL* 23: 511 B, 363 D; 25, 504 B–C.

[121] *PL* 22: 919, 923; 24, 513 B; 26, 341 B.

[122] *PL* 25, 505 A.

[123] *PL* 25, 512 D.

[124] *PL* 23, 634 B.

[125] *PL* 25, 575 C.

[126] Cf. Harnack, "Porphyrius *Gegen die Christen*," pp. 5 and 31.

[127] This is the opinion of Harnack, "Porphyrius *Gegen die Christen*," p. 7, and of Labriolle, *La réaction païenne*, p. 292. The principal passages where Jerome makes these refutations are *PL* 22: 502, 666; 25: 491 B, 492 B, 493 A, 548 B, 575 A, 580 A; 26, 178 A.

[128] *Epist. ad Augustinum* III.6 (*PL* 22, 919): "Hanc autem explanationem quam primus Origenes in decimo *Stromateon* libro, ubi epistulam Pauli ad Galatas interpretatur, et ceteri deinceps interpretes sunt secuti, illa vel maxime causa subintroducunt, ut Porphyrio respondeant blasphemanti . . . Quid dicam de Ioanne qui dudum in pontificali gradu Constantinopolitanam rexit Ecclesiam, et proprie super hoc capitulo latissimum exaravit librum, in qua Origenis et veterum sententiam est secutus? Si igitur me reprehendis errantem, patere me, quaeso, errare cum talibus."

[129] Lataix, "Le commentaire de s. Jérôme sur Daniel," p. 165.

[130] *In Danielem, praef.* (*PL* 25, 494 A): "Ad intellegendas autem extremas partes Danielis, multiplex Graecorum historia necessaria est: Sutorii videlicet Callinici, Diodori, Hieronymi, Polybii, Posidonii, Claudii Theonis et Andronici cognomento Alipii, quos et Porphyrius esse secutum se dicit; Iosephi quoque et eorum quos ponit Iosephus, praecipueque nostri Livii et Pompeii Trogi atque Iustini."

[131] *In Dan.* 11.21 (*PL* 25, 566 D): "Haec Porphyrius sequens, Sutorium sermone laciniosissimo prosecutus est, quae nos brevi compendio diximus."

[132] *In Dan.* 11.36 (*PL* 25, 570 C–D): "Porphyrius autem et ceteri qui sequuntur eum de Antiocho Epiphane dici arbitrantur . . . quodque sequitur *et diriget, donec compleatur ira, quia in ipso erit consummatio* sic intellegunt, tam diu eum posse, donec irascatur ei Deus et ipsum interfici iubeat. Siquidem Polybius et Diodorus qui Bibliothecarum scribunt hi-

If Jerome did not himself read Porphyry's Κατὰ χριστιανῶν, at least he is one of the few writers to have a precise idea of its contents.[133] He is also, better than anyone, abreast of the antichristian polemics among the Hellenizing circles. Celsus, Porphyry, and Julian are in his eyes the three symbols of impiety.[134] Even if he does not have at his disposal the basic texts that have been lost, he at least knows Celsus through Origen,[135] and Porphyry through Methodius, Eusebius, and Apollinaris. As for the Emperor Julian's work *Against the Galileans*, Jerome mentions it and quotes it[136] and for a moment thinks perhaps of refuting it, along with Porphyry.[137] But it is difficult to decide whether he read it in the actual text[138] or knew it only through the

---

storias, narrant eum non solum contra Deum fecisse Iudaeae, sed avaritiae facibus accensum etiam templum Dianae in Elimaide, quod erat ditissimum, spoliare conatum." The probable borrowings made from Polybius through the intermediary of Porphyry were brought to light by R. von Scala, "Ueber neue Polybiusbruchstücke bei Hieronymus," *Verhandl. der 42. Philologenversammlung* (Leipzig 1894) 357–358. He notes that these borrowings, when compared with those made by Livy, are more faithful in Porphyry-Jerome than in Livy.

133 Harnack, "Porphyrius *Gegen die Christen*," p. 8 n. 4. On the refutation of Porphyry by Pacatus, cf. below, p. 226.

134 *Epist. ad Pammachium* 57.9 (*PL* 22, 575): "Hoc quippe impiorum est Celsi, Porphyrii, Iuliani." *De vir. inl., praef.* (*PL* 23, 634 B): "Discant ergo Celsus, Porphyrius, Iulianus rabidi adversus Christum canes, discant eorum sectatores (qui putant Ecclesiam nullos philosophos et eloquentes, nullos habuisse doctores) quanti et quales viri eam fundaverint, exstruxerint et adornaverint."

135 *Epist. ad Magnum* 70.3 (*PL* 22, 666): "Scripserunt contra nos Celsus atque Porphyrius: priori Origenes, alteri Methodius, Eusebius et Apollinaris fortissime responderunt. Quorum Origenes octo scripsit libros." *Epist. ad Pammachium* 48.13 (*PL* 22, 502): "Origenes, Methodius, Eusebius, Apollinaris multis versuum milibus scribunt adversus Celsum et Porphyrium"; cf. *Adv. Rufin.* 2.33 (*PL* 23, 476 B) and 3.42 (*PL* 23, 511 B): "Adversum impiissimos Celsum atque Porphyrium quanti scripsere nostrorum?"

136 *In Matth.* 1.2.16 (*PL* 26, 23 B): "Hoc loco obiecit nobis Iulianus Augustus dissonantiam Evangelistarum, cur evangelista Matthaeus Ioseph dixerit filium Iacob, et Lucas eum filium appellarit Heli," and 1.9.9 (*PL* 26, 56 A): "Arguit in hoc loco Porphyrius et Iulianus Augustus vel imperitiam historici mentientis, vel stultitiam eorum qui statim secuti sint Salvatorem."

137 *Epist. ad Magnum* 70.3 (*PL* 22, 666): "Iulianus Augustus septem libros in expeditione Parthica adversum Christum evomuit et iuxta fabulas poetarum suo se ense laceravit. Si contra hunc scribere tentavero, puto, interdices mihi ne rabidum canem Philosophorum et Stoicorum doctrinis, id est Herculis clava percutiam?" and *In Hoseam* 3.11.1 (*PL* 25, 915 B): "Hunc locum in septimo volumine Iulianus Augustus, quod adversum nos, id est Christianos, evomuit, calumniatur et dicit: quod de Israel scriptum est, Matthaeus evangelista ad Christum transtulit (*Matth.* 2.15), ut simplicitati eorum qui de gentibus crediderant, inluderet."

138 The work was recent. Gregory of Nazianzus, Jerome's master, had composed two *Invectives* against him (cf. Labriolle, *La réaction païenne*, p. 427) and the *Ambrosiaster* challenges his influence, which was still profound in Rome around 375, as F. Cumont has shown, "La polémique de l'Ambrosiaster," pp. 427–431. Jerome himself notes *In Abacuc*

refutation made by Apollinaris of Laodicea.[139] For all his invectives, Jerome displays a lively interest in the religious works of the Neoplatonists. Not only did he read Porphyry's *Life of Pythagoras* and the *De abstinentia* with such an eager concern that he plagiarized them, but he boasts of having read Iamblichus' commentary on Porphyry's Χρυσᾶ παραγγέλματα, that is, chapter 21 of his *Adhortatio ad philosophiam*.[140] He makes a very succinct summary of Philostratus' *Life of Apollonius of Tyana*,[141] a work of which he speaks with admiration, although he does not know that Porphyry compared the miracles of Apollonius with those of Christ and the Apostles.[142] It is not

2.3.14 (*PL* 25, 1329 D) what a revolution Julian's death had provoked: "Dum adhuc essem puer, et in grammaticae ludo exercerer, omnesque urbes victimarum sanguine polluerentur, ac subito in ipso persecutionis ardore Iuliani nuntiatus esset interitus, eleganter unus de ethnicis: Quo modo, inquit, Christiani dicunt Deum suum esse patientem et ἀνεξίκακον? Nihil iracundius, nihil hoc furore praesentius: ne modico quidem spatio indignationem suam differre potuit. Hoc ille ludens dixerit."

[139] It is surprising that Jerome assigns seven books to *Against the Galileans*, which was really in three books. According to the conjecture of the editor, Neumann, p. 100, Jerome's mistake was due to his having read a rebuttal in seven books. On Julian's rebuttal by Apollinaris, cf. Puech, *Hist. de la litt. grecque chrét.*, vol. 3, p. 634.

[140] *Adv. Rufin.* 3.39 (*PL* 23, 507 A): "Cuius enim sunt illa Χρυσᾶ παραγγέλματα? Nonne Pythagorae? In quibus omnia eius breviter dogmata continentur et in quae latissimo opere philosophus commentatus est Iamblichus, imitatus ex parte Moderatum virum eloquentissimum et Archippum ac Lysidem Pythagorae auditores." He is here referring to the commentary *Symbola Pythagorica* that concludes Iamblichus' *Protreptica* (ed. Th. Kiessling [Leipzig 1813] 307–379) and not to a lost commentary on the *Golden Verses*, as Zeller thinks, *Die Philosophie der Griechen*, 3, 2, 2, p. 739 n. 1.

[141] *Epist. ad Paulinum* 53.1 (*PL* 22, 541): "Apollonius (sive ille Magus, ut vulgus loquitur, sive philosophus, ut Pythagorici tradunt) intravit Persas, pertransivit Caucasum" (2.2). There follows a summary of his travels among the Brahmins (3.10); he converses with Iarchas, who is sitting on a golden throne (3.16) and drinking the water of Tantalus (3.32), discoursing of nature (3.34), the stars (3.41). He next goes to Alexandria (5.24), then consults the Gymnosophists in Ethiopia (6.4ff). Jerome concludes: "Invenit ille vir ubique quod disceret, et semper proficiens semper se melior fieret. Scripsit super hoc plenissime octo voluminibus Philostratus." The editor Hilberg, vol. 1, p. 445, is wrong, in my opinion, in considering as an interpolation this last sentence, which appears in all the manuscripts and is in Jerome's style. It will be noted that about the time when Jerome wrote, Philostratus' *Life of Apollonius* was translated into Latin by Virius Nicomachus Flavianus (cf. above, chap. 1 sec. 1 n. 23) and Apollonius of Tyana was discussed also by St. Augustine (cf. Labriolle, *La réaction païenne*, p. 455).

[142] *Tract. de Ps.* 81 (*Anecd. Mareds.* 3, 2, p. 80 = frag. 4 in Harnack's collection, p. 46): "Hoc enim dicit Porphyrius: Homines rusticani et pauperes, quoniam nihil habebant, magicis artibus operati sunt quaedam signa. Non est autem grande facere signa. Nam fecerunt signa et in Aegypto magi contra Moysen. Fecit et Apollonius, fecit et Apuleius: et infinita signa fecerunt," and *Adv. Ioann. Hieros.* 34 (*PL* 23, 404 C): "Apollonius Tyaneus scribitur, cum ante Domitianum staret in consistorio, repente non comparuisse. Noli potentiam Domini magorum praestigiis adaequare." Cf. Philostr. 8.5, Porphyry, frag. 63 (ed. Harnack, p. 85), Lactantius *Inst.* 5.3. Jerome is severe not against Apollonius but against Porphyry, who draws conclusions from this episode in Apollonius' life.

surprising that Jerome, temperamentally a polemist, should have displayed a lively interest in the age-old controversy between pagans and Christians. It is, however, curious to note that this critic who scorned Plato indulgently evaluated and read with such interest several religious works of the Neoplatonists. On the other hand, Jerome has no indulgence for the Oriental religions, particularly for the Mithraic cult, which he appears to know better than the others.[143]

Jerome also makes use of the Greek historians, but he is far from having read all those that he mentions. In the first place, a reference to Greek history does not necessarily imply that Jerome has a Greek source before him, nor even a historian. For instance, he refers to Greek history in connection with the education of Alexander the Great, but his direct source is certainly Quintilian.[144] It is questionable whether such a rhetorical passage, in which Jerome invokes the testimony of Greek and Roman history, really presupposes a Greek source.[145] On the other hand, as we have already ascertained in the case of Porphyry,[146] when Jerome makes a display of learning and assembles quotations from ancient historians, it is a sign that he takes them from

---

[143] *Epist. ad Laetam* 107.2 (*PL* 22, 869): "Ante paucos annos propinquus vester Graccus . . . cum praefecturam gereret urbanam, nonne specum Mithrae et omnia portentosa simulacra quibus Corax, Nymphus, Miles, Leo, Perses, Helios, Dromo, Pater initiantur, subvertit, fregit, excussit? . . . Iam Aegyptius Serapis factus est Christianus. Marnas Gazae luget inclusus et eversionem templi iugiter pertimescit." Jerome also mentions the conversion of the Hindus, Persians, Ethiopians, Armenians, Huns, Scythians, Goths, but he knows nothing of their ancient religion.

[144] Quint. *Inst. or.* 1.1.9:   *Epist. ad Laetam* 107.4 (*PL* 22, 872):

Si quidem Leonides Alexandri paeda-   *Graeca narrat historia* Alexandrum po-
gogus, *ut a Babylonio Diogene traditur*, qui-   tentissimum regem orbisque domitorem,
busdam eum vitiis imbuit, quae robustum   et in moribus, et in incessu, Leonidis pae-
quoque et iam maximum regem ab illa in-   dagogi sui non potuisse carere vitiis, qui-
stitutione puerili sunt prosecuta.   bus adhuc parvulus esset infectus.

The borrowing from Quintilian is proved certain by the context. See above, n. 95.

[145] For example, *Epist. ad Vitalem* 72.2 (*PL* 22, 674): "Legamus veteres historias et maxime Graecas ac Latinas, et inveniemus lustralibus hostiis secundum errorem veterum portentuosas soboles tam in hominibus quam in armentis ac pecudibus expiatas."

[146] See above, p. 73. It is also probably through an intermediary that Jerome knows Phlegon of Tralles and Nicolaus of Damascus in the following passages: *Quaest. Hebr. in Gen.* 10.4 (*PL* 23, 1001 A): "Legamus Varronis *De Antiquitatibus* libros et Sisinnii Capitonis et Graecum Phlegonta, ceterosque eruditissimos viros, et videbimus omnes paene insulas et totius orbis litora terrasque mari vicinas Graecis accolis occupatas." Cf. *Chron. ann. ab Abr.* 2047 (*PL* 27, 571), where Jerome quotes Phlegon's thirteenth book from Eusebius. The intermediary is a commentator on Ezekiel in *In Ezechielem* 8.26.6 (*PL* 25, 242 C): "Graecas et Phoenicum maximeque Nicolai Damasceni et alias Barbarorum aiunt se, qui huic historiae contradicunt, legisse historias, et nihil super oppugnatione a Chaldaeis invenisse Tyriae civitatis, cum probare possimus multa dici in Scripturis facta, quae in Graecis voluminibus non inveniantur; nec debere nos eorum auctoritati adquiescere, quorum perfidiam et mendacia detestantur."

an intermediary. It is therefore far from certain that he read all the Greek historians that he lists in the preface of his *De viris inlustribus*: Hermippus the Peripatetic, Antigonus of Carystus, Satyrus, Aristoxenes the musician,[147] and not even the Greek Apollonius whom he imitated,[148] according to his own admission. He probably borrows these names from the lost preface of Suetonius' *De viris inlustribus*.[149]

To be frank, Jerome appears to have read among the Greek historians only those who were directly useful to him for the study of the Scriptures. The name of Thucydides occurs to him only for display,[150] and the only quotation from this author that Jerome uses is a maxim that had become proverbial and of whose authorship Jerome seems to be unaware.[151] He is more familiar with Herodotus,[152] although several times he quotes him merely for literary or moral interest. These quotations, at second hand, come from Plutarch[153] or Clement of Alexandria.[154] The allusion that Jerome makes to the episode

---

[147] *De vir. inl., prol.* (PL 23, 631 A): "Fecerunt hoc idem apud Graecos Hermippus Peripateticus, Antigonus Carystius, Satyrus doctus vir et longe omnium doctissimus Aristoxenus musicus, apud Latinos autem Varro, Santra, Nepos, Hyginus et ad cuius exemplum nos provocas, Tranquillus."

[148] *Epist. ad Desiderium* 47.3 (PL 22, 493): "Scripsi librum de inlustribus viris, ab Apostolis usque ad nostram aetatem, imitatus Tranquillum Graecumque Apollonium."

[149] Cf. Bickel, *Diatribe*, p. 136 n. 1. Bernoulli, *Der Schriftstellerkatalog des Hieronymus* (Freiburg im Breisgau 1895) 75, had already doubted that Jerome had read all these writers.

[150] *Epist. ad Paulinum* 58.5 (PL 22, 583). "Historici (proponant sibi) Thucydidem, Sallustium, Herodotum, Livium," and *ad Heliod.* 60.16 (PL 22, 601): "Alioquin ad haec merito explicanda et Thucydides et Sallustius muti sint."

[151] *Epist. ad Evangelum* 73.9 (PL 22, 681): "Tanto supercilio et auctoritate Melchisedech Spiritum sanctum pronuntiavit, ut illud verissimum comprobarit, quod apud Graecos canitur: *Imperitia confidentiam, eruditio timorem creat.*" Thucydides 2.40.3 puts these words in Pericles' mouth: ἀμαθία μὲν θράσος, λογισμὸς δὲ ὄκνον φέρει. This quotation appears again in Pliny the Younger *Epist.* 4.7.3: "ac sicut ἀμαθία μὲν θράσος, λογισμὸς δὲ ὄκνον φέρει, ita recta ingenia debilitat verecundia, perversa confirmat audacia."

[152] *Epist. ad Paulinum* 58.5 (above, n. 150) and *In Abdiam* 1.15 (PL 25, 1110 B): "Legamus Herodotum et Graecas barbarasque historias, et videbimus quo modo sub Babyloniis et Assyriis impletum sit quod dicitur."

[153] *Adv. Iovin.* 1.48 (PL 23, 292 B): "Scribit Herodotus quod mulier cum veste deponat et verecundiam." Cf. Herodotus 1.8: ῞Αμα δὲ χιτῶνι ἐκδυομένῳ συνεκδύεται καὶ τὴν αἰδῶ γυνή, and Plutarch *Praec. coniug.* 10: Οὐκ ὀρθῶς ῾Ηρόδοτος εἶπεν, ὅτι ἡ γυνὴ ἅμα τῷ χιτῶνι ἐκδύεται καὶ τὴν αἰδῶ. This entire discussion by Jerome is largely borrowed from Plutarch (cf. above, p. 72).

[154] *Epist. ad Heliod.* 60.14 (PL 22, 598): "Hesiodus [read Herodotus] natales hominum plangens gaudet in funere"; Herodotus 1.31 concludes the story of Cleobis and Biton with these words: διέδεξέ τε ἐν τούτοις ὁ θεός, ὡς ἄμεινον εἴη ἀνθρώπῳ τεθνάναι μᾶλλον ἢ ζώειν; Clement *Stromateis* 3.3 (PG 8, 1120 A) says that Herodotus in this story οὐκ ἄλλο τι βούλεται, ἀλλ' ἢ ψέγειν μὲν τὴν γένεσιν, τὸν θάνατον δὲ ἐπαινεῖν. If Jerome's text is not corrupt, it is because he himself read *Hesiod* for *Herodotus* in his copy of Clement. This famous episode had previously been mentioned, under Herodotus' name, by Cicero *Tusc.* 1.47.

famous in literature, regarding Xerxes' tears, might have a similar source, Greek or Latin.[155] The historical data that Jerome declares he finds in Herodotus seem, however, to presuppose a direct reading of the text, although he is mistaken in attributing to facts reported by Herodotus an erroneous date.[156] He assumes in Herodotus, in his description of Babylon, units of measure that Herodotus did not use.[157] He also takes from Josephus Herodotus' account of the siege of Pelusium by Sennacherib.[158] At least he

---

[155] *Epist. ad Heliod.* 60.18 (*PL* 22, 601). Cf. Herodotus 7.45–46. The fact that Jerome does not mention the author of this anecdote inclines one to believe that he read it in an intermediary, for instance, Pliny the Younger *Epist.* 3.7.13.

[156] *Epist. ad Oceanum* 77.8 (*PL* 22, 695) and *In Ionam, prol.* (*PL* 25, 1119 B): "quantum ad historias tam Hebraeas quam Graecas pertinet, et maxime Herodotum." Cf. Herodotus 1.104–106. Jerome sets in the reign of Darius the facts that Herodotus set in the reign of Cyaxares, and in Cyaxares' reign the facts that Herodotus set in the reign of Astyages. Jerome is therefore quoting from memory, unless he is following a different chronology.

[157] Herodotus 1.178 and *In Isaiam* 5.14 (*PL* 24, 164 A). It is true that Jerome's reference, "Refert Herodotus et multi alii qui Graecas historias conscripserunt," is very vague.

[158] Herodotus 2.141:

μετὰ δὲ ἐπ' Αἴγυπτον ἐλαύνειν στρατὸν μέγαν Σαναχάριβον βασιλέα Ἀραβίων τε καὶ Ἀσσυρίων ... στρατοπεδεύσασθαι ἐν Πηλουσίῳ (Αἰγυπτίους).
(Herodotus adds only that Sennacherib's army was put to rout in one night by rats.)

In Isaiam 9.37 (*PL* 24, 385 B):

Pugnasse autem Sennacherib regem Assyriorum contra Aegyptios et obsedisse Pelusium, iamque exstructis aggeribus urbi capiendae venisse Taracham regem Aethiopum in auxilium et una nocte iuxta Ierusalem CLXXXV milia exercitus Assyrii pestilentia corruisse, narrat Herodotus et plenissime Berosus, Chaldaicae scriptor historiae, quorum fides de propriis libris petenda est.

Josephus *Ant.* 10.2.4, ed. G. Dindorf (Paris 1865), p. 368, 46:

Πολὺς αὐτῷ χρόνος διετρίβετο πρὸς τὴν τοῦ Πηλουσίου πολιορκίαν, καὶ τῶν χωμάτων ἤδη μετεώρων ὄντων, ἃ πρὸς τοῖς τείχεσιν ἤγειρε καὶ ὅσον οὔπω μέλλοντος προσβαλεῖν αὐτοῖς, ἀκούει τὸν τῶν Αἰθιόπων βασιλέα Θαρσίκην πολλὴν ἄγοντα δύναμιν ἐπὶ συμμαχίαν τοῖς Αἰγυπτίοις ἥκειν ... Μυῶν γὰρ πλῆθός φησι (Ἡρόδοτος) μιᾷ νυκτὶ καὶ τὰ τόξα καὶ τὰ λοιπὰ ὅπλα διαφαγεῖν τῶν Ἀσσυρίων καὶ διὰ τοῦτο μὴ ἔχοντα τόξα τὸν βασιλέα τὴν στρατιὰν ἀπάγειν ἀπὸ τοῦ Πηλουσίου. Καὶ Ἡρόδοτος μὲν οὕτως ἱστορεῖ ἀλλὰ καὶ Βηρωσὸς ὁ τὰ Χαλδαϊκὰ συγγραψάμενος μνημονεύει τοῦ βασιλέως τοῦ Σεναχηρίβου.

certainly read in Herodotus the description of Egypt and the detailed account of the death of Cambyses.[159] With regard to Xenophon, whom Jerome mentions several times,[160] he read the *Oeconomicus* in Cicero's translation.[161] He probably did not read the *Symposium*, for his only reference to this work seems borrowed from the same source that furnished him with an entire discussion on the thriftiness of Antisthenes and Diogenes and that may possibly be the lost conclusion of Porphyry's *De abstinentia*.[162] To counterbalance this, he read in the text and knew intimately the *Cyropedia*, to which he several times refers the reader in the course of his commentaries.[163] Jerome also frequently uses the two Jewish writers Philo and Josephus, devoting to each of them a notice in his *De viris*. Actually, Jerome's remarks on Philo are pure plagiarism from Eusebius,[164] although he pretends that he had in his possession all Philo's books that he mentions.[165] Sychowski thence

[159] Herodotus 2.5ff and 3.4ff, 27–30, and 64. Cf. *In Ezechielem* 9.29 (*PL* 25, 285 C): "Plenissime hanc historiam narrat Herodotus, ubi et omnis Aegyptus per pagos et castella et vicos describitur, et Nili origo gentisque illius populi, et mensura terrae per circuitum usque ad desertum Aethiopiae et litora magni maris, Libiaeque et Arabiae confinia demonstrantur." Similarly, *Epist.* 53.1 *ad Paulinum* (*PL* 22, 541), Jerome mentions in Ethiopia the *famosissimam Solis mensam . . . in sabulo*, not from Philostratus but from Herodotus 3.18.

[160] *Epist. ad Pammachium* 48.13 (*PL* 22, 502): "Legite Platonem, Theophrastum, Xenophontem"; *In Amos* 1.1 (*PL* 25, 993 B): "In ore philosophorum semper Socrates et Plato, Xenophon et Theophrastus . . . versantur."

[161] See above, n. 14.

[162] *Adv. Iovin.* 2.14 (*PL* 23, 318 A): "Paupertatis eius (Antisthenis) et laboris, et Xenophon testis est in Symposio." It will be observed that Diogenes Laertius in his *Life of Antisthenes* 1.13 and 15 (ed. Cobet, pp. 136–137) refers to Xenophon's *Symposium*. On Jerome's borrowing from Porphyry's *De abstinentia*, see above, p. 73. Bickel, *Diatribe*, p. 418, thinks however that this passage was inserted by Jerome in the Porphyrian context.

[163] *In Isaiam* 12.45 (*PL* 24, 441 B): "Legamus Xenophontis octo librorum Cyri maioris historiam, et prophetiam Isaiae cernemus expletam"; *In Danielem* 5.1 (*PL* 25, 518 C), regarding the destruction of the Chaldean empire by Cyrus: "Quod quidem et Xenophon in Cyri maioris scribit infantia, et Pompeius Trogus et multi alii qui barbaras scripsere historias" (cf. Xenophon *Cyrop.* 7.5.15ff); *In Ezechielem* 8.27.10 (*PL* 25, 251 D): "Lydos quoque illo tempore inter gentes robustissimas reputatos, quorum rex Croesus ab eodem Cyro captus sit, Xenophon scribit plenissime" (cf. Xenophon *Cyrop.* 7.2.3ff). On Persian thriftiness, cf. Xenophon *Cyrop.* 1.2.8; Cicero *Tusc.* 5.34.99; *Adv. Iovin.* 2.13 (*PL* 23, 316 A); *In Danielem* 7.5 (*PL* 25, 529 A), a parallel commented on by Bickel, *Diatribe*, p. 88, proving that Jerome read direct from Xenophon; similarly Xenophon *Cyrop.* 7.3.14 = *Adv. Iovin.* 1.45 (*PL* 23, 287 C). Cf. Bickel, *Diatribe*, p. 325. Lastly, the passage *Tract. in Ps.* (*Anecd. Mareds.* 3, 2, p. 276, 26) uses Xenophon *Cyrop.* 3.1 without naming him.

[164] Cf. Bernoulli, *Schriftstellerkatalog*, pp. 15 and 115, and S. von Sychowski, *Hieronymus als Litterarhistoriker, eine quellenkritische Untersuchung der Schrift des hl. Hieronymus "de viris inlustribus,"* Kirchengeschichtliche Studien, vol. 2, 2 (Münster 1894) pp. 95ff.

[165] *De vir. inl.* 11 (*PL* 23, 659 B): "Sunt et alia eius monumenta ingenii, quae in nostras manus non pervenerunt."

concludes that Jerome has read nothing of Philo and that his only personal contribution is the scholastic formula: ἢ Πλάτων φιλωνίζει ἢ Φίλων πλατωνίζει.[166] This conclusion is too hasty. To be sure, Jerome regularly mentions Philo along with Josephus and each time repeats the same vague praise of his Platonic erudition.[167] He knows, however, that Philo described in a certain book the life of the Essenes.[168] He refers to Philo for the interpretation of the Jewish priestly dress.[169] He probably makes use of his De praemiis et honoribus sacerdotum for the descriptions of Hebraic sacrifices.[170] He read Philo's De mundi opificio, from which he learned of the Platonic theory of the seven ages of life.[171] In conclusion, Jerome's De nominibus Hebraicis is merely, as he informs us, a translation of a Hebrew lexicon revised by Origen,[172] and we note further that he borrows from Philo's De somniis the explanation of a Hebrew word.[173] In all, Philo is thus, particularly for

[166] Sychowski, Hieronymus, p. 69. This formula reappears in the notices by Photius and Suidas on Philo.

[167] Epist. ad Eustachium 22.35 (PL 22, 421): "Tales Philo Platonici sermonis imitator, tales Iosephus, Graecus Livius, in secunda Iudaicae captivitatis historia, Essenos refert"; ad Magnum 70.3 (PL 22, 666) after mention of Josephus' Against Apion: "Quid loquar de Philone, quem vel alterum, vel Iudaeum Platonem critici pronuntiant?"

[168] Cf., besides the text quoted in the preceding note, Adv. Iovin. II.14 (PL 23, 317 A): "(Esseni) super quorum vita et Philo vir doctissimus proprium volumen edidit." It will be observed that this sentence, inserted in an entire discussion plagiarized from Porphyry's De abstinentia (cf. above, n. 113), certainly represents a personal knowledge on Jerome's part. For this information he is indebted to the reading either of Philo's treatise Quod liber sit quisquis virtuti studet, in which the life of the Essenes is studied, or of the preface of the De vita contemplativa, which refers to this treatise.

[169] Epist. ad Marcellam 29.7 (PL 22, 441): "Iosephus ac Philo, viri doctissimi Iudaeorum, multique de nostris id persecuti sunt, quorum, ut aiunt, voce audies me." Cf. Epist. ad Fabiolam 64 (PL 22, 607–622).

[170] Epist. ad Fabiolam 64.1 (PL 22, 608 and n. g).

[171] Dial. contra Pelagianos 3.6 (PL 23, 603 B): "Quid dicemus de utriusque sexus aetate diversa, quae iuxta Philonem et prudentissimum philosophorum (Platonem in Timaeo?) ab infantia usque ad decrepitam senectutem, septenario ordine devolvitur, dum sibi sic invicem aetatum incrementa succedunt, ut quando de alia transeamus ad aliam, sentire minime valeamus?" Cf. De mundi opificio chap. 36 (ed. Cohn-Wendland, vol. I, p. 37, 10).

[172] De nominibus Hebraicis, praef. (PL 23, 815 A): "Philo, vir disertissimus Iudaeorum, Origenis quoque testimonio comprobatur edidisse librum Hebraicorum nominum, eorumque etymologias iuxta ordinem litterarum e latere copulasse. Qui cum vulgo habeatur a Graecis et bibliothecas orbis impleverit, studii nostri fuit in Latinam linguam vertere ... inter cetera enim ingenii sui praeclara monumenta etiam in hoc laboravit (Origenes), ut quod Philo quasi Iudaeus omiserat, hic ... ut Christianus impleret." Jerome therefore had at his disposal only Origen's revision of Philo. Cf. Schanz, vol. 4, I, p. 468.

[173] Philo De somniis 1.77:
'Ραμεσσή ... ἑρμηνεύεται ... σεισμὸς σητός.

Epist. ad Fabiolam 78.3 (PL 22, 700):
Ramesses a quibusdam interpretatur: Commotio turbulenta.

Jerome, a tool, and his interest in Philo is more that of the historian than the philosopher.

The only pagan historian that Jerome knows thoroughly and from whom he can draw continuously for his historical commentaries on the Scriptures is Josephus. He considers him the Greek Livy[174] and reserves a place for him in his *De viris* because he spoke of Christ.[175] Jerome's predilection for Josephus is so marked that during his lifetime it was thought that he had translated Josephus. Despite his denials,[176] part of the manuscript tradition attributes to him the authorship of a Latin translation of Josephus' *History of the Jewish War*.[177] Most of Jerome's explanations of the *Quaestiones Hebraicae in Genesim* are taken textually from Book 1 of the *Antiquities*, although he avoids the mention of Josephus, except to criticize him.[178] After admitting into his *Quaestiones Hebraicae* a mistaken interpretation on Josephus' part, he later on corrects it.[179] He will again have to criticize Josephus for a voluntary omission.[180] For all these strictures, Jerome owes to Josephus his knowledge of Hebraic history and civilization. If he needs information on metrics[181] or on the priestly dress of the Jews,[182] he derives it from the *Antiquities*. He refers to it too whenever a point of history has to be cleared up, whether it is

---

[174] See above, n. 4.

[175] *De vir. inl.* 13 (PL 23, 662–663).

[176] *Epist. ad Lucinium* 71.5 (PL 22, 671): "Porro Iosephi libros et sanctorum Papiae et Polycarpi volumina, falsus ad te rumor pertulit a me esse translata: quia nec otii mei, nec virium est, tantas res eadem in alteram linguam exprimere venustate."

[177] Cf. Cassiodorus *Inst. div.* 17 (ed. Mynors, p. 55, 22): "(Iosephus) etiam et alios septem libros *Captivitatis Iudaicae* mirabili nitore conscripsit, quam translationem alii Hieronymo, alii Ambrosio, alii deputant Rufino." On this translation, see Schanz, vol. 4, 1, p. 423.

[178] See the notes on the *Hebraicae Quaestiones* in PL 23, 983ff. Josephus is mentioned in 985 B, 1001 A, and particularly 1038 B: "Iosephus in primo *Antiquitatum* libro, Israel ideo appellatum putat, quod adversum Angelum steterit; quod diligenter excutiens, in Hebraeo penitus invenire non potui." Jerome thus criticizes, wrongly too, the etymology given by Josephus *Ant.* 1.20.2 (ed. Dindorf, p. 38, 16): σημαίνει δὲ τοῦτο κατὰ τὴν Ἑβραίων γλῶτταν, τὸν ἀντιστάντα ἀγγέλῳ.

[179] He thinks at first, *Hebr. Quaest. in Gen.* 10.4 (PL 23, 1001 A), with Josephus *Ant.* 1.6.1, that the word *Tharsis* in Scripture designates the city of *Tarsus*; then he changes his mind. Cf. *Epist. ad Marcellam* 37.2 (PL 22, 462), *In Isaiam* 1.2.16 (PL 24, 53 A and 666 D), *In Danielem* 10.6 (PL 25, 554 D), *In Ionam* 1.1 (PL 25, 1122), and *Anecd. Mareds.* 3, 1, p. 48, 13.

[180] *Commentarioli in Ps.* 105 (*Anecd. Mareds.* 3, 1, p. 78): "Et *fecerunt in Oreb et adoraverunt sculptile* . . . Hunc locum consulte Iosephus in Archaeologiae libris praetergreditur."

[181] *Commentarioli in Ps.* 108 (*Anecd. Mareds.* 3, 1, p. 85, 5: "Iosephus autem refert in libris Ἀρχαιολογίας hunc psalmum et Deuteronomii canticum uno metro esse compositum et putat elegiacum metrum in utroque posse reprehendi." Cf. Josephus *Ant.* 2.16.4, 4.8.44, and 7.12.3.

[182] See above, n. 169.

a question of chronology[183] or a confused genealogy.[184] Jerome himself often takes care to translate textually any passage from Josephus that clarifies the commentary on the Holy Scriptures.[185] Lastly, he equips himself with Josephus' erudition by borrowing from him, often without any acknowledgment, many a quotation from ancient writers. On the question where Noah landed after the Flood, he quotes Berosus, Jerome the Egyptian, Mnaseas, and Nicolaus of Damascus but acknowledges that he is merely translating Josephus.[186] Elsewhere, on the etymology of the word *Africa*, he quotes Alexander Polyhistor and Cleodemus Malchus, without specifying that his only source is Josephus.[187] On several occasions, again, he quotes Berosus, once acknowledging that Josephus is the intermediary,[188] then again claiming to have read the text.[189] With regard to the *History of the Jewish War*, its chief interest for Jerome is that it shows the fulfillment of the prophecies.[190] He has also read the *Contra Apionem*[191] and the *De Machabaeis*.[192] Jerome then had in his possession the Greek text of Josephus' complete works. To him this text was almost his bedside book. However, he works with such speed that he quotes them without consulting the references. Again and again he

---

[183] *In Danielem* 8.14 (*PL* 25, 537 B): "Legamus Machabaeorum libros et Iosephi historiam ibique scriptum reperiemus, centesimo quadragesimo tertio anno a Seleuco . . . ingressum Antiochum Ierosolymam." Cf. Josephus *Ant.* 12.5.3.

[184] *In Matth.* 1.2.22 (*PL* 26, 28 C): "Herodes ille . . . huius Herodis filius est . . . Lege Iosephi historiam." Cf. Josephus *Ant.* 18.7.2.

[185] Among others, *In Danielem* 2.1 and 6.1 (*PL* 25, 498 B and 522 D), translating Josephus *Ant.* 10.10.3 and 10.11.4.

[186] *De situ et nom. loc. Hebr.* Ararat (*PL* 23, 905 B–D), translating Josephus *Ant.* 1.3.6 (ed. Dindorf, p. 11).

[187] *Hebr. Quaest. in Gen.* 25.1 (*PL* 23, 1026 A), translating Josephus *Ant.* 1.15 (ed. Dindorf, p. 27, 11).

[188] *In Danielem* 5.1 (*PL* 25, 518 B): "sed iuxta Berosum qui Chaldaeam scripsit historiam et Iosephum qui Berosum sequitur" = Josephus *Adv. Apionem* 1.20 (ed. Dindorf, vol. 2, p. 350).

[189] See the texts quoted above, n. 158.

[190] *In Zachariam* 3.11.6 and 3.14.1 (*PL* 25, 1504 C and 1522 C); *In Isaiam* 17.64.8 (*PL* 24, 626 B): "ad tempus Romanae victoriae universa referimus, quae Iosephus Iudaicae scriptor historiae septem explicat voluminibus quibus imposuit titulum *Captivitatis Iudaicae*, id est Περὶ ἁλώσεως."

[191] *Epist. ad Magnum* 70.3 (*PL* 22, 666): "Iosephus antiquitatem adprobans Iudaici populi, duos libros scripsit contra Apionem Alexandrinum grammaticum: et tanta saecularium profert testimonia, ut mihi miraculum subeat, quo modo vir Hebraeus et ab infantia sacris litteris eruditus cunctam Graecorum Bibliothecam evolverit."

[192] *Dial. contra Pelagianos* 2.6 (*PL* 23, 567 A): "Unde et Iosephus Machabaeorum scriptor historiae, frangi et regi posse dixit perturbationes animi, non eradicari." Cf. Josephus *De Machab.* 3 (ed. Dindorf, vol. 2, p. 394, 50). Jerome also lists Josephus' works in his notice in the *De vir. inl.* But this notice would not be sufficient to prove that he had read them, since it derives entirely from Eusebius, as Bernoulli, *Schriftstellerkatalog*, pp. 16 and 117, and Sychowski, *Hieronymus*, p. 99, have shown.

assures the reader that, according to Josephus, the miracle of the divine powers noisily leaving the Temple of Jerusalem took place at Easter.[193] Actually, Josephus dates the destruction of the Temple[194] from this omen. Jerome was led astray when he compiled his *Chronicle* with the aid of Eusebius' *Chronicle*, whose reliability he did not verify. It was only later, in his *Commentary on Isaiah*, that he corrected the anachronism.[195] Similarly, Jerome is mistaken when he declares, with a vast display of references, that according to Josephus the Essenes abstained from wine and meat and fasted daily.[196] Josephus makes no such assertion.[197] This proves that Jerome, who in this passage plagiarizes Porphyry's *De abstinentia*, did not take the trouble to consult the references mentioned by Porphyry.

Jerome then read, among the Greek historians, only the few who could be of immediate service for his commentary on the Scriptures, that is, Herodotus, Xenophon's *Cyropedia*, a few treatises by Philo, Josephus' works. The

---

[193] *Chron. ann. ab. Abr.* 2047 (*PL* 27, 571): "Iosephus etiam vernaculus Iudaeorum scriptor, circa haec tempora, die Pentecostes, sacerdotes primum commotiones locorum et quosdam sonitus sensisse testatur, deinde ex adyto Templi repentinam subito erupisse vocem dicentium: Transmigremus ex his sedibus." This mistake is repeated *PL* 22, 367 and 992; 26, 213 A; etc. First Jerome connects these miracles with the death of Christ, then again with Easter.

[194] *Capt. Iud.* 6.5.3 (ed. Dindorf, vol. 2, p. 293, 2). Similarly Jerome *Tract. in Ps.* (*Anecd. Mareds.* 3, 2, p. 387, 7) quoted incorrectly *Capt. Iud.* 6.9.3.

[195] *In Isaiam* 18.66.6 (*PL* 24, 657 A): "Haud dubium quin Ierusalem significet Romano exercitu circumdatam . . . quando praesides templi consona Angeli voce dixerunt: 'Transeamus his sedibus.' De quibus non solum Iosephus, Iudaicae scriptor historiae, sed multis prius saeculis Psalmista testatur." Cf. *PL* 25, 1186 A.

[196] Porphyry *De abstinentia* 4.11 (Bidez, p. 75, 51):

τῶν τε παρ' αὐτοῖς φιλοσοφῶν τριτταὶ ἰδέαι ἦσαν, καὶ τῆς μὲν προΐσταντο Φαρισαῖοι, τῆς δὲ Σαδδουκαῖοι, τῆς δὲ τρίτης, ἣ καὶ ἐδόκει σεμνοτάτη εἶναι, Ἐσσαῖοι. Οἱ οὖν τρίτοι τοιοῦτον ἐποιοῦντο τὸ πολίτευμα, ὡς πολλαχοῦ Ἰώσηππος τῶν πραγματειῶν ἀνέγραψε, καὶ γὰρ ἐν τῷ δευτέρῳ τῆς Ἰουδαϊκῆς Ἱστορίας, ἣν δι' ἑπτὰ βιβλίων συνεπλήρωσε, καὶ ἐν τῷ ὀκτωκαιδεκάτῳ τῆς Ἀρχαιολογίας, ἣν διὰ εἴκοσι βιβλίων ἐπραγματεύσατο καὶ ἐν τῷ δευτέρῳ τῷ πρὸς τοὺς Ἕλληνας, εἰσὶ δὲ δύο τὰ βιβλία.

Jerome *Adv. Iovin.* 2.14 (*PL* 23, 316 C):

Iosephus in secunda *Iudaicae captivitatis* historia et in octavo decimo *Antiquitatum* libro et *Contra Apionem* duobus voluminibus, tria describit dogmata Iudaeorum: Pharisaeos, Sadducaeos, Essaenos. Quorum novissimos miris effert laudibus, quod et ab uxoribus et vino et carnibus semper abstinuerint et quotidianum ieiunium verterint in naturam.

In chap. 14 Porphyry speaks of the Essenes' abstinence from flesh.

[197] *Capt. Iud.* 2.8.2 and *Ant.* 18.1.5 (ed. Dindorf, vol. 2, p. 96, and 1, p. 694). Jerome's principal references to Josephus, besides those already mentioned, are *Antiquities*, *PL* 24, 441 B; 25: 52 A, 55 D, 505 B, 520 C, 522 B, 535 A, 559 C; 26, 98 C; *History of the Jewish War*, *PL* 24, 64 B; 25: 952 A, 1350 D, 1509 A.

other historians whom he quotes are known to him only through Josephus. And although he is quite familiar with this historian, he sometimes makes mistakes, on his own account, for lack of a rigorous historical method.

Jerome assures us that he read medical treatises for the interpretation of certain passages in the Scriptures.[198] What does he know about Greek medicine? He knows the standard categories of medicine[199] and makes several vague references to Hippocrates that do not in any sense presuppose that Jerome read his works. Pease has shown besides that Jerome took from Origen most of his medical references or metaphors.[200] Actually, Galen is the only source on medical questions. It is from Galen's Περὶ ὑγιεινῶν λόγων[201] and from the commentary on the *Aphorisms*[202] that he borrows his occasional

[198] See the text quoted above, n. 2.

[199] *Epist. ad Paulinum* 53.6 (*PL* 22, 544): "Taceo de . . . medicis, quorum scientia mortalibus vel utilissima est in tres partes scinditur: τὸ δόγμα, τὴν μέθοδον, τὴν ἐμπειρίαν." Galen *De sectis* 1 distinguishes three schools: the *Empirici*, the *Methodici*, and the *Logici* or *Dogmatici*.

[200] *Adv. Vigilantium* 4 (*PL* 23, 357 B): "Galliae . . . hominem moti capitis, atque Hippocratis vinculis adligandum, sedentem cernunt in Ecclesia," and *Adv. Iovin.* 1.3 (*PL* 23, 222 B): "Nonne vel febrem somniare eum putes, vel adreptum morbo phrenetico, Hippocratis vinculis adligandum?" The point is the insulting expression signifying "fit to be tied." *In Ezech.* 1.1.7 (*PL* 25, 22 C): "Sunt qui simpliciter in quattuor animalibus, iuxta Hippocratis sententiam, quattuor arbitrantur elementa mundi monstrari, de quibus constant omnia: ignem, aerem, aquam, terram." Cf. Galen Περὶ τῶν καθ᾽ Ἱπποκράτην στοιχείων. *Epist. ad Nepotianum* 52.15 (*PL* 22, 539): "Hippocrates adiurat discipulos suos, antequam doceat, et in verba sua iurare compellit: extorquetque sacramento silentium, sermonem, incessum, habitum moresque praescribit." This is a reference to the Ἱπποκράτους ὅρκος, ed. Kuehn, vol. 1, p. 1. On Jerome's borrowing medical information from Origen, cf. A. S. Pease, "Medical Allusions in the Works of St. Jerome," *Harvard Studies in Classical Philology* 25 (1914) 73–86.

[201] Galen Περὶ ὑγιεινῶν λόγων 1.7 (ed. Kuehn, vol. 6, p. 34):

Ἐχρῆν δὲ αὐτοὺς μὴ τοῦτο μόνον Ἱπποκράτους ἀνεγνωκέναι τε καὶ μνημονεύειν, ὡς τὰ ἐναντία τῶν ἐναντίων ἐστὶν ἰάματα.

Epist. ad Algasiam 121, praef. (*PL* 22, 1007): Vidi ego nauseam, et capitis vertiginem antidoto, quae appellatur πικρά, saepe sanari, et iuxta Hippocratem contrariorum contraria esse remedia. [On the πικρά, cf. *PL* 22, 703.]

Cf. *Epist. ad Furiam* 54.9 (*PL* 22, 554): "Aiunt medici et qui de humanorum corporum scripsere naturis, praecipueque Galenus in libris quorum titulus Περὶ ὑγιεινῶν, puerorum et iuvenum ac perfectae aetatis virorum mulierumque corpora insito calore fervere, et noxios esse his aetatibus cibos, qui calorem augeant; sanitatique conducere frigida quaeque in esu et potu sumere. Sicut e contrario senibus, qui pituita laborant et frigore, calidos cibos et vetera vina prodesse." This is a summary of Galen Περὶ ὑγιεινῶν 1.11 and 5.5.

[202] *Adv. Iovin.* 2.11 (*PL* 23, 313 C): "Hippocrates in *Aphorismis* docet crassa et obesa corpora, quae crescendi mensuram compleverint, nisi ablatione sanguinis cito imminuantur, in paralysim et pessima morborum genera erumpere, et idcirco necessariam esse demptionem, ut rursum habeant in quae possint crescere. Non enim manere in uno statu naturam corporum, sed aut crescere semper, aut decrescere, nec posse vivere animal, nisi crescendi capax sit." Cf. Ἱπποκράτους ἀφορισμοὶ καὶ Γαλήνου εἰς αὐτοὺς ὑπομνήματα 1.3 (ed. Kuehn, vol. 17, 2, p. 413).

quotations from Hippocrates. For his treatise *Adversus Iovinianum,* Jerome used, besides this *Commentary on the Aphorisms,* Galen's *Protrepticus*[203] and his Περὶ τῆς τῶν ἁπλῶν φαρμάκων κράσεως καὶ δυνάμεως.[204] He does not even hesitate, in his exegetical works, to appeal to Galen's medical authority in order to establish the power of the number *Seven.*[205] Finally, he occasionally embellishes his letters with medical aphorisms taken from Galen.[206] He had thus at his disposal Galen's principal works and he read them himself, for his references are very exact. He uses them particularly against Iovinianus to show that Galen, a pagan writer, furnishes a scientific basis for the supporters of asceticism.

With regard to the natural sciences, Jerome has frequent recourse to them to explain some Biblical metaphor or to deduce a moral axiom therefrom. Fonck collected the principal passages where Jerome speaks of the curiosities of nature but did not make a critical investigation of his sources.[207] Jerome affects to having read the principal Greek naturalists. Among these he quotes Aristotle, Theophrastus, Marcellus of Side, Dioscorides,[208] and

[203] *Adv. Iovin.* 2.11: "Unde et Galenus, vir doctissimus, Hippocratis interpres, athletas quorum vita et ars sagina est, dicit in *Exhortatione medicinae* nec vivere posse diu, nec sanos esse, animasque eorum ita nimio sanguine et adipibus, quasi luto involutas, nihil tenue, nihil caeleste, sed semper de carnibus et ructu et ventris ingluvie cogitare." Cf. Galen Προτρεπτικὸς λόγος ἐπὶ τὰς τέχνας 11 (ed. Kuehn, vol. 1, p. 27).

[204] *Adv. Iovin.* 2.6 (PL 23, 306 A): "Et (quod forsitan legendum mirum sit) hominis fimus quantis curationibus proficiat Galenus ἐν ἁπλοῖς docet." Actually, not only this remark, but Jerome's entire discussion of the medical usefulness of objects that are apparently useless in nature is taken from this treatise by Galen 10.13.19 and 20 (ed. Kuehn, vol. 12, pp. 270, 292, 293).

[205] *In Amos* 2.5 (PL 25, 1037 C): "Novit et hoc saecularis philosophia, et medicorum libri, quorum Galenus disertissimus atque doctissimus scripsit ternos libros κρίσεων καὶ τῶν κριτικῶν ἡμερῶν, in quibus septenarii numeri ostendens potentiam, ardentissimas febres septimo dicit solvi die: aut si tanta humoris noxii et pituitae fuerit magnitudo, ut primae hebdomadis nequaquam fervore consumpta sit, secundae hebdomadis ultimus exspectatur dies, id est quartus decimus. Quod si hunc, ut iuxta Hippocratem loquar, νόσος vicerit, transeunt ad vicesimam primam diem, hoc est ad finem tertiae hebdomadis." Cf. Galen Περὶ κρισίμων ἡμερῶν 1.4 (ed. Kuehn, vol. 9, p. 784).

[206] *Epist. ad Nepotianum* 52.11 (PL 22, 537): "Pulchre dicitur apud Graecos, et nescio an apud nos aeque resonet: Pinguis venter non gignit sensum tenuem." Cf. Galen Πρὸς Θρασύβουλον βιβλίῳ πότερον ἰατρικῆς ἢ γυμναστικῆς ἐστι τὸ ὑγιεινόν, chap. 37 (ed. Kuehn, vol. 5, p. 878) and *Com. Att. fragmenta* (ed. Koch, vol. 3, p. 613, frag. 1234): παχεῖα γαστὴρ λεπτὸν οὐ τίκτει νόον.

[207] Léopold Fonck, "Hieronymi scientia naturalis exemplis illustratur," *Biblica* 1 (1920) 481–499.

[208] *Adv. Iovin.* 2.6 (PL 23, 306 B): "Legat qui vult Aristotelem et Theophrastum prosa, Marcellum Sidetem et nostrum Flavium hexametris versibus disserentes, Plinium quoque Secundum et Dioscoridem et ceteros tam physicos quam medicos, qui nullam herbam, nullum lapidem, nullum animal tam reptile quam volatile et natatile, non ad suae artis utilitatem referunt." This is the conclusion of the discussion on the usefulness of creatures, borrowed, as we have just seen, from Galen alone.

Oppian.[209] Did he actually read them? It may be doubted a priori, for the use of "similitudes" is not new in Christian literature. Doubt becomes certainty when each particular case is examined. The information that Jerome claims to take from Oppian on the 153 species of fish certainly stems from some Christian commentary on the miracle of the fishes where Simon Peter, according to St. John,[210] caught 153 fishes. Jerome merely inserted in this passage, to add to the authoritative nature of his information, the remarks on Oppian that he took from Eusebius' *Chronicle*.[211] Most of the facts that he asserts were taken from the *physiologi*[212] he owes to the Greek or Latin ecclesiastical writers who had used the same similitude. For instance, to arouse the reader to repentance, he mentions how swallows use celandine and goats dittany, but he is merely plagiarizing Tertullian or Pacianus. The similitude of the partridge does not come from Aristotle, or Theophrastus, or Pliny, whom Jerome quotes on this topic, but from St. Ambrose.[213] That of the

[209] *In Ezechielem* 14.47.6 (*PL* 25, 474 C): "Aiunt autem qui de animantium scripsere naturis et proprietate, qui ἁλιευτικά tam Latino quam Graeco didicere sermone, de quibus Oppianus Cilix est, poeta doctissimus, centum quinquaginta tria esse genera piscium, quae omnia capta sunt ab Apostolis."

[210] *Ioann.* 21.11. According to Pliny *Hist. Nat.* 32.53, there are 174 species of fish. According to Oppian *De piscatione* 1.80 (ed. Lehrs [Paris 1862], p. 40), they are numberless.

[211] *Chron. ann. ab Abr.* 2188 (*PL* 27, 629): "Oppianus Cilix poeta cognoscitur, qui Halieutica miro splendore conscribit."

[212] Among others, on the love of eagles for their young (*In Is.* 66.13: *PL* 24, 662 A); on the suckling of she-lions (*In Danielem* 7.4: *PL* 25, 528 B); on the ferocity of she-bears (*In Hos.* 13.7: *PL* 25, 935 A); on dragons and ostriches (*In Mich.* 1.1.16: *PL* 25, 1157 B); on the effects of the plant ἀγνός (*In Zach.* 14.16: *PL* 25, 1537 B).

[213] Cf. Tertullian *De paenitentia* 12 (*PL* 1, 1248 A):

Cervus sagitta transfixus, ut ferrum et inrevocabiles moras eius de vulnere expellat, scit sibi dictamno medendum. Hirundo, si excaecaverit pullos, novit illos oculare rursus de sua chelidonia. Peccator restituendo sibi institutam a Domino exomologesin praeteribit illam quae Babylonium regem in regna restituit?

Pacianus *Paraenesis* 11 (*PL* 13, 1088 B):

Caprae ferae, ut dicunt, remedia sua noverunt: confixas quippe, audio, venenatis sagittis, saltus peragrare Dictaeos, quoad Dictami caule detonso, salutarium virulento latice succorum, pulsa decutiant tela corporibus ... Excaecatos hirundo pullos novit oculare de sua chelidonia: nos, lumina mentis amissa, nulla malae tractationis radice tractabimus?

Jerome *In Ecclesiastem* 7.18 (*PL* 23, 1122 A):

Si enim, iuxta eos qui de physicis disputant, novit hirundo pullos de sua oculare chelidonia, et dictamnum capreae adpetunt vulneratae, cur nos ignoremus medicinam paenitentiae propositam esse peccantibus?

Tertullian himself probably took these examples from Pliny *Hist. Nat.* 8.27 (*alias* 41). For the similitude of the partridge, cf.:

Ambrose *Hexaem.* 6.3 (*PL* 14, 246 C):

Perdicem astutam, quae aliena ova diri-

In Ieremiam 17.11 (*PL* 24, 789 C):

Aiunt scriptores naturalis historiae, tam

turtle, which Jerome reinforces with the pagan authority of the *physiologi*, is taken from Epiphanius of Cyprus' *Physiologus*, a veritable repository of similitudes for the use of Christian commentators.[214] Jerome is equally indebted for most of his knowledge of mineralogy to Epiphanius, several times mentioning with the highest praise his treatise Περὶ τῶν δώδεκα λίθων.[215] Thus, although he read Pliny the Elder, Jerome knows the pagan Greek naturalists only by name. He borrows from the Greek or Latin ecclesiastical writers the notions on the natural sciences that are indispensable for his commentaries.

---

piat, hoc est perdicis alterius, et corpore foveat suo: sed fraudis suae fructum habere non posse, quia cum eduxerit pullos suos, amittit eos; quia ubi vocem eius audierint, quae ova generavit, relicta ea, ad illam se naturali quodam munere et amore conferunt, quam veram sibi matrem ovorum generatione cognoverint, significantes hanc nutricis fungi officio, illam parentis . . . Unde et Hieremias ait: "Clamavit perdix." Huius imitator est diabolus, qui generationes creatoris aeterni rapere contendit.

bestiarum et volucrum quam arborum herbarumque (quorum principes Aristoteles et Theophrastus, apud nos Plinius Secundus) hanc perdicis esse naturam ut ova alterius perdicis, id est aliena furetur et eis incubet foveatque, cumque fetus adoleverit, avolare ab eo, et alienum parentem relinquere. Huiusce modi divites fiunt, qui aliena diripiunt.

Origen *Hom. in Ier.* 17.1 (translated by Jerome, *PL* 25, 616 A) took from this passage another similitude introduced by the words: "Ex natura volucris dignum videtur quandam historiam commemorare." Similarly, Epiphanius *Physiologus* 9 (*PG* 43, 526 A).

[214] Epiphanius *Physiologus* 10 (*PG* 43, 526 B) *de turture*:

ἀποζευχθέντων δὲ αὐτῶν, φυλάττουσι τὴν μονογαμίαν, ἕως τέλους τῆς ζωῆς αὐτῶν.

Adv. Iovin. 1.30 (*PL* 23, 263 D):

Legamus physiologos et reperiemus turturis hanc esse naturam, ut si parem perdiderit, alteri non iungatur: ut intellegamus digamiam etiam a mutis avibus reprobari.

The origin of this similitude is the Song of Songs 2.12. Cf. also Basil *Hexaem.* 8.6 (*PG* 29, 178 C) and Dionysius *De avibus* 1.24 (ed. Lehrs [Paris 1862], p. 112).

[215] *Epist. ad Fabiolam* 64.22 (*PL* 22, 621): "Sufficiat quod et sanctus papa Epiphanius egregium super hoc volumen edidit, quod si legere volueris, plenissimam scientiam consequeris" (Jerome uses concurrently Epiphanius, Josephus, and Philo in this letter on the Jewish priestly dress); *In Isaiam* 15.54.11 (*PL* 24, 523 C–D): "De natura autem duodecim lapidum atque gemmarum, duos tantum nominabo, virum sanctae et venerabilis memoriae episcopum Epiphanium, qui insigne nobis ingenii et eruditionis suae reliquit volumen, quod inscripsit Περὶ λίθων, et Plinium Secundum" (Epiphanius is translated word for word 24, 525 A); *In Ezechielem* 9.28.11 (*PL* 25, 271 C): "Super quibus et vir sanctus Epiphanius episcopus proprium volumen mihi praesens tradidit, et XXXVII liber Plinii Secundi *Naturalis historiae*, post multiplicem omnium rerum scientiam, de gemmis et lapidibus disputat." I do not know the source of the long quotation from Xenocrates on the stone *adamas* that Jerome cites *In Amos* 3.7.7 (*PL* 25, 1073 A).

3. Jerome and Greek Patristics

One of the most noticeable characteristics of St. Jerome's Greek pagan culture is in fact that he acquired it with a view to exegetical works and quite often by way of ecclesiastical writers. It will therefore be no surprise that his works reveal, in a much more direct manner than his reading among pagan authors, his reading in Greek Christian writers. If one studies without preconceptions the *De viris inlustribus*, one is struck, as were Facundus of Hermione[1] and after him most of the medieval writers of the West, by the large number of Greek writers that Jerome appears to have read. In his letters also he kindly lists for his correspondents in the West a great number of Greek Fathers. The traditional attitude is to admire Jerome's Greek learning and to be amazed at his capacity to assemble such a complete library. The critical research conducted by Sychowski and Bernoulli[2] shattered this fine confidence. They showed that the seventy-eight notices in the *De viris inlustribus* of writers prior to Eusebius of Caesarea were plagiarized, often literally, and always awkwardly, from Eusebius' *Ecclesiastical History*, supplemented when necessary by the *Chronicle*. Jerome never verified Eusebius' assumptions. He read him very rapidly, translated him carelessly. What is worse, he tried to conceal this plagiarism by offering Eusebius' comments as if they were his own.[3] If we add that the long list of Greek writers that Jerome enumerates in his *Letter to Magnus* refers solely to the *De viris inlustribus*, whose sequence it follows, reproducing the observations most frequently verbatim,[4] we are inclined to accept Harnack's striking principle that asserts, to show their different cultural levels, that Jerome uses Eusebius' *Ecclesiastical History* just as Eusebius uses the library at Caesarea.[5]

Such an estimate is certainly unjust, unless we are careful to limit its implication. We have already established, with regard to Philo and Josephus,

---

[1] Facundus of Hermione *Defensio trium capitulorum* 4.2 (*PL* 67, 619 D): "Hieronymus quoque noster, vir admodum doctus, qui etiam tantae fuerat lectionis, ut omnes aut paene omnes, sive in Graeco sive in Latino eloquio divinarum Scripturarum tractatores legeret, scripsit librum, cuius est titulus *De viris inlustribus*, in quo non solum catholicos, sed etiam haereticos memoravit, qui de Scripturis sanctis in utraque lingua aliquid conscripserunt"; Gennadius *De scriptoribus ecclesiasticis* 1 (*PL* 58, 1061 A), however, notes lacunae, but not insofar as concerns the Greek Fathers: "Hunc virum (Iacobum Nisibenum) beatus Hieronymus in libro χρονικῶν velut magnarum virtutum hominem nominans, in Catalogo cur non posuerit, facile excusabitur, si consideremus, quod ipsos tres vel quattuor Syros quos posuit, et interpretatos in Graecum se legisse testatur."

[2] Bernoulli, *Schriftstellerkatalog*.

[3] Sychowski, *Hieronymus*, pp. 68–71.

[4] *Epist. ad Magnum* 70.4 (*PL* 22, 667); the order is inverted only for Origen and Miltiades, Apollonius and Hippolytus, and lastly Malchion. The only original notice with regard to the *De vir. inl.* concerns Origen.

[5] Harnack, *Altchr. Literatur*, vol. I, p. L, n. I.

that Jerome, although he borrowed his accounts in the *De viris inlustribus* from Eusebius, himself read several treatises by Philo and also Josephus' complete works.[6] The fact that Jerome plagiarizes from Eusebius for a particular account does not consequently force us to think that he personally knows nothing of the author in question. Moreover, Bernoulli himself identifies a few personal additions by Jerome in the first part of the *De viris inlustribus*, while the second part seems entirely his own. In conclusion, Jerome's literary activity was still almost at the beginning in 392, when he compiled the *De viris inlustribus*, and he had still twenty-eight years of intense work to complete his reading of the Greek Fathers. The researches of Bernoulli and Sychowski render an immense but negative service. They note the comments taken from Eusebius that cannot be evaluated in calculating the extent of Jerome's reading. But it remains for us to compare, with the original observations in the *De viris inlustribus*, Jerome's entire output, in order to achieve a balanced estimate of the level of his patristic culture.[7]

Devoting his life to the commentary on the canonical writings of the Old and the New Testament, Jerome does not seem to have made much use of the Apostolic Fathers and is indebted to Eusebius for the accounts in the *De viris inlustribus* relating to them.[8] To be sure, he claims that he knows Ignatius and Polycarp,[9] and the rumor spread in the West that he had translated Polycarp and Papias. He denies this unwarranted rumor, assuring us that such a task is beyond his strength, but he lets it be understood that he has their works at his disposal.[10] It is surprising in this instance that he never quotes Polycarp and that he makes serious mistakes about Ignatius. A textual quotation from the *Epistle to the Smyrnians* is attributed by him to the *Epistle to Polycarp*.[11] Another quotation that he makes as coming from

---

[6] See above, pp. 81–86.

[7] To my knowledge, this task has never been attempted, for Luebeck confined his study to Jerome's reading among the pagan writers. There are, however, some observations on Jerome's Christian reading in Bernoulli, *Schriftstellerkatalog*, pp. 287–293.

[8] *De vir. inl.* 6 (Barnabas), 10 (Hermas), 15 (Clement), 16 (Ignatius), 17 (Polycarp), 18 (Papias). Cf. Bernoulli, *Schriftstellerkatalog*, pp. 112–122, and Sychowski, *Hieronymus*, pp. 84–107.

[9] *Adv. Helvidium* 17 (PL 23, 212 A): "Numquid non possum tibi totam veterum scriptorum seriem commovere: Ignatium, Polycarpum, Irenaeum, Iustinum martyrem multosque alios apostolicos et eloquentes viros, qui adversus Ebionem et Theodotum Byzantium, Valentinum, haec eadem sentientes, plena sapientiae volumina scripserunt? Quae si legisses aliquando, plus saperes." Cf. *Anecd. Mareds.* 3, 2, p. 5, 24, where Jerome declares that Irenaeus, Polycarp, and Dionysius acknowledge the authenticity of the Apocalypse.

[10] Text quoted sec. 2 n. 176.

[11] *De vir. inl.* 16 (PL 23, 666 B). This mistake shows Jerome's ignorance of Ignatius, according to Bernoulli, *Schriftstellerkatalog*, p. 289.

Ignatius is actually a passage from Barnabas' *Epistle*.[12] The first mistake is explained by a careless use of Eusebius, from whom Jerome borrows this quotation;[13] the second assumes that Jerome quoted from memory, probably from an intermediate writer.[14] A third quotation from Ignatius is certainly borrowed from a homily by Origen that Jerome had just translated.[15] If he did not read Ignatius' *Epistles*, did he read Barnabas' *Epistle*? Once he mistakenly quotes a passage from it, as we have seen, as coming from Ignatius, but probably following Origen.[16] He quotes it again twice, but whereas he studies it after the canonical Epistles in the *De nominibus Hebraicis*,[17] he includes it among the apocrypha in his *Commentary on Ezekiel*.[18] We are

---

[12] Barnabas *Epist.* 5.9 (ed. F. X. Funk, *Opera Patr. apost.*, vol. 1, p. 14 = *PG* 2, 736 A):

Ὅτε δὲ τοὺς ἰδίους ἀποστόλους τοὺς μέλλοντας κηρύσσειν τὸ εὐαγγέλιον αὐτοῦ ἐξελέξατο, ὄντας ὑπὲρ πᾶσαν ἁμαρτίαν ἀνομωτέρους.

Dial. contra Pelagianos 3.2 (*PL* 23, 598 A):

Ignatius vir apostolicus et martyr scribit audacter: Elegit Dominus apostolos, qui super omnes homines peccatores erant.

[13] Cf. Sychowski, *Hieronymus*, p. 103 n. 6. Either Jerome thought that the *Epistle to the Smyrnians* and the *Epistle to Polycarp* were one and the same letter addressed to several recipients, or (and this seems to me more probable) the words "et proprie ad Polycarpum, commendans illi Antiochensem ecclesiam" are a marginal addition that was unfortunately inserted in the middle of the quotation from the *Epistle to the Smyrnians*.

[14] For example, Origen *Contra Celsum* 1.63 (*PG* 11, 777 B): Γέγραπται δὴ ἐν τῇ Βαρνάβα καθολικῇ ἐπιστολῇ (ὅθεν ὁ Κέλσος λαβὼν τάχα εἶπεν εἶναι ἐπιρρήτους καὶ πονηροτάτους τοὺς ἀποστόλους), ὅτι ἐξελέξατο τοὺς ἰδίους ἀποστόλους Ἰησοῦς, ὄντας ὑπὲρ πᾶσαν ἀνομίαν ἀνομωτέρους.

[15] Ignatius *Epist. ad Ephes.* 19.1 (ed. Funk, p. 186 = *PG* 5, 660 A):

Καὶ ἔλαθε τὸν ἄρχοντα τοῦ αἰῶνος τούτου ἡ παρθενία Μαρίας καὶ ὁ τοκετὸς αὐτῆς, ὁμοίως καὶ ὁ θάνατος τοῦ Κυρίου.

Origen *Hom. 6 in Lucam* (*PG* 13, 1814 C):

Unde eleganter in cuiusdam Martyris epistula scriptum repperi, Ignatium dico episcopum Antiocheae post Petrum secundum qui in persecutione Romae pugnavit ad bestias: Principem saeculi huius latuit virginitas Mariae, latuit propter Ioseph, latuit propter nuptias.

Jerome *In Matth.* 1.1.18 (*PL* 26, 24 B):

Martyr Ignatius etiam quartam addidit causam, cur a desponsata conceptus sit: ut partus, inquiens, eius celaretur diabolo, dum eum putat non de Virgine sed de uxore generatum.

It will be noted that this quotation appears again in Eusebius *Quaestiones ad Stephanum* 1.2 (*PG* 22, 881 C).

[16] See nn. 12 and 14.

[17] *De nominibus Hebraicis, ad finem* (*PL* 23, 904). We know that this work is a translation or an adaptation of Origen.

[18] *Barnabae epistula* 8.2 (ed. Funk, p. 26 = *PG* 2, 748 B):

Ὁ μόσχος ὁ Ἰησοῦς ἐστίν, οἱ προσ-

Jerome *In Ezech.* 13.43.19 (*PL* 25, 425 A):

Vitulum autem qui pro nobis immolatus est, et multa Scripturarum loca et

thus tempted to think that in each instance he is accepting the view of a different source, intermediate between the text and himself.[19] In conclusion, Jerome seems to admit in the *De viris inlustribus* that he does not know Papias[20] from direct contact; furthermore, he never quotes him.

He appears on the other hand to have read St. Clement of Rome's first *Epistle to the Corinthians*, from which he quotes three times verbatim. He read it in Greek, for he does not follow the text of the old Latin translation.[21] It is moreover possible that the second of these quotations was borrowed, not directly from Clement's text, but from a discussion by Origen on the Antipodes.[22] Jerome also mentions, without questioning their authenticity, the *Letters on Chastity* attributed to St. Clement, which he probably secured

---

φέροντες ἄνδρες ἁμαρτωλοί, οἱ προσ-   praecipue Barnabas epistula, quae habetur
ενέγκαντες αὐτὸν ἐπὶ τὴν σφαγήν.   inter scripturas apocryphas, nominat.

[19] I have at any rate verified that Jerome did not read the Epistle of Barnabas in the old Latin version.

[20] *De vir. inl.* 18 (*PL* 23, 670 B): "Hic *dicitur* mille annorum Iudaicam edidisse δευτέρωσιν, quem secuti sunt Irenaeus et Apollinarius et ceteri." Cf. Sychowski, *Hieronymus*, p. 107 n. 7, and Bernoulli, *Schriftstellerkatalog*, p. 290.

[21] Clement *I Epist. ad Cor-*   *Versio Lat. antiquiss.* (ed.   *In Isaiam* 52.13 (*PL* 24,
inthios 16.2 (ed. Funk, p. 80   Morin, *Anecd. Mareds.* 2   505 A):
= *PG* 1, 240 A):   [1894], p. VI):   de quo et Clemens, vir
    Τὸ σκῆπτρον τῆς μεγα-   Sceptrum *maiestatis* Dei   apostolicus, qui post Petrum
λωσύνης τοῦ Θεοῦ, ὁ κύριος   Dominus Iesus Christus   Romanam rexit ecclesiam,
Ἰησοῦς Χριστὸς οὐκ ἦλθεν   non venit *cum sono glo-*   scribit ad Corinthios: Scep-
ἐν κόμπῳ ἀλαζονείας οὐδὲ   *riae, quamvis poterat,* sed   trum Dei Dominus Iesus
ὑπερηφανίας, καίπερ δυνά-   *cum* humilitate.   Christus non venit *in iactan-*
μενος, ἀλλὰ ταπεινοφρό-   *tia superbiae, cum possit omnia,*
νων.   sed *in* humilitate.

Ibid., 20.8 (Funk, p. 88 =   *Ibid.*:   *In Epist. ad Ephes.* 2.2 (*PL* 26,
PG 1, 249 B):   Oceanus . . . et *omnis or-*   465 C):
   Ὠκεανὸς ἀπέραντος ἀν-   *bis terrarum.*   (mundi) . . . de quibus et
θρώποις καὶ οἱ μετ' αὐτὸν   Clemens in epistula sua scri-
κόσμοι.   bit: Oceanus, et *mundi qui*
                                             trans ipsum sunt.

Ibid., 49. 2 (Funk, p. 122 =   *Ibid.*:   *Ibid.*, 4.1 (*PL* 26, 492 D):
PG 1, 309 A):   Vinculum caritatis Dei   Cuius rei et Clemens ad
   Τὸν δεσμὸν τῆς ἀγάπης   quis *potest* enarrare?   Corinthios testis est scribens:
τοῦ Θεοῦ τίς δύναται   Vinculum charitatis Dei quis
ἐξηγήσασθαι;   *poterit* enarrare?

[22] Origen *De principiis* 2.3.6 (*PG* 11, 194 C): "Meminit sane Clemens apostolorum discipulus etiam eorum quos ἀντίχθονας Graeci nominarunt . . . quos et ipsos mundos appellavit, cum ait: Oceanus intransmeabilis est hominibus, et hi qui trans ipsum sunt mundi" (this text is preserved only in the translation by Rufinus). The same quotation appears in Origen *Selecta in Ezech.* 8 (*PG* 13, 796 C) and previously in Clement of Alexandria *Stromateis* 5.12 (*PG* 9, 117 B).

when he was compiling a voluminous dossier to show, in opposition to Iovinianus, the outstanding merit of chastity.[23] He knows, lastly, the tales, attributed to Clement, that describe the life of St. Peter, but he does not name them without irony.[24]

With regard to Hermas' *The Shepherd*, Jerome borrows from Eusebius the laudatory notice that he devotes to him in the *De viris inlustribus*, and confines himself to the addition on his own account that this work is almost unknown among the Latins.[25] He therefore does not know of the existence of Latin translations.[26] Although he mentions it or quotes it in three other passages, there is no assurance that he read it in the original text. In fact, in these passages he considers it as stupid and dangerous apocryphal writing.[27]

[23] *Adv. Iovin.* 1.12 (*PL* 23, 239 B): "Ad hos (eunuchos) et Clemens successor Apostoli Petri, cuius Apostolus Petrus meminit, scribit epistulas omnemque paene sermonem suum de virginitatis puritate contexit." On the identification and the authenticity of these letters, cf. Bernoulli, *Schriftstellerkatalog*, p. 289, and Puech, *Litt. gr. chrét.*, vol. 2, p. 44. The letters are edited in *PG* 1, 379–452 and in Funk, *Op. Patr. apost.*, vol. 2, pp. 1–27. The only writer who mentions these letters, apart from Jerome, is Epiphanius *Adv. haer.* 30.15 (*PG* 41, 431 A); but he can scarcely be Jerome's source.

[24] *In Epist. ad Galat.* 1.1.18 (*PL* 26, 329 B): "*Veni Ierosolymam videre Petrum.* Non ut oculos, genas vultumque eius adspiceret . . . et utrum frontem vestiret coma, an (ut Clemens in *Periodis* eius refert), calvitiem haberet in capite," and *Adv. Rufinum* 2.17 (*PL* 23, 459 B): "Clemens, inquit (Rufinus), apostolorum discipulus, qui Romanae ecclesiae post apostolos episcopus et martyr fuit, libros edidit, qui appellantur ἀναγνωρισμός, id est *recognitio*, in quibus, cum ex persona Petri apostoli doctrina, quasi vere apostolica, in quam plurimis exponatur, in aliquibus . . . Eunomii dogma inseritur." On Rufinus' translation of Clement's *Recognitiones*, cf. Schanz, vol. 4, 1, p. 420. The first of these two quotations might have been borrowed by Jerome from Origen's lost *Commentary on the Epistle to the Galatians*, for in Origen, book 3 *In Genesim*, chap. 14 (*PG* 12, 85 A) Clement Romanus' *Recognitiones* are also quoted under the title ἐν ταῖς περιόδοις.

[25] *De vir. inl.* 10 (*PL* 23, 658 A): "sed apud Latinos paene ignotus est." This statement is disputed. Actually, if we except the Muratorian Fragment, Tertullian is the only one in the West prior to Jerome who expresses an opinion on the *Shepherd* (*De orat.* 16 = *PL* 1, 1172 A and *De pudic.* 10 and 20 = *PL* 2, 1000 A and 1021 A); Pseudo-Cyprian *De aleatoribus* 2 and 4 (*PL* 4, 829–830) and Philastrius *De haeres.* 80 (*PL* 12, 1192) make use of it without mentioning it by name.

[26] On the two Latin translations, the *Palatina* and the *Vulgata*, cf. Schanz, vol. 4, 1, pp. 427–428. The older of these two translations is possibly not anterior to Jerome.

[27] *Hermae Pastor*, *Vis.* 4.2.4 (Funk, vol. 1, p. 382):

Διὰ τοῦτο ὁ Κύριος ἀπέστειλεν τὸν ἄγγελον αὐτοῦ τὸν ἐπὶ τῶν θηρίων ὄντα, οὗ τὸ ὄνομά ἐστιν Θεγρί.

Vis. 1.2.2 (Funk, vol. 1, p. 338):
καὶ ἦλθεν γυνὴ πρεσβῦτις.

Vis. 4.2.1 (Funk, vol. 1, p. 380):
Ὑπαντᾷ μοι παρθένος κεκοσμημένη

Jerome *In Habakkuk* 1.14 (*PL* 25, 1286 B):
Ex quo liber ille apocryphus stultitiae condemnandus est, in quo scriptum est, quendam angelum nomine Tyri (*read* Thegri) praeesse reptilibus.

In Hoseam 2.7.8 (*PL* 25, 878 A):
Unde et in libro *Pastoris* (si cui tamen placet illius recipere lectionem) Hermae primum videtur Ecclesia cano capite,

Did he then change his opinion from time to time? That is improbable, since the *Commentary on Habakkuk* where he expresses his unfavorable opinion of *The Shepherd* is palpably contemporaneous with the *De viris inlustribus*.[28] The most probable explanation is that Jerome did not himself read *The Shepherd* and that he criticized it severely under Origen's influence[29] just as he praised it following Eusebius.

Just as Jerome did not read the Apostolic Fathers, except perhaps Clement, he has only an imperfect knowledge of Christian literature in the second century. He neither read nor knows, except through Eusebius, the majority of Greek writers prior to Origen that he mentions in the *De viris inlustribus*: Justus of Tiberias,[30] Quadratus,[31] Aristides,[32] Agrippa Castor,[33] Hegesippus, Melito, Apollinaris of Hierapolis, Dionysius of Corinth, Pinytus of Cnossos, Philip of Gortyna, Musanus, Modestus,[34] Bardesanes,[35] Pantae-

---

ὡς ἐκ νυμφῶνος ἐκπορευομένη ... εἶχεν   deinde adulescentula, et sponsa crinibus
δὲ τὰς τρίχας αὐτῆς λευκάς. Ἔγνων   adornata.
ἐγὼ ἐκ τῶν προτέρων ὁραμάτων, ὅτι ἡ
Ἐκκλησία ἐστίν.
Cf. *Praefatio Hieronymi in libros Samuel et Malachim* (PL 28, 556 A): "Igitur Sapientia, quae vulgo Salomonis inscribitur, et Iesu filii Syrach liber, et Iudith, et Tobias, et *Pastor* non sunt in canone."

[28] Both works are usually dated in the year 392.

[29] Origen *De principiis* 4.11 (PG 11, 365 A): ἐν τῷ ὑπό τινων καταφρονουμένῳ βιβλίῳ τῷ Ποιμένι; *In Numeros, hom.* 8.1 (translated by Rufinus in PG 12, 622 C): "in libello *Pastoris*, si cui tamen scriptura illa recipienda videtur"; particularly *In Matth. comm. series* 53 (PG 13, 683): "in aliqua parabola refertur *Pastoris*, si cui placeat etiam illum legere librum." Origen rarely mentions the work without reservation (cf. *Selecta in Ps., hom.* 1 in Ps. 37 = PG 12, 1372 B, and *In Matth.* 14.21 = PG 13, 1240 C), except *In Epist. ad Rom.* 10.31 (PG 14, 1282 B): "quae scriptura valde mihi utilis videtur," and several other similar passages.

[30] *De vir. inl.* 14 (PL 23, 663 B). Jerome's only personal statement in this notice, according to which Justus might have written "quosdam commentariolos de Scripturis," is valueless. Cf. Sychowski, *Hieronymus*, p. 61, and Bernoulli, *Schriftstellerkatalog*, p. 238.

[31] The passage in the *Epist. ad Magnum* 70.4 (PL 22, 667) on Quadratus is an arrangement of the *De vir. inl.* 19 and of the *Chron. ann. ab Abr.* 2141 (PL 27, 615).

[32] Jerome's additions to Eusebius in the *De vir. inl.* 20 and *Epist. ad Magnum* 70.4 on Aristides are valueless, as Sychowski has shown, *Hieronymus*, p. 109 n. 2.

[33] On Jerome's addition to Eusebius in his notice on Agrippa *De vir. inl.* 21, "et Deum maximum eius Abraxas, qui quasi annum continens iuxta Graecorum numerum supputatur," cf. below, n. 49.

[34] *De vir. inl.* 32 (PL 23, 679 C). Bernoulli, *Schriftstellerkatalog*, p. 198, shows that even the statement on Modestus' spurious writings, although it appears original, actually goes back to Eusebius.

[35] *De vir. inl.* 33 (PL 23, 682 A). Sychowski, *Hieronymus*, p. 121 n. 6, shows that the last statement of this notice, where Jerome appraises Bardesanes' style, is a pretext intended to inspire the belief that Jerome had read him. The only quotation from this writer that he uses is through Porphyry; cf. above, sec. 2 n. 110.

nus,[36] Rhodon,[37] Miltiades, Apollonius, Serapion, Theophilus of Caesarea, Bacchylus of Corinth, Polycrates of Ephesus,[38] Heraclitus, Maximus, Candidus, Apion, Sextus, Arabianus, Judas. According to Bernoulli, this is even the part of Jerome's work in which he is least original, often confining himself to a literal translation of Eusebius.[39]

Is he at least acquainted with the principal writers? In his notice of St. John, Jerome mentions a commentary by Justin Martyr on the Apocalypse.[40] But this information is erroneous. Jerome carelessly takes it from Eusebius' words.[41] There is no evidence either that Jerome read the *Apologies*.[42] Probably he is making a very clear reference to Justin's treatise *Against All Heresies*, but he knew of its existence through Eusebius.[43] Harnack had previously decided that Jerome had not himself read Justin's works.[44]

He seems to be more familiar with the work of Irenaeus, although he takes from Eusebius his notice in the *De viris inlustribus*[45] and several times mentions the existence of a commentary by Irenaeus on the Apocalypse through a mistaken interpretation of a passage in Eusebius.[46] He knows, however,

---

[36] *De vir. inl.* 36 (*PL* 23, 683 B). Sychowski, *Hieronymus*, p. 63, has shown that even the account of Pantaenus' voyage to India, which appears original, is based on Eusebius.

[37] *De vir. inl.* 37 (*PL* 23, 686 A). Even the mention "adversus Cataphrygas insigne opus," which seems original, is a gratuitous conjecture, on Jerome's part, from Eusebius; Sychowski, *Hieronymus*, p. 128 n. 3, and Bernoulli, *Schriftstellerkatalog*, p. 203.

[38] *De vir. inl.* 45 (*PL* 23, 691 C). The mention of "haec propterea posui, ut ingenium et auctoritatem viri ex parvo opusculo demonstrarem" is intended to make the reader think that Jerome quotes from the text and not from Eusebius. Cf. Sychowski, *Hieronymus*, p. 138 n. 6, and Bernoulli, *Schriftstellerkatalog*, p. 228.

[39] Bernoulli, *Schriftstellerkatalog*, p. 297.

[40] *De vir. inl.* 9 (*PL* 23, 655 B): "(Ioannes) . . . scripsit Apocalypsim, quam interpretatur Iustinus martyr et Irenaeus."

[41] Sychowski, *Hieronymus*, p. 60, and Bernoulli, *Schriftstellerkatalog*, pp. 114 and 172.

[42] The only indication that might lead one to think so is very slight. This is (cf. Bernoulli, *Schriftstellerkatalog*, pp. 195 and 291) the fact that Jerome corrects Eusebius' statement, 4.11, which seems to quote this passage as being from *Against Marcio* and not from the *Apology*. But perhaps, despite carelessness on Jerome's part, it turns out well, for Eusebius speaks of this *Apology* immediately afterward.

[43] Text quoted above, n. 9. Cf. Eusebius *Historia ecclesiastica* 4.11 (*PG* 20, 331 A).

[44] Harnack, *Altchr. Literatur*, p. 104, quoted by Bernoulli, *Schriftstellerkatalog*, p. 291.

[45] Including the mention of several of Irenaeus' letters to Pope Victor relating to the date of Easter, although Eusebius speaks of only one letter. Cf. Sychowski, *Hieronymus*, p. 65, and Bernoulli, *Schriftstellerkatalog*, p. 153.

[46]

Eusebius *Hist. eccl.* 3.39. 12–13 (*PG* 20, 299 A–B):	*De vir. inl.* 18 (*PL* 23, 670 B):	*Tract. in Ps.*, *Anecd. Mareds.* 3, 2, p. 5, 24, with reference to the Apocalypse:	*In Isaiam* 18, *prol.* (*PL* 24, 627 B):	*In Ezechielem* 11. 26.1 (*PL* 25, 339 B):
Καὶ χιλιάδα τινά φησιν ἐτῶν ἔσεσθαι μετὰ	Hic (Papias) dicitur mille annorum Iudaicorum edidisse δευτέρωσιν,	Nam et vete-	Apocalypsis Ioannis, quam si iuxta litteram accipimus, Iuda-	Neque enim iuxta Iudaicas fabulas, quas illi δευτερώσεις

that Irenaeus' treatise *Against Heresies* is a polemic against the Valentinian heresy.[47] An allusion made by Jerome to Stesichorus' *Palinode* seems to derive, as we have seen,[48] from the chapter in this treatise dealing with Simon Magus. Above all, Jerome appears to get from Irenaeus his information on the heresy of Basilides, who attributed divine motive to the 365 days of the year.[49] He also refers expressly to Irenaeus when speaking of the Marcosian

---

τὴν ἐκ νεκρῶν ἀνάστασιν, σωματικῶς τῆς τοῦ Χριστοῦ βασιλείας ἐπὶ ταυτησὶ τῆς γῆς ὑποστησομένης ... καὶ τοῖς μετ' αὐτὸν πλείστοις ὅσοις τῶν ἐκκλησιαστικῶν, τῆς ὁμοίας αὐτῷ δόξης παραίτιος γέγονε, τὴν ἀρχαιότητα τἀνδρὸς προβεβλημένοις ὥσπερ οὖν Εἰρηναίῳ καὶ εἴ τις ἄλλος τὰ ὅμοια φρονῶν ἀναπέφηνεν.

quem secuti sunt Irenaeus et Apollinarius et ceteri qui post resurrectionem aiunt in carne cum sacctis Dominum regnaturum. Tertullianus auoque in libro De spe fidelium et Victorinus Petabionensis et Lactantius hac opinione ducuntur.

res ecclesiastici viri e quibus Irenaeus et Polycarpus et Dionysius et alii Romani interpretes, de quibus est et Cyprianus sanctus recipiunt librum et interpretantur.

izandum est, si spiritualiter, ut scripta est, multorum veterum videbimur opinionibus contraire: Latinorum Tertulliani, Victorini, Lactantii; Graecorum, ut ceteros praetermittam, Irenaei tantum Lugdunensis episcopi faciam mentionem, adversum quem vir eloquentissimus Dionysius Alexandrinae ecclesiae pontifex elegantem scribit librum, inridens mille annorum fabulam ... Cui duobus voluminibus respondit Apollinarius.

appellant, gemmatam et auream de caelo exspectamus Ierusalem ... Quod et multi nostrorum et praecipue Tertulliani liber qui inscribitur *De spe fidelium* et Lactantii *Institutionum* volumen septimum pollicetur, et Victorini Petabionensis episcopi crebrae expositiones, et nuper Severus noster in dialogo cui *Gallo* nomen imposuit. Et ut Graecos nominem et primum extremumque coniungam, Irenaeus et Apollinarius.

---

[47] Text quoted above, n. 9. Cf. Irenaeus' preface on the *Valentini* (PG 7, 442 A).

[48] See above, sec. 2 nn. 34 and 80. Cf. *Epist. ad Ctesiphontem* 133.4 (PL 22, 1153): "Simon Magus haeresim condidit, Helenae meretricis adiutus auxilio."

[49] Irenaeus *Adv. haer.* 1.24.7 (PG 7, 680 A, with 671 B, Jerome's own reference to the disciples of Basilides and their theories): esse autem principem illorum Ἀβράξας et propter hoc trecentos sexaginta quin-   *De vir. inl.* 21 (PL 23, addition to Eusebius' notice on Agrippa, who refuted Basilides): Deum maximum eius Ἀβράξας, qui quasi annum   *In Amos* 1.3.9 (PL 25, 1018 D): Basilides, qui omnipotentem Deum portentoso nomine appellat Ἀβράξας et eundem secundum Graecas litteras et annui cursus nu-

heresy.[50] Actually, there is nothing to prove that Jerome read Irenaeus. In fact, the chapter in Irenaeus relating to the Marcosian heretics to which Jerome refers was repeated verbatim in the form of a very long excerpt by Epiphanius of Cyprus, who also repeated, in a form that was almost verbatim, Irenaeus' chapter on Basilides.[51] In addition, the theories on Melchisedek, which Jerome assures us stem from Irenaeus,[52] do not appear in Irenaeus' extant works but in a chapter by Epiphanius on the Melchisedian heresy.[53] I am therefore not so certain as Bernoulli that Jerome had at hand Irenaeus' chief work.[54] He probably did not know it except through Epiphanius.[55]

Jerome declares that he read a commentary by Theophilus of Antioch on

---

que numeros habere in se.

continens, si iuxta Graecorum numerum supputetur.

merum dicit in solis circulo contineri, quem ethnici sub eodem numero aliarum litterarum vocant Μείθραν.

Cf. also *Anecd. Mareds.* 3, 3, p. 36, 11.

[50] *De vir. inl.* 121 (*PL* 23, 750 C):

Gnosticae, id est Basilidis et Marci, de quibus Irenaeus scripsit, haereseos accusatur (Priscillianus).

Epist. ad Theodoram 75.3 (*PL* 22, 687):

Refert Irenaeus, vir apostolicorum temporum et Papiae auditoris evangelistae discipulus, episcopusque Ecclesiae Lugdunensis, quod Marcus quidam de Basilidis Gnostici stirpe descendens primum ad Gallias venerit.

In Isaiam 17.64.4 (*PL* 24, 622 D):

de quibus diligentissime vir apostolicus scribit Irenaeus episcopus Lugdunensis et martyr, multarum origines explicans haereseon et maxime Gnosticorum, qui per Marcum Aegyptium, Galliarum primum circa Rhodanum ... nobiles feminas deceperunt.

[51] Epiphanius *Adv. haer.* 1.3.14 (*PG* 41, 583–624) = Irenaeus *Adv. haer.* 1.13–21 (*PG* 7, 579–666). Cf. Epiphanius *Adv. haer.* 1.2.4 (*PG* 41, 316 B): λέγει δὲ τὴν ὑπεράνω τούτων δύναμιν εἶναι καὶ ἀρχὴν ᾿Αβρασὰξ διὰ τὸ τὴν ψῆφον τοῦ ᾿Αβρασὰξ ἔχειν τριακοσιοστὸν ἑξηκοστὸν πέμπτον ἀριθμόν. He quotes Irenaeus 316 C.

[52] *Epist. ad Evangelum* 73.2 (*PL* 22, 677): "Verti me ad Hippolytum, Irenaeum, Eusebium Caesariensem et Emisenum, Apollinarem quoque et Eustathium nostrum, qui primus Antiochenae ecclesiae episcopus contra Arium clarissima tuba bellicum cecinit, et deprehendi horum omnium opiniones, diversis argumentationibus ac diverticulis ad unum compitum pervenisse, ut dicerent Melchisedech hominem fuisse Chananaeum ... (679) Haec legi in Graecorum voluminibus."

[53] Epiphanius *Adv. haer.* 2.1.35 (*PG* 41, 970 A).

[54] Bernoulli, *Schriftstellerkatalog*, p. 292. According to this writer, pp. 147 and 210, it was probably a cursory reading of Irenaeus 5.8.10 that made Jerome declare in his notice on Origen in the *De vir. inl.* that Theodotion of Ephesus was a disciple of Ebion (*PL* 23, 702 A; cf. 25, 493 A). Another indication might be the reference, of which I have spoken, to the Palinode by Stesichorus, which does not appear in Epiphanius. But perhaps Jerome borrows it from Tertullian *De anima* 34 (*PL* 2, 709 A) and not from Irenaeus.

[55] On Jerome and Epiphanius, cf. above, pp. 50 and 89, and below, p. 123.

the Gospels and another on Proverbs.[56] This assertion, original with regard to Eusebius, is confirmed by two texts where Jerome mentions or quotes the commentary on the Gospels. But their authenticity seemed to him suspect.[57]

The only writer prior to Origen that Jerome used a little less cursorily was Clement of Alexandria. In actual truth, the notice on Clement in the *De viris inlustribus* comes entirely from Eusebius[58] and the occasional mention of his works by Jerome is often so indirect that I should not venture to decide whether he read the *Pedagogus* and the *Protrepticus*.[59] At least he makes use of the *Stromateis*. He is indebted to it for a few pagan quotations from ancient writers,[60] and refers to it in connection with the properties of odd numbers[61] and the calculation of the seventy weeks of years of which Daniel speaks.[62]

It can be seen how Jerome's reading, insofar as concerns the Fathers of the first two centuries, was rare and discursive. It is all the more surprising to assert that he quite positively read, although he does not mention it in the

[56] *De vir. inl.* 25 (*PL* 23, 678 A): "Legi sub nomine eius in Evangelium et in Proverbia Salomonis commentarios, qui mihi cum superiorum voluminum elegantia et phrasi non videntur congruere." Sychowski, *Hieronymus*, p. 117 n. 3, observes with good reason that this statement is no proof whatever that Jerome read Theophilus' other works.

[57] *In Matthaeum, prol.* (*PL* 26, 20 B): "Legisse me fateor ante annos plurimos in Matthaeum Origenis viginti quinque volumina et totidem eius homilias commaticumque interpretationis genus, et Theophili Antiochenae urbis episcopi commentarios, Hippolyti quoque martyris et Theodori Heracleotae Apollinarisque Laodiceni ac Didymi Alexandrini," and *Epist. ad Algasiam* 121.6 (*PL* 22, 1020): "Theophilus Antiochenae ecclesiae septimus post Petrum apostolum episcopus, qui quattuor Evangelistarum in unum opus dicta compingens, ingenii monumenta dimisit, haec super hac parabola in suis commentariis locutus est: Dives qui habuerat villicum." Cf. *Theophili in Evangelia libri IV*, ed. Zahn, *Forschungen zur Geschichte des neutestamentlichen Kanons*, vol. 2, p. 77, 23ff.

The commentary on the Gospels bearing the name of Theophilus of Antioch is a Latin compilation dating in the sixth century (cf. Puech, *Litt. gr. chrét.*, vol. 2, pp. 212–213, and Schanz, vol. 4, 2, p. 567) and could not possibly be the work mentioned by Jerome.

[58] Cf. Sychowski, *Hieronymus*, pp. 129–130.

[59] See above, sec. 2 nn. 30 and 39.

[60] See above, sec 2 nn. 26, 81, and 154.

[61] *Epist. ad Pammachium* 48.13 (*PL* 22, 509): "Scilicet enumerandum mihi est qui Ecclesiasticorum de impari numero disputarint: Clemens, Hippolytus, Origenes, Dionysius, Eusebius, Didymus." Cf. Clem. Alex. *Stromateis* 6.16 (*PG* 8, 364ff).

[62] *In Danielem* 9.24 (*PL* 25, 549 A): "Clemens vir eruditissimus, presbyter Alexandrinae ecclesiae, parvi pendens annorum numerum, a Cyro, rege Persarum, usque ad Vespasianum et Titum imperatores Romanos, septuaginta annorum hebdomadas dicit esse completas." Cf. *In Isaiam* 11.36, *prol.* (*PL* 24, 377 B) and Clem. Alex. *Stromateis* 1.21 (*PG* 8, 853–889). Perhaps Jerome is also indebted for what he knows of the heretic Cassianus, of whom he speaks *In Epist. ad Galat.* 3.6.8 (*PL* 26, 431 A), to the exposition by Clement *Stromateis* 3.13 (*PG* 8, 1191ff). But the parallel is not conclusive and Jerome's use would then be a very free one. Jerome says, *Adv. Rufin.* 1.13 (*PL* 23, 426 B), that Clement usually received help from a Jew, probably following *Stromateis* 1.11.2, as Puech suggests.

De viris inlustribus, an ancient work whose author is unknown to him. This is the *Altercatio Iasonis et Papisci* by Ariston of Pella. It is a dialogue on Judaism that served as a model for the dialogues of Justin Martyr, but is scarcely known.[63] It is quite probable that Jerome was interested in this work and diligently sought for it because Origen, in his controversy with Celsus, recommended its reading.[64]

Jerome in fact read and used Origen's works with such care that he neglected the ancient Fathers. The fact is certain, although the notice in the *De viris inlustribus* on Origen is almost entirely plagiarized from Eusebius.[65] At first glance it is surprising that a fulminating polemist like Jerome, who declared himself Origen's enemy in his dispute with Rufinus, should be an industrious reader of the heretic. Cavallera had already noted very properly, when studying Jerome's attitude toward Origen before, during, and after this quarrel, that at the height of the crisis, while actually applying the most violent epithets to Origen, Jerome never questions the scientific value of Origen as an exegete.[66] Without discussing the question from a doctrinal viewpoint, I shall confine myself to an estimate of the extent of Jerome's reading of Origen.

It must be observed that not all Origen's works interest Jerome in the same degree. Jerome himself divides them into three categories: the *excerpta* that he also calls *enchiridion*, σχόλια, or σημειώσεις, the running explanation of difficult passages; the homilies; the *volumina* or τόμοι, real *summae* that comment exhaustively on the Holy Scriptures.[67] Since the time when Jerome stayed in Constantinople, one of his Latin correspondents, Vincentius, who probably did not realize the extent of Origen's works, had been asking Jerome to

---

[63] *Liber Hebr. quaest. in Genesim* 1.1 (*PL* 23, 986 C): "Plerique existimant, sicut in altercatione quoque Iasonis et Papisci scriptum est . . . in Hebraeo haberi: *In filio fecit Deus caelum et terram*," and *In Epist. ad Galat.* 3.14 (*PL* 26, 361 C): "Memini me in Altercatione Iasonis et Papisci, quae Graeco sermone conscripta est, ita repperisse: λοιδορία Θεοῦ ὁ κρεμάμενος, id est: *Maledictio Dei qui appensus est*." A Latin translation of this work was made at an unknown date by a certain Celsus; the preface is extant (*PL* 6, 55 A).

[64] Origen *Contra Celsum* 4.52 (*PG* 11, 1116 A). Cf. Puech, *Litt. gr. chrét.*, vol. 2, pp. 157–159.

[65] Sychowski's hypothesis, *Hieronymus*, p. 146 n. 17, that Jerome used for this notice a commentary by Symmachus on Matthew is without foundation. He assumes the existence of this commentary through a wrong interpretation of Eusebius; cf. Bernoulli, *Schriftstellerkatalog*, p. 210.

[66] Cavallera, *Saint Jérôme*, I, 2, pp. 121–123. The entire note Q, pp. 122–127, is devoted to "Jérôme et Origène."

[67] *Transl. homiliarum Origenis in Ieremiam et Ezech., prol. ad Vincentium* (*PL* 25, 585 A), *In Isaiam, prol.* (*PL* 24, 21 A), *In Psalm.* (*Anecd. Mareds.* 3, 1, pp. 1–2). On the precise interpretation of these terms, cf. Mgr Devreesse's article "Chaînes exégétiques," *Supplément au Dictionnaire de la Bible*, p. 1106.

translate all Origen.[68] Jerome makes an excuse, not about the vast labor involved, but about the state of his eyesight and the lack of copyists. He sends his correspondent only twenty-eight homilies in translation, fourteen on Jeremiah and fourteen on Ezekiel, but he promises that later on he will translate, if possible, Origen's entire output.[69] On his return to Rome, Jerome was again asked to translate Origen's bulky commentaries. He requested Pope Damasus to excuse him if he translates for him only the two homilies on the Song of Songs, and not the commentary in ten volumes. Such a task is beyond his strength, would take too long, and would be very expensive.[70] For the same reasons, he cannot satisfy Blaesilla, who asked him to translate Origen's twenty-five volumes on Matthew, his five volumes on Luke, and his thirty-two volumes on John.[71] He cannot devote any more of his life to his first plan to translate all Origen, since Damasus commissioned him with the Hebrew revision of the Holy Scriptures. He appears determined, however, to translate at least the homilies. At Bethlehem too, he translated Origen's thirty-nine homilies on Luke as a continuation of Ambrose's commentary, then nine homilies on Isaiah.[72] In this undertaking, which thenceforth ran the risk of compromising Jerome, it was only the outbreak of the Origenist crisis that interrupted him. Rufinus was to take a malicious delight, indeed, in the preface to his translation of the Περὶ ἀρχῶν, in posing as a continuator of Jerome's vast design, namely, to translate, in accordance with the general wish, all Origen into Latin. He is amazed at the considerable number of seventy homilies by Origen translated by Jerome and he compares, with a show of feigned innocence, Jerome's commentaries on Paul's Epistles with simple translations of Origen's volumes.[73] Jerome

---

[68] *Trans. hom. Orig. in Ierem. et Ezech.*, prol. *ad Vincentium* (PL 25, 583 D): "Magnum est quidem, amice, quod postulas, ut Origenem faciam Latinum et hominem iuxta Didymi Videntis sententiam, alterum post Apostolum ecclesiarum magistrum etiam Romanis auribus donem . . . (586 A) Scio te cupere ut omne genus transferam dictionis."

[69] *Ibid.* (PL 25, 586 A): "Hoc tamen spondeo, quia si, orante te, Iesus reddiderit sanitatem, non dicam cuncta, sed permulta sum translaturus."

[70] *Interp. homiliarum duarum Origenis in Canticum*, prol. *ad Damasum* (PL 23, 1173): "illo opere praetermisso, quia ingentis est otii, laboris et sumptuum, tantas res, tamquam dignum in Latinum transferre sermonem."

[71] *Trans. homiliarum XXXIX Origenis in Lucam*, prol. (PL 26, 219 A): "Si quidem illud quod olim sancta Blaesilla flagitaverat, ut viginti quinque tomos illius in Matthaeum et quinque alios in Lucam et triginta duos in Ioannem, nostrae linguae traderem, nec virium mearum, nec otii, nec laboris est."

[72] PL 26, 219–306, and 24, 901–936. Cf. Schanz, vol. 4, 1, pp. 457–458. The date of the translation of the homilies on Isaiah is discussed.

[73] Rufinus *Praefatio in libros Περὶ ἀρχῶν* 1–2 (PL 22, 733): "Scio quam plurimos fratrum scientiae Scripturarum desiderio provocatos, poposcisse ab aliquantis eruditis viris et Graecarum litterarum peritis, ut Origenem Romanum facerent . . . (Hieronymus) pollicetur sane in ipsa praefatione se et ipsos in Cantica canticorum libros, et alios quam plurimos Origenis, Romanis auribus largiturum . . . qui cum ultra septuaginta libellos

vigorously protests that he has never translated Origen's doctrinal works: the *De resurrectione*, the Περὶ ἀρχῶν, the *Stromateis*, nor even a single "tome."[74] He will still translate the Περὶ ἀρχῶν, but for the sole purpose of proclaiming the danger of Rufinus' translation, which, by corrupting this text, renders Origen's heretical thought innocuous.[75]

If Jerome no longer translated Origen as in the past, he did not stop reading him and using him in his commentaries. He does not conceal this fact, since he regularly mentions his source, at least once in the course of his commentary. But he purposely dissembles, for instance in his *Commentary on the Epistle to the Ephesians*,[76] the importance of his borrowings from Origen. It is Rufinus' insistence, and necessarily so, that forces Jerome to acknowledge that this commentary is a compilation from various Greek writers, particularly from Origen.[77] Klostermann has shown by means of numerous convincing parallels that after his quarrel with Rufinus, Jerome continued to employ exactly the same method and depended on Origen even in the *Commentary on Jeremiah*, his last work.[78] Although refuting Origen's doctrines, Jerome no longer mentions him except in a past sense, but he identifies him clearly by the words "allegoricus interpres."[79] Thus Jerome stopped translating first Origen's "tomes," then his homilies. But in his original purpose to publicize in the Latin world Origen's exegetical work he persevered until his death, although he had become one of the most bitter enemies of Origen's doctrine.

If Origen exerted, either positively or by a reaction, such an influence over

---

Origenis, quos Homiliticos appellavit, aliquantos etiam de Tomis in Apostolum scriptis transtulisset in Latinum, in quibus cum aliquanta offendicula inveniantur in Graeco, ita elimavit omnia interpretando atque purgavit, ut nihil in illis, quod a fide nostra discrepat, Latinus lector inveniat."

[74] *Epist. ad Pammachium et Oceanum* 84.7 (PL 22, 749): "Centum quinquaginta anni prope sunt, ex quo Origenes mortuus est Tyri. Quis Latinorum ausus est umquam transferre libros eius *de resurrectione*, περὶ ἀρχῶν, στρωματέας et τόμους?"

[75] On the Origenist quarrel, cf. J. Brochet, *Saint Jérôme et ses ennemis* (diss. Paris 1905) 208ff, and Villain, "Rufin d'Aquilée," 23ff. The former supports Jerome, the latter Rufinus. Cf. also Bardy, *Recherches sur l'histoire du texte et des versions latines du "De principiis" d'Origène.* To the bibliography therein must be added K. Mueller, "Zu den Auszügen des Hieronymus (ad Avitum) aus des Origenes Περὶ ἀρχῶν," *Sitzungsberichte der preuss. Akad.* (1919) 616–631.

[76] *In Epist. ad Ephes.*, prol. (PL 26, 442 C): "Illud quoque in praefatione commoneo, ut sciatis Origenem tria volumina in hanc epistulam conscripsisse, quem et nos ex parte secuti sumus."

[77] *Adv. Rufin.* 1.24 (PL 23, 436 B): "nos triplicem expositionem posuimus: in prima quid nobis videretur, in secunda quid Origenes opponeret, in tertia quid Apollinarius simpliciter explanaret; quorum si nomina non posui, ignosce verecundiae meae," and 1.25 (PL 23, 437 B).

[78] E. Klostermann, "Die Ueberlieferung der Jeremiahomilien des Origenes," *Texte und Untersuchungen* 1, 3 (Gebhardt-Harnack) 66–75.

[79] Klostermann, p. 65.

St. Jerome, it was because the latter knew his work so well. It is reasonable to assume with Cavallera that this work was revealed to him from the time of his stay in Constantinople by Gregory of Nazianzus, the author of the *Philocalia*.[80] In any case, he drew up in Rome, it is thought, a catalogue of Origen's complete works, inserted in his letter to Paula. His intention was to show that Origen's productivity exceeded that of the greatest pagan scholars: Varro and Didymus Chalcenterus.[81] How did Jerome compile such a catalogue? Did he merely copy an earlier catalogue or were all the books that he mentions actually at his disposal? This nice problem was broached by Klostermann, without his being able to flatter himself that he had resolved it.[82] We know that Origen's complete works were preserved in Caesarea, that they were classified and catalogued there by Pamphilus the martyr, and that Eusebius of Caesarea had inserted this catalogue in Book 3 of his *Life of Pamphilus*, which is no longer extant. Now Jerome possessed Eusebius' book.[83] One is therefore inclined to think that his *Letter to Paula* simply reproduces Pamphilus' catalogue.[84] However, Pamphilus' catalogue, on Jerome's own admission,[85] came to almost 2,000 items, whereas Jerome's catalogue scarcely reaches 800 listings.[86] In addition, the order in which Jerome's catalogue lists these works is strange. Origen's dogmatic writings are inserted between his commentaries on the Old and the New Testament. The order followed by the numbering of the "tomes" is the same only for the homilies. These are so many indications of revisions.[87] On the other

[80] Cavallera, *Saint Jérôme*, I, 2, p. 116.

[81] *Epist. ad Paulam* 33.1 (PL 22, 447).

[82] E. Klostermann, "Die Schriften des Origenes in Hieronymus' Brief an Paula," *Sitzungsber. der kön. preuss. Akad. der Wissenschaften zu Berlin* 2 (1897) 855–870. This catalogue also appears in Hilberg's edition of the Vienna *Corpus*, but not in *PL*.

[83] Cf. Eusebius *Hist. eccles.* 6.32.3.

[84] *De vir. inl.* 81 (PL 23, 727 A): "de vita Pamphili libri tres," and *Epist. ad Marcellam* 34.1 (PL 22, 448): "Hic (Pamphilus) cum multa reppererit et inventorum nobis indicem dereliquerit, centesimi vicesimi sexti Psalmi commentarium et Phe litterae tractatum, ex eo quod non inscripsit, confessus est non repertum. Non quod talis tantusque vir (Adamantium dicimus) aliquid praeterierit, sed quod neglegentia posterorum ad nostram usque memoriam non durarit. Hoc ideo dixi, ut quia de eodem Psalmo mihi proposuisti quid esset *panis doloris* . . . ostenderem me de Origenis commentariis quid senserit non habere." Jerome quotes a passage from Book 3, *Adv. Rufin.* 1.9 (PL 23, 422 B). Cf. Bernoulli, *Schriftstellerkatalog*, p. 292, and Klostermann, "Die Schriften des Origenes," p. 858. It will be noted that the commentary on Psalm 126, which was missing in Pamphilus' catalogue, is also missing in Jerome's.

[85] *Adv. Rufin.* 2.22 (PL 23, 466 D): "Numera indices librorum eius, qui in tertio volumine Eusebii in quo scripsit vitam Pamphili, continentur: et non dico sex milia, sed tertiam partem non reperies."

[86] Klostermann, "Die Schriften des Origenes," p. 858.

[87] *Ibid.*, p. 859. I should even be prepared to believe, if the letter to Paula was written at Rome, that it has reached us under a later, revised form.

hand, Jerome prides himself on having assembled a great number of Origen's writings.[88] He worked in Caesarea itself, where he consulted the *Hexapla*,[89] the *Epistle to the Hebrews*,[90] and the *Apology for Origen*.[91] He even borrowed from the library at Caesarea copies of Origen's works, in Pamphilus' handwriting.[92] If therefore the sequence of Jerome's catalogue corresponds to the books by Origen that he mentions in his other works, this will prove that this catalogue reflects the library that Jerome used so effectively. He probably compiled it with the aid of Pamphilus' catalogue, suppressing however all Origen's writings that he had not himself read. These latter works must have been lost at the time when the papyri in Pamphilus' library were destroyed before being recopied on parchment by Acacius and Euzoius.[93]

In fact, Origen's homilies that Jerome included in his catalogue are the same as those he mentions or quotes in his other works.[94] Among the dogmatic treatises, he read the Περὶ ἀρχῶν,[95] the four books of the *De resur-*

[88] *Epist. ad Pammachium et Oceanum* 84.3 (*PL* 22, 745): "Quod autem opponunt, congregasse me libros illius super cunctos homines: utinam omnium Tractatorum haberem volumina ... Congregavi libros eius, fateor; et ideo errores non sequor, quia scio universa quae scripsit." On Jerome's own library, cf. Bernoulli, *Schriftstellerkatalog*, p. 294.

[89] Cf. the texts quoted by Bernoulli, *Schriftstellerkatalog*, p. 294, and Cavallera, *Saint Jérôme*, 1, 2, p. 88 n. H ("Saint Jérôme et la bibliothèque de Césarée"), especially *De vir. inl.* 54 (*PL* 23, 702 A): "Praeterea quintam et sextam et septimam editionem, quas etiam nos de eius bibliotheca habemus, miro labore repperit et cum ceteris editionibus comparavit," and *In Psalm.* 1 (*Anecd. Mareds.* 3, 1, p. 5): "*non sic* in Hebraeis voluminibus non habetur, sed ne in ipsis quidem LXX interpretibus, nam ἑξαπλοῦς Origenis in Caesariensi bibliotheca relegens, semel tantum scriptum repperi," and (p. 12) "Cum vetustum Origenis hexaplum Psalterium revolverem, quod ipsius manu fuerat emendatum."

[90] *De vir. inl.* 3 (*PL* 23, 643 B): "Porro ipsum Hebraicum habetur usque hodie in Caesariensi bibliotheca," and *Dial. contra Pelagianos* 3.2 (*PL* 23, 597 B): "In Evangelio iuxta Hebraeos ... quod et in Caesariensi habetur bibliotheca."

[91] *Adv. Rufin.* 3.12 (*PL* 23, 486 D): "Postea vero per interpretationem tuam quaestione contra Origenem toto orbe commota, in quaerendis exemplaribus diligentior fui et in Caesariensi bibliotheca Eusebii sex volumina repperi Ἀπολογίας ὑπὲρ Ὠριγένους."

[92] *De vir. inl.* 75 (*PL* 23, 722 A): "Pamphilus ... tanto Bibliothecae divinae amore flagravit, ut maximam partem Origenis voluminum sua manu descripserit, quae usque hodie in Caesariensi bibliotheca habentur. Sed et in duodecim prophetas viginti quinque Ἐξηγήσεων Origenis volumina manu eius exarata repperi, quae tanto amplector et servo gaudio, ut Croesi opes habere me credam." It is quite clear that, if Jerome had this volume in his possession at the time of writing this notice in the *De vir. inl.*, it was because he was engaged in composing his commentary on the twelve minor prophets and that he borrowed it for this purpose (cf. *De vir. inl.* 135 and *In Ionam, prol.* (*PL* 25, 1117 A).

[93] Cf. *Epist. ad Marcellam* 34.1 (*PL* 22, 448): "quam (bibliothecam) ex parte corruptam Acacius dehinc et Euzoius eiusdem ecclesiae sacerdotes in membranis instaurare conati sunt."

[94] I shall indicate the numbering of the books in Jerome's catalogue in Klostermann's edition by the sigil Kl. followed by a figure representing Klostermann's numbering arrangement.

[95] Kl. 77 "Peri archon libri IIII." On his translation, cf. above, p. 102.

rectione,[96] the *Dialogue against Candidus the Valentinian.*[97] Among the exegetical treatises, he translated the homilies and used preferably the tomes in his commentaries. He is quite familiar with the *Stromateis.* This is certainly one of the main sources of his knowledge of Greek philosophy.[98] He borrows from Book 6 a long quotation from Plato that gave him an opportunity to characterize Origen as a theoretician of falsehood.[99] He knows that Origen's theories on the resurrection reappear in the *Stromateis.*[100] The danger inherent in the book does not prevent Jerome from consulting it very frequently for the exposition of the Epistle to the Galatians,[101] Daniel,[102] and even Jeremiah.[103] Jerome also read Origen's exegesis on Genesis, which he mentions in his catalogue, the fourteen books[104] and the seventeen homilies,[105]

[96] Kl. 78 "de resurrectione libros II"; 79 "et alios de resurrectione dialogos II." Cf. the text quoted above, n. 74, and *Adv. Ioann. Hieros.* 25 (*PL* 23, 392 A): "Dicit ergo Origenes in pluribus locis et maxime in libro *De resurrectione* quarto et in expositione primi Psalmi et in *Stromatibus* duplicem errorem versari in Ecclesia: nostrorum et haereticorum."

[97] Kl. 81; cf. *Adv. Rufin.* 2.18–19 (*PL* 23, 461 B and 463 A) where Jerome gives a rapid analysis of the work. With regard to the *De martyrio* (Kl. 82) Jerome's reference *De vir. inl.* 56 (*PL* 23, 703 B) does not prove that he read it, for he is plagiarizing Eusebius 6.28.1; cf. Bernoulli, *Schriftstellerkatalog,* p. 149.

[98] Kl. 11; cf. *Epist. ad Magnum* 70.4 (*PL* 22, 667): "Hunc (Clementem Alexandrinum) imitatus Origenes decem scripsit Stromateas, Christianorum et philosophorum inter se sententias comparans et omnia nostrae religionis dogmata de Platone et Aristotele, Numenio Cornutoque confirmans," and *Dial. contra Pelagianos* 1 (*PL* 23, 518 A): "(Stoici et Peripatetici) quorum sententias ... Origenes ecclesiasticae veritati in *Stromatibus* suis miscere conatur."

[99] Text quoted above, sec. 2 n. 88, and *Epist. ad Pammachium et Oceanum* 84.3 (*PL* 22, 746): "Quod autem periuriorum atque mendacii inter se orgiis foederentur, sextus *Stromateon* liber (in quo Platonis sententiae nostrum dogma componit) planissime docet."

[100] Text quoted above, n. 96.

[101] The tenth book of the *Stromateis* is used by Jerome *In Epist. ad Galat., prol.* 3.5.13 and 3.5.19 (*PL* 26: 309 A, 406 C–408 B, a long textual quotation, 414 D), and again *Epist. ad Augustinum* 112.4–6 (*PL* 22, 918–919); text quoted above, sec. 2 n. 128.

[102] *In Danielem* 4.6, 9.24, 13.1 (*PL* 25: 514 A, 549 B, 580 B) quoting the ninth and tenth books of the *Stromateis.* On the extent of these borrowings, cf. Lataix, "Le commentaire de s. Jérôme sur Daniel," 268–274: "Opinions d'Origène."

[103] *In Ierem.* 4.22.24ff (*PL* 24, 817 C–D): "Nunc dico ... magistrum eorum Origenem hunc locum referre ad Christum ... Scribit autem hoc, ne discipuli eius negare audeant, in quinto *Stromatum.*"

[104] Kl. 7; cf. *Epist. ad Damasum* 36.9 (*PL* 22, 456): "sciens Origenem duodecimum et tertium decimum in Genesim librum de hac tantum quaestione dictasse (de septem vindictis Cain)." Jerome *Epist. ad Pammachium et Oceanum* 84.7 (*PL* 22, 749) also calls it *Hexaemeron.* On the exact number of books in this commentary, cf. Klostermann's note to the passage indicated in Kl. 7.

[105] Kl. 98; cf. the text above, n. 351. The context indicating that there is a question of odd numbers in the matter of Noah's ark seems to refer to Origen-Rufinus *Hom. 2 in Genesim* (*PG* 12, 171–172).

as well as the two books of mystical homilies.[106] He must have read also the homilies on Exodus, Leviticus, Numbers, Deuteronomy, Joshua, Judges, which Rufinus possessed[107] and Jerome used on several occasions.[108] He likewise uses Origen to comment on Ecclesiastes, without one's being able to determine whether they are homilies or *excerpta*.[109] He prizes particularly Origen's works on the Song of Songs. He translates his two homilies[110] and regrets his inability to do the same for the ten books. But he used these ten books, for he considers them indispensable to every commentator of the Song of Songs. He knows the exact number of verses and is even acquainted with the first edition in two volumes, written by Origen in his youth.[111] The works on the Psalms, which Dom Morin discovered, prove that Jerome knew just as well Origen's corresponding works that are mentioned in his catalogue. Not only did he read the text of the Psalms in a manuscript corrected in Origen's own handwriting,[112] but he made a commentary on it when compiling Origen's *Enchiridion*,[113] a huge number of his tomes,[114] and his homilies.[115] Elsewhere, Jerome also refers several times to Origen's exposi-

---

[106] Kl. 8, a plausible conjecture that the homily on Melchizedek mentioned by Jerome *Epist.* 73.2 (*PL* 22, 677) *in fronte Geneseos* was part of this collection.

[107] Kl. 99–104. On the translations of Rufinus, cf. Schanz, vol. 4, 1, p. 419. The homilies on Deuteronomy are the only ones left unfinished in translation on account of Jerome's death.

[108] *Epist. ad Damasum* 36.1 (*PL* 22, 453): "(Origenes) de mundis atque immundis animalibus in *Levitico* plura disseruit, ut si ipse invenire nihil possem, de eius tamen fontibus mutuarer." Cf. Origen-Rufinus *In Levit.*, hom. 7.4–7 *de mundis et immundis animalibus* (*PG* 12, 483 C–492 B). On the other hand, *Epist. ad Fabiolam* 78 (*PL* 22, 698–724) *de XLII mansionibus Israelitarum in deserto* repeatedly uses the twenty-seventh homily of Origen-Rufinus on Numbers (*PG* 12, 780ff).

[109] Kl. 71 and 109; cf. Jerome *In Ecclesiasten* 4.13 (*PL* 23, 1103 C) where Jerome shows that he compared Victorinus' text with his source Origen. On the use made of Origen in this commentary, although Jerome declares in the preface (*PL* 23, 1062 B) "nullius auctoritatem secutus sum," cf. Gruetzmacher, *Hieronymus*, vol. 2, p. 52.

[110] Kl. 110; cf. *PL* 23, 1173–1196.

[111] Kl. 72–73; cf. *PL* 23, 1173: "decem voluminibus explicitis, quae ad viginti usque versuum milia paene perveniunt," and *Epist. ad Marcellam* 37.3 (*PL* 22, 463): "Rogo, non habuerat decem Origenis volumina?" On the first edition of this commentary, cf. *In Abdiam, prol.* (*PL* 25, 1098 C) and *PG* 13, 36 and 59.

[112] Text quoted above, n. 89.

[113] Kl. 178; cf. *Anecd. Mareds.* 3, 1, *prol.* p. 1 (= *PL* 26, 821): "Proxime cum Origenis *Psalterium*, quod *Enchiridion* ille vocabat, strictis et necessariis interpretationibus adnotatum in commune legeremus, simul uterque deprehendimus non nulla eum vel praestrinxisse leviter, vel intacta penitus reliquisse, de quibus in alio opere latissime disputavit; ... studiose et sedule postulasti, ut ... in Psalterii opere latissimo quasi praeteriens aliqua perstringerem ... ea quae in tomis vel in omiliis ipse disseruit, vel ego digna arbitror lectione, in hunc angustum commentariolum referam."

[114] Kl. 27–69. It is this work that Jerome refers to again *Epist. ad Augustinum* 112.20 (*PL* 22, 929).

[115] Kl. 114–117.

tions of the Psalms.[116] He likewise possessed a very complete file of Origen on the Prophets. His *Commentary on Isaiah* brings together the homilies by Origen mentioned in his catalogue: thirty volumes,[117] σημειώσεις or *excerpta* and twenty-five homilies of which Jerome translated nine.[118] On Jeremiah, Jerome translated fourteen of Origen's homilies[119] and he used them concurrently with his five volumes for a commentary on Jeremiah.[120] Sometimes he follows Origen's text so literally that, when Origen quotes the opinion of his Hebrew masters, Jerome too quotes them as if they had been his own masters.[121] He translated in the same manner fourteen homilies on Ezekiel[122] and in his commentary used without mention the corresponding commentary by Origen in twenty-five books.[123] We are at last very well informed about the material that Jerome used for his commentary on the twelve minor prophets. In the *De viris inlustribus* he declares he is as rich as Croesus because he possesses, out of the twenty-five books of Origen's commentaries, Pamphilus' autograph copy, which he borrowed from the

---

[116] *Epist. ad Ctesiphontem* 133.3 (*PL* 22, 1152). Cf. Origen *In Ps.* 15.7 (*PG* 12, 1213 C). *Adv. Ioann. Hieros.* 25 (*PL* 23, 392 B): "in expositione primi psalmi"; cf. Origen *Selecta in Ps.* 1.5 (*PG* 12, 1091–1098). *Adv. Rufin.* 1.13 (*PL* 23, 426 C): "Octogesimum quoque nonum psalmum qui scribitur: *Oratio Moysi hominis Dei* et reliquos undecim qui non habent titulos, secundum Huilli expositionem, eiusdem Moysi putat (Origenes); cf. Origen *Ex comm. in Ps.* (*PG* 12, 1056 B–C).

[117] Kl. 12. The note indicates that the number 36 is a mistake in transcription. Cf. *In Isaiam, prol.* (*PL* 24, 21 A): "Scripsit enim in hunc prophetam iuxta editiones quattuor, usque ad Visionem quadrupedum in deserto, Origenes triginta volumina, e quibus vicesimus sextus non invenitur. Feruntur et alii sub nomine eius de visione τετραπόδων duo ad Gratam libri, qui pseudographi putantur, et viginti quinque homiliae et Σημειώσεις quas nos *excerpta* possumus appellare." Jerome regularly follows the commentary in thirty books, while criticizing its allegorical interpretations, *PL* 24, 94 C (cf. *Epist. ad Pammachium et Oceanum* 84.3, *PL* 22, 745), 99 A: "in octavo volumine explanationum Isaiae," 154 C, and *Adv. Rufin.* 1.13 (*PL* 23. 426 C): "tricesimum tomum in Isaiam."

[118] Kl. 13 and Kl. 111. The note indicates that the number 32 in the catalogue is an error in transcription. A translation of these nine homilies may be found edited in *PL* 24, 901–936.

[119] Kl. 112; cf. *PL* 25, 585–692. Jerome uses these homilies likewise in his *Epist. ad Damasum* 18, as is shown by the parallels established by Klostermann, "Die Ueberlieferung der Jeremiahomilien," pp. 76–83.

[120] Kl. 75. In my opinion, most of the passages in Jerome's commentary on Jeremiah mentioned by Klostermann ("Die Ueberlieferung der Jeremiahomilien," pp. 72–75) that do not refer to Origen's homilies on Jeremiah are derived from these books. Origen is regularly referred to in these words: *quidam, allegoricus,* or *pravus interpres.*

[121] Klostermann, *ibid.,* p. 83, and G. Bardy, "Saint Jérôme et ses maîtres hébreux," *RB* 46 (1934) 145–164.

[122] Kl. 113. The number 12 in the catalogue is an error in transcription; cf. *PL* 25, 691–786.

[123] Kl. 26. The number 29 in the catalogue is an error in transcription; cf. *In Ezech.* 9.4 (*PL* 25, 88 Aff). This is a word-for-word translation of Origen's *Selecta in Ezech.,* *PG* 13, 799 D. On the sources of this commentary, cf. Gruetzmacher, *Hieronymus,* 3, p. 200.

library at Caesarea.[124] This number coincides exactly with the numbers in the catalogue.[125] He mentions, too, quite specifically, the point at which Origen's two books on Zachariah stopped,[126] and in his commentary on Hosea he uses two distinct homilies by Origen.[127] It will therefore not be surprising if the commentaries on the minor prophets brought and still bring on Jerome the charge of being Origen's compiler.[128]

Jerome read with the same care Origen's works on the New Testament. He continually uses, as Zahn has shown,[129] Origen's twenty-five homilies and his twenty-five volumes on Matthew, although he pretends that he had not read them for a long time.[130] He has translated the thirty-five homilies,[131] and he also knows the six volumes on Luke,[132] as well as the thirty-two books on John.[133]

He appears to have had at his disposal a complete collection of Origen's commentaries on Paul's Epistles, for he quotes his commentary on the Epistle to the Romans,[134] the first Epistle to the Thessalonians,[135] the Epistle to the

[124] Text quoted above, n. 92.

[125] Kl. 15–25. It must therefore be admitted that Jerome's mention, *In Malach., prol.* (*PL* 25, 1543 A), "Scripsit in hunc librum Origenes tria volumina," is erroneous, for then the total number of books on the twelve minor prophets would be twenty-six.

[126] Kl. 24 "In principio Zachariae libros II"; cf. *In Hoseam, prol.* (*PL* 25, 820): "in ipsum (Zachariam) duo tantum Origenes scripsit volumina, vix tertiam partem a principio libri usque ad visionem quadrigarum edisserens," and *In Zach., prol.* (*PL* 25, 1418 A): "Scripsit in hunc prophetam Origenes duo volumina, usque ad tertiam partem libri a principio."

[127] Kl. 14 "In Hosea de Effraim librum I"; 15, "In Hoseam commentarium." Cf. *In Hoseam, prol.* (*PL* 25, 819 A): "Origenes parvum de hoc propheta scripsit libellum cui hunc titulum imposuit: Περὶ τοῦ πῶς ὠνομάσθη ἐν τῷ Ὡσῆε Ἐφραίμ, hoc est: *quare appellatur in Hosea Ephraim*, volens ostendere quaecumque contra eum dicuntur, ad haereticorum referenda personam. Et aliud volumen ἀκέφαλον καὶ ἀτέλεστον, quod et capite careat et fine."

[128] *In Mich.* 2, *prol.* (*PL* 25, 1189 C): "dicunt Origenis me volumina compilare." Cf. Gruetzmacher, *Hieronymus*, 2, pp. 114 and 196.

[129] Th. Zahn, *Forschungen zur Geschichte des neutestamentlichen Kanons*, vol. 2 (Erlangen 1883) 275–281: "Origenes und Hieronymus zu Matthäus."

[130] Kl. 84 and 180; cf. texts quoted above, nn. 57 and 71.

[131] Kl. 181; cf. *PL* 26, 219–306.

[132] Kl. 87. The number 15 in the catalogue is an error in transcription; cf. the text quoted above, n. 71.

[133] Kl. 85. Cf. the text quoted above, n. 71.

[134] Kl. 88. Cf. *Epist. ad Damasum* 36.1 (*PL* 22, 453): "Nam et Origenes in quarto Pauli ad Romanos ἐξηγήσεων tomo de circumcisione magnifice disputavit" = Origen-Rufinus *In Epist. ad Romanos* 4.2 (*PG* 14, 966ff) and *Epist. ad Algasiam* 121.8 (*PL* 22, 1024). This is a word-for-word translation, without mentioning Origen, of a fragment of the *Philocalia* taken from book 9, chap. 9 on the *Epist. ad Romanos* = Origen-Rufinus *In Epist. ad Romanos* 6.8 (*PG* 14, 1076 and n. 86).

[135] Kl. 93 "In epistula ad Thessalonicenses Iᵃ libros III." Cf. *Epist. ad Minervium et*

Ephesians,[136] the commentary and the homilies on the Epistle to the Galatians,[137] the homilies on the Epistle to the Corinthians.[138] It is quite probable that he possessed a complete set of Origen's works on Paul and that, if he does not mention them all in the course of his writings, it is because some were less important than others.[139]

The manuscript tradition is defective for the remaining items in the catalogue, which cannot be positively identified.[140] But Jerome also possessed several collections of Origen's correspondence, like those that he mentions at the end of his catalogue:[141] a collection in nine books,[142] another in two books, in which the replies of Origen's correspondents appear,[143] and a third collection containing letters of Origen, Julius Africanus, and Gregory Thaumaturgus.[144] These are probably the collections that supplied all the information for Jerome's *De viris inlustribus* that did not come from Eusebius on Origen's contemporaries, as Bernoulli has previously assumed, although he did not know the contents of the catalogue.[145] The collections consisted of Origen's correspondence with Ambrose,[146] Tryphon,[147]

Alexandrum 119.9 (*PL* 22, 974): "Origenes in tertio volumine ἐξηγητικῶν Epistulae Pauli ad Thessalonicenses primae," and *PG* 14, 1297 D–1304 A.

[136] Kl. 90. Cf. text quoted above, n. 76, and *Adv. Rufin.* 1.21 (*PL* 23, 438 D = *PG* 14, 1297 B): "Ponamus tamen ipsa verba quae in Origenis libro tertio continentur." On Jerome's use of this commentary, cf. Klostermann, "Die Ueberlieferung der Jeremiahomilien," p. 64 n. 3.

[137] Kl. 89. Cf. *In Epist. ad Galat., prol.* (*PL* 26, 308 B): "Origenis commentarios sum secutus; scripsit enim ille vir in epistulam Pauli ad Galatas quinque proprie volumina et decimum Stromatum suorum librum commatico super explanatione eius sermone complevit; tractatus quoque varios et excerpta quae vel sola possint sufficere, composuit," 2.5.28 and 3.5.24 (*PL* 26, 392 A and 421 C) and *Epist. ad Augustin.* 112.4 (*PL* 22, 918). These *tractatus varii* probably refer to the seven homilies on the Epistle to the Galatians (Kl. 185).

[138] Kl. 183. Cf. the text quoted below, n. 177.

[139] Kl. 91, 92, 94–96, 184, 186, 187.

[140] Kl. 188–191.

[141] Kl. 192–197.

[142] Kl. 195 "Epistularum eius ad diversos libri VIIII." Cf. *Adv. Rufin.* 2.18 (*PL* 23, 461 A) quoting from Rufinus *De adulteratione libr. Orig.* (*PG* 17, 624) Origen's letter *ad quosdam caros suos Alexandriam,* taken *ex libro epistularum Origenis quarto.*

[143] Kl. 193 "Item excerpta Origenis et diversarum ad eum epistularum libri II."

[144] Kl. 192 "Origenis, Africani et Gregorii."

[145] Bernoulli, *Schriftstellerkatalog,* p. 293.

[146] *De vir. inl.* 56 (*PL* 23, 703 B): "(Ambrosius) . . . non inelegantis ingenii fuit, sicut eius ad Origenem epistulae indicio sunt," and 61 (*PL* 23, 707 B): "unde et in quadam epistula ἐργοδιώκτην eum (Ambrosium) Origenes vocat," and *Epist. ad Marcellam* 43.1 (*PL* 23, 478): "in quadam epistula quam ad eundem (Ambrosium) de Athenis scripserat (Origenes)." Cf. Sychowski, *Hieronymus,* p. 148, and Bernoulli, *Schriftstellerkatalog,* pp. 270–271.

[147] *De vir. inl.* 57 (*PL* 23, 703 B): "Tryphon, Origenis auditor, ad quem non nullae eius exstant epistulae." Cf. Bernoulli, *Schriftstellerkatalog,* p. 310. Tryphon's homilies

Beryllus,[148] Alexander of Jerusalem,[149] Julius Africanus,[150] and Gregory Thaumaturgus.[151] Finally, Jerome owned the letter written by Origen to Pope Fabian in defense of his works.[152]

Thus Jerome's entire output confirms the fact that he knew all Origen's books that he mentions in his catalogue and that he used them constantly. The rare exceptions to this rule are more apparent than real. The question rests on *excerpta*[153] that Jerome could quite conceivably have possessed and read without mentioning them in his commentaries that preferably used the more learned "tomes." Or it may be a question of Origen's homilies on the books in Scripture for which Jerome did not write any commentary.[154] Inversely, it is certain that Jerome read a few more of Origen's books than those that appear in the catalogue, whether he omitted them through carelessness or whether manuscript tradition of the catalogue is defective.[155] This involves the Κατὰ Κέλσον,[156] the *De nominibus Hebraicis*,[157] and *excerpta* on

---

mentioned by Jerome seem to me to be merely letters that discuss some points of exegesis on specific passages of Scripture.

[148] *De vir. inl.* 60 (*PL* 23, 706 C): "Beryllus . . . scripsit varia opuscula et maxime epistulas in quibus Origeni gratias agit. Sed et Origenis ad eum litterae sunt." Cf. Sychowski, *Hieronymus*, p. 150.

[149] *De vir. inl.* 62 (*PL* 23, 710 B): "Alexander . . . scripsit . . . ad Origenem." Cf. Sychowski, *Hieronymus*, p. 155 n. 5, and Bernoulli, *Schriftstellerkatalog*, p. 293. I believe with Sychowski, *Hieronymus*, p. 156 n. 6, that the statement "Sed et aliae eius ad diversos feruntur epistulae" does not necessarily imply a direct knowledge of these letters on Jerome's part.

[150] *De vir. inl.* 63 (*PL* 23, 710 C) and *Praef. in Danielem* (*PL* 28, 1293 A). Cf. *PG* 11, 45. Also *In Ieremiam* 5.29.21ff (*PL* 24, 862ff). Jerome relates a Hebraic tradition from Origen's letter addressed to Africanus *De historia Susannae* 7–8 (*PG* 11, 63). Cf. Sychowski, *Hieronymus*, p. 157 n. 3, and Bernoulli, *Schriftstellerkatalog*, p. 276.

[151] *De vir. inl.* 65 (*PL* 23, 711 B): "Πανηγυρικὸν εὐχαριστίας scripsit Origenes . . . qui usque hodie exstat (= *PG* 10, 1049–1104). Scripsit et μετάφρασιν in Ecclesiasten, brevem quidem, sed valde utilem, et aliae huius vulgo feruntur epistulae." Cf. *In Ecclesiasten* 4.13 (*PL* 23, 1103 A): "Vir sanctus Gregorius Ponti episcopus Origenis auditor in Metaphrasi Ecclesiastae ita hunc locum intellexit," quoting Gregory's text, *In Ecclesiasten* 4.13–16 (*PG* 10, 1000 A). This short treatise could have been included among the *Letters*. Cf. Bernoulli, *Schriftstellerkatalog*, p. 293. One of Origen's letters to Gregory has been preserved (*Philocalia*, chap. 13 = *PG* 11, 87).

[152] Kl. 197 "Item epistula pro apologia operum suorum libri II." Cf. *Epist. ad Pammachium et Oceanum* 84.10 (*PL* 22, 751): "Ipse Origenes in epistula quam scribit ad Fabianum Romanae urbis episcopum paenitentiam agit, cur talia scripserit, et causas temeritatis in Ambrosium refert, quod secreto edita in publicum protulerit."

[153] Kl. 9, 10, 86.

[154] Kl. 70, 80, 105–108, 182.

[155] Cf. Klostermann, "Die Schriften des Origenes," pp. 858 and 870.

[156] Cf. the texts quoted above, sec. 2 n. 135.

[157] Cf. the texts quoted above, sec. 2 n. 172. Perhaps Jerome does not include it in his catalogue of Origen's works because it is only a revision of one of Philo's treatises.

Matthew[158] and on the Epistle to the Galatians.[159] But I believe that this catalogue, far from being completely plagiarized from Pamphilus' catalogue, gives us information, in a very precise way, on Origen's works represented in Jerome's library. It is also significant that, if Jerome does not, exceptionally, indicate the number of books in Origen's commentary on Hosea, it is because the copy that he has before him is mutilated at the beginning and at the end.[160] The range of his reading in Origen is therefore extensive and his knowledge of this writer far exceeds our own, since the majority of Origen's works are lost. To Jerome, Origen appears as the indispensable source. If he writes a commentary on a book or merely on a verse of Scripture, Jerome searches out a corresponding homily by Origen on such a book or verse. If by chance he cannot find such a homily, for instance in commenting on a passage of Psalm 126, he apologizes, saying that Pamphilus no longer possessed the homily. But he regrets the thought that Origen did write it and that time destroyed it.[161] Similarly, he notes that the twenty-sixth of Origen's thirty books on Isaiah cannot be found[162] and that Origen's homilies on Luke do not contain any commentary on the parable of the unjust steward. But he assumes that Origen did not omit this parable and that time has destroyed the commentary.[163] If Jerome knows that Origen did not make any particular commentary on a book of Scripture, for instance the Book of Daniel, he looks for explanations in another of Origen's works, namely the *Stromateis*.[164] But he feels particularly satisfied when he has at his disposal for a single subject (as in the case of the Psalms,[165] Isaiah,[166] and Hosea[167]) a large amount of Origen's works to compile. It is therefore not

---

[158] Cf. the text quoted above, n. 57.

[159] Cf. the text quoted above, n. 137. The catalogue omits, besides the *Περὶ εὐχῆς* (cf. *Epist.* 96.14, *PL* 22, 784 and n. d; but did Jerome know it otherwise than from the extracts quoted by Theophilus of Alexandria?), the *Phe litterae tractatus* (*Epist. ad Marcellam* 34.1, *PL* 22, 448), but it is uncertain whether these words refer to a particular work by Origen or only the commentary on verses 129–136 of Psalm 118. Cf. Ambrose *In Ps.* 118, *sermo* 17 (*PL* 15, 1440) and the two books to Grata on Isaiah. These two books, however, are apocryphal (text quoted above, n. 117).

[160] Texts quoted above, n. 127.

[161] Text quoted above, n. 84. Jerome's catalogue in fact does not mention any homily on Psalm 126.

[162] Text quoted above, n. 117.

[163] *Epist. ad Algasiam* 121.6 (*PL* 22, 1021): "Origenis et Didymi in hanc parabolam [Luke 16.1] explanationem invenire non potui; et utrum abolita sit temporum vetustate, an ipsi non scripserint, incertum habeo." We must assume that Origen's homilies on Luke (now lost, but in Jerome's possession) did not expound this parable. We can verify the fact that the homilies on Luke translated by Jerome do not expound it either.

[164] See above, n. 102.

[165] See above, p. 106.

[166] See above, p. 107.

[167] See above, p. 108.

surprising that Jerome's contemporaries were even then charging him with compiling Origen and that they realized that his method of working was to "contaminate" various Greek Fathers. Jerome does not deny the fact. On the contrary, he prides himself on it and invokes the illustrious reputation of the pagan Latin writers who imitated the Greeks and of the ecclesiastical writers who used Origen's erudition before him.[168] What did him harm was particularly his continuing to plagiarize an author of whom he had become the avowed enemy. Why, asks Rufinus, does Jerome attack the adherents of Origen, when he himself is one of them? Jerome replies, not without presumption, that he has praised Origen only twice,[169] and he adds with more reason that he follows Origen as an exegete and not as a theologian.[170] Why then, if Jerome condemns him, does he reproduce in his commentaries, without giving the name of the author, Origen's interpretations? Jerome answers Rufinus and Pelagius that he reproduces these interpretations as a matter of information, without accepting them, and that he omits Origen's name through Christian charity.[171] Lastly, St. Augustine himself is stunned and shocked to see the opponent of Origen's and Pelagius' adherents protecting himself, in defense of a daring interpretation, with Origen's authority.[172]

[168] *In Michaeam* 2, *prol.* (*PL* 25, 1189 D): "Nam quod dicunt Origenis me volumina compilare, et contaminare non decere veterum scripta, quod illi maledictum vehemens esse existimant, eandem laudem ego maximam duco, cum illum imitari volo, quem cunctis prudentibus et vobis placere non dubito. Si enim criminis est Graecorum bene dicta transferre, accusetur Ennius et Maro, Plautus, Caecilius et Terentius, Tullius quoque . . . Sed et Hilarius noster furti reus sit." Rufinus *Apol.* 2.25 (*PL* 21, 604 B) indignantly points to these words of Jerome as an admission of plagiarism. Jerome repeats them *Adv. Rufin.* 1.24 (*PL* 23, 436 B). Again and again he cites as his predecessors in the art of using the Greek Fathers, and particularly Origen, for Scriptural commentary Hilarius, Eusebius of Vercelli, Victorinus of Pettau, and Ambrose (*Epist.* 61.2 and 84.7, *PL* 22, 603 and 749, and *Adv. Rufin.* 1.2, *PL* 23, 417 B).

[169] *Epist. ad Pammachium et Oceanum* 84.2 (*PL* 22, 744): "Ni fallor, duo loca sunt, in quibus eum laudavi: praefatiuncula ad Damasum in homilias Cantici Canticorum et Prologus in librum Hebraicorum nominum."

[170] *Ibid.*, "Laudavi interpretem, non dogmatisten, ingenium, non fidem, philosophum, non apostolum." Cf. *Epist. ad Theophilum* 82.7 (*PL* 22, 740): "sicut enim interpretationem et idiomata Scripturarum Origeni semper attribui, ita dogmatum constantissime abstuli veritatem."

[171] *In Ieremiam* 4.22.24 (*PL* 24, 817 B–C): "Soleo in commentariis et explanationibus, quorum mos est diversas sententias ponere interpretum, huiusce modi ponere sermonem: *quidam hoc dicunt, alii hoc autumant, non nulli sic sentiunt.* Quod et ipse miserabilis Grunnius, et post multos annos discipuli Ioviniani, et illius, calumniati sunt et calumniantur me sub alienis nominibus proprias sententias ponere, quod ego causa benevolentiae facio, ne aliquem certo nomine videar lacerare. Quia igitur benignitas versa est in calumniam, nunc dico et illi qui mortuus est, et isti qui vivit, et haeresim illius instaurare conatur, magistrum eorum Origenem hunc locum referre ad Christum."

[172] Augustine *Epist. ad Hieron.* 116.23 (*PL* 22, 947) = 82: "Origenem vero ac

If, therefore, the bulk of Jerome's knowledge of the Fathers of the first two centuries is slight, his debt to Origen on the other hand is very great. It will be still more apparent when Jerome's works are compared systematically with the fragments of Origen, particularly those that preserve continuity.[173]

I have shown that, thanks to several epistolary collections, Jerome also knew Origen's principal correspondents and the environment in which he lived.[174] He knows equally well Pierius, one of Origen's first successors at the school in Alexandria. Jerome's own addition in his notice in the *De viris inlustribus* mentions various treatises by Pierius, especially a homily on Hosea,[175] which Jerome uses for his own commentary.[176] He also quotes Pierius' homily on the First Epistle to the Corinthians[177] and uses his recension of Matthew.[178] Probably he had in his possession the collection of Pierius' twelve λόγοι that Photius still read.[179]

Jerome was also the only person in the West who had read several works by Hippolytus, the other great exegete of the third century. Although Hippolytus himself belonged to the West, it was certainly through the East that Jerome came to know this Greek-speaking writer.[180] Does that mean that Jerome read the nineteen books by Hippolytus, of which he offers a catalogue in his notice in the *De viris*? Of these nineteen titles, seven simply reproduce Eusebius' notice.[181] It is not even certain that he read all the others. It is

---

Didymum reprehensos abs te lego in recentioribus quaestionibus, quamvis Origenem mirabiliter ante laudaveris. Cum his ergo errare puto, quia nec te ipse patieris."

[173] With regard to a papyrus fragment, a detailed study of this genre was made by R. Reitzenstein, "Origenes und Hieronymus," *Zeitschrift für neutestamentl. Wissenschaft* (1921) 91–93.

[174] See above, p. 109.

[175] *De vir. inl.* 76 (PL 23, 722 C): "Huius est longissimus tractatus de propheta Hosea, quem in vigilia Paschae habitum ipse sermo demonstrat." Cf. Bernoulli, *Schriftstellerkatalog*, p. 282.

[176] *In Hoseam, prol.* (PL 25, 819 B): "Pierii quoque legi tractatum longissimum, quem in exordio huius prophetae die vigiliarum Dominicae passionis extemporali et diserto sermone profudit."

[177] *Epist. ad Pammachium* 49.3 (PL 22, 511): "Origenes, Dionysius, Pierius, Eusebius Caesariensis, Didymus, Apollinaris latissime hanc epistulam interpretati sunt: quorum Pierius, cum sensum Apostoli ventilaret atque edisseret, et proposuisset illud exponere: *volo autem omnes esse sicut meipsum* [I Cor. 1.7], adiecit: ταῦτα λέγων ὁ Παῦλος ἀντικρὺς ἀγαμίαν κηρύσσει."

[178] *In Matth.* 4.24.36 (PL 26, 181 A): "In quibusdam Latinis codicibus additum est *neque Filius*, cum in Graecis et maxime Adamantii et Pierii exemplaribus hoc non habeatur adscriptum."

[179] Puech, *Litt. gr. chrét.*, vol. 2, p. 463. One of the twelve speeches read by Photius had the precise title "On Easter and the Prophet Hosea."

[180] On the fate of Hippolytus' writings, cf. Puech, *Litt. gr. chrét.*, vol. 2, pp. 551–552, and Bernoulli, *Schriftstellerkatalog*, p. 272.

[181] *De vir. inl.* 61 (PL 23, 707 A) and Eusebius *Hist. eccles.* 6.20 and 22. Cf. Sychowski,

surprising, for instance, that Jerome mentions in the *De viris* a homily by Hippolytus on the Psalms, but omits it in a list of the commentators on the Psalms that Jerome purposely enumerates very fully in order to dazzle Augustine with his Greek erudition.[182] In any case, he read at least Hippolytus' commentaries on Genesis,[183], Zachariah,[184] and Daniel.[185] He also read several homilies by Hippolytus that do not appear in his catalogue in the *De viris*: the homily Εἰς τὰς εὐλογίας Ἰσάακ,[186] a commentary on Matthew,[187] and tracts *De sabbato* and *De eucharistia*.[188] Only these exegetical commentaries interest Jerome in the works of Hippolytus. Nor does he refer to them except when a point of detail calls for additional information.

It is surprising that, while Jerome is so familiar with Origen's and Pierius' works, he scarcely read Dionysius of Alexandria, who directed their school. On Jerome's part, there is no personal information in the notice assigned to him in the *De viris*.[189] He does not know of the existence of his polemic *Against the Sabellians*[190] except through Rufinus. Two references to the second book of his treatise *On Promises* are no evidence whatever that he read it. It was one of the long fragments preserved by Eusebius that apprized him of the fact that Dionysius did not reject the canonical status of the Apocalypse,[191] and it was probably Apollinaris' refutation that furnished him with a comprehensive conspectus of the chapters in this work that were

---

Hieronymus, p. 153 n. 4, and Bernoulli, *Schriftstellerkatalog*, p. 151. Hans Achelis, "Hippolytstudien," *Texte und Untersuchungen*, n.s. 1, 4 (Leipzig 1897) 12, assures us, however, that Jerome was the ancient Christian writer who knew Hippolytus best.

[182] *Epist. ad Augustin.* 112.20 (PL 22, 929); cf. Achelis, "Hippolytstudien," p. 125.

[183] *Epist. ad Pammachium et Oceanum* 84.7 (PL 22, 749): "Nuper sanctus Ambrosius sic Hexaemeron illius (Origenis) compilavit, ut magis Hippolyti sententias Basiliique sequeretur." Cf. texts quoted above, n. 52, and Achelis, "Hippolytstudien," pp. 109–110.

[184] *In Zach., prol.* (PL 25, 1418 A): "in hunc prophetam . . . Hippolytus quoque edidit commentarios."

[185] *In Dan.* 9.24 (PL 25, 547 D): "Hippolytus autem de eisdem hebdomadibus opinatus est ita." Cf. *In Isaiam, lib.* 11, *prol.* (PL 24, 377 B) and Hippolytus *Frag.* 7 *In Dan.* (PG 10, 648 B).

[186] *Epist. ad Damasum* 36.16 (PL 22, 460): "Hippolyti martyris verba ponamus, a quo et Victorinus noster non plurimum discrepat . . .: 'Isaac portat imaginem Dei Patris, Rebecca Spiritus sancti.'" Cf. Achelis, "Hippolytstudien," p. 110.

[187] Text quoted above, n. 52.

[188] *Epist. ad Lucinium* 71.6 (PL 22, 672): "De sabbato quod quaeris, utrum ieiunandum sit, et de eucharistia, an accipienda quotidie, scripsit quidem et Hippolytus vir disertissimus."

[189] *De vir. inl.* 69. Cf. Sychowski, *Hieronymus*, p. 163 n. 3, proving that Eusebius is the only source for the entire notice.

[190] *Adv. Rufin.* 2.17 (PL 23, 459 D): "(Scribit Rufinus) . . . Dionysium Alexandrinae urbis episcopum, virum eruditissimum, contra Sabellium quattuor voluminibus disputantem in Arianum dogma delabi." Cf. Rufinus *De adult. libr. Orig.*, PG 17, 622 A.

[191] *Tract. in Ps.* (*Anecd. Mareds.* 3, 2, p. 5, 24), text quoted above, n. 46. Cf. Eusebius *Hist. eccl.* 7.25 (PG 20, 697).

opposed to chiliasm.[192] If Jerome read anything in Dionysius, it was a commentary on Genesis[193] and another on the First Epistle to the Corinthians,[194] which were otherwise quite unknown.

The same condition holds with regard to the notice in the *De viris* on Methodius of Olympia, one of Origen's first opponents. Although this notice does not derive from Eusebius, who avoids mention of Methodius,[195] Jerome does not appear to have read any of the seven homilies by Methodius named in the *De viris*. Only the tract *Against Porphyry* is several times mentioned in Jerome's works. But although he is acquainted with its length,[196] he does not seem to know the contents.[197]

With regard to the other Greek writers of the period comprised between Origen and Eusebius, Jerome knows them only through Eusebius,[198] although he may perhaps have read a few of the pieces of Lucian of Samosata.[199] We have seen to what considerable extent the *De viris* borrowed from the *Ecclesiastical History* of Eusebius of Caesarea.[200] This is not all. Jerome is indebted also to Eusebius for the matter of his *Chronicle* and his

---

[192] *In Isaiam* 18, *prol.* (PL 24, 627 B), text quoted above, n. 46. Note too that Dionysius' treatise refutes Nepos, and not Irenaeus, as Jerome seems to think.

[193] Text quoted above, n. 61.

[194] Text quoted above, n. 177.

[195] *De vir. inl.* 83. Cf. Puech, *Litt. gr. chrét.*, vol. 2, p. 511.

[196] *Epist. ad Magnum* 70.3 (PL 22, 666): "Methodius usque ad decem milia procedit versuum."

[197] Add to the texts quoted above, sec. 2 n. 135, *In Isaiam, prol.* (PL 25, 491 A): "Cui (Porphyrio de *Daniele*) solertissime responderunt Eusebius Caesariensis episcopus tribus voluminibus, id est octavo decimo et nono decimo et vicesimo, Apollinarius quoque uno grandi libro, id est vicesimo sexto, et ante hos ex parte Methodius"; *In Isaiam* 12.13 (PL 25, 580 A): "Cuius calumniae plenius responderunt Eusebius Caesariensis et Apollinarius Laodicensis et ex parte disertissimus vir martyr Methodius, quae qui scire voluerit, in ipsorum libris poterit invenire," and *Praef. in Danielem* (PL 28, 1294 B). Jerome seems unable to give a precise reference to Methodius and he appears to quote him through the other two refutations. Of his other works, he appears to know only the titles, perhaps Eusebius-Pamphilus' *Apology for Origen*. Cf. *Adv. Rufin.* 1.11 (PL 23, 423 C). Observe in the notice in the *De vir. inl.* the expression *ut alii adfirmant*, which seems to prove that Jerome wrote this notice with the help of several intermediary sources.

[198] He uses exclusively the *Ecclesiastical History* for the notices on Gaius, Malchion, Anatolius of Alexandria, and Phileas, and the *Chronicle* for the notice on Geminus.

[199] *De vir. inl.* 77 (PL 23, 723 A): "tantum in Scripturarum studio laboravit, ut usque nunc quaedam exemplaria Scripturarum Luciani martyris nuncupentur. Feruntur eius de fide libelli et breves ad non nullos epistulae." On the recension of the Scriptures by Lucian, cf. also *Adv. Rufin.* 2.27 (PL 23, 471 D), *Epist. ad Sunniam et Fretelam* 106.2 (PL 22, 838), *Praef. in librum Paralipomenon* (PL 28, 1325 A), and *Praef. in IV Evangelia* (PL 29, 527 B). The existence of the other treatises is uncertain.

[200] Cf., besides the works of Sychowski and Bernoulli *passim*, Schanz, vol. 4, 1, p. 449, and *Epist. ad Pammachium et Oceanum* 84.2 (PL 22, 744): "Ecclesiasticam pulchre Eusebius historiam texuit."

Liber de situ et nominibus locorum Hebraicorum. Neither of them is anything more than an adaptation, for the use of the Latin world, of Eusebius' corresponding works.[201] Apart from these works, the notice in the *De viris* on Eusebius mentions a number of other works that Jerome uses as well: the *Evangelical Demonstration*,[202] the *De Evangeliorum diaphonia*,[203] the commentaries on Isaiah[204] and the Psalms,[205] the polemic *Against Porphyry*, the *Apology for Origen*,[206] and the *Life of Pamphilus*.[207] The only works that appear in the *De viris* whose perusal is not definitely attested by Jerome's other works are the *Evangelical Preparation*, the *Theophany*, and the *De martyribus*. But it is probable that Jerome possessed Eusebius' complete works, for he incidentally

[201] Cf. Schanz, vol. 4, pp. 444 and 467.

[202] *De vir. inl.* 81 (*PL* 23, 727 A): "Εὐαγγελικῆς ἀποδείξεως libri XX"; *In Hoseam, prol.* (*PL* 25, 819 B): "Eusebius Caesariensis in octavo decimo libro Εὐαγγελικῆς ἀποδείξεως quaedam de Hosea propheta disputat"; *In Dan.* 9.24 (*PL* 25, 544 B): "Transeamus ad Eusebium Pamphili qui in octavo libro Εὐαγγελικῆς ἀποδείξεως tale nescio quid suspicatur: non mihi videtur frustra septuaginta hebdomadarum facta divisio" (cf. *In Isaiam* 11, *PL* 24, 377 B), quoting almost verbatim Eusebius *Demonstr. Evang.* 8.2 (*PG* 22, 612 B–617 C). Book 18 is lost, but *In Dan.* 9.24 (*PL* 25, 542 C) quotes verbatim the opinion of Julius Africanus "in quinto temporum volumine" on the seventy weeks of the year according to Eusebius *Demonstr. Evang.* 8.2 (*PG* 22, 608 D–612 A). Cf. also the text quoted above, n. 52, with Eusebius *Demonstr. Evang.* 5.3 (*PG* 22, 365 A).

[203] *De vir. inl.* 81 and *In Matth.* 1.1.16 (*PL* 26, 23 B): "super hoc et Africanus temporum scriptor et Eusebius Caesariensis in libris διαφωνίας εὐαγγελίων plenius disputarunt." This statement on the *Letter to Aristides* by Julius Africanus was transmitted to Jerome by Eusebius *Hist. eccl.* 1.7 (*PG* 20, 89 B).

[204] *De vir. inl.* 81: "In Isaiam libri X," *In Isaiam, prol.* (*PL* 24, 21 A): "Eusebius quoque Pamphili iuxta historicam explanationem XV (?) edidit volumina." Cf. *PL* 24: 154 C, 179 B, 180 D. Jerome criticizes this commentary for filling in the lacunae of its historical information with allegories in the style of Origen. Cf. *PG* 24, 89ff.

[205] *De vir. inl.* 81 and *Epist. ad Augustinum* 112.20 (*PL* 22, 929). Jerome also knows the revised translation of this commentary by Eusebius of Vercelli. Cf. *De vir. inl.* 96 and *Epist. ad Vigilantium* 61.2 (*PL* 22, 603).

[206] Texts quoted above, sec. 2 n. 135 and sec. 3 n. 197. According to Lataix, "Le commentaire de s. Jérôme sur Daniel," p. 165, Eusebius supplied Jerome with the soundest part of his information on Porphyry. The text *De vir. inl.* 81, "contra Porphyrium . . . ut quidam putant, libri XXX ⟨de quibus ad me XX tantum pervenerunt⟩," is interesting, for it deals with an addition by Jerome posterior to his first edition. Note that Jerome *Epist. ad Magnum* 70.3 (*PL* 22, 666) writes that this commentary is in twenty-five books. On this question of editions, cf. A. Feder, "Zusätze zum Schriftstellerkatalog des hl. Hieronymus," *Biblica* 1 (1920) 500–513, and *Studien zum Schriftstellerkatalog des hl. Hieronymus* (Freiburg im Breisgau 1927).

On the *Apology*, cf. Sychowski, *Hieronymus*, p. 168 n. 1, and Bernoulli, *Schriftstellerkatalog*, p. 219. We know that the question of ascertaining whether this book is by Pamphilus or by Eusebius was one of the principal points in the controversy between Jerome and Rufinus. Cf. *In Ezech.* 6.18.5 (*PL* 25, 173 D), *Epist.* 84.11 (*PL* 22, 752), 133.3 (*PL* 22, 1152), and *Adv. Rufin.* 1.8–11; 2.15, 16, 23; 3.12, 24, 37, especially the text quoted above, n. 91.

[207] Texts quoted above, nn. 84 and 85.

refers to certain of his commentaries whose titles do not appear in the *De viris*.[208] It was also through Eusebius that Jerome knew the *Chronography* of Julius Africanus, his *Letter to Aristides*,[209] and the *Evangelical Canons* by Ammonius.[210] Eusebius is therefore to Jerome one of the most indispensable working tools in the Latin world. Jerome is indebted to him for the better part of his historical information on the modern period, while at the same time he distrusts Eusebius as soon as he steps out of a factual context. If Jerome knows Eusebius' works so well, it is because he was in close association with the library at Caesarea, as has already been established in connection with his reading in Origen.[211] He is equally very well informed on Eusebius' successors at Caesarea, namely, Acacius, Euzoius, and Gelasius. He knows the care they expended on this library.[212] He read in Acacius at least the *Miscellaneous Questions*.[213] He knows that at Caesarea one may read the works of the obscure Euzoius, otherwise completely unknown;[214] and even that Gelasius is a prolific writer, but publishes nothing.[215]

It is quite a simple matter to establish which contemporary writers Jerome really read. He himself declares that at Antioch he studied the Holy Scriptures under Apollinaris of Laodicea.[216] This master exerted a marked influence on Jerome. Even if his work came to be suspected of heresy, Jerome advises its perusal,[217] while scrupulously omitting in the *De viris*[218] any mention of Apollinaris' dogmatic works. He does not hesitate either to criticize his theories[219] and even his exegetical method,[220] when the need arises, but

---

[208] On Genesis, cf. the text quoted above, n. 61, and on the First Epistle to the Corinthians, n. 177.

[209] Texts quoted above, nn. 202 and 203.

[210] *De vir. inl.* 55 (*PL* 23, 703 A): "Evangelicos canones excogitavit, quos postea secutus est Eusebius Caesariensis." Cf. *Praef. in IV Evangelia* (*PL* 29, 528 A). This confusion (for the canons are those of Eusebius himself) is due to an erroneous interpretation by Jerome of Eusebius' letter to Carpianos (*PG* 22, 1276 = *PL* 29, 529 C). Cf. Bernoulli, *Schriftstellerkatalog*, p. 269.

[211] See above, p. 104.

[212] Text quoted above, n. 93.

[213] *De vir. inl.* 98 (*PL* 23, 738 A): "(volumina) Συμμίκτων ζητημάτων sex," *Epist. ad Minervium et Alexandrum* 119.6 (*PL* 22, 970): "Acacius Caesareae . . . post Eusebium Pamphili episcopus, in quarto Συμμίκτων ζητημάτων libro proponens sibi hanc eandem quaestionem (I Cor. 15.5) latius disputavit . . . et sic locutus est."

[214] This is how I interpret the statement in *De vir. inl.* 113 (*PL* 23, 746 B): "Feruntur eius varii multiplicesque tractatus, quos nosse perfacile est."

[215] *De vir. inl.* 130 (*PL* 23, 754 B): "accurati limatique sermonis fertur quaedam scribere, sed celare."

[216] See above, sec. 1 n. 9.

[217] *Epist. ad Vigilantium* 61.1 and *ad Tranquillinum* 62.2 (*PL* 23, 602 and 606).

[218] *De vir. inl.* 104. Cf. Sychowski, *Hieronymus*, p. 184.

[219] Theory of impeccability, *Anecd. Mareds.* 3, 2, p. 197, 1: "Si ergo voluerint nobis dicere: Propterea non dicimus eum habuisse sensum, ut non videatur habere peccatum,

usually without mentioning him by name. Still, he considers Apollinaris as one of the most useful commentators on Scripture and he borrows from him frequently. He even regrets that his commentaries are not more detailed.[221] He read very carefully his commentaries on Paul's Epistles: the First Epistle to the Corinthians,[222] the First Epistle to the Thessalonians,[223] the Epistle to the Galatians,[224] and particularly the Epistle to the Ephesians.[225] He likewise comments, with Apollinaris' aid, on the Prophets,[226] Ecclesiastes,[227] Matthew,[228] and he has at his disposal Apollinaris' commentary on the Psalms,[229] and probably a commentary on Genesis.[230] He knows, besides, his polemical

---

nos illis respondeamus" (Dom Morin refers to Apollinaris; cf. *Anecd. Mareds.* 3, 2, p. 398, 1, and 3, 3, p. 28, 11), and the theory of the soul, *Epist. ad Marcellinum et Anapsychiam* 126.1 (*PL* 22, 1086): "An certe ex traduce, ut Tertullianus, Apollinaris et maxima pars Occidentalium autumant . . . ?"

[220] *Praef. in Ezram* (*PL* 28, 1405 A): "Quod etiam sapientissimo cuidam nuper apud Graecos accidit, ut interdum Scripturae sensum relinquens, uniuscuiusque interpretis sequeretur errorem." Cf. *In Ecclesiasten* 12.7 (*PL* 23, 1167 C) and *Adv. Rufin.* 2.34 (*PL* 23, 477 A).

[221] Texts quoted below, nn. 226 and 227.

[222] Text quoted above, n. 177, and *Epist. ad Minervium et Alexandrum* 119.4 (*PL* 22, 968), with regard to I Cor. 15.5: "Apollinarius, licet aliis verbis, eadem quae Theodorus adseruit: quosdam non esse morituros."

[223] *Epist. ad Minervium et Alexandrum* 119.8 (*PL* 22, 974): "Super quo [I Thess. 4.15] ... dicendum est quid videatur aliis, Theodoro videlicet, Apollinario et Diodoro, qui unam sequuntur sententiam."

[224] *In Epist. ad Galat., prol.* (*PL* 26, 309 A): "Praetermitto Didymum videntem meum et Laodicenum de Ecclesia nuper egressum, et Alexandrum veterem haereticum, Eusebium quoque Emesenum et Theodorum Heracleoten, qui et ipsi non nullos super hac re commentariolos reliquerunt." Cf. *PL* 22, 918 and 947.

[225] *In Epist. ad Ephes., prol.* (*PL* 26, 442 C): "Apollinarium etiam et Didymum quosdam commentariolos edidisse, e quibus licet pauca decerpsimus." A more honest admission *Adv. Rufin.* 1.16, 21, 24, 25 (*PL* 23: 428 B, 433 B, 436 B, 437 B).

[226] *In Hoseam, prol.* (*PL* 25, 819 A): "apud Graecos repperi Apollinarem Laodicenum, qui cum in adulescentia sua breves et in hunc et in alios prophetas commentariolos reliquisset, tangens magis sensus, quam explicans, rogatus est postea, ut in Hoseam plenius scriberet, qui liber venit in nostras manus; sed et ipse nimia brevitate ad perfectam intellegentiam lectorem ducere non potest." Cf. *In Malach., prol.* (*PL* 25, 1544 A) and *In Isaiam, prol.* (*PL* 24, 21 A).

[227] *In Ecclesiasten* 4.13 (*PL* 23, 1103 B): "Laodicenus interpres res magnas brevi sermone exprimere contendens, more sibi solito etiam hic locutus est."

[228] Text quoted above, n. 57.

[229] *Epist. ad Augustin.* 112.20 (*PL* 22, 929): "superfluum est te voluisse disserere, quod illos latere non potuit: maxime in explanatione Psalmorum, quos apud Graecos interpretati sunt multis voluminibus primus Origenes, secundus Eusebius Caesariensis, tertius Theodorus Heracleotes, quartus Asterius Scythopolitanus, quintus Apollinaris Laodicenus, sextus Didymus Alexandrinus. Feruntur et diversorum in paucos Psalmos opuscula, sed nunc de integro Psalmorum corpore dicimus."

[230] Cf. text quoted above, n. 52.

works, mentioning a tract of his entitled *Against Marcellus of Ancyra*,[231] another *Against Eunomius*,[232] and especially his great tract in thirty books *Against Porphyry*, which he constantly makes use of, notably for an evaluation of the weeks of the year according to Daniel that appears in the twenty-sixth book.[233] In conclusion, he quotes the special work in two books, in which Apollinaris supported the old millenarian doctrine.[234]

It was in all probability at Antioch and through Apollinaris' intercession that Jerome made contacts with several ecclesiastical writers and procured their works. He is informed on the life of Eustathius of Antioch,[235] mentions a number of his writings,[236] and read at least his letter on Melchizedek.[237] With regard to Eustathius' friend Eusebius of Emesa, whose career was spent at Antioch, where Jerome saw his tomb,[238] he read at least the commentaries on Genesis[239] and the Epistle to the Galatians.[240] He read likewise the commentaries on Paul's Epistles by his disciple Diodorus of Tarsus[241] and charges him with ignorance, although he was a great scholar, because Diodorus, a priest of Antioch, had been Apollinaris' adversary.[242] Similarly, if Jerome asserts in the *De viris* that he had read John Chrysostom's *De sacerdotio* only, although both men had lived at the same time at Antioch, it was because one had been a pupil of Diodorus, and the other of Apolli-

---

[231] *De vir. inl.* 86.

[232] *De vir. inl.* 120.

[233] Add to the texts quoted above, sec. 2 n. 135 and sec. 3 n. 197, *Epist. ad Pammachium et Oceanum* 84.2 and 7 (*PL* 22, 744 and 748); *In Matth.* 4.24.16 (*PL* 26, 178 A); *In Dan.*, *prol.* (*PL* 25, 491 A): "Apollinarius quoque uno grandi libro, hoc est vicesimo sexto," and 9.24 (*PL* 25, 548 A–D; cf. 575 A and 590 A); *In Isaiam lib.* 11, *prol.* (*PL* 24, 377 B).

[234] Text quoted above, n. 46.

[235] A biographical detail, *Adv. Rufin.* 3.42 (*PL* 23, 511 A).

[236] *De vir. inl.* 83.

[237] Text quoted above, n. 52. To be precise, one of his letters addressed to Alexander of Alexandria deals with Melchizedek: cf. Puech, *Litt. gr. chrét.*, vol. 3, p. 441, and *PG* 18, 696 B.

[238] *De vir. inl.* 91 (*PL* 23, 734 A): "mortuus, Antiochiae sepultus est."

[239] *Liber Hebr. quaest. in Gen.* 22.13 (*PL* 23, 1020 A): "Ridiculam rem in hoc loco Emisenus Eusebius est locutus: *Sabech*, inquiens, dicitur *hircus* qui rectis cornibus et ad carpendas arboris frondes sublimis attollitur." Cf. also the text quoted above, n. 52, and Dom A. Wilmart, "Le souvenir d'Eusèbe d'Emèse," *Analecta Bollandiana* 38 (1920) 242.

[240] *De vir. inl.* 91 (*PL* 23, 734 A): "ad Galatas libri X," and *In Epist. ad Galat.*, *prol.* (*PL* 26, 309 A; cf. *PL* 22, 918 and 947).

[241] *De vir. inl.* 119 (*PL* 23, 750 A): "in Apostolum commentarii." Cf. *Epist. ad Minervium et Alexandrum* 119.3 (*PL* 22, 968), with reference to the First Epistle to the Corinthians: "Diodorus Tarsensis episcopus praeterito hoc capitulo in consequentibus breviter adnotavit," and 119.8 (*PL* 22, 974), with reference to the First Epistle to the Thessalonians: "Diodorus haec conscripsit."

[242] *De vir. inl.* 119: "(Eusebii Emiseni) eloquentiam imitari non potuit propter ignorantiam saecularium litterarum." On his rivalry with the school of Apollinaris, cf. Puech, *Litt. gr. chrét.*, vol. 3, p. 447.

naris.[243] Later, when John Chrysostom became famous, Jerome was to read one of his homilies and appreciate it better.[244] If, on the other hand, Jerome had read the complete works of the obscure Theodorus of Heraclea,[245] it was doubtless under Apollinaris' influence, for he repeatedly mentions their commentaries side by side, noting that their ideas coincide.[246] In conclusion, Jerome maintained personal relations at Antioch with Evagrius.[247] He highly appreciates and quotes his translation of St. Athanasius' *Life of Anthony*, which he takes as a model in its genre[248] and uses for his *Life of Paul of Thebes*.[249]

His residence at Constantinople acquainted Jerome with the Cappadocians,[250] but seems to have influenced him much less markedly. He has a lively admiration for Gregory of Nazianzus, boasts of having been his pupil, and retains the memory of his oral instruction and his oratorical successes.[251] But while cognizant of the extent of his works,[252] he virtually never makes use of them.[253] Under Gregory of Nazianzus, Jerome heard

---

[243] *De vir. inl.* 129 (PL 23, 754): "Ioannes Antiochenae ecclesiae presbyter, Eusebii Emiseni Diodorique sectator, multa componere dicitur, de quibus Περὶ ἱερωσύνης tantum legi." Facundus of Hermione (PL 67, 678) even assures us that Jerome translated a book by the patriarch Theophilus of Alexandria against Chrysostom. Cf. *PL* 22, 933, and Dom Chr. Baur, "S. Jérôme et s. Chrysostome," *RB* 23 (1906) 430–436.

[244] Text quoted above, sec. 2 n. 128. Cf. *PG* 51, 371–388, and Baur, "L'entrée littéraire de s. Chrysostome dans le monde latin," *RHE* 8 (1907) 249–265.

[245] *De vir. inl.* 90 (PL 23, 734 A): "in Matthaeum, et in Ioannem et in Apostolum et in Psalterium." Jerome asserts that he read the first of these commentaries, *In Matth., prol.* (PL 26, 20 B); quotes the third, *In Epist. ad Galat., prol.* (PL 26, 309 A; cf. *PL* 22, 918 and 947) and *Epist.* 119.2 (PL 22, 967; cf. 974); and mentions the fourth, *Epist. ad Augustin.* 112.20 (PL 22, 929). Cf. the texts quoted above, nn. 57, 224, and 229.

[246] Texts quoted above, nn. 222 and 223.

[247] *De vir. inl.* 125 (PL 23, 751 B): "Cum adhuc esset presbyter, diversarum hypotheseon tractatus mihi legit, quos necdum edidit."

[248] *Ibid.*, "Vitam quoque beati Antonii de Graeco Athanasii in sermonem nostrum transtulit." Jerome quotes its preface, *Epist. ad Pammachium* 57.6 (PL 22, 572 = PG 26, 83).

[249] Cf. Schanz, vol. 4, 1, p. 438.

[250] Cf. *Epist. ad Magnum* 70.4 (PL 22, 667): "Cappadocumque Basilii, Gregorii, Amphilochii."

[251] See the texts quoted above, sec. 1 n. 10. Cf. Puech, *Litt. gr. chrét.*, vol. 3, p. 338.

[252] *De vir. inl.* 117 (PL 23, 747 B): "ad triginta milia versuum omnia opera sua composuit."

[253] It will be observed that, in the notice in the *De vir. inl.*, Jerome does not even mention his voluminous correspondence. The only one of Gregory's works that Jerome uses with certainty is the poem *In laudem virginitatis* (PG 37, 522) indicated in *De vir. inl.* 117 as "liber hexametro versu Virginitatis et nuptiarum contra se disserentium," and *Adv. Iovin.* 1.13 (PL 23, 241 B): "Et praeceptor meus Gregorius Nazianzenus virginitatem et nuptias disserens Graecis versibus explicavit." In my view, in the *Epist. ad Damasum* 18.9 (PL 22, 367), the "quidam Graecorum in Scripturis apprime eruditus," which deals with the seraphs, refers not to Gregory of Nazianzus *Oratio* 38 *in Theophania* (PG 36, 320), but to the author referred to by Gregory in the same terms. This agrees with Jerome's state-

Gregory of Nyssa's[254] tract *Against Eunomius* being read and probably that of his brother St. Basil.[255] But he appears ignorant of Gregory of Nyssa's other works,[256] and, if he read the *Hexaemeron*[257] or the *Commentary on Isaiah* by Basil,[258] he mentions the former only incidentally and criticizes the latter. It was also at the Council of Constantinople in 381 that Jerome came in contact with Amphilochius of Iconium, who read to him his tract *De Spiritu sancto*.[259] It is probable that, from this time, Jerome conceived and prepared a treatise on the Holy Ghost, for he then had at his disposal a voluminous mass of material on this subject. This consisted of Basil's tract,[260] Ephrem's treatise, of which he procured a translation from Syriac into Greek,[261] and a tract by Didymus of Alexandria. But discouraged, whether as a result of the death of Pope Damasus, who had commissioned this work, or on account of the publication of St. Ambrose's treatise in rebuttal, or through philosophical incapability, Jerome finally renounced this task and confined himself to the publication, after many delays, of a translation of Didymus' tract,[262] which was intended to bring to light Ambrose's plagiarisms.[263]

---

ment *In Isaiam* 6.1 (*PL* 24, 91 D) that he had composed this letter when he was studying under Gregory. This identification confirms Cavallera's opinion, *Saint Jérôme*, vol. 1, 2, pp. 81ff, against Amelli on the identity of *Epist.* 18 with the *subitus tractatus*.

[254] Text quoted above, sec. I n. 11.

[255] *De vir. inl.* 116 (*PL* 23, 747 A): "Contra Eunomium elaboravit libros et de Spiritu sancto volumen et in Hexaemeron homilias novem," and 120 (*PL* 23, 750 B): "Responderunt ei Apollinarius, Didymus, Basilius Caesariensis, Gregorius Nazianzenus et Gregorius Nyssenus."

[256] *Ibid.*, 128 (*PL* 23, 754 A): "qui et multa alia scripsisse et scribere dicitur."

[257] Text quoted above, n. 183.

[258] Basil *In Isaiam* 5.26 (*PG* 30, 425 A):

Τὸ μὲν οὖν σύσσημον ἐν τοῖς ἔθνεσιν ἤρθη· τουτέστι, τὸ σημεῖον τοῦ σταυροῦ τοῦ ἀναδειχθέντος.

Jerome *In Isaiam* 5.26 (*PL* 24, 90 D):

Legi in cuiusdam commentariis hoc quod dicitur: *Levabit signum in nationibus procul, et sibilabit ad eum de finibus terrae* de vocatione gentium debere intellegi, quod elevato signo Crucis, et depositis oneribus peccatorum, velociter venerint atque crediderint. Sed nescio quo modo sensui possint congruere quae sequuntur.

[259] *De vir. inl.* 133 (*PL* 23, 755 A): "Amphilochius Iconii episcopus nuper mihi librum legit de Spiritu sancto."

[260] Text quoted above, n. 255.

[261] *De vir. inl.* 115 (*PL* 23, 747 A): "Legi eius *De Spiritu sancto* Graecum volumen, quod quidam de Syriaca lingua verterant, et acumen sublimis ingenii etiam in translatione cognovi."

[262] *Praef. ad Paulinianum* (*PL* 23, 107 A): "volui garrire aliquid de Spiritu sancto et coeptum opusculum eiusdem urbis pontifici (Damaso) dedicare." Cf. Schanz, vol. 1, p. 482.

[263] *Ibid.* (*PL* 23, 109 A): "Certe qui hunc legerit, Latinorum furta cognoscet et contemnet rivulos, cum coeperit haurire de fontibus."

The fact is that, in the interval, Jerome betook himself to Alexandria and possibly became acquainted with Didymus.[264] Although he stayed only one month at Alexandria, he boasts of being Didymus' pupil. Not only is he proud of being able to report one of the anecdotes Didymus confided to him,[265] but he uses it constantly. With his help Jerome comments on the Epistle to the Galatians,[266] the First Epistle to the Corinthians,[267] especially the Epistle to the Ephesians,[268] and also the Gospel according to St. Matthew,[269] and the prophets Isaiah,[270] Hosea,[271] Zachariah.[272] He read, besides, his commentaries on the Psalms[273] and perhaps on Genesis[274] and also mentions many others. If he wishes to comment on a parable of St. Luke's, he regrets not having been able to find any commentary on the subject by Didymus.[275] Although Jerome has the highest respect for Didymus and is perhaps indebted to him even for his exegetical method,[276] he does not refrain, at the time of his dispute with Rufinus, from taxing Didymus with a tendency toward Origen, particularly in his commentary on Origen's Περὶ ἀρχῶν.[277] Lastly, it was during his stay with Didymus that Jerome probably read the tract *Against Apollinaris*[278] by his pupil Ambrose of Alexandria.

[264] Texts quoted above, sec. 1 n. 14. Cf. Cavallera, *Saint Jérôme*, vol. 1, 2, pp. 127–130, n. R: "Didyme et saint Jérôme."

[265] *Epist. ad Castrutium* 68.2 (PL 22, 652). This anecdote about Anthony and Didymus is also reported by Socrates *Hist. eccl.* 4.25 (PG 67, 528 A). It was possible to compose the notice *De vir. inl.* 87 and 88 on Athanasius and Anthony, thanks to the contacts between Jerome and Didymus or Evagrius of Antioch.

[266] Text quoted above, n. 224.

[267] Text quoted above, n. 177, and *Epist. ad Minervium et Alexandrum* 119.5 (PL 22, 968–970, a long textual quotation).

[268] Texts quoted above, n. 225.

[269] *De vir. inl.* 109 (PL 23, 743 B) and the text quoted above, n. 57.

[270] *In Isaiam, prol.* (PL 24, 21 A): "Didymus, cuius amicitiis nuper usi sumus, ab eo loco ubi scriptum est: *Consolamini, consolamini populum meum, sacerdotes: loquimini ad cor Ierusalem* [Is. 40.1] usque ad finem voluminis decem et octo edidit tomos."

[271] Text quoted above, sec. 1 n. 14, and *Adv. Rufin.* 3.28 (PL 23, 500 C).

[272] *In Zach., prol.* (PL 25, 1418 A): "in hunc prophetam ... Didymus quoque explanationum libros me rogante dictavit, quos cum aliis tribus in Hoseam et mihi προσεφώνησε."

[273] Text quoted above, n. 229.

[274] Text quoted above, n. 61. Certain extant fragments of Didymus on Genesis (PG 39, 1111 A) deal in fact with numbers.

[275] Text quoted above, n. 163.

[276] *Epist. ad Hedibiam* 120.12 (PL 22, 1005): "Triplex in corde nostro descriptio et regula Scripturarum est: prima, ut intellegamus eas iuxta historias, secunda iuxta tropologiam, tertia iuxta intellegentiam spiritualem." On Didymus' exegetical method, cf. Puech, *Litt. gr. chrét.*, vol. 3, p. 160 and n. 5.

[277] *Adv. Rufin.* 1.6 and 2.11 (PL 23, 420 A and 454 C) and *Epist.* 84.10 (PL 22, 751).

[278] *De vir. inl.* 126.

The four great centers of Greek culture that influenced Jerome are, then, as follows: Constantinople, Antioch, Alexandria, and Caesarea. I have been able to relate all his reading activities to these centers, which Jerome frequented successively. The exceptions are rare. These are the works of Epiphanius[279] and Tryphillio's commentary[280] on the Song of Songs, which Jerome must have read when he disembarked at Cyprus,[281] the works of Cyril of Jerusalem[282] and of Sophronius,[283] which Jerome had at hand in his monastery at Bethlehem. The only real exception is the commentary on the Psalms by the Arian Asterius,[284] unless Jerome is claiming that he possesses it while knowing of its existence only through a quotation by Eusebius.[285] As for the other writers mentioned by Jerome in the *De viris*, there is nothing to prove that he read them, although he mentions the titles of a number of their works. It will be observed on the other hand that all these writers—Archelaus, Marcellus of Ancyra, Photinus, Lucius, Eunomius, Maximus, Serapion, Titus of Bostra—[286] are involved in the heretical controversies of the fourth century. The question will arise whether Jerome, who scarcely seems to have been affected by these ancient disputes,[287] does not derive most of his information from some history of heresies such as Epiphanius' *summa*.[288] Apart from this, he

---

[279] *De vir. inl.* 114. See above, p. 89, what I have said about his reading of the *Περὶ λίθων* and Epiphanius' *Physiologus*. Cf. also the *Vita s. Hilarionis, prol.* (PL 23, 29 C): "Quamquam enim sanctus Epiphanius Salaminae Cypri episcopus, qui cum Hilarione plurimum versatus est, laudem eius brevi epistula scripserit, quae vulgo legitur, tamen aliud est locis communibus laudare defunctum, aliud defuncti proprias narrare virtutes." This letter of Epiphanius' is lost. On other letters by Epiphanius, cf. *Adv. Ioann. Hieros.* (PL 23, 412 D).

[280] *De vir. inl.* 92 (PL 23, 734 B): "Legi eius in Cantica canticorum commentarios. Et multa alia composuisse fertur, quae in nostras manus minime pervenerunt."

[281] Texts quoted above, sec. 1 n. 12.

[282] *De vir. inl.* 112.

[283] *De vir. inl.* 134.

[284] *De vir. inl.* 94 and the text quoted above, n. 229. Jerome here displays his erudition for Augustine.

[285] Eusebius *Comm. in Ps.* 4 (PG 23, 112 A).

[286] *De vir. inl.* 72, 86, 89, 107, 118, 120, 127, 99, 102.

[287] Although he had refused to compile a catalogue of heresies at Augustine's request, a few years after his death an unfounded rumor was prevalent that he had composed such a catalogue. St. Augustine, *De haeresibus*, chap. 88, heard this rumor, but was even then doubtful of its truth (PL 42, 49).

[288] For example, Marcellus of Ancyra's *Letter on Faith*, of which Jerome speaks in his notice, appears in Epiphanius *Adv. haer.* 3.1.72 (PG 42, 384 C). On Archelaus, cf. Epiphanius *Adv. haer.* 2.2.66.7–11 (PG 42, 39–46); Puech, *Litt. gr. chrét.*, vol. 3, p. 550; and Schanz, vol. 4, 1, p. 429. On the Arian Lucius, cf. Epiphanius *Adv. haer.* 3.2.68 (PG 42, 201 A). Recourse to a history of heresies is still more probable for the ancient heretics whom Jerome lists: PL 22, 1153; 23, 186 D (= *Dial. adv. Lucif.* 23); 25: 880 C, 1018 D, 1235 B, 1269 D.

admits that he knows nothing about a particular work except through hearsay.[289]

We can now estimate, from an understanding of its sources, the significance of Jerome's Greek culture and the manner in which he acquired it. Although in the West he was considered a great Hellenist, perhaps accusingly,[290] and although he had spent the best part of his life in the East, with the result that his spoken language was pervaded by Hellenisms, still serious omissions are noticeable in his Greek culture. He did not read the old pagan literature, except perhaps a few of Plato's dialogues with the help of a translation. The most significant part of his knowledge of classical Greek literature derives either from his Western Greco-Roman studies, particularly his reading in Cicero, or from more recent writers, notably Plutarch and Porphyry. He did not read the masterpieces of the fifth century. Of the important writers he knows not their thought but a few anecdotes about their lives or some of their aphorisms. The only books of this period that Jerome used are Herodotus and Xenophon's *Cyropedia*, because they were useful for his exegetical work. For the same reason, Philo and Josephus are the pagan writers whom he prefers. He has also a certain curiosity with regard to the pagan cults and the controversy between pagans and Christians that leads him to read Philostratus, Iamblichus, Porphyry, and Julian. In conclusion, he shows an interest in medicine and read Galen.

Such are his pagan sources. But Jerome is always inclined to be silent about his actual source and to mention, as if he had read them, those writers that he knew only through an intermediate source. He thus lends his works an erudite tone that easily deceived his contemporaries in the West. Furthermore, he does not know a very large number of pagan writers, and particularly the naturalists, except from ecclesiastical writers. I believe therefore that we must not underestimate the confession contained in the famous account of Jerome's *Dream*, whatever its literary artifice may be.[291] During his long residence in the East, Jerome did not acquire a taste for Greek pagan literature, either from religious scruples, or through natural indifference; perhaps also because texts had become rare. The *Letter to Magnus*[292] reflects, I believe, his true

[289] *De vir. inl.* 131 on Theotimus the Scythian. Add that in the *De vir. inl.* Jerome refrains from writing a notice on Evagrius Ponticus, whose works he knows, if only from Rufinus' translations (*PL* 22, 1151 and 24, 794 D).

[290] Cf. *Epist. ad Domnionem* 50.2 (*PL* 22, 513): "Nec mirum si me absentem iam diu et absque usu Latinae linguae, semigraeculum barbarumque, homo latinissimus et facundissimus superet."

[291] Cf. P. de Labriolle, "Le songe de s. Jérôme," *Miscellanea Geronimiana* (Rome 1920) 217–239, and A. S. Pease, "The Attitude of Jerome towards Pagan Literature," *Transactions and Proceedings of the American Philological Association* 50 (1919) 150–167. According to Pease, Jerome presumably returned to pagan literature after having scorned it.

[292] *Epist.* 70 (*PL* 22, 664).

attitude to the pagan writers: he uses only those that are of direct service for commentary or demonstration.

His clerical erudition, although infinitely more assured and firsthand, has its limitations. Jerome read nothing of the entire Greek Christian literary output prior to Origen, except a few works by Clement of Rome and Clement of Alexandria. He derives his knowledge of them from intermediary writers. His culture is really the product of his frequent sojourns at Constantinople, Antioch, Alexandria, and Caesarea. Nor did the Council of Constantinople, although it brought Jerome in contact with several eminent contemporaries, exert a deep influence on him. On the other hand, Apollinaris' visits to Antioch and Didymus' visits to Alexandria made a profound impact on his exegetical works, while the library at Caesarea supplied him with the complete works of Origen and Eusebius. For it is intriguing to postulate that Jerome, if he was instrumental in the condemnation of Origen and in the disappearance of his doctrinal works, nonetheless preserved a considerable part of his exegetical work, either through his translations, or through his commentaries. The influence of Didymus and Apollinaris on Jerome's exegesis is not less certain and would be still more evident, had not most of their works been lost. His commentary on the Epistle to the Ephesians, for instance, is merely, as Jerome himself must acknowledge, a compilation of relevant commentaries by each of these three writers under suspicion of heresy.[293] That is due, as he assures us in his defense, not to his participation in their heresies, but to the very nature of sacred commentary, which must posit the opinions of the principal exegetes.

Jerome's aim, then, as a Hellenist, is to acquaint the West with the status of Greek exegesis. He strove toward abundant documentation. "Would to heaven," he exclaims humorously,[294] "that I had all the commentators!" Actually, in the course of his travels, and thanks to his connections, he acquired quite a large number. When he wanted to take the trouble, he demonstrated his possession of a very well-grounded erudition, derived from firsthand sources.[295] And so he was no less proud of his Greek culture than he was proud of writing or translating in Ciceronian Latin. He had the highest regard for those Western scholars who knew Greek, and urged them to turn to the original Greek texts.[296] On the other hand, he had only scorn for those

---

[293] *Adv. Rufin.* 1.16–26 (particularly *PL* 23: 428 B, 433 B, 436 B, 437 B).

[294] Text quoted above, n. 88.

[295] For example, for the explanation of the seventy weeks of years, *In Dan.* 9.24 (*PL* 25, 542–553) or in his *Epist.* 119 *ad Minervium et Alexandrum*, Jerome collects the most diverse textual quotations.

[296] Cf. *Epist. ad Paulam* 39.1 (*PL* 22, 465), *ad Paulinum* 85.3 (*PL* 22, 753), with reference to his own translation of the Περὶ ἀρχῶν: "licet tibi Graeca sufficiant et non debeas turbidos nostri ingenioli rivulos quaerere, qui de ipsis fontibus bibis." Cf. below, chap. 3 sec. 2 n. 20.

who thought they could write commentaries on Scripture without the aid of the Greeks. Reticius of Autun dared to speak of the Song of Songs without having read Origen's ten books on the subject![297] Imagine St. Augustine's commentary on the Psalms being an original work![298] Jerome took a malicious delight in listing for St. Augustine all the Greek writers that he ought to have read before taking his pen in hand. That would have eliminated a host of mistakes.[299] Sometimes Jerome was even bantering and unfair to Latin writers trying to produce original work instead of turning back to the sources.[300] As for himself, he felt incapable of continuing his exegesis, now that his weak eyes prevented him from deciphering the manuscripts of the Greek commentators.[301] One might therefore rebuke him in the same manner as he reproached St. Ambrose: the reader will observe that he is pillaging from the Greeks and will disregard this stream after having drunk from the sources.[302] It is true that the Latin writers, his contemporaries, were altogether prevented from doing so, as we ourselves still are.

Jerome's principal defect derives from his contempt for pagan culture considered as such, and his disinterestedness in the evolution of human thought. The dogmas of the philosophers are rejected as the products of overweening pride, sheer nonsense. His culture is essentially exegetical and ascetic, as is evidenced by his attitude toward Porphyry. Although Porphyry's philosophy was the dominant philosophy, Jerome is not slow to criticize it, and is content to hurl invectives at it; for instance, on the occasion of the death of Praetextatus.[303] The only works by Porphyry that hold Jerome's attention are the Κατὰ χριστιανῶν, lending itself as it does to Scriptural discussions, and the *De abstinentia*, because it is an apology for asceticism.[304] Jerome almost refuted the former and plagiarized the latter. But he considers

[297] *Epist. ad Marcellam* 37.3 (*PL* 22, 463): "Rogo, non habuerat decem Origenis volumina? non ceteros interpretes?"

[298] *Epist. ad Augustinum* 105.5 (*PL* 22, 837): "commentarios in Psalmos, quos si vellem discutere, non dicam a me, qui nihil sum, sed a veterum Graecorum docerem interpretationibus discrepare."

[299] Text quoted above, n. 229, and ending with the words: "Respondeat mihi prudentia tua qua re tu post tantos et tales interpretes in explanatione Psalmorum diversa senseris."

[300] *In Matth.* 3.22.15 (*PL* 26, 162 B): "Quidam Latinorum ridicule Herodianos putant, qui Herodem Christum esse credebant, quod nusquam omnino legimus." Jerome derives his better interpretation from Origen (Origen *In Matth.* 17.26, *PG* 13, 1553 A), but Epiphanius had already made the mistake (*Adv. haer.* 1.1.20, *PG* 41, 269 B) that Jerome attributes to the Latin writers only.

[301] *In Ezech.* 7, *praef.* (*PL* 25, 199 C): "Sed et Graecorum commentarios fratrum tantum voce cognoscimus."

[302] Text quoted above, n. 263.

[303] See above, p. 47.

[304] With regard to Porphyry's *Life of Pythagoras* and Iamblichus' *Protreptica*, he is interested only in the Pythagorean ascetic precepts.

every serious opposition of Christian thought to pagan Hellenism as useless and dangerous, for to him the authority of Scripture is the only valid argument. Hence his constant assaults on the philosophy of Origen, although he owes so much to Origen on the exegetical basis. Hence, too, his scorn for Marius Victorinus, who interprets Scripture as a philosopher.[305] Rufinus is quite wrong in accusing Jerome of indulgence to pagan literature: this illusion arises from the fact that, by a kind of "inferiority complex," Jerome prides himself in having a thorough knowledge of pagan literature in order to prove that Christian literature is still richer and more prolific.[306] Actually, the Hellenism that he commends is strictly monastic and has no value except in terms of the *lectio divina*.[307] This type of culture, which was to prevail in the Middle Ages, is very circumscribed: pagan literature is merely an instrument in the service of the exegete.

In the name of Christians, Jerome accuses Origen of having interpreted Scripture in the light of the pagan doctrines, as Porphyry, in the name of the pagans, had already reproached him for applying the allegorical method of the Greek philosophers to the Judaic fables.[308] Pagan Hellenism and Christian Hellenism, as represented in the eyes of Western readers by Macrobius, Porphyry's disciple, and by St. Jerome respectively, must, it seems, remain forever mutually impenetrable.

Some far-thinking minds, however, conceived a dramatic confrontation between Neoplatonic thought and Christian thought springing from the Patristic tradition. It was the progeny of Marius Victorinus that, despite the decline of Greek culture in the fifth century, extended into Italy, Africa, Gaul. Manlius Theodorus, St. Augustine, Claudianus Mamertus decided, while submitting Porphyrian philosophy to the control of their Christian faith, to enrich their religious life with the spiritual resources of Neoplatonism.

---

[305] Jerome *In Epist. ad Galat., prol. (PL* 26, 308 A): "Non quod ignorem C. Marium Victorinum, qui Romae me puero rhetoricam docuit, edidisse commentarios in Apostolum, sed quod occupatus ille eruditione saecularium litterarum Scripturas omnino sanctas ignoraverit et nemo possit quamvis eloquens de eo bene disputare quod nesciat." The same attitude appears in the *De vir. inl.* 101 with regard to Victorinus' books *Adversus Arium* "more dialectico valde obscuros, qui nisi ab eruditis non intelleguntur."

[306] Cf. the text quoted above, sec. 2 n. 134.

[307] Cf. Gorce, *La lectio divina*, p. 221.

[308] Cf. Porphyry, *apud Eusebium Hist. eccl.* 6.19 *(PG* 20, 565 A): Συνῆν τε γὰρ ἀεὶ τῷ Πλάτωνι, τοῖς τε Νουμηνίου καὶ Κρονίου, Ἀπολλοφάνους τε καὶ Λογγίνου καὶ Μοδεράτου, Νικομάχου τε καὶ τῶν ἐν τοῖς Πυθαγορείοις ἐλλογίμων ἀνδρῶν ὡμίλει συγγράμμασιν· ἐχρῆτο δὲ καὶ Χαιρήμονος τοῦ Στωϊκοῦ, Κορνούτου τε ταῖς βίβλοις. It is interesting to note that, like Jerome (text quoted above, n. 98), Porphyry has a grievance against Origen for using Plato, Numenius, and Cornutus.

PART TWO

ATTEMPTS AT CONFRONTATION AND THE DECLINE OF HELLENISM IN THE FIFTH CENTURY

Chapter 3

GREEK STUDIES IN ITALY

1. MILAN AND CHRISTIAN NEOPLATONISM

With the death of Theodosius, the East and the West were rent by rivalry that persisted for four years. In the West it was directed by Stilicho, Honorius' minister, and in the East by Arcadius' ministers Rufinus, then Eutropius.[1] Stilicho's claims to the tutorship of Arcadius[2] and Gildo's revolt in Africa, fomented by the East, were the instigating causes. A gulf separated the two halves of the Empire. Eutropius was not acknowledged as consul in the West.[3] Not all the measures taken by Arcadius had the force of law.[4] Even the interchange of news between Constantinople and the West became extremely difficult.[5]

The poems of Claudian, Stilicho's official panegyrist, reveal the attitude of the Roman elements that were hostile to Constantinople. The unity of the Empire subsists in theory, but the Greeks inspire hate. It was the intrigues of the Greek ministers, declares Claudian, who motivated this rivalry between the two imperial brothers.[6] Constantinople distrusts Rome.[7] The Greeks make bad soldiers and appeal for support from Honorius' Gauls.[8] They play like children when their father, Stilicho, is away but call upon him immediately they are threatened.[9] Effeminate Asiatic customs have been introduced into the Eastern court, which dared to name the eunuch Eutropius[10] as consul. The Byzantine senate had debased itself to the point of erecting a statue

[1] Cf. Lot, *Les destinées*, pp. 24–25.
[2] Cf. Claudian, ed. Koch (Leipzig 1893), *In III cons. Hon.* 151ff; *In VI cons. Hon.* 80ff; *In Rufin.* 2.4–6.
[3] Claudian *In Eutrop.* 2.123–137; *De cons. Stil.* 2.279–283, 295, 304, 385.
[4] *Codex Theodosianus*, ed. Mommsen-Meyer (Berlin 1905), 12.1.158.
[5] Eunapius, frag. 74, ed. C. Mueller, *FHG* 4, p. 46.
[6] Claudian *Laus Stil.* 2.78ff; *In Eutrop.* 1.281 and 396.
[7] Claudian *Bell. Gildon.* 1.60.
[8] Claudian *In IV cons. Hon.* 459 and 473; *In Eutrop.* 2.406ff.
[9] *In Eutrop.* 2.509ff and 527: "Tendit ad Italiam supplex Aurora potentem."
[10] *In Eutrop.* 1.151, 371, 414, 427, and 2.406.

to him.[11] The nobility is concerned with nothing but lavish living, perfumes, witty repartee, the theater, dancing, racing; and it despises Rome.[12] Stilicho, on the other hand, promotes arts and letters in the West.[13] Such laments over the luxury and the indolence of the Oriental cities were usual at that time, for similar comments appear in Ausonius.[14] While Stilicho was alive, the tension persisted. It was increased by the fact that Pope Innocent had taken the part of John Chrysostom, who was exiled by Arcadius. A warning letter written by Honorius to his brother resulted in the recrudescence of harshness against John's supporters, many of whom fled to Italy.[15] The threat of war was imminent. Stilicho went so far as to close the Italian ports to the traders from the East, who were considered as spies.[16]

However, until the capture of Rome by Alaric, the prestige of Greek culture remained unimpaired in the West. Claudian himself, who was trained in Alexandria and came to Italy only on the chance of an administrative career,[17] had a great respect for Greek antiquity.[18] In his youth he composed poems in Greek, as was recalled by the inscription that adorned the base of his statue standing in Trajan's Forum. This inscription praises him for uniting in himself Vergil and Homer.[19] Even his Latin poems are full of reminiscences of the ancient philosophers[20] and especially of the Greek poets.[21] His greatest praise for Honorius' queen is to say that she was nourished on the Homeric, Orphic, and Sapphic poems.[22] He himself uses an Orphic poem in

[11] *In Eutrop.* 2, *praef.* 57, and 2.74 and 135.

[12] *In Eutrop.* 2.322ff, particularly 339: "Romam contemnere sueti," and 534: "Tantane te nostri ceperunt taedia mundi?"

[13] Claudian *De cons. Stil.* 2.126.

[14] Ausonius *Ordo urbium nobilium* 17 and *Gratiarum actio ad Gratianum* 7.34, ed. Peiper (Leipzig 1886), pp. 145 and 362.

[15] Cf. Seeck, *PW* s.v. Honorius 2281.

[16] *Cod. Theod.* 7.16.1.

[17] Cf. P. Fargues, *Claudien, études sur sa poésie et son temps* (diss. Paris 1933) 6–10. This work has been reviewed, notably by J. Marouzeau, *REL* 12 (1934) 224–225.

[18] Claudian *In IV cons. Hon.* 398 and *In cons. Prob. et Olybr.* 196–197:
> Talem nulla refert antiquis pagina libris
> nec Latiae cecinere tubae, nec Graia vetustas.

[19] Cf. Kaibel, *Epigrammata Graeca*, no. 879, pp. 363 and 535, and Schanz, vol. 4, 2, p. 4.

[20] C. Pascal, *Graecia capta* (Florence 1905) 138, believed that he had discovered an Empedoclean echo in Claudian *Laus Stil.* 2.6ff. E. Bignone, "Parmenide e Claudiano, In laud. Stil. II, 6 sgg.," *Bolletino di filol. class.* 23 (1917) 212–214, associates this passage with a fragment from Parmenides. Cf. Fargues, *Claudien*, pp. 247–248, and for the listing of philosophers, taken from the manual by Manlius Theodorus, cf. below, n. 42.

[21] Th. Birt's edition of Claudian, *MGH, Auct. ant.* 10, p. LXXII, mentions a host of reminiscences, particularly from Homer, Hesiod, Callimachus, Oppian, etc. But this list requires scrupulous verification.

[22] Claudian *De nupt. Hon.* 231–235:
> . . . exemplaque discit
> prisca pudicitiae, Latios nec volvere libros

the *De raptu Proserpinae*.[23] Together with Macrobius he is the first Latin writer to testify to the spread of Orphic literature in the West.[24] His rhetoric stems from the Second Sophistic.[25] His philosophy is inspired by Neoplatonism. He conceives Theodosius' divination in astrological form as an ascent through the concentric circles of the heavens.[26] He accepts the Platonic tripartite division of the soul.[27] He adopts the theory of metempsychosis into the bodies of animals and believes that purifications in the waters of Lethe, after 3,000 years, result in the recovery of the human form.[28] It is not reasonable to see him as an adherent of Hellenism,[29] but this political enemy of the Greeks is none the less steeped in pagan Greek culture. While carefully avoiding all allusion to Christianity, he readily refers to the rites of the Oriental cults [30] and poetically develops the philosophical themes of Neopythagoreanism and Neoplatonism.[31]

> desinit aut Graios, ipsa genitrice magistra,
> Maeonius quaecumque senex, aut Thracius Orpheus,
> aut Mytilenaeo modulatur pectine Sappho.

[23] Cf. L. Cerrato, "De Claudii Claudiani fontibus in poemate *De raptu Proserpinae*," *Riv. di filol. class.* 9 (1881) 273–395; Fargues, *Claudien*, pp. 259–266; and especially E. Bernert, "Die Quellen Claudians in *De raptu Proserpinae*," *Philologus* 93 (1939) 352–376, who finds the sources in an Alexandrian poem and an Orphic poem.

[24] Cf. A. Boulanger, "L'orphisme à Rome," *REL* 15 (1937) 134–135. He does not, however, think that the *De raptu Proserpinae* assumes an Orphic source.

[25] He probably read some epideictic speeches by Aristides, Themistius, and Libanius, according to Fargues, *Claudien*, pp. 47 and 54. In his chapters 6 and 7 Fargues has made use of the works of A. Parravicini, *Studio di retorica sulle opere di Claudiano* (Milan 1905); L. B. Struthers, "Quo modo Cl. Claudianus praeceptis rhetoricis in laudationibus scribendis usus sit quaeritur," *Harvard Studies in Classical Philology* 27 (1916) 171–172, and "The Rhetorical Structure of the Encomia of Cl. Claudianus," *ibid.*, 30 (1919) 49–87. Fargues has clearly shown that Claudian's design of the panegyrics and the invectives conforms to the model laid down by the Greek rhetoricians, especially in the manuals attributed to Menander and in Aphthonius' *Progymnasmata*.

[26] Claudian *In III cons. Hon.* 162–170. On astronomy and astrology in Claudian, cf. *In VI cons. Hon.* 18; Fargues, *Claudien*, pp. 174–183, and W. H. Semple, "Notes on Some Astronomical Passages of Claudian," *Classical Quarterly* 37 (1937) 161–169.

[27] Claudian *In IV cons. Hon.* 228–256.

[28] Claudian *In Rufin.* 2.483–493. Cf. O. Ferrari, "Il mondo degl'inferi in Claudiano," *Athenaeum* 4 (1916) 335–338. The ultimate sources must be *Phaedo* 82a–b, mentioned by Servius *In Aen.* 6.703, where he comments on Vergil's lines dealing with Lethe, and *Phaedrus* 249a–b on the three millenary options. But the additions to Plato and the combination of the two passages show that Claudian here follows a Neoplatonic commentator. Despite Birt's views, in the edition mentioned, p. 52, several Neoplatonic writings accept reincarnation of the soul into the bodies of animals. See the texts cited in chap. 1 sec. 3 n. 32.

[29] Cf. Fargues, *Claudien*, p. 166.

[30] The cult of Cybele, *De raptu Proserpinae* 1.202–213, *In Eutrop.* 1.278 and 2.279–303; the cult of Mithra, *De cons. Stil.* 1.63, the cult of Apis, *In IV cons. Hon.* 570ff.

[31] Cf. Fargues, *Claudien*, p. 329.

Claudian lacks the philosophical habit, but he is informative on Manlius Theodorus, one of the greatest contemporary philosophers. The distinguished role that this philosopher played has not been brought into public notice, owing to the fact that his works are lost.[32] Still, Claudian's panegyric and the statements of St. Augustine permit us to evaluate his literary activity and the position he has held in the history of Roman Hellenism. In Claudian's view, Theodorus secured eternal glory for himself, not only by his brilliant career, but through the numerous books that he published before his consulship.[33] He was a Neoplatonic philosopher[34] who taught both ethics[35] and physics.[36] He produced a history of philosophy in which he expounded the views of the principal philosophers of Greek Antiquity.[37] He also wrote on the origin of the universe, on the parts of the soul,[38] and on astronomical questions.[39]

[32] His name does not even appear in the index of Father Henry's *Plotin et l'Occident* or in Labriolle's *Litt. lat. chrét.* The only surviving text of Theodorus is the epitaph on his sister (*CIL* 5, 6240), which I examine in an article published in 1944 in the *REA*.

[33] Claudian *Paneg. Manl. Theod.* 115: "nascentes ibant in saecula libri," and 333–335:

> Consul per populos idemque gravissimus auctor
> eloquii, duplici vita subnixus in aevum
> procedat pariter libris fastisque legendus.

[34] *Ibid.*, 94: "In Latium spretis Academia migrat Athenis," and 149: "Scilicet illa *tui* patriam praecepta Platonis / erexere."

[35] *Ibid.*, 95–99.

[36] *Ibid.*, 100–112. Cf. 10: "Te quoque naturae sacris mundique vacantem."

[37] *Ibid.*, 67–69:

> Omnia Cecropiae relegis secreta senectae
> discutiens, quid quisque novum mandaverit aevo
> quantaque diversae producant agmina sectae,

and 84–86:

> Graiorum obscuras Romanis floribus artes
> inradias, vicibus gratis formare loquentes
> suetus et alterno verum contexere nodo.

I am not at all convinced that we are dealing with historical *dialogues*, in which the various philosophers would be the interlocutors, as Claudian's poetic rhetoric would suggest. The theories of these philosophers were to be expounded in sequence, as Claudian does in lines 70–83. At the most, these expositions were in the form of historical apothegms by means of which each philosopher was thought to reply to his opponents, as in the *Sayings of the Seven Wise Men*. It may be recalled that Flavianus, a contemporary of Theodorus and like him a Platonic philosopher, had also written a *De dogmate philosophorum* (cf. above, chap. 1 sec. 1 n. 24) and that a similar work is mentioned by Jerome (see above, chap. 2 sec. 2 n. 38).

[38] Claudian *Paneg. Manl. Theod.* 253–255:

> Qualem te *legimus* teneri primordia mundi
> scribentem aut partes animae, per singula talem
> cernimus et similes agnoscit pagina mores.

[39] *Ibid.*, 273–275:

> Uranie redimita comas, qua saepe magistra
> Manlius igniferos radio descripserat axes,
> sic alias hortata deas . . . [cf. 125–132].

The rhetorical and poetic character of the discussion compels us to verify these references. When Claudian enumerates all the questions on ethics and physics that we learn about from contact with Theodorus, we must not necessarily conclude that Theodorus wrote a special treatise on each of these topics. Claudian is merely discussing a rhetorical commonplace. On the other hand, the works of St. Augustine confirm and substantiate the other references supplied by Claudian. Augustine calls Theodorus a fervent admirer of Plotinus.[40] He does not refer to his history of philosophy, but I shall show that he had at his disposal, at a time when he knew no Greek, Celsinus' Greek manual, which he read in translation.[41] One will be inclined to think that this translation was the work of Theodorus that is summarized by Claudian in his panegyric. In point of fact, this translation, according to Claudian, contained a series of notices on Anaximenes, Thales, Heraclitus, Empedocles, Democritus, Epicurus, Plato, Anaximander.[42] Now the manual followed by Augustine in Book 8 of the *De civitate Dei* contains a series of notices on Pythagoras, Thales, Anaximander, Anaximenes, Anaxagoras, Diogenes of Apollonia, Archelaus, Socrates, Plato.[43] The order adopted by Claudian is poetic and lacks precision, whereas Augustine follows the historical order. But their notices on Anaximander coincide textually:

Claudian *In laud. Manl. Theod.* 79–81:	Augustine *De civ. Dei* 8.2, ed. Dombart,
Ille ferox unoque tegi non passus Olympo	p. 322, 15:
immensum per inane volat finemque	Huic successit Anaximander eius auditor,
perosus	mutavitque de rerum natura opinionem.
parturit *innumeros* angusto pectore *mun-*	Non enim ex una re sicut Thales ex
dos.	umore, sed ex suis propriis principiis
	quasque res nasci putavit. Quae rerum
	principia singularum esse credidit infi-
	nita, et *innumerabiles mundos* gignere et
	quaecumque in eis oriuntur; eosque mun-

On a Milanese diptych dating in Stilicho's time there is a representation of an austere figure in converse with a Muse. Is this not Theodorus, the philosopher and consul, rather than the poet Claudian, as K. Weitzmann and S. Schultz assumed, "Zur Bestimmung des Dichters auf dem Musendiptychon von Monza," *Jahrb. des archäol. Instituts* 49 (1934) 128–138?

[40] Augustine *De beata vita* 1.4, ed. Knoell, *CSEL* 63 (Vienna 1922), p. 92, 8: "Lectis autem Plotini paucissimis libris, cuius te esse studiosissimum accepi." Father Henry, *Plotin et l'Occident*, pp. 82–88, has shown that the only acceptable reading is *Plotini*, and not *Platonis*, which Migne still retains, *PL* 32, 961.

[41] See below, pp. 192–194.

[42] Cf. Fargues, *Claudien*, p. 172, who sees in it merely a trivial list of names. On the other hand, in my hypothesis, Celsinus' work translated by Theodorus was based on the model of the lists of philosophers furnished by Plutarch *De placitis philos.* 1.3 or by Stobaeus *Ecl.* 1.10.12.

[43] Augustine *De civ. Dei* 8.2, ed. Dombart, vol. 1, pp. 321–323.

> dos modo dissolvi, modo iterum gigni
> existimavit, quanta quisque aetate sua
> manere potuerit; nec ipse aliquid divinae
> menti in his rerum operibus tribuens.

This very manual must have inspired Sidonius Apollinaris, who agrees with Augustine but is more detailed on certain points.[44]

Another of Theodorus' works is expressly mentioned by Augustine. This is an essay on the genesis of the human soul and its appearance on earth. Theodorus hesitates among several hypotheses: is the soul that is sent by the divinity produced by Nature, or by a fatalism? Or does it come of its own motion?[45] If one compares this reference with those of Claudian, no doubt remains that Theodorus wrote at least one Neoplatonic work on Nature, wherein he examined the genesis of the universe and the genesis of the soul and discussed astronomical questions. This prose treatise even survived for a long time in its entirety or in part. Gerbert seems to have known a copy in the tenth century,[46] and a number of reliable testimonies assure us of having

[44] See below, p. 256. Sidonius' notice, *Carm.* 15.83–86, on Anaximander runs as follows:

> Huius discipuli versa est sententia dicens
> principiis propriis semper res quasque creari,
> singula qui quosdam fontes decernit habere
> aeternum inriguos ac rerum semine plenos.

[45] Augustine *De beata vita* 1.1, p. 89, 7: "Cum enim in hunc mundum sive deus, sive natura, sive necessitas, sive voluntas nostra, sive coniuncta horum aliqua sive simul omnia,—res enim multum obscura est, sed tamen *a te iam inlustranda suscepta*,—velut in quoddam procellosum salum nos quasi temere passimque proiecerit." The panegyric on Theodosius by Drepanius Pacatus, pronounced in 389, ed. Baehrens, *XII Panegyrici Latini* (Leipzig 1874), p. 276, 9, shows how these problems were in current vogue: "Non frustra plane opinione *sapientium*, qui naturalium momenta causarum subtilius sciscitati arcanis caelestibus nobiles curas intulerunt, augustissima quaeque species plurimum creditur trahere de caelo. Sive enim divinus ille animus venturus in corpus dignum prius metatur hospitium, sive, cum venerit, pro habitu suo fingit habitaculum, sive aliud ex altero crescit et, cum se paria coniunxerunt, utraque meliora sunt: parcam arcanum caeleste rimari. Tibi istud soli pateat, imperator, cum deo consorte secretum. Illud dicam quod intellexisse hominem et dixisse fas est: talem esse debere qui gentibus adoratur, cui toto orbe terrarum privata vel publica vota redduntur, a quo petit navigaturus serenum, peregrinaturus reditum, pugnaturus auspicium." It is justifiable to ask whether the *sapientes* of whom Pacatus speaks do not refer to Theodorus and his book on the origin and the nature of the soul.

[46] Gerbert *Epist.* 130 *ad Rainardum monachum* (anno 988), ed. J. Havet (Paris 1889), p. 117: "Age ergo et te solo conscio ex tuis sumptibus fac ut mihi scribantur M. Manlius *de astrologia*, Victorius *de rhetorica*, Demostenis *Optalmicus*." Havet, p. 118 n. 1, thinks that the reference cannot be to Manilius but assumes that Boethius' astronomy is meant (Manlius Boethius). This hypothesis is improbable, for Gerbert *Epist.* 8 (anno 983), p. 6, mentions that he had already discovered "VIII volumina Boetii de astrologia." This is evidently a different work of which he here calls for a copy, as the different name of the author indicates.

seen manuscripts of the treatise at the close of the sixteenth century, particularly one in the library of the jurist Cujas.[47]

This treatise was read by Augustine and must have influenced his writings at Cassiciacum. But Theodorus' personal influence was assuredly still more considerable. At the time of his stay in Milan, during a period when he was preparing for his conversion and attended Ambrose's sermons, Augustine had several discussions with Theodorus on metaphysics, particularly one discussion on the corporeal nature of the soul and of God,[48] and one on beatitude.[49] This latter discussion was the starting point of the *De beata vita*, which Augustine dedicated to Theodorus. Furthermore, Augustine meditated, together with his mother Monica, on the sentiments that Theodorus had

---

[47] Cf. Reifferscheid, *Suetonii reliquiae*, p. 447, note, referring to Saumaise, *Praef. ad Ampelium* (Leiden 1638), p. 301; Claverius, *Adnot. ad Claudian.*; Fabricius, *Bibl. Lat.*, ed. Ernesti, vol. I, p. 501. H. Omont, "Catalogue des manuscrits de la bibliothèque de Cujas (1574)," *Nouvelle revue hist. de droit français et étranger* 9 (1885) 233–237, and "Inventaire des manuscrits de la bibliothèque de Cujas," *ibid.*, 12 (1888) 632–641, gives no confirmation. No work of Manlius Theodorus is mentioned in these inventories, but several manuscripts designated under vague titles, such as *Physica, Liber de anima, Varia opera variorum autorum*, or "Some twenty books written by hand, almost all defective, without beginning or end," may correspond to it. J. Koch, *De codicibus Cujacianis quibus in edendo Claudiano Claverius usus est* (diss. Marburg 1889), pp. 8 and 40, states that this library was dispersed in 1590. One of the manuscripts from this library reappears in the Ambrosian Library, another at Göttingen. It seems that the Ambrosian Library acquired an entire collection. It is therefore not impossible that the Cujas manuscript of Theodorus, which, according to Fabricius, missed being edited by Jacques-Philippe de Maussac, still lies today, unidentified, in the Ambrosian in Milan.

[48] Augustine *De beata vita* 1.4, p. 92, 1: "Animadverti enim et saepe in sacerdotis nostri et aliquando in sermonibus tuis, cum de deo cogitaretur, nihil omnino corporis esse cogitandum, neque cum de anima; nam id est unum in rebus proximum Deo." The expression *sacerdos noster* refers to Ambrose, Bishop of Milan, where Theodorus lived. Cf. Claudian *Paneg. Manl. Theod.* 124: "Illa per occultum Ligurum se moenibus infert." I have shown in an article, "Plotin et s. Ambroise," *Revue de philologie* (1950) 29–56, that Ambrose's sermons had led Augustine toward Neoplatonism.

[49] Augustine *De beata vita* 1.5, p. 92, 22: "Quid enim solidum tenui, *cui adhuc de anima quaestio nutat et fluctuat*? Quare obsecro te per virtutem tuam, per humanitatem, *per animarum inter se vinculum atque commercium*, ut dexteram porrigas, hoc autem est, ut me ames et a me vicissim te amari credas carumque haberi. Quod si impetravero, *ad ipsam beatam vitam, cui te iam haerere praesumo*, parvo conatu facile accedam. Quid autem agam quove modo ad istum portum necessarios meos congregem ut cognoscas et ex eo animum meum,—neque enim alia signa invenio, quibus me ostendam,—plenius intellegas, disputationum mearum quod mihi videtur religiosius evasisse atque tuo titulo dignius, ad te scribendum putavi et ipso tuo nomine dedicandum; aptissime sane; nam *de beata vita quaesivimus inter nos* nihilque aliud video, quod magis *Dei donum* vocandum sit" (a pun on *Theodorus = Dei donum*). Cf. 1.4, p. 91, 9: "accipe, mi Theodore . . . abs te cuius modi auxilium certus exspectem." On Augustine's hesitation with regard to the soul and its origin, cf. H. de Leusse, "Le problème de la préexistence des âmes chez M. Victorinus Afer," *RSR* 29 (1939) 236–237.

revealed to him in the course of these discussions.[50] Their contact was so close that Augustine calls it a converse of souls and begs for Theodorus' aid in solving the problem of the fate of the human soul. He is in no doubt that Theodorus already enjoys this beatitude, this gift of God that he himself has not yet received. Was it not through Theodorus' example that he decided to go into retreat in the countryside around Milan?[51]

If Theodorus' influence on Augustine has never been revealed, it was because Augustine himself mentions not a single word about it in the *Confessions*. But this omission is deliberate. Let us examine Augustine's evolution, as he describes it, after an interval of twelve years, in the *De beata vita* and in the *Confessions*. In both these works the same stages are mentioned: the reading of the *Hortensius*,[52] a Manichean period,[53] an interval of academic scepticism,[54] the influence of Ambrose's sermons,[55] delays due to his attachment to his mistress and to his professorial chair as rhetorician,[56] the reading of Neoplatonic treatises and the confrontation of their doctrine with the prologue of St. John.[57] But whereas the preface to the *De beata vita* emphasized the part that Theodorus had taken in his conversion, leading him toward Neoplatonism with a Christian tendency, the very name of Theodorus does not appear in the *Confessions*. Augustine rests satisfied with mentioning the literary influence exerted on him by certain Neoplatonic treatises, as though they had fallen haphazardly into his hands. He is silent about the name of "the man swollen with prodigious pride" who gave them to him to read in Milan.[58]

The proud Milanese who made Augustine read these treatises was, in my opinion, Manlius Theodorus. This reading matter, in fact, as we shall see, consisted of one or several treatises of Plotinus' *Enneads* and Porphyry's *De regressu animae*.[59] Now Theodorus was, as Augustine knew and even

[50] Augustine *De ordine* 1.11.31, ed. Knoell, p. 143, 8: "quem bene ipsa nosti." This statement merely means that Monica knows Theodorus from having read his books. But perhaps Augustine had even introduced his mother to him.

[51] Theodorus says (*apud Claudianum In laud. Theod.* 174):

Agrestem dudum me, diva, reverti
cogis et infectum longa rubigine *ruris*
ad tua signa revocas.

[52] *Conf.* 3.4 = *De beata vita* 1.4, p. 91, 14.

[53] *Conf.* 4.1 = *De beata vita*, p. 91, 21.

[54] *Conf.* 5.10.19 = *De beata vita*, p. 91, 24.

[55] *Conf.* 5.13.23 and 6.3.4 = *De beata vita*, p. 92, 2.

[56] *Conf.* 6.15.25 = *De beata vita*, p. 92, 5: "uxoris honorisque inlecebra detinebar." Cf. my "Premières Confessions de s. Augustin," *REL* 22 (1945) 155–174.

[57] *Conf.* 7.9 = *De beata vita*, p. 92, 8.

[58] *Conf.* 7.9.13, ed. Labriolle, p. 158 (addressing God): "Procurasti mihi per quendam hominem immanissimo tyfo turgidum quosdam Platonicorum libros ex Graeca lingua in Latinam versos."

[59] See below, pp. 173–180.

admitted, a fervent adherent of Plotinus, and their discussions had centered on the soul's return to beatitude. He dazzled Augustine, at the time of the *De beata vita*, with the distinguished career that he had deliberately renounced in 383 in order to devote himself to philosophy.[60] But this is not Augustine's definitive attitude with regard to Theodorus. His admiration declined rapidly. In the *De beata vita* Augustine, a recent convert, does not dwell on Theodorus' great good fortune and the esteem that he enjoys.[61] In the *De ordine* he takes Theodorus as a type of those philosophers whose literary renown is for the use of proud men and he declares that, as for himself, he seeks no such acclaim.[62] In conclusion, in the *Retractationes*, Augustine regrets the eulogies that he had formerly bestowed on Theodorus when praising his eminent good fortune and conferring on him the enjoyment of beatitude on earth.[63] There is nothing surprising in the fact that, in the *Confessions*, Augustine avoids mention of Theodorus among his spiritual benefactors and accords him merely this scornful reference to his pride. For at the time of the writing of the *Confessions*, Theodorus had just abandoned his philosophic retreat in order to resume a career in public office. He also wanted to hear his consulship praised in the letters of Symmachus, chief of the pagan party in the senate,[64] and in the panegyric of Claudian, whom Augustine also considered

---

[60] Cf. W. Ensslin, *PW* s.v. Theodorus 70.

[61] *De beata vita* I.1, p. 89, 2: "vir humanissime atque magne Theodore"; I.5, p. 93, 7: "eloquentia tua territus non sum; quidquid enim amo, quamvis non adsequar, timere non possum; fortunae vero sublimitatem multo minus; apud to enim vere, quamvis sit magna, secunda est; nam quibus dominatur, eosdem secundos facit."

[62] *De ordine* I.11.31, p. 142, 24 (Augustine replies to Monica): "Non valde curo, inquam, superborum imperitorumque iudicia, qui similiter in legendos libros atque in salutandos homines inruunt. Non enim cogitant quales ipsi, sed qualibus induti vestibus sint et quanta pompa rerum fortunaeque praefulgeant. Isti enim in litteris non multum attendunt, aut unde sit quaestio, aut quo pervenire disserentes moliantur, quidve ab eis explicatum atque confectum sit. In quibus tamen quia non nulli reperiuntur, quorum animi contemnendi non sunt,—aspersi sunt enim condimentis humanitatis et facile per aureas depictasque ianuas ad sacrosancta philosophiae penetralia perducuntur,—satis eis fecerunt et maiores nostri, quorum libros tibi nobis legentibus notos esse video, et his temporibus,—ut omittam ceteros,—vir et ingenio et eloquentia et ipsis insignibus muneribusque fortunae et,—quod ante omnia est,—mente praestantissimus Theodorus, quem bene ipsa nosti, id agit, ut et nunc et apud posteros nullum genus hominum de litteris nostrorum temporum iure conqueratur."

[63] *Retract.* I.2 (*PL* 32, 588): "Displicet autem illic, quod Manlio Theodoro, ad quem librum ipsum scripsi, quamvis docto et Christiano viro, plus tribui quam deberem, et quod Fortunam etiam illic saepe nominavi, et quod tempore vitae huius in solo animo sapientis dixi habitare vitam beatam, quomodolibet se habeat corpus eius, cum perfectam cognitionem Dei, hoc est qua homini maior esse non possit, speret Apostolus, quae sola beata vita dicenda est."

[64] It was in 398, on the occasion of his consulate, that Symmachus sent him the letters 5.5, 6, 10, 11, ed. Seeck, *MGH, Auct. ant.* 6, 1, pp. 125–127. These letters are full of congratulations and friendly compliments.

as a pagan.[65] Such a return to secular life, when Augustine was more and more enamored of asceticism, must have had on him the effect of a kind of cowardice and treason. Perhaps, too, he was afraid, if he mentioned Theodorus among his spiritual fathers, of being compromised by this name and of exposing himself to his detractors.[66]

Manlius Theodorus' example shows that, at the time of Theodosius' death, apart from the Macrobian type of pagan Neoplatonism, there existed a Christian Neoplatonism. This was the tradition of Marius Victorinus, which aimed to reconcile the data of reason and of faith. The path traced by Theodorus' works was not followed by Augustine solely. The mysterious Aponius, who appears to have been a cleric early in the fifth century, applies this method to exegesis. In his *Commentary on the Song of Songs* he shows that he knows pagan philosophy, and he attempts with considerable audacity to confront it with the Scriptures. His knowledge seems to stem from the same manual on history and philosophy that Augustine and Sidonius read:

Aponius *In Cant.* 3.5, ed. H. Bottino and J. Martini, Rome 1843, p. 95:	Augustine *De civ. Dei* 8.2, ed. Dombart, p. 322, 7:
In priore enim "filiarum Ierusalem adiuratione caprearum et cervarum" per-	Iste autem Thales, ut successores etiam propagaret, rerum naturam scrutatus

[65] The *Confessions* were composed in 398, according to Labriolle's edition, p. VI; in 400, according to Schanz, vol. 4, 2, p. 407. Theodorus was consul designate in 398 and the official *recitatio* of Claudian's panegyric took place in Milan at the beginning of the year 399, according to the editor Birt, *MGH, Auct. ant.* 10, p. XXXIX. Theodorus' literary activity lies between the two occasions of his magistracy, that is, between 383 and 397. Augustine *De civ. Dei* 5.26, Dombart, p. 239, 21, says of Claudian: "Unde et poeta Claudianus, quamvis *a Christi nomine alienus*, in eius (Theodosii) tamen laudibus dixit"; this epithet establishes him with certainty as a pagan, as has been well pointed out by Fargues, *Claudien*, p. 156, against Birt, *MGH, Auct. ant.* 10, p. LXIII.

[66] Theodorus seems to me even suspect of indulgence toward the pagan party. In 399, in his consulship, a pagan reaction replaced the statue of Victory in the Senate (cf. Claudian *De cons. Stil.* 3.202–216 and especially *De VI cons. Hon.* 597–602 and 653; Seeck, *PW* s.v. Honorius 2280; Birt, *MGH, Auct. ant.* 10, p. LVIII n. 1; Palanque, *Saint Ambroise* (above, chap. I sec. I n. 2) 307. See, however, Palanque's change of view, *RHE* 35 (1939) 298, following the work of Mlle L. Malunovicz, *De ara Victoriae in curia Romana quo modo decertatum sit* (Wilno 1937). It is virtually a rejoinder for Symmachus, the unfortunate champion of the Victory, a few years before, against St. Ambrose. This countermove, successfully made two years after Ambrose's death, would explain the laudatory letters addressed by Symmachus to Theodorus. The destruction of the pagan temples at Carthage, which took place on March 19, 399, was merely the belated execution of Stilicho's decree issued in the preceding year (*Cod. Theod.* 16.10.15 and 19). Augustine *De civ. Dei* 18.54.1, *PL* 41, 620, who mentions the incident in a discussion on the successes of Christianity, appears to avoid describing what happened in Rome in the same year: "Porro sequenti anno, consule Manlio Theodoro, quando iam secundum illud oraculum daemonum aut figmentum hominum nulla esse debuit religio Christiana, quid per alias terrarum partes forsitan factum sit, non fuit necesse perquirere."

sonas Thalesianae et Ferecidensis philosophiae intellegi diximus ... De quibus
Thales nomine *initium* omnium *rerum
aquam* in suo dogmate pronuntiavit, *et
inde omnia* facta *subsistere* ab inviso et
magno. Causam vero motus aquae spiritum insidentem confirmat; simulque
geometricam artem perspicaci sensu
prior invenit, per quam suspicatus est
rerum omnium creatorem. Ferecides
autem vocabulo *animam* hominis prior
omnibus *immortalem auditoribus* suis tradi-
disse docetur et eam esse vitam corporis,
et unum nobis de caelo spiritum, alterum
credidit terrenis seminibus comparatum.
Deorum vero naturam et originem ante
omnes descripsit. Quod opus multum
religioni nostrae conferre probatur, ut
noverit turpiter natos turpioremque
vitam duxisse, dedecorosius mortuos,
quos idolatriae cultor deos adfirmat.

suasque disputationes litteris mandans
eminuit maximeque admirabilis extitit,
quod astrologiae numeris comprehensis
defectus solis et lunae etiam praedicere
potuit. *Aquam* tamen putavit *rerum* esse
principium et hinc omnia elementa mundi
ipsumque mundum et quae in eo gig-
nuntur *existere*. Nihil autem huic operi
quod mundo considerato tam mirabile
aspicimus, ex divina mente praeposuit.[67]

Contra Academicos 3.17.37, ed. Knoell,
p. 75, 27:
Pythagoras ... postquam commotus
Pherecydae cuiusdam Syri disputationibus *immortalem* esse *animum* credidit,
multos sapientes etiam longe lateque
peregrinatus audierat.

Aponius uses allegorical exegesis so accommodatingly that he discovers in
the Song of Songs a reference to the philosophy of Thales and Pherecydes.
But in particular, with much less critical acumen than St. Augustine, he
recognizes in these ancient philosophers the two principles of Christian
philosophy: the creation of the universe and the immortality of the soul. It
is evident how boldly the Christian Philhellenes reconciled philosophy and
faith.

2. THE DECLINE

Pagan Hellenism was thus still in the ascendant at the beginning of the fifth
century, despite the political dissensions that divided East and West. Macrobius' Porphyrian philosophy, Theodorus' Christian Platonism, and Claudian's literary culture attest that at this date minds were still imbued with
Hellenism. The teaching of philosophy too still continued in Italy.[1] This

---

[67] Cf. Claudian *Paneg. Theod.* 71: "*Hic* confidit aquis," and Sidonius *Carm.* 15.89–92:
      Thales hic etiam numeris perquirit et astris
      defectum ut Phoebi nec non Lunaeque laborem
      nuntiet anterius: sed *rebus* inutile ponit
      principium, dum credit *aquis subsistere* mundum.

[1] A subscription to Sedulius' poems, written between 425 and 450, states: "(Sedulius)
in Italia philosophiam didicit." Cf. Schanz, vol. 4, 2, p. 368. Perhaps he had attachments
in Greece, for he ended his days there. However, he detested the "poison of Cecrops."

culture did not survive after the capture of Rome by Alaric. Not that all
Oriental influence could not flourish henceforth. On the contrary, since Stilicho's death, the frailty of the emperor of the West forced him to accept a
kind of tutelage of the East that was destined to increase in the course of the
fifth century. Honorius sustained Alaric's siege of Ravenna only with the aid
of the troops sent from the East.[2] His successor Valentinian III, the royal
friend of magicians and astrologers,[3] was crowned by his Byzantine colleague, Theodosius II;[4] but he was to acknowledge Marcian, Theodosius
II's successor, without having been able to offer his counsel on the succession.[5]
It was useless for Avitus, Majorian, Severus, on their assumption of power in
the West, to solicit the favor of the emperor of the East.[6] The latter was not
to be reconciled until the day when he placed on the throne of the West his
own creatures, Anthemius (467), then Julius Nepos (474). But, for all the
political prestige that the emperor of the East retained, Greek literature was
no longer pursued in Italy during the fifth century. The reorganization of
public education in 425 did not affect Rome.[7] A few instances of readjust-
ment under Anthemius must not delude us.[8] At the close of the century certain persons were to go to the length of ridiculing the sober studies and the
eminent names of Hellenism.[9]

The only surviving seats of culture were clerical. The impulse was given,
in the field of sacred literature, by St. Jerome, but there still remained also
other Hellenists. His enemy Rufinus, who was able to improve his Greek
through a long stay in Egypt and Palestine, was a no less elegant translator.[10]
He revealed to the West a host of works of the first order.[11] He became the
champion of the Origenist doctrine with his translation of the Περὶ ἀρχῶν
and a number of Origen's homilies, the *Apology for Origen* by Pamphilus of

<hr>

[2] Cf. Lot, *Les destinées* (above, Introduction n. 8) 36.

[3] Procopius *Bell. Vand.* 1.3, *CSHB*, p. 321, 19: φαρμακεῦσί τε γὰρ τὰ πολλὰ καὶ
τοῖς ἐς τὰ ἄστρα περιέργως ὡμίλει.

[4] *Ibid.*, p. 321, 8.

[5] Cf. Ensslin, *PW* s.v. Marcianos.

[6] Cf. Lot, *Les destinées*, p. 79, and Ensslin, *PW* s.v. Leo.

[7] This constitution of Theodosius II and Valentinian III (*Cod. Theod.* 14.9.3, ed.
Mommsen-Krueger, p. 787) organizes the university of Constantinople (cf. C. Diehl
and G. Marçais, *Le monde oriental de 395 à 1081* [Paris 1936] 9) and does not apply to
Rome, as Schanz mistakenly believes, vol. 4, 2, p. 314.

[8] See below, pp. 261–262.

[9] This tendency is attested by Ennodius 438 (*Opusc.* 5), ed. F. Vogel, *MGH, Auct. ant.*
7, p. 301, 40. The virtues of the saints, he declares, cure better than medicine "illa saecularis pompae philosophia Hippocratis et Galeni contrita subsidiis."

[10] H. Hoppe, "Griechisches bei Rufin," 132–144, has shown that Hellenisms were
comparatively rare in Rufinus. His art in translation is much more akin to Jerome's than
to the literalism characteristic of the translators of Irenaeus or the *Acta Archelai*. Hellenisms hardly appear in Rufinus except in passages where he quotes the *Vetus Latina*.

[11] On Rufinus' translations, cf. Schanz, vol. 4, 1, pp. 415–423.

Caesarea, and the *Dialogues of Adamantius*. He established a basis for historical studies with his translation of Eusebius' *Church History*, the *History of the Monks of Egypt*, and probably Josephus' *Jewish War*. He spread the taste for the Christian tale by translating Clement's *Recognitions* and *Letter to James*. He encouraged asceticism with his translations of the *Sententiae* of Evagrius Ponticus and Sextus' Pythagorean maxims. Lastly, he made several of the homilies of St. Basil and St. Gregory of Nazianzus available to Western readers. All these translations, as we shall see, were read and reread in the course of the sixth and seventh centuries, and exerted considerable influence, especially on the monks of Lérins.[12] Rufinus' personal writings show also that he readily consulted the Greek text of the Scriptures or the Greek writers.[13] However, his rigorous asceticism led him to a very narrow conception of culture. At one moment he charges Jerome with not having read the Greek pagan writers whom he quotes;[14] while again, on the other hand, he taxes Jerome with teaching them to the young monks of Bethlehem.[15] This hatred of pagan Hellenism was to become widespread in ascetic circles.

St. Jerome and Rufinus encouraged the taste for Greek exegesis in the smaller cultured circles. Melania the Elder, Rufinus' protectress, had read, we are told, "300 myriads of Origen, 25 myriads of Gregory, Stephen, Pierius, Basil, and some others."[16] St. Paula, Jerome's protectress, ended, after long years of residence in Bethlehem, by using Greek for regular conversation.[17] Her entire family, even the members who stayed in Rome, like Pammachius, knew Greek.[18] We must, however, refrain from thinking, as Bardy does, that every time Jerome inserts a Greek word or a Greek proverb into a

[12] See below, pp. 231ff.

[13] Cf. *PL* 21: 299, 302 A (Septuagint), 302 B (Josephus *Antiq.*), 478 A, 517 A (cf. Socrates *Eccles. hist.* 4.25.9–10 on Anthony).

[14] Rufinus *Apol. in Hieron.* 2.7, *PL* 21, 588 D: "Iam vero Chrysippum et Aristidem, Empedoclem et cetera Graecorum auctorum nomina, ut doctus videatur et plurimae lectionis, tamquam fumos et nebulas lectoribus spargit; denique inter cetera etiam Pythagorae libros legisse se iactat, quos ne exstare quidem eruditi homines adserunt."

[15] Text quoted above, chap. 2 sec. 1 n. 15.

[16] Palladius *Hist. Laus.* 55.3, ed. A. Lucot (Paris 1912), p. 349. The correctness of this information may be questionable, as far as concerns the writers read by Melania, for Palladius 11.4, p. 84 and n. 4, attributes to Ammonius also the reading of 600 myriads of Origen, Didymus, Pierius, and Stephanus. This Stephanus is otherwise unknown.

[17] Jerome *Epist. ad Eustochium* 108.28, *PL* 22, 904: on her deathbed "Graeco sermone respondit nihil se habere molestiae."

[18] See the texts collected by G. Bardy, "La culture grecque," pp. 41–45, on the knowledge of Greek that Eustochium, Blaesilla, Toxotius, and Pammachius had; the text o Jerome quoted by Bardy, p. 42 n. 3, with reference to the education of Laeta's daughter ("Discat Graecorum versuum numerum; sequatur statim Latina eruditio") applies in my opinion to the elementary teaching of the Greek *grammaticus* who made the pupils read Homer and Menander.

letter this is an indication that the recipient understood this language.[19]
Knowledge of Greek was not so very widespread. A cultured person such as
Paulinus of Nola, whom Jerome believed capable of reading Origen's *De
principiis* in the original text,[20] seemed to have forgotten his Greek since he
left the secular scene.[21] At the very most he refers very rarely to the Septuagint[22] or quotes Greek etymologies or current Greek expressions.[23] If he
reads Eusebius' *Chronica*, it is in Jerome's translation.[24] In any case, he has a
veritable horror of pagan Hellenism. He detests astrology.[25] For him, the
myth of Necessity in Plato's *Republic* is nothing but a vulgar falsehood, contrary to Providence.[26] He considers the doctrine of the universe infinite in
time as an offense directed against the omnipotence of the Creator.[27] He
taxes Jovius, one of his relatives, with a taste for the pagan writers and for
Greek literature: reading Demosthenes, Xenophon, or Plato is so much time
wasted for eternal salvation.[28] One of his poems directed against the philo-

---

[19] Thus Jerome's letters to Fabiola, Principia, Vigilantius, Ctesiphon, and Demetriades
must not necessarily imply that these correspondents knew Greek, as Bardy says, "La
culture grecque," pp. 48–50.

[20] Jerome *Epist. ad Paulinum* 85.3, PL 22, 753 : " Quorum exemplaria a supradicto fratre
(Pammachio) poteris mutuari, licet tibi Graeca sufficiant, et non debeas turbidos nostri
ingenioli rivulos quaerere, qui de ipsis fontibus bibis." This is possibly just a polite formula.

[21] He even says (*Epist. ad Rufin.* 46, PL 51, 397 B): "Nam quo modo profectum capere
potero sermonis ignoti, si desit a quo ignorata condiscam?" On this point Fabre is of the
same opinion as myself, but this letter is perhaps by another Paulinus, who might have
undertaken to translate a genuine or apocryphal work by St. Clement. Cf. Bardy, "La
culture grecque," p. 46 nn. 1 and 2, and Schanz, vol. 4, 1, p. 272.

[22] PL 61, 195 B.

[23] For example, PL 61: 371 C, 405 B, 623 B, 693 A, 707 A.

[24] Paulinus *Epist. ad Alypium* 3, PL 61, 162 D. Yet he does not have the work in his
possession, since he asks Domnion to send it to Alypius.

[25] Paulinus *Carm.* 22.125, mentioning Aratus and Manetho. Cf. La Ville de Mirmont,
"L'astrologie," 286–293.

[26] Paulinus *Epist. ad Iovium* 16, PL 61, 230 B: "Quod deliramentum ne vulgo impute-
mus, aut nimium philosophos admiremur, Platone etiam delirante narratur qui in
gremio anus pensum Necessitatis exponit, et tres ei filias addit concinentes, et versantes
fusum, et per fila ludentes, hoc scilicet lanificio autumans eas conficere res hominum et
tempora cuique signate detexere. Tantum abusus est humanis auribus adrogantia inanis
facundiae, ut ridiculam anilis fabulae cantilenam non erubesceret scriptis suis, quibus de
divina etiam natura quasi conscius disputare audebat, inserere." Cf. Plato *Republic*
10.617b–c.

[27] PL 61, 229 A.

[28] Paulinus *Epist. ad Iovium*, PL 61, 232 A: "Omnium poetarum floribus spiras,
omnium fluminibus exundas, philosophiae quoque fontibus inrigaris, peregrinis etiam
dives litteris, Romanum os Atticis favis imples. Quaeso te, ubi tunc tributa sunt, cum
Tullium et Demosthenen perlegis? Vel iam usitatiorum de saturitate fastidiens lectionum, Xenophontem, Platonem, Catonem Varronemque perlectos revolvis, multosque
praeterea, quorum nos forte nec nomina, tu etiam volumina tenes." In all probability,
these names were chosen for the rhyme!

sophers is scarcely a proof that he made use of them. He merely knows that Plato wrote a treatise *On the Soul*, which has no value.[29] This semischolar who jeers at the Platonists of his day had a reputation as the most effective adversary of Plato. St. Augustine consults him to ask for Ambrose's *De philosophia*, which attacked the Platonic theory of metempsychosis. On the basis of a false rumor he believes that Paulinus is preparing a refutation of the philosophers.[30] Paulinus would have had difficulty in writing such a work. His intentions exceeded his capacity. He is the enemy of Greek culture because he is so ignorant of it.

After Alaric's invasion, the Pelagian heresy, spreading from the East to the West between 415 and 430, contributed nevertheless in extending the knowledge of Greek Christian literature.[31] Pelagius was ignorant of Greek when he wrote his *Commentary on the Epistles of St. Paul*,[32] but he spoke a little Greek later on, after four years' residence in the East: for it was in Greek that he made his defense before the Synod of Diospolis.[33] He quoted John Chrysostom in several of his works.[34] His warmest supporter in the West, Julian, bishop of Eclana, was a distinguished Hellenist who, after expulsion from his bishopric, sought refuge with Theodore of Mopsuestia, then in Constantinople.[35] Julian's *Commentary on Hosea, Joel, Amos* proposed to rectify an omission in Latin exegesis and to substitute the method of literal exegesis, in

---

[29] Paulinus *Carm.* 35.35, PL 61, 693 A:

> Sunt et sectantes incerti dogma Platonis
> quos quaesita diu animae substantia turbat,
> tractantes semper, nec definire valentes;
> unde Platonis amant *de anima* describere librum
> qui praeter titulum nil certi continet intus.

[30] Augustine *Epist. ad Paulinum* 31.8, PL 33, 125: "Adversus paganos te scribere didici ex fratribus ... mitte ut legamus ... Libros beatissimi papae Ambrosii credo habere sanctitatem tuam; eos autem multum desidero, quos adversus non nullos imperitissimos et superbissimos, qui de Platonis libris Dominum profecisse contendunt, diligentissime et copiosissime scripsit." He vainly repeats his first request in *Epist.* 42 and 45.2, PL 33, 159 and 181.

[31] Cf. G. de Plinval, *Pélage, ses écrits, sa vie et sa réforme* (Lausanne 1943), pp. 85–86, 134, 140 n. 1, 206 n. 2, on Pelagius' Greek culture.

[32] C. H. J. Chapman, "Pélage et le texte de s. Paul," *RHE* 18 (1922) 472–476. There is no reason therefore to assume that he learned it in Ireland.

[33] Augustine *De gestis Pelagii* 1.2.4, PL 44, 322: "eius responsionem Graeco sermone prolatam."

[34] Particularly in his *De natura*. Cf. Augustine *De natura et gratia* 64.76, PL 44, 285. He also uses him in his *Commentary on the Epistles of St. Paul* as well as the Latin translation of the commentaries of Origen and Theodore of Mopsuestia on Paul. Cf. A. Souter, *The Earliest Latin Commentaries on the Epistles of St. Paul* (Oxford 1927) 227–229, summarizing the conclusions of previous research, and E. Dinkler, *PW* s.v. Pelagius 230.

[35] Cf. Schanz, vol. 4, 2, pp. 507–509; Gennadius *De viris* 46 (45), PL 58, 1084, calls him "Graeca et Latina lingua scholasticus."

line with the school of Antioch, for Origen's allegorical exegesis.[36] The
Commentary on the Psalms, which is attributed with probability to Julian of
Eclana, seems to be an adaptation of the commentary by Theodore of Mop-
suestia.[37] The *Commentary on Job* follows step by step the commentary of
Polychronios of Apamea, brother of Theodore of Mopsuestia, and also borrows occasionally from John Chrysostom.[38] In his book *To Florus*, Julian
designated in fact, as the three greatest names in Catholicism, John Chrysostom, Basil of Caesarea, and Theodore of Mopsuestia.[39] In the service of the
Pelagian cause, Anian the deacon of Celeda specializes in the art of translating
Chrysostom. He declares that Chrysostom surpasses all the Greek Fathers,
even Basil, Gregory, and Antiochus of Ptolemais, and that only the pupils of
the rhetoricians will not appreciate him perhaps, because he is more useful
than florid.[40] But at the same time he links him to Pelagianism and offers him
as a guarantee of the orthodoxy of the movement.[41] This dispute over dogma

[36] Pseudo-Rufinus *In Hoseam, Ioel, Amos, praef.*, PL 21, 962 A: "Iam vero cum apud
Latinos in explanandis maxime prophetis, quamvis tam fuerit continuata, ut videretur
etiam coniurata taciturnitas, tamen apud Graecos et apud Syros extitere non nulli qui
scripta eorum disserere niterentur. Ex quibus mihi sane pauca aliqua sancti Ioannis
Constantinopolitae episcopi legere contigit, sed suo more, id est exhortationi magis
quam expositioni totam paene operam commodantis. Origenes autem proprio tenore
decurrens allegoriarum magis lepida, quam historicorum explanationum solida et
tenenda componit." On the method adopted, cf. also 964 A, 965 A, and G. Morin, "Un
ouvrage restitué à Julien d'Eclanum: Le commentaire du Pseudo-Rufin sur les prophètes
Osée, Joel et Amos," *RB* 30 (1913) 19.

[37] Cf. A. d'Alès, "Julien d'Eclane exégète," *RSR* 7 (1916) 323–324; R. Devreesse,
"Le commentaire de Théodore de Mopsueste sur les Psaumes," *Revue biblique* 37 (1928)
365–366, announcing his edition of this commentary, which appeared in *Studi e testi*,
vol. 93 (1939).

[38] Cf. A. Vaccari, *Un commento a Giobbe di Giuliano di Eclana* (Rome 1915), chap. 4,
and d'Alès, "Julien d'Eclane exégète," pp. 314–322.

[39] Julian *Ad Florum* 3, apud *Augustinum Op. imperf. contra Iulian.* III, PL 45, 1295: "dis-
putatores catholica sanitate fulgentes Ioannes, Basilius, Theodorus."

[40] Anianus *Epist. ad Orontium*, PG 58, 975: "Certe quod ab aliis quoque plurimis
audire potuisti, omnes iam ecclesiasticae Graecorum bibliothecae, post tam varias
veterum scriptorum splendidasque divitias, post tot insignium magistrorum tam clara
lumina, huius praecipue voluminibus ornantur. Denique et sancti Basilii admirabilem
illam curam loquendi, et Antiochi plausibilem pompam, et sublimem illum Gregorii
cothurnum, facile intellegas hac Ioannis medietate superata. Ita enim stylum suum, in-
violata, ut diximus, facultate regnantem, Scripturarum ubique et sapore imbuit et tingit
colore: ut illi quidem de apparatu eloquii remittere, iste vero de maiestate Scripturarum
coruscare videatur. Solae ab eo forsitan adulescentulorum minus blandae mulceantur
aures, quibus in ludo positis litterarum non tam placent solida, quam picta, quique
pulchra potius, quam utilia sectantur, nec tam agentia diligunt, quam sonantia, magisque
gaudent florum amoenitate conspergi, quam frugum ubertate nutriri."

[41] He cries out with compunction, in the preface of his translation of the seven *Homilies on St. Paul*, PG 50, 472: "Quantum vero nobis consolationis exoritur, cum cernimus
tam erudito tamque inlustri Orientis magistro, eam quam in nobis Traducianus oppugnat,

resulted in making Chrysostom a renowned figure in the West. Augustine himself, who is hardly in touch with Greek ecclesiastical literature, will later be forced, in order to refute the Pelagian heresies, to read carefully, in the original Greek, several works by Chrysostom.[42]

Beginning with the first third of the fifth century, all trace of literary culture disappeared in Italy. Unquestionably, some persons still knew Greek. The necessity of taking part in theological disputations obliged one to resort to Greek when the acts of the Councils were not bilingual.[43] Again, the relations between the clergy of Rome and of Constantinople, and the presence of Roman nuncios at the court of Byzantium must incline one to believe that Greek was known in pontifical circles. As Steinacker has shown, Pope Celestine and his legates did not know Greek, and Leo the Great was forced to ask a Greek, Bishop Julian of Cos, for a translation of the *Acts* of the Council of Chalcedon.[44] This explains the intransigent attitude of the Roman Church, which adhered to the formulas of Augustinian theology without always being able to enter thoroughly into the theological debates of the East.[45] The Holy See had at its disposal only a few specialists. Arnobius the Younger was able, in his *Commentary on the Psalms*, to find help in the Septuagint[46] and, in his dogmatic writings, to translate a particular letter of Cyril of Alexandria.[47] Marius Mercator, who wrote an entire treatise in Greek, collected and translated a number of texts by Nestorius, Cyril, and Theodore of Mopsuestia. These translations were serviceable in promoting an understanding of the condemnation of Pelagianism or Nestorianism.[48] His translations, however, were far from literary. He forces himself, in his concern for accuracy, to a narrow literalness, and is not even afraid of a solecism.[49] Leo the Great, too,

---

astrui veritatem, quam certe beatus Ioannes, ut in omnibus libris suis, ita hic quoque ab omni munitam latere custodit, armat, accendit, ut videatur non tam praesentes informasse discipulos, quam nobis contra verae fidei oppugnationem auxilia praeparasse." On Anianus' translations of Chrysostom, notably the *Homily to Neophytes,* cf. Schanz, vol. 4, 2, p. 511.

[42] Cf. Baur, "L'entrée littéraire de s. Chrysostome," and below, pp. 104–105.

[43] Cf. E. Schwartz, "Zweisprachigkeit in den Konzilakten," *Philologus* 88 (1933) 245–253.

[44] H. Steinacker, "Die römische Kirche und die griechischen Sprachkenntnisse des Frühmittelalters," *Festschrift Th. Gomperz* (Vienna 1902) 333–334.

[45] Steinacker, *ibid.,* p. 340, extends this decline of the Greek language to the sixth century and makes the renaissance begin in the clerical circles of the seventh century. This means disregarding the tremendous effort made in the time of Dionysius Exiguus and Rusticus, an effort contemporaneous with the renaissance of pagan literature under Theodoric.

[46] Cf. *PL* 53: 518 B, 552 C, 553 A, 562 B.

[47] Cf. *PL* 53: 290 C, 294 C, and G. Morin, "Etude d'ensemble sur Arnobe le jeune," *RB* 28 (1911) 158–160.

[48] The list of his works may be found in Schanz, vol. 4, 2, pp. 482–483.

[49] Cf. Mercator, preface to the *Sermones Nestorii, PL* 48, 756 A: "Scio etiam ab istis

requires translations to be scrupulously faithful.[50] In fact, he tries, in order to justify his doctrinal position, to assemble an entire dossier of the Greek Fathers. But he was probably incapable of working otherwise than with translations.[51]

We may measure the sharp decline that the invasions of the barbarians produced in succeeding generations and the danger to which culture, recently still so flourishing, was exposed. It is no exaggeration to say that in the middle of the fifth century, apart from a few experts, the most cultured men in Italy, whether lay or cleric, had become incapable of reading Greek and that the concept of culture itself was compromised thereby. No literary work— so mediocre was culture—reveals any traces of Hellenism therein, as was to be the case in Africa and above all in Gaul. There was nothing to foretell the splendid outburst of Greek literature induced by the reign of Theodoric at the beginning of the sixth century.

---

exprobranda nobis esse aliqua dicta vitiosa, quae nobis vis servandae Graecae proprietatis extorsit." Cf. 755 A.

[50] What he calls "absolutissima interpretatio." Cf. F. Blatt, "Remarques sur l'histoire des traductions latines," p. 221.

[51] This compilation, which serves as documentary evidence for two famous dogmatic letters (*Epist.* 28 and 165, *PL* 54, 755 and 1173) quotes Athanasius from the old translation of the *Conlectio Quesnelliana* (*PL* 54, 1178 B = *PL* 56, 666 A); John Chrysostom from the Pelagian translation *incerti interpretis*, ed. Steelsius (Antwerp 1553), pp. 42 and 98; Theophilus of Alexandria from Jerome's translation (*PL* 54, 1184 A and 1185 A = *PL* 22, 794 and 776); Gregory of Nazianzus from Rufinus' translation (*PL* 54, 1185 B = *CSEL* 46, 100.23 and 103.7). The first of these two passages from Rufinus had already been quoted in Cassianus' *Contra Nestorium*, dedicated specifically to Leo. Cf. below, chap. 5 sec. 1 n. 21. Cyril of Alexandria is quoted from Mercator's translation (*PL* 54, 1186 A–B = *PL* 48: 1008 D, 1017 A, 1026 C) and from the *Conlectio Quesnelliana* (*PL* 54, 1187 A = *PL* 56, 742 A). Cf. Baur, "L'entrée littéraire," p. 265 n. 1, and L. Saltet, "Les sources de l' ’Ερανιστής de Théodoret," *RHE* 6 (1905) 290–303. To the same class of studies belongs perhaps the translation of the homilies of Eusebius of Emesa. This dates in the fifth century, according to A. Wilmart, "Le souvenir d'Eusèbe d'Emèse," p. 252, and E. M. Buytaert, "L'authenticité des dix-sept opuscules contenus dans le manuscrit T 523 sous le nom d'Eusèbe d'Emèse, *RHE* 43 (1948) 5–89.

Chapter 4

ST. AUGUSTINE AND
HELLENISM IN AFRICA

1. Augustine and the Greek Language

St. Augustine's Greek culture cannot sustain comparison with that of St. Jerome. Augustine considers him a very great scholar, thoroughly versed in the Greek and Latin ecclesiastical writers. Jerome's reading is infinitely more extensive than his own,[1] for he has read virtually everything.[2] Augustine himself does not hide the fact that he never set foot in any Greek-speaking country.[3] So the question has been asked for at least a century whether St. Augustine knew Greek. This question has even become trite, since some dozen writers have already treated it. But they are far from agreeing on Augustine's Greek culture, as well as on his ignorance of Hebrew or his knowledge of Punic.[4] Some insist on Augustine's ignorance,[5] others on his

[1] Augustine *De peccatorum meritis et remissione* 3.6.12 (PL 44, 192), referring to original sin: "Hunc doctissimum virum si facile interrogare possemus, quam multos utriusque linguae divinarum Scripturarum tractatores et Christianarum disputationum scriptores commemoraret, qui non aliud, ex quo Christi Ecclesia est constituta, senserunt, non aliud a maioribus acceperunt, non aliud posteris tradiderunt. Ego quidem, quamvis longe pauciora legerim, non memini me aliud audivisse a Christianis . . . non memini me aliud legisse apud eos, quos de his rebus aliquid scribentes legere potui."

[2] *Contra Iulianum* 1.7.34 (PL 44, 665): "Nec sanctum Hieronymum, quia presbyter fuit, contemnendum arbitreris, qui Graeco et Latino, insuper et Hebraeo eruditus eloquio, ex occidentali ad orientalem transiens Ecclesiam, in locis sanctis atque in litteris sacris usque ad decrepitam vixit aetatem, omnesque vel paene omnes qui ante illum aliquid ex utraque parte orbis de doctrina ecclesiastica scripserant legit."

[3] Cf. *Epist. ad Consentium* 120.2.10 (PL 33, 457): "Nam Antiochiam cogito incognitam, sed non sicut Carthaginem cognitam," and *De Trinitate* 9.6.10 (PL 42, 966): "Nam et cum recolo Carthaginis moenia quae vidi et cum fingo Alexandriae quae non vidi."

[4] Cf. O. Rottmanner, "Zur Sprachenkenntnis des hl. Augustinus," *Theologische Quartalschrift* 77 (1895) 269–276.

[5] H. N. Clausen, *Aurelius Augustinus sacrae Scripturae interpres* (Hauniae 1826) 30–39; O. Rottmanner (see preceding note) 270–271; J. Draeseke, "Zur Frage nach den Quellen von Augustins Kenntnis der griechischen Philosophie," *Theologische Studien und Kritiken* 89 (1916) 541–562; P. Alfaric, *L'évolution intellectuelle de s. Augustin* (Paris 1918) 18; G. Combès, *Saint Augustin et la culture classique* (diss. Paris 1929) 1–7; P. Guilloux, "Saint Augustin savait-il le grec?" *RHE* 21 (1925) 79–83; H. I. Marrou, *Saint Augustin et la fin*

knowledge, of Greek,[6] although the majority adopt a middle solution and venture to affirm neither his total ignorance nor his perfect knowledge. Is it possible after so many discussions to offer some new feature on the subject? Three facts strike me. In the first place, both sides have tended to discuss indefinitely a small number of texts, those in which St. Augustine speaks of himself, instead of trying to establish a complete documentation. Only Angus and Marrou have felt it necessary to support their thesis with several of Augustine's works. But a large number of texts still remain to be examined with regard to the problem. This has not yet been done. In addition, it would be necessary to distinguish several possible investigations that would shed light on each other. The inquiry on Augustine's knowledge of Greek has been carried much further than the inquiry relating to his Greek culture. Now, particularly at a time when translations are abundant, a writer's meager knowledge of Greek may not mean that his Hellenic culture is necessarily superficial. Inversely, his culture may be extensive yet he may not necessarily know the language.[7] Lastly, and above all, the best studies on the subject show a serious omission, particularly apparent in the most recent article by Berthold Altaner. This omission is the lack of chronology. It is not sufficient to make, as Angus does, a statistical abstract of the Greek expressions used by Augustine. In fact, a language is learned and forgotten; a culture is acquired and depreciates in the course of time. Did Augustine know Greek better at the age of twenty or at seventy-six? Did he learn slowly or did he forget slowly in the course of his long life? That is the question that interests us. I shall try, therefore, instead of recommending after so many others a new proportioning between his knowledge and his ignorance of

---

de la culture antique, pp. 28–37 and 418–421; M. Comeau, *Saint Augustin exégète du IVe Évangile* (diss. Paris 1930) 46–48 and 58–69; B. Altaner, "Augustinus und die griechische Sprache," *Pisciculi, Studien zur Religion und Kultur des Altertums, F. J. Doelger zum 60. Geburtstage dargeboten* (Münster 1939) 19–40.

   [6] H. Reuter, *Augustinische Studien, IV*: "Augustin und der katholische Orient" (Gotha 1887) 171–230; S. Angus, *The Sources of the First Ten Books of Augustine's De Civitate Dei* (Princeton 1906) 236–276; H. Becker, *Augustin, Studien zu seiner geistigen Entwickelung* (Leipzig 1908) 120–138; E. Rolfes, "Hat Augustin Plato nicht gelesen?" *Divus Thomas* 5 (1918) 17–39; S. Salaville, "La connaissance du grec chez s. Augustin," *Echos d'Orient* 25 (1922) 387–393, and "Saint Augustin et l'Orient," *Angelicum* 8 (1931) 3–23; A. C. Vega, "El helenismo de s. Agustin; llegó s. Agustin a dominar el griego?" *Religion y cultura* 2 (1928) 34–45; Henry, *Plotin et l'Occident*, pp. 133–137; Bardy, "La culture grecque," pp. 24–31.

   [7] Alfaric in particular is guilty of this confusion when he writes, *L'évolution intellectuelle*, p. 18: "He himself admitted that he was incapable of reading an entire book written in this language [*De Trinitate* 3.1] and in an expansive moment he went so far as to say, quite frankly, that he had no knowledge of it at all [*Contra litt. Petil.* 2.91]. In short, he was virtually completely ignorant of the literature of Greece, whether pagan or ecclesiastical."

Greek, to determine the principal stages of his Greek studies. Such an aim is not excessive, since the chronology of his works is practically determined.[8]

A guide in this inquiry presents itself in Augustine's use, throughout his literary career, of the Greek text of the Scriptures. Without going so far as to speak, as Dom De Bruyne does, of an almost complete revision of the two Testaments based on the Greek text,[9] it is certain that Augustine prefers the Greek to the Hebrew text,[10] and, among the various Greek versions, those of the Septuagint.[11] He readily refers to it and even has several copies and occasionally mentions the variant readings.[12]

Angus and Marrou have made a thorough study of Augustine's attitude toward the Septuagint. They have properly noted that recourse to the Greek is quite irregular in Augustine according to his different commentaries. Sometimes he resorts to it quite frequently; then again, rarely; and still at other times, not at all. But they have not succeeded in explaining this fact and have drawn no conclusion from it. Marrou considers that it is a *surprise* for the historian,[13] and discovers in Augustine "a lack of precision in the application of his method,"[14] which was probably a sign of decadence.

This anomaly is explained, I believe, if one examines the date of these commentaries. Those that do not use, or that use in quite exceptional cases, the Greek text, are the earlier ones. These are the *De Genesi contra Manichaeos* (389/390), *De Genesi ad litteram imperfectus liber, De sermone Domini in monte,*

---

[8] It is appreciably the same in Schanz, vol. 4, 2, p. 406, and Labriolle, *Litt. lat. chrét.*, table 8. Cf. also P. Zarb, "Chronologia operum s. Augustini secundum ordinem Retractationum digesta," *Angelicum* 10 (1933) 359–396, 478–512; and 11 (1934) 72–91. Note that the interest of such an inquiry was already perceived by Henry, *Plotin et l'Occident*, p. 134.

[9] Dom D. de Bruyne, "Saint Augustin réviseur de la Bible," *Miscellanea Agostiniana* 2 (Rome 1931) 521–606. I fully subscribe to the important reservations formulated on his theory by J. Lagrange, "De quelques opinions sur le Psautier latin," *Revue biblique* 41 (1932) 161–186, and Marrou, *Saint Augustin*, p. 441 n. 3.

[10] See the text quoted below, sec. 4 n. 1. There Augustine explains to Jerome the inconveniences caused by using his translation made from the Hebrew text.

[11] See the text quoted by Marrou, *Saint Augustin*, p. 436.

[12] *Enarr. in Ps.* 67.34 (PL 36, 839) on the variants χεῖρα αὐτῆς and χειρὰς αὐτῆς; *Quaest. in Hept.* 6.12 (PL 34, 781) on the variants ὤμων and ὄνων; on the fact that he has several Greek manuscripts of the Septuagint, cf. *Enarr. in Ps.* 105.1 (PL 37, 1405): "Paucissimi codices sunt (quod quidem in nullo Graecorum repperi, quos inspicere potui) qui habeant *Alleluia* in fine centesimi et quinquagesimi Psalmi"; *In Ps.* 118.14.45 (PL 37, 1539): "*Non nulli* autem codices non habent *mandata*, sed *testimonia*; sed *mandata* in pluribus inveni, et maxime Graecis: cui linguae, tamquam praecedenti unde ad nos ista translata sunt, magis credendum esse quis ambigat?" *In Ps.* 118.10.26 (PL 37, 1526) and *Contra Cresconium Donatistam* 1.14.18 (PL 43, 457): "inspice codices Graecos in eisdem testimoniis sanctarum Scripturarum, et videbis unde sit appellata *dialectica.*"

[13] Marrou, *Saint Augustin*, p. 437: "A surprise here awaits the historian."

[14] *Ibid.*, p. 439.

and the three commentaries on the Epistles of St. Paul (394/395), *De diversis quaestionibus LXXXIII* (389/396), *De diversis quaestionibus ad Simplicianum* (396/397), *Quaestiones Evangeliorum, Adnotationes in Job*, and *De consensu Evangelistarum* (around the year 400), *De Genesi ad litteram* (401/415).

Does Augustine not use the Greek text at this period because he had not yet succeeded in procuring it? The objection breaks down, since we find that he sometimes does refer to it. To be specific, the very rare comments that the Greek text suggests to him are those that he might have suggested to someone who knew no Greek except the alphabet and the most rudimentary elements and yet tried to derive some benefit from the comparison between the Latin translation and the Greek text: *per gloriam vestram*, a translation of νὴ τὴν καύχησιν, is a kind of oath, often uttered by the Greeks.[15] The term *Mazuroth* is not translated in the Greek text any more than in the Latin text.[16] The word *palam* does not appear in the Greek text.[17] The rendering *agrum* is preferable to the rendering *villam*, for the Greek text has ἀγρόν.[18] Is it conceivable that Augustine, if he knew Greek, would consult the Greek text only for comments of this type, which are so simple and even silly, and would not consult it when he encounters insurmountable difficulties in interpretation that a knowledge of the Greek text would have elucidated?[19]

If one examines St. Augustine's non-exegetical treatises during the same period, one observes that he, like every Roman who had studied Cicero and Varro, certainly knows some Greek words. But it is an exclusively bookish knowledge. In fact, the word he is searching for sometimes eludes his stubborn memory.[20] If he finds it, he does not dare slip it into his text without the

---

[15] *In Epist. ad Galat.* 9 (PL 35, 2110): "*per gloriam vestram* quam Graeca exemplaria manifestissimam iurationem esse convincunt"; *De sermone Domini in monte* 17.51 (PL 34, 1255): "Graeca exemplaria diiudicant νὴ τὴν καύχησιν ὑμετέραν, quod non nisi a iurante dicitur"; cf. *Sermo* 180.5.5 (PL 38, 974): "*per vestram gloriam.* Ambiguitatem Graecus sermo dissolvit. Inspicitur in Epistula Graeca, et invenitur ibi iuratio quae non est ambigua: νὴ τὴν ὑμετέραν καύχησιν. Νὴ τὸν Θεόν, ubi dixerit Graecus, iurat. Quotidie auditis Graecos, et qui Graece nostis: νὴ τὸν Θεόν; quando dicit νὴ τὸν Θεόν iuratio est."

[16] *Adnotationes in Iob* 38.32 (PL 34, 877): "*Mazuroth* . . . interpretatum nec in Graeca lingua invenimus."

[17] *De sermone Domini in monte* 2.2.9 (PL 34, 1274): "Quia in Graecis quae priora sunt, non invenimus *palam*, non putavimus hinc esse disserendum." Other instances of resorting to the Greek text without result: *ibid.*, 1.11.31 and 1.19.60 (PL 34, 1244 and 1261); further on, Augustine avoids committing himself: ought one in the *Pater Noster* to say *et ne nos inferas* or *et ne nos inducas*? "Tantumdem valere arbitror, nam ex uno Graeco quod dictum est εἰσενέγκῃς utrumque translatum est" (*ibid.*, 2.9.30, PL 34, 1282).

[18] *De consensu Evangelistarum* 3.25.71 (PL 34, 1206): "et in codicibus quidem Graecis magis *agrum* invenimus quam *villam*"; another very simple comment, *ibid.*, 2.70.137 (PL 34, 1144).

[19] *Ibid.*, 2.80.157 and 3.7.27 (PL 34, 1156 and 1174).

[20] *De ordine* 2.12.35 (PL 32, 1012): "nata est librariorum et calculonum professio, velut

utmost precautions, even when it is a current expression.[21] He is unable to decide whether the term *Raca* is Greek or Hebrew: some say it is Greek, but then the sense of the sentence is hardly satisfactory. Augustine thinks then that *more probably* it is Hebrew, as a Jew has assured him.[22] Can such uncertainty be explained in a man who knows even a modicum of Greek?[23]

In the light of these remarks, unless I am mistaken, the texts that have been discussed so often and that offer an evaluation of Augustine's own knowledge of Greek become clear. Between 390 and 400, he can just barely read Greek and a few elementary expressions. That is all he has retained from his Greek studies during his boyhood, for he admits that he pursued listlessly and without benefit the courses of the Greek *grammaticus*.[24] He has not studied it since then. Before receiving baptism, at the time of the *Contra Academicos* (386), he thought Licentius' taste for Greek poetry was ridiculous, for Augustine himself understood not a word of it.[25] Five years later, after being instructed in the faith, he excuses his use of the words *historia, aetiologia, analogia, allegoria*. Let no one brand him with the foolish imputation of wanting to act the Hellenist: these are technical terms used by the ecclesiastical writers.[26] Simi-

---

quaedam grammaticae infantia, quam Varro litterationem vocat; Graece autem quo modo appelletur, non satis in praesentia recolo." The word Augustine is looking for is Γραμματιστική , for cf. Martianus Capella, *De nupt.* 3.229, ed. Dick, p. 85, 1 (Grammar is speaking): "hincque mihi Romulus *Litteraturae* nomen adscripsit, quamvis infantem me *Litterationem* voluerit nuncupare, sicut apud Graecos Γραμματιστική primitus vocitabar."

[21] *De Genesi contra Manichaeos* 1.5.9 (PL 34, 178): "Primo ergo materia facta est confusa et informis, unde omnia fierent quae distincta atque formata sunt, quod credo a Graecis *chaos* appellari."

[22] *De serm. Dom. in mon.* 9.23 (PL 34, 1240): "Non nulli autem de Graeco voluerunt interpretationem huius vocis putantes *pannosum* dici *Racha*, quoniam Graece ῥάκος *pannus* dicitur . . . Probabilius est ergo quod audivi a quodam Hebraeo, cum id interrogassem . . ."

[23] More erudite and more intelligent comments may be found in the *De Genesi ad litteram*, for example 2.15.32, 7.1.2, 8.10.19 (PL 34: 277, 356, 380), but then this treatise is later (401/415). It would be interesting to know in exactly what year these lines were written.

[24] *Conf.* 1.13.20, p. 17 Lab.: "Quid autem erat causae, cur Graecas litteras oderam, quibus puerulus imbuebar, ne nunc quidem mihi satis exploratum est," and 1.14.23, p. 20 Lab.: "Videlicet difficultas, difficultas omnino ediscendae linguae peregrinae quasi felle aspergebat omnes suavitates Graecas fabulosarum narrationum. Nulla enim verba noveram."

[25] *Contra Acad.* 3.4.7 (PL 32, 937): "Deinde cum sis bene canorus, malim auribus nostris inculces tuos versus, quam ut in illis Graecis tragoediis, more avicularum quas in caveis inclusas videmus, verba quae non intellegis cantes. Admoneo tamen ut pergas potum, si voles, et ad scholam redeas nostram, si tamen aliquid iam te Hortensius et philosophia meretur." I do not understand how Altaner, "Augustinus," p. 29, can conclude from this passage that Augustine was very proud of his Greek at this date!

[26] *De utilitate credendi* 3.5 (PL 42, 68): "Ne me ineptum putes, Graecis nominibus

larly, in the *De musica*, published around 391, he apologizes for using Greek words. If he does so, it is because they are technical terms belonging in the vocabulary of music. As there is no Latin equivalent, they have passed without change into the language.[27] Ten years later, in the *Contra Faustum Manichaeum* (400), in the *Contra litteras Petiliani* (401/403), he still aligns himself in the category of those who barely know Greek. This is neither an excess of humility nor irony, as might have been thought. He is just barely able to give the etymology of the word *Evangel*[28] or the term *Catholic*[29] or deciphers from the Greek that *Beatus vir* translates Μακάριος ἀνήρ.[30] In 403 he is still not competent enough to evaluate critically the translation of the Gospels made by Jerome from the Greek. He tries nevertheless to verify it with reference to the Greek text but finds almost no defect whatsoever in it.[31]

Now one can better understand why St. Augustine exhorted Jerome in 394, in the name of the African clergy and in his own name, to translate the Greek commentators of the Scriptures.[32] The same conclusion is drawn from

---

utentem. Primum quia sic accepi, nec tibi hoc aliter audeo intimare, quam accepi. Deinde tu quoque animadvertis, non esse harum rerum apud nos usitata nomina; quae si fabricassem interpretando, essem profecto ineptior; si autem circumloquerer, minus essem in disserendo expeditus. Id tantum oro credas, quoquo modo errem, nihil a me inflato ac tumido fieri."

[27] *De musica* 1.12.23 (*PL* 32, 1097): "illa unitas quam te amare dixisti, in rebus ordinatis hac una effici potest, cuius Graecum nomen ἀναλογία est, nostri quidam *proportionem* vocaverunt, quo nomine utamur si placet: non enim libenter, nisi necessitate, Graeca vocabula in Latino sermone usurpaverim." He will later on, however, prefer, *De musica* 3.1.2 (*PL* 32, 1115), *rythmus* and *metrum* to *numerus* and *mensura*, because the Greek terms are clearer: "sed quoniam haec apud nos late patent et cavendum est ne ambigue loquamur, commodius utimur Graecis."

[28] *Contra Faustum Manichaeum* 2.6 (*PL* 42, 214): "Certe omnes qui Graece vel tenuiter noverunt, Evangelium *bonum nuntium* aut *bonam adnuntiationem* interpretantur." He himself resorts to Greek, *De Genesi ad litteram* 11.4 (*PL* 34, 248), to justify the translation of *factus* in preference to *natus*. The etymology also of *Ecclesia* and *Synagoga* may be found in *In Epist. ad Rom. expos. inchoata* 2 (*PL* 35, 2089).

[29] *Contra litteras Petiliani* 2.38.91 (*PL* 43, 292): "Ego quidem Graecae linguae perparum adsecutus sum et prope nihil; non tamen impudenter dico, me nosse ὅλον non esse *unum*, sed *totum*, et καθ' ὅλον *secundum totum*, unde Catholica nomen accepit." Cf. *Contra Gaudentium* 2.2 (*PL* 43, 741).

[30] *Contra litt. Petil.* 2.46.108 (*PL* 43, 296): "Verum tamen admoneo ut istum primum Psalmum Graece legas ... Quod enim scriptum est Latine *Beatus vir*, Graece habet Μακάριος ἀνήρ."

[31] *Epist. ad Hieron.* 71.4.6 (*PL* 33, 243): "Proinde non parvas Deo gratias agimus de opere tuo, quo Evangelium ex Graeco interpretatus es, quia paene in omnibus nulla offensio est, cum Scripturam Graecam contulerimus." The value of this text must not, however, be exaggerated, for Augustine is evidently trying to compliment Jerome, and Jerome's translation is really good.

[32] *Epist. ad Hieron.* 28.2.2 (*PL* 33, 112): "Petimus ergo et nobiscum petit omnis Africanarum Ecclesiarum societas, ut interpretandis eorum libris, qui Graece Scripturas nostras

the preface to Book 3 of the *De Trinitate*, but this difficult text was so rarely translated, so often interpreted rather freely, that it must be translated in its entirety in order to appreciate it properly:

I should like you very much to believe that I prefer work that entails reading to dictating matter to be read. Those who do not care to believe this but have the means and the desire to test it should give me books to read that answer my inquiries or the questions of others. These questions I must listen to, in view of my personal service in Christ and of the zeal that inflames me to defend our faith against the error of carnal and bestial men; and they will see how easily I would withdraw from this task, and how joyfully I can take a respite from my pen.

But what we have read about these subjects is either not completely published in Latin or is not available, or at least not available to us except with difficulty. And we do not have such a ready command of Greek as to make us in any sense competent to read and understand books dealing with such matters. From the little that has been interpreted for us I am sure that this literary genre contains answers to all the questions that we can profitably ask. Furthermore, I cannot resist the pleas of my brethren since I have sworn an oath in their service to aid their praiseworthy studies in Christ as far as lies in my power, by word of mouth and by my pen—two means that the charity in me inspires. I confess too that through my writing I have learned a great deal that I did not know. This labor of mine, therefore, ought not to seem superfluous to anyone, whether idler or profound scholar, since it is in great part necessary to many hard workers and many unlearned men, among whom I consider myself. Hence, aided and supported to a very large extent by the writers whose books on this subject we have now read, I have undertaken to investigate and discuss, at God's prompting and with his help, those questions that I think may piously be investigated and treated, with regard to the Trinity, the one supreme and supremely beneficent God. If there are no other writings of this kind, let those who have the desire and the ability have this to read. If however there are already such writings, it will be easier to find some, the more numerous they become.[33]

---

quam optime tractaverunt, curam atque operam impendere non graveris. Potes enim efficere, ut nos quoque habeamus tales illos viros, et unum potissimum, quem tu libentius in tuis litteris sonas. De vertendis autem in Latinam linguam sanctis Litteris canonicis laborare te nollem."

[33] *De Trinitate* 3, *prooemium* 1 (PL 42, 867): "Credant qui volunt, malle me legendo quam legenda dictando laborare. Qui autem hoc nolunt credere, experiri autem et possunt et volunt, dent quae legendo vel meis inquisitionibus respondeantur vel interrogationibus aliorum, quas pro mea persona quam in servitio Christi gero, et pro studio quo fidem nostram adversum errorem carnalium et animalium hominum muniri inardesco, necesse est me pati: et videant quam facile ab isto labore me temperem et quanto etiam gaudio stilum possim habere feriatum. Quod si ea quae legimus de his rebus, sufficienter edita in Latino sermone aut non sunt, aut non inveniuntur, aut certe difficile a nobis inveniri queunt, Graecae autem linguae non sit nobis tantus habitus, ut talium rerum libris legendis et intellegendis ullo modo reperiamur idonei, quo genere litterarum ex iis quae nobis pauca interpretata sunt, non dubito cuncta quae utiliter quaerere possumus contineri; fratribus autem non valeam resistere, iure quo eis servus factus sum flagitantibus, ut eorum in Christo laudabilibus studiis lingua ac stilo meo,—quas bigas in me charitas

It is evident that Augustine is defending himself against a criticism directed against his first two books of the *De Trinitate*. It was said that this new treatise was useless, since many excellent works on the subject already existed. Augustine was wrong, instead of reading these books and consulting them, to claim that he was producing an original work. These are the same charges that Jerome was to make a few years later against the *Enarrationes in Psalmos*.[34] Augustine retorts that his book is useful precisely because Greek theological literature has scarcely been translated into Latin or because these translations are not available. The little he has read in translation appeared to him quite interesting, and he would seriously take it into account, but he has no time to wait for more complete information. His ministry requires him to reply with urgency and in his own way to the questions submitted to him. I think, therefore, that shortly after the year 400 Augustine was as incapable of reading the Greek theologians as he was incapable in the year 394 of reading the Greek exegetes. His only sources were either excerpts whose translation he had commissioned, or rather the rare translations that he was able to secure (I am thinking, for instance, of Didymus' *De Spiritu sancto*, translated by Jerome, which Augustine had actually read).[35] We know besides that he had been very moved to see Jerome renounce his monumental plan to translate the Greek writers in order to devote his life to translating the Hebrew text of the Scriptures.[36]

---

agitat,—maxime serviam, egoque ipse multa quae nesciebam scribendo me didicisse confitear: non debet hic labor meus cuiquam pigro aut multum docto videri superfluus, cum multis impigris multisque indoctis, inter quos etiam mihi, non parva ex parte sit necessarius. Ex his igitur quae ab aliis de hac re scripta iam legimus, plurimum adminiculati et adiuti, ea quae de Trinitate, uno summo summeque bono Deo, pie quaeri et disseri posse arbitror, ipso exhortante quaerenda atque adiuvante disserenda suscepi: ut si alia non sunt huius modi scripta, sit quod habeant et legant qui voluerint et valuerint; si autem iam sunt, tanto facilius aliqua inveniantur, quanto talia plura esse potuerint." Contrary interpretations of this text may be found in Reuter, p. 171; Angus, p. 238; Henry, p. 135; Altaner, p. 26; etc.

34 See text quoted above, chap. 2 sec. 3 n. 229.

35 See below, sec. 3 n. 30. It is certain that the passing of the "I" to the "we" creates an ambiguity in this text. The most responsible commentator on this passage, Father Henry, *Plotin et l'Occident*, p. 135 n. 2, understands by "we" the Latin writers and concludes that Augustine did not have these works specially translated for him. I am quite prepared to believe this. But he is wrong, in my judgment, to conclude that in this passage there is no admission of ignorance on Augustine's part. Augustine includes himself here, as in the letter to Jerome, among the Latin writers. The expression "ex iis quae *nobis* pauca interpretata sunt, *non dubito* cuncta quae utiliter quaerere *possumus* contineri" proves that Augustine is personally reduced to *conjecture* the value of Greek literature from rare translations.

36 Text quoted above, n. 32. On this important change in Jerome's literary career, cf. above, p. 101.

We must then, unless I am mistaken, abandon Becker's theory that an examination of the Greek expressions used by Augustine in his works prior to the year 400 gave proof, in his view, of an extensive knowledge of Greek.[37] We must also reject Guilloux's and Salaville's gratuitous hypothesis that Augustine perfected his Greek between 391 and 396 through contact with his bishop Valerius.[38] The Greek expressions that Becker found in Augustine amount to a few elementary words, a few simple etymologies, a few technical terms, a few ecclesiastical Hellenisms.[39] Augustine memorizes them: a method, as he himself admits, employed by those who know no Greek.[40] If then he so rarely uses, and always without great benefit, the Greek text of the Septuagint that he nevertheless has before him, it is because he cannot do better.

Perhaps it was the scarcity of translations and the criticisms that his first books *De Trinitate* and his first *Enarrationes in Psalmos* had aroused that decided Augustine to turn to Greek. In fact, some fifteen years later, he declares that this language is the most beautiful in the world.[41] His progress in the language is attested by the publication of the *Enarrationes in Psalmos* and the *Tractatus in Ioannem* in 416, and the *Quaestiones* and *Locutiones in Heptateuchum* in 419, wherein his recourse to Greek is either frequent or customary. One catches Augustine off guard very often, giving what are virtually short courses in Greek on the cases,[42] genders,[43] numbers,[44] syntax,[45] semantics,[46]

[37] Becker, *Augustin*, p. 238, concludes his inquiry with the remark that Augustine knew Greek "nicht nur oberflächlich, sondern ziemlich genau." Alfaric, *L'évolution intellectuelle*, p. 18 n. 2, had already criticized this conclusion.

[38] Guilloux, "Saint Augustin savait-il le grec?" p. 80, and Salaville, "La connaissance du grec," p. 390.

[39] I borrow this excellent classification from Marrou, *Saint Augustin*, pp. 32–33, but I consider that it nearly exhausts St. Augustine's Greek vocabulary only for this first period. For instance, the Greek terms of the *De magistro* 15 (PL 32, 1203) are evidently borrowed from a Latin grammar handbook on the parts of speech. The investigation of C. I. Balmus, *Etude sur le style de s. Augustin dans les Confessions et la Cité de Dieu* (Paris 1930) 87–92, shows besides that Augustine did not introduce any Hellenism into the Latin language.

[40] *De Trinitate* 13.19.26 (PL 42, 1035): "sicut solent qui Graece nesciunt, Graeca verba tenere memoriter."

[41] *Quaest. in Heptat.* 7.37 (PL 34, 805): "in linguis gentium Graeca ita excellat, ut per hanc omnes decenter significentur." Cf. *De civ. Dei* 8.2 (PL 41, 225): "Quantum autem adtinet ad litteras Graecas, quae lingua inter ceteras gentium clarior habetur"; 8.10 (PL 41, 235): "Graeci, quorum lingua in gentibus praeeminet"; and 18.37 (PL 41, 597): "Quantum ad Graecos adtinet, in qua lingua huius saeculi maxime ferbuerunt."

[42] For example, *Enarr. in Ps.* 67.16 (PL 36, 827): "Ambiguus est autem in Graeco casus, utrum sit nominativus, an accusativus; quoniam in ea lingua *mons* neutri generis est, non masculini."

[43] For example, *Enarr. in Ps.* 118.15.56 (PL 37, 1543); *Tract. in Ioann.* 38.11 (PL 35, 1681): "Apud Graecos enim feminini generis est *principium*, sicut apud nos *lex* generis feminini est, quae apud illos est masculini; sicut *sapientia* et apud nos, et apud illos, generis

the breathings,[47] the numerical value of the letters of the Greek alphabet,[48] as though he were quite proud of his new knowledge. It is only now that he can make distinctions among the number of Greek synonyms.[49] He has even become sufficiently acquainted with the Greek of the Scriptures to collate and compare all the passages where the word πνοή is taken in different senses.[50] He considers the Latin language poor in comparison with Greek.[51]

feminini est. Consuetudo locutionis ideo per diversas linguas variat genera vocabulorum, quia in ipsis rebus non invenis sexum"; *Quaest. in Heptat.* 2.11 (*PL* 34, 600): "in Graeco autem in feminino genere dicitur αὐτῆς, masculino et neutro αὐτοῦ, et habet codex Graecus αὐτοῦ."

[44] For example, *Enarr. in Ps.* 67.14 (*PL* 36, 822): the Greek text mentions that *pennae* cannot be a genitive singular but does not specify whether it is a nominative or a vocative plural.

[45] *Enarr. in Ps.* 104.13 (*PL* 37, 1395): "Graeca autem locutio est: *nocere illos*, Latina vero: *nocere illis*" ; *Quaest. in Heptat.* 3.20 (*PL* 34, 681): "Sic enim Graecus dicit *non curo*: οὐ μέλει μοι."

[46] *Enarr. in Ps.* 123.5 (*PL* 37, 1644): "Primo quid est: *Forsitan pertransiit anima nostra*; quo modo potuerunt enim, Latini expresserunt quod Graeci dicunt ἄρα. Sic enim Graeca habent exemplaria: ἄρα; quia dubitantis verbum est, expressum est quidem dubitationis verbo, quod est *fortasse*; sed non omnino hoc est. Possumus illud verbo dicere minus quidem Latine coniuncto, sed apto ad intellegentias vestras. Quod Punici dicunt *iar*, non *lignum*, sed quando dubitant, hoc Graeci ἄρα: hoc Latini possunt vel solent dicere: *putas*, cum ita loquuntur: *Putas, evasi hoc?* Si forte dicatur: *forsitan evasi*, videtis quia non hoc sonat; sed quod dixi *putas*, usitate dicitur; Latine non ita dicitur. Et potui illud dicere, cum tracto vobis; saepe enim et verba non Latina dico, ut vos intellegatis. In Scriptura autem non potuit hoc poni, quod Latinum non esset; et deficiente Latinitate, positum est pro eo, quod non hoc sonaret." Note Augustine's effort to express very slight shades of meaning. Similarly with αἰών and αἰώνιον. Cf. *Ad Orosium contra Priscill. et Orig.* 5.5 (*PL* 42, 672), *Enarr. in Ps.* 78.21, 92.2, 104.8 (*PL* 36, 1020; 37, 1187 and 1383), and *Quaest. in Heptat.* 1.31 (*PL* 34, 556).

[47] *Quaest. in Heptat.* 1.162 (*PL* 34, 592): "Fallit eos enim verbum Graecum, quod eisdem litteris scribitur, sive *eius*, sive *suae*, sed accentus dispares sunt, et ab eis qui ista noverunt, in codicibus non contemnuntur; valent enim ad magnam discretionem. Quamvis et unam plus litteram habere posset, si esset *suae*, ut non esset αὐτοῦ, sed ἑαυτοῦ." On accents, cf. *Epist. ad Paulinum Nolanum* 149.4 (*PL* 33, 632) with reference to ὗς and υἱός: "diligentiora exemplaria per accentus notam eiusdem verbi Graeci ambiguitatem Graeco scribendi more dissolvunt."

[48] *Tract. in Ioann.* 10.12 (*PL* 35, 1473): "Ad litteras numeros computant Graeci. Quod nos facimus *a* litteram, ipsi lingua sua ponunt alpha α et vocatur alpha α *unum*." The rest of this demonstration shows that the total of the letters in Adam's name represents forty-six. Cf. *De haeresibus* 4 (*PL* 42, 26), a similar demonstration to show that the word ἄβρασαξ represents the number 365. This discussion belongs to Augustine alone: he added it to the text of Epiphanius' *Anacephalaeosis*.

[49] None of the examples quoted by Angus, *Sources*, pp. 234–244, is prior to this period.

[50] Cf. *De anima et eius origine* (c. 419) 14.19 (*PL* 44, 485) and *De civ. Dei* 13.24.3 (*PL* 41, 400–401).

[51] For example, *Quaest. in Heptat.* 2.116 (*PL* 39, 637): "Quod Latini *rationale* interpretati sunt, inopia linguae fecit. Graecus enim habet λόγιον, non λογικόν. Rationale autem

He ventures remarks on the comparative grammar of both languages.[52] In
addition, he feels qualified to appreciate the comparative value of the translators,[53] for his philosophy on the art of translation is diametrically opposed
to St. Jerome's philosophy. In his opinion, a translation wherein the Greek
word is rendered by a Latin word, when the Hellenism has been introduced
into the language, is an antiquated translation.[54] The most literal translation is the best, and may go, if necessary, as far as a barbarism,[55] provided
that it remains intelligible.[56] He himself occasionally ventures on a neo-

---

solemus appellare, quod Graeci dicunt λογικόν." Cf. 2.154 (PL 34, 649): Latin does not
have two verbs to translate ἐλεήσω and οἰκτειρήσω.

[52] *Enarr. in Ps.* 118.152 (PL 37, 1588): "Latinae autem linguae illud potius usitatum est,
ut *ab initio*, vel *initio* dicatur quod κατ᾽ ἀρχάς Graece, quasi pluraliter, sed adverbialiter
dicitur. Quale est cum dicimus: *alias hoc facio*, pluralem numerum feminini generis dicere
videmur, sed adverbium est et significat: *alio tempore*."

[53] *Epist. ad Paul. Nol.* (in 414) 149.12 (PL 33, 635): "Illa plane difficillime discernuntur,
ubi ad Timotheum scribens ait: *Obsecro itaque primum omnium fieri obsecrationes, orationes,
interpellationes, gratiarum actiones* [I Tim. 2.1]. Secundum Graecum enim eloquium dis-
cernenda sunt: nam nostri interpretes vix reperiuntur, qui ea diligenter et scienter transferre curaverint."

[54] *Sermo* 319.3 (PL 38, 1441): "*Ubi ego sum, illic et minister meus* [Ioann. 12.26]. Graecum
codicem legite et *diaconum* invenietis. Quod enim interpretatus est Latinus: *minister,*
Graecus habet: *diaconus*; quia vere *diaconus* Graece, *minister* est Latine, quo modo *martyr*
Graece, *testis* Latine, *apostolus* Graece, *missus* Latine. Sed iam consuevimus nominibus
Graecis uti pro Latinis." Cf. *Contra duas epistulas Pelagianorum* 1.16.32 (PL 44, 564) regarding Adam's and Eve's clothing when they were driven out of Paradise: "Neque enim
sibi tunicas, ut totum corpus tegerent post peccatum, sed succinctoria consuerunt, quae
non nulli interpretes nostri minus diligentes *tegmina* interpretati sunt. Quod quidem
verum est: sed generale nomen est *tegmen*, quo indumentum et operimentum omne
possit intellegi. Et ideo debuit ambiguitas evitari, ut quem ad modum Graecus περιζώ-
ματα posuit, quibus non teguntur nisi pudendae corporis partes, sic et Latinus aut ipsum
Graecum poneret, quia et ipso consuetudo iam utitur pro Latino, vel sicut quidam *succinctoria* vel sicut alii melius *campestria* nominarunt."

[55] *Enarr. in Ps.* 50.16 (PL 36, 597): "*Erue me de sanguinibus, Deus, Deus salutis meae.*
Expressit Latinus interpres verbo minus Latino proprietatem tamen ex Graeco. Nam
omnes novimus Latine non dici *sanguines* nec *sanguina*; tamen quia ita Graecus posuit
plurali numero, non sine causa, nisi quia hoc invenit in prima lingua Hebraea, maluit pius
interpres minus Latine aliquid dicere, quam minus proprie"; *In Ps.* 118.13.43 (PL 37,
1537): "Sequitur: *quia in iudiciis tuis speravi*, vel sicut de Graeco quidam diligentius expressit: *superspernavi*: quod verbum, etsi minus usitate compositum est, tamen implet
veritatis interpretandae necessitatem"; *In Ps.* 118.23.3 (PL 37, 1568): "Non nulli uno
verbo volentes dicere quod uno verbo in Graeco positum est, *haereditavi* interpretati
sunt. Quod, etsi Latinum esse posset, magis significaret eum qui dedit haereditatem quam
eum qui accepit."

[56] *Enarr. in Ps.* 104.12 (PL 37, 1395): "Non nulli autem codices habent, non *paucissimi
et incolae*, sed *paucissimos et incolas*. Ubi apparet eos qui ista ita interpretati sunt, Graecam
fuisse locutionem secutos, quae transferri non potest in Latinum, nisi cum ea absurditate
quae ferri omnino non possit. Quod enim totam ipsam locutionem transferre conemur,
dicturi sumus: *In eo esse illos numero brevi paucissimos et incolas in ea*. Quod autem ait

logism.[57] Or, if he cannot find the Latin equivalent of a Greek word that has not yet entered the language, he collects the synonyms that allow him to determine the more essential meaning.[58] If no translator has found the precise term, he does not hesitate to offer one.[59] In short, on occasion, he can explain and correct a mistake of the translators through textual criticism of the Greek manuscripts.[60]

It will be granted that here we are far from Augustine's first gropings in Greek that we have hitherto examined. This practice of resorting to Greek coincides remarkably with the method advocated in the *De doctrina Christiana* for the study of the Holy Scriptures. According to this method, the Latin translations constitute the starting point for the exegete. As they do not always agree, the Greek or the Hebrew alone will allow him to discriminate between the translators and to correct the translator who gives a wrong meaning as a result of the *ambiguitas* of the Greek language[61] or who takes one word for another.[62] Resorting to Greek will also help to clarify the Latin translation when it presents an ambiguity[63] that the context or a

---

Graecus: *in eo esse illos,* hoc est Latine: *cum essent,* quod verbum non potest casus accusativus sequi, sed nominativus. Quis enim dicat: *Cum essent paucissimos?* Sed: *cum essent paucissimi.*"

[57] *De civ. Dei* 14.9.4 (*PL* 41, 415): "illa quae ἀπάθεια Graece dicitur, quae, si Latine posset, *impassibilitas* diceretur."

[58] *De Trinitate* 4.2.4 (*PL* 42, 889): "Haec enim congruentia, sive convenientia, vel concinentia, vel consonantia, vel si quid commodius dicitur, quod unum est ad duo, in omni compaginatione vel si melius dicitur coaptatione creaturae, valet plurimum. Hanc enim coaptationem, sicut mihi nunc occurrit dicere, quam Graeci ἁρμονίαν vocant"; *Quaest. in Heptat.* 2.47 (*PL* 34, 610): "*Excepto instructu,* vel *censu,* vel si quo alio verbo melius interpretatur ἀποσκευή."

[59] *Enarr. in Ps.* 118.26.121 (*PL* 37, 1577): "Nam etiam quidam codices habent: *Ne tradas me persequentibus*; quod enim Graece dictum est ἀντιδικοῦσι, quidam interpretati sunt *nocentibus,* quidam *persequentibus,* quidam *calumniantibus.* Miror autem omnium quos in promptu habere potui codicum nusquam me legisse *adversantibus,* cum sine controversia quod Graece ἀντίδικος, hoc Latine *adversarius* appelletur."

[60] *Quaest. in Heptat.* 3.90 (*PL* 34, 715): the translation *confirmationem* is explained by a confusion on the part of the Greek copyists between βεβήλωσις and βεβαίωσις.

[61] *De doctrina Christiana* 2.11.16 (*PL* 34, 42): "Et Latinae quidem linguae homines, quos nunc instruendos suscepimus, duabus aliis ad Scripturarum divinarum cognitionem opus habent, Hebraea scilicet et Graeca, ut ad exemplaria praecedentia recurratur, si quam dubitationem attulerit Latinorum interpretum infinita varietas"; Augustine gives as an example of a wrong meaning, *De doctrina Christiana* 2.12.17 (*PL* 34, 43), those who translated ὀξύς by *acutus* and not *velox,* as required by the context.

[62] *Ibid.,* 2.12.17. For example, those who translated μοσχεύματα as *vitulamina* (on account of μόσχος: *vitulus*) and not as *plantationes.*

[63] *Ibid.,* 3.3.7 (*PL* 34, 68): "Si tantum dixisset *quae praedico vobis* neque subiunxisset *sicut praedixi,* non nisi ad codicem praecedentis linguae recurrendum esset, ut cognosceremus utrum in eo quod dixit *praedico,* producenda an corripienda esset media syllaba: nunc autem manifestum est producendam esse; non enim ait *sicut praedicavi,* sed *sicut praedixi.*"

comparison of the translators is not sufficient to resolve.[64] If one is ignorant of Greek, let him then adhere to the most literal translators. Those who are concerned with thought more than with the words and who, in their fear of falling into a solecism or a barbarism, render a Greek expression by a Latin expression run the risk of distorting the holy writer's thought.[65] Purism is misplaced selfishness in a Christian.[66] A lucid translation in the vulgar tongue is preferable to an elegant but obscure translation.[67] Naturally, it is better, if possible, to check it with the Greek, either by questioning those who speak Greek or by learning it oneself.[68]

I can scarcely believe that this theory about resorting to Greek was propounded by Augustine in the year 397, as is commonly said. How could he, at this time, when he was ignorant of Greek as we have seen him to be, elaborate this method? Unless he borrowed it entirely, with examples, from a previous writer, it would be very unlikely for him to have such a precise idea of exegetical work before having had any experience of it. In all probability, he also had a theory of resorting to Hebrew, although he did not know this language. But Dom De Bruyne has shown[69] that the *De doctrina*

---

[64] Cf. *ibid.*, 3.4.8 (*PL* 34, 68): "Rarissime igitur et difficillime inveniri potest ambiguitas in propriis verbis, quantum ad libros divinarum Scripturarum spectat, quam non aut circumstantia ipsa sermonis qua cognoscitur scriptorum intentio, sed interpretum conlatio, aut praecedentis linguae solvat inspectio."

[65] *Ibid.*, 2.13.19 (*PL* 34, 44): "Aut linguarum illarum, ex quibus in Latinam Scriptura pervenit, petenda cognitio est, aut habendae interpretationes eorum qui se verbis nimis obstrinxerunt, non quia sufficiunt, sed ut ex eis veritas vel error detegatur aliorum, qui non magis verba quam sententias interpretando sequi maluerunt. Nam non solum verba singula, sed etiam locutiones saepe transferuntur, quae omnino in Latinae linguae usum, si quis consuetudinem veterum qui Latine locuti sunt, tenere voluerit, transire non possunt." See also the rest of the chapter.

[66] *Ibid.*, 2.13.20 (*PL* 34, 44): "eo magis inde offenduntur homines, quo infirmiores sunt; et eo sunt infirmiores, quo doctiores videri volunt, non rerum scientia qua aedificamur, sed signorum qua non inflari omnino difficile est."

[67] *Ibid.*, 3.3.7 (*PL* 34, 68): "Unde plerumque loquendi consuetudo vulgaris utilior est significandis rebus, quam integritas litterata. Mallem quippe cum barbarismo dici: non est *absconditum a te ossum meum* [instead of *os*, Ps. 138.15], quam ut ideo esset minus apertum, quia magis Latinum est." Inversely, the literal translation *sapientius est hominum* is not accepted by Augustine, *De doct. Christ.* 2.13.20 (*PL* 34, 45), because this Greek turn of phrase is unintelligible to speakers of Latin.

[68] *Ibid.*, 2.14.21 (*PL* 34, 45): "quae, si ex alienis linguis, veniunt, aut quaerenda sunt ab earum linguarum hominibus, aut eaedem linguae, si et otium est et ingenium, ediscendae, aut plurium interpretum consulenda conlatio est." Marrou, *Saint Augustin*, p. 440, is mistaken, in my view, when he takes *earum linguarum hominibus* to mean the *scholars*. I think it is simply a matter of questioning Greeks or Jews, as St. Augustine so often did.

[69] De Bruyne, "L'Itala de s. Augustin," *RB* 30 (1913) 301ff, puts this revision about the year 427 and notes traces of it in precisely the passage that concerns us, 2.16–22. His comments are still valuable, in my opinion, despite the harsh criticisms of F. Cavallera, "Saint Augustin et le texte biblique de l'Itala," *Bulletin de litt. ecclés.* (1915/1916) 420–428,

Christiana was completely revised, and not merely finished, for publication.[70] It is therefore more simple to assume that the pages dealing with the theory of consultation of the Greek were not published before the years 416/419. At this date, Augustine decided to learn Greek and made notable progress in the language, but he had not yet mastered it. He happened to suggest a translation without confirming it: is ἀδολεσχῆσαι taken, in a particular passage in Genesis, in a laudatory or depreciatory sense? Augustine states his feeling about it, but leaves it to more learned scholars to decide.[71] Elsewhere, on the special meaning of the word Θεός without the article, he refers to those who know Greek.[72] Is he worried about the etymology of the term *Paschal*? He has certainly read in the commentators that *Pascha* signifies *Transitus* in Hebrew, but the word reminds him of πάσχειν. To clear up any doubt, he asks some Greeks. The test is decisive and shows his mistake.[73] Finally, in

---

even if we do not accept De Bruyne's conclusions on the *Itala*. When Cavallera, p. 423, denies that Augustine ever revised a single work of his because "the work was already in the hands of the public," this argument is invalid for the first draft of the *De doctrina Christiana*, which had not been published.

[70] Augustine's expression, *Retractationes* 2.4.1 (PL 34, 631): "Libros de doctrina Christiana, cum imperfectos comperissem, perficere malui ... Complevi ergo tertium... Addidi etiam novissimum librum," does not appear to me necessarily to contradict this interpretation. Cf. Schanz, vol. 4, 2, p. 446.

[71] *Quaest. in Heptat.* 1.69 (PL 34, 565): "Quod scriptum est: *et exiit Isaac exerceri in campo a meridie* [Gen. 24.63]; qui verbum de hac re Graecum nesciunt, exercitationem corporis putant. Scriptum est autem Graece ἀδολεσχῆσαι: ἀδολεσχεῖν vero ad animi exercitationem pertinet et saepe vitio deputatur; more tamen Scripturarum plerumque in bono ponitur. Pro isto verbo quidam interpretati sunt *exercitationem*, quidam *garrulitatem*, quasi *verbositatem*, quae in bono, quantum ad Latinum eloquium pertinet, vix aut numquam invenitur; sed ut dixi in Scripturis plerumque in bono dicitur; et videtur mihi significare animi affectum studiosissime aliquid cogitantis cum delectatione cogitationis, nisi aliud sentiunt qui haec verba Graeca melius intellegunt."

[72] *Ibid.*, 1.105 (PL 34, 575): "*Propter hoc vidi faciem tuam quem ad modum cum videt aliquis faciem Dei* [Gen. 33.10] ... sine articulo in Graeco dictum est; quo articulo evidentissime solet veri Dei unius fieri significatio. Non enim dixit πρόσωπον τοῦ Θεοῦ, sed dixit πρόσωπον Θεοῦ: facile autem hoc intellegunt, qua distantia dicatur, qui Graecorum eloquium audire atque intellegere solent."

[73] *Enarr. in Ps.* 140.25 (PL 37, 1832): "Secundum Graecam locutionem *Pascha* videtur *passionem* significare; πάσχειν enim *pati* dicitur; secundum Hebraeam linguam, sicut interpretati sunt qui noverunt, Pascha *Transitus* interpretatur. Nam et si interrogetis bene Graecos, negant Graecum esse Pascha. Sonat ibi quidem πάσχειν, id est *pati*, sed non solet sic deflecti: *passio* enim πάθος Graece dicitur, non *pascha*." It is true that Augustine had made this inquiry before 400, for cf. *Epist. ad Ianuarium* 55.2 (PL 33, 205): "Pascha ... non Graecum, sicut vulgo videri solet, sed Hebraeum esse dicunt qui linguam utramque noverunt." But the relation between *Pascha* and πάσχειν strikes him again in the *Tract. in Ioann.* 55.1 (PL 35, 1784): "*Pascha*, fratres, non sicut quidam existimant, Graecum nomen est, sed Hebraeum; opportunissime tamen occurrit in hoc nomine quaedam congruentia utrarumque linguarum."

exceptional cases, he also fails to comprehend some Greek construction.[74] It would be very difficult for him, in 416, despite his desire to make himself understood, to write in Greek to John of Jerusalem.[75] He knows then at this time enough Greek to verify the Latin renderings with the aid of the Septuagint, but this knowledge is largely a bookish knowledge. He uses abundantly both grammars and lexica, for he does not have a fluent knowledge of the language and does not have sufficient comprehension of the Greek to dispense, in difficult cases, with consulting those who speak it.[76]

The Pelagian controversy was destined to oblige Augustine to read a large number of Greek texts that were to make his knowledge of the language more perfect. In fact, his attitude toward the Pelagians is that of a master who resolves difficulties on the authority of the Greek text. In the *Contra Iulianum*, he now aligns himself with those who know Greek,[77] and gravely censures

---

[74] *Locut. in Heptat.* 2.24 (*PL* 34, 512). By mistake he combines τὰ ἀλυσιδωτά with what precedes and explains this unusual construction in a perfunctory way. Cf. Angus, *Sources*, p. 253. Augustine also suggests false etymologies; for example, *Quaest. in Heptat.* 1.91 (*PL* 34, 571): "Unde videtur et in Graeca lingua resonare, quod dicunt, τάχα velut ab eo quod est τύχη." But this is no proof of ignorance, for the greatest scholars in antiquity are also prolific in fanciful etymologies.

[75] *Epist. ad Ioann. Hieros.* 179.5 (*PL* 33, 775): "Quid pluribus agam apud sanctitatem vestram? Quandoquidem me onerosum sentio, maxime quia per interpretem audis litteras meas."

[76] I have hitherto not explained why the *Tract. in Ioann.* and the *X Tract. in Epist. Ioann. ad Parthos* resort less frequently to Greek than the *Enarr. in Ps.* or the *Quaest. in Gen.*, which are contemporary. Was it a lack of precision in the Augustinian method? Possibly. Was it not especially the fact that these homilies were addressed not to the clergy but to a wide public, the large majority of whom did not know the first word of Greek? This is Comeau's opinion, *Saint Augustin exégète*, pp. 58–69, and the didactic tone assumed by Augustine will be observed in his explanation that *martyr* means *testis*, *In Epist. Ioann. ad Parthos tract.* 1.2 (*PL* 35, 1979): "Forte aliqui fratrum nesciunt, qui Graece non norunt, quod sint *testes* Graece: et usitatum nomen est omnibus et religiosum; quos enim *testes* Latine dicimus, Graece *martyres* sunt." It seems to me that in our own days many persons who do not know Greek still know the meaning of the word *martyr*, at least if they have pursued the elementary courses in the catechism. In the context itself of the *Enarr. in Ps.* does not the very irregular frequency of resorting to Greek vary according to the date and to the question of whether each *Enarratio* was originally a sermon or not? Thus the *Enarratio in Ps.* 118, which was certainly a written treatise, and one of the last in date (cf. Possidius *Indiculus*, *PL* 46, 12: "Reliqui omnes, excepto centesimo decimo octavo, in populo disputati sunt"), is one of those where recourse to Greek was most frequent. Similarly with the *Enarr. in Ps.* 67, 71, and 77 dictated in 415; cf. *Epist. ad Evodium* 169.1 (*PL* 33, 743) and B. Capelle, "Le texte du Psautier latin en Afrique," *Collectanea Biblica Latina* 4 (Rome 1913) 158. On the other hand, recourse to Greek is extremely rare in Augustine's *Sermons*.

[77] *Contra Iulianum* 5.2.7 (*PL* 44, 785): "In eo vero quod aisti: Si illi interpretationi, quae *perizomata*, id est *praecinctoria*, posuit, favetur, latera magis dicam tecta fuisse, quam femora, primum doleo sic te abuti eorum ignorantia qui Graece nesciunt, ut eorum qui sciunt iudicium reveritus non sis."

the wrong meanings in Julian,[78] *Graecorum consideratione verborum*. That same year, he entitles, with a Greek word, *Enchiridion*, his treatise *De fide, spe et charitate*. In 426/427, the perusal of his youthful works for his *Retractationes* shows him the mistakes that his ignorance of Greek had then made him commit. In his *De moribus ecclesiae catholicae* (388/389), he commented on several passages of Scripture in a corrupt text because he did not refer to the Greek manuscripts and was still ignorant of the language of Scripture.[79] In certain passages of the *De sermone Domini in monte*,[80] the *Contra epistulam Parmeniani* (composed in 400),[81] the *De Genesi ad litteram*,[82] he took no account of the Greek text, which would have allowed him to correct a defective translation. In conclusion, we see Augustine in his extreme old age inserting in his prose a Greek turn to express a philosophical notion that is inadequately rendered in Latin.[83] This is not all. He now translates directly from the Greek the extracts from the authors that he has just read. He assumes the same role of Hellenist for the African clergy and, at the express request of Quodvultdeus, he agrees to translate in its entirety a short work by Epiphanius.[84]

An examination of these translations gives us an idea of the knowledge of Greek that Augustine acquired in his old age, after long efforts for years. He copies the Greek word rather than seek its equivalent in the Latin language: e.g. χειρόγραφος, *chirographus*. He even takes care to reproduce the etymologies: προσετάχθης, *ordinatus es*.[85] His translation of Epiphanius is also literal, but it is not any more adequate. It reveals actually wrong meanings, and one feels that Augustine has often vainly sought for the equivalent of the Greek expression.[86]

These belated attempts show us that Augustinian literalism is not merely a

---

[78] *Ibid.*, 4.16.80 (*PL* 44, 780). See other examples below, p. 205.

[79] *Retract.* 1.7.2–3 (*PL* 32, 592): "Mendositas nostri codicis me fefellit minus memorem Scripturarum, in quibus nondum adsuetus eram . . . Has autem quattuor virtutes in eodem libro Sapientiae suis nominibus appellatas, sicut a Graecis vocantur, longe postea repperimus in codicibus Graecis."

[80] *Ibid.*, 1.19.4 (*PL* 32, 615).

[81] *Ibid.*, 2.17 (*PL* 32, 637).

[82] *Ibid.*, 2.24.2 (*PL* 32, 640).

[83] *Opus imperf. contra Iulianum* 5.44 (*PL* 45, 1481): "Fecit ergo Deus cuncta de nihilo, id est omnia quae ut essent fecit, si eorum originem primam respiciamus, ex his quae non erant fecit: hoc Graeci dicunt: ἐξ οὐκ ὄντων."

[84] See below, pp. 206–207.

[85] The texts for these examples may be found below, sec. 3 nn. 42 and 47.

[86] Here are some examples: *De haeresibus* 3 (*PL* 42, 26) = Epiphanius *Anacephalaiosis* (*PG* 42, 856 B): "(Saturninus) . . . mundum solos angelos septem praeter *conscientiam* Dei Patris fecisse dicebat." *Sententiam*, not *conscientiam*, would have been expected, to translate γνώμην. *De haer.* 42 (*PL* 42, 33) = Epiphanius *Anaceph.* (*PG* 42, 868 A): "*Turpis* autem sunt *operationis* (Origeniani); isti sunt *inenarrabilia* facientes" = αἰσχροποιοὶ δὲ οὗτοί εἰσιν, ἀρρητοποιοῦντες. The proper term is *nefanda*, and *turpis operationis* is an awkward expression.

theory applicable to the Scriptures. It implies an inherent inability in Augustine, for all his laboriously acquired knowledge of Greek, to achieve Jerome's elegance. Greek always remained for him a language learned from books.[87] How then was Augustine able to rectify this omission? Must it be concluded, with Marrou, that "Augustine's intellectual culture is entirely a culture in the Latin language?"[88] Had he just an indirect and superficial knowledge of Greek literature, whether pagan or ecclesiastical?

2. AUGUSTINE AND GREEK PAGAN CULTURE

Gustave Combès has already shown Augustine's slight acquaintance with the Greek classics,[1] but most frequently without specifying his actual sources. Augustine read Homer in his classes with the Greek *grammaticus* without acquiring any taste for the text.[2] One episode in the *Iliad*, where Poseidon foretells to Aeneas the future of his race,[3] another episode in the *Odyssey*, where Ulysses' dog recognizes its master,[4] are probably the only recollections that his memory retained, unless of course he borrowed them from some commentator on Vergil.[5] He also quotes two lines from Homer relating to divination, in the translation that Cicero had made,[6] and charges him,

---

[87] The text of *Sermo* 225.3.3 (*PL* 38, 1097): "Inveni te Latinum, Latinum tibi proferendum est verbum. Si autem Graecus esses, Graece tibi loqui deberem et proferre ad te verbum Graecum. Illud verbum in corde nec Latinum est, nec Graecum: prorsus antecedit linguas istas quod est in corde meo," does not at all prove, as Reuter suggests, *Augustinische Studien*, p. 180, that Augustine spoke Greek when necessary. We find in *Sermo* 288.3 (*PL* 38, 1305) the same reasoning applied to Latin, Greek, Punic, Hebrew, Egyptian, Indian. Is it necessary to conclude that Augustine spoke all these languages? It is, however, not more correct to say with Altaner, "Augustinus," p. 38, that the contrary to fact conditions, *esses, deberem*, indicate that Augustine could not speak Greek. These unreal conditions merely signify that the protasis, "Si Graecus esses," is contrary to fact. On the other hand, Gunnar Rudberg, "Till Augustinus' ortografi," *Eranos* 25 (1927) 222–229, notes that Augustine was not in the least concerned, in the course of his career, with Greek orthography.

[88] Marrou, *Saint Augustin*, p. 37.

[1] Combès, *Saint Augustin*, pp. 12ff.

[2] *Conf.* 1.14.23, p. 19 Lab.: "Nam et Homerus peritus texere tales fabellas et dulcissime vanus est et mihi tamen vanus erat puero."

[3] *Il.* 20.303; cf. *De civ. Dei* 3.2 (*PL* 41, 80): "Nam hunc [Neptunum] Homerus de stirpe Aeneae . . . inducit magnum aliquid divinantem."

[4] *Od.* 17.291ff; cf. *De quant. animae* 26.50 and 28.54 (*PL* 32, 1064 and 1066): "Sciebat enim, ut opinor, dominum suum canis, quem post viginti annos recognovisse perhibetur," and *De musica* 1.4.8 (*PL* 32, 1087): "Et canis heroem dominum, iam suis hominibus oblitum, recognovisse praedicatur"; Cicero *Epist. ad fam.* 1.10 refers to the same passage.

[5] With regard to the first episode, Augustine quotes Vergil *Aen.* 5.810; with reference to the second, *Georg.* 3.316.

[6] *Od.* 18.136–137; cf. *De civ. Dei* 5.8 (*PL* 41, 148). This Ciceronian passage is lost.

following the *Tusculanae disputationes*, with having attributed human desires to the gods.[7] He knows from Varro that Homer calls the planet Venus *Hesperos*.[8] Pliny the Elder taught him that Homer complained that men had lost their giant stature.[9] A Neoplatonist informs him that Homer sometimes calls the gods *daemones*.[10] Of the Homeric poems, therefore, he has neither any direct knowledge nor a general comprehension, and probably read in his youth only rare excerpts. He knows the other Greek poets even less well. Varro tells him that Hesiod gave the Muses[11] their names: but Orpheus, Linus, Musaeus,[12] Asclepiades, Archilochus, and Sappho are to him mere empty names.[13] He knows that Aesop is a fabulist[14] and that Socrates deigned to versify some of his pieces, but he is probably acquainted, like St. Jerome,[15] with the Aesopic fables only through the Latin fabulists.[16] Without knowing the Greek theater,[17] Augustine, on Cicero's word,[18] scorns it. He has read neither the classical Greek historians[19] nor the orators. From Cicero

---

[7] *Conf.* 1.16.25, p. 21 Lab., and *De civ. Dei* 4.26 (*PL* 41, 132), quoting *Tusc.* 1.26.56.

[8] *De civ. Dei* 21.8.2 (*PL* 41, 720), quoting Varro *De gente populi Romani*.

[9] *De civ. Dei* 15.9 (*PL* 41, 448), quoting Pliny *Nat. hist.* 7.16.

[10] *De civ. Dei* 9.1 (*PL* 41, 256): "Illi qui deos quosdam bonos, quosdam malos esse, dixerunt, daemones quoque appellaverunt nomine deorum, quamquam et deos, sed rarius, nomine daemonum; ita ut ipsum Iovem, quem volunt esse regem ac principem ceterorum, ab Homero fateantur daemonem nuncupatum." Cf. Plutarch *De defectu oraculorum* 10, p. 415 B (quoted by Eusebius *Praep. Evang.* 5, *PG* 21, 320 A): Ἑλλήνων δὲ Ὅμηρος μὲν ἔτι φαίνεται κοινῶς ἀμφοτέροις χρώμενος τοῖς ὀνόμασι, καὶ τοὺς θεοὺς ἔστιν ὅτε δαίμονας προσαγορεύων.

[11] *De doctr. Christ.* 2.17.27 (*PL* 34, 49).

[12] *De civ. Dei* 18.14 and 37 (*PL* 41, 572 and 597).

[13] *De musica* 2.7.14 (*PL* 32, 1107): "Quem versum dici voluit Asclepiades nescio qui, aut Archilochus, poetae scilicet veteres, aut Sappho poetria, et ceteri quorum etiam nominibus versuum genera vocantur, quae primi animadvertentes cecinerunt."

[14] *Contra Acad.* 2.3.7 (*PL* 32, 922): "Quam totam fabulam (nam subito Aesopus factus sum) . . ." and *Contra mendacium* 13.28 (*PL* 40, 538): "unde et Aesopi tales fabulas ad eum finem relatas nullus tam ineruditus fuit, qui putaret appellanda mendacia."

[15] Jerome *Epist.* 108.15 (*PL* 22, 890): "cornicem Aesopi alienis coloribus adornare," and *Epist.* 29.7 (*PL* 22, 441): "iuxta Aesopici canis fabulam, dum magna sectamur, etiam minora perdentes." Cf. Phaedrus *Fabulae* 1.3 and 4.

[16] *De consensu Evangelistarum* 1.7.11 (*PL* 34, 1048): "Socrates . . . Aesopi fabulas pauculis versibus persecutus est." Cf. Avianus *Fabulae, prol. ad Theodosium*: "Huius ergo materiae ducem nobis Aesopum noveris . . . Verum has pro exemplo fabulas et Socrates divinis operibus indidit," from Plato *Phaedo* 60d.

[17] Text quoted above, sec. 1 n. 25.

[18] *De civ. Dei* 2.9 and 11 (*PL*, 41, 53 and 55), quoting Cicero *De re publica* 4. Plutarch's text, quoted by Combès, *Saint Augustin*, p. 12, is not then necessarily the actual source.

[19] The story of the legend of Arion (*De civ. Dei* 1.14), the anecdotes relating to the death of Cato (*De civ. Dei* 1.24), Marius and Sulla (*De civ. Dei* 3.27), and Cato the Younger (*De civ. Dei* 5.12.4) are in a sense in the public domain in Latin literature. It is therefore futile to think, as Combès does, *Saint Augustin*, p. 13, that Augustine sought them out in Herodotus or Plutarch!

alone he discovered that Demosthenes made pronunciation the basis of rhetoric.[20] To him, as to St. Jerome, Cicero made available *On the Crown*,[21] which he had translated and published following his *De optimo genere oratorum.*[22]

It was also Cicero who supplied St. Augustine with the most lucid information on ancient Greek philosophy. Furthermore, Augustine studied him very conscientiously. The *De natura deorum* furnished Augustine with information on Anaximenes, Anaximander, Anaxagoras, Diogenes of Apollonia, Democritus, Euhemerus.[23] The *De finibus* enlightened him on the succession of the philosophers Arcesilaus, Polemon, Xenocrates.[24] From the *Tusculanae disputationes* he learned about Pythagoras[25] and Dinomachus;[26] and from the *De fato*, about Posidonius.[27] It was also through Cicero that he became acquainted with the astronomers Aratus and Eudoxus[28] and probably the geometrician Archimedes,[29] for his scientific culture virtually seems to be the reading of a few very elementary Latin treatises.[30]

Varro supplies Augustine with valuable additional information on

[20] *Epist. ad Dioscorum* 118.3.22 (*PL* 33, 442). Cf. Cicero *De oratore* 1.61.260.

[21] *Contra Cresconium* 2.1.2 (*PL* 43, 468): "Si enim Demosthenes clarissimus oratorum, quibus verborum tanta fuit cura, quanta rerum auctoribus nostris, cum tamen ei non nullam locutionis insolentiam obiecisset Aeschines, negavit ille in eo positas esse fortunas Graeciae, illone an illo verbo usus fuerit, et huc an illuc manum porrexerit, quanto minus nos laborare debemus de regulis derivandorum nominum?"

[22] See above, chap. 2 sec. 2 n. 14.

[23] On the first four, cf. *Conf.* 10.6.9, p. 246 Lab., *Epist. ad Dioscorum* 118.23–25 (*PL* 33, 443–444), *Contra Iulianum* 4.75 (*PL* 44, 776–777), and Cicero *De natura deorum* 1.10–12. On Democritus, cf. *Contra Acad.* 3.10.23 (*PL* 32, 945), *Epist.* 118.4.28–29, and Cicero *De nat. deor.* 1.12 and 25–26. On Euhemerus, cf. *De cons. Evang.* 1.23.32 (*PL* 34, 1056) and *De civ. Dei* 7.27 (*PL* 41, 217) and Cicero *De nat. deor.* 1.42.

[24] On Arcesilaus, Polemon, Xenocrates, cf. *Epist.* 118.3.16 and 144.2 (*PL* 33, 440 and 591), *Contra Iulianum* 1.4.12 (*PL* 44, 647), and Cicero *De finibus* 5.31, *Acad.* 2.42.

[25] Cf. *Epist.* 137.3.12 (*PL* 33, 521) and *Tusc.* 1.16 on Pythagoras, disciple of Pherecydes; *Op. imperf. contra Iulianum* 5.1 (*PL* 45, 1432) and *Tusc.* 1.25 on the esteem in which Pythagoras held the inventor of the names of objects; in addition, Augustine *Contra Iulianum* 5.5.23 (*PL* 44, 797) quotes an anecdote from Cicero's lost *De consiliis* about the intoxicated young men who were calmed by the solemn music that Pythagoras called for.

[26] Cf. *Contra Iulian.* 5.15.76 (*PL* 44, 777) and Cicero *Tusc.* 5.30, *De finibus* 5.8.

[27] Cf. *De civ. Dei* 5.2 and 5 (*PL* 41, 142 and 145) and Cicero *De fato* 3.

[28] *De civ. Dei* 16.23 (*PL* 41, 500); cf. Cicero *De re publica* 1.14.

[29] *De utilitate credendi* 6.13 (*PL* 42, 74); Archimedes is often mentioned by Cicero.

[30] Cf. Marrou, *Saint Augustin*, p. 253 n. 1 and p. 266 n. 1. A large number of other references made by Augustine to the Epicureans appear in Alfaric, *L'évolution intellectuelle*, p. 232 n. 4, and Combès, *Saint Augustin*, p. 15. References to the Sceptics too occur in Alfaric, pp. 349–352, and Combès, p. 16. I do not stress this point, since Cicero's considerable influence on Augustinian thought is universally recognized and sufficiently proved.

Pythagoras,[31] Xenophanes,[32] Heraclitus,[33] Adrastus, and Dio;[34] and it was in all likelihood in Varro that he read Alexander the Great's apocryphal letter to his mother Olympias, in which was described the Egyptian priest Leo's view on the human origin of the gods.[35] In conclusion, he found in Cornelius Nepos a particular item on Crates;[36] in Seneca, a quotation from Straton;[37] in Aulus Gellius, an analysis of Epictetus' *Enchiridion*.[38]

It is true that Augustine states that he had read, at the age of about twenty, Aristotle's *Categories*,[39] which were available in the translation by Marius Victorinus,[40] but he does not appear to have read any other work of his.[41] He once quotes Aristotle from Cicero's *Hortensius*[42] and he knows only from Cicero that Aristotle calls the soul the fifth element.[43] In other respects, he considers his theories obscure[44] and charges the Pelagians with imitating the *Categories*[45] in their dialectical passion.

Did he read Plato? The reading in a number of manuscripts of the *De beata vita*, "lectis Platonis paucissimis libris," for a long time gave this impression, and Rolfes still maintained it not long since.[46] But Father Henry proved that

---

[31] *De ordine* 2.20.54 (*PL* 32, 1020) and *De civ. Dei* 7.35 (*PL* 41, 223), where Varro is quoted.

[32] *De civ. Dei* 7.17 (*PL* 41, 208).

[33] *Ibid.*, 6.5.2 (*PL* 41, 181).

[34] *Ibid.*, 21.8.2 (*PL* 41, 720).

[35] *De cons. Evang.* 1.23.33 (*PL* 34, 1057) and *De civ. Dei* 8.5 and 27; 12.10.2 (*PL* 41: 229, 256, 358) The Augustinian context lets it be assumed that Varro is the source. Now Aulus Gellius 13.4.2 clearly observes that this letter appeared in Varro.

[36] *Op. imperf. contra Iulian.* 4.43 (*PL* 45, 1362).

[37] *De civ. Dei* 6.10.1 (*PL* 41, 190).

[38] *Quaest. in Heptat.* 1.30 (*PL* 34, 556).

[39] *Conf.* 4.16.28, p. 86 Lab.

[40] Boemer, *Der lateinische Neuplatonismus*, pp. 87–96, has shown that Augustine had certainly read them in this translation.

[41] The references noted by Combès, *Saint Augustin*, pp. 14–15, to Aristotle's *De interpretatione*, *Topics*, and *De mundo* are of no value in proving that Augustine read these treatises. Marrou, *Saint Augustin*, p. 34 n. 7, already recognized this for the first two treatises, but allowed himself to be led into an error, n. 10, by Combès, in the matter of the third treatise. Combès says, p. 14, that Augustine wrongly attributes to Plato a passage in Aristotle's *De mundo*; but it is Combès, not Augustine, who is mistaken, for this passage (*Sermo* 241.8.8, *PL* 38, 1138) is a passage from the *Timaeus*, in Cicero's translation 11.16. On the other hand, Augustine certainly read the *De mundo*, but he does not regard it as a work of Aristotle's, for he quotes it, *De civ. Dei* 4.2 (*PL* 41, 113), not under Aristotle's name but under the name of Apuleius, the Latin adapter.

[42] *Contra Iulian.* 5.15.78 (*PL* 44, 778).

[43] *De civ. Dei* 22.11.2 (*PL* 41, 773). Cf. Cicero *Acad.* 1.7 and *Tusc.* 1.10.22 and Alfaric, *L'évolution intellectuelle*, p. 232 n. 2.

[44] *De utilitate credendi* 6.13 (*PL* 42, 74).

[45] *Contra Iulian.* 1.4.12, 2.10.37, 3.2.7, 5.14.51 (*PL* 44: 647, 700, 705, 812) and *Op. imperf. contra Iulian.* 2.51 (*PL* 45, 1163).

[46] Rolfes, "Hat Augustin Plato nicht gelesen?" (above, sec. 1 n. 6) 17–39.

this reading was corrupt and that the reading should be *Plotini*, not *Platonis*.[47] It seems nowadays to be accepted that Augustine did not have the Greek text of the *Dialogues* at his disposal.[48] On the other hand, before the year 400 he read the part of the *Timaeus* that Cicero had translated. In the *De consensu Evangelistarum* and the *De Trinitate* he quotes from it the definition of eternity.[49] He also quotes from it on three occasions the same passage on the address of the supreme deity to the gods that he has just created,[50] and he frequently returns to this chapter. The gods were created by God;[51] they in turn created mortal beings.[52] The universe and the gods, although having a beginning, will not have an end.[53] The creation of mortals is indispensable to the perfection of the universe.[54] He also quotes from the Ciceronian translation two passages relating to the creation of the world[55] and probably borrows from it the notion that the universe is an animal[56] and that God rejoices in the beauty of creation.[57] I nowhere find that Augustine made use of

---

[47] *De beata vita* 1.4 (*PL* 32, 961). Cf. Henry, *Plotin et l'Occident*, pp. 82–88. This reading had already been adopted by the editor Knoell.

[48] Cf. Cl. Baeumker, "Der Platonismus im Mittelalter," *Festrede in der Münch. Akad. der Wissenschaften* (1916), p. 21; Henry, *Plotin et l'Occident*, pp. 125–126; Marrou, *Saint Augustin*, p. 34.

[49] *De cons. Evang.* 1.35.53 (*PL* 34, 1070) and *De Trinitate* 4.18.24 (*PL* 42, 904) = Plato *Timaeus* 29c = Cicero *Tim.* 3: "Quantum enim ad id quod ortum est aeternitas valet, tantum ad fidem veritas."

[50] *De civ. Dei* 13.16.1 (*PL* 41, 388): "Nempe Platonis haec verba sunt, sicut ea Cicero in Latinum transtulit," and 22.26 (*PL* 41, 794) and *Sermo* 241.8.8 (*PL* 38, 1138): "in libro quodam quem scripsit *de constitutione mundi*," quoting textually Cicero *Tim.* 11.16 (ed. Mullach, *Fragm. philos. Graec.*, vol. 2, p. 169).

[51] *De civ. Dei* 6.1.1. and 9.23.1 (*PL* 41, 175 and 275).

[52] *Ibid.*, 12.24 and 26 (*PL* 41, 373 and 375). Cf. Cicero *Tim.* 11: "vos ad id quod erit immortale, partem attexitote mortalem."

[53] *De civ. Dei* 10.31, 12.18, 13.18 (*PL* 41: 311, 391, 368).

[54] *Ibid.*, 12.26 (*PL* 41, 375). Cf. Cicero *Tim.* 11: "Tria nobis genera reliqua sunt, eaque mortalia; quibus praetermissis, caeli absolutio perfecta non erit."

[55] Cicero *Tim.* 3:   *De civ. Dei* 11.21 (*PL* 41, 334):

  Haec nimirum gignendi *mundi causa iustissima.* Nam cum constituisset Deus *bonis* omnibus explere mundum ...

  Hanc etiam Plato *causam* condendi *mundi iustissimam* dicit, ut a bono Deo *bona* opera fierent.

Ibid., 4.11 (p. 161 Mullach):   *Ibid.*, 8.11 (*PL* 41, 236):

  Quam ob rem mundum efficere moliens *Deus terram primum ignemque iungebat.*

  In *Timaeo* autem Plato, quem librum *de mundi constitutione* conscripsit, *Deum* dicit in illo opere *terram primo ignemque iunxisse* (cf. also *ibid.*, 22.11.4–5, *PL* 41, 773–774).

[56] *De civ. Dei* 10.29.2 (*PL* 41, 309) and *Retract.* 1.11 (*PL* 32, 602). Cf. Cicero *Tim.* 4: "animal unum ... effecit."

[57] *De civ. Dei* 11.21 (*PL* 41, 334). Cf. Cicero *Tim.* 3: "Sic ratus est opus illud effectum esse pulcherrimum."

Chalcidius' translation, as has been reiterated by Alfaric, Combès, and Marrou.[58] To my knowledge, the only passage quoted by Augustine that does not appear in the Ciceronian version corresponds to a lacuna several pages long in the Ciceronian text and merely proves that when Augustine read this text, it was not yet corrupt.[59]

There is also nothing to prove that Augustine read Apuleius' lost translation of the *Phaedo*, as has been stated several times.[60] The rare references that he makes to this dialogue seem indirect. One of them derives from Porphyry;[61] another, from some commentator on Vergil;[62] still another is a literary allusion to the famous passage relating to Socrates' daemon, which is the subject of Apuleius' treatise *De deo Socratis*, so often quoted by Augustine.[63] Lastly, it was from the *Tusculans* that Augustine relates the anecdote about Cleombrotes' committing suicide after reading the *Phaedo*.[64] Similarly, two references to the *Symposium* in no sense prove that Augustine read this dialogue. One of these references is a textual quotation from Apuleius' *De deo Socratis*;[65] the other, relating to the apologue of Πενία and Πόρος, is borrowed

---

[58] Alfaric, *L'évolution intellectuelle*, p. 231 and n. 4; Combès, *Saint Augustin*, p. 14; Marrou, *Saint Augustin*, p. 34 and n. 3.

[59] This is the passage in the *De civ. Dei* 13.18 (*PL* 41, 391): "Si dii minores, quibus inter animalia terrestria cetera etiam hominem faciendum commisit Plato, potuerunt, sicut dicit, ab igne removere urendi qualitatem, lucendi relinquere quae per oculos emicaret . . ." Cf. Plato *Tim.* 45b: Τοῦ πυρὸς ὅσον τὸ μὲν κάειν οὐκ ἔσχε, τὸ δὲ παρέχειν φῶς ἥμερον οἰκεῖον ἑκάστης ἡμέρας σῶμα ἐμηχανήσαντο γίγνεσθαι. Now the lacuna in the Ciceronian text extends from *Tim.* 43b to 46a. It seems to me, therefore, certain that Augustine here preserves a few words of Cicero's lost text.

[60] Alfaric, *L'évolution intellectuelle*, p. 231 and n. 5; Combès, *Saint Augustin*, p. 14; Marrou, *Saint Augustin*, p. 34 and n. 4. Boemer, *Der lateinische Neuplatonismus*, pp. 28–30, had however already done justice to the texts proposed by Alfaric, but without specifying the actual sources.

[61] *De civ. Dei* 10.30 (*PL* 41, 310): "(Porphyrius) . . . abstulit, quod esse Platonicum maxime *perhibetur*, ut mortuos ex vivis, ita vivos ex mortuis semper fieri"; cf. *Phaedo* 70c.

[62] *De civ. Dei* 13.19 (*PL* 41, 392): "Optime autem cum hominibus agi arbitratur Plato, si tamen hanc vitam pie iusteque peregerint, ut a suis corporibus separati, in ipsorum deorum, qui sua corpora numquam deserunt, recipiantur sinum:
     Scilicet immemores supera ut convexa revisant,
       rursus et incipiant in corpore velle reverti [*Aen.* 6.750–751].
Quod Vergilius ex Platonico dogmate dixisse laudatur." Cf. *Phaedo* 108c. The text *De civ. Dei* 8.3 (*PL* 41, 227), which Combès referred also to this passage from the *Phaedo*, is still more indirect.

[63] *De cons. Evang.* 1.7.12 (*PL* 34, 1048). Cf. *Phaedo* 60d–e and Apuleius' interpretation, *De deo Socratis, passim*. It will be noted that Augustine, however, linked this passage from the *Phaedo* with the next passage on Aesop's fables: texts quoted above, n. 16.

[64] *De civ. Dei* 1.22.1 (*PL* 41, 36). Cf. Cicero *Tusc.* 1.34 and Lact. *Inst.* 3.18.

[65] *De civ. Dei* 8.18 (*PL* 41, 243): "Quoniam *nullus deus miscetur homini*, quod *Platonem dixisse* perhibent . . ." Cf. Apuleius *De deo Socratis*, ed. Thomas, p. 11, 10: "ut idem *Plato ait, nullus deus miscetur hominibus*," and Plato *Symp.* 203a.

from some Neoplatonist, probably Porphyry.[66] In conclusion, Augustine quotes from the *Tusculans* the anecdote in the *Meno* about the child who by himself discovered geometry[67] and the anecdote about Alcibiades' tears.[68] He knows only from Cicero's *De re publica* the notion expressed by Plato in his *Republic* that all the gods are beneficent[69] and the episode of the resurrection of Er of Pamphylia.[70] I think therefore that from Plato's *Timaeus* Augustine read only the section that Cicero had translated. But he is abundantly informed on his philosophy, partly through the Romans—Cicero,[71] Varro,[72] Apuleius,[73] Cyprian,[74] Ambrose[75]—and partly through the Greek Neoplatonists.

In fact, there is no doubt that Augustine had a direct knowledge of these Neoplatonists. I shall not undertake after so many others to examine the history of his conversion and to determine the part played in this conversion by Platonic writings. We know that, in accordance with the personal inclinations of the writers who have discussed the question, Augustine's conversion seems like a conversion to Neoplatonism or to Christianity.[76] There is the same uncertainty in the matter of his Neoplatonic sources. Some critics, like Theiler, insist on the Porphyrian influence that Augustine experienced;[77] others, among them Father Henry, on the Plotinian influence.[78] Even the methods differ. Theiler gives warning that he is not trying to prove a textual association between Augustine and Porphyry, but merely a doctrinal connection between the theories of the pagan philosopher and those of

---

[66] *Epist. ad Nebridium* 3.2 (*PL* 33, 64): "merito *philosophi* in rebus intellegibilibus divitias ponunt, in sensibilibus egestatem." Cf. *Symp.* 203b and Theiler, *Porphyrios und Augustin*, pp. 26–27, referring among others to Porphyry *Sententiae* 33.17.

[67] *De Trin.* 12.15.24 (*PL* 42, 1011). Cf. Plato *Meno* 81e–84a and Cicero *Tusc.* 1.24.56.

[68] *De civ. Dei* 14.8.3 (*PL* 41, 413). Cf. Cicero *Tusc.* 3.32.77.

[69] *De civ. Dei* 4.18 (*PL* 41, 126): "Hoc Plato dicit, hoc alii philosophi, hoc excellentes rei publicae populorumque rectores." Cf. *De civ. Dei* 8.13 (*PL* 41, 237).

[70] *Ibid.*, 22.28 (*PL* 41, 795); cf. Plato *Repub.* 614b. The corresponding passage in Cicero's *De re publica* is lost, but Macrobius *Somn. Scip.* 1.1.9 gives Cicero's opinion of it.

[71] See also *Epist. ad Dioscorum* 118.3.20 (*PL* 33, 441).

[72] *De civ. Dei* 7.28 (*PL* 41, 218), quoting Varro.

[73] *De utilitate credendi* 7.17 (*PL* 42, 77): "Alexim puerum in quem Plato etiam carmen amatorium fecisse dicitur." Cf. Apuleius *Apol.* 10.8: "Disce igitur versus Platonis philosophi . . . in Alexin Phaedrumque pueros coniuncto carmine."

[74] Cf. *PL* 43, 224, where Plato is quoted from St. Cyprian's *De idolorum vanitate.*

[75] Cf. *PL* 34, 56: Augustine borrows from Ambrose the notion that Plato was taught by the prophet Jeremiah.

[76] The two rival theories are those of Alfaric, *L'évolution intellectuelle*, and of Boyer, *Christianisme et néo-platonisme dans la formation de s. Augustin* (Paris 1920). Cf. Schanz, vol. 4, 2, p. 403; Boyer, pp. 1–7, and Marrou, *Saint Augustin*, p. xiii, n. 1. Add: Sister M. P. Garvey, *Saint Augustine: Christian or Neo-platonist?* (diss. Milwaukee 1939). I have shown in my article "Plotin et s. Ambroise" the error in such an alternative.

[77] Theiler, *Porphyrios und Augustin*.

[78] Henry, *Plotin et l'Occident*.

the recently converted Augustine.[79] Father Henry, on the other hand, attaches the greatest significance to the discovery of a textual connection, however slight, and draws important conclusions from this fact.[80]

Theiler starts from the principle that, since most of Porphyry's work is lost, it is impossible to determine the textual nature of Augustine's dependence in terms of this lost text. However, the relationship of the Augustinian theories to the Porphyrian theories can be demonstrated, he believes, from the works or fragments of Porphyry and of later Platonists that have been preserved: that is, Proclus, Aeneas of Gaza, Sallust, Hierocles, Olympiodorus, Damascius, Dionysius the Areopagite. This association of ideas would prove that Augustine, contrary to the admitted belief, did not read Plotinus and knew him only from a commentary by Porphyry on the *Enneads*. He owes everything to Porphyry, whose treatise Περὶ ἀγνείας and the Πρὸς Νημέρτιον[81] he had also read.

This definitive conclusion far exceeds the results of Theiler's inquiry, for he practically confines himself to an analysis of the *De vera religione*.[82] Even his method is open to criticism. There is no denying the conjectural character of this reconstruction of Porphyry's lost works with the aid of later treatises whose authors are not even direct and faithful heirs of Porphyrian doctrine. Nor is it any more certain that Porphyry ever wrote a treatise entitled Περὶ ἀγνείας.[83] Let us assume however that the method is valid. It would not be applicable in any case unless Theiler found in Augustine and Porphyry a common doctrine opposed to the Plotinian doctrine. Now this is not the case, as Theiler himself must agree. There are, he declares, occasional resemblances between Augustine and Plotinus, but Porphyry's lost text systematized, as Augustine's text does, the Plotinian theses.[84] Here we are in the region of pure conjecture. Many doctrinal resemblances that Winter, following the same defective method, had thought he had established between Augustine and Plotinus[85] prove, according to Theiler, Augustine's reliance

[79] Theiler, *Porph. und Aug.*, pp. 4–5: "Almost the entire Augustinian philosophy may be considered as Porphyrian."

[80] Henry, *Plotin et l'Occident*, pp. 18ff and p. 68.

[81] Theiler, *Porph. und Aug.*, p. 48.

[82] See the reservations postulated in P. de Labriolle's review, *Revue critique* 101 (1934) 139–142.

[83] Neither Suidas nor Bidez's catalogue in his *Vie de Porphyre*, pp. 65*–73*, mentions it. The title Περὶ ἀγνείας or Περὶ ἀγνοῦ βίου is a conjectural reconstruction by Bickel, *Diatribe*, vol. I, p. 213. He assumes that this unknown work by Porphyry is the source of St. Jerome's *Adversus Iovinianum*. Cf. above, p. 72.

[84] Theiler, *Porph. und Aug.*, pp. 32 and 35. He is also obliged to note analogies between Augustine and Plotinus, pp. 14, 47 (n. 1), 49, 60, 62, and to reject them deliberately. See the previous comments by Henry, *Plotin et l'Occident*, pp. 71ff and 130 n. 2, on such a method.

[85] Aem. Winter, *De doctrinae neoplatonicae in Augustini civitate Dei vestigiis* (diss. Freiburg im Breisgau 1928) 17–29.

on Porphyry. Lastly, Theiler also takes little account of the numerous quotations from Plotinus that Augustine uses in his later works, notably in the *De civitate Dei*, but appears to imply that Augustine never read Plotinus, even in his later years. Does he at least prove an unquestionable connection between Augustinian doctrine and Neoplatonic doctrine, whether Plotinian or Porphyrian? Certain resemblances are far from convincing. For instance, the thesis on the inherent goodness of man appears in Cicero as well as in the Neoplatonists.[86] The notion that God is not jealous of man is not specifically Neoplatonic but goes back to the *Timaeus*, which Augustine had read in Cicero's translation.[87] Again, certain views, such as that on the soul that meditates, are as much Christian as pagan, and it seems hazardous to maintain that Porphyry inspires Augustine with his religious sentiments.[88] Could it not just as well be maintained, as Augustine does, that Christianity revealed this spiritual richness to Porphyry himself? Theiler's bias appears when he assures us that Augustine is not original and that his sole merit lies in having tried to save the ancient treasures in a decadent age.[89] This is actually a denial of the sincere and personal character of Augustine's religion.

Productive and rigorous in a different sense is Father Henry's inquiry. He begins by indicating all the Augustinian texts relating to the Greek writers translated by Victorinus that Augustine asserts he had read at the time of his conversion.[90] He observes that the only one among the *Platonici* that Augustine designates by name is Plotinus, whereas Porphyry's name does not appear in any work prior to the *De consensu Evangelistarum*.[91] On the other hand, in the *De civitate Dei* Augustine uses several textual quotations from Plotinus' treatise *On the Beautiful*,[92] just as he used this treatise, without mentioning it by name, in the passage of the *Confessions* that summarizes his earlier Neoplatonic reading.[93] Augustine also quotes in the *De civitate Dei* the Περὶ ψυχῆς ἀποριῶν [94] and the treatises *On Providence*,[95] *On the Three Principal Hypostases*,[96] *On What is beyond Being*,[97] and probably *On Happiness*.[98]

---

[86] Theiler acknowledges it, *Porph. und Aug.*, p. 13.

[87] Cf. *ibid.*, p. 25.

[88] *Ibid.*, p. 66.

[89] *Ibid.*, p. 57.

[90] Henry, *Plotin et l'Occident*, pp. 79–82.

[91] *Ibid.*, p. 70.

[92] *Ibid.*, p. 107.

[93] *Ibid.*, pp. 107 and 112. In *La vision d'Ostie, sa place dans la vie et l'œuvre de s. Augustin* (diss. Paris 1938), chap. 2, Father Henry has shown, in addition, the Plotinian character of the Augustinian mystique.

[94] Henry, *Plotin et l'Occident*, p. 123.

[95] *Ibid.*, p. 122.

[96] *Ibid.*, p. 127.

[97] *Ibid.*, pp. 129–130.

[98] *Ibid.*, p. 138.

Father Henry is thus reduced to admitting that Augustine read in the year 386 only the treatise *On the Beautiful* in Marius Victorinus' version,[99] but that in 415 he read in the original text all the *Enneads*.[100]

These conclusions seem cogent,[101] and it is useless to discuss further, after Father Henry, all that Augustine owes to Plotinus. It will suffice to indicate the passage in the *De consensu Evangelistarum* that has escaped Father Henry's perspicacity; it permits us to observe how Augustine assimilated Plotinian thought while adapting it to Christian purposes, with the result that it became changed into the recital of the ecstasy at Ostia. It was not, properly speaking, the ecstasy at Ostia that was Plotinian. But at the time when he wrote the account Augustine had just reread, in the *De consensu*, these lines from Plotinus.[102] He translates into Plotinian terms his first experience:

Plotinus *Enn.* 5.1.4, ed. Bréhier, p. 19:	Augustine *De consensu Evang.* 1.23.35 (*PL* 34, 1058):	Conf. 9.10.24, p. 228, 10:
Ἐπὶ τὸ ἀρχέτυπον αὐτοῦ καὶ τὸ ἀληθινώτερον ἀναβὰς κἀκεῖ πάντα ἰδέτω νοητὰ καὶ παρ' αὐτῷ ἀίδια ἐν οἰκείᾳ συνέσει καὶ ζωῇ καὶ τούτων τὸν ἀκήρατον νοῦν προστάτην, καὶ σοφίαν ἀμήχανον, καὶ τὸν ὡς ἀληθῶς ἐπὶ Κρόνου βίον θεοῦ κόρου καὶ νοῦ ὄντος. Πάντα γὰρ ἐν	Erubuerunt hinc philosophi Platonici, qui iam Christianis temporibus fuerunt; et Saturnum aliter *interpretari* conati sunt, dicentes appellatum *Κρόνον velut a satietate intellectus*, eo quod Graece satietas *κόρος*, intellectus autem sive mens *νοῦς*	Et venimus in *mentes* nostras et *transcendimus* eas, ut attingeremus regionem *ubertatis* indeficientis, ubi pascis Israel in aeternum *veritatis* pabulo, *et ibi vita sapientia* est, per quam fiunt omnia ista, et quae fuerunt et quae futura sunt, et ipsa non fit, sed sic est, ut fuit, et sic erit semper.[103]

---

[99] He does not venture, p. 128 n. 3, to assert this insofar as concerns the treatise *On the Three Principal Hypostases*. In a preceding chapter Henry established that Marius Victorinus had in fact read the *Enneads*.

[100] Henry, *Plotin et l'Occident*, p. 137.

[101] Despite Nicolau's review, *REL* 13 (1935) 410–414, denying the possibility that Augustine, at any period of his life, was able to read the *Enneads* in the Greek text. Altaner, "Augustinus," p. 36 n. 53, goes further and thinks that Augustine could not even compare the translation of the *Enneads* with the original text. It would also be necessary to prove that a complete translation of the *Enneads* in Latin ever existed at this date, which is a very dubious point. It is self-evident that, in all respects, Augustine must have had the greatest trouble in reading this difficult text.

[102] Both texts must have been composed about the year 398.

[103] Henry, *La vision d'Ostie*, pp. 23 and 39, though unaware of the parallel in the *De consensu*, had already discovered, from the context, the Plotinian tone in this passage of the *Confessions*. Note particularly that in changing the νοητά to *mentes nostras* Augustine is careful not to assign divine qualities to the Intelligibles and changes the entire progression of the ascent toward God. For him, divinity is revealed in the inmost recesses of the human conscience, "in the *fine pointe*," as the mystics of the seventeenth century were to say.

αὐτῷ τὰ ἀθάνατα περι-
έχει, νοῦν πάντα, θεὸν
πάντα, ψυχὴν πᾶσαν,
ἑστῶτα ἀεί.

Ibid., 5.1.7, p. 25:
ὡς τὰ μυστήρια καὶ οἱ
μῦθοι οἱ περὶ θεῶν αἰνίτ-
τονται Κρόνον μὲν θεὸν
σοφώτατον πρὸ τοῦ Διὸς
γενέσθαι ‹διὰ τὸ› ἃ γεννᾷ
πάλιν ἐν ἑαυτῷ ἔχειν, ᾗ
καὶ πλήρης καὶ νοῦς ἐν
κόρῳ· μετὰ δὲ ταῦτά φασι
Δία γεννᾶν κόρον ἤδη
ὄντα· ψυχὴν γὰρ γεννᾷ
νοῦς, νοῦς ὢν τέλειος.

dicitur; cui videtur suffra-
gari et Latinum nomen,
quasi ex prima Latina
parte et Graeca posteriore
compositum, ut diceretur
Saturnus quasi satur esset
vous. Viderunt enim
quam esset absurdum, si
filius temporis Iuppiter
haberetur, quem deum
aeternum vel putabant vel
putari volebant. At vero
secundum istam novellam
interpretationem, quam
veteres eorum si habuis-
sent, mirum si Ciceronem
Varronemque latuisset,
Saturni filium Iovem dicunt,
tamquam *ab illa summa
mente profluentem* spiritum,
quem volunt esse velut
animam mundi huius, om-
nia caelestia et terrena
corpora implentem ...
Numquid non, si possent
isti, sicut ipsam interpretationem, ita etiam super-
stitionem hominum com-
mutarent et aut nulla
simulacra, aut certe Sa-
turno potius quam Iovi
Capitolia constituerent?

Augustine joyfully accepts the etymology proposed by Plotinus.
But whereas Plotinus sought primarily for a rationalistic justification
of the myths, Augustine finds in these lines a condemnation of the cult
dedicated to Jupiter. Plotinus is involved in polytheism. Logically,
according to his interpretation, the cult of Jupiter should yield to the
cult of Saturn, the supreme intelligence. To this cult alone should statues
be erected.[104] Without expressing himself for or against the theory
of the Soul of the universe, associated with this interpreta-

---

[104] Augustine *De consensu* 1.23.36 (PL 34, 1058): "qui secundum istam suam novam
opinionem et summas arces, si quidquam in his rebus potestatis habuissent, Saturno
potius dedicarent, et mathematicos vel genethliacos maxime delerent, qui Saturnum
quem sapientum effectorem isti dicerent, maleficum deum inter alia sidera constitue-
runt."

tion,[105] Augustine declares that this precedence accorded to Saturn over Jupiter despite astrology can lead from paganism to Christianity, since the supreme Intelligence is identified with the Wisdom of the God of Israel.[106]

We may observe how Augustine was able to take full advantage of the passages in the treatise *On the Three Principal Hypostases* that appeared to be as remote as possible from Christian faith. Now, the *De consensu*, which dates in the year 400, was written at a time when St. Augustine, as we have seen, did not yet read Greek at sight. We shall be obliged to believe that at that time, as Father Henry was already inclined to think, this treatise was among Plotinus' *paucissimi libri*, translated by Victorinus, that had such a great influence on Augustine's conversion.

I no longer agree with Father Henry when he suggests that the Platonic studies that prepared Augustine for conversion were confined to one or two treatises of the *Enneads*, to the exclusion of Porphyry's treatises.[107] However, Augustine, when speaking of these studies, seems to indicate clearly several works and even several writers.[108] The fact that he never quotes Porphyry in the writings contemporary with his conversion does not prove that he did not read him; for, although he *names* Plotinus, he does not quote another line from Plotinus,[109] as Father Henry acknowledges. Father Henry shows considerable ingenuity in making it seem probable that, when Augustine protests in the *Confessions* against having tasted Egyptian food, he thereby

---

[105] *Ibid.*, 1.23.35: "utrum autem universa ista corporalis moles, quae mundus appellatur, habeat quandam animam, vel quasi animam suam, id est rationalem vitam, qua ita regatur sicut unumquodque animal, magna atque abdita quaestio est; nec adfirmari debet ista opinio, nisi comperta quod vera sit, nec refelli nisi comperta quod falsa sit."

[106] *Ibid.:* "nos vero esse quandam summam Dei sapientiam, cuius participatione fit sapiens quaecumque anima fit vere sapiens, non tantum concedimus, verum etiam maxime praedicamus."

[107] Henry, *Plotin et l'Occident*, pp. 73 and 91, and "Augustine and Plotinus," p. 20.

[108] *Conf.* 7.9.13 (p. 158 Lab.): "Procurasti mihi per quendam hominem immanissimo tyfo turgidum *quosdam Platonicorum libros* ex Graeca lingua in Latinam versos, et ibi legi non quidem his verbis, sed hoc idem omnino *multis et multiplicibus* suaderi rationibus, quod *in principio erat Verbum, et Verbum erat apud Deum, et Deus erat Verbum*"; 7.9.14 (p. 159 Lab.): "Indagavi quippe *in illis litteris varie dictum et multis modis*, quod sit Filius in forma Patris non rapinam arbitratus esse aequalis Deo"; 7.20.26 (p. 169 Lab.): "lectis *Platonicorum ullis libris*"; 8.2.3 (p. 177 Lab.): "ubi autem commemoravi legisse me *quosdam libros Platonicorum*, quos Victorinus quondam rhetor urbis Romae, quem Christianum defunctum esse audieram, in Latinam linguam transtulisset, gratulatus est mihi (Simplicianus), quod non in aliorum philosophorum scripta incidissem plena fallaciarum et deceptionum secundum elementa huius mundi, in *istis* autem *omnibus modis* insinuari Deum et eius Verbum. Deinde . . . Victorinum ipsum recordatus est, quem Romae cum esset, familiarissime noverat." On the other hand, the expression in the *De beata vita* 1.4 (*PL* 32, 961): "lectis autem Plotini paucissimis libris," proves that he had read at that date only a very limited number of Plotinus' treatises.

[109] Henry, *Plotin et l'Occident*, p. 120.

designates the works of Plotinus alone, who was born at Lycopolis in Egypt.[110] It would be surprising for Augustine to have had in mind specifically Plotinus' native country, for even we know his place of birth only from the later sources of Eunapius and Suidas,[111] while the *Life* written by Porphyry is silent on this point. But more than that, the Augustinian context, "And there also did I read that they had changed the glory of thy incorruptible nature into idols, and divers shapes, into the likeness of the image of corruptible man, and birds, and beasts, and serpents,"[112] hardly applies to Plotinus, who can scarcely pass as the champion of these idols, and would rather incline one to think of his disciple Porphyry or Iamblichus, or again of the hermetic writings such as the *Asclepius* attributed by Augustine to Hermes Trismegistus. On the other hand, Augustine points out in the *De civitate Dei*, when he confronts Plotinus' pagan lineage with his Christian lineage, that is, with Marius the convert,[113] that he understands by *Platonici*, apart from Plotinus, his disciples Porphyry and Iamblichus. Did he not read any of them after his conversion?

Adolf Dyroff is of this opinion, and brings forward two names: Amelius and Porphyry. He rightly makes the observation that Augustine was not the first to have confronted the Johannine prologue with Neoplatonic doctrine. Augustine himself asserts that he has it from Simplicianus that a Neoplatonist would have wanted to see this prologue carved on the walls of Christian churches.[114] Dyroff conjectures with probability that this Neoplatonist is Marius Victorinus, who followed the tradition established by Amelius, a pupil of Plotinus.[115] May one conclude with him that Augustine read treatises by Amelius, translated by Victorinus? It is a rash assumption, for nothing proves that these treatises were ever translated. It is still more hazardous, and even quite improbable, to assume with Dyroff that Augustine read a translation of Porphyry's treatise *Against the Christians* that contained such an

[110] *Ibid.*, p. 98 n. 1; Henry himself does not seem very sure of the value of his demonstration. He could substantiate it by quoting Cumont, "Le culte égyptien et le mysticisme de Plotin," *Monuments Piot* 25 (1921/1922) 77–92.

[111] Eunapius *Vitae philosophorum ac sophistarum*, p. 6, ed. Boissonade (1822), and Suidas s.v. Πλωτῖνος. It is true that Eunapius' work appeared several years before the *Confessions*, but there is no reason to believe that Augustine had read it.

[112] *Conf.* 7.9.15, p. 160 Lab. Cf. Boyer, *Christianisme et néo-platonisme*, p. 81, and A. Dyroff, "Zum Prolog des Johannes Evangeliums," *Doelger Festschrift* (Münster 1939) 90.

[113] *De civ. Dei* 8.12 (*PL* 41, 237): "(Platonicos) ex quibus sunt valde nobilitati Graeci Plotinus, Iamblichus, Porphyrius." Cf. *Epist.* 118.5.33 (*PL* 33, 448): "Tunc Plotini schola Romae floruit, habuitque condiscipulos multos *acutissimos et solertissimos viros*. Sed aliqui eorum magicarum artium curiositate depravati sunt, aliqui Dominum Iesum Christum ipsius veritatis atque sapientiae incommutabilis, quam conabantur attingere, cognoscentes gestare personam, in eius militiam transierunt."

[114] Cf. below, n. 144.

[115] Cf. Dyroff, "Zum Prolog," pp. 88–89.

interpretation of the Johannine prologue. Augustine, as I shall show, never read this treatise,[116] and it is not easy to see how he could have been drawn to Christianity by such study! To suppose that Porphyry, in this treatise, had demonstrated the accord between the Johannine prologue and Platonic doctrine would have been a virtual denial of the originality of Christianity and a declaration that the so-called inspired texts merely abolished distinctions among the pagan philosophies. Amelius himself tried only to show that the Christian religion, characterized as barbarous, had developed in the dogma of the Incarnation the Platonic views of the Hellenic philosophers on the descent of the soul into the body.[117]

However, a slight detail informs us that Augustine read in the work of a pupil of Plotinus' at the time of the *Contra Academicos*, for he borrows from him a very scholastic expression about the master: Plotinus is so close to Plato that one might think them contemporaries, but Plotinus is so distant from him in time that it must be admitted that one is a reincarnation of the other.[118] This saying would be quite appropriate in Porphyry's *Vita Plotini*. Actually, it does not appear there, but it might have been taken from the prolegomena to Porphyry's commentary on the *Enneads*. It is surprising too that Theiler did not examine this carefully in order to confirm his theories. Immediately after this saying about Plotinus, Augustine declares that "acutissimi et solertissimi viri," by demonstrating harmony between Aristotle and Plato, created a single philosophy.[119] One cannot help thinking of Porphyry's treatise Περὶ τοῦ μίαν εἶναι τὴν Πλάτωνος καὶ ᾿Αριστοτέλους αἵρεσιν,[120] all the more so as later on Augustine was to apply these very epithets to Plotinus' pupils.[121] One may also admit, with Theiler, a relationship either in viewpoint or in terminology between Porphyry and the Augustinian writings of this period. For instance, the notion of *aversio a terrenis et in unum Deum conversio*,[122] the idea of *ordo*, equivalent to

---

[116] Cf. below, n. 176.

[117] Cf. the fragment from Amelius quoted by Eusebius *Praep. Evang.* 11.19.1 (PG 21, 900 B); Cyril *Contra Iulian.* 8 (PG 76, 936 A), and Theodoret *Curatio Graec. adfect.* 4 (PG 83, 852 C).

[118] *Contra Acad.* 3.18.41 (PL 32, 956): "os illud Platonis ... emicuit maxime in Plotino, qui Platonicus philosophus ita eius similis *iudicatus est*, ut simul eos vixisse, tantum autem interest temporis, ut in hoc ille revixisse putandus sit." We have noted above, pp. 81–82, that Jerome too quotes an analogous scholastic formula, applied to Philo.

[119] *Contra Acad.* 3.19.42 (PL 32, 956): "Non defuerunt *acutissimi et solertissimi viri*, qui docerent disputationibus suis Aristotelem ac Platonem ita sibi concinere, ut imperitis minusque attentis dissentire videantur; multis quidem saeculis multisque contentionibus, sed tamen eliquata est, ut opinor, una verissimae philosophiae disciplina."

[120] This is no. 32 in the catalogue of Porphyry's works drawn up by Bidez, *Vie de Porphyre*, p. 68*.

[121] Text quoted above, n. 113.

[122] Theiler, *Porph. und Aug.*, p. 8.

the Porphyrian term τάξις,[123] the concept of punishment immanent in sin,[124] psychology applied to the search for God,[125] and above all—what has escaped Theiler—the concept of demons, maleficent spirits that inhabit the air.[126] I believe with Father Henry and contrary to Theiler that the putative textual quotation from Porphyry's *Introduction to the Intelligibles* in Augustine's *De musica* can just as readily refer to Plotinus.[127] But there are a number of Augustinian passages, contemporary with his conversion, that Theiler and Father Henry failed to note and whose Porphyrian echoes are certain, since Augustine himself indicates them in the *Retractationes*, where he admits several of his Neoplatonic lapses. He had been wrong, he asserts, in speaking in the *Contra Academicos* of the return of the soul to heaven.[128] He had been wrong

[123] *Ibid.*, pp. 17ff.

[124] *Ibid.*, p. 31.

[125] *Ibid.*, p. 49.

[126] *Contra Acad.* 1.7.20 (*PL* 32, 916): "versum alienum etiam imperitissimis canere ac pronuntiare concessum est. Ideoque talia cum in memoriam nostram incurrerint, non mirum est, si sentiri possunt ab huius aeris animalibus quibusdam vilissimis, quos daemonas vocant, a quibus nos superari acumine ac subtilitate sensuum posse concedo, ratione autem nego . . . Quam ob rem ad extremum hortabatur, ut animos suos ii qui talia didicissent, illi divinationi sine dubitatione praeferrent, darentque operam his disciplinis instruere atque adminiculari suam mentem quibus aeriam istam invisibilium animantium naturam transilire et eam supervolare contingeret." This conception of demons in no sense corresponds to the notion expounded by Plotinus *Enn.* 3.4.3 and 3.5.6, but to Porphyry's (cf. *De philosophia ex oraculis haurienda*, ed. Wolff, pp. 147–149 and 225–227), which Eusebius *Praep. Evang.* 4.6 (*PL* 21, 249 B) defined thus: the friend, the scholar, the apostle of demons. A more complete exposition of these theories may be found in Augustine's *De divinatione daemonum* 3.7 and 4.8 (*PL* 40, 584–585). From the fact that the demons dwell in the air, they have a triple superiority over men: keenness of senses (*acrimonia sensus*), rapidity of movement (*celeritate motus*), long experience (*diuturna rerum experientia*). There is therefore nothing surprising in their ability to predict the future or perform prodigies, although they have no divine power. It will be observed that the *De div. daem.* begins with an oracle through which Serapis had predicted the destruction of his own temple at Alexandria. The statement in *De div. daem.* 7.11 (*PL* 40, 588): "Iuno autem ab istis potestas aeria praedicatur," refers, as will be seen below (n. 157), to Porphyry's *De imaginibus*. Serapis was, to Porphyry, the chief of the evil spirits. On his demonology, cf. Wolff's ed., pp. 223–229, and T. Hopfner, *Griechisch-Aegyptischer Offenbarungszauber*, Studien zur Palaeographie und Papyruskunde, vol. 21, p. 12. On the speed of demons, cf. Porphyry *De abstin.* 2.39, ed. Hercher, p. 39, 31.

[127] Porph. *Sent.* 40.5 = Aug. *De mus.* 6.13.40. Cf. Henry, *Plot. et l'Occid.*, pp. 71–72, who repeats Winter, *De doctrinae neoplatonicae . . . vestigiis*, p. 51, without realizing it.

[128] *Retract.* 1.1.3 (*PL* 32, 587): "Alio loco de animo cum agerem dixi: *Securior rediturus in caelum* [*Contra Acad.* 2.9.22, *PL* 32, 930]. *Iturus* autem quam *rediturus* dixissem securius, propter eos qui putant animos humanos pro meritis peccatorum suorum de caelo lapsos sive deiectos in corpora ista detrudi." Augustine had said the same thing, *De beata vita* 36 (*PL* 32, 976): "si vobis cordi est ad Deum *reditus* noster," and *Solil.* 1.1.5 (*PL* 32, 872): "ad te mihi *redeundum* esse sentio." Cf. *Retract.* 1.8.2 (*PL* 32, 594) with reference to an allusion in the *De animae quantitate* 20.34 (*PL* 32, 1055) to the theory of preexistence.

to appear to take into account, in the *Soliloquies,* Porphyry's formula: "Omne corpus est fugiendum."[129] This formula, which Augustine discusses at great length in the *De civitate Dei,* he himself there admits having read in Porphyry's *De regressu animae.*[130] This proves that he had already read and assimilated this treatise at the time of his conversion. I believe therefore, contrary to Father Henry, that Augustine had read, at the time of his conversion, besides Plotinus' Περὶ καλοῦ, at least one work of Porphyry's; and, contrary to Theiler, that, if he had then read a single work by Porphyry in Victorinus' translation, it was the *De regressu animae.*[131] The *libri Platonicorum* refer to both writers conjointly.

This is an important conclusion. It obliges us to abandon the idea, formulated by Father Henry,[132] of an Augustine who favored Neoplatonism, reading only Plotinus, of whom he was an enthusiastic pupil, but becoming hostile to the movement later on, when his study of Porphyry had opened his eyes. Actually, do we not see Augustine, in the *De civitate Dei,* deciding in favor of Porphyry against Plotinus, on a problem as important as the

---

[129] *Retract.* 1.4.3 (*PL* 32, 590): "In eo quod ibi dictum est: *Penitus esse ista sensibilia fugienda* [*Solil.* 1.14.24, *PL* 32, 882], cavendum fuit, ne putaremur illam Porphyrii falsi philosophi tenere sententiam, qua dixit: Omne corpus esse fugiendum." The same *mea culpa* occurs with reference to the same idea expressed in the *Contra Academicos* (*Retr.* 1.1.2, *PL* 32, 586): "Sed eorum more tunc loquebar, qui sensum non nisi corporis dicunt, et sensibilia non nisi corporalia," in the *De musica* (*Retr.* 1.11.2, *PL* 32, 601), and in the *De ordine* (*Retr.* 1.3.2, *PL* 32, 588): "[mihi displicet] quod non addebam *corporis* quando sensus corporis nominavi." Cf. *De ordine* 1.1.3, *PL* 32, 979: "Qui tamen, ut se noscat, magna opus habet consuetudine recedendi a sensibus."

[130] *De civ. Dei* 10.29.2 (*PL* 41, 308): "Hoc fortasse credere recusatis intuentes Porphyrium in his ipsis libris, ex quibus multa posui, quos *de regressu animae* scripsit, tam crebro praecipere: *Omne corpus esse fugiendum,* ut anima possit beata permanere cum Deo." The passages where Augustine returns to this Porphyrian formula may be found collected in Boemer, *Der lateinische Neuplatonismus,* p. 76, to which should be added the passages mentioned by Winter, *De doctrinae neoplatonicae . . . vestigiis,* pp. 44–45.

[131] Boemer, *Der lat. Neuplat.,* p. 83, quotes the statement *De civ. Dei* 22.26, *PL* 41, 794: "Sed Porphyrius ait, *inquiunt,* ut beata sit anima corpus esse omne fugiendum," to prove that Augustine is using Victorinus' translation. It is not a valid argument. The subject of *inquiunt* is not Victorinus, but the opponents whom Augustine is trying to convince and who cast at him the Porphyrian formula as a reproach.

[132] Henry, *Plot. et l'Occid.,* p. 73: "It is not proved that St. Augustine, when composing his first dialogues, already knew Porphyry's works," and p. 90: "It was only much later, toward the end of his days, when he examined his conscience and composed his *Retractiones,* in 427, when the glamor of Neoplatonism had worn off before the dazzling splendor of Grace, that Augustine assumed the blame of having given too much praise to 'these impious men,' to whom, however, he was indebted for so much. But at this date, between Plotinus and himself, Porphyry had cast his shadow." Henry, *La vision d'Ostie,* p. 119, is nevertheless forced to observe that "in a curious text . . . Augustine makes surprising concessions to Porphyry." But he also seems to believe that the case was unique.

problem of metempsychosis?[133] It would not be correct to believe with Alfaric that Augustine became first of all a convert to Neoplatonism, then gradually detached himself as his duties as bishop imposed on him a more rigid Christianity. Is it not apparent that in 390, the very year when he wrote the *De vera religione*, Augustine was considered by the Neoplatonist Maximus of Madaura as a member who had left the sect?[134] I think with Abbot Boyer that his "attitude . . . toward the philosophers retained more unity than is sometimes stated."[135] His supreme apologetic effort in the *De civitate Dei* consisted, unless I am mistaken, in contemplating the sequence of his own conversion in order to lead Porphyry's disciples to Christianity.

The translation of the *De regressu animae* by Victorinus probably prepared the synthesis that Augustine was to attempt between Christianity and Neoplatonism, and an article has shrewdly noted the flavor of Victorinus in Augustine's theories on the preexistence of the soul, before he had evolved toward Creationism.[136] He himself was very impressed by Marius Victorinus' conversion. Since the *De vera religione*, he thought that the Platonists had only to change a few ideas or expressions to become Christians, as most of them did.[137] He does not express himself differently in the *Letter to Dioscorus* in 410[138] or in the last book of the *De civitate Dei*, written shortly before his death.[139] At the most, it may be noted with Winter that Augustine's tone with regard to the Platonists became harsh toward the end of the *De civitate*

[133] *De civ. Dei* 10.30 (*PL* 41, 310): "Nam Platonem animas hominum post mortem revolvi usque ad corpora bestiarum scripsisse certissimum est. Hanc sententiam Porphyrii doctor tenuit et Plotinus, Porphyrio tamen iure displicuit."

[134] Maximus *Epist. ad Augustinum* 16.4, *PL* 33, 82, calls Augustine: "vir eximie qui a mea secta deviasti."

[135] Boyer, *Christian. et néo-platon.*, p. 112 n. 3.

[136] H. de Leusse, "Le problème," pp. 236–237. However, the question of knowing to what extent Victorinus' theological thought influenced Augustine remains controversial. Cf. Schanz, vol. 4, 1, p. 160.

[137] *De vera relig.* 4.7 (*PL* 34, 126): "Itaque si hanc vitam illi viri nobiscum rursus agere potuissent, viderent profecto cuius auctoritate facilius consuleretur hominibus, et *paucis mutatis verbis atque sententiis* Christiani fierent, sicut plerique recentiorum nostrorumque temporum Platonici fecerunt." The word *recentiorum* applies to Marius Victorinus and to his generation, the term *nostrorum* to Manlius Theodorus and his generation.

[138] *Epist.* 118.3.21 (*PL* 33, 442): "Certamina tamen de loquacissimis Graecorum gymnasiis eradicata atque compressa sunt, ita ut si qua nunc erroris secta contra veritatem, hoc est contra Ecclesiam Christi emerserit, nisi nomine cooperta Christiano ad pugnandum prosilire non audeat. Ex quo intellegitur ipsos quoque Platonicae gentis philosophos, *paucis mutatis* quae Christiana improbat disciplina, invictissimo uni regi Christo pias cervices oportere submittere et intellegere Verbum Dei homine indutum."

[139] *De civ. Dei* 22.25 (*PL* 41, 792): "Verum de animi bonis, quibus post hanc vitam beatissimus perfruetur, *non a nobis dissentiunt* philosophi nobiles: de carnis resurrectione contendunt; hanc, quantum possunt, negant. Sed credentes multi, negantes paucissimos reliquerunt et ad Christum . . . fideli corde conversi sunt."

Dei, while in the first ten books, prior to 416, he had nothing but praise or moderate criticism for them.[140]

The very fact that Porphyry's Κατὰ χριστιανῶν was not known to Augustine allows him to assume more readily that Porphyry's philosophy can lead to Christianity. Victorinus' impressive conversion already showed that the barriers between Hellenism and Christianity could be transcended. The circle that Augustine frequented before his conversion, with Hermogenianus and Zenobius, was completely permeated with Platonism.[141] He himself was initiated into this circle, if my conjectures are valid, by the Christian philosopher Manlius Theodorus.[142] Even clerics like Simplicianus, who had a reputation for saintliness and was to succeed Ambrose, were in no sense disturbed to see him reading in Victorinus' translation the _libri Platonici_, that is, Plotinus' treatise _On the Beautiful_ or Porphyry's _De regressu animae_.[143] Did not Simplicianus know a Platonist according to whom the Churches should engrave in letters of gold and set on high places the prologue of the Gospel according to St. John?[144] The desire to find a harmony between the prevalent philosophy and the new religion was then a general feeling among Christians in the West, except among the ascetics, who a priori rejected the entire pagan culture.

Augustine is aware nevertheless that Porphyry's disciples are the principal defenders of paganism. In the _De civitate Dei_ he quite specifically addresses "those who exalt and cherish Porphyry" but, from their denial of the Incarnation, are reduced to searching in the magic arts for some derivative that appeals to their taste for the divine;[145] or again "those of his contemporaries

[140] Winter, _De doctr. neoplaton._, pp. 9–15.

[141] Cf. Alfaric, _L'évol. intell._, p. 373.

[142] See above, pp. 137–139.

[143] Text quoted above, n. 108. St. Ambrose _Epist. ad Simplicianum_ 65.1 (_PL_ 16, 1222 C) recalls that Simplicianus had traveled over the world for his education and that he was a determined worker "acri praesertim ingenio etiam intellegibilia complectens, utpote qui etiam philosophiae libros quam a vero sint devii demonstrare soleas et _plerosque_ tam inanes esse, ut prius scribentium in suis scriptis sermo, quam vita eorum defecerit." The word _plerosque_ signifies, in my opinion, that the Neoplatonists were excluded from this condemnation.

[144] _De civ. Dei_ 10.29.2 (_PL_ 41, 308): "Quod initium sancti Evangelii, cui nomen est _secundum Ioannem_, quidam Platonicus, sicut a sancto sene Simpliciano qui postea Mediolanensi Ecclesiae praesedit episcopus, solebamus audire, aureis litteris conscribendum et per omnes Ecclesias in locis eminentissimis proponendum esse dicebat." It would be interesting if archaeology could reveal whether this actually took place.

[145] _Ibid._, 10.29.1 (_PL_ 41, 308), an apostrophe to Porphyry: "O si cognovisses Dei gratiam per Iesum Christum Dominum nostrum ipsamque eius incarnationem . . . Scio me frustra loqui mortuo: sed quantum ad te adtinet; quantum autem ad eos qui te magnipendunt et te vel qualicumque amore sapientiae, vel curiositate artium quas non debuisti discere, diligunt, quos potius in tua compellatione adloquor, fortasse non frustra."

who cherish Plato and Porphyry" but deny the resurrection of the flesh in the name of the Porphyrian principle of the *De regressu animae*: "Omne corpus est fugiendum."[146] By this he means that Porphyry's adherents were numerous. It was not merely a question of the small circle of Macrobius' friends: an entire section of the cultured public in the West remained aloof from Christ.[147]

But Porphyry himself, in Augustine's view, experienced Christian influence and was ashamed of certain pagan theories, such as the Platonic theory that the soul, through love of the body, was reincarnated in animals.[148] Augustine read the principal treatises that marked the turning points in Porphyry's thought and found in him an evolution, regrets, as though he felt drawn to Christianity but turned aside with horror.[149]

He read, in fact, some of Porphyry's youthful writings, certainly the *Philosophy of the Oracles*, and probably the *De imaginibus*. These two treatises that antedate Plotinus' influence on Porphyry seem very remote from Christian thought.[150] Augustine read the former in a translation.[151] He quotes a long extract from it, notably a Delphic oracle revealing that the gods fear the god of the Jews.[152] While interpreting this oracle as pagan homage

[146] *Ibid.*, 22.28 (*PL* 41, 796): "quicumque illos diligunt et adhuc vivunt."

[147] The letters of Maximus of Madaura or of Longinianus, in the Augustinian collection (*Epist.* 16 and 234, *PL* 33, 81 and 1030), inform us of some of these pagans in Augustine's circle, some sympathetic, others hostile to Christianity. Cf. Labriolle, *La réaction païenne*, pp. 445–446.

[148] Cf. *Sermo* 241.7.7 (*PL* 38, 1137): "Sed tamen ab ipsis deliramentis erubescendo, a Christianis ex aliqua parte correptus, dixit, scripsit: *Corpus est omne fugiendum.*" Cf. *De civ. Dei* 13.19 (*PL* 41, 392) with reference to the migration of souls into the bodies of animals: "de quo Platonico dogmate iam in libris superioribus [10.30, quoted above, n. 133] diximus Christiano tempore erubuisse Porphyrium."

[149] *De civ. Dei* 10.28 (*PL* 41, 306): "Quam (sapientiam) si vere ac fideliter amasses, Christum Dei virtutem et Dei sapientiam cognovisses, nec ab eius saluberrima humilitate tumore inflatus vanae scientiae resiluisses." I interpret thus with Labriolle, *La réaction païenne*, p. 232, the *resiluisses*, as against the old editors who saw therein a reference to the legend of Porphyry as an apostate.

[150] Cf. Bidez, *Vie de Porphyre*, chap. 3.

[151] *De civ. Dei* 19.23.1 (*PL* 41, 650): "Nam in libris quos ἐκ λογίων φιλοσοφίας appellat, in quibus exsequitur atque conscribit rerum ad philosophiam pertinentium velut divina responsa, ut ipsa verba eius, quem ad modum ex lingua Graeca in Latinam interpretata sunt, ponam ... Deinde post hos versus Apollinis qui non stante metro Latine interpretati sunt, subiunxit atque ait ..." The words "qui non stante metro Latine interpretati sunt" (as well as the words "nescio quos versus Graecos" in the text quoted below, n. 155) incline one to believe, however, that, following his usual exegetical method, Augustine collated the translation with the Greek text.

[152] *Ibid.* (*PL* 41, 651): "In Deum, inquit, generatorem et in regem ante omnia, quem tremit et caelum et terra atque mare et infernorum abdita, et ipsa numina perhorrescunt; quorum lex est Pater," quem valde sancti honorant Hebraei." ⟨Cf. Apuleius' Prayer to Isis, *Met.* 11.24–25. TRANS.⟩ According to the editor Wolff, p. 142, this oracle appeared

rendered to the true God, Augustine is quite aware that Porphyry contrasts Jews with Christians: in fact, another oracle asserts that Christ is a god, justly put to death by the Jews.[153] Similarly, when Porphyry quotes an oracle that declares that the gods have judged Christ to be very devout and immortal, Augustine is aware that it is done in order to contrast him with the sinfulness of the Christians.[154] The malefic operations of St. Peter, says an oracle, are the only reason that the Christian religion was due to last for 365 years.[155] Augustine takes up arms violently against such assertions.

---

at the end of the first book of the *Philosophy of Oracles*. Lactantius *De ira* 23.12 supplies the Greek text of the first three verses:

Ἐς δὲ θεὸν βασιλῆα, καὶ ἐς γενετῆρα προπάντων,
ὃν τρομέει καὶ γαῖα καὶ οὐρανὸς ἠδὲ θάλασσα
Ταρτάριοί τε μυχοί, καὶ δαίμονες ἐκφρίσσουσι.

St. Augustine returns several times to these last three words, particularly in the *De civ. Dei* 20.24.1; 22.3; 22.25 (*PL* 41: 696, 754, 793). This oracle was probably followed by an oracle from Jupiter, charging the Christians with stupidity because they believed in the end of the world. Cf. *De civ. Dei* 20.24.1 and Winter, *De doctr. neoplaton.*, p. 30.

[153] Porph. *Phil. of Oracles*, book 3, ed. Wolff, p. 183 = *De civ. Dei* 19.23.1 (*PL* 41, 650).

[154] Porph. (see preceding note), p. 180 (= Eusebius *Demonstr. Evang.* 3.7.1):

Παράδοξον ἴσως δόξειεν ἄν τισιν εἶναι τὸ μέλλον λέγεσθαι ὑφ' ἡμῶν. Τὸν γὰρ Χριστὸν οἱ θεοὶ εὐσεβέστατον ἀπεφήσαντο καὶ ἀθάνατον γεγονότα, εὐφήμως τε αὐτοῦ μνημονεύουσι.

Augustine *De civ. Dei* 19.23.2 (*PL* 41, 652):

Praeter opinionem, inquit, profecto quibusdam videatur esse quod dicturi sumus. Christum enim dii piissimum pronuntiaverunt et immortalem factum, et cum bona praedicatione eius meminerunt; Christianos vero pollutos, inquit, et contaminatos et errore implicatos esse dicunt; et multis talibus adversus eos blasphemiis utuntur.

The parallel between Eusebius and Augustine is continued at great length, but Augustine does not quote Porphyry from Eusebius, for he is more complete than Eusebius. He had long meditated on this passage; for cf. *De civ. Dei* 10.27 (*PL* 41, 305): "Non enim te decepisset, quem vestra, ut tu ipse scribis, oracula sanctum immortalemque confessa sunt," and, in the year 400, *De cons. Evang.* 1.15.23 (*PL* 34, 1052): "quidam philosophi eorum, sicut in libris suis Porphyrius Siculus prodidit, consuluerunt deos suos quid de Christo responderent; illi autem oraculis suis Christum laudare compulsi sunt."

[155] *De civ. Dei* 18.53.2 (*PL* 41, 617):

Cum enim viderent nec tot tantisque persecutionibus eam potuisse consumi, sed his potius mira incrementa sumpsisse, excogitaverunt *nescio quos versus Graecos,* tamquam consulenti cuidam, divino oraculo effusos, ubi Christum quidem ab huius tamquam sacrilegii crimine faciunt innocentem, Petrum autem maleficiis fecisse subiungunt, ut coleretur Christi nomen per trecentos sexaginta quinque

De civ. Dei 22.25 (*PL* 41, 795):

Neque enim Petri maleficiis eam cum laude credentium tanto ante praenuntiare compulsus est (Deus). Ille est enim Deus quem ... confitente Porphyrio atque id oraculis deorum suorum probare cupiente, ipsa numina perhorrescunt.

He borrows probably from Porphyry's *De imaginibus* a number of rational-istic explanations of the names of the gods. Attis castrated derives his name from the spring flowers that die without bearing fruit.[156] The Heroes who dwell in the air take their name from Hera, whose etymology is ἀήρ.[157] Against these names Augustine sets the Christian martyrs. He may have read this treatise in a Latin translation, for he does not know merely a few frag-ments but has a general comprehension of the whole work. He quite under-stands the danger of naturalistic symbolism, thanks to which Porphyry has revived the old myths and given them a philosophical intent.[158]

The *Letter to Anebo*[159] has still more interest for Augustine. He sees therein

---

annos, deinde completo memorato nu-mero annorum, sine mora sumeret finem.

It seems to me quite clear, given the context, that this fragment comes from the *Philosophy of Oracles*, although the editor Wolff omitted it.

[156] *De imag.*, frag. 7, ed. Bidez, p. 10* (= Eusebius *Praep. Evang.* 3.11, PG 21, 197 C):

Ἀλλ' ὁ μὲν Ἄττις τῶν κατὰ τὸ ἔαρ προφαινομένων ἀνθῶν, καὶ πρὶν τελε-σιογονῆσαι διαρρεόντων. Ὅθεν καὶ τὴν τῶν αἰδοίων ἀποκοπὴν αὐτῷ προσ-ανέθεσαν, μὴ φθασάντων ἐλθεῖν τῶν καρπῶν εἰς τὴν σπερματικὴν τελείω-σιν.

De civ. Dei 7.25 (PL 41, 215):

Propter vernalem quippe faciem terrae, quae ceteris temporibus est pulchrior, Por-phyrius philosophus nobilis Atyn flores significare perhibuit; et ideo abscisum, quia flos decidit ante fructum.

Augustine declares that he resorts to Porphyry because Varro was silent on this point.

[157] *De imag.*, frag. 5, p. 7* (= PG 21, 196 C):

Καὶ τοῦ μὲν παντὸς ἀέρος ἡ δύναμις Ἥρα τοὔνομα ἀπὸ τοῦ ἀέρος κεκλη-μένη.

De civ. Dei 10.21 (PL 41, 299):

Hoc enim nomen (Heroas) a Iunone dicitur tractum, quod Graece Iuno Ἥρα appellatur; et ideo nescio quis filius eius secundum Graecorum fabulas Heros fuerit nuncupatus: hoc videlicet veluti mysticum significante fabula, quod aer Iunoni depu-tetur, bui volunt cum daemonibus heroas habitare.

[158] *Enarr. in Ps.* 113.2.4 (PL 37, 1483): "Videntur autem sibi purgatioris esse religionis qui dicunt: nec simulacrum, nec daemonium colo, sed per effigiem corporalem eius rei signum intueor, quam colere debeo. Ita vero interpretantur simulacra, ut alio dicant significari terram, unde templum solent appellare Telluris [= Eusebius *Praep. Evang.* 3.11.15], alio mare sicut Neptuni ⟨simulacro⟩ [*ibid.*, 3.11.22], alio aerem sicut Iunonis [*ibid.*, 3.11.2], alio ignem sicut Vulcani [*ibid.*, 3.11.23], alio Luciferum sicut Veneris [*ibid.*, 3.11.40], alio solem, alio lunam [*ibid.*, 3.11.24], quorum simulacris eadem nomina sicut Telluris imponunt ... de quibus rursus cum exagitari coeperint, quod corpora colant, maximeque terram et mare et aerem et ignem ... respondere audent non se ipsa corpora colere, sed quae illis regendis praesint numina." Cf. also *De doctr. Christ.* 3.7.11; similari-ties noted by C. Reinhardt, *De Graecorum theologia*, p. 113 n. 1.

[159] And not *to Anubis*, as written by Alfaric, *L'évol. intell.*, p. 375 n. 3, and Combès, *Saint Aug.*, p. 17 (is this not an indication that this latter work is frequently based on secondary sources?), nor *to Aurelius*, as Bardy states, "La culture grecque," p. 30.

a criticism of paganism and produces a detailed analysis.[160] Porphyry seems to shrink from admitting, on his own account, a category of good spirits.[161] He is surprised that the gods enjoy sacrifices, pay heed to human pleas; that the stars, which are bodies, are called gods. He assumes that divination and portents are mystifications caused by maleficent spirits. If the gods are good, why do they listen to unjust requests made by man? And why do they demand from their priests abstinence from meat, though they themselves welcome the smoke of sacrificial victims? The cult of Isis and Osiris, as Chaeremon describes it, assumes that man can act even upon the ethereal gods. As Eusebius had done, Augustine delights in this criticism of paganism by a pagan, and he is kind enough or simple enough to believe that, if Porphyry is not more violent against the old religions, it is probably so that he can the better convince Anebo.

With regard to the *De regressu animae*, we have seen how this treatise impressed Augustine's mind even before his conversion. He was then on the very point of adopting the formula "Omne corpus est fugiendum," which flattered his first leanings toward Manicheanism. Afterward, he perceived that this theory was irreconcilable with the Christian dogma of the resurrection of the flesh and that it prevented many pagans from becoming converts.[162] He believed however that this dogma was not contrary to reason. The hypothesis of an incorruptible body reconciled Plato's theory that the soul cannot subsist without the body, with Porphyry's theory that condemned metempsychosis, as Plato and Plotinus understood it. And he ingenuously thinks that if Plato and Porphyry could have known each other, they would perhaps have become Christians.[163] Augustine praises Porphyry in particular for his discovery that the purified soul returns to the Father.[164] Nevertheless he attacks, with the aid of the *Timaeus*, which assigns a temporal beginning to the universe and to the gods, the theory that the soul, since it is imperishable, has no beginning either. There is no point in asserting that the genesis of which Plato speaks is a causal genesis, and not a temporal genesis;[165] for,

---

[160] *De civ. Dei* 10.11.1–2 (*PL* 41, 288), which reproduces almost textually the Greek fragment from Porphyry preserved by Eusebius *Praep. Evang.* 5.10 (*PG* 21, 341 B).

[161] *De civ. Dei* 10.11.2 (*PL* 41, 290): "sub aliorum opinatione," and 10.21 (*PL* 41, 299): "quamvis non ex sua sententia, sed ex aliorum." Cf. *De abstin.* 2.37, ed. Hercher, p. 38, 30.

[162] In addition to the texts quoted above, nn. 128–130, cf. *De civ. Dei* 10.24 and especially 22.26–28.

[163] *De civ. Dei* 22.27 (*PL* 41, 795): "Singula quaedam dixerunt Plato atque Porphyrius, quae si inter se communicare potuissent, facti essent fortasse Christiani." Cf. 10.30 (*PL* 41, 310).

[164] *Ibid.*, 10.30 (*PL* 41, 311): "Vidit hoc Porphyrius purgatamque animam ob hoc reverti dixit ad Patrem, ne aliquando iam malorum polluta contagione teneatur."

[165] *Ibid.*, 10.31 (*PL* 41, 311): "Verum id quo modo intellegant, invenerunt, non esse

as Porphyry himself acknowledges, the beatitude of the purified soul has a beginning but no end.[166] Christianity offers a way to salvation that, as Porphyry acknowledges at the end of the first book of the *De regressu animae*, he has never been able to find either in any philosophy or in the wisdom of the Indians and the Chaldeans.[167] If he did not see this, it was because he lived in the time of Diocletian's persecutions and thought that Christianity was approaching its end.[168] Augustine commends Porphyry for having distinguished between theurgy and magic, which invokes obscene spirits, and for confining the operations of theurgy to the purification of the "pneumatic" soul or the *anima spiritualis* as opposed to the *anima intellectualis*.[169] This was the indication that secretly Porphyry was ashamed of theurgy,[170] whose effects too, as he acknowledges, were sometimes unpleasant.[171] He had the credit of

---

hoc videlicet temporis, sed substitutionis initium: sicut enim, inquiunt, si pes ex aeternitate semper fuisset in pulvere, semper ei subesset vestigium; quod tamen vestigium a calcante factum nemo dubitaret, nec alterum altero prius esset, quamvis alterum ab altero factum esset: sic, inquiunt, et mundus atque in illo dii creati, et semper fuerunt semper existente qui fecit, et tamen facti sunt." I assume that we are here dealing with a textual fragment of the *De regressu animae*, although Bidez omits it in his edition. The argument will be resumed later on by Boethius and refuted by Philopon. Cf. below, pp. 313–314. The expression τὰ ἴχνη τῶν εἰδῶν with reference to the creation of the world is attested by Proclus in Porphyry *In Tim.* 30 A, ed. Diehl, 1, p. 383, 19, and Philopon *De aeternitate mundi*, ed. Rabe, p. 547, 8. The expression corresponds, I think, to the metaphor of the imprint of the foot (*vestigium*) mentioned by Augustine. Guitton, *Le temps et l'éternité chez Plotin et s. Augustin* (diss. Paris 1933) 160, and Winter, *De doctr. neoplaton.*, p. 58, were unaware of the source.

[166] *De civ. Dei* 10.31 (*PL* 41, 312): "Beatitudo quoque eius post experimentum malorum firmior et sine fine mansura, *sicut iste confitetur*, procul dubio coepit ex tempore, et tamen semper erit, cum antea non fuerit."

[167] Text quoted below, p. 245. We know that Porphyry also asked in his *Letter to Anebo*: "quae sit ad beatitudinem via ex Aegyptia sapientia" (*De civ. Dei* 10.11.2, *PL* 41, 290). What an evolution since the time when he declared in the *Philosophy of Oracles* (ed. Wolff, p. 141 = Eusebius *Praep. Evang.* 9.10 and 14.10, *PG* 21, 697 A and 1220 C): Τὴν δ' εὕρεσιν (σωτηρίας) Αἰγυπτίοις ὁ θεὸς ἐμαρτύρησε, Φοίνιξί τε καὶ Χαλδαίοις ('Ασσύριοι γὰρ οὗτοι), Λυδοῖς τε καὶ 'Εβραίοις.

[168] *De civ. Dei* 10.31 (*PL* 41, 313): "Videbat ergo ista Porphyrius et per huius modi persecutiones cito istam viam perituram, et propterea non esse ipsam liberandae animae universalem putabat." This statement confirms my hypothesis (above, p. 184 and n. 155) that we must refer the oracle that predicts the dissolution of the Christian Church 365 years after its institution to Porphyry's *Philosophy of Oracles*.

[169] Augustine *De Gen. ad litt.* 12.24.50 (*PL* 34, 474) accepts this Porphyrian division of the soul into intellectual, spiritual, corporeal.

[170] *De civ. Dei* 10.26 (*PL* 41, 303): "Nescio quo modo (quantum mihi videtur) amicis suis theurgis erubescebat Porphyrius." As a matter of fact, after criticizing sacrifices, Porphyry (*De abstin.* 2.60, ed. Hercher, p. 46, 39) goes on to say: θεοῖς δὲ ἀρίστη μὲν ἀπαρχὴ νοῦς καθαρὸς καὶ ψυχὴ ἀπαθής.

[171] For more details on the attitude of Porphyry and Augustine toward theurgy, cf. *De civ. Dei* 10.9.1–2; *De regressu animae*, frag. 2, ed. Bidez, pp. 27*–31*.

distinguishing between the angels, who dwell in the ether, and the demons, who dwell in the air.[172] He also comprehended the dogma of the Trinity, naming at least the Father and the Son ($\pi\alpha\tau\rho\iota\kappa\grave{o}s$ $\nuο\hat{u}s$),[173] and even the dogma of Grace.[174] But in his arrogance he refused to recognize the Son incarnate in Christ.[175]

It is evident how carefully Augustine read and analyzed Porphyry's principal works, except the $K\alpha\tau\grave{\alpha}$ $\chi\rho\iota\sigma\tau\iota\alpha\nu\hat{\omega}\nu$[176] and the *De abstinentia*.[177] How

---

[172] *De civ. Dei* 10.9.2 (*PL* 41, 287).

[173] *Ibid.*, 10.23 and 28, 10.29.1, 19.23.4 = frags. 7–10, ed. Bidez. The expression $\pi\alpha\tau\rho\iota\kappa\grave{o}s$ $\nuο\hat{u}s$ is not peculiar to Porphyry but was borrowed by him from the Chaldeans. Cf. Kroll, *De orac. Chald.*, p. 6, and below, at sec. 4 n. 80.

[174] *De civ. Dei* 10.29.1 (*PL* 41, 307): "Confiteris tamen gratiam, quando quidem ad Deum per virtutem intellegentiae pervenire, paucis dicis esse concessum." Augustine must be referring to a formula similar to the formula used by Porphyry, *Philos. of Oracles* (= Eusebius *Praep.* 6.4, *PG* 21, 412 A): $\dot{\eta}$ $\mu\alpha\gamma\varepsilon\acute{\iota}\alpha$ $\dot{\varepsilon}\nu$ $\tau\hat{\omega}$ $\lambda\acute{u}\varepsilon\iota\nu$ $\tau\grave{\alpha}$ $\tau\hat{\eta}s$ $\varepsilon\dot{\iota}\mu\alpha\rho\mu\acute{\varepsilon}\nu\eta s$ $\pi\alpha\rho\grave{\alpha}$ $\theta\varepsilon\hat{\omega}\nu$ $\dot{\varepsilon}\delta\acute{o}\theta\eta$ $\varepsilon\dot{\iota}s$ $\tau\grave{o}$ $\dot{o}\pi\omega\sigma\omega\hat{u}\nu$ $\tau\alpha\acute{u}\tau\eta\nu$ $\pi\alpha\rho\alpha\tau\rho\acute{\varepsilon}\pi\varepsilon\iota\nu$. Cf. above, pp. 37–38.

[175] *De civ. Dei* 10.28 (*PL* 41, 307): "Hunc autem Christum esse non credis: contemnis enim eum propter corpus ex femina acceptum et propter crucis opprobrium." It will be observed that, in the passages analyzed, the *De regressu animae* is certainly the source, even if it is not quoted each time. Augustine informs us of this in *De civ. Dei* 10.29.2 (*PL* 41, 308): "in his ipsis libris, ex quibus multa posui *De regressu animae*."

[176] Such is the view endorsed by Harnack, "Porphyrius *Gegen die Christen*," pp. 25–41 (followed by Winter, *De doctr. neoplaton.*, pp. 49–50), that Augustine did not even know the $K\alpha\tau\grave{\alpha}$ $\chi\rho\iota\sigma\tau\iota\alpha\nu\hat{\omega}\nu$ from the Greek refutations, as Jerome did. Augustine heard merely a very indirect echo of it from the antichristian rebuttals of a Carthaginian pagan, sent to him by Deogratias. (Cf. Augustine *Epist. ad Deogratias* 102, *PL* 33, 370). On the Porphyrian origin of these rebuttals, cf. below, at sec. 4 n. 14. Augustine is nevertheless wrong in denying that the Porphyry who was the author of these rebuttals is to be identified with Porphyry the Sicilian, several of whose works he read. Cf. *Retract.* 2.31 (*PL* 32, 643): "non nullas earum (quaestionum) a Porphyrio philosopho propositas dixit. Sed non eum esse arbitror Porphyrium Siculum illum cuius celeberrima est fama." This proves that at the date of the *Retractationes* Augustine did not yet suspect that Porphyry, so many works of whom he had read, was also the author of a treatise against the Christians.

[177] None of the doctrinal similarities that have been noted between Augustine and the *De abstinentia* is sufficient to establish that Augustine knew Porphyry's ascetic theories from the *De abstinentia* rather than from the lost parts of the *Letter to Anebo*. Cf. Winter's interesting demonstration, *De doctr. neoplaton.*, pp. 33–41, restoring passages in this letter by comparing Augustine's text with Iamblichus' *De mysteriis*. On the other hand, the following parallel suggests that Augustine had read his *Life of Plotinus*:

Porph. *Vita Plotini* 22:	*De cons. Evang.* 1.7.12 (*PL* 34, 1048; cf.
$^{\prime}O$ $\gamma\grave{\alpha}\rho$ $\delta\grave{\eta}$ $^{\prime}A\pi\acute{o}\lambda\lambda\omega\nu$ . . . $\dot{o}$ $\tauο\sigmaο\hat{u}\tau\sigma\nu$	1053):
$\varepsilon\dot{\iota}\pi\grave{\omega}\nu$ $\pi\varepsilon\rho\grave{\iota}$ $\Sigma\omega\kappa\rho\acute{\alpha}\tau\sigma\upsilon s\cdot$ $^{\prime}A\nu\delta\rho\hat{\omega}\nu$ $\dot{\alpha}\pi\acute{\alpha}\nu$-	Socrates autem quem rursus in activa,
$\tau\omega\nu$ $\Sigma\omega\kappa\rho\acute{\alpha}\tau\eta s$ $\sigmaο\phi\acute{\omega}\tau\alpha\tau\sigmaς$.	qua mores informantur, omnibus praetulerunt, ita ut testimonio quoque dei sui *Apollinis omnium sapientissimum* pronuntiatum esse non taceant.

Father Henry, *Plotin et l'Occident*, pp. 30–42 and 199, has shown that Porphyry's *Life of Plotinus* had been read in the West by Firmicus Maternus and Ammianus Marcellinus.

sympathetically too, for the blasphemies that he encounters against the Christians in the *Philosophy of the Oracles* do not deter him from reading Porphyry and judging him indulgently. He is not satisfied, like Eusebius, with using his criticism of paganism like artillery. It is Porphyry's philosophy that seems to him, on the whole, reconcilable with Christian doctrine. Furthermore, it leads to a recognition of several dogmas: the act of divine Grace, the Trinity, angels and demons, and even, despite appearances, the resurrection of the flesh. Porphyry is then partly enlightened by the true God. It is his philosophical pride that alone prevents him from adoring the Word made flesh and crucified.

It seems to me impossible to confine the Neoplatonic influence experienced by Augustine to Plotinus, as Father Henry does. Porphyry's influence is at least just as evident. It began to be felt before the conversion, but I do not see that it was less effective at the time of the *De civitate Dei*. Augustine is very interested in this philosophy and is convinced that it is one of the ways that may lead to Christ, as it led Victorinus or himself. Far from thinking with Alfaric or Theiler that Augustine the neophyte was converted to Plotinus' or Porphyry's Neoplatonism and later on withdrew from it, I believe that Augustine used the experience of his own conversion for his apologetics. In the *De civitate Dei* he has no intention of denying the tendencies common to the pagan philosophy and the Christian religion of his time, since he utilizes this harmony for the purpose of converting his opponents. But he discovered what was irreducible: the excessive scorn of the flesh among philosophers, and pride of spirit. So he became more circumspect in his vocabulary in order to avoid any Neoplatonic lapse.

Augustine does not confine himself to reading the works of Plotinus and Porphyry, which had had such a strong influence on his thought. He is equally familiar with the principal works that exert a religious influence on his contemporaries. He knows that the pagans confront the miracles of Christ with those of Apuleius and of Apollonius of Tyana.[178] Like Jerome, he had to read for himself the *Life of Apollonius* by Philostratus, for he considers him a worthy man.[179] We know that Philostratus' aim was to present

---

[178] *Epist. ad Deogratias* 102.6.32 (*PL* 33, 383): "Et tamen si hoc quod de Iona scriptum est, Apuleius Madaurensis vel Apollonius Tyaneus fecisse diceretur, quorum multa mira nullo fideli auctore iactitant . . . non iam in buccis creparet risus, sed typhus," and *Epist. ad Marcellinum* 136.1 (*PL* 33, 514): "Apollonium si quidem suum nobis et Apuleium, aliosque magicae artis homines in medium proferunt, quorum maiora contendunt exstitisse miracula." Porphyry already linked together Apollonius and Apuleius (cf. above, at chap. 2 sec. 2 n. 142), and Lactantius (*Inst.* 5.3, *PL* 6, 557 B) is surprised that, in his book against the Christians, Hierocles speaks of Apollonius without mentioning Apuleius.

[179] *Epist. ad Marcellinum* 138.4.18 (*PL* 33, 533): "multo enim melior, quod fatendum est, Apollonius fuit, quam tot stuprorum auctor et perpetrator, quem Iovem nominant."

Apollonius as a philosopher, not as a magician.[180] Augustine perhaps possessed the translation of Philostratus that Virius Nicomachus Flavianus[181] had
just published a few years previously. With regard to Apuleius, Augustine
knows that he writes books in Greek,[182] but there is nothing to prove that he
had read them, although he uses Apuleius' Latin works and even his translation of an Aristotelian Περὶ κόσμου.[183] He also read *Asclepius*, a hermetic
dialogue, in the translation that was for a long time wrongly attributed to
Apuleius, and he quotes quite frequently from it. This dialogue, in his
opinion, represents Egyptian wisdom, since it is an apology for idolatry.
Augustine notes with particular interest the prediction where Hermes Trismegistus proclaims and laments the end of the ancient cults. He knew then
the perishable gods![184] As for the Sibylline oracles, Augustine read first of all
some of them relating to Christ, in an anonymous translation that paid no
attention to meter.[185] It is possible that this was the translation of the *Philosophy of the Oracles*, which related oracles concerned with Christ, in connection with which Augustine makes a similar comment.[186] Later on, a certain
Flaccianus supplies him with the complete Greek text and calls to his attention
that one part was in acrostics. Augustine reproduces this piece in a translation
in Latin verse. He does not mention the translator by name, but he is very
careful to show that the Latin verses respect the acrostic scheme, despite the
difficulty of this *tour de force*. He is also so insistent on the mystic properties of
the number of these twenty-seven verses that I wonder whether he is not the
author of this translation. If he is not, it is one of his close friends.[187] What
leads us to think that Augustine was the author is that, in his enthusiasm for
the Christian character of these oracles, Augustine took pains to assemble all

---

[180] On Philostratus' intentions, cf. Labriolle, *La réaction païenne*, pp. 177–180.

[181] See above, chap. I sec. I n. 22.

[182] *De civ. Dei* 8.12 (*PL* 41, 237): "in utraque autem lingua, id est Graeca et Latina,
Apuleius Afer exstitit Platonicus nobilis."

[183] *Ibid.*, 4.2 (*PL* 41, 113): "quae uno loco Apuleius breviter stringit in eo libro quem
de mundo scripsit."

[184] *Ibid.*, 8.23–26 (*PL* 41, 247–254; cf. 42, 281 and 43, 224) = Asclepius 9ff.

[185] *Ibid.*, 18.23.1 (*PL* 41, 579): "Haec sane Erythraea Sibylla quaedam de Christo
manifesta conscripsit: quod etiam nos prius in Latina lingua *versibus male Latinis et non
stantibus* legimus, per nescio cuius interpretis imperitiam, sicut post cognovimus."

[186] Text quoted above, n. 151.

[187] *De civ. Dei* 18.23.1 (*PL* 41, 579): "vir clarissimus Flaccianus qui etiam proconsul
fuit ... Graecum nobis codicem protulit ... Hi autem versus, quorum primae litterae
istum sensum, quem diximus, reddunt, sicut eos quidam Latinis et stantibus versibus est
interpretatus, hoc continent ... In his Latinis versibus de Graeco utcumque translatis, ibi
non potuit ille sensus occurrere, qui fit cum litterae, quae sunt in eorum capitibus, con-
nectuntur, ubi Y littera in Graeco posita est; quia non potuerunt verba Latina inveniri,
quae ab eadem littera inciperent, et sententiae convenirent." Marrou, *Saint Aug.*, p. 36,
thinks that this translation is not by Augustine, but would Flaccianus have offered Augustine his Greek manuscript if Augustine had not been able to understand it?

those that Lactantius quoted in Greek and to translate them himself into Latin.[188] Such enthusiasm can be explained, for Augustine considers the

[188] Here is an interesting specimen of Augustine's art of translation:

Lactantius *Inst.* 4.18–19 (*PL* 6, 506 A = CSEL 19, p. 352, 3):

De civ. Dei 18.23.2 (*PL* 41, 580):

Εἰς ἀνόμους χεῖρας καὶ ἀπίστων
       ὕστερον ἥξει
δώσουσιν δὲ θεῷ ῥαπίσματα χερσὶν
       ἀνάγνοις,
καὶ στόμασιν μιαροῖς ἐμπτύσματα
       φαρμακόεντα
δώσει δ' εἰς μάστιγας ἁπλῶς ἁγνὸν
       τότε νῶτον.

In manus iniquas infidelium postea veniet: dabunt autem Deo alapas manibus incestis et impurato ore exspuent venenatos sputus: dabit vero ad verbera simpliciter sanctum dorsum.

Καὶ κολαφιζόμενος σιγήσει, μή τις
       ἐπιγνῶ
τίς λόγος ἢ πόθεν ἦλθεν, ἵνα φθιμέ-
       νοισι λαλήσει
καὶ στέφανον φορέσει τὸν ἀκάνθινον.

Et colaphos accipiens tacebit, ne quis agnoscat quod verbum, vel unde venit ut inferis loquatur, et corona spinea coronetur.

(p. 354, 6 = 507 A):

Εἰς δὲ τὸ βρῶμα χολήν, κεῖς δίψαν
       ὄξος ἔδωκαν
τῆς ἀφιλοξενίης ταύτην δείξουσι τρά-
       πεζαν.

Ad cibum autem fel, et ad sitim acetum dederunt: inhospitalitatis hanc monstrabunt mensam.

Αὐτὴ γὰρ δύσφρων τὸν σὸν θεὸν οὐκ
       ἐνόησας
παίζοντα θνητοῖσι νοήμασιν, ἀλλ' ἀπ'
       ἀκάνθης
ἔστεψας στεφάνῳ φοβερήν τε χολὴν
       ἐκέρασσας.

Ipsa enim insipiens tuum Deum non intellexisti, ludentem mortalium mentibus; sed spinis coronasti, et horridum fel miscuisti.

(p. 361, 8 = 511 A):

Ναοῦ δὲ σχισθῇ τὸ πέτασμα καὶ ἥμα-
       τι μέσσῳ
νὺξ ἔσται σκοτόεσσα πελώριος ἐν τρι-
       σὶν ὥραις.

Templi vero velum scindetur: et medio die nox erit tenebrosa nimis in tribus horis.

(p. 363, 10 = 513 A):

Καὶ θανάτου μοῖραν τελέσει, τρίτον
       ἦμαρ ὑπνώσας,
καὶ τότ' ἀπὸ φθιμένων, ἀναλύσας εἰς
       φάος ἥξει
πρῶτος ἀναστάσεως κλητοῖς ἀρχὴν
       ὑποδείξας.

Et morte morietur tribus diebus somno suscepto: et tunc ab inferis regressus ad lucem veniet primus, resurrectionis principio revocatis ostenso.

It is incorrect to say, with Marrou, *Saint Aug.*, p. 36, that Augustine reproduces Lactantius' translation. The latter does not translate but merely comments on the Greek verses, quoting some parallel passages from Scripture.

pagan oracles relating to Christ much more adapted than the Jewish prophecies to lead pagan spirits toward the true faith.[189]

Thus, although Augustine's culture was founded solely with the help of books written in Latin, he is far from despising the Greek writers. We have observed him collecting a large number of translations and resorting, when necessary, to the Greek original. In 410 he himself severely rebukes the young Greek Dioscorus who claims instruction from Augustine: it is foolish to want to study Greek philosophy from Cicero, when he can read the original texts.[190] Augustine displays in this letter a fine scorn for philosophers, except the Platonists. But he has in his own possession a *compendium*, in six books, of extracts from the Greek philosophers. There has been debate regarding the work indicated by Augustine. In the *De haeresibus*, composed toward the end of his life, he names the author: "quidam Celsus."[191] Schanz has maintained that, from an examination of the context, this work referred to a list of sects later than Christ, like the *De haeresibus*, and that it was impossible to identify it with the philosophical section of Cornelius Celsus' encyclopedia. In his view, it is a question of the Συναγωγὴ δογμάτων πάσης αἱρέσεως φιλοσόφου, a Greek work by a certain Celsinus of Castabala in Cappadocia, whose name has been preserved in Suidas.[192] Schwabe and Dyroff have disputed this view and think that the book may well be Cornelius Celsus' Latin encyclopedia.[193]

[189] See however in *Contra Faustum Manichaeum* 13.1 (*PL* 42, 281; cf. 282 and 292) the criticisms that Augustine previously directed against Faustus' argument: "Sane si sunt aliqua, ut fama est, Sibyllae de Christo praesagia, aut Hermetis quem dicunt Trismegistum, aut Orphei aliorumque in gentilitate vatum, haec nos aliquanto ad fidem iuvare poterunt, qui ex gentibus efficimur Christiani." We must assume that he had not yet read the Sibylline Oracles at this date. We know that a considerable number of these collections were Christian-inspired apocrypha. Cf. Rzach, *PW* s.v. Sibyllinische Orakel, 2117–2119.

[190] *Epist. ad Dioscorum* 108.2.10 (*PL* 41, 437): "Deinde iam exulcerati et irati (Graeci) quam cito te, quod nimis non vis, et hebetem iudicabunt, qui Graecorum philosophorum dogmata, vel potius dogmatum particulas quasdam discerptas atque dispersas in Latinis dialogis, quam in ipsorum auctorum libris Graecis tota atque contexta discere maluisti."

[191] *De haeresibus*, prol. (*PL* 42, 23): "Opiniones omnium philosophorum, qui sectas varias condiderunt usque ad tempora sua (neque enim plus poterat), sex non parvis voluminibus quidam Celsus absolvit. Nec redarguit aliquem, sed tantum quid sentirent aperuit, ea brevitate sermonis, ut tantum adhiberet eloquii quantum rei nec laudandae nec vituperandae, nec adfirmandae aut defendendae, sed aperiendae indicandaeque sufficeret; cum ferme centum philosophos nominasset, quorum non omnes instituerunt *haereses* proprias; quoniam nec illos tacendos putavit, qui suos magistros sine ulla dissensione secuti sunt."

[192] M. Schanz, "Ueber die Schriften des Cornelius Celsus," *Rheinisches Museum* 36 (1881) 369–371. Cf. Suidas, s.v. Κελσίνος Εὐδώρου Κασταβαλεὺς φιλόσοφος, and Stephanus Byzantinus, s.v. Καστάβαλα.

[193] L. Schwabe, "Die *Opiniones philosophorum* des Celsus," *Hermes* 19 (1884) 385–392, and A. Dyroff, "Der philosophische Teil der Encyclopädie des Cornelius Celsus," *Rheinisches Museum* 88 (1939) 7–18. Schanz-Hosius, 2, p. 724, is hesitant to take sides.

How can one decide? Schwabe is right in observing that Augustine here refers to some pagan work on the philosophical sects, not to a treatise on
Christian heresy that was his source.[194] But, to maintain his thesis, he is
obliged to assume that Quintilian's statement about Celsus' philosophical
writings does not apply to his encyclopedia.[195] The only way to decide is to
discover whether Augustine, in his earlier works, made use of Celsus or Celsinus. He quotes Cornelius Celsus in the *Soliloquies*, as Dyroff has noted.[196]
But this quotation gives us reason to think that Augustine does not mean
Cornelius Celsus in the *De haeresibus*. In fact, it shows that Cornelius Celsus
developed his own ideas or at least took sides between the sects, while the
work mentioned in the *De haeresibus* was, according to Augustine's formal
evidence, an objective catalogue of philosophers. It will be observed, also,
that in the *Soliloquies* Augustine explicitly mentions Cornelius Celsus as a
well-known writer, whereas the "quidam Celsus" of the *De haeresibus*
appears to be almost unknown.[197]

Now, Augustine also happens to mention Celsinus. This Celsinus, he says
in the *Contra Academicos*, called the Neoplatonic books that Augustine read
at the time of his conversion, that is, Plotinus and Porphyry, "substantial"
books.[198] This quotation agrees perfectly with the catalogue of sects mentioned by Suidas. If Augustine, in the *De haeresibus*, notes that the author of
this catalogue has gone "usque ad sua tempora," it was because this catalogue

---

[194] Augustine's only sources are Philastrius, Epiphanius of Cyprus, and Pseudo-
Jerome's *Indiculus de haeresibus*, which Augustine possesses as an anonymous work. Cf.
G. Bardy, "Le *De haeresibus* et ses sources," *Misc. Agost.* 2 (1931) 397–416, and Schanz,
vol. 4, 2, p. 439. On the other hand, Augustine associates this "quidam Celsus" with
"noster Epiphanius."

[195] Quintilian *Inst. orat.* 10.1.124: "Scripsit non parum multa Cornelius Celsus Sextios
secutus, non sine cultu ac nitore."

[196] Augustine *Solil.* 1.12.21 (*PL* 32, 881): "Cogor interdum Cornelio Celso adsentiri,
qui ait summum bonum esse sapientiam, summum autem malum dolorem corporis."

[197] Dyroff, "Der philos. Teil," p. 8, seems to have observed how embarrassing this
"quidam Celsus" was for his theory.

[198] Augustine *Contra Acad.* 2.2.5, ed. Knoell, CSEL 63, p. 26, 19 = *PL* 32, 921: "Et
quoniam nondum aderat ea flamma, quae summa nos adreptura erat, illam qualem
aestuabamus arbitrabamur esse vel maximam, cum ecce tibi *libri quidam pleni,* ut ait
Celsinus, bonas res Arabicas ubi exhalarunt in nos, ubi illi flammulae instillarunt pretio-
sissimi unguenti guttas paucissimas, incredibile, Romaniane, incredibile et ultra quam de
me fortasse et tu credis,—quid amplius dicam?—etiam mihi ipsi de me ipso incredibile
incendium concitarunt." Henry, *Plotin et l'Occident,* p. 79, quotes this text without any
explanation regarding Celsinus. Knoell's edition, in the Index, proposes to identify him
with the person "immanissimo tyfo turgidum" who, according to *Conf.* 7.9.13, supplied
Augustine with these Neoplatonic writings; but Knoell offers not the slightest evidence
to justify his conjecture. Dyroff, "Der philos. Teil," p. 15, discards this text as unfavorable to his theory by declaring that the question merely involves the oral expression of a
certain Celsinus, a friend of Augustine's otherwise completely unknown. Cf. *De ordine*
2.28: "libri plenissimi."

included even the Neoplatonists. Augustine must have taken from him the
term "sect" relating to Plotinus and various other items of information on
the history of philosophy that he included a little later on in the *Contra Academicos*.[199] Similarly, when Augustine, in Book 8 of the *De civitate Dei*, reviews the various philosophical sects, as far as and including Plotinus,
Porphyry, and Iamblichus, he is probably following Celsinus' manual. In
point of fact, he could not have known Iamblichus except from this manual,
since he never uses him and had read nothing by him. In other respects, he
shows clearly that he is following a manual entitled *Opiniones omnium philosophorum*, but that he makes excisions;[200] and this entire discussion has its
parallel in Claudian and Sidonius Apollinaris. They have then a common
source in the Latin translation of Celsinus' handbook.[201] Perhaps it was the
reading of this manual that made Augustine, during his stay in Milan, read
the Neoplatonists. In any case, he had not yet forgotten it toward the end of
his life.[202]

Augustine's reading in medical literature shows that, when the opportunity occurs, he is even trying to supplement his Greek knowledge from the
original texts. He first heard about Hippocrates through the eminent physician Vindicianus, in the course of their conversations,[203] and he knows that a

[199] Texts quoted above, n. 118 and p. 141. Dyroff, "Der philos. Teil," p. 13, notes that
this comment on Pythagoras and Pherecydes does not stem from any extant Latin
writer.

[200] Cf. *De civ. Dei* 8.1, ed. Dombart, p. 320, 25: "Ex omnibus quorum sententias
litteris nosse potuimus, eligendi sunt cum quibus non indigna quaestio ista tractetur.
Neque enim hoc opere omnes *omnium philosophorum* vanas *opiniones* refutare suscepi";
8.2, p. 323, 7: "perhibetur"; 8.3, p. 323, 12: "memoratur" and "sicut de illo *quidam*
benevolentius suspicatur"; p. 324, 24: "sic alii atque alii aliud atque aliud opinati sunt,
quos commemorare longum est"; 8.4, p. 325, 20: "memoratur," 325, 23: "laudatur,"
325, 30: "quid autem in his vel de his singulis partibus Plato senserit . . . disserendo
explicare et longum esse arbitror et temere adfirmandum esse non arbitror," p. 326, 18:
"laudantur"; 8.5, p. 328, 13: "quicumque alii, quorum enumeratione immorari non est
necesse." The title *Opiniones omnium philosophorum* is the title of Celsus' work (above,
n. 191) and agrees with the Greek title: δόγματα πάσης αἱρέσεως φιλοσόφου. Augustine shows clearly in this text that the author called the philosophical sects *haereses*; and he
does not follow Cicero *De natura deorum* 1.10–12.

[201] On Claudian, cf. above, p. 135. On Sidonius Apollinaris, below, p. 257. Who can
this Greek Celsinus be who is posterior to Iamblichus? Of all the ancient writers who
have borne this name (cf. *PW* and the *Thesaurus ling. Lat.*, *suppl.*, s.v. Celsinus) the only
one who seems to fit is Julian the Apostate's son-in-law, who is mentioned in several of
Libanius' letters and was active in the literary field at Beirut. Since Augustine did not
read Greek fluently at the date of the *Contra Acad.*, it must be admitted that this manual
had been translated by some Latin Neoplatonist in the fourth century, probably by
Theodorus himself, from whom he received the *libri Platonici*.

[202] Despite his lapse in writing *Celsus* for *Celsinus*, which may be due to a failing
memory for proper names in his old age.

[203] *Conf.* 4.3.5, p. 69 Lab.

large number of apocrypha circulate under the name of Hippocrates.[204] Cicero, on the other hand, furnishes him with the Hippocratic anecdote about the concurrent illnesses of twins.[205] But in his last days Augustine read the texts. He quotes a Hippocratic aphorism,[206] perhaps in translation,[207] and certainly read Soranus' *Gynaeceia* in Greek. In his *Quaestiones in Heptateuchum* Augustine quoted from memory and quite inaccurately a passage under the name of Hippocrates and, in the *Contra Iulianum*, the same passage under the name of Soranus, but again incorrectly. He returned a third time to this subject in the *Retractationes*, and this time he consulted the text in order to correct his mistake.[208] We are convinced that Augustine read this passage in Greek, for Muscio's translation, a simple practical manual for midwives, much abridged in relation to the Greek, does not apply to this section of the *Gynaeceia* and does not contain this specific passage.[209] There

---

[204] *Contra Faustum Manich.* 33.6 (*PL* 42, 514).

[205] *De civ. Dei* 5.2 (*PL* 41, 142). The reference is probably to a lost passage in the *De fato*.

[206] *De civ. Dei* 22.8.3 (*PL* 41, 763): "Ut aliquanto homo diutius vivat, tamen inde morte quamlibet tardius adfutura, secundum Hippocratis, ut ferunt, sententiam, omnis est omittenda curatio" = Hippocrates *Aphor.* 6.83.

[207] On these translations, cf. Kuehlewein, in *Hermes* 17 (1882) 484, and Fuchs, "Anecdota Hippocratea," *Philologus* 58, n.s. 12 (1899) 414.

[208]

Soranus *Gy-naeceia* 1.10.39, *CMG* 4, p. 27 = ed. V. Rose, p. 206, 16:	*Quaest. in Heptat.* 1.93 (*PL* 34, 572, *in Gen.* 30.37–42):	*Contra Iulian.* 5.14. (*PL* 44, 813 *in Gen.* 30.37–42):	*Retract.* 2.62 (*PL* 32, 655):
ʿΟ δὲ τῶν Κυπρί-ων τύραννος κακό-μορφος ὢν εἰς ἀγάλ-ματα περικαλλῆ κατὰ τοὺς πλησια-σμοὺς τὴν γυναῖκα βλέπειν ἀναγκάζων, πατὴρ εὐμόρφων ἐγένετο παίδων.	Sed et mulieri ac-cidisse traditur, et scriptum reperitur in libris antiquissimi et peritissimi medici Hippocratis, quod suspicione adulterii fuerat punienda cum puerum pul-cherrimum peperis-set, utrique parenti generique dissimi-lem, nisi memoratus medicus solvisset quaestionem, illis admonitis quaerere ne forte aliqua talis pictura esset in cubi-culo; qua inventa mulier a suspicione liberata est.	Tale vero aliquid etiam in fetibus hu-manis posse con-tingere, Soranus medicinae auctor nobilissimus scribit, et exemplo confir-mat historiae. Nam Dionysium tyran-num narrat, eo quod ipse deformis esset, nec tales habere fili-os vellet, uxori quae in concubitu formo-sam proponere so-lere picturam, cuius pulchritudinem con-cupiscendo quodam modo raperet, et in prolem quam con-cipiebat adficiendo transmitteret.	Verum in huius tanti tamque elabo-rati operis quinto vo-lumine, ubi comme-moravi deformem maritum coniugi suae, ne deformes pareret, proponere in concubitu formo-sam solere picturam, nomen hominis qui hoc facere solebat, quasi certum posui, cum sit incertum, quia memoria me fefellit. Hoc autem Soranus auctor medicinae scripsit regem Cyprium facere solere, sed no-men eius proprium non expressit.

[209] In contradiction to Marrou, *Saint Aug.*, p. 142 n. 5. Cf. Muscio *Sorani gynaeceiorum*

is evident then in Augustine a growing need to make direct contact with the Greek pagan writers. This evolution seems to correspond to the laborious progress that I have noted in his knowledge of the Greek language. From the time of his adolescence, the reading of a few translations by Victorinus had a decisive influence on the course of his life. It was natural that, when he knew a little Greek, he should think of referring to the original texts. For a long time he seemed to go on reading them with the help, whenever necessary, of a translation. But toward the end of his life he had no longer any need even of this aid and read at sight all kinds of Greek works.

3. Augustine and Greek Patristics

A study of Augustine's Greek ecclesiastical culture will confirm this conclusion. This culture is rather circumscribed, but perhaps less so than has been stated. Doubtless, when Augustine quotes in the *De doctrina Christiana* the "countless Greeks" who utilized the treasures of Egypt for the glory of Christ, he does not want to imply that he read all of them. Actually this passage, I think, is merely a reference to St. Jerome's *Letter to Magnus*, where all these writers were listed.[1]

On the other hand, if he rarely quotes authorities, it is because he does not approach his treatises in the way that Jerome approached his commentaries. For him, it is not a matter of listing the various interpretations of a given passage in the sacred text or the different solutions of a given difficulty that had already been suggested. His task is too individual to require so much reading, although he frequently uses the Latin historians and has sufficient texts of Tertullian, Hilary, and particularly Ambrose and Cyprian.[2]

Furthermore, Augustine is convinced of the fundamental unity of the Church. He believes that the faith is precisely the same among the Greeks and the Latins.[3] Thus he does not feel the need, as a general rule, to appeal to

---

vetus translatio Latina, ed. V. Rose (Leipzig 1882), who does not translate Book 1 of Soranus. I have verified the fact that the anecdote, moreover, appears neither in the *Gynaeceia* of Vindicianus nor in that of Caelius Aurelianus.

[1] *De doctr. Christ.* 2.40.61 (*PL* 34, 63): "Nonne aspicimus quanto auro et argento et veste suffarcinatus exierit de Aegypto Cyprianus doctor suavissimus et martyr beatissimus? quanto Lactantius? quanto Victorinus, Optatus, Hilarius, ut de vivis taceam? quanto innumerabiles Graeci?" Jerome *Epist. ad Magnum* 70 (*PL* 22, 667) listed a number of Greek ecclesiastical writers; then, among the Latin writers, Tertullian, Minucius Felix, Arnobius, Lactantius, Victorinus, Cyprian, Hilary, and he concluded: "de ceteris vel mortuis vel viventibus taceo." See above, p. 90.

[2] Marrou, *Saint Aug.*, pp. 418–421.

[3] *Contra Iulian.* 1.4.13–14 (*PL* 44, 648): "An ideo contemnendos putas, quia Occidentalis ecclesiae sunt omnes, nec ullus est in eis commemoratus a nobis Orientis episcopus? Quid ergo faciemus, cum illi Graeci sint, nos Latini? Puto tibi eam partem orbis sufficere debere, in qua primum Apostolorum suorum voluit Dominus gloriosissimo martyrio

Greek authorities for his Latin readers. He does not depart from this method except on two occasions that are quite exceptional. The first time, to bring back to the Catholic faith some obscure bishop, he draws his argument from the authority of the Greek and Roman Fathers where these agree.[4] On another occasion, it is because the Pelagians support their heretical theories with several Greek texts that Augustine follows them on this ground and considers it his duty to quote the principal Greek writers who have treated the question.[5] It is therefore not necessary to think that Augustine is unacquainted with, or systematically disregards, Greek ecclesiastical literature. What strikes me, on the contrary, is the effort he makes to get to know it, either through translations or even from the original texts. Did he not urge Jerome in 394 to complete the translation of the Greek commentators, as he had started to do in his commentaries on St. Paul's Epistles, inspired by Origen, rather than to devote himself to the translation of the Hebrew text of the Scriptures?[6]

Augustine mentions Philo and Josephus. I do not think that he had read Philo in the Greek, but he knows that certain writings by St. Ambrose stem from him; so much so that when some point in Ambrose appears to him to deserve censure, he quotes him under Philo's name.[7] With regard to Josephus,

---

coronare . . . Non est ergo cur provoces ad Orientis antistites, quia et ipsi utique Christiani sunt et utriusque partis terrarum fides ista una est." See in addition the texts assembled by Reuter, *Augustinische Studien, IV*: "Augustin und der katholische Orient," pp. 165–166.

[4] *Epist. ad Fortunatianum* 148.15 (*PL* 33, 618) after having quoted Jerome, Ambrose, Athanasius, Basil: "Haec omnia de litteris eorum et Latinorum et Graecorum, qui priores nobis in catholica Ecclesia viventes divina eloquia tractaverunt, ideo commemoranda arbitratus sum, ut sciat iste frater . . ."

[5] See below, p. 205.

[6] Text quoted above, chap. 4 sec. 1 n. 32.

[7] *Contra Faustum Manich.* 12.39 (*PL* 42, 274): "Vidit hoc Philo quidam, vir liberaliter eruditissimus, unus illorum, cuius eloquium Graeci Platoni aequare non dubitant . . . Ut enim quiddam eiusdem Philonis commemorem, arcam diluvii secundum rationem humani corporis fabricatam volens intellegi, tamquam membratim omnia pertractabat. Cui subtilissime numerorum etiam regulas consulenti, congruenter occurrebant omnia quae ad intellegendum Christum nihil impedirent quoniam in corpore humano etiam ille humani generis Salvator apparuit, nec tamen cogerent quia corpus humanum est utique et hominum ceterorum. At ubi ventum est ad ostium, quod in arcae latere factum est, omnis humani ingenii coniectura defecit. Ut tamen aliquid diceret, inferiores corporis partes, *per quas* urina et fimus *egeruntur*, illo ostio significari ausus est credere." Without naming Philo, Ambrose adopts his interpretation of the ark, *De Noe et arca* 8 (*PL* 14, 372 A): "Pulchre autem addidit: *Ostium ex adverso facies* [Gen. 6.16], eam partem declarans corporis, *per quam* cibos *egerere* consuevimus; ut quae putamus ignobiliora esse corporis, his honorem abundantiorem circumdaret." Augustine read this treatise of Ambrose's in a more complete text than our present text (cf. *Contra Iulian.* 2.2 [*PL* 44, 674] and *Contra duas epist. Pel.* 4.11.29 [*PL* 44, 632], where he quotes passages that do not

before 419 he had read the *De excidio Ierusalem*, perhaps in translation,[8] and before 425 the *Antiquities*, of which we see him using at least the synopses.[9] Now, this work had not yet been translated into Latin.

Among the ancient Greek Fathers, Augustine liked Irenaeus. He read him in the Latin translation that has preserved his treatise *Against Heresies*, for he quoted two passages from it.[10] He reckoned Irenaeus among the Western authorities, along with the Latin writers Cyprian, Reticius, Olympius, Hilary, and Ambrose. This proves that he made no distinction in the Church between the Greek Church and the Latin Church.

Augustine also knew Origen, whom he considered a heretic. But what exactly did he read of Origen's writings? At the time of the Origenist quarrel between Jerome and Rufinus, he tried particularly to discover the purpose of the dispute. In fact, Jerome's *De viris* contained only a literary notice on Origen, without any evaluation of his doctrine. Augustine asked Jerome to write a special treatise on Origen's errors, or even, if possible, on the principal Greek heresies "for the instruction of those who have no leisure, on account of their other occupations, or who have not the capacity, as the language is foreign to them, to read and study so much."[11] It was then at this date, in 397, that Augustine was not able to read Origen in Greek. Jerome

appear in the present text). It is unlikely that his reference to Philo *Quaest. in Gen.* 2.6 is a direct reference, for no ancient Latin translation of this work is known. Aucher's modern translation, made from the Armenian language, has: "Non obscure ostendit humanum aedificium porta illa ex latere, quam decenter adnotavit lateralem vocans, per quam excrementa stercoris foras expelluntur" (*Philonis opera*, ed. Richter, vol. 6, Leipzig 1829) 311. Cf. *Exam.* 6.9.72, p. 259, 7.

[8] *Epist. ad Hesychium* 199.9.30 (*PL* 33, 916): "Nam Iosephus qui Iudaicam scripsit historiam, talia mala dicit illi populo tunc accidisse, ut vix credibilia videantur: unde non immerito dictum est, talem tribulationem nec fuisse a creaturae initio, nec futuram." Cf. Marrou, *Saint Aug.*, p. 36 n. 5 and p. 418 n. 4. Augustine refers either to the translation by Pseudo-Hegesippus or to the translation attributed to Rufinus. Cf. Schanz, vol. 4, 1, p. 423.

[9] *De civ. Dei* 18.45.2–3 (*PL* 41, 606–607). This chapter on the history of Israel from the building of the Temple to the birth of Christ is an almost textual copy of the summaries of Books 11 to 14 of the *Antiquities*. Augustine's only personal contribution is the statement: "Tunc iam Roma subiugaverat Africam," which notes a synchronism with the history of Rome.

[10] *Contra Iulian.* 1.3.5 (*PL* 44, 644), quoting word for word Irenaeus *Adv. haer.* 4.2.7 (*PG* 7, 979 B) and 5.19.1 (*PG* 7, 1175 B): "Irenaeus Lugdunensis episcopus non longe a temporibus Apostolorum fuit: iste ait: 'Non aliter salvari homines ab antiqua serpentis plaga . . . et vivificavit mortuos.' Item idem ipse: 'Quem ad modum adstrictum est, inquit . . . per quae adligati eramus morti.'" Augustine returns to these quotations in *PL* 44, 662.

[11] *Epist. ad Hieron.* 40.6 (*PL* 33, 158): "in notitiam eorum quibus aut non vacat propter aliena negotia, aut non valent propter alienam linguam tam multa legere atque cognoscere."

made him distinctly aware of this, for, without acceding to his wish, he replied sharply to a criticism that Augustine had directed against his *Comment-ary on the Epistle to the Galatians*. Augustine had only to read Origen: he would then have seen that the opinion attributed to Jerome was Origen's and that Jerome reproduced it without adopting it.[12] Some twenty years later, Augustine had certainly read at least Origen's *Homilies on Genesis*, in Rufinus' translation,[13] and very probably the *De principiis*, in Jerome's translation.[14] In fact, although Augustine admired Origen's erudi-

---

[12] Jerome *Epist. ad Augustinum* 75.4 (*PL* 33, 253): " Si quid igitur reprehensione dignum putaveras in explanatione nostra, eruditionis tuae fuerat quaerere utrum ea quae scripsi-mus haberentur in Graecis, ut, si illi non dixissent, tunc meam proprie sententiam con-demnares, praesertim cum libere in praefatione confessus sim, Origenis commentarios me esse secutum et vel mea vel aliena dictasse." Similarly, Augustine should know that the title *Epitaphium* does not coincide with Jerome's *De vir. inl.*, *Epist. ad Aug.* 75.3 (*PL* 33, 252): "Legisti enim et Graecos et Latinos, qui vitas virorum inlustrium descripserunt, quod numquam *Epitaphium* huic operi scripserint, sed *De inlustribus viris*."

[13] Origen–Rufinus *In Genesim, hom.* 2.2 (*PG* 12, 166 A–B):

(Apelles) ... dicit nullo modo fieri potuisse, ut tam breve spatium tot *animalium* genera eorumque cibos qui per totum annum sufficerent, *capere* potuisset... Sed ad haec nos quae a prudenti-bus viris et Hebraicarum traditionum gnaris atque a veteribus magistris didici-mus, ad auditorum notitiam deferemus. Aiebant ergo maiores *quod Moyses* qui, ut de eo Scriptura testatur, *omni sapientia Aegyptiorum fuerat eruditus*, secundum artem geometricam, quam praeci-pue Aegyptii callent, cubi-torum numerum in hoc loco posuit. Apud *geometras* enim secundum eam ratio-nem quae apud eos virtus vocatur ex solido et quad-rato vel in *sex cubitos* unus deputatur, si generaliter, vel trecentos, si minutatim de-ducatur.

In Quaest. in Heptat. 1.4 (*PL* 34, 549):

De arca Noe quaeri solet utrum tanta *capacitate* quanta describitur, *anima-lia* omnia quae in eam in-gressa dicuntur, et escas eorum ferre potuerit. Quam quaestionem cubito geometrico solvit Ori-genes, adserens non frustra Scripturam dixisse *quod Moyses omni sapientia Aegyptiorum fuerit eruditus*, qui geometricam dilexe-runt. *Cubitum* autem geo-*metricum* dicit tantum valere quantum nostra *cubita sex* valent.

De civ. Dei 15.27.3 (*PL* 41, 474):

Si autem cogitemus quod Origenes non ineleganter adstruxit, *Moysen* scilicet ho-minem Dei eruditum, sicut scriptum est, *omni sapientia Aegyptiorum*, qui geometri-cam dilexerunt, *geometrica cubita* significare potuisse, ubi unum quantum *sex* no-stra valere adseverant.

[14] *De civ. Dei* 11.23.1 (*PL* 41, 336), with reference to the descent of the souls into bodies: "Hinc Origenes iure culpatur. In libris enim quos appellat Περὶ ἀρχῶν, id est

tion,[15] he was cognizant of his major errors. In 415, he replied to Orosius' appeal, alarmed at the progress of Origenism in Spain, and refuted Origen's theories on the temporal character of the punishment of evil angels, the preexistence of creatures in the Word, the degradation of creatures according to their sins, the souls of heavenly bodies.[16] In the *De civitate Dei* he repeated his arguments against preexistence and the degradation of souls[17] and, without mentioning Origen, added objections against the theory of the salvation of Satan,[18] the cyclic concept of the universe,[19] and the theory of the spiritual conversion of resurrected bodies.[20] In his *De haeresibus* he again returned to these theories of cycles and the salvation of Satan, and he noted that Epiphanius had forgotten to indicate these theories as the essential mistake on Origen's part.[21] He seemed then to have known in particular Origen's theories from the controversy between Jerome and Rufinus and through consultation with Orosius, and he confined himself to the objections that were to result in Origen's definitive condemnation under Justinian.

Augustine was more familiar with the two major works of Eusebius of Caesarea: the *Chronica* and the *Church History*. These were working tools that he used, the first one in Jerome's translation, the second in Rufinus' translation. He was able to secure the *Chronica* as early as 394, when his colleague Alypius received it from Paulinus of Nola, who had had it reproduced on a copy of Domnion, Jerome's correspondent.[22] He considered it indispensable for any work on exegesis and frequently referred to it himself, sometimes under the name of Eusebius only, and again under the names of

---

De principiis, hoc sensit, hoc scripsit." It was naturally Jerome's translation rather than Rufinus' that, for Augustine, shed full light on Origen's errors, which Augustine refuted. In the text quoted below, n. 19, the Augustinian text of the words of Ecclesiastes is, all in all, much closer to Jerome's translation (preserved in this fragment) than to the translation by Rufinus.

[15] *De civ. Dei* 11.23.1: "Miror hominem in ecclesiasticis litteris tam doctum et exercitatum non attendisse, primum quam hoc esset contrarium Scripturae huius tantae auctoritatis intentioni."

[16] *Ad Orosium contra Priscillianistas et Origenistas* 4–11 (PL 42, 671–678). It will be observed that this refutation repeats point by point the Origenist theories on which Orosius asked Augustine's view, but it does not assume in Augustine a personal knowledge of Origen.

[17] *De civ. Dei* 11.23 (PL 41, 336–337). Cf. *Epist. ad Optatum* 202(a), 4.8 (PL 33, 932).

[18] *De civ. Dei* 21.17 (PL 41, 731): he refutes this theory in chap. 23. Cf. *Op. imperf. contra Iulian.* 5.47 and 6.10 (PL 45, 1484 and 1518).

[19] *De civ. Dei* 12.13.2 (PL 41, 361) with reference to the interpretation of Ecclesiastes 1.9–10. Cf. *Retract.* 1.6.6 (PL 32, 593) and Origen *De principiis* 1.4.5 and 3.5.3 (PG 11, 328 A).

[20] *De civ. Dei* 13.20 (PL 41, 393) with reference to the interpretation of I Cor. 15.32. Cf. Origen *De principiis* 2.10.1 (PG 11, 234 A).

[21] *De haer.* 43 (PL 42, 33), with mention of the *defensores Origenis*.

[22] *Paulini Epist. ad Alypium* 24.3 (PL 33, 99).

Eusebius and Jerome.[23] With regard to the *Church History*, he took from it an anecdote to illustrate his meaning,[24] or an additional item,[25] or a correction to Epiphanius' assertions on heretics.[26] Lastly, it was through the *Church History* that he knew the text of Julius Africanus' letter to Aristides, in which Christ's dual genealogy was explained.[27] Augustine also read Anthony's *Life* by Athanasius, in the translation by Evagrius of Antioch.[28] He even thought he had, in translation, Athanasius' treatise against the Arians. But his quotation from it on the invisibility of God proves that he had in his possession merely some apocryphal treatise composed in Latin.[29] In Didymus, he read

[23] *De doctr. Christ.* 2.39.59 (*PL* 34, 62): "... quod Eusebius fecit de temporum historia propter divinorum librorum quaestiones, quae usum eius flagitant." Cf. his quotations under the name of Eusebius: *Quaest. in Heptat.* 2.47 (*PL* 34, 612), *De civ. Dei* 16.16 and 18.25 (*PL* 41, 497 and 582), the latter under the names of Eusebius and Jerome; *De civ. Dei* 18.8, 18.10, and 18.31 (*PL* 41: 566, 568, 587).

[24] *De cura pro mortuis gerenda* 6.8 (*PL* 40, 597): "Legimus in Ecclesiastica historia, quam Graece scripsit Eusebius et in Latinam linguam vertit Rufinus, martyrum corpora in Gallia canibus exposita" (= *Hist. eccl.* 5.1). Cf. *De civ. Dei* 21.6.1 (*PL* 41, 717) = Eusebius-Rufinus, *Hist. eccl.* 2.23.

[25] *De haer.* 83 (*PL* 42, 46) = *Hist. eccl.* 6.37.

[26] *De haer.* 10 and 22 (*PL* 42, 27 and 28) = *Hist. eccl.* 6.38 and 5.13.

[27] *Retract.* 2.7.3 (*PL* 32, 633): "Nam etiam nomen eiusdem mulieris quae peperit Iacob ... et de marito posteriore Melchi peperit Heli, cuius erat adoptivus Ioseph, non tacuit Africanus. Quod quidem, cum Fausto responderem, nondum legeram." Julius Africanus *Epist. ad Aristidem* 3 (*PG* 10, 57 B) *apud* Eusebius *Hist. eccl.* 1.7 (*PL* 20, 93 B) in fact mentions this woman who was called Estha. Augustine had been unable to read this text in 400, the date of the *Contra Faustum*, because Rufinus' *Hist. eccl.* had not yet appeared. It is assumed in fact that Rufinus wrote it in 403.

[28] Augustine *Conf.*, p. 200 Lab. = Athanasius *Vita Antonii* 2 (*PG* 26, 841 B); *De doctr. Christ.*, prol. (*PL* 34, 17) = Athanasius *Vita Anton.* 4 (*PG* 26, 845 A), where one may find Evagrius' translation facing the Greek text. Cf. also G. Garitte, *Un témoin important du texte de la vie de s. Antoine par s. Athanase: La version latine inédite des Archives du chapitre de Saint-Pierre de Rome* (Institut historique belge de Rome, Etudes de philologie, d'archéologie et d'histoire anciennes, vol. 3, Brussels 1939), and P. Monceaux, "Saint Augustin et saint Antoine, contribution à l'histoire du monachisme," *Miscellanea Agostiniana* 2 (1931) 61–89. Augustine appears rather to follow Evagrius.

[29] Pseudo-Athanasius *De Trinitate* 10 (*PL* 42, 294 C):

(Arianis) in primo respondendum est Filium Dei *non ita visum ut Deus* erat, sed ut homo capi poterat.

Ibid., 11 (*PL* 42, 299 D):

Ariani dicunt Patrem solum *invisibilem* Deum, et maiorem, et ideo solum colendum atque adorandum. Ego credo secundum divinam substantiam ac maiestatem, Spiritum Filium, Spiritum quoque Spiritum sanctum, Domino in Evangelio

Augustine *Epist. ad Fortunatianum* 148.10 (*PL* 33, 626):

Beatissimus quoque Athanasius Alexandrinus episcopus, cum ageret adversus *Arianos*, qui tantum modo Deum *Patrem invisibilem dicunt*, Filium vero et Spiritum sanctum visibiles putant, aequalem Trinitatis invisibilitatem Scripturarum sanctarum testimoniis, et diligentia suae disputationis adseruit, instantissime suadens *Deum non esse visum*, nisi adsumptione creaturae, *secundum* Deitatis autem suae proprietatem omnino Deum esse *in-*

the *De Spiritu sancto*, translated by Jerome,[30] but he had read nothing of Apollinaris of Laodicea. In fact, he was incapable of recognizing one of Jerome's references to Apollinaris' commentary on the Epistle to the Galatians.[31] He knew only that his heresy consisted of denying the human soul in Christ, an error toward which Alypius[32] leant for a moment, and he understood from Epiphanius the various sects of Apollinarists.[33] He protested vociferously against Julian of Eclana, who treated him as an Apollinarist because he refused to admit that Christ was subject to the lusts of the flesh,[34] but he did not know whether there were still Apollinarists.[35]

The three Greek writers whom the dispute with Julian obliged Augustine to study less cursorily were Gregory of Nazianzus, Basil, and John Chrysostom. To tell the truth, Augustine was barely familiar with Gregory's work, so much so that he did not even have at hand Rufinus' translation. In fact, we find him, in 413, quoting, as though it came from Gregory of Nazianzus, a Latin text by Gregory of Elvira.[36] Some years later, in his treatises against

---

dicente: *Spiritus est Deus* [*Ioann.* 4.24]. Et ideo, ut dixi, *secundum* divinam substantiam *invisibilem* confiteor *Patrem*, invisibilem *Filium*, invisibilem *Spiritum sanctum*: et neque maius aliquid, neque minus in Deitatis substantia credo.

visibilem, id est *Patrem* et *Filium* et *Spiritum sanctum*, nisi quantum mente ac spiritu nosci potest.

This *De Trinitate*, which in the manuscripts bears the name of Athanasius, is not a translation, but an original Latin text, probably by Gregory of Elvira. Cf. Schanz, vol. 4, 1, p. 309. Furthermore, these ideas are borrowed from Athanasius *Orat. adv. Arianos* 3.14 and 4.36, *PG* 26, 351 B and 524 C.

[30] *Quaest. in Exodum* 2.25 (*PL* 34, 604) = Didymus *De Spiritu sancto* (interpr. Hieronymo) 2 (*PG* 39, 1033 C).

[31] Jerome *Epist. ad Aug.* 3 (*PL* 33, 252): Praetermitto . . . Laodicenum, de Ecclesia nuper egressum.

Augustine *Epist. ad Hieron.* 82.3.23 (*PL* 33, 286): Nam Laodicenum, cuius nomen taces, de Ecclesia dicis nuper egressum.

[32] *Conf.* 7.19.25, p. 169 Lab. Cf. *Epist.* 140.12 (*PL* 33, 542), *De haer.* 55 (*PL* 42, 40), *Contra sermonem Arianorum* 5.5 (*PL* 42, 686), *Sermo V de Paschate* 7 (*PL* 46, 833).

[33] *Op. imperf. contra Iulian.* 47 (*PL* 45, 1366), translating word for word Epiphanius *Anaceph.* 3.2.1 (*PG* 42, 873 C).

[34] *Contra Iulian.* 5.15.55 (*PL* 44, 814). Cf. *De div. quaest.* 83, quaest. 81.1 (*PL* 40, 93).

[35] *Enarr. in Ps.* 29.2 (*PL* 36, 217).

[36] Gregory of Elvira *De fide orthodoxa contra Arianos* (*PL* 17, 365 D and 564 D): Huc accedit quod sic Filium Dei ut iam dictum est, *visum a patribus* adprobamus, ut non totum in illo, quod Deus est, videretur . . . Et utique haec omnia Filii verba defendimus, quem in monte Sina cum Moyse locutum fuisse scimus [*Exod.* 31.18], qui agendis explicandisque rebus a

Augustine *Epist. ad Fortunatianum* 148.10 (*PL* 33, 626): Gregorius etiam sanctus episcopus Orientalis, apertissime dicit Deum natura invisibilem, quando *patribus visus* est, sicut Moysi, cum quo facie ad faciem loquebatur, *alicuius conspicabilis materiae dispositione adsumpta, salva* sua *invisibilitate* videri potuisse.

Julian, he quoted seven passages from a translation of Gregory of Nazianzus, as he expressly acknowledged.[37] The translation he used was none other than the translation of the nine sermons by Rufinus.[38] There is nothing to prove that Augustine had read anything whatever of Gregory of Nazianzus, apart from this translation, and he even appears to have confused him with Gregory of Nyssa, St. Basil's brother.[39] He was more familiar with Basil. We find him using, for his monumental commentary on Genesis, Basil's homilies on the *Hexaemeron*, in Eustathius' translation.[40] He also quoted other passages from Basil in his treatise against Julian. He read some of them, as he himself admitted, in Julian of Eclana,[41] but he also quoted from the Greek text that he himself translated with the aid of an unknown translation.[42] What is very

---

Patre advenerat ... Et tamen sic visus accipitur, ut *alicuius conspicabilis*, ut dixi, *materiae dispositione adsumpta* videretur, *salva* scilicet *invisibilitate* eius.

    This text of Gregory of Elvira is edited under the name of Gregory of Nazianzus (*PG* 36, 669), Ambrose (*PL* 17, 549), Phoebadius (*PL* 20, 31), or Vigilius of Thapsus (*PL* 62, 449). But Dom Wilmart, "Les tractatus sur le cantique attribués à Grégoire d'Elvire," *Bulletin de littérature ecclésiastique* (1906), pp. 233–299, proved that the author was Gregory of Elvira. Cf. Schanz, vol. 4, I, p. 308. Augustine's mistake stems probably from the fact that, in his manuscript, this text was already inserted into the collection of the nine homilies of Gregory of Nazianzus, translated by Rufinus. Cf. "Rufini orationum Gregorii Nazianzeni novem interpretatio," ed. Engelbrecht, *CSEL* 46, pp. IX–XVI. This interpolation is in all likelihood the work of Rufinus himself, according to Wilmart, p. 282.

[37] *Contra Iulian.* 1.5.15 (*PL* 44, 649): "Sed non tibi deerit magni nominis et fama celeberrima inlustris episcopus etiam de partibus Orientis, cuius eloquia ingentis merito gratiae, etiam in linguam Latinam translata usquequaque claruerunt."

[38] *Ibid.*, 1.5.15 and 2.3.7 (*PL* 44: 649, 650, 677). The quotations are repeated in *Op. imperf. in Iulian.* 1.67, 69, 70 (*PL* 45: 1075, 1077, 1092, 1093) and *De dono perseverantiae* 19.49 (*PL* 45, 1024). The table of parallels appears in Rufinus' translation, ed. Engelbrecht, *CSEL* 46, I, p. 288.

[39] *Contra Iulian.* 1.5.19 (*PL* 44, 652): "Vide iam utrum sufficiant tibi ex Orientis partibus duo isti tam insignes viri, et tam clara praediti sanctitate, et, sicut fertur, etiam carne germani."

[40] Basil *Hom.* 2 *in Hexaem.* (*PG* 29, 44 A); Eustathius *Hexaem. metaphrasis* 2.6 (*PL* 30, 888 C); Augustine *De Gen. ad litt.* 1.18.36 (*PL* 34, 260). Cf. Altaner, "Eustathius," *Zeitschrift für neutestamentliche Wissenschaft* 39 (1940) 161–170.

[41] *Contra Iulian.* 1.5.16–17 (*PL* 44, 650–651).

[42] Basil *De ieiunio*, hom. 1.3 (*PG* 31, 168 A):

Νηστεία ἐν τῷ παραδείσῳ ἐνομοθετήθη. Τὴν πρώτην τὴν ἐντολὴν ἔλαβεν Ἀδάμ· "Ἀπὸ τοῦ ξύλου τοῦ γινώσκειν καλὸν καὶ πονηρὸν οὐ φάγεσθε." Τὸ δὲ οὐ φάγεσθε νηστείας ἐστὶ καὶ ἐγκρατείας νομοθεσία. Εἰ ἐνήστευσεν ἀπὸ

Augustine *Contra Iulian.* 1.5.18 (*PL* 44, 652):

    Sed audi quod ad rem praesentem spectat, quid de peccato primi hominis ad nos etiam pertinente dicat iste sanctus sine ulla ambiguitate Basilius. Quod etsi repperi interpretatum, tamen propter diligentiorem veri fidem verbum e verbo malui

strange is that, in the course of the treatise, Augustine made another quotation from Basil but wrongly assigned it to John Chrysostom.[43] The only conclusion that can be reached is that Augustine's manuscript contained both treatises by Basil and others by Chrysostom and that the omission or the disappearance of an *incipit* did not always allow Augustine to identify the author of each homily. Most of them must have been by Chrysostom, for it was with him that Augustine was most familiar, as he had the most voluminous information about him. As a matter of fact, he learned to know him only rather late and still, in 402, seemed unable to comprehend a very specific reference that Jerome had made to his works.[44] Even in 414 he seemed to

τοῦ ξύλου ἡ Εὔα, οὐκ ἂν ταύτης νῦν ἐδεόμεθα τῆς νηστείας. Οὐ γὰρ χρείαν ἔχουσιν οἱ ἰσχύοντες ἰατροῦ, ἀλλ' οἱ κακῶς ἔχοντες. Ἐκακώθημεν διὰ τῆς ἁμαρτίας· ἰαθῶμεν διὰ τῆς μετανοίας· μετάνοια δὲ χωρὶς νηστείας ἀργή. "Ἐπικατάρατος ἡ γῆ, ἀκάνθας καὶ τριβόλους ἀνατελεῖ σοι." Στυγνάζειν προσετάχθης, μὴ γὰρ τρυφᾶν.

Hom. 1.4 (*PL* 31, 168 B): Ἐπειδὴ οὐκ ἐνηστεύσαμεν, ἐξεπέσαμεν τοῦ παραδείσου· νηστεύσωμεν τοίνυν ἵνα πρὸς αὐτὸν ἐπανέλθωμεν.

transferre de Graeco. In sermone de ieiunio: "Ieiunium, inquit, in paradiso lege constitutum est. Primum enim mandatum accepit Adam. *A ligno sciendi bonum et malum non manducabitis* [Gen. 2.17]. *Non manducabitis* autem ieiunium est et legis constitutionis initium. Si ieiunasset a ligno Eva, non isto indigeremus ieiunio. Non enim opus habent valentes medico, sed male habentes. Aegrotavimus per peccatum, sanemur per paenitentiam. Paenitentia vero sine ieiunio vacua est. *Maledicta terra spinas et tribulos pariet* [Gen. 3.17–18). Contristari ordinatus es, numquid deliciari?" Et paulo post in eodem sermone idem ipse: "Quia non ieiunavimus, inquit, decidimus de paradiso. Ieiunemus ergo, ut ad eum redeamus."

This second part of the quotation is reproduced by Augustine *Op. imperf. contra Iulian.* 1.52 (*PL* 45, 1075). Rufinus did not translate this homily of Basil's.

[43] Basil *Hom.* 13 *in sanctum baptisma* (*PG* 31, 428 A):
    Γεύσασθε καὶ ἴδετε . . . Ὁ Ἰουδαῖος τὴν περιτομὴν οὐχ ὑπερτίθεται διὰ τὴν ἀπειλήν, ὅτι πᾶσα ψυχὴ ἥτις οὐ περιτμηθήσεται τῇ ἡμέρᾳ τῇ ὀγδόῃ ἐξολοθρευθήσεται ἐκ τοῦ λαοῦ αὐτῆς· σὺ δὲ τὴν ἀχειροποίητον περιτομὴν ἀναβάλλῃ ἐν τῇ ἀπεκδύσει τῆς σαρκός, ἐν τῷ βαπτίσματι τελειουμένην, αὐτοῦ τοῦ Κυρίου ἀκούσας. "Ἀμὴν ἀμὴν λέγω ὑμῖν, ἐὰν μή τις γεννηθῇ δι' ὕδατος καὶ Πνεύματος, οὐ μὴ εἰσέλθῃ εἰς τὴν βασιλείαν τοῦ θεοῦ."

Contra Iulian. 2.6.17 (*PL* 44, 685):
    Merito idem Ioannes etiam ipse sicut et martyr Cyprianus, circumcisionem carnis in signo praeceptam commendat esse baptismatis: Et vide quo modo Iudaeus, inquit, circumcisionem non differt propter comminationem, quia omnis anima quaecumque non fuerit circumcisa die octavo exterminabitur de populo suo [Gen. 17.14]. Tu autem, inquit, non manufactam circumcisionem differs, quae in exspoliatione carnis in corpore perficitur, ipsum Dominum audiens dicentem: "Amen amen dico vobis, nisi quis renatus fuerit ex aqua et spiritu, non introibit in regnum caelorum [*Ioann.* 3.5]"?

[44] Jerome *Epist. ad Aug.* 75.6 (*PL* 33, 253):

Augustine *Epist. ad Hieron.* 82.3.23 (*PL* 33, 286):

know him only through the quotation that Pelagius had made in his *De gratia*.[45] It was the controversy with Julian of Eclana that made him start inquiring about him. In his fourth book addressed to Turbantius, Julian of Eclana used for Pelagian purposes the *Homily to Neophytes*.[46] He thus covered up his heresy with the authority of the Eastern Church. Confronted with such a danger, Augustine secured a Greek manuscript of Chrysostom, quoted it in Greek, translated it word for word, compared this translation with the Pelagian translation, and showed that the latter falsified Chrysostom's meaning. He added his own translation of another passage in the same homily, where the dogma of original sin was affirmed but softened down in the Pelagian translation.[47] Several of the other passages in Chrysostom that

---

Quid dicam de Ioanne, qui dudum in pontificali gradu Constantinopolitanam rexit ecclesiam et proprie super hoc capitulo latissimum exaravit librum, in quo Origenis et veterum sententiam est secutus?

Tres igitur restant, Eusebius Emisenus, Theodorus Heracleotes et quem paulo post commemoras Ioannes qui dudum in pontificali gradu Constantinopolitanam rexit ecclesiam.

Cf. Baur, "L'entrée littéraire," p. 251; B. Altaner, "Beiträge zur Geschichte der altlateinischen Uebersetzungen von Väterschriften (Basilius der Grosse und Johannes Chrysostomus)," *Historisches Jahrbuch* 61 (1941) 213; and G. Bardy, "Grecs et latins dans les premières controverses pélagiennes," *Bulletin de littérature ecclésiastique* 49 (1948) 3ff, and *La question des langues dans l'église ancienne*, vol. 1 (Paris 1948).

[45] Augustine *De natura et gratia* 64.76 (*PL* 44, 285). Cf. Baur, "L'entrée littéraire," p. 253.

[46] Translated probably by Anianus of Celeda. Cf. Baur, "L'entrée littéraire," p. 254; and Schanz, vol. 4, 2, p. 511, referring to S. Haidacher, "Eine unbeachtete Rede des hl. Chrysostomus an Neugetaufte," *Zeitschrift für kath. Theol.* 28 (1904) 168. On Julian of Eclana, cf. above, pp. 145–146.

[47] I have found this Pelagian translation in MS Paris. BN Lat. 10593, fols. 10ʳ–17ʳ, of the 6th cent. It is therefore probable that the collection of translations by Basil and Chrysostom that appears in this manuscript is of Pelagian derivation. Here are the texts:

Chrysostom *Hom. ad Neoph.* (*apud* Aug. *Contra Iulian.* 1.6.22 and 26, *PL* 44, 656 and 658):

Διὰ τοῦτο καὶ τὰ παιδία βαπτίζομεν, καίτοι, ἁμαρτήματα οὐκ ἔχοντα.

Pelagian translation (*apud* Aug. *Contra Iulian.* 1.6.21, *PL* 44, 655 = MS 10593, fol. 11ʳ):

Hac de causa etiam infantes baptizamus, *cum non sint coinquinati peccato.*

Augustine's translation, *Contra Iulian.* 1.6.22 and 26, *PL* 44, 656 and 658):

Ideo et infantes baptizamus, *quamvis peccata non habentes.*

(MS 10593, fol. 15ʳ = *Libellus fidei*):

"Ερχεται ἅπαξ ὁ Χριστός, εὗρεν ἡμῶν χειρόγραφον πατρῶον, ὅτι ἔγραψεν ὁ 'Αδάμ. 'Εκεῖνος τὴν ἀρχὴν εἰσήγαγε τοῦ χρείους, ἡμεῖς τὸν δανεισμὸν ηὐξήσαμεν ταῖς μεταγενεστέραις ἁμαρτίαις.

Venit semel Christus et paternis nos cautionibus invenit adstrictos, quas conscripsit Adam. Ille initium obligationis ostendit, peccatis nostris faenus adcrevit.

Venit semel Christus, invenit nostrum chirographum paternum, quod scripsit Adam. Ille initium induxit debiti, nos faenus auximus posterioribus peccatis.

Augustine also quoted against the Pelagians are probably his own translations as well, for he assured his readers that he possessed all the homilies and made his own excerpts; and it is not likely that the Pelagians had translated so literally texts that showed them in the wrong.[48]

During the same period Augustine had also at least one other manuscript of the Greek Fathers. In fact, when Quodvultdeus had asked him in 427 to write for the clergy of Carthage a brief exposition of the principal heresies, Augustine, who twenty years before had vainly begged Jerome to write such a book, refused and proposed sending him a book by Epiphanius of Cyprus. This work, known for its orthodoxy, discussed eighty heresies and was far more documented than the similar work of the Latin Philastrius. The work under discussion was undoubtedly a book Augustine had read in Greek, for he could not supply Quodvultdeus with a translation. He did not even have at his disposal a translator, and suggested sending the original Greek for Quodvultdeus to get translated in Carthage.[49] The latter apologizes for not accepting the offer. He himself knew no Greek. He realized the scarcity of translators. He therefore begged Augustine to carry out the task himself.[50] Augustine finally consented. He knew that Epiphanius had been dead only a few years, although this information did not appear in Jerome's *De viris*,[51] but he seemed quite misinformed about his work. In fact, he seemed to be unaware that Epiphanius composed a very voluminous treatise, the *Panarion*, in which he refuted the eighty heresies. Actually, Augustine translated only a

---

[48] The texts follow:

Contra Iulian. 1.6.24 (PL 44, 656)	= *Epist. ad Olympiadem* (PG 52, 574 C).
	= *Hom. de Lazaro resuscitato* (Chrysostom, ed. Feller [Antwerp 1614] 3, p. 109; actually by Potamius).
Contra Iulian. 1.6.25 (PL 44, 657)	= *Hom. 3 in Genesim* (PG 53, 592 A–B).
Contra Iulian. 1.6.27 (PL 44, 658–659)	= *Hom. 10 in Epist. ad Rom.* (PG 60: 475 B, 476 C, 480 A).
Contra Iulian. 2.6.17 (PL 44, 685)	= *Hom. in Crucem* (PG 50, 820 C).

The *Hom. in Crucem*, quoted also by Cassiodorus, *PL* 70, 50 D, appears in MS Paris BN, new Latin acquisitions 1599 (7th/8th cent.), fols. 1ʳ–5ᵛ. Cf. Wilmart, "La collection des 38 homélies latines de s. Jean Chrysostome," *Journal of Theological Studies* 19 (1917/ 1918) 305–328.

[49] *Epist. ad Quodvultdeum* 222.2 (PL 33, 999): "Vide ergo ne forte librum sancti Epiphanii tibi mittere debeam ... qui possit apud Carthaginem in Latinam linguam verti facilius atque commodius, ut tu potius praestes nobis quod quaeris a nobis."

[50] Quodvultdeus *Epist. ad Aug.* 223.2 (PL 33, 1000): "Frustra etiam homini qui Latina non didicit, Graeca facundia delegatur ... Quid autem Venerationem tuam de interpretum non solum difficultate, sed etiam obscuritate admoneam, cum ipse hoc magis ac plene diiudices?"

[51] Augustine *De haer., prol.* (PL 42, 23): "abhinc non longe humanis rebus exemptus." Epiphanius was still living when Jerome wrote the *De vir. inl.*

short synopsis of the *Panarion*.[52] His translation showed that this synopsis displayed strong similarities to the *Anacephalaeosis*, without being identical. In point of fact, the Greek manuscript translated by Augustine contained six books only, whereas the *Anacephalaeosis* reproduced the arrangement of the *Panarion* in seven volumes.[53] In addition, certain details common to the *Panarion* and to Augustine's manuscript do not appear in the *Anacephalaeosis* in their current form.[54] In any case, this mediocre synopsis composed by some disciple of Epiphanius was, in Augustine's opinion, a very precious document on account of the extreme scarcity of Greek books. Augustine's translation, itself mediocre,[55] was an indispensable addition to the culture of the clergy of Carthage.

Augustine then had the utmost difficulty in keeping abreast of Greek ecclesiastical literature. In 405 he was still extremely ignorant of this literature and was not capable of contending with St. Jerome on the basis of ecclesiastical knowledge. The latter, defending some rash interpretation, had cited seven Greek writers. In his reply, Augustine was perhaps ironical in assuming ignorance of the very names of Apollinaris of Laodicea and John Chrysostom. But he was sincere when he assured his readers that he had not read them, any more than he had read Alexander, Eusebius of Emesa, and Theodore of Heraclea, and that he knew Origen and Didymus only by hearsay.[56] Afterward, he made a heroic effort to know the Fathers of the Eastern

---

[52] *Ibid.*: "De octoginta haeresibus loquens sex libros etiam ipse conscripsit, historica narratione memorans omnia, nulla disputatione adversus falsitatem pro veritate decertans. Breves sane sunt hi libelli . . . Tu namque, quamvis breviter, perstricte atque summatim, tamen vis etiam responderi commemoratis haeresibus: quod ille non fecit." Yet J. Draeseke, "Zu Augustinus' *De civ. Dei* XVIII, 42, eine Quellenuntersuchung," *Zeitschrift für wissenschaftliche Theologie* 32 (1889) 230–248, believes he has proof that this chapter of Augustine's directly follows Epiphanius, and not Aristaeus or Josephus. I am not convinced.

[53] Apart from the text quoted above, cf. *De haer.* 57 (*PL* 42, 41): "Proinde ille de octoginta haeresibus, separatis viginti, quas ante Domini adventum exstitisse, sicut ei visum est, computavit, reliquas post Domini ascensum natas sexaginta, brevissimis libris quinque comprehendit, atque omnes sex libros totius eiusdem sui operis fecit."

[54] For example, *De haer.* 17 (*PL* 42, 28) on the serpent that distributes the Eucharist among the sect of the *Ophitae* = *Panarion* (*PG* 41, 648 D); *De haer.* 32 (*PL* 42, 31): *Elki* = *Panarion* (*PG* 41, 900 A).

[55] See above, chap 4 sec. 1 n. 86. It is this same summary = *Anaceph.* 3.2.1 (*PG* 42, 873 C) that Augustine reproduces word for word, *Op. imperf. contra Iulian.* 4.47 (*PL* 42, 1366), in preference to his own notice on the Apollinarists, *De haer.* 55 (*PL* 42, 40).

[56] *Epist. ad Hieron.* 82.3.23 (*PL* 33, 286): "Flagitas a me ut aliquem saltem unum ostendam, cuius in hac re sententiam sim secutus, cum tu tam plures commemoraveris, qui te in eo quod adstruis praecesserunt; petens ut in eo, si te reprehendo errantem, patiar te errare cum talibus, *quorum ego, fateor, neminem legi*; sed cum sint ferme sex vel septem, horum quattuor auctoritatem quoque infringis. Nam Laodicenum, cuius nomen taces, de Ecclesia dicis nuper egressum; Alexandrum autem veterem haereticum; Origenem

Church. We have observed him collecting in his library a large number of translations. Sometimes he did not even select them with sufficient discrimination, since, relying on a wrong *incipit*, he mistook two Latin works of Gregory of Elvira for treatises by Athanasius and Gregory of Nazianzus. But he displayed a marked eclectic sense. He collected Jerome's translations (Origen's *De principiis*, Eusebius' *Chronica*, Didymus' *De Spiritu sancto*) as well as those of Rufinus (Origen's *Homilies on Genesis*, Eusebius' *Church History*, Gregory of Nazianzus' *Novem orationes*). He took an interest in the older writers, like Irenaeus, as well as in contemporaries like Basil, Gregory, Chrysostom. He even felt the need, at the time of the Pelagian dispute, of getting Greek texts of Basil and Chrysostom. Finally, toward his last days, he had a reputation as a great Hellenist in the eyes of the African clergy, who were very ignorant of Greek, and in his old age the famous scholar translated, not without difficulty or mistakes, Epiphanius' slim book on the Greek heresies, which probably he alone possessed.

An examination of Augustine's reading in the Greek writers confirms the conclusions that I have reached on the slowness of his linguistic progress. For a very considerable time he was just barely able to comprehend translations from the Greek. He had to wait until later years to achieve the ability to read Greek fluently. The influence that pagan and ecclesiastical literature exerted on him was, all in all, very unequal. Very soon Plotinus and Porphyry exercised a decisive influence on the development of his philosophical thought. His theological culture was, on the other hand, much more individual, and his belated reading of the Greek Fathers helped only to confirm and direct the orthodoxy of original views.

4. Pagan Hellenism in Africa

St. Augustine's powerful personality shows how difficult it was to learn Greek in North Africa at the beginning of the fifth century. There was however in quite a number of cities a Greek-speaking colony, which sometimes exerted an influence. Such were those Greeks of Oea who contributed by their clamors to the maintenance of the old Latin translations from the Septuagint in preference to Jerome's Vulgate translated from Hebrew.[1] Carthage

---

vero ac Didymum reprehensos abs te lego in recentioribus opusculis . . . Tres igitur restant Eusebius Emisenus, Theodorus Heracleotes et quem paulo post commemoras Ioannes qui dudum in pontificali gradu Constantinopolitanam rexit ecclesiam."

[1] Augustine *Epist. ad Hieron.* 71.3 (*PL* 33, 242): "Nam quidam frater noster episcopus, cum lectitari instituisset in ecclesia cui praeest, interpretationem tuam, movit quiddam longe alter abs te positum apud Ionam prophetam, quam erat omnium sensibus memoriaeque inveteratum, et tot aetatum successionibus decantatum. Factus est tantus tumultus in plebe, maxime Graecis arguentibus et inclamantibus calumniam falsitatis, ut cogeretur episcopus (Oea quippe civitas erat) Iudaeorum testimonium flagitare." Cf. also *De civ.*

in particular claimed a reputation as a cosmopolitan city in which all languages were spoken.[2] But the influence of these colonies must not be exaggerated. They were merchants and their number was not high, to judge from epigraphical remains. According to Monceaux, who studied Christian epigraphy in Northern Africa, the inscriptions in Greek date almost all from the Byzantine Empire, and there is not one that can be shown to be anterior to the Vandal Conquest.[3] This is an indication that the Greek-speaking colonies, in the days of Augustine, were reduced or markedly Latinized. With regard to Augustine himself, it cannot be said that he promoted Greek studies in his circle.[4] Their decline was already perceptible.

However, the Hellenic tradition persisted, at least in pagan areas, and if Augustine, in the *De civitate Dei*, is still interested in Porphyry, it is because the latter inspired antichristian polemics and added fuel to pagan religiosity.

The influence of the Κατὰ χριστιανῶν was still alive, as is proved by a treatise *De physicis* that was wrongly attributed to Marius Victorinus and must have been by one of his African disciples at the close of the fourth century or the beginning of the fifth.[5] Under the plural "quidam," the author refutes a

---

Dei 22.8.17 and 22 (*PL* 41, 767 and 769) on miracles that took place at Hippo, concerning the Syrian Bassus and two brothers who were natives of Caesarea in Cappadocia, and 22.8.3 (*PL* 41, 762) on the presence in Carthage of a surgeon from Alexandria. Other references are noted by Bardy, "La culture grecque," p. 26.

[2] Salvian *De gub. Dei* 7.17 (*PL* 53, 143 B): "Illic enim omnia officiorum publicorum instrumenta, illic artium liberalium scholae, illic philosophorum officinae, cuncta denique vel linguarum gymnasia vel morum." The rhetorical character of this argument, whose purpose was to denounce Carthage as a modern Babylon, makes one hesitate to put too much faith in it.

[3] P. Monceaux, "Enquête sur l'épigraphie chrétienne d'Afrique," *Revue archéologique*, 4th series, 2 (1903) 65. W. Thieling's dissertation, *Der Hellenismus in Kleinafrika*, p. 164, cannot invalidate Monceaux's conclusions insofar as concerns the fourth and fifth centuries. This work appeared to me, at least in the literary section, unconvincing and based on secondary sources.

[4] His disciple Favonius Eulogius, who had some notion of Neoplatonic theories, seems to have written his *Commentary on Scipio's Dream* particularly from Latin sources. Cf. above, p. 36 and chap. 1 sec. 3 n. 67. Orosius, who wrote his *Historiae adv. paganos*, ed. Zangemeister, *CSEL*, vol. 5, on Augustine's invitation in 417, quotes as Greek writers only Plato (p. 54, 4), Palaephatos (p. 62, 7; p. 63, 10), Phanocles (p. 61, 13), Josephus (p. 451, 7; p. 460, 17)—all of these from Eusebius' *Chronicle* translated by Jerome—and Polybius (p. 261, 4; p. 282, 6) from Livy. Quodvultdeus of Carthage, the putative author of the *Liber de promissionibus et praedictionibus Dei* by Pseudo-Prosper, and the one who begged Augustine for a translation of the *De haer.* (cf. Schanz, vol. 4, 2, p. 471) quotes Origen, *In Levit.*, Hermes, the Sibylline Oracles (*PL* 51, 818 Dff) from the *De civ. Dei* 18.23. From Lactantius he quotes Josephus' *Antiquities* and this saying that he attributes to Plato: "Si initium mundo dedit, dedit et finem" (*PL* 51, 838 A). Cf. Franses, *Die Werke des hl. Quodvultdeus*, pp. 69ff.

[5] Cf. Monceaux, *Hist. litt. de l'Afr. chrét.*, vol. 3, p. 399. He observes that the Biblical quotations are clearly African.

very specific opponent who criticized in the name of reason the fundamental dogmas of Christianity. The narrative of the original Fall appeared to him a tissue of absurdities. Why did God, who knows the future, give Adam an order, knowing it would be violated? Why did he make a tree grow that would arouse desire? Was he then powerless to create man without sin, or to keep him from temptation? Why, after creating man immortal, does he condemn him, in a fit of rage, to die? And the Christians believe that this same God, who did not want to forgive at once, came afterward to suffer for the salvation of men![6] The immaculate birth of Christ is contrary to nature.[7] The flesh is an impurity unworthy of a God.[8] It is improbable that at his birth the angels, ethereal beings, greeted this man of flesh with the name of king.[9] The death of a God is an inconceivable phenomenon.[10] The beatific life of the resurrected is an unjust reward, for God would grant man more than the return to his first nature, that is, to the humanity of the earthly paradise.[11] We can recognize the favorite themes of Porphyry, who in the Κατὰ χριστιανῶν certainly discussed the episode of Adam's sin.[12] I am surprised also that neither Harnack nor Labriolle thought of referring these texts to this book.[13] It probably seems astonishing at first sight that the Κατὰ χριστιανῶν was still read in Africa around the year 400, whereas Augustine never had it in his possession. But Augustine's correspondence informs us that compilations of rebuttals circulated in Africa. Several of these rebuttals were submitted to him by the deacon of Carthage, Deogratias, who had them from a pagan friend. At least four of these were put under Porphyry's instigation.[14]

---

[6] *De physicis* 9 (*PL* 8, 1300 B–D).

[7] *Ibid.*, 17 (*PL* 8, 1304 C).

[8] *Ibid.*, 16 and 19 (*PL* 8, 1304 A and 1305 C).

[9] *Ibid.*, 22 (*PL* 8, 1306 D).

[10] *Ibid.*, 20 (*PL* 8, 1306 A).

[11] *Ibid.*, 27 (*PL* 8, 1310 A).

[12] Cf. frag. 42 in Harnack's collection, "Porphyrius *Gegen die Christen*," p. 67 = Severianus of Gabales *De mundi creatione, hom.* 6.3 (*PG* 56, 487; cf. 495). Why, said Porphyry, did God forbid man the knowledge of good and evil? Why is the serpent accursed, if the real tempter was Satan? Similar arguments on Genesis appeared in Julian's *Contra Galilaeos*, ed. Neumann, p. 167, 9, and already in Celsus, *apud* Origen *Contra Celsum* 6.49ff, *PG* 11, 1373.

[13] They would have a place, if not in the collection of the fragments of Porphyry, at least in Labriolle's study, *La réaction païenne*. But Monceaux, *Hist. litt. de l'Afr. chrét.*, had confined himself, in the *De physicis*, to the mention of the weakness of the refutation, not the force of the objections.

[14] After discussing them, Augustine introduces the fifth objection with the words (*Epist.* 102.28, *PL* 33, 381): "Post hanc quaestionem, qui eas ex Porphyrio proposuit, hoc adiunxit," and the sixth objection with the words (*PL* 33, 382): "Postrema quaestio proposita est de Iona, nec ipsa quasi ex Porphyrio, sed tamquam ex irrisione paganorum." In spite of Labriolle's contrary view, *La réaction païenne*, p. 250, I believe with Harnack, p. 74, that this last criticism, the improbability of the story of Jonah and the whale, un-

Why are the faithful promised a resurrection that has nothing in common with Christ's or Lazarus' resurrection? Why did Christ come so late, excluding so many generations from salvation? Why are pagan rites condemned, whereas bloody sacrifices have persisted for so long in the Jewish religion? Why does Christ assign the unfaithful to eternal punishment, while he also says, "For with the same measure that ye mete withal it shall be measured to you again?" Other arguments, raised by the pagan whose brusque intervention in the middle of a philosophical discussion had perturbed young Volusianus so deeply, seem to stem from the same compilation. Immaculate conception is contrary to reason. The incarnation of a god who gives up his royal progress for a petty little body (*corpusculum*) is a blasphemy against divinity. Many others apart from Christ drove out spirits, healed the sick, resurrected the dead without attempting to appear gods.[15] Why are the sacrifices of the Old Testament scorned by the New Testament, although the Christians identify Jesus with the god of the Jews? Does not Christian morality, which consists of returning good for evil, run the risk of bringing destruction on a State threatened by so many enemies?[16] Augustine cannot believe that the antichristian Porphyry, to whom certain of these objections are referred, is the philosopher Porphyry of Sicily, whose theories on the return of the soul attracted him in his youth.[17] But the identity of the two Porphyrys leaves no one in doubt today. His antichristian influence must have been no less marked in Gaul, where Pacatus, as we shall see, thought it necessary to compose a refutation to the Κατὰ χριστιανῶν.[18]

If, beyond this antichristian attitude, we try to find out what the culture and the positive beliefs of the Hellenizers possibly were at the time of Augustine, Martianus Capella's *De nuptiis* can shed light on the matter.[19] The

---

questionably stems from the Κατὰ χριστιανῶν; for Jerome *In Ionam* 2.1 refers to it. If Augustine is unaware of its Porphyrian origin, it is because, in the African collection of criticisms, the origin of each objection was not specified every time, but most of them, if not all, went back to Porphyry. Cf. above, at sec. 2 n. 176.

[15] Volusianus *Epist. ad Augustinum* 135.2, *PL* 33, 513. The last argument involves the miracles of Apollonius of Tyana and of Apuleius, as Marcellinus specifies, *Epist. ad Aug.* 136.1, *PL* 33, 514. Now this argument is Porphyrian; cf. the texts quoted above, sec. 2 n. 178.

[16] Marcellinus *Epist. ad Aug.* 136.2, *PL* 33, 515. It was Marcellinus who referred these objections to Augustine, for they had disturbed Volusianus so deeply that he did not venture to submit them himself.

[17] Text quoted above, sec. 2 n. 176.

[18] See below, p. 226.

[19] The exact date of the work is in dispute. The traditional view places it between 410 and 439 (cf. Schanz, vol. 4, 2, p. 169). Wessner, *PW* s.v. Martianus, 2004, assigns it to the close of the fourth century. I think that the reasons proposed in A. Dick's edition (Leipzig 1925), p. xxv, n. 1, for putting back the date still further toward the third century are without value. The African origin is certain, but the expression in *De nupt.* 6.637, p. 311, 12, "quamdiu viguit (Roma)," is ambiguous. It may be understood thus: "etiam nunc

general scheme of this encyclopedia conforms to the Latin tradition established by Varro's treatise *On the Disciplines*.[20] But Martianus voluntarily omits medicine and architecture, on account of their empirical character.[21] He thus coincides with the Hellenistic tradition of the seven liberal arts.[22] He prides himself in fact on his Hellenic culture. He readily inserts Greek words[23] in his text, likes to give Greek names to his allegorical characters, and declines them according to Greek rules.[24] On one occasion he even risks a Greek sentence, but this would not prove that the writer spoke this language fluently, for the sentence contains two proverbs joined together.[25] He does not forget to indicate the Greek origin of each discipline, which he regularly describes in the form of a woman robed in the pallium.[26] Most of the disciplines have as patrons famous Greek names: Aristotle, Chrysippus, Carneades for dialectic;[27] Demosthenes for rhetoric;[28] Archimedes and Euclid for geometry;[29] Pythagoras for arithmetic;[30] Pythagoras, Plato, Eratosthenes, Ptolemy, Hipparchus for astronomy;[31] Orpheus, Amphion, Arion for music.[32] Martianus also lists, among the dwellers in heaven, a whole series of Greek writers: Linus and Homer, Orpheus and Aristoxenes, Plato and Archimedes, Heraclitus, Thales and Democritus, Pythagoras, Aristotle, Epicurus, Zeno, Arcesilaus.[33] The manner in which the philosophy of

---

viget" (date prior to the invasion of Alaric in 410), or: "non iam viget" (date posterior to 410). I should incline to the second hypothesis.

[20] It is even from Martianus that Ritschl, *De M. Varronis disciplinarum libris*, Progr. Bonn 1845 (= *Opusc. philol.*, vol. 3 [Leipzig 1887] 357–402), reconstructs Varro's scheme.

[21] *De nupt.* 9.891, p. 471, 23. We have already noted above, p. 27, that in Macrobius medicine was excluded from the philosophical disciplines. Augustine too conceived of seven disciplines only. Cf. *Retract.* 1.6, *PL* 32, 591, and B. Fischer, *De Augustini disciplinarum libro qui est de dialectica* (diss. Jena 1912).

[22] On the origins of this cycle, cf. Marrou, *Saint Augustin*, pp. 211–235.

[23] Cf. among others p. 4, 14 and p. 483, 14 *egersimon*; p. 285, 15 *agalmata* (these two words are *hapax legomena* in the Latin language); p. 4, 11; p. 39, 15; p. 44, 21, and *passim*.

[24] For example, p. 6, 20 *Sophian*; p. 7, 5 and 6 *Manticen, Pronoees*; pp. 472ff *Phronesis, Genethliace*; *Symbolice, Oeonistice*.

[25] *De nupt.* 8.807, p. 426, 10: "ni ὄνος λύρας ⟨ἀκούων⟩, καιρὸν γνῶθι."

[26] For grammar, p. 82, 15; dialectic, p. 152, 1 and p. 153, 3; rhetoric, p. 212, 6; for the scientific disciplines, p. 286, 20: "Inspiraris nobis Graias Latiariter artes," and p. 291, 19: "illi etiam Helladica tantum modo facultate, nihil effantes Latiariter atticissant." Cf. p. 421, 15; p. 430, 4.

[27] *De nupt.*, p. 151, 6ff.

[28] *Ibid.*, p. 212, 24ff.

[29] *Ibid.*, p. 291, 14.

[30] *Ibid.*, p. 366, 9.

[31] *Ibid.*, p. 422, 8 and p. 430, 5.

[32] *Ibid.*, p. 480, 15.

[33] *Ibid.*, p. 78, 10. The theme of the "paradise of the intellectuals" was then common. Cf. above, at chap. 1 sec. 3 n. 87, and Cumont, *Recherches sur le symbolisme funéraire*, p. 275 n. 2 and p. 315.

each of them is characterized in one word recalls the enumeration of philosophers made by Claudian, Augustine, Sidonius. The origin of this method is,
as has been seen, a Greek manual translated into Latin.[34] One must be careful
therefore not to fall into the belief that Martianus had had any direct association with all these writers, certain of whom are, besides, fictitious. Their
names are mere ornamentation. When Martianus claims that he is quoting
accurately from a Greek text, he very often takes it from a Latin writer.[35] His
indebtedness to Varro, even if he did not know him directly, is immense.[36]
His Hellenic culture is superficial and very unequal with respect to the disciplines. As is natural, he follows only the Latin theorists for grammar. For
dialectic, apart from his Latin sources, he reads Aristotle's *Categories*, but in a
Latin adaptation, as is shown by the examples taken from Vergil and
Cicero.[37] Similarly, for geometry and arithmetic, he follows closely Euclid's
Elements, probably in a Latin adaptation.[38] For astronomy, also, despite the
contacts with the manuals of Geminus, Cleomedes, Theon, there is nothing
to warrant a statement whether he is drawing from a Greek source. On the
other hand, for his chapter on rhetoric, he had at hand a biography of Demosthenes, to which was appended a line from the *Iliad*.[39] The discussion on
"narrative," in which Martianus quotes Theodorus of Byzantium,[40] reproduces the doctrine of the later Greek theorists, which is opposed to Ciceronian
doctrine.[41] With regard to music, after a prologue on its moral usefulness,
derived from Varro,[42] Martianus Capella most frequently copies word for
word the treatise by Aristides Quintilianus,[43] the Neoplatonist of the third or

[34] See above, pp. 135 and 192–194.

[35] For example, the quotations from Dicaearchus, Anaxagoras, Pytheas, Ptolemy,
Artemidorus, and Isidore in a geographical discussion plagiarized from Pliny the Elder.
Cf. the references in Dick's ed., pp. 292–304.

[36] Cf. Eyssenhardt's ed. of the *De nuptiis* (Leipzig 1866), pp. XXXI–LVIII. Wessner, *PW*
s.v. Martianus, 2007–2012, has judiciously reduced these borrowings and thinks that
Martianus knew the Varronian doctrine only from late treatises.

[37] Pages 164ff. It will be observed that according to Fischer, *De Augustini disciplinarum
libro*, Martianus' teaching is very much akin to that of Augustine. Cassiodorus, *Inst.* ed.
Mynors, p. 119, 13, also mentions a dialectician of the fifth century(?): Tullius Marcellus
of Carthage, who composed seven books on syllogisms.

[38] Cf. *De nupt.*, pp. 352–362 and 376–421.

[39] *De nupt.* 5.430, p. 213, 9: "denique de illo versus huius modo ferebatur: δεινὸς
ἀνήρ· τάχα κεν καὶ ἀναίτιον αἰτιόῳτο [*Il.* 11.654]." I have not found this detail in any
of the numerous extant biographies of Demosthenes.

[40] *De nupt.* 5.552, p. 274, 18.

[41] This conclusion is reached from the parallels established between Martianus and the
Anonymus Seguerianus by H. W. Fischer, *Untersuchungen über die Quellen der Rhetorik des
Mart. Cap.* (diss. Breslau 1936) 115–116.

[42] Cf. the similarities noted by C. Schmidt, *Quaestiones de mus. script. Rom.* (diss.
Darmstadt 1899) 53–56.

[43] Cf. R. Westphal, *Griechische Rhythmik und Harmonik nebst der Gesch. der drei*

fourth century who adopted Porphyry's theory on the descent of the soul.[44] This puts us on the track of the philosophical and religious influences that Martianus could have experienced from Greek writers. Although a pagan, he does not believe any more than the Christians in the ancient conception of Greek mythology.[45] On the other hand, it seems that he had read the same work that Macrobius had read on Apollo's epithets, a book whose erudition went back, as has been seen, to Porphyry's treatise *On the Sun*.[46] I suspect also that his allegorical descriptions of the various gods, with their numberless attributes, were taken from some Neoplatonic treatise Περὶ ἀγαλμάτων that described the symbolical value of the slightest details.[47] But there is something further. The allegory of the marriage of Mercury and Philology owes its dramatic character, I think, to the fact that Martianus is describing mysteries that were presented in the form of *tableaux vivants*. He himself appeals to the tradition of the Milesian tales and is inspired by the episode of the marriage of Cupid and Psyche in Apuleius' *Metamorphoses*.[48] The model he

musischen Disciplinen, vol. 1 (Leipzig 1867), Suppl. pp. 26–40, and Deiters, *Ueber das Verhältnis des Mart. Cap. zu Aristides Quintilianus* (Progr. Posen 1881).

[44] Cf. Jan, *PW* s.v. Aristides Quintilianus.

[45] Compare Martianus' formula, *De nupt.* 8.817, p. 432, 14: "*fabulosisque commentis Grai complevere caelum*," with that of the Christian Fulgentius *Mitol.* 1.21, ed. Helm (Leipzig 1898), p. 11, 16: "*sepulto mendacis Graeciae fabuloso commento* quid misticum in his sapere debeat cerebrum agnoscamus."

[46] Macrobius *Sat.* 1.17.47, p. 99, 1:

Apollo Χρυσοκόμας cognominatur a fulgore radiorum quos vocant comas aureas solis, unde et ᾿Ακερσεκόμης, quod numquam radii possunt a fonte lucis avelli, item ᾿Αργυρότοξος.

Mart. Cap. *De nupt.* 1.12, p. 11, 12:

Nec mirum, quod Apollinis silva ita rata modificatione congrueret, cum caeli quoque orbes Delius moduletur in sole, hincque esse, quod illic Phoebus et hic vocitetur *Auricomus* (nam Solis augustum caput radiis perfusum circumactumque flammantibus velut auratam caesariem rutili verticis imitatur), hinc quoque *Sagittarius*.

Ibid., 1.19, p. 15, 5:

(Virtus) . . . caeci poetae Graium versum Mercurio comprobante commemorat: Φοῖβος ἀκερσεκόμης λοιμοῦ νεφέλην ἀπερύκει, ex quo pestem fugari posse Mercurius, si voces primae vestigiis eius accederent, admonebat.

Cf. above, p. 30. Cf. also the hymn of Martianus, where the sun is invoked under all sorts of names: 2.190, p. 74, 8.

[47] *De nupt.* 6.567, p. 285, 15 (with reference to Pallas): "quam docto adsimulant habitu qui *agalmata* firmant." This word is unique in Latinity. See also, pp. 30–31, the detailed description of the ornaments of Jupiter and Juno.

[48] Apuleius *Metam.* 6.23. The Milesian tradition is invoked by Apuleius *Metam.* 1.1 *prol.* and Mart. Cap. *De nupt.* 2.100, p. 43, 2.

adopted helped him to describe an initiation ceremony, just as Apuleius, in Book 11, had described an initiation into the rites of Isis.[49] From the very first words, Martianus appears as a priest guarding a secret.[50] This secret is the story of Philology's heavenly ascent and apotheosis on the occasion of her marriage to Mercury.

Martianus imagines this episode as a ritual ceremony, consisting of various Orphic, Neopythagorean, and Chaldean elements. To test whether this divine marriage is fitting for her, Philology resorts to learned calculations on the nuptial number[51] and on the numbers that correspond to her secret name and that of her bridegroom. In these calculations the letter Y appears, a Neopythagorean symbol,[52] and the Pythagorean formula of the oath μὰ τὴν τετράδα.[53] To avoid being consumed by the heat given off by the heavenly spheres, she smears herself with a magic ointment, in whose composition there seems to enter the Pythagorean herb called "to the hundred heads."[54] The dress that she puts on is that of a neophyte who is trying to avoid all defilement.[55] Several rites make her lose contact with her mortal condition (ἀπαθανατισμός). An emetic cleanses her of all her former knowledge.[56] Then she consumes the Orphic egg that transfigures her,[57] and she is crowned, according to the Pythagorean rite, with the Leucas, the herb of immortality.[58] After sacrificing to Athanasia, she may mount the litter that has been

---

[49] Apuleius *Metam.* 11.23. On the different interpretations and the dual dramatic and ecstatic character of the ceremony, cf. Cumont, *Les religions orientales*, p. 245 n. 106.

[50] His son asks, *De nupt.* 1.2, p. 4, 9: "Quid istud, mi pater, quod nondum vulgata materie cantare deproperas et ritu nictantis antistitis, priusquam fores aditumque reseraris, ὑμνολογίζεις?" Cf. the famous Orphic formula: φθέγξομαι οἷς θέμις ἐστί, θύρας δ᾽ ἐπίθεσθε, βέβηλοι (O. Kern, *Orphicorum fragmenta* [Leipzig 1922], p. 257).

[51] *De nupt.* 2.101, p. 43, 6. On the nuptial number, cf. P. Tannery, "Le nombre nuptial de Platon," *Mémoires scientifiques* 1, 12–38, and A. Diès, "Le nombre de Platon, essai d'exégèse et d'histoire," *Mémoires présentés . . . à l'Académie des Inscriptions* 14 (Paris 1936).

[52] *De nupt.* 2.102, p. 43, 17. On this symbol, cf. chap. 1 sec. 3 n. 62 and chap. 2 sec. 2 n. 63.

[53] *Ibid.*, 2.107, p. 44, 21. On this oath, cf. above, chap. 1 sec. 3 n. 46.

[54] *Ibid.*, 2.110, p. 46, 15. Cf. P. Boyancé, "Une allusion à l'œuf orphique," *MEFR* 52 (1935) 95–96. He offers a noteworthy commentary on this passage and the pages following.

[55] Note particularly *De nupt.* 2.115, p. 48, 16: "calceos praeterea ex papyro textili subligavit, ne quid eius membra pollueret morticinum."

[56] *Ibid.*, 2.135, p. 59. She ejects particularly a book containing hieroglyphics!

[57] *Ibid.*, 2.140, p. 60, 18. Cf. 1.68, p. 32, 5. Cf. Boyancé, "Une allusion à l'œuf orphique," pp. 97–112, and "Le disque de Brindisi et l'apothéose de Sémélé," *REA* 44 (1942) 210 n. 2.

[58] *De nupt.* 2.141, p. 61, 11. Cf. Boyancé, "Leucas," *Revue archéologique* 30 (1929) 211–219. I adopt his emendation. Others read ἀείζως.

prepared for her astral ascent.[59] We know that the astral ascent was represented in the liturgy of the mysteries of Isis and Mithras and that this rite had a purificatory function.[60] Reaching the circle of Juno, she asks for a first revelation of beatitude.[61] She advances from star to star, with various incidents each of which must have a mystic significance,[62] to the circle of Jupiter. But, arriving at the boundary, she is not unaware that the supreme divinity is still beyond, and she worships it silently. "She also prays to the virgin-source and, according to the Platonic mysteries, the powers *Ἅπαξ* and *Δὶς ἐπέκεινα*."[63] These latter words give the clue to the setting. In fact, Psellus, who expounds the doctrine of the Chaldean oracles dear to Plotinus, Porphyry, Iamblichus, and Proclus,[64] explains that, in the hierarchy of the celestial powers, there were to be noted the *πηγαί* and the *ἀρχαί*. Those that were called the *πηγαῖοι πατέρες* were *Ἅπαξ ἐπέκεινα*, Hecate, and *Δὶς ἐπέκεινα*.[65] Hecate is the virgin who gives birth to souls.[66]

Now it was in a sanctuary of Hecate that the theurgist Maximus of Ephesus, in the time of Julian the Apostate, practiced the Neoplatonic mysteries.[67] Photagogic rites played an important part in these mysteries. The recitation of a formula and the offering of a pinch of incense to the divinity produced its epiphany. The statue seemed to smile and a flame burst out

[59] *De nupt.* 2.133, p. 58, 13: "cum sonitu introfertur lectica interstincta sideribus, cui ritu mystico crepitus praecinebant." Is this a concrete representation of the "chariot of the soul"?

[60] Cf. P. Collomp, "Per omnia elementa," *Revue de philologie* 36 (1912) 196–201.

[61] *De nupt.* 2.149, p. 64, 12: "iam fas puto quicquid *περὶ εὐδαιμονίας* lectitans intellexeram conspicari."

[62] Cf. *ibid.*, 2.142, p. 62, 1, on the *simulacrum animae*; and Servius *In Aen.* 4.654, ed. Thilo, 1, p. 577, 8ff, particularly: "sciendum simulacra haec esse etiam eorum qui per apotheosin dii facti sunt; unde aut visi esse apud inferos aut illuc descendisse dicuntur." The Neoplatonists derived this theory from Homer. Cf. Plotinus *Enneads* 1.1.12, ed. Bréhier, vol. 1, p. 48.

[63] *De nupt.* 2.205, p. 77, 7: "quandam etiam fontanam virginem deprecatur, secundum Platonis quoque mysteria *Ἅπαξ καὶ Δὶς ἐπέκεινα* potestates." The interest of this passage has already been noted by Bidez, "Un faux dieu des oracles chaldaïques," *Revue de philologie* 27 (1903) 79 n. 1, and "Le philosophe Jamblique," p. 40 n. 3.

[64] Psellus *Brevis dogmatum Chaldaicorum expositio*, PG 122, 1153 B.

[65] *Ibid.*, 1152 A: *μετὰ δὲ τούτους, οἱ πηγαῖοι πατέρες, οἱ καλούμενοι καὶ κοσμαγωγοί· ὧν ὁ πρῶτος ὁ Ἅπαξ ἐπέκεινα λεγόμενος· μεθ' ὃν ἡ Ἑκάτη, εἶτα ὁ Δὶς ἐπέκεινα.* Cf. other texts on these divinities, quoted by Kroll, *De oraculis Chaldaicis*, pp. 16–17, who rightly thinks that these divinities did not appear in the original doctrine of the *Chaldean Oracles*.

[66] Psellus *Expos. orac. Chald.*, PG 122, 1136 B: *Καὶ ἐν μὲν τοῖς δεξιοῖς αὐτῆς μέρεσι τιθέασι (οἱ Χαλδαῖοι) τὴν πηγὴν τῶν ψυχῶν· ἐν δὲ τοῖς ἀριστεροῖς τὴν πηγὴν τῶν ἀγαθῶν, καί φασιν, ὅτι ἡ μὲν πηγὴ τῶν ψυχῶν ἕτοιμός ἐστιν εἰς τὰς ἀπογεννήσεις· ἡ δὲ πηγὴ τῶν ἀρετῶν ἐν ὅροις μένει ἔνδον τῆς ἰδίας οὐσίας καὶ οἷον παρθένος ἐστὶ καὶ ἀμιγής.* Cf. Kroll, *De orac. Chald.*, pp. 27ff.

[67] Eunapius *Vit. sophist.*, *Maximus*, ed. Boissonade (Paris 1849), p. 475, 12.

from the torches that it held in its hands.[68] Martianus knows these rites and describes them in connection with the council of the gods. The rays of Jupiter, the spheres that he holds in his hand, suddenly burst into flame, as well as Juno's crown, while the goddess' countenance remains invisible to the dazzled onlookers.[69]

How was this liturgy accessible to Martianus? Through a ritual tradition or a literary tradition?[70] The ritual tradition could quite well have been extended to the time of Martianus. In fact, the mysteries of Hecate were in vogue at the close of the fourth century in Macrobius' circle. They were celebrated in Rome in a vault situated under the *arx* of the Capitol. Praetextatus was a hierophant, and his wife a priestess.[71] Only Stilicho's edict put an end to the cult and excluded the faithful from the vault.[72] Elsewhere, the pagan mysteries were still celebrated secretly in the fifth century.[73] But the Neoplatonic liturgy itself was founded on the literary texts that had created these mysteries artificially, by the intermixture of various older rites. In the West at least, these texts were, I think, not by Iamblichus but by Porphyry.[74]

---

[68] Cf. Cumont, "Le culte égyptien," p. 89; Bidez, "Note sur les mystères platoniciens," *RBPH* 7 (1928) 1478. On the meaning of the ἔλλαμψις in the mysteries, cf. P. Boyancé, *Le culte des Muses chez les philosophes grecs* (diss. Paris 1936) 57. On these nocturnal rites in the time of Quodvultdeus, cf. *PL* 40, 703.

[69] *De nupt.* 1.73–75, p. 33, 24: "ast ubi primos honorati capitis radios ingressurus immisit, ipse etiam Iuppiter paululum retrogressus sub immensi nitoris numine caligavit; sphaerae vero orbesque, quos dextera sustinebat, veluti speculo cognati luminis refulsere."

[70] The question regarding the Orphic egg has already been posed by Boyancé, "Une allusion à l'œuf orphique," p. 99. Contrary to Cumont's view, he is inclined to admit a ritualistic tradition.

[71] On the funerary inscription *CIL* 6, 1779.28, Praetextatus' widow says to him: "Hecates ministram trina secreta edoces." She herself declares that she is "sacrata apud Aeginam Hecatae."

[72] Cf. Cumont, *Textes et monuments figurés relatifs aux mystères de Mithra*, vol. 1 (Brussels 1899), pp. 351–352, n. A: "La légende de s. Silvestre et le Mitreum du Capitole."

[73] Cf. U. Wilcken, "Heidnisches und Christliches aus Aegypten, II: Heidnische Vereine in christlicher Zeit," *Archiv für Papyrusforschung* 1 (1901) 407–419.

[74] In my view, there is no justification in contrasting Iamblichus, the theurgist, and Porphyry, the rationalist philosopher, as Bidez does, "Le philosophe Jamblique," p. 36. K. Praechter, "Richtungen und Schulen im Neuplatonismus," p. 116, has clearly shown that there is at least as much continuity as opposition between the two. Iamblichus does not appear to have been read in the West. Still, on the other hand, Pseudo-Dunchad comments on *De nupt.* 2.192, p. 74, 12, in accordance with a passage in Porphyry's *De imaginibus* quoted by Augustine: "Attin Porphyrius flores significare perhibuit." Cf. Manitius, vol. 1, p. 525, and Augustine's text quoted above, chap. 4 sec. 2 n. 156. The Carolingian commentator therefore still feels that Martianus' philosophy is Porphyrian. But the question will not be finally settled until the "Syrus quidam" quoted by Martianus, p. 62, 1 and p. 71, 6, has been identified. P. Boyancé informs me that he proposes to identify this "Syrus quidam" with Pherecydes of Syros, whom Augustine designates in the same terms in the text quoted on p. 141.

In fact, the followers of these mysteries were those very people who on the philosophical level derived from Porphyry. Martianus shares their beliefs. It is in the Milky Way, the abode of the princes of the elements, angels, the blessed, that the apotheosis of Philology takes place.[75] But the supreme divinity, the invisible sun, the impenetrable νοῦς, lies beyond that, outside the barriers of the astral world.[76] The gods themselves worship it, preserving a mystic silence.[77] St. Augustine also mentions Porphyry as responsible for the theurgic practices, particularly the epiphanies that were still prevalent in his day.[78] The major charge against Porphyry is that he adopted and propagated Chaldean theology.[79] Still, he does not suspect that the Porphyrian Triad, so similar, he believes, to the Christian Trinity, is likewise of Chaldean origin.[80] But he is quite well aware that the philosophical doctrine of the

---

[75] *De nupt.* 1.97, p. 41, 11. The gods are convoked "in *palatia* quae in Galaxia Iovis arbitri habitationem potissimam faciunt"; 2.108, p. 77, 15: "iter in Galaxium flectit, ubi senatum deum a Iove noverat congregatum . . . elementorum quoque praesides angelicique populi pulcherrima multitudo animaeque praeterea beatorum veterum, quae iam caeli templa meruerant, gressus Maiugenae sequebantur." On the *palatia* of the Milky Way, cf. the text quoted above, chap. 1 sec. 3 n. 87.

[76] *Ibid.*, 2.185, p. 73, 14, a hymn to the sun: "*ultramundanum* fas est cui cernere patrem"; 2.202, p. 76, 17: "tanti operis tantaeque rationis patrem deumque non ⟨ne⟩sciens ab ipsa etiam deorum notitia secessisse, quoniam *extramundanas* beatitudines eum transcendisse cognoverat, empyrio quodam intellectualique mundo gaudentem." Cf. also the formula "νοῦς sacer" that recurs on p. 39, 15 and p. 285, 11, applied to Mercury and Pallas, the interpreters of divinity.

[77] *Ibid.*, 9.910, p. 483, 9: "ipseque tunc Iuppiter caelestesque divi superioris melodiae agnita granditate, quae in honorem cuiusdam ignis arcani ac flammae insopibilis fundebatur, reveriti intimum patrimumque carmen paululum in venerationem *extramundanae* omnes intellegentiae surrexerunt." On the mystic value of silence, cf. Kroll, *De orac. Chald.*, p. 16.

[78] Augustine *De civ. Dei* 10.9, ed. Dombart, p. 415, 30, says that Porphyry reserved theurgy for the purification of the *anima spiritalis*: "Hanc enim dicit per quasdam consecrationes theurgicas, quas teletas vocant, idoneam fieri atque aptam susceptioni spirituum et angelorum et ad videndos deos." Cf. 10.10, 10.23, 10.26, where Augustine particularly emphasizes the notion that Porphyry recognized the inability of theurgy to reveal the supreme Intelligence. But Martianus does not think differently! Augustine *De civ. Dei* 10.10, ed. Dombart, p. 418, 3, refers quite clearly to the epiphanies: "Quod enim qui has sordidas purgationes sacrilegis ritibus operantur quasdam mirabiliter pulchras, sicut iste commemorat, vel angelorum imagines vel deorum tamquam purgato spiritu vident (si tamen vel tale aliquid vident): illud est, quod apostolus dicit: *Quoniam Satanas transfigurat se velut angelum lucis.*"

[79] *Ibid.*, 10.32, Dombart, p. 455, 29: "utique se a Chaldaeis oracula divina sumpsisse, quorum adsiduam commemorationem facit, tacere non potuit." Augustine continues, contrasting Porphyry with Abraham, who abandoned the superstitions of Chaldea to show us the true way: Christ, who purifies us entirely, the *anima intellectualis*, the *anima spiritalis*, and the body.

[80] See above, p. 188. Psellus *Expos. orac. Chald.*, *PG* 122, 1140 D, also notes the analogy with the Christian Trinity but observes that the νοῦς πατρικός of the *Chaldean Oracles*

return of the soul is reproduced, among the pagans, by a religious mystery,[81] in which Hecate plays the preponderant role.[82]

Hellenic culture and beliefs that were still prevalent, despite the decline of Greek, in St. Augustine's day[83] were seriously affected by the Vandal Conquest. Africa found itself suddenly cut off from Rome and Constantinople.[84] The Arian invader persecuted Catholics suspected of loyalty to the emperor. Byzantine policy with regard to the Vandal kings was weak in the extreme.

---

is not the creator of the universe, contrary to the Word of God in Christian dogma. The third person of the Chaldean triad is this πηγαῖα ψυχή, also mentioned by Favonius Eulogius, whence flow all the souls that descend upon the earth through the nine circles according to Porphyry's doctrine of the Περὶ Στυγός. Text quoted above, chap. 1 sec. 3 n. 67. On Augustine's attitude with regard to this ψυχή, which he hesitates to identify with the Holy Spirit, cf. below, pp. 241–246.

[81] On the adherents to the theurgic rites recommended by the De regressu animae, cf. chap. 4 sec. 2 n. 145. On the Neoplatonic interpretations in the pagan temples, cf. Augustine Epist. 91 (202), PL 33, 315.

[82] With regard to the formula of the De regressu animae: "Omne corpus est fugiendum," which challenges the dogma of the resurrection of the flesh, Augustine adds, Sermo 242.7, PL 38, 1137: "Sed nolo hic diutius disputare, libros vestros lego: mundum istum animal dicitis . . . id est habere animam suam, sed sensus corporis non habere, quia extrinsecus nihil est quod sentiri possit: habere tamen intellectum, haerere Deo; et ipsam animam mundi vocari Iovem, vel vocari Hecatem, id est quasi animam universalem mundum regentem, et unum quoddam animal facientem. Eundemque mundum aeternum esse dicitis, semper futurum, finem non habiturum. Si ergo aeternus est mundus, et sine fine manet mundus, et animal est mundus, anima ista semper tenetur in mundo: certe corpus est omne fugiendum? Quid est quod dicebas: Corpus est omne fugiendum? Ego dico beatas animas incorruptibilia corpora semper habituras. Tu qui dicis: corpus est omne fugiendum, occide mundum. Tu dicis ut fugiam de carne mea: fugiat Iuppiter tuus de caelo et terra." It is therefore probable that, in the De regressu animae, Porphyry expounded the Plotinian theory of Jupiter as the world soul (cf. above, p. 175). Then he expounded the Chaldean theory of Hecate as the world soul. Cf. Kroll, De orac. Chald., p. 69, who compares this Augustinian text with a Chaldean oracle mentioned by Porphyry. On the role of Hecate in the theophanies, cf. Proclus' texts assembled by Kroll, De orac. Chald., p. 49.

[83] It will be observed, however, that in Martianus the religious mystery tends to be interlarded with allegory. The rite becomes a literary device. Martianus is also a compiler, as is evident from the discussion on the sixteen heavenly regions, p. 27, 8ff. Here, following Nigidius Figulus (cf. C. Thulin, Die Götter des Mart. Cap. und der Bronzeleber von Piacenza, Religionsgesch. Versuche und Vorarbeiten, vol. 3, 1, Giessen 1906), he reproduces the Etruscan doctrine, and Juno's revelation regarding demons, pp. 64ff, which assumes a Latin source.

[84] Genseric banished Bishop Felix of Hadhramaut for having given shelter to a monk from overseas (cf. Victor of Vita Hist. Pers. 1.23, ed. Petschenig, CSEL 7, p. 11, 10). Huneric demanded an oath from the bishops of Africa in 484: "nullus vestrum ad regiones transmarinas epistulas diriget" (ibid., 3.19, p. 80, 17). The influence of Diadochus in Africa can be explained, according to Marrou, only if he was led captive from Epirus to Carthage, at the time of a Vandal raid between 467 and 474. Cf. my Hist. litt. des grandes invasions germaniques, pp. 91–113 and 151–165.

It involved negotiations at any cost in order to arrest the persecution. The rare impulses toward war were not pursued effectively, except the war that ended in the disaster of Basiliscus under Leo I (468). His successor Zeno found himself suddenly forced to conclude a treaty of perpetual peace with Genseric (475) and to leave the Romans in Africa to their sorry lot.[85] They did not, however, stop directing their glances toward the emperor of the East. It was to Constantinople and the Eastern provinces that most of the refugees and exiles swarmed, victims of the persecutions of Genseric and Huneric.[86] Thanks to a lull in the persecution, under King Gunthamund, the poet Dracontius ventured to eulogize the emperor. He was thrown into prison.[87] It was only at the close of the century, under King Trasamund (496–523), that a literary renaissance, contemporary with the Italian renaissance under Theodoric, was able to blossom forth.[88] But whereas the Italian renaissance was to influence every discipline and follow the model of the East,[89] the African renaissance, restricted to rhetoric and courtly poetry, proceeded within confined limits. The works of the poet Fulgentius,[90] who had read Martianus Capella,[91] shows us this rapid hardening of the cultural process.[92]

[85] For the story of these relations, cf. L. Schmidt, *Gesch. der Wandalen* (Leipzig 1901); F. Martroye, *Genséric* (Paris 1907); E. F. Gautier, *Genséric* (Paris 1932).

[86] For the refugees, cf. Theodoret *Epist.* 29–36 and 70, *PG* 83, 1208–1213 and 1240; *Acta sanctorum* Jan. 8th, vol. 1, p. 483; Theophanes, *a.* 5964; Victor of Vita *Hist. Pers.* 3.30, p. 87, 15; Procopius *Bell. Vand.* 2.5, *CSHB*, p. 431, 5. On the exiles, cf. Theodoret *Epist.* 52–53, *PG* 83, 1228; Martroye, *Genséric*, p. 340.

[87] Cf. Dracontius *Satisfactio*, and Schanz, vol. 4, 2, p. 59.

[88] On this renaissance, cf. Schmidt, *Gesch. der Wand.*, pp. 195–200, who has a tendency to minimize the misdeeds of the Vandals, and E. Provana, "Blossio Emilio Draconzio, studio biografico e letterario," *Memorie della r. Accad. della scienze di Torino*, sc. mor. stor. e filol., ser. 2, vol. 62 (1912) 39–47.

[89] Cf. below, pp. 273ff.

[90] It is not only in order to simplify the exposition that I identify the mythographer Fulgentius with Bishop Fulgentius of Ruspe, although this identification is disputed. Cf. Schanz, vol. 4, 2, p. 205. I consider that the problem is analogous to the question of Boethius' *Opuscula theologica*, long regarded as spurious. On the one hand, it is a completely profane work, that is, pagan in attitude. On the other hand, it is the work of a Christian theologian. For lack of perspective, it is difficult to believe in a single author. The stylistic differences that have been brought out by O. Friebel, *Fulgentius der Mythograph und Bischof, mit Beitr. zur Syntax des Spätlateins*, Studien zur Gesch. und Kultur des Altertums, vol. 5 (Paderborn 1911), do not prevent him from believing in a single author, according to the demonstration by R. Helm, "Der Bischof Fulgentius und der Mythograph," *Rhein. Mus.* 54 (1899) 111–134.

[91] He quotes him in his *Sermones antiqui*, ed. Helm (Leipzig 1898), p. 123, 4.

[92] The numerous quotations from the Greek Fathers appearing in Book 4 of Vigilius of Thapsus' *Contra Eutychetem*, a work intended for readers in the East and perhaps written in exile in Constantinople, must not induce one to think that Vigilius knew Greek. All these extracts are taken from Leo's *Tome*.

Fulgentius, however, had learned the elements of Greek before Latin, according to the scholastic tradition[93] devotedly preserved in this aristocratic family. On the evidence of his biographer Ferrandus, he could "recite from memory the whole of Homer and understand a great part of Menander as he read the text . . . His mother wanted him, as he was destined to live among Africans, to be able to speak Greek more easily by observing the rough breathings, as if he had been brought up in Greece . . . Even a long time after he had lost the habit of speaking and reading it, he pronounced Greek with such a pure accent that one would have said he lived almost daily among Greeks."[94] As Ferrandus did not know Greek, he was a bad judge of Fulgentius' talents, and his pious praise is valueless. On the other hand we should accept his involuntary admissions. There was no longer then in Africa any Greek-speaking colony. Fulgentius himself very soon stopped speaking and reading Greek. Let us therefore be circumspect in assuming, as Father Lapeyre does, that he read all the Greek theologians in the original![95] The putative text is nothing more than a rhetorical list of the Greek and Latin Fathers who defended the Church against the heretics.[96] It was his study of Latin works— Rufinus' *Historia monachorum*, Cassianus' *Institutiones* and *Conlationes*—that decided Fulgentius' ecclesiastical vocation.[97] He knew of Origen's theories only from hearsay.[98] His theology is strictly Augustinian.[99] His correspondence with the "Scythian monks" of Constantinople is Latin, and these monks

[93] Despite the statements of Father G. G. Lapeyre, *Saint Fulgence de Ruspe*, pp. 90ff. On Greek as a spoken language in sixth-century Africa, he relies on inscriptions of the third century!

[94] Ferrandus, *Vie de s. Fulgence de Ruspe*, ed. and trans. Lapeyre, p. 10. It would be more correct to translate: "*although* he was destined."

[95] Lapeyre, *Saint Fulgence*, p. 264.

[96] Fulgentius *De verit. praedestin.*, PL 65, 649 D: "Quis vero neget beatos episcopos Innocentium Romanum, Athanasium Alexandrinum, Eustachium Antiochenum, Gregorium Nazianzenum, Basilium Caesariensem, Ambrosium Mediolanensem, Hilarium Pictaviensem, Constantinopolitanum Ioannem, Aurelium Carthaginensem, Augustinum Hipponensem ceterosque pontifices qui ecclesias Dei vigilantissime gubernantes aut nascentibus aut iam natis haereticis habitante Spiritu sancto restiterunt . . . quid inquam istos neget vasa misericordiae quae Deus praeparavit in gloriam? Sed quis usque adeo divinae fidei et caritatis inimicus, ut Paulum, Antonium, Ioannem, Hilarionem, Macarium aliosque similis vitae ac sanctitatis monachos . . . vasa contumeliae non metuat appellare?" The first list of names was probably borrowed from some translated conciliar text, the second from Rufinus' *Hist. mon.*

[97] Ferrandus *Vit. Fulg.*, ed. Lapeyre, p. 46.

[98] Fulgentius *De verit. praedestin.* 3.22, PL 65, 669 B: "quod sensisse dicitur Origenes."

[99] Add to Schanz, vol. 4, 2, p. 577 B: B. Nisters, "Die Christologie des hl. Fulgentius von Ruspe," *Münsterische Beiträge zur Theologie*, part 16 (Münster 1930), and M. Schmauss, "Die Trinitätslehre des Fulgentius von Ruspe," *Charisteria, A. Rzach zum 80. Geburtstag dargebracht* (Reichenberg 1930).

tried to teach him by means of the texts of the Greek Fathers, of which he was ignorant.[100] At the very most he could decipher the Septuagint with the help of Latin translations or indicate the meaning of a few ecclesiastical Hellenisms.[101] John Scot Erigena had good reason therefore to observe that there was nothing in Fulgentius' theological work to indicate any direct contact with the Greek Fathers. Prudentius of Troyes agreed with him on this point but noted that the pagan works of his youth testified to some knowledge of Greek on Fulgentius' part.[102]

In his youth Fulgentius boasted to his readers, in fact, of being a Hellenist.[103] He affected a jargon teeming with words derived from Greek and liked to collect Greek etymologies.[104] He proclaimed his Christian faith but delighted in the Greek legends.[105] His allegorical prologue was inspired by Martianus Capella: Calliope declares that after dwelling in Athens, then Rome, she sought refuge in Alexandria at the time of Alaric's invasion. But Galen's medical school, all-powerful in that city, drove her to flee to Africa.[106] She introduces Fulgentius to Philosophy and Urania and promises, if he follows them, that they will confer on him astral immortality, as they did on Plato, through the revelation of the mysteries. The book, then, is

---

[100] Cf. Schanz, vol. 4, 2, p. 579, and *PL* 65, 442ff.

[101] Cf. Fulgentius *Contra Fabianum* and *PL* 65, 752–768. Even ten years after the Byzantine conquest, the African Bishop Pontianus of Thenae replies to Justinian, who proposes to condemn Theodore of Mopsuestia, Ibas, and Theodoret: "eorum dicta ad nos usque nunc minime pervenerunt" (*PL* 67, 997 A).

[102] Prudentius *Epist. ad Ioann. Scot.*, *PL* 95, 1310 A: "quem si Atticae linguae scientiam habuisse aut ignoras aut negas, lege libros illius, qui Mythologiarum seu Vergilianae continentiae inscribuntur, et invenies ei maximam illius linguae adfuisse peritiam."

[103] Fulgentius *Sermones antiqui*, p. 116, 14: "Unde et Demostenes *pro Philippo* ait,— sed nequid te Graecum turbet exemplum, ego pro hoc tibi Latinum feram,—ait enim . . ."

[104] Helm, *Fulgentii opera*, pp. viff.

[105] Text quoted above, n. 45. Cf. p. 30, 13 "pagani"; 30, 22; 32, 20 "ornatrix Graecia"; 55, 18 "sicut nihil Latina gratiosius veritate, ita nihil Graeca falsitate ornatius"; 64, 2 "decepta Graecia credulitate demonum potius quam deorum."

[106] Fulgentius *Mit.*, pp. 8–9. On the reputation of the Alexandrian physicians, cf. Ammianus Marcellinus, ed. Gardthausen (Leipzig 1874), p. 305, 28: "medicinae autem . . . ita studia augentur in dies, ut licet opus ipsum refellat, pro omni tamen experimento sufficiat medico ad commendandam artis auctoritatem, si Alexandriae se dixerit eruditum." The physician Magnus, whose commentary on Hippocrates' *Aphorisms* was quoted in 447 by the African Cassius Felix, *De medicina*, ed. V. Rose, p. 48, 4 and p. 182, 9, is probably Magnus of Nisibis, a physician resident in Alexandria in the fourth century. Cf. Christ, *Griech. Litteraturgesch.*, 2, 2, p. 1096. Similarly, another Alexandrian commentary on the *Aphorisms* was to survive in Italy after the disappearance of Hellenism. Cf. below, p. 408. It will be observed that Eunapius *Vit. Sophist.*, ed. Boissonade, p. 493, says, with reference to the rhetorician Eusebius of Alexandria (fourth century), that his Egyptian origin is sufficient to prove his art of speaking, and he adds, p. 493, 19: Τὸ δὲ ἔθνος ἐπὶ ποιητικῇ μὲν σφόδρα μαίνονται, ὁ δὲ σπουδαῖος Ἑρμῆς αὐτῶν ἀποκεχώρηκεν.

presented as a revelation of the secret nature of the gods.[107] But this setting should not induce a belief in any survival whatever of the Platonic mysteries that Martianus Capella still knew. Fulgentius' erudition is completely bookish. More than this, the Greek erudition of which he makes such a display is deceptive. His quotations are sometimes invented, so much so that he could be considered a charlatan.[108] Even when he mentions actual writers, he pretends to have read them, although these names are taken from an intermediate Latin source.[109] His numerous instances of confusion about the names of writers or the titles of the books from which he quotes textually are due, I believe, to the fact that he is using Greco-Latin glossaries.[110] This method is sometimes evident. To explain the etymology of Bellerophon he looks in his glossary for a similar word and finds under the word βουληφόρος a quotation from Homer and one from Menander.[111] Still more, he often repeats himself. For the etymology of Clio, then for the etymology of Heracles, he referred to the word κλέος and found the same fragment from Homer, with the translation, which he reproduces word for word both times.[112] It is evident to what a level his Greek culture is reduced: to the bits and pieces of ancient writers indicated by his dictionary. Hellenic culture was quite dead under the Vandals. Fulgentius himself, educated in a privileged environment that was passionately devoted to Hellenism, presents merely a caricature of that Hellenism.

[107] Fulgentius *Mit.*, p. 14, 22: "quarum sequax si fueris, celeri te raptu ex mortali caelestem efficient, astrisque te, non ut Neronem poeticis laudibus sed ut Platonem misticis interserent rationibus"; p. 15, 10: "Ergo nunc de deorum primum natura, unde tanta malae credulitatis lues stultis mentibus inoleverit, edicamus."

[108] Skutsch, *PW* s.v. Fulgentius, 219.

[109] Fulgentius *Mit.*, p. 24, 17, quoting Antiphon, Philochorus, Artemon, and Serapion Ascalonites from Tertullian *De anima* 46, ed. Wissowa, *CSEL* 22, p. 337, 3, or a common source. The distinction between actual and invented quotations was made by Zink, *Der Mytholog Fulgentius* (Würzburg 1867) 62ff. A number of quotations from Hermes Trismegistus will be noted.

[110] On the Greco-Latin glossaries and the expansion of glossography in the fifth century, cf. Schanz, vol. 4, 2, pp. 251–252.

[111] Fulgentius *Mit.*, p. 59, 9–13.

[112] *Mit.*, p. 25, 19:
prima Clio quasi cogitatio prima discendi—cleos enim Graece fama dicitur, unde et Homerus: κλέος οἶον ἀκούσαμεν, id est famam solam audivimus.

Mit., p. 41, 12:
Hercules enim Eracles Graece dicitur, id est eroncleos quod nos Latine virorum fortium famam dicimus, unde et Homerus ait: κλέος οἶον ἀκούσαμεν, hoc est: famam solam audivimus.

The Homeric text, *Il.* 2.486, has ἀκούομεν.

Chapter 5

GREEK CULTURE IN GAUL

1. Hellenism at Stake

The Hellenic pagan culture of which Macrobius is the best illustration was not confined to any individual or to any one province. The same form and the same ideal appear again at the beginning of the fifth century in Rutilius Namatianus, a native of the southwest of Gaul who became a high official in the Western Empire.[1] The poem *On His Return*, which describes his journey from Rome and was completed in 417,[2] is the work of a sensitive writer who prides himself on competing with Greek poetry.[3] He resorts to Greek sources; for, as Carlo Pascal noted,[4] Rutilius' entire theme of the eternal nature of Rome was inspired, item for item, by a speech of Aelius Aristides on the same topic. In all probability, the textual parallels between the two works are not absolutely convincing, owing to the fact that Rutilius transposes into verse what was a project in prose, but the length and the continuity

---

[1] The question of Greek culture in Gaul has never received special treatment, but some suggestions may be found in O. Denk, *Geschichte des gallo-fränkischen Unterrichts- und Bildungswesens von den ältesten Zeiten bis auf Karl den Grossen, mit Berücksichtigung der literarischen Verhältnisse* (Mainz 1892), chaps. 4–7; M. Roger, *L'enseignement des lettres classiques d'Ausone à Alcuin* (diss. Paris 1905); T. Haarhoff, *Schools of Gaul, A Study of Pagan and Christian Education in the Last Century of the Western Empire* (Oxford 1920); and Jullian, *Histoire de la Gaule*, vol. 8, 2, pp. 255–259.

[2] On his native country there is a question between Poitiers, Toulouse, and Narbonne. Cf. Schanz, vol. 4, 2, pp. 38–41. On the date of his trip, cf. J. Carcopino, "A propos du poème de Rutilius Namatianus," *REL* 6 (1928) 180–200.

[3] Rutilius *De reditu suo* 1.99–100 (ed. Vessereau-Préchac, Paris 1933), with reference to the aqueducts of Rome:

> Hos potius dicas crevisse in sidera montes
> tale Gigantem Graecia laudet opus.

and 1.263:

> Ardua non solos deceant miracula Graios.

[4] Pascal, "Una probabile fonte di Rutilio Namaziano," *Rendiconti della r. Accademia di archeologia ... di Napoli*, 1903, reprinted in *Graecia capta, saggi sopra alcune fonti greche di scrittori latini* (Florence 1905) 163–177. The question involves the twenty-sixth speech of Aelius Aristides, ed. Keil (Berlin 1898), vol. 2, pp. 91ff.

of the parallel incline one to believe, as Pascal does, that there is more than the thematic link in common and that Aelius Aristides' speech is Rutilius' specific source.[5] Furthermore, Rutilius is equally imbued with Greek poetry. The theme of the recognition of beloved places indubitably evokes, for him, as later on for Du Bellay, Homer's line describing smoke rising above a roof and symbolizing to Ulysses his distant homeland.[6] Further on, Rutilius compares the ascetic life of the early monks, which he discovers with amazement, to the melancholy of Bellerophon, which Homer describes in the *Iliad*.[7] Such reminiscences should not cause surprise in Rutilius, for Ausonius' grandson, Paulinus of Pella, who belongs to the same generation and who was brought up at Bordeaux, testifies to having studied the *Iliad* and the *Odyssey* in his youth.[8]

[5] A. Boulanger, *Aelius Aristide et la sophistique* (diss. Paris 1923) 360 n. 5, is of the contrary opinion, but does not elaborate on his reasons.

[6] Rutilius *De reditu* 1.193–196:

> Nec locus ille mihi cognoscitur indice fumo,
> qui dominas arces et caput orbis habet,
> quamquam signa levis fumi commendat Homerus,
> dilecto quotiens surgit in astra solo.

Cf. *Odyssey* 1.57–59:

> . . . αὐτὰρ 'Οδυσσεύς,
> ἱέμενος καὶ καπνὸν ἀποθρῴσκοντα νοῆσαι
> ἧς γαίης, θανέειν ἱμείρεται.

The same lines had already struck Ovid, *Pont.* 1.3.33.

[7] Rutilius *De reditu* 1.447–452:

> Sive suas repetunt factorum ergastula poenas,
> tristia seu nigro viscera felle tument.
> Sic nimiae bilis morbum adsignavit Homerus
> Bellerophonteis sollicitudinibus.
> Nam iuveni offenso saevi post tela doloris
> dicitur humanum displicuisse genus.

Cf. *Iliad* 6.200–202:

> 'Αλλ' ὅτε δὴ καὶ κεῖνος ἀπήχθετο πᾶσι θεοῖσιν,
> ἤτοι ὁ κὰπ πεδίον τὸ 'Αλήϊον οἶος ἀλᾶτο,
> ὃν θυμὸν κατέδων, πάτον ἀνθρώπων ἀλεείνων.

Vessereau points out that the Homeric text does not speak of bile as the cause of the sickness. I think that Rutilius probably and mistakenly applied to Bellerophon line 166, which actually refers to Proitos:

> "Ως φάτο· τὸν δὲ ἄνακτα χόλος λάβεν οἷον ἄκουσε.

[8] Paulinus of Pella *Eucharisticos* (ed. G. Brandes, *CSEL*, vol. 16, 1), p. 294, lines 72–74:

> Nec sero exacto primi mox tempore lustri
> dogmata Socratus et bellica plasmata Homeri
> erroresque legens cognoscere cogor Ulixis.

The *dogmata Socratus* denote, I assume, not philosophical study of the Platonic dialogues, but the perusal of a collection of the Socratic *placita* similar to Flavianus' *De dogmate philosophorum* mentioned above, chap. 1 sec. 1 n. 24. The context indicates in fact that Paulinus is here speaking of the elementary studies pursued before the Latin course, as the custom was, under the Greek *grammaticus*.

In contrast to Rutilius Namatianus, who was imbued with pagan Hellenism although he was perhaps a Christian[9] and who recalls Macrobius, the Aquitainian orator Latinius Pacatus Drepanius, who attacks Hellenism, rather recalls St. Jerome. In fact, he executes the plan that was previously nursed but not carried out by Jerome. This was a refutation of Porphyry's Κατὰ χριστιανῶν.[10] His treatise, of which only scanty fragments are extant, had a long life, since it was excerpted, under the name of Polycarp, by Victor of Capua in the middle of the sixth century.[11] It must be admitted that, in spite of imperial decrees, Porphyry's great antichristian work was still in vogue in Gaul at the beginning of the fifth century, at least in the form of a manual of objections,[12] and that it caused spiritual consternation for Pacatus to have been anxious to refute it. Such a refutation, whose loss cannot be sufficiently deplored, assumes in its author a high degree of culture and a sound knowledge of the Greek language. We must not therefore attach too wide a significance to Ausonius' evidence on the decline of Greek culture in Gaul.[13]

Apart from these theoretical discussions, practical morality brought into conflict supporters and opponents of traditional pagan Hellenism. Rutilius was enraged to find on the island of Capraria those men who dignified themselves with the Greek name of "monks."[14] It was in fact a new type of literature,

[9] In support of Rutilius' paganism, see the forceful but not quite decisive arguments of Labriolle, "Rutilius Claudius Namatianus et les moines," *REL* 6 (1928) 30–41.

[10] The fragments of this work appear in John the Deacon's *catena* on the Heptateuch (6th cent.?). This *catena* is preserved in Paris. Lat. 12309, 11th cent., fol. 13ᵛ, ed. Pitra, *Spicil. Solesm.* 1 (Paris 1852) 266–301. Cf. pp. L–LIV. I adopt the identification of Pacatus as proposed by Harnack, "Neue Fragmente des Werkes des Porphyrius *Gegen die Christen*, die Pseudo-Polycarpiana und die Schrift des Rhetors Pacatus," *Sitzungsber. der preuss. Akad. der Wiss.*, phil.-hist. Klasse (1921) 1, pp. 266–284 and 834–835, despite the strictures of W. A. Baehrens, "Pacatus," *Hermes* 56 (1921) 443–445, reproduced by Labriolle, *La réaction païenne*, p. 249. The argument from grammar that the language of the fragments is posterior to the beginning of the fifth century is not valid; for these fragments are minimal, and how can one know that they were not revised by the sixth- or ninth-century compiler? The very fact that a refutation of the Κατὰ χριστιανῶν seemed to St. Jerome a useful work (text quoted above, chap. 2 sec. 2 n. 118) supports the identification suggested by Harnack. Perhaps it was because Pacatus wrote this refutation that Jerome abandoned his plan to write one himself. It is therefore futile to think, as Angély does, *Un apologiste gaulois du Vᵉ siècle: Pacatus* (Agen 1927), or, with Baehrens, that this was another Pacatus, the son or father of the orator. If it is assumed that Pacatus had recently been converted from Hellenism to Christianity, we have a still better explanation for his realization of the extreme danger of Porphyry's treatise and for his desire to mitigate it.

[11] On Victor and on John the Deacon, cf. below, chap. 7, p. 359.

[12] It has been noted above, pp. 210ff, that such a collection of Porphyrian accusations was then current in Africa.

[13] Ausonius *Commemoratio prof. Burdig.* 8 (*Grammatici Graeci Burdigalenses*), ed. Peiper (Leipzig 1886), p. 57, line 6: "fructus exilis tenuisque sermo," and lines 13ff.

[14] Rutilius *De reditu* 1.441–442:

although also of Greek origin, that was to introduce and develop the ascetic ideal in Gaul and the entire West.

I do not think that Cassianus, whose writings propagated this new ideal in Gaul, knew Greek as his mother tongue,[15] but he spoke it fluently. He was even able to appreciate the elegance with which some Father of the Desert would express himself in Greek, and it was in Greek, either directly or through an interpreter, that he gathered the information about the Egyptian ascetics, the majority of whom spoke only Coptic.[16] His works prove besides that he read Greek texts. He frequently resorts to the Greek text of the Scriptures to elucidate the meaning of the Latin translation.[17] He produced Greek ecclesiastical literature. His treatise *Against Nestorius* quotes several Nestorian formulas[18] and starts with a summary of the heresies that existed at the beginning of the Nestorian heresy.[19] The refutation of this heresy constitutes an entire compilation of the Greek Fathers on the Incarnation. Like Augustine addressing Julian of Eclana, Cassianus in fact considers that their authority will have more weight for Nestorians than the authority of the Latin Fathers.[20]

       Ipsi se monachos Graïo nomine dicunt
       quod soli nullo vivere teste volunt.

[15] We know how controversial the question of Cassianus' native country is: "natione Scytha," says Gennadius *De vir. inl.* 62 (61). The most varied emendations and interpretations have been advanced: Scythia minor, Syria, Gaul. Apart from the bibliography listed by Schanz, vol. 4, 2, p. 512, cf. A. Ménager, "La patrie de Cassien," *Echos d'Orient* 24 (1921) 330–358, and J. Thibaut, "Autour de la patrie de Cassien," *ibid.*, pp. 447–449. Although these two writers return to the hypothesis of a Syrian origin, I do not consider their arguments definitive. As a matter of fact, most of the Greek terms pointed out by Ménager, p. 335, to prove that Greek was really Cassianus' mother tongue, were borrowed by Cassianus from Evagrius Ponticus (cf. below, p. 230). Moreover, Cassianus made use of the Latin poets, whom he occasionally quotes. I think that the simplest hypothesis is the most likely one: *Scytha* denotes *Scythia minor*, a hypothesis reproduced brilliantly by H. I. Marrou, "Jean Cassien à Marseille," *Revue du Moyen Age latin* 1 (1945) 5–17. Cf. also Marrou, "La patrie de Jean Cassien," *Orientalia Christiana periodica* 13 (1947) 588–596.

[16] Cassianus *Conlationes* 16.1 (ed. Petschenig, *CSEL* 13, p. 439, 4): "(Ioseph) . . . ita non solum Aegyptia sed etiam Graeca facundia diligenter edoctus ut vel nobis vel his qui Aegyptiam linguam penitus ignorabant, non ut ceteri per interpretem, sed per semetipsum elegantissime disputaret." On the ignorance of Greek among the first Fathers of the Desert, cf. *Inst.* 5.33, p. 106, 19, and Puech, *Litt. gr. chrét.* 3, pp. 135–136.

[17] Cf. the references in Petschenig's edition to the words *Graece, Graeci, Graecus*, in the *Index nominum*.

[18] Cf. *ibid.*, p. 392, *Index scriptorum* s.v. *Nestorii fragmenta.*

[19] Cassianus *Contra Nestorium* 1.2 (from Ebion to Apollinaris).

[20] *Ibid.*, 7.28.1, p. 386, 13: "Sed forte, quia hi quos enumeravimus viri in diversis mundi partibus fuerunt, minus probabiles tibi auctoritate videantur: ridiculum id quidem, quia loco fides non imminuitur, et quid sit quis, non ubi sit considerandum, praesertim cum religio omnes uniat et hi qui in fide una sunt in corpore quoque uno esse

He quotes textually two speeches by Gregory of Nazianzus in Rufinus' translation,[21] Athanasius' *Contra Arianos*,[22] and a homily by John Chrysostom,[23] whom he knew personally and whose faithful disciple he boasted of being. Cassianus' other works show that he also read a biography of Basil of Caesarea, of whom he relates two apothegms in his *Institutiones*.[24] In the *Conlationes* Cassianus even supports his theory of free will on the authority of Hermas' *Pastor*,[25] whose value Prosper of Aquitaine, in his refutation, was to deny.[26] It is quite probable that Cassianus had nevertheless not read the *Pastor* and knew it only from Origen, who returns several times to the same passage and underlines its importance.[27] In fact, while avoiding any mention of him, Cassianus borrows frequently from Origen, of whom he had read at least the *De principiis*, the *Commentary on the Song of Songs*, and the homilies on Genesis and Exodus.[28]

Nor is Cassianus a stranger to Greek pagan culture, although he in no sense

---

noscantur; sed tamen aliquos tibi, quos non despicias, etiam de orientalibus proferemus." It is interesting to compare Cassianus' attitude with Augustine's; text quoted above, chap. 4 sec. 3 n. 3.

[21] *Ibid.*, 7.28, quoting Gregory of Nazianzus *De epiphaniis* 13 and *De luminibus* 13 (ed. Engelbrecht, *CSEL* 46, p. 100, 23 and p. 123, 18). Neither Rufinus' editor nor Cassianus' brought out this comparison.

[22] *Ibid.*, 7.29, quoting Athanasius *Contra Arianos orationes IV*. On Athanasius, cf. also *Conl.* 18.14.1.

[23] *Ibid.*, 7.30. It was from this passage in Cassianus that Cassiodorus *In Ps.* 17.13 (*PL* 70, 127 B) borrowed his quotation from Chrysostom.

[24] *Inst.* 6.19, p. 125, 26: "Fertur sancti Basilii Caesariensis episcopi districta sententia: et mulierem, inquit, ignoro et virgo non sum"; and 7.19, p. 143, 20: "Fertur sententia sancti Basilii Caesariensis episcopi ad quendam prolata Syncletium tali quo diximus tepore torpentem ... et senatorem, inquit, Syncletium perdidisti et monachum non fecisti." On the esteem in which Basil was held by Cassianus, cf. *Inst., praef.* 5.

[25] *Conl.* 8.17.2, p. 233, 25: "de utrisque vero (angelis) liber Pastoris plenissime docet"; and 13.12.7, p. 380, 25: "adiacere autem homini in quamlibet partem arbitrii libertatem etiam liber ille qui dicitur Pastoris apertissime docet, in quo duo angeli unicuique nostrum adhaerere dicuntur, id est bonus ac malus, in hominis vero optione consistere, ut eligat quem sequatur." It will be observed that the author of the *Vita s. Genovefae*, who must date in the sixth century, also quotes the *Pastor* in the Palatine Version. Cf. the edition of B. Krusch, *MGH, Script. rer. Mer.* 3, p. 221, 11 and n. 1. The *Pastor* is also quoted in the fifth century by the Arian author of the *Opus imperf. in Matth.* 19.28 (*PG* 56, 814 A).

[26] Prosper *Liber contra conlatorem* 13.6 (*al.* 30), *PL* 51, 250 C: "Post illud autem nullius auctoritatis testimonium quod disputationi suae de libello Pastoris inseruit."

[27] *Hermae Pastor* 2, *mand.* 6 quoted by Origen *Hom. in Luc.* 35 (translated by Jerome, *PG* 13, 1889 C) and *De principiis* 3.2 (translated by Rufinus, *PG* 11, 309 B).

[28] See the textual parallels established by Dom Salvatore Marsili, *Giovanni Cassiano ed Evagrio Pontico, dottrina sulla carità e contemplazione*, Studia Anselmiana, vol. 5 (Rome 1936) 150–158, and the few reservations advanced in Capelle's review, *RHE* 35 (1939) 554–556.

attempts to boast of it but rather affects to scorn it. However, he incidentally quotes a pagan maxim that had become proverbial.[29] He also shows that he had read a collection of aphorisms of the philosophers, for he quotes in Greek a Socratic aphorism and another by Diogenes in order to contrast the continence of the monks with the philosophers' wantonness.[30] Lastly, he puts into the mouth of the abbot Serenus a definition of νοῦς that was borrowed from the Neoplatonic school.[31]

There is still another point. The ascetic ideal that Cassianus presents for the admiration of the West, far from being taken directly from the Egyptian Fathers, as Cassianus claims, reproduced the teaching of a very cultured Greek, Evagrius Ponticus. He had settled toward the end of his days in the Desert of Skiathis, then in the Desert of Cells. This supremely important fact has only recently been brought to light. But Dom Marsili's demonstration that Cassianus was merely the Latin translator of Evagrius Ponticus' elaborate theories appears to me highly convincing. Jerome had already complained of the influence that Evagrius was beginning to exert in the West, since the time that Rufinus had translated some of his works,[32] and accused Evagrius of being one of those responsible for the growing Pelagian heresy.[33] Dom Marsili has shown that Cassianus had done still far more than Rufinus for the spread of Evagrius' doctrine, to which he was indebted for his theories on the

---

[29] *Conl.* 2.16.1, p. 59, 17: "Vetus namque sententia est: ἀκρότητες ἰσότητες, id est, nimietates aequales sunt." In his *Letters*, Jerome had quoted a similar maxim, *PL* 22, 898: μεσότης ἡ ἀρετή, ὑπερβολὴ κακία, and 22, 1116: μεσότητας ἀρετάς, ὑπερβολὰς κακίας εἶναι.

[30] *Conl.* 13.5.3–4, p. 366, 6: "Denique famosissimus ille ipsorum Socrates hoc, ut ipsi concelebrant, de se non erubuit profiteri; nam cum intuens eum quidam φυσιογνώμων dixisset: ὄμματα παιδεραστοῦ, hoc est *oculi corruptoris puerorum*, et inruentes in eum discipuli inlatum magistro vellent ultum ire convicium, indignationem eorum hac dicitur compressisse sententia: παύσασθε, ἑταῖροι· εἰμὶ γάρ, ἐπέχω δέ, id est: *quiescite, o sodales*; etenim sum, sed contineo . . . Cum quo autem horrore proferenda est illa sententia Diogenis? Factum enim, quod philosophos mundi huius . . . velut quiddam memorabile non puduit . . . nam cuidam in adulterii crimine puniendo, ut ferunt, ait: τὸ δωρεὰν πολούμενον, θανάτῳ μὴ ἀγόραζε, id est: *quod gratis venditur, morte non emas*." I have searched in vain for these anecdotes in Diogenes Laertius and in the extant fragments of Porphyry's Φιλόσοφος ἱστορία. Is Porphyry's Περὶ ἁγνείας the source? Cf. above, p. 72.

[31] *Conl.* 7.4.2, p. 183, 5: "νοῦς itaque, id est *mens*, ἀεικίνητος καὶ πολυκίνητος definitur, id est *semper mobilis et multum mobilis*."

[32] The *Centum sententiae* and the *Sentences for Virgins*; cf. Schanz, vol. 4, 1, p. 421, and A. Wilmart, "Les versions latines des Sentences d'Evagre pour les vierges," *RB* 28 (1911) 143–153. He points out that we have two different Latin translations of this text.

[33] Jerome *Epist. ad Ctesiphontem* 133.3 (*PL* 22, 1151): "Evagrius Ponticus Hyperborita, qui scribit ad virgines, scribit ad monachos, scribit ad eam cuius nomen nigredinis testatur perfidiae tenebras [*Melania*!] edidit librum et sententias περὶ ἀπαθείας . . . Huius libros per Orientem Graecos et interpretante discipulo eius Rufino Latinos plerique in Occidente disputant."

connection between charity and contemplation. He must have known Evagrius personally in the Egyptian Desert between 385 and 399 and, although he preserves a careful silence about his source, he makes unquestionable reference to Evagrius at least once.[34]

The textual relations between the two works are striking and numerous. Cassianus borrows from Evagrius the description of the different items of monastic dress and their symbolical interpretation.[35] It is from Evagrius that he knows a particular aphorism of Macarius.[36] Or again, he claims to have heard from the lips of Abbot Moses a general rule proclaimed by Evagrius.[37] We can observe the extent of literary fiction in Cassianus' ascetic works. His doctrine is manifestly elaborated. The classification and the definitions of the various vices[38] or the various practices of the spiritual life[39] are the work of Evagrius, and not of the illiterate monks of the Desert. Evagrius' method, reproduced by Cassianus, even shows markedly the effects of pagan scholasticism. The soul is divided into λογικόν, θυμικόν, ἐπιθυμητικόν.[40] Monastic wisdom, as opposed to pagan philosophy, or ψευδώνυμος γνῶσις, is similarly divided into ethical or practical, physical, and theoretical or theological.[41] The purpose (*scopos*) of asceticism is the purity of the soul that is achieved through three successive renunciations: worldly goods, passions, all perceptible things. Cassianus is only careful not to accept on his own account the theory of ἀπάθεια whose Pelagian tone St. Jerome had condemned.[42] But he knows the five successive stages of contemplation that Evagrius had enumerated.[43]

Cassianus' originality was then very slight, and Dom Marsili can conclude that actually it was the teaching of the Didascalia of Alexandria that was transmitted to the West[44] by Evagrius and Cassianus, at least as much as was

[34] *Inst.* 5.32, p. 105. Cf. Marsili, *Giovanni Cassiano ed Evagrio Pontico*, pp. 82–85.

[35] Marsili, *Giov. Cass.*, pp. 87–88. On the hood, symbol of the return to childhood in Christ, on the ἀνάλαβος, symbol of work, and on the μηλωτίς, symbol of mortification, cf. Cassianus *Inst.* 1.3, 1.5, 1.7, and Evagrius *Pract. ad Anat., praef.* (PG 40: 1220 C, 1221 A, 1221 B).

[36] *Inst.* 5.41 = Evagrius *Pract.* 2.29 (PG 40, 1244 B); cf. Marsili, *Giov. Cass.*, p. 90.

[37] *Inst.* 10.25 = Evagrius *Pract.* 1.19 (PG 40, 1225 C); cf. Marsili, *Giov. Cass.*, p. 91.

[38] Cf. the numerous parallels drawn up by Marsili, *Giov. Cass.*, pp. 90–92, particularly on ἀκηδία and κενοδοξία.

[39] Marsili, *Giov. Cass.*, pp. 98–101.

[40] *Conl.* 24.15.3 = Evagrius *Pract.* 1.61 (PG 40, 1236 A); cf. Marsili, *Giov. Cass.*, p. 103.

[41] Cf. Marsili, pp. 93, 102, 105–110.

[42] *Ibid.*, pp. 110–121.

[43] *Ibid.*, pp. 121–128.

[44] *Ibid.*, p. 163. M. Viller, "Aux sources de la spiritualité de s. Maxime, les œuvres d'Evagre le Pontique," *Revue d'ascétique et de mystique* 11 (1930) 156–184, 239–268, 331–336, had already shown the role of Evagrius as the source of Byzantine spirituality through the intermediary Maximus the Confessor.

the example of the Fathers of the Desert. The monastic areas in southern Gaul were to persist during the entire fifth century under the influence of this doctrine. While displaying a profound scorn for the Greek culture and the Greek philosophy of which they were ignorant, the monks of Lérins adopted without reserve the ascetic ideal propagated by Cassianus and developed by Evagrius, without suspecting that this method of progressive detachment from material goods was very similar to Neoplatonic asceticism.[45] The work of Eucherius, the monk of Lérins to whom Cassianus dedicated the second part of his *Conlationes*, shows to what level Greek culture in this region had been reduced. His letter to Valerianus, written in 432, exposes the recipient to the scorn of the world and of pagan philosophy, exhorts him to lead a philosophical life rather than continue to read the philosophers,[46] and announces that he intends to refute them in a forthcoming book.[47] This work, if it was actually written, is not extant, but the little that Eucherius tells about Aristippus and the books previously read by Valerianus inclines one to believe that with regard to Greek philosophy he knew only a few literary commonplaces or at the most a collection of *placita*. The instances of notable conversions that he takes from Greek Christian literature do not even prove that he knew this literature. In Clement of Rome he read, not the authentic works, but the romanticized biography that Rufinus had translated.[48] Similarly, he is indebted for his biographical information on Gregory Thaumaturgus to Rufinus' *Ecclesiastical History*, which inserted those very two miracles in Eusebius of Caesarea's narrative.[49] As for the anecdote of Basil of Cae-

---

[45] It would be interesting to study the parallelism between the exposition of demonology in the Fathers of the Desert and in the Neoplatonists.

[46] Eucherius *Epist. paraenetica ad Valerianum cognatum de contemptu mundi et saecularis philosophiae* (*PL* 50, 724 A): "Quin tu, repudiatis illis philosophorum praeceptis quorum lectioni operam ac ingenium accommodas, ad imbibenda Christiani dogmatis studia animum adicis . . . Unde licet dicere philosophiae alios nomen usurpasse, nos vitam."

[47] *Ibid.*, 724 B: "Anne aliquis ex illa Aristippi schola veritatem videbit, qui ingenio suo a suibus aut pecore nihil differt, cum beatitudinem in corporis voluptate constituat: *Cui Deus venter est et gloria* in pudendis eius? . . . Sed alius adversus philosophos dicendi locus reservetur . . . Omitte iam illas, quibus oblectaris, maxime generales eorum sententias, *breviter ex omni disputationis genere conlectas*." From these last words, it is probable that Eucherius is thinking of a collection of philosophers' *sententiae* that was popular in Gaul.

[48] *Ibid.*, 718 C: "Clemens vetusta prosapia senatorum atque etiam ex stirpe Caesarum, omni scientia refertus omniumque liberalium artium peritissimus, ad hanc iustorum viam transiit; itaque etiam in ea excellenter effloruit, ut principi quoque apostolorum successor exstiterit." On the *Recognitiones Clementis* translated by Rufinus (*PG* 1, 1157) and Clement's inventive genealogy, cf. Puech, *Litt. gr. chrét.* 2, p. 33. On Clement's studies, cf. *Recogn.* 1.3 (*PG* 1, 1208). In his *Praef. ad Gaudentium*, Rufinus explains how Clement can be called the successor of St. Peter, from the fact that Linus and Cletus had been bishops of Rome in Peter's lifetime.

[49] Eucherius, *ibid.*: "Gregorius e Ponto sacerdos, philosophia primus apud mundum et eloquentia praestans; sed postea maior praestantiorque virtutibus, adeo ut (sicut de hoc

sarea's conversion by Gregory of Nazianzus,[50] it assumes a knowledge not of the writings of these two saints (for they show that Gregory of Nazianzus' conversion was posterior to Basil's),[51] but of some pious biography, perhaps the same one from which Cassianus had already taken two of Basil's apothegms.[52] Eucherius also seems to cite, in a rhetorical list, the names of Evagrius and John Chrysostom.[53] Actually, there is nothing in his *Formulae* and his *Instructiones* to prove a sound knowledge of Greek. Probably he knew the etymology and the meaning of the Greek terms that passed into ecclesiastical vocabulary,[54] but he took them from Jerome's *Onomasticum*.[55] Despite this ignorance, a Greek writer did exert a profound influence on him, perhaps without his knowledge. This was Evagrius Ponticus, whose doctrine was known to him from Cassianus. On the island of Lérins, he thinks, dwell the true disciples of the Egyptian ascetics.[56] But the method that he outlines at the beginning of his *Formulae* is Evagrius' scholastic method transmitted by Cassianus. This meant an adaptation to the sacred studies of the pagan schema: practice and theory, and division into physical, ethical, logical, to which corresponds the study of Scripture *secundum historiam, secundum tropologiam, secundum anagogen.*[57]

---

historiae nostrae fides loquitur) inter reliqua admirabilium signa meritorum, precibus huius atque orationibus mons referatur secessisse, lacus exaruisse." These two miracles are reproduced in Rufinus' own addition to Eusebius' *Church History* 7.28.2 (ed. Schwartz-Mommsen in the *Eusebius Werke* (*Griech. christl. Schriftsteller*) 2, 1, pp. 953–954.

[50] *Ibid.:* "Alius item sanctus atque eiusdem nominis Gregorius, aeque litteris ac philosophiae deditus, caelestem hanc philosophiam concupivit. Cuius etiam, quod ad rem pertinet, nequaquam silendum videtur, quod Basilium studiis prius saecularibus familiarem sibi et rhetorices adhuc professioni vacantem, auditorium eius ingressus, manu hunc apprehensum abduxit, dicens: Omitte ista et da saluti operam. Et postea uterque memorabilis sacerdos reliquit utique in Ecclesiae nostrae libris ingenii sui praeclara monimenta."

[51] Cf. P. Allard, *Saint Basile*, 3rd ed. 1899, pp. 22–23, and Puech, *Litt. gr. chrét.* 3, pp. 322–323.

[52] Cf. above, n. 24. There is nothing similar in Pseudo-Amphilochius' *Vita s. Basilii*, *PG* 29, pp. ccxcivff; but cf. P. Peeters, "Un miracle des ss. Serge et Théodore et la vie de s. Basile dans Fauste de Byzance," *Anal. Bolland.* 39 (1921) 88 n. 1, on the subject of a lost life of St. Basil by his disciple Helladius. It was possibly from a Latin translation of this life that Cassianus and Eucherius borrowed their anecdotes.

[53] Eucherius *Epist. ad Valerianum* (*PL* 50, 719 A). The reading is uncertain between *Hilarium* and *Evagrium* and the name of John appears without any qualification.

[54] Cf. particularly *Instr.* 2.15 *de Graecis nominibus.*

[55] F. Wutz, *Onomastica sacra*, p. xxiv. Cf. Schanz, vol. 4, 2, p. 519.

[56] Eucherius *De laude eremi* 42 (*PL* 50, 711 B = ed. Wotke, *CSEL* 31, p. 193, 2): "Haec nunc habet sanctos senes illos, qui divisis cellulis Aegyptios Patres Gallis nostris intulerunt."

[57] Eucherius *Formulae, praef.* (*PL* 50, 728 = Wotke, pp. 4–5). Cf. Cassianus *Conl.* 14.1 and 2 and 8. The following parallel is particularly conclusive:

Vincent of Lérins, Eucherius' companion, does not seem to be any better informed at first hand about Greek literature. In the *Commonitorium primum* he reviews the most distinguished names in Christian literature to prove that heresy depends on the novelty of a doctrine, whatever the reputation and the erudition of those who profess it. But this enumeration has a very marked rhetorical character and, whenever Vincent refers to a Greek work, he shows unconsciously that he had not read it. For Nestorius, he mentions no work whatever. For Apollinaris of Laodicea, he mentions the treatise *Against Porphyry*, in thirty books, but the context shows that Vincent takes this information from Jerome's *De viris*.[58] He composed a brilliant critique on Origen but manifestly had read nothing by him.[59] The biographical information that he himself had was taken from Eusebius' *Church History*, in Rufinus' translation.[60] When he boasted, in order to confirm Origen's eminent erudition, of quoting the testimony of the pagan Porphyry, it was to the same Latin and ecclesiastical source that he referred. Led into mistakes by Rufinus' text, he also committed a gross blunder in chronology with regard to Porphyry's life.[61] Rufinus was also the author of the thesis, mentioned by Vincent, that

---

Evagrius *Pract.* 1.50 (*PG* 40, 1233 A):	Cassianus *Conl.* 14.1.3, p. 398, 25:	Eucherius *Form.*, *praef.*, p. 5, 22:
Πρακτική ἐστι μέθοδος πνευματική, τὸ παθητι- κὸν μέρος τῆς ψυχῆς ἐκκαθαίρουσα.	prima πρακτική, id est actualis, quae emenda- tione morum et vitiorum purgatione perficitur.	unam (practicen) quae ac- tualem vitam morum emen- datione consumet.

[58] Jerome *De vir. inl.* 104:

Apollinarius Laodicenus ... innumera-bilia scribens volumina sub Theodosio imperatore obiit. Exstant eius adversus Porphyrium triginta libri qui inter cetera eius opera vel maxime probantur.

Vincent *Common.* 1.11 (*PL* 50, 653):

Quam multos ille haereses multis volu-minibus oppresserit, quot inimicos fidei confutaverit errores, indicio est opus illud triginta non minus librorum nobilissimum ac maximum, quo insanas Porphyrii calumnias magna probationum mole con-fudit. Longum est universa ipsius opera commemorare.

[59] Vincent *Common.* 1.17 (*PL* 50, 662): "Sed credo pauca conscripsit? Nemo mor-talium plura; ut mihi sua omnia non solum non perlegi, sed ne inveniri quidem posse videantur."

[60] *Ibid.*: "Quam autem non solum privatae conditioni, sed ipsi quoque fuerit reveren-dus imperio declarant historiae." There follow the anecdote of Origen and Mamaea, mother of Alexander Severus (= Rufinus *Hist. eccl.* 6.21.3, p. 569, 2 Mommsen) and mention of Origen's letter to the Emperor Philip (Rufinus *Hist. eccl.* 6.36.3, p. 591, 21).

[61] Rufinus *Hist. eccl.* 6.19.5, p. 559, 20 Mommsen, quoting Porphyry:

Huius autem absurdae expositionis ini-tium processit a viro quem etiam ego, adhuc cum essem valde parvulus *vidi arcem totius* eruditionis tenentem, sicut etiam ex his quae posteritatis memoriae

Vincent *Common.* 1.17 (*PL* 50, 663):

De cuius (Origenis) incredibili quadam scientia si quis referentibus nobis Christia-num non accipit testimonium, saltem testificantibus philosophis gentilem re-cipiat confessionem. Ait namque ille Porphyrius excitum se fama ipsius Alex-

Origen's books had been corrupted by an interpolator.[62] So, when he invites his reader to skim through the works of Paul of Samosata, we should not think that he himself has before him a text of this ancient heretic, who was very soon forgotten in the West.[63] He must have found this name in one of the numerous collections of heresies, such as Augustine's *De haeresibus*. Vincent's second *Commonitorium*, as far as can be judged from the extant fragment, seems far better documented, but it was composed solely with the aid of the texts quoted at the Council of Ephesus that had been held three years previously.

The same absence of direct, personal contact with Greek literature appears in Salvian, who belongs to this circle of Lérins, although his last days were spent at Marseilles. He probably prided himself on his Greek culture while professing to disdain it. At the beginning of the *De gubernatione Dei* he quotes a Pythagorean text on the soul of the universe, but this text is borrowed from Lactantius, who took it from Cicero.[64] Another borrowing from Lactantius indicates the degree of Salvian's maladroitness or ignorance. The words that in Lactantius describe Socrates' teaching, in Plato's *Republic*, on having women in common, are presented by Salvian as a textual quotation from

---

tradidit voluminibus comprobatur. Origenes hic est.

p. 563, 24: per idem vero tempus cum apud Alexandriam in verbi Dei studiis exerceretur . . .

andriam fere perrexisse, ibique eum *vidisse iam senem*, sed plane talem tantumque qui *arcem totius* scientiae condidisset.

The metaphor of *arcem* that recurs in both writers is an assurance that Vincent closely follows Rufinus' Latin text, not Eusebius' Greek text, which has only σφόδρα εὐδο-κιμήσαντος. Bidez, *Vie de Porphyre*, p. 11 n. 2, has already shown that Porphyry could not have met Origen, *already an old man*, at Alexandria, as Vincent wrongly concludes from Rufinus' text.

[62] Vincent *Common.* 1.17 (*PL* 50, 664): "sed dicet aliquis corruptos esse Origenis libros." The reference to Rufinus' *De adulteratione librorum Origenis* is transparent.

[63] Vincent *Common.* 1.25 (*PL* 50, 672), where the imperative *Lege* is in fact the equivalent of a conditional clause: "*Lege* Pauli Samosateni opuscula, Priscilliani, Eunomii, Ioviniani reliquarumque pestium; cernas infinita exemplorum congeriem, prope nullam omitti paginam quae non novi et veteris Testamenti sententiis fucata et colorata sit." The statement is correct insofar as it relates to Paul of Samosata (cf. the index of Biblical quotations in Bardy, *Paul de Samosate*, diss. Bruges 1923, p. 550; he forgets, p. 45, to mention Vincent among the rare scholars in the West who refer to Paul of Samosata by name). But Vincent might certainly generalize.

[64] *De gub. Dei* 1.1.2 (ed. Pauly, *CSEL* 8, p. 3, 12 = *PL* 53, 29 B): "Pythagoras philosophus, quem quasi magistrum suum philosophia ipsa suspexit, de natura ac beneficiis Dei disserens sic locutus est: Animus per omnes mundi partes commeans atque diffusus, ex quo omnia quae nascuntur animalia vitam capiunt." Cf. Lactantius *Inst.* 1.5 (*PL* 6, 134 A) and Cicero *De natura deorum* 1.11.27. Salvian's direct source is certainly Lactantius, as is proved by the context, which quotes Vergil *Georg.* 4.221 and Cicero *Tusc.* 1.27.66.

Socrates as though Socrates himself had written the *Republic*.[65] Salvian, however, has some very general data on the various schools of Greek philosophers and apparently obtained this information from some little *compendium*, perhaps the same as Eucherius'.[66] But the rare expressions or etymologies taken by Salvian from Greek are not sufficient to credit him with knowing this language.[67] Similarly, in the extant writings of Faustus of Riez, who was also trained at Lérins, the sole Greek source that was mentioned was Origen's *De principiis*, in Rufinus' translation.[68]

Thus the men of Lérins, which was the principal center of monastic culture in fifth-century Gaul, were quite unfamiliar with Greek literature and culture. They did not have even a remote conception of this culture except through the aid of the translators Rufinus and Cassianus. Nor does it seem probable that Greek was taught in any other monastery.[69] On the contrary, certain monks, like Sulpicius Severus, the friend of Paulinus of Nola, pushed

---

[65] Lactantius *Inst.* 3.21 (*PL* 6, 417–418):
Videamus tamen quid illum Socrates docuerit ... *Matrimonia* quoque, inquit, *communia esse debebunt* ... *sic*, inquit, *civitas concors erit* et amoris mutuis constricta vinculis, *si omnes omnium* fuerint et mariti et patres et uxores et liberi.

Salvian *De gub. Dei* 7.23, p. 188, 25 = *PL* 53, 150 D:
Videamus ergo quas Socrates de pudicitia leges sanxerit et quas illi de quibus loquimur. Uxorem, inquit Socrates, propriam nullus habeat, *matrimonia* enim cunctis *debent esse communia*; sic namque maior *erit concordia civitatum, si omnes* viri feminis sine discretione *omnibus* misceantur ... Ecce quae sunt et Romanae et Atticae sapientiae exempla ... Sed vicit tamen Socrates, qui de hac re et libros condidit et memoriae haec pudenda mandavit.

[66] On the Platonists and the Stoics, cf. *De gub. Dei* 1.1.3, p. 3, 19 = *PL* 53, 29 B: "Plato et omnes Platonicorum scholae moderatorem rerum omnium confitentur Deum; Stoici eum gubernatoris vice intra id quod regat semper manere testantur." On Epicurus, cf. *De gub. Dei* 1.1.5, p. 5, 11 = *PL* 53, 30 C: "et sane invenire aliquos qui ab istorum iudicio discrepaverint, praeter Epicureorum vel quorundam epicurizantium deliramenta non possum, qui sicut voluptatem cum virtute, sic Deum cum incuria et torpore iunxerunt." On the *Graeci quidam sapientiae sectatores* (Crates?), cf. *De gub. Dei* 1.2.12, p. 8, 19 = *PL* 53, 33 B. On the biography of Socrates, cf. *De gub. Dei* 7.23, *passim*. On several mistakes made by Salvian, cf. J. P. Waltzing, "Tertullien et Salvien," *Le musée belge* 19–24, no. 1 (1920) 39–43.

[67] Cf. Schanz, vol. 4, 2, p. 526 n. 4.

[68] Cf. C. Weyman, "Zu Herondas V, 14," *Philologus* 54 (1895) 185.

[69] Cf. *Vita s. Eugendi* 4, ed. Krusch, *MGH, Script. rer. Merov.* 3, p. 155, 28: "lectione namque in tantum se die noctuque, expletis consummatisque omnibus quae a proposito vel abbate iniuncta sunt, dedit et impendit, ut praeter Latinis voluminibus etiam Graeca facundia redderetur instructus." Even if this text contains correct information, it does not invalidate my thesis, for it presents St. Eugendus, a monk at Condat in the Jura in the fifth century, as an exceptional case and as self-taught.

their hatred of Hellenism[70] to the point of distrusting Oriental monasticism.[71] It must therefore be admitted that there was a renaissance of Greek culture in Gaul in the last third of the fifth century: for Gennadius and Claudianus Mamertus were notable Hellenists, and Sidonius Apollinaris describes the existence of an aristocratic circle where Greek literature and philosophy were still a living force.

2. THE RENAISSANCE OF 470

Gennadius of Marseilles presents the image of a great Hellenist among his associates. Several of his lost writings—eight books against all heresies, five books against Nestorius, ten books against Eutyches, a treatise entitled *De mille annis*—suggest that he had a profound knowledge of the theological debates of the East,[1] and his *De ecclesiasticis dogmatibus* shows us in fact a well-informed heresiologist. He is even familiar with the most recent disputes, since he translated Timotheus Aelurus' letter addressed to the Emperor Leo, while Timotheus was still alive.[2] Furthermore, Gennadius testifies how much Greek ascetic literature, as Cassianus had made it known, was still appreciated. In fact he translated four of Evagrius Ponticus' treatises and even took the trouble to retranslate the *Centum sententiae*, correcting Rufinus' old translation, which seemed to him inaccurate.[3]

---

[70] Sulpicius Severus *Vita s. Martini* 1.3, ed. Halm, *CSEL* 1 (Vienna 1866), p. 110, 19: "aut quid posteritas emolumenti tulit legendo Hectorem bellantem aut Socratem philosophantem? Cum eos non solum imitari stultitia sit, sed non acerrime etiam impugnare dementia. Quippe qui humanam vitam praesentibus tantum actibus aestimantes spes suas fabulis, animas sepulcris dederint"; *Dial.* 3.17.6, p. 216, 1: "Sciat Corinthus, sciant Athenae non sapientiorem in Academia Platonem nec Socratem in carcere fortiorem." Thus Martin is wiser than Socrates, who probably thought that the soul was mortal! We can estimate the ignorance of Sulpicius Severus. He evidently knows nothing about Origen either, except that he was refuted by Jerome. Cf. *Dial.* 1.6.1, p. 157, 27: "(Origenes) tractator Scripturarum sacrarum peritissimus *habebatur.*"

[71] He contrasts the monks of the West with the monks of the East, *Dial.* 1.8.5, p. 160, 8, and 3.2.2, p. 199, 22, and he asserts the superiority of St. Martin to the Egyptian monks, *Dial.* 1.26.1, p. 178, 13. Cf. Schanz, vol. 4, 2, p. 474.

[1] Cf. Schanz, vol. 4, 2, p. 552.

[2] Gennadius *De vir. inl.* 72 (*PL* 58, 1102 A): "Vivere adhuc iam haeresiarcha dicitur et habetur. Hunc ipsum libellum noscendi gratia ego, rogatus a fratribus, in Latinum transtuli et cavendum praetitulavi." On the role and the heresy of Timotheus Aelurus, cf. L. Duchesne, *Histoire ancienne de l'église* 3, chap. 12, "Les Monophysites."

[3] Gennadius *De vir. inl.* 11 (*PL* 58, 1067 A): "Composuit et anachoretis simpliciter viventibus librum *Centum sententiarum* per capitula digestum, et eruditis ac studiosis *Quinquaginta sententiarum,* quem ego Latinum primus feci. Nam superiorem olim translatum, quia vitiatum et per tempus confusum vidi, partim reinterpretando, partim emendando, auctoris veritati restitui." Cf. Schanz, vol. 4, 2, p. 552.

It is no longer possible to appreciate Gennadius' translations, which are now lost, but it appears from his *De viris* that he was well versed in Greek. Gennadius shows that he had read a considerable number of Greek books, on the contents of which he gives exact details, while on the other hand his comments on Syriac literature are more vague and at second hand.[4] He even goes so far as to reject as spurious, on account of its style, a treatise by Theophilus of Alexandria.[5] A study of Gennadius' reading establishes the trends of his time. He devotes a series of notices to the Fathers of the Desert: Pachomius, Theodore, Horsiesi, Macarius the Egyptian, Evagrius.[6] Of the first three, who spoke Coptic,[7] his knowledge is rather vague. Possibly he had read only Pachomius' Rule, which was very soon translated into Greek, then into Latin by Jerome. With regard to Macarius, he also read nothing but one single letter. On the other hand, he had in his possession and translated quite a number of the works of Evagrius, who was evidently his chief source for Egyptian asceticism.[8]

In addition, Gennadius studied the theological problems that stirred the Eastern Churches during the fifth century. In Theodore of Mopsuestia he read the monumental work on Incarnation, in fifteen books,[9] and several treatises[10] of John Chrysostom's two opponents, Antiochus of Ptolemais and Severianus of Gabales. He was familiar with Origenistic controversy between John of Jerusalem and Theophilus of Alexandria.[11] Lastly, he had read a number of works relating to the Nestorian heresy: those by Nestorius himself, and others by Atticus of Constantinople, Theodore of Ancyra, Cyril of Alexandria, Cyrus of Alexandria, John of Antioch.[12] All this reading must have helped him to work on his treatise *Against Nestorius*, which had to be well documented even if he had not read Nestorius' or Cyril's "infiniti tractatus diversarum ὑποθέσεων," as he wanted to imply.[13] Hagiography had an

---

[4] Cf. B. Czapla, *Gennadius als Litterarhistoriker*, as printed in *Kirchengeschichtliche Studien* 4, 1 (Münster [Westphalia] 1898), p. 8 (I follow the pagination of the offprint containing the conclusions).

[5] Gennadius *De vir. inl.* 33 (PL 58, 1079 A): "Legi et tres de Fide libros sub nomine eius titulatos; sed quia lingua inconsonans est, non valde credidi."

[6] *Ibid.*, 7–11.

[7] Puech, *Litt. gr. chrét.* 3, p. 135.

[8] Apart from the two works mentioned above, Gennadius also translated Evagrius' *Adversus octo principalium vitiorum suggestiones* and *Sententiolae*.

[9] Gennadius *De vir. inl.* 12.

[10] *Ibid.*, 20–21. On the esteem in which certain circles in the West held Antiochus, cf. the text quoted above, chap. 3 sec. 2 n. 40. On the other hand, the chapter on John Chrysostom that appears in certain manuscripts is not by Gennadius. Cf. Schanz, vol. 4, 2, p. 554.

[11] Gennadius *De vir. inl.* 30 and 33.

[12] *Ibid.*, 52, 53, 55, 57, 81, 93.

[13] *Ibid.*, 53 and 57. Cf. Czapla, *Gennadius*, p. 15.

equal interest for him. He read the story of the finding of the relics of St. Stephen by Lucian of Caphar Gamala, a story that became known in the West from a translation, by Avitus of Bracara, that was brought from the Holy Places by Orosius.[14]

The only Greek works that Gennadius knew from hearsay, without having read them, are Theodoret's *Church History* and the *Eranistes*, for he made serious blunders about them.[15] Possibly he also knew of the works of Gennadius of Constantinople, about which details are lacking.[16] But in general Gennadius' *De viris* is a source book for Greek literature, and the author makes no attempt to appear a greater scholar than he is, as Jerome did in his catalogue.[17] Above all, his desire is to render a service to his public: he is eager both to turn to the sources of asceticism and to make himself familiar with the Nestorian controversy.

Quite different is the direction taken by the men belonging in the group of Claudianus Mamertus and Sidonius. They reveal the existence of a cultured society intensely interested in the pagan philosophy and literature of the Greeks.

Claudianus' letter to the rhetorician Sapaudus shows what the prestige of Greece still meant to him. Greece, he declares, teaches all the arts and all the disciplines. Her culture has spread throughout almost the entire world.[18] Her thinkers have studied physics and metaphysics thoroughly.[19] It was to Greece that Cicero went for instruction. As for Plato, he combined Socrates' Greek wisdom with the wisdom of the Egyptians, the Indians, and the Pythagoreans.[20] The modern period, in which all the disciplines are neglected, in which the Romans do not even venture any longer to speak Latin, is a period of decadence. But Sapaudus, who had read the good writers, trains in his school pupils imbued with the Greek disciplines and nourished on Attic

---

[14] *Ibid.*, 46. Cf. Schanz, vol. 4, 2, p. 485.

[15] *Ibid.*, 89. Cf. Czapla, *Gennadius*, p. 22.

[16] *Ibid.*, 90.

[17] Cf. Czapla, *Gennadius*, pp. 39–42.

[18] Claud. Mam. *Epist. ad Sapaudum*, ed. A. Engelbrecht, *CSEL* 11 (Vienna 1885), p. 203, 1: "Disciplinarum omnium atque artium magistra Graecia idcirco maxime nobilibus studiis provecta est atque orbem paene totum multiplicibus complexa doctrinis, quoniam nemo illic omnium fuit, qui quidquam bonae frugis ferret, cui non par merito honos siet."

[19] *Ibid.*, p. 203, 7: "hinc non nulli mortales naturam paene supergressi mortalium extentis usquequaque excellentium ingeniorum viribus infatigabilibus curis rerum abdita rimantes repositas primordiorum causas et temporaliter fluentium substantiarum praefixos aevo terminos indage et arte complexi non modo intra mundanum, sed supercaeleste etiam introiere secretum."

[20] *Ibid.*, p. 204, 6–14. On the Neoplatonic and probably Porphyrian origin of the tradition of Plato's having traveled to India, cf. Boemer, *Der lateinische Neuplatonismus*, pp. 96–103.

honey.[21] Since we do not know Sapaudus' entire output, we cannot judge to what degree this eulogy, in which rhetorical exaggeration seems evident, is deserved. It assumes at least in Claudianus Mamertus a real love for Greek culture and a notion of its value. The *De statu animae*, which he wrote around 470, was to give his view of the meaning of this culture. Certain references to Greek writers are manifestly just formulaic, as we have already noted in Jerome. St. Augustine, asserts Claudianus, has the demonstrative force of a Chrysippus, the subtlety of a Zeno. On the other hand, the supporters of the theories of Faustus of Riez are the Epicureans or the Cynics of modern times.[22] Claudianus Mamertus has however a general knowledge of the great schools of philosophy. He refers to Plato's theory of ideas,[23] to the scepticism of the New Academy,[24] or to Epicurus' atomic doctrine.[25] He has studied dialectic and read Aristotle's *Categories*,[26] but most probably in a Latin commentary by Marius Victorinus, as Franz Boemer has clearly shown.[27] Finally, he likes to clarify his exposition, to use Greek words taken from the vocabulary of philosophy, geometry, or medicine.[28] These words may

[21] Claud. Mam. *Epist. ad Sapaudum*, p. 205, 15: "discipulorum tibimet velut filiorum numerositas dilecta formatur, quae Graecarum quoque disciplinarum nectare imbuta ac si melle Attico pasta." On Sapaudus of Vienne, see Schanz, vol. 4, 2, p. 269.

[22] Claud. Mam. *De statu animae* 2.9, p. 133, 10: "Aurelius Augustinus ... veluti quidam Chrysippus argumentandi virtute aut Zenon sensuum subtilitate aut Varro noster voluminum magnitudine et qui profecto talis natura adtentione disciplinis exstiterit, ut non immerito ab istis corporalibus nostri saeculi Epicureis aut Cynicis spiritalis sophista dissenserit, libro ad Hieronymum de origine animae sic pronuntiat ..."

[23] *Ibid.*, 2.4, p. 112, 6: "sic et in his principalibus formis ratio par est, quas Plato ideas nominat."

[24] *Ibid.*, 3.3, p. 158, 3: "Vereor ne et istic opinatus videaris novus Academicus, qui et cum Academicis nihil scias et de his quae nescis sine cunctatione definias"; and 3.13, p. 180, 14: "Verum si bene scriptorum tuorum recolis, animadvertere simul potes proposuisse te potius de quibus disputandum foret, quam de propositis disputasse nec te Academicorum seniorum more nescientiam tuam scisse, sed iuxta sectae ipsius iuniores utrum scires aliquid ignorasse."

[25] *Ibid.*, 2.12, p. 146, 7: "aut si unus mundus plures porro non habet caelos, aliquos tibi cum Epicuro mundos atomorum minuta parturiant, ut tertium caelum Paulus inveniat."

[26] *Ibid.*, 1.19, p. 69, 4: "ex illis Aristotelicis categoriis nulli prorsus subiacet essentia divina, rursus anima humana non omnibus subiacet, porro corpus quodlibet subiacet omnibus."

[27] Boemer, *Der latein. Neuplaton.*, pp. 87–96. I do not reproduce Boemer's demonstration, which appears convincing. The order in which Claudianus Mamertus, p. 69, 4, and Augustine *De Trin.* 5.1.2 (*PL* 42, 912) list the Categories differs from the order adopted by Aristotle and Porphyry. The notion of God transcending the Categories does not yet appear in Porphyry. As Claudianus Mamertus does not depend on Augustine, their common source must be Marius Victorinus, the author of a commentary on the *Categories*, as Cassiodorus testifies.

[28] Philosophical vocabulary, p. 45, 19: "illi elemento compos, quod Graeci vocant *aethera*," and p. 106, 4: "quod est et absque corpore est, incorporeum esse necesse est, quod Graeci elegantius ἀσώματον vocant"; geometrical vocabulary, p. 89, 4: "Haec

however have come from Latin technical manuals; but they are inserted in discussions that testify in Claudianus to a certain Hellenic culture, at least indirectly.

Book 2 of the *De statu animae* shows that he has a much more profound knowledge of certain Greek philosophers. In fact, in order to refute the theories of Faustus of Riez, who maintained that the soul is corporeal and that God alone is incorporeal, Claudianus Mamertus appeals in succession to the authority of the pagan philosophers, the doctors of the Church, and the Holy Scriptures. He is not particularly interested in the Greek ecclesiastical writers; for, although he quotes quite a number of Latin Fathers—Ambrose, Augustine, Hilary, Eucherius—he mentions only one Greek work, Gregory of Nazianzus' *Apologeticus*, which he had been able to read in Rufinus' translation.[29] On the other hand, among the pagan philosophers, he will quote very accurately Plato and the Pythagoreans.[30]

Boemer thought that, from a grammatical and stylistic study of these quotations, he could determine what the true source was: whether it was the original Greek or a Latin translation. He thought he could thus prove that the quotation from the *Phaedo* was taken from a complete translation of the dialogue, a first-century translation that was different from the one made by Apuleius.[31] The quotation from a Περὶ φυσικῆς by Plato would refer to a Latin *De physicis* whose source would be Apuleius.[32] The quotation from the *Phaedrus* would have come from a Platonic or Neoplatonic commentator,

---

ergo de qua loqui institueram longitudo cum fuerit puncto inchoata punctoque finita, a Graecis γραμμή, a nostris linea dicitur; iam nunc, si quid sit longitudo sine latitudine cognoscere valuisti et lineam longitudine finita formasti, duas aequales lineas sibimet ἀντιστάτας e regione constitue"; medical vocabulary, p. 63, 12: "nam et cum flamus et reflamus, particulas eius haurimus et reddimus, quas in pastum totius corporis venae illae capiunt, quas ἀρτηρίας Graeci vocant."

[29] Claud. Mam. *De statu animae* 2.9, p. 131, 8: "Gregorius Nazianzenus in apologetico magnum videlicet inter animam et corpus clamat esse discrimen atque ut corpus corporalibus pasci, sic animam incorporeis saginari." Cf. Gregory, translated by Rufinus, *Apologeticus* 1.7, ed. Engelbrecht, *CSEL* 46 (Vienna 1910), p. 11, 9: "Nihil enim re vera mihi ad beatam vitam praestantius videbatur quam velut clausis carnalibus sensibus, et extra carnem mundumque effectum quempiam in semet ipsum converti, id est suos sensus atque animos conspicari," and 1.16–17. I do not know who this "quidam nobilissimus tractator sanctarum Scripturarum" may be, whose saying is quoted by Claudianus Mamertus *De statu animae*, epilogus, p. 196, 6: "quattuor pones dilectionis regulas, quod supra nos, quod iuxta nos, quod nos, quod infra nos." Probably this "quidam" was a Latin scholar.

[30] Claud. Mam. *De statu animae* 2.3, p. 105, 1: "Ex his igitur quos contra veritatem vocat (Faustus), vocem veritatis accipiat et geminae primum Graeciae classicum multisona Pythagoreorum tuba et lituum Platonis exaudiat."

[31] Boemer, *Der latein. Neuplaton.*, pp. 1–30.

[32] *Ibid.*, pp. 34–42.

perhaps Marius Victorinus.[33] The quotation from Porphyry's *De regressu animae* would be taken from Marius Victorinus' translation.[34] On the other hand, all the Pythagorean quotations from Philolaus, Archytes, Hippon, and the Sextii would be Claudianus Mamertus' own translations, made from the Greek text that he had read in some Pythagorean who was anterior to Neoplatonism.[35]

Boemer's method is ingenious and subtle. It allows us to build conjectures important for the history of ideas on the study of a word and the various connotations that it has undergone. For instance, the history of the different uses of the word *inlocalitas* (ἀδιαστασία) would permit us to note an evolution of the meaning parallel to the history of ideas, and to assign an approximate date to the text in which it appears. But it is impossible to disguise the slenderness of these conjectures. The only quotation whose length, it appears, would allow one to reach more cogent conclusions on the style is from the *Phaedo*. But it raises serious problems among philologists. The majority were tempted to see this quotation as a fragment of Apuleius' translation of the *Phaedo*, mentioned specifically by Sidonius Apollinaris, a friend of Claudianus'.[36] Boemer, on the other hand, finds in it the style of an anonymous writer of the first century, but Hårleman refutes this and recognizes Claudianus Mamertus' style.[37] Such a disagreement, involving five centuries, can make one question the value of stylistic criteria, applied to such short fragments.

It has not occurred to anyone to note how the quotations from Plato are inserted, in some way, into a Porphyrian context. This fact, which springs from making a parallel between these pages and some chapters of Augustine's *De civitate Dei*, will guide us to Claudianus' true sources. Both analyze Porphyry and faithfully reproduce the turns of his thought:

Porphyry *Hist. phil.* 4, *apud* Cyril of Alexandria *Contra Iulianum* 1 (PG 76, 553 B):	Augustine *De civitate Dei* 10.23 (*PL* 41, 300) = *De regressu animae*, frag. 8, ed. Bidez, p. 36*:	Claud. Mam. *De statu animae* 2.7, ed. Engelbrecht, *CSEL* 11, p. 122, 6:
Πορφύριος γάρ φησι, Πλάτωνος ἐκτιθέμενος δόξαν· Ἄχρι τριῶν ὑποστάσεων τὴν τοῦ Θείου προελθεῖν οὐσίαν, εἶναι δὲ τὸν μὲν ἀνωτάτω Θεὸν τἀγαθόν· μετ' αὐτὸν δὲ	Quae autem dicat (Porphyrius) esse principia, tamquam Platonicus, novimus. Dicit enim *Deum Patrem* et *Deum Filium*, quem Graece appellat	Igitur *Platon* procedat in medium a quo vere claret quam magnum in semet bonum genus humanum neglegat ... Quo fit ut mirari admodum digne nequeam huius Platonis ani-

[33] *Ibid.*, pp. 61–70.

[34] *Ibid.*, pp. 74–96.

[35] *Ibid.*, pp. 132–153.

[36] Cf. Schanz, vol. 3, p. 129, and vol. 4, 2, p. 549.

[37] Einar Hårleman, *De Claudiano Mamerto Gallicae Latinitatis scriptore quaestiones* (Uppsala 1938) 57–80. Cf. the review, favorable to his thesis, by A. Ernout, *Revue de Philologie* 14 (1940) 78–79.

καὶ δεύτερον τὸν δημιουρ- γόν· τρίτον δὲ καὶ τὴν τοῦ κόσμου ψυχήν· ἄχρι γὰρ ψυχῆς τὴν θειότητα προ- ελθεῖν.
(Cf. also Didymus *De Trin.* 2.27, *PG* 39, 760 B.)

paternum intellectum vel paternam *mentem*; de Spi- ritu autem sancto aut nihil aut non aperte aliquid dicit; quamvis quem alium dicat horum medium, non intellego.
(Cf. *De civ. Dei* 10.27 [*PL* 41, 307]: "πατρικὸν νοῦν, id est paternam mentem sive intellectum qui paternae est voluntatis conscius.")

mum, qui tantis equidem saeculis ante puerperium virginis, ante incarnationem Dei, ante hominis resurrec- tionem, ante praedicatam summae Trinitatis in genti- bus unitatem ineffabilem una tres in divinitate per- sonas laudabili ausu, mira- bili ingenio, inimitabili eloquio quaesivit, invenit, prodidit, *Patrem Deum pater- namque mentem*, artem sive consilium et utriusque horum amorem mutuum unam summam aequiter- nam indivisam divinitatem non solum ita credi opor- tere docuit, sed ita esse convicit.

This comparison, which has never been made[38] and which clarifies a par- ticularly important point of Porphyrian doctrine, is vital for my demonstra- tion. It shows that Porphyry attributed to Plato a theory of the Trinity that comprised God the Father, the πατρικὸς νοῦς, and a third intermediate hypo- stasis that united them. Porphyry set this triad under Plato's authority; this explains the fact that, while Claudianus Mamertus attributed to Plato the discovery of this Trinity, Augustine more correctly assigned it to Porphyry *tamquam Platonicus.* Then Porphyry quoted several passages from Plato relat- ing to the soul, notably the page in the *Phaedo* where Plato shows that the body diverts us from the truth in this life, but that the soul after death will be able to enjoy it. Claudianus translated this passage textually while Augustine summarized it:

Augustine *De civ. Dei* 10.29 (*PL* 41, 307):
ad Deum per virtutem in- tellegentiae pervenire pau- cis dicis esse concessum ... Uteris etiam hoc verbo apertius, ubi Platonis sen- tentiam sequens nec ipse

Plato *Phaedo* 66b:
"Ἕως ἂν τὸ σῶμα ἔχω- μεν καὶ συμπεφυρμένη ᾖ ἡμῶν ἡ ψυχὴ μετὰ τοῦ τοιούτου κακοῦ, οὐ μή ποτε κτησώμεθα ἱκανῶς οὗ ἐπιθυμοῦμεν· φαμὲν

Claud. Mam. *De statu animae*, p. 125, 14:
Donec corpus habeamus permixtusque sit tali malo noster animus, numquam nos id quod iam olim con- cupiscimus satis plene con- secuturos. Concupiscimus

[38] Boemer, *Der latein. Neuplaton.*, p. 72, did not recognize it and wrongly compares this text with *De civ. Dei* 11.25. Bidez, who assembled the fragments of the *De regressu animae*, does not mention Claudianus Mamertus.

dubitas in hac vita homi- δὲ τοῦτο εἶναι τὸ ἀλη- autem veri scientiam . . .
nem nullo modo ad perfec- θές . . .
tionem sapientiae pervenire, 67a: Καὶ ἐν ᾧ ἂν p. 126, 22: eo autem tem-
secundum intellectum ta- ζῶμεν, οὕτως, ὡς ἔοι- pore quo vivimus, ita de-
men viventibus omne quod κεν, ἐγγυτάτω ἐσόμεθα mum adpropinquabimus ad-
deest providentia Dei et τοῦ εἰδέναι, ἐὰν ὅτι μά- plicabimurque scientiae, si
gratia post hanc vitam λιστα μηδὲν ὁμιλῶμεν nihil aut quam minimum
posse compleri. τῷ σώματι μηδὲ κοινω- corpore utamur neque in
νῶμεν, ὅτι μὴ πᾶσα societate eius, nisi quatenus
ἀνάγκη, μηδὲ ἀναπιμ- necesse est, animum dimit-
πλώμεθα τῆς τούτου tamus. Ita enim minime
φύσεως, ἀλλὰ καθαρεύω- replebimur vitiosa turbu-
μεν ἀπ' αὐτοῦ, ἕως ἂν ὁ lentaque natura corporis,
θεὸς αὐτὸς ἀπολύσῃ sed puri a contagione eius,
ἡμᾶς. in quantum facere possu-
mus, erimus.

This quotation from the *Phaedo* must have been inserted in Porphyry's *De regressu animae* among other quotations from Plato relating to the soul and taken from the dialogues quoted or mentioned by Claudianus Mamertus. These dialogues were the *Phaedrus*, a Περὶ φυσικῆς, the *Hipparchus*, the *Laches*, the *Symposium*, the *Alcibiades*, the *Gorgias*, the *Crito*.[39] There is, too, a reference to the *Phaedrus* in the Augustinian context.[40] Porphyry probably concluded the list of Platonic dialogues with a quotation from the *Timaeus*, with regard to which he asserted that the soul is coeternal with God:

De civ. Dei 10.31 (*PL* 41, 311; cf. *De civ. Dei* 22.11):
Ut enim hoc Platonici nollent credere hanc utique causam idoneam sibi videbantur adferre, quia nisi quod semper antea fuisset, sempiternum deinceps esse non posset. Quamquam et de mundo et de his quos in mundo deos a Deo factos scribit Plato, apertissime dicat eos esse

De statu animae, p. 128, 1:
Quid in *Timaeo* etiam arce quadam et quodam philosophiae vertice de anima pronuntiaverit, placitae brevitatis gratia missum facio.

---

[39] *De statu animae* 2.7, p. 127, 21: "verum quid hic idem Platon in Hipparcho, quid in Lachete, in Protagora, in Symposio, in Alcibiade, in Gorgia, in Critone . . . de anima pronuntiaverit, placitae brevitatis gratia missum facio." Previously, p. 123, 7, Claudianus had referred to the ψόγος Λυσίου (*Phaedrus* 234d–236e) and had quoted textually *Phaedrus* 245c. I shall presently examine his quotation from the Περὶ φυσικῆς, p. 124, 17. On the quotation from the *Phaedo*, cf. the text already quoted from Macrobius, above, pp. 37–38.

[40] *De civ. Dei* 10.30 (*PL* 41, 310): "Nam Platonem animas hominum post mortem revolvi usque ad corpora bestiarum scripsisse certissimum est. Hanc sententiam Porphyrii doctor tenuit et Plotinus, Porphyrio tamen iure displicuit." The context shows that Augustine borrows from Porphyry's *De regressu animae* this reference to *Phaedrus* 249.

coepisse et habere initium, finem tamen
non habituros, sed per conditoris poten-
tissimam voluntatem in aeternum per-
mansuros esse perhibeat.[41]

Augustine, challenging Porphyry, refutes this point at great length. On
the other hand, Claudianus Mamertus, who was to eulogize Porphyry, refrains from raising the problem. Porphyry then notes that the soul must shun
everything corporeal in order to achieve beatitude:

De civ. Dei 10.29 (*PL* 41, 308):
An vero quod ipsum corpus morte
depositum et in melius resurrectione mu-
tatum iam incorruptibile neque mortale
in superna subvexit? Hoc fortasse credere
recusatis, intuentes Porphyrium in his
ipsis libris, ex quibus multa posui, quos
De regressu animae scripsit, tam crebro
praecipere: *omne corpus esse fugiendum, ut
anima possit beata permanere cum Deo.*

De statu animae, p. 128, 13:
Sed nec Porphyrius Platonicus multis
post saeculis a magistro uspiam in hac
eadem causa dissensit. Inlustri quippe
voce genus humanum suae dignitatis admonuit: *Si beati*, inquit, *esse volumus,
corpus est omne fugiendum.* Est ergo incorporeum quiddam in nobis, cui adversa
corporis universi contagio est, et quid
istud erit, nisi imago Dei, et quid imago
Dei, nisi humanus animus?

Finally Porphyry enumerated all the religious philosophies that claim to
show the way to salvation and asserted that he had not found it. For Augustine, as for Claudianus, the transition from pagan philosophy to Christian
doctrine is quite natural:

De civ. Dei 10.32.1 (*PL* 41, 312) = *De
regressu animae*, frag. 12, ed. Bidez, p. 42*:
Cum autem dicit Porphyrius in primo

De statu animae, p. 130, 10:
Quid ego nunc Zoroastris, quid Brach-
manum ex *India*, quid Anacharsidis ex

---

[41] The rest of this text will be found quoted above, chap 4 sec. 2 n. 165. Contrary to
Winter, *De doctrinae Neoplatonicae . . . vestigiis*, p. 57, I do not think that Augustine borrows this passage from a commentary on the *Timaeus*, not even from a commentary by
Porphyry, for I have shown that Augustine quoted from the text of the *Timaeus* only the
few chapters translated by Cicero. Cf. above, p. 170. A commentary on the *Timaeus*
would have furnished him with the entire text of the dialogue. On the other hand,
although Augustine discusses the problem of the soul in chap. 31, it certainly appeared in
his source between the quotation from the *Phaedo* and the formula "Corpus omne
fugiendum." In fact, the problem is already raised in chap. 29.2 (*PL* 41, 308): "Vos certe
tantum tribuitis animae intellectuali, quae anima utique humana est, ut eam consubstan-
tialem paternae illi menti, quem Dei Filium confitemini, fieri posse dicatis." Similarly,
chap. 31 is entitled: *Contra argumentum Platonicorum, quo animam humanam Deo adserunt
esse coaeternam.*

Claudianus' reference, p. 188, 8: "neget quispiam sphaeram esse mundum: uno quidem ille verbo negaverit, sed non id uno item verbo vel Timaeus adstruxerit," in no sense
assumes any direct knowledge of the *Timaeus*; a fortiori, the more remote references
noted by Boemer, *Der latein. Neoplaton.*, p. 71.

iuxta finem *De regressu animae* libro nondum receptam unam quandam sectam,
quae universalem contineat viam animae
liberandae, vel a philosophia verissima
aliqua vel ab *Indorum* moribus ac disciplina aut inductione Chaldaeorum aut
alia qualibet via, nondumque in suam
notitiam eandem viam historiali cognitione perlatam. Procul dubio confitetur
esse aliquam, sed nondum in suam venisse notitiam. Ita ei non sufficiebat quicquid de anima liberanda studiosissime di-
dicerat, sibique vel potius aliis, nosse ac tenere videbatur. Sentiebat enim adhuc sibi
deesse aliquam praestantissimam auctoritatem, quam de re tanta sequi oporteret.[42]

Scythia . . . in defensionem veri sententias adferam?

p. 131, 3: Facile profecto hoc idem factu
mihi esset, nisi adici quempiam coacta
testium turba non sineret et divina iam
nunc oracula pandere vel tempus foret
vel ratio commoneret.

(There follow the quotations from Gregory of Nazianzus, Ambrose, Augustine,
Eucherius.)

The entire extent of the parallel between Augustine and Claudianus
Mamertus is evident. It permits us to reconstruct the process of Porphyrian
speculation in the course of the first book of the *De regressu animae*. It is not
necessary for all that to think that Claudianus is dependent on Augustine. The
latter attributes to Porphyry, and the former to Plato, the theory of the Trinity that Porphyry had discovered but placed under Plato's authority. Claudianus defines what the first hypostasis of this Trinity is, not much of which
Augustine asserted that he had understood. Augustine analyzes Porphyry's
notions, while Claudianus retains in particular the formulas and the quotations, and displays this knowledge to good account, to imply that he had read
all Plato. In the quotation from the *Phaedo*, Claudianus refrains from translating the short clause: ἕως ἂν ὁ θεὸς αὐτὸς ἀπολύσῃ ἡμᾶς. Augustine on the
other hand finds therein an entire theory of Grace in Plato and Porphyry.
When the theory of the soul coeternal with God seems difficult to reconcile
with Christianity, Claudianus avoids the difficulty, while Augustine devotes
a special chapter to it. In conclusion, Claudianus enthusiastically adopts the
Porphyrian theory "Omne corpus fugiendum" that Augustine, after having
adopted it as his own in his youth, indignantly rejected in the *De civitate Dei*,
because it was incompatible with the dogma of the resurrection of the flesh.
If we admit that all of Claudianus' Platonic quotations were taken from
Porphyry's *De regressu animae*, an explanation at once appears for the singular

[42] Boemer, *Der latein. Neuplaton.*, p. 85, already established this parallel and seemingly
admits that Porphyry is the common source, through Marius Victorinus as the intermediary, but he contradicts himself, pp. 104–109, by demonstrating at great length that
the question concerns the commonplace of the wisdom of the Barbarians and that there
is no need to think that Porphyry is the source. He forgets, however, to note Sidonius
Apollinaris' reference, *Carm.* 2.165, to Anacharsis' residence in Scythia.

mistake that makes Claudianus say that Plato wrote a treatise Περὶ φυσικῆς. In fact, the similarity between his quotation from the putative Περὶ φυσικῆς and a passage in Apuleius can be explained differently from Boemer's explanation:[43]

Apuleius *De Platone*, ed. Thomas, p. 86, 6:
Nam quoniam tres partes philosophiae congruere inter se primus obtinuit, nos quoque separatim dicemus de singulis *a naturali philosophia* facientes exordium.

Claudianus Mamertus *De statu animae*, p. 124, 17:
Idem Plato in libro quem Περὶ φυσικῆς scripsit:

Ibid., 1.9, p. 91, 20:
Animam vero animantium omnium non esse corpoream nec sane perituram, cum corpore fuerit absoluta ... ipsamque semper et per se moveri, agitatricem aliorum quae natura sui inmota sunt atque pigra.

anima, inquit, animantium omnium corporalis non est ipsaque se movet, aliorum quoque agitatrix, quae naturaliter inmota sunt.

Boemer has well observed that Claudianus Mamertus' quotation has as its source neither Plato, where these exact words do not appear, nor Apuleius, as Engelbrecht thought. Boemer admits that this similarity is explained either by a common source, or a post-Apuleian Latin intermediary.[44] He accepts this second hypothesis because Claudianus Mamertus, in this quotation, uses the word *anima* in the sense of *animus*, a use that does not antedate Apuleius.[45] The argument is not tenable. In fact, Boemer acknowledges, on the other hand, that Claudianus regularly and indifferently uses *animus* and *anima*.[46] He could then just as well himself have translated this passage from Greek. It would moreover be surprising, if Claudianus derived from Apuleius through the intermediary of a Latin *De physicis*, that he should mention his source as a Greek work bearing a Greek title: Plato's Περὶ φυσικῆς. Everything is clear, on the other hand, if it is admitted that Claudianus here translated Porphyry. The source common to Apuleius and Claudianus is not difficult to discover. In fact, Sinko has shown that Apuleius' *De Platone* presented lengthy passages, parallel to Albinus' *Didaskalikos*;[47] and it is readily

[43] Boemer, *Der latein. Neuplaton.*, p. 35, observed only the second half of the parallel. Hence he mistakenly writes, p. 36, that there is no trace of the title Περὶ φυσικῆς to be found in Apuleius.

[44] Boemer, *Der latein. Neuplaton.*, p. 36.

[45] *Ibid.*, pp. 37, 20ff.

[46] *Ibid.*, p. 21.

[47] Th. Sinko, *De Apulei et Albini doctrinae Platonicae adumbratione* (Cracow 1905), especially p. 3, where he examines the tripartition into natural, moral, and dialectic philosophy. Cf. Schanz, vol. 3, p. 121.

acknowledged that Apuleius is here plagiarizing a Greek work, either Albinus' Περὶ τῶν Πλάτωνι ἀρεσκόντων, or the course given by their common master Gaius.[48] There is nothing surprising in the fact that Claudianus used this Greek work through the intermediary of Porphyry's *De regressu animae* and that he took as a textual quotation from a Περὶ φυσικῆς by Plato a passage from a part of this work that indirectly expounded Plato's dogmas Περὶ φυσικῆς, just as Book I of Apuleius' *De Platone* indirectly expounded his *naturalis philosophia*.[49]

The lengthy parallel between the *De civitate Dei* and the *De statu animae* requires us, then, to reject many of Boemer's conclusions on Claudianus' sources. The quotation from the *Phaedo* was not taken either from an anonymous translation of the first century or from Apuleius' translation. The quotation from the Περὶ φυσικῆς did not come from some Latin *De physicis* whose source was Apuleius. Both quotations were taken from Porphyry's *De regressu animae*, which Claudianus here plagiarized in its entirety. Only the conjecture of a Neoplatonic intermediary, which Boemer had proposed for the quotation from the *Phaedrus*, is confirmed, since this intermediary was Porphyry.[50] The only question that remains is to know whether Claudianus himself translated from the Greek text or whether he followed Marius Victorinus' translation. Augustine, as we have seen, read the *De regressu animae* in Victorinus' translation.[51] Now Claudianus never coincides word for word with him. What is more, he claims that he is making his own *excerptum* from the *Phaedo*, which he condensed when he made a longer extract quoted by Porphyry. The title Περὶ φυσικῆς also indicates that Claudianus followed the Greek text and not a translation. Lastly, Hårleman establishes by a study of his style that Claudianus himself translated his quotation from the *Phaedo*. All these indications agree in assuming that Claudianus read the *De regressu animae* in Greek, and not in Victorinus' translation.

The *De statu animae* contains also quite a different series of quotations from Greek writers. These quotations are Pythagorean. A study of the chapters indisputably taken from Porphyry indicates that we should not take Claudianus' assertions literally. Just as he boasted of having read an entire series of

[48] Cf. Praechter, s.v. Gaios, *PW*, Suppl. 3, 536.

[49] We have seen above, chap. 5 sec. 1 n. 65, that Salvian made a similar mistake in using Lactantius. He took for a textual Socratic quotation the theories of the *Republic* that Lactantius summarized in *oratio obliqua*.

[50] Note, however, that Oxyrhynchus Papyrus 1016 (dating in the beginning of the third century A.D.) clearly has αὐτοκίνητον and not ἀεικίνητον, and Robin, editor of the *Phaedrus*, 245c, adopts this reading of αὐτοκίνητον, which seems to him to be a better explanation of Plato's syllogism (cf. his notice, p. LXXVII n. 1 and p. 33 n. 3). Boemer, *Der latein. Neuplaton.*, p. 61, should have pointed out this rendering. I believe, however, that this form does not weaken his conclusions, for I admit, against Robin, that this reading of the third-century papyrus is the correction of a Neoplatonic commentator.

[51] Cf. above, p. 180.

Plato's dialogues, he quotes Philolaus, Archytas, Hippon, and the two Sextii as though he had read their works,[52] and he assures us that he read similarly Archippus, Epaminondas, Aristaeus, Gorgiades, Diodorus, and all the Pythagoreans.[53] Boemer, who believes in a plurality of sources for the Platonic quotations, acknowledges a single source for these Pythagorean quotations.[54] He strives to demonstrate that Claudianus translated these quotations straight from the Greek and that he took them from some Neopythagorean prior to Neoplatonism. The fact of admitting a unique source for the Pythagorean quotations seems to me all the more probable as the Platonic quotations, as I have shown, have also a unique source, that is, Porphyry's *De regressu animae*. On the other hand, it is difficult for me to believe that this source was anterior to Neoplatonism. Boemer's only argument that has any weight in my view is the fact that the Sextii are never quoted in the extant Neoplatonic works.[55] It must also be admitted, since these words are posited on the authority of the two Sextii, father and son, at the same time,[56] that Claudianus did not himself read a work of any one of them. He took their common dogma from a later intermediate source, probably the same as the one that transmitted to him the dogmas of the other Pythagorean writers. Must we believe that this collection is anterior to Neoplatonism because the concept of the *inlocalitas animae* is anterior to it? The argument is inconclusive, for, as Boemer himself acknowledges, this Neopythagorean concept at first acquired all its importance only when the Neoplatonists had appropriated it for themselves.[57] Now the custom of drawing up the catalogue of Pythagorean writers was peculiar to the Neoplatonists. Porphyry and Iamblichus each did so in his *Life of Pythagoras*. Thus in Iamblichus' *Life of Pythagoras* these names appear: Archippus of Tarentum,[58] Epaminondas,[59]

[52] On Philolaus, cf. *De statu animae* 2.3 and 7, p. 105, 7 and 120, 12. On Archytas, *ibid.*, p. 121, 5. On Hippon, *ibid.*, p. 121, 14. On the Sextii, *ibid.*, 2.8, p. 129, 11.

[53] *Ibid.*, 2.7, p. 121, 19: "sed non ita nunc omnium philosophorum Pythagoricae familiae sententias persequor, ut easdem copiosius aggerando de alienis admodum voluminibus meum faciam, satis arbitrans memet principium Pythagorici gymnasii de praesenti quaestione scita evidentia protulisse, certus scilicet neminem refutare doctorum, quin hoc idem senserint scriptoque prodiderint Archippus, Epaminondas, Aristaeus, Gorgiades, Diodorus et omnes Pythagorae posteri, quorum videlicet nominum, ne dicam sententiarum multitudine, si eadem prodita velim, volumen efficerem."

[54] Boemer, *Der latein. Neuplaton.*, p. 162.

[55] *Ibid.*, p. 136 and n. 2.

[56] *De statu animae* 2.8, p. 129, 10: "Romanos etiam eosdemque philosophos testes citemus, apud quos Sextius pater Sextiusque filius propenso in exercitium sapientiae studio adprime philosophati sunt atque hanc super omni anima tulere sententiam: incorporalis, inquiunt, omnis est anima et inlocalis atque indeprehensa vis quaedam, quae sine spatio capax corpus haurit et continet."

[57] Boemer, p. 164.

[58] Iamblichus *Vita Pythag.* 249ff.

[59] *Ibid.*, 35 and 250.

Aristaeus of Crotona,[60] Diodorus of Aspendus.[61] Of the Pythagoreans listed by Claudianus Mamertus, only Gorgiades does not appear in this catalogue, but he is completely unknown otherwise.[62] As for the definitions of the soul according to Philolaus, Archytas, Hippon, quoted by Claudianus, did he not borrow them from some Neoplatonic treatise on the soul? I am inclined to think that he is indebted for them to Porphyry's *De regressu animae*, which would be the only source then of his knowledge of Greek. There is nothing in the fragments of the *De regressu animae* preserved by Augustine that confirms this conjecture. But Macrobius' chapters taken from the *De regressu animae* are very suggestive. They contain a list of definitions of the soul according to the different philosophers, notably Pythagoras and Philolaus, and Macrobius ends this list with the conclusion that the two essential dogmas on the soul that stand out are incorporeality and immortality.[63] Furthermore, Franz Cumont has already observed the relation existing between the definition of the soul by Pseudo-Philolaus and Numenius' doctrine, the chief source for the *De regressu animae*, which interpreted the soul's prison mentioned in the *Phaedo* as designating pleasure.[64] Now this definition by Pseudo-Philolaus has been preserved precisely by Claudianus Mamertus.[65] There are therefore cogent reasons for believing that the *De regressu animae* contained a whole collection of quotations relating to the incorporeality of the soul or to immortality. Claudianus Mamertus very scrupulously repeats the first series, in which Porphyry treated both the Platonic tradition and the Pythagorean tradition.[66]

[60] *Ibid.*, 104 and 265.

[61] *Ibid.*, 266.

[62] Cf. Boemer, p. 130; Zeller, *Philosophie der Griechen* 3, 2, p. 118; *PW* 7, 1597. However, this name perhaps appears in Diogenes Laertius, 1.1.14, ed. Cobet, p. 10, 21. After the historian Leandrius, Gorgiades counts among the seven wise men of Greece: Λεώφαντον Γορσιάδα, Λεβέδιον ἢ ᾿Εφέσιον (= *FHG* 2, 336 = Diels, *Vorsokratiker*, p. 519, 2, who with Reiske corrects Γορσιάδα to Γοργιάδα).

[63] Macrobius *In Somn.* 1.14.19, p. 531, 21. See above, chap. 1 sec. 3 n. 72. In Stobaeus *Ecl.* 1.41.1, ed. Meineke, p. 225, there is a similar collection of definitions of the soul, but Stobaeus does not indicate the author of this collection, and there is no complete identity between the two lists.

[64] Cumont, "Comment Plotin détourna Porphyre du suicide," p. 119 n. 2. Cf. the text of Olympiodorus quoted above, chap. 1 sec. 3 n. 71.

[65] Claudianus Mamertus *De statu animae* 2.7, p. 120, 17: "(Philolaus) sic loquitur . . . diligitur corpus ab anima, quia sine eo non potest uti sensibus; a quo postquam morte deducta est, agit in mundo incorporalem vitam." It will be observed that an entire paragraph of Priscianus Lydus' chap. 1 of the *Solutiones ad Chosroem* discusses the question that preoccupies Claudianus and could well serve as a title for his work (p. 44, 15): *De eo quod anima incorporea sit*. Now Priscianus Lydus, ed. Bywater, *Supplementum Aristotelicum* 1, p. 42, 17, notes that the sources for this chapter are Porphyry's *Quaestiones commixtae* and Iamblichus' *De anima*. Cf. Bywater, p. xii.

[66] Add that the Peripatetic Adrastus, mentioned by Claudianus, p. 88, 21, was one of

Claudianus not only read Porphyry's *De regressu animae* but was imbued with his doctrine of the incorporeal soul and defended it against Faustus of Riez.[67] The opponent who was attacked in Faustus' letter was probably a Platonist imbued with Pythagoreanism.[68] Claudianus, for his part, was an enthusiast. He was amazed that pagan philosophy based on reason coincided with Christian truth.[69] The human spirit penetrated the secret of the hidden divinity.[70] It studied first of all the body, subject to time and place; then it examined itself; then it realized that it was not God, since it moved in time and it sought for God.[71] God being incapable of being body, and the soul being made in his resemblance, "it rightly preferred, on account of its resemblance to the Creator, to exalt the creatures rather than humiliate the Creator," and concluded that the soul was incorporeal like God.[72] Claudianus adhered unreservedly to the Neoplatonic concept of the return of the soul to God.[73] He probably supported his theory with St. Paul's remark: "They knew God,"[74] but he did not make the prudent reservations to Porphyry's system that St. Augustine had made in the *De civitate Dei*. Porphyry scorns the body to such an extent that he cannot, in his pride, accept the scandalous Incarnation or the dogma of the resurrection of the flesh. The same formula "Omne corpus fugiendum" that Augustine as bishop had reproved in the

---

Plotinus' bedside books (cf. Porphyry *Vita Plot.*, p. 109, 46). With regard to the geometrician Hermophilus, mentioned on p. 173, 23, he is unknown. Cf. Boemer, p. 131.

    [67] *De statu animae* 1.12, p. 52, 15: "Istud ego tamen philosophos reperio dicere, qui non nullis disputationibus adstruunt et ipsos lunae vel solis globos incorporeis videlicet spiritibus sub divina quadam mente vegetari. Sed oportet agnoscas hoc idem testimonium non solum pro sententia tua contra nos nihil, sed adversus eandem pro nobis valere plurimum ... Cum vero illi non dubitanter, sed scienter, non corporeos, sed corporatos spiritus dixerint, nonne dinoscitur quodcumque est corporatum non esse corporeum?" Such argumentation assumes a personal study of the philosophers. These are the philosophers of whom Jerome spoke, *In Iob* 25. Faustus *Epist.*, p. 9, 9, ed. Engelbrecht, had quoted them in support of his thesis on the immortal soul.

    [68] Faustus *Epist.* 3, ed. Engelbrecht, p. 9, 13: "sed inter haec ideo tu animam negas esse corpoream, quia iuxta aliquorum opinionem nec localis sit, nec qualitate aut quantitate subsistat."

    [69] *De statu animae* 2.7, p. 124, 22: "cum videamus illic valde consentanea nostrisque oppido convenientia pronuntiari, quae non solum praeiudicio auctoritatis utuntur, sed virtute rationis adminiculantur."

    [70] *Ibid.*, 2.2, p. 101, 19: "ingressa est divinitatis abditae mens humana secretum."

    [71] I summarize here the contents of chap. 2.2.

    [72] *Ibid.*, p. 104, 1: "iusteque maluit propter similitudinem creatoris sublimare creaturam quam propter eandem similitudinem humiliare creatorem."

    [73] He appears here to suggest besides that this chap. 2.2 has as its source the *De regressu animae*; for he concludes, 2.3, p. 104, 14: "Huius modi igitur rationibus utentium philosophorum quoad potui voluminibus perdagatis ignobilium plebe reiecta potiores quosque delegi, qui veritati in praesentiarum testificarentur."

    [74] *De statu animae* 2.2, quoting Rom. 1.21 "cum cognovissent Deum."

name of dogma, Claudianus adopted fervently, in spite of the warnings in the *De civitate Dei*. This imprudent fervor recalls the fervor of Augustine, recently converted, when he spoke of the return of the soul and scorned the flesh.[75]

Were this pagan curiosity and this bold attitude peculiar to Claudianus Mamertus? Sidonius Apollinaris' works prove that certain cultured circles in Gaul, about the year 470, remained attached to Greek literature and philosophy. Frankly, it is difficult to determine Sidonius' degree of Greek culture. He rarely speaks of it without circumlocution, and the numerous references that he makes, notably in his verse, to literature, mythology, and the geography of Greece are most frequently recollections of Latin classical writers.[76] He prides himself nevertheless on his learning, as is shown by the numerous Greek writers that he mentions in comparing them with one or another of his contemporaries. Which of these writers did he know, and by what means?

The letter in which Sidonius thanks Claudianus Mamertus for having dedicated to him the *De statu animae* gives us an idea of the Greek ecclesiastical writers that he used. Claudianus, he declares, is the equal of the writers in both Latin and Greek.[77] He is humble like John, he rebukes like Basil, he consoles like Gregory, he narrates like Eusebius.[78] The juxtaposition of the three great names is to be noted: John Chrysostom, Basil of Caesarea, Gregory of Nazianzus, who were then the only Greek Fathers that Augustine knew by direct contact. Furthermore, Sidonius had unquestionably read Eusebius' *Chronica*, at least in Jerome's adaptation, since he sent a copy to his friend Namatius.[79] He shows equal interest in the Fathers of the Desert. In one letter he mentions Paul, Anthony, Hilarion, Macarius as models of the monastic life.[80] In his *Euchariston*, dedicated to Faustus of Riez, he had already enumer-

---

[75] See above, pp. 179–180.

[76] Cf. E. Geisler, *De Apollinaris Sidonii studiis* (diss. Breslau 1885) and "Loci similes auctorum Sidonio anteriorum," *Apollinaris Sidonii epistulae et carmina*, ed. C. Luetjohann (Berlin 1887), *MGH, Auct. ant.* 8, pp. 351 and 416. I shall quote Sidonius Apollinaris from this edition. H. Rutherford's thesis, *Sidonius Apollinaris, étude d'une figure gallo-romaine du Ve siècle* (Clermont-Ferrand 1938), is very superficial in the matter of Sidonius' culture. Cf. A. Loyen, *Sidoine Apollinaire et l'esprit précieux*, pp. 12–17 and 26–30. In my opinion, he underestimates the Greek and philosophical cultural equipment of Sidonius and his friends. I have been unable to procure the article by A. Jaeger, "Sidonius Apollinaris, ein Beitrag zu vormittelalterl. Bildungskrise," *Pharus* 19 (1928) 241–266.

[77] Sid. Apoll. *Epist.* 4.3.6, p. 55, 19: "ad extremum nemo saeculo meo quae voluit adfirmare sic valuit. Si quidem dum sese adversus eum, quem contra loquitur, exertat, morum ac studiorum linguae utriusque symbolam iure sibi vindicat."

[78] *Ibid.*, 4.3.7, p. 55, 27: "submittitur ut Iohannes, ut Basilius corripit, ut Gregorius consolatur . . . ut Eusebius narrat."

[79] *Epist.* 8.6.18, p. 133, 14: "Varronem logistoricum, sicut poposceras, et Eusebium chronographum misi."

[80] *Epist.* 7.9.9, p. 114, 9: "si quempiam nominavero monachorum, quamvis illum Paulis, Antoniis, Hilarionibus, Macariis conferendum, sectatae anachoreseos praerogativa

ated the important hermits whose virtues Faustus imitated: Helias, John, the two Macarii, Paphnutius, Or, Ammon, Sarmata, Hilarion, Anthony.[81] It is probable that Sidonius had read Athanasius' *Life of Anthony* in a Latin translation,[82] and the *Life of Paul* and the *Life of Hilarion*, both written by Jerome,[83] and that he was knowledgeable about the other hermits through Rufinus' *Historia monachorum*.[84] But he had still another source, now lost, for we know nothing about Sarmata, a disciple of Anthony, except from a very brief mention in Jerome's *Chronicle*,[85] and it would be quite surprising for Sidonius to have thought of mentioning him among so many illustrious names, if he too had not been the subject of a *Life* translated into Latin.

Despite this inquisitiveness regarding the location of the Egyptian ascetics, an attitude that was common in fifth-century Gaul, Sidonius' cultural ecclesiastical erudition does not appear to be very profound. This is explained in part since he did not abandon his secular life for an ecclesiastical career until 469, scarcely ten years before his death. Even then he appeared much more interested in literature than in theology. The use that he made of the great Cappadocians or of the Fathers of the Desert was purely literary, as was the use that he was to make of the Greek artists and philosophers. He bestows hyperbolical praise equally on Faustus of Riez as on Claudianus Mamertus, without being concerned to take sides in their controversy. Once, however, he seems to be aroused about the old disputes, when chance led him to discover in the library of his hosts Ferreolus and Apollinaris a treatise by Origen translated by Rufinus and discussions arose about it. Sidonius, who had no doubt about the authenticity of this treatise, although it was spurious, supported Origen and maintained against Jerome's adherents that Rufinus'

---

comitetur, aures ilico meas in condito tumultu circumstrepitas ignobilium pumilionum murmur everberat."

[81] *Carm.* 16.99–103:

> Qua nunc Helias, nunc te iubet ire Iohannes,
> nunc duo Macarii, nunc et Paphnutius heros,
> nunc Or, nunc Ammon, nunc Sarmata, nunc Hilarion,
> nunc vocat in tunica nudus te Antonius illa,
> quam fecit palmae foliis manus alma magistri.

[82] It may be the translation by Evagrius of Antioch or the Latin translation anterior to Evagrius' that was mentioned by Dom Wilmart, "Une version latine inédite de la vie de s. Antoine," *RB* 31 (1914/1919) 163–173, and published by G. Garitte. Cf. above, chap. 4 sec. 3 n. 28.

[83] Cf. Schanz, vol. 4, 1, pp. 435–438.

[84] Cf. *ibid.*, p. 421. Rufinus devotes a notice to Helias (chap. 12), to John (chap. 1), to the two Macarii (chaps. 28–29), to Paphnutius (chap. 16), to Or and Ammon (chaps. 2–3).

[85] Jerome *Chron. anno* 359 (*PL* 27, 687): "Sarmata, Amatas et Macarius discipuli Antonii insignes habentur . . . Sarraceni monasterium beati Antonii inruentes Sarmatam interficiunt." Cf. *Acta SS. Bolland.*, *Octobr.*, vol. 5, pp. 603–605. Sarmata is not mentioned in the *Vitae Patrum*.

translation was accurate with regard both to meaning and expression.[86]

Sidonius' pagan culture is more diversified, but at first sight does not appear very assured. He likes to show that he is an expert in art, but, if he names Mentor, Praxiteles, Scopas, Polyclitus, Phidias, Apelles,[87] that does not at all prove that he knows them otherwise than by name. Similarly, his ideas of Greek literature are purely rhetorical. Homer is always paired with Vergil,[88] Alcaeus with Horace,[89] Demosthenes with Cicero.[90] With one word Sidonius characterizes Hesiod, Pindar, Menander, Archilochus, Stesichorus, Sappho;[91] and elsewhere he considers Orpheus, Euripides, Sophocles, Menander, Homer, and Herodotus as models of different literary genres.[92] When he wants to speak of Seneca's tragedies, a periphrasis turns to Greek literature: Seneca practiced the art of Euripides and Aeschylus, which

---

[86] *Epist.* 2.9.5, p. 31, 20: "quos inter Adamantius Origenes Turranio Rufino interpretatus sedulo fidei nostrae lectoribus inspiciebatur; pariter et, prout singulis cordi, diversa censentes sermocinabamur, cur a quibusdam protomystarum tamquam scaevus cavendusque tractator improbaretur, quamquam sic esset ad verbum sententiamque translatus, ut nec Apuleius Phaedonem sic Platonis, neque Tullius Ctesiphontem sic Demosthenis in usum regulamque Romani sermonis exscripserint." The text discovered by Sidonius was none other than the Περὶ τῆς εἰς Θεὸν ὀρθῆς πίστεως, translated by Rufinus (ed. Bakhuyzen, Leipzig 1901). It is a series of dialogues conducted by Adamantius with the Gnostics (cf. Schanz, vol. 4, 1, p. 421). We must assume that Sidonius had an opportunity to make a personal comparison between the text and the translation of these *Dialogues*, but his argument is not logical, for it is with reference to the translation of the Περὶ ἀρχῶν that Rufinus' accuracy was impugned.

[87] *Carm.* 23. 50–56:

> Post quas nos tua pocula et tuarum
> Musarum medius torus tenebat,
> quales nec statuas imaginesque
> aere aut marmoribus coloribusque
> Mentor, Praxiteles, Scopas dederunt,
> quantas nec Polycletus ipse finxit
> nec fit Fidiaco figura caelo.

Cf. *Epist.* 7.3.1, p. 106, 24: "hac temeritate Apelles peniculo, caelo Fidias, malleo Polyclitum muneraremur."

[88] *Epist.* 5.17.1, p. 89, 24; 9.15.1, line 48, and *Carm.* 9.217.

[89] *Epist.* 8.11.3, line 23.

[90] *Epist.* 8.1.2, p. 126, 10, and 8.2.2, p. 127, 7. His only exact knowledge is that Demosthenes was criticized by Demades.

[91] *Carm.* 9.211–216:

> Non hic Hesiodea pinguis Ascrae
> spectes carmina Pindarique chordas;
> non hic socciferi iocos Menandri,
> non laesi Archilochi feros iambos,
> vel plus Stesichori graves Camenas,
> aut quod composuit puella Lesbis.

On Pindar, cf. *Epist.* 9.15.1, line 26.

[92] *Carm.* 23.120–135.

Sidonius defines in accordance with some lines from Horace's *Ars poetica*.[93]
As for Demosthenes and Aeschines, who suggest each other, Sidonius knows
only their speeches *On the Crown* and *Against Ctesiphon* respectively, which
had been translated by Cicero.[94] Like the various arts and the different literary genres, the sciences too are placed under the aegis of an illustrious Greek
writer, either historical or legendary, and supplied with a symbol.[95] Such
lists are the mark of a rhetorical training that had become scholastic and arti-
ficial. Let us therefore not entertain the slightest belief that Sidonius used all
these writers. But inversely it would be a mistake to conclude that Sidonius
had had no direct contact with the Greek language and literature. The empty
display of learning that gives him such pleasure must not make us forget that
he knew Greek. In fact, we have no reason to doubt his word when he describes, in a friendly letter free from all declamatory flourishes, that he is
starting to teach his son. The son reads aloud Terence's *Hecyra*; the father,
Menander's *The Arbitration*.[96] Doubtless the fact that a father resumes his
Greek on the occasion of his son's studies is not unique,[97] but it would be
difficult to see in this a theme for declamation that does not conceal some
reality. Sidonius' statement is all the more probable in that Menander, along
with Homer, was the supreme classical author, not only in the East where
Choricius of Gaza and Aristaenetus still quoted him,[98] but in the Latin West
of the fifth century.[99] *The Arbitration*, which was the best preserved among

[93] *Carm.* 9.234–236:

> Orchestram quatit alter Euripidis,
> pictum faecibus Aeschylon secutus
> aut plaustris solitum sonare Thespin.

Cf. Horace *Ars poet.* 276ff.

[94] *Epist.* 4.3.6, p. 55, 22: "ut Aeschines blanditur, ut Demosthenes irascitur." Cf. the
text quoted above, n. 90. Sidonius knows, however, at least by name, Demosthenes'
Philippics, *Carm.* 23.139.

[95] *Epist.* 4.3.5, p. 55, 15: "(doctrina Claudiani) . . . quae si fors exigit tenere non abnuit
cum Orpheo plectrum cum Aesculapio baculum, cum Archimede radium cum Euphrate
horoscopium, cum Perdice circinum cum Vitruvio perpendiculum quaeque numquam
investigare destiterit cum Thalete tempora, cum Atlante sidera, cum Zeto pondera, cum
Chrysippo numeros, cum Euclide mensuras."

[96] *Epist.* 4.12.1, p. 64, 11: "nuper ego filiusque communis Terentianae *Hecyrae* sales
ruminabamus; studenti adsidebam naturae meminens et professionis oblitus quoque
absolutius rhythmos comicos incitata docilitate sequeretur, ipse etiam fabulam similis
argumenti, id est *Epitrepontem* Menandri in manibus habebam; legebamus pariter,
laudabamus iocabamurque et, quae vota communia sunt, illum lectio, me ille capie-
bat."

[97] This is the case with Symmachus. Cf. above, chap. 1 sec. 1 n. 10.

[98] Cf. A. Koerte, *PW* s.v. Menandros, 717 and 737–743.

[99] Cf. Ausonius *Protrept. ad nepot.* 13.46–47:

> Conditor Iliados et amabilis orsa Menandri
> evolvenda tibi,

and Ferrandus of Carthage *Vita Fulgentii* 1.4, trans. Lapeyre, p. 10. Cf. above, p. 221,

Menander's plays, was probably the most frequently read. Sidonius' testimony wrongly appeared to be suspect, because *The Arbitration* does not deal with the same subject as the *Hecyra*.[100] Lafaye has clearly shown that Sidonius is speaking only of a similarity of subject (*similis argumenti*). The exercise that he is working on with his son is the rhetorical exercise of the parallel, and not a philological comparison of the two texts.[101] This exercise is carried on *alternis lectionibus* in line with the old method that Aulus Gellius had already noted.[102] The parallel between *The Arbitration* and the *Hecyra* was not conceived by Sidonius. He must have been teaching in the usual manner. Sidonius was then capable of reading with understanding the Greek text of Menander and of appreciating the subtle humorous points, even without the aid of a Latin translation or adaptation, since the *Hecyra* is not an adaptation of *The Arbitration*.

This knowledge of Greek, however slight it might be, should not be a surprise in the aristocratic circles of Gaul at this period. One of Sidonius' friends, Consentius of Narbonne, was certainly even much more learned in this language than Sidonius. Whatever share declamation had in the eulogies that Sidonius bestows on him, he informs us that Consentius spoke Greek fluently and on this account executed several diplomatic missions at the court of Byzantium.[103] He was versed in Greek poetry and must have aroused the

---

and Schanz, vol. 4, 2, p. 313 n. 8. Menander's ʼΕπιτρέποντες was already quoted by Quintilian *Inst. or.* 10.1.169 as a classic.

[100] P. E. Legrand, "Pour l'histoire de la Comédie nouvelle, Le Δύσκολος et les ʼΕπιτρέποντες de Ménandre," *REG* 15 (1902) 363.

[101] G. Lafaye, "Le modèle de l'Hécyre," *REG* 40 (1916) 22–25. Cf. Wilamowitz, *Menander, das Schiedsgericht* (Berlin 1925) 133.

[102] Aulus Gellius, *Noct. Att.* 2.23.3, ed. Hertz (Leipzig 1871), p. 98, 4. The entire chapter is a parallel between Caecilius' *Plocium* and Menander's, intended to prove the superiority of the Greek comedy writer.

[103] *Carm.* 23.228–240:

> Tum si forte fuit quod imperator
> Eoas soceri venire in aures
> fido interprete vellet et perito,
> te commercia duplicis loquelae
> doctum solvere protinus legebat.
> O, sodes, quotiens tibi loquenti
> Byzantina sophos dedere regna,
> et te seu Latialiter sonantem
> tamquam Romulea satum Subura,
> seu linguae Argolicae rotunditate
> undantem Marathone ceu creatum
> plaudentes stupuere Bosphorani
> mirati minus Atticos alumnos?

On the other hand, Sidonius *Epist.* 9.13.2, lines 22–23:

> declamans gemini pondere sub stili
> coram discipulis Burdigalensibus,

admiration of the Byzantines.[104]

A study of Sidonius' philosophical culture permits one to assert that he had also at hand a manual that contained brief views on the various Greek philosophers. In fact, we find on three occasions, from his own hand, the list of the same philosophers, characterized almost in the same terms. Each time, Sidonius begins by reviewing the seven wise men of Greece. The poetic device consists of summarizing in one line the doctrine of each philosopher, whose native country is invariably mentioned.[105] This device was not new. It was practiced with greater elaboration by Ausonius[106] and by several anonymous writers.[107] It was in vogue in the schools in Sidonius' time and these variations on the same theme must have started with a collection of Greek apothegms. In fact, Ausonius quotes in Greek the maxims of the seven wise men, and a poem in the *Palatine Anthology* has preserved a technique of this kind, expressed in Greek.[108] This compilation of apothegms, whether translated or not, appears to be Sidonius' source.

The same source must have furnished him with the list of the principal Greek philosophers, carefully catalogued and numbered,[109] that appears in *Carmen* 15 following the list of the seven wise men: Thales, Anaximander, Anaximenes, Anaxagoras, Diogenes of Apollonia, Arcesilas (Archelaus), Socrates, Plato. Diels has already observed that this list reproduces the order adopted by St. Augustine in the *De civitate Dei* for his nomenclature of the

---

signifies, not that Lampridius taught Latin and Greek, as Roger thought, *L'enseignement des lettres classiques*, p. 71, but only that he wrote both prose and poetry in Latin.

[104] *Epist.* 9.15, lines 19–28:

> ... sed istud aptius paraverit
> Leo Leonis aut secutus orbitas
> cantu in Latino, cum prior sit Attico
> Consentiorum qui superstes est patri,
> fide, voce, metris ad fluenta Pegasi
> cecinisse dictus omniforme canticum,
> quotiensque verba Graia carminaverit,
> tenuisse celsa iunctus astra Pindaro
> montemque victor isse per biverticem
> nullis secundus inter antra Delphica.

[105] *Carm.* 2.157–163, 15.44–50, 23.101–110.

[106] Ausonius *Ludus septem sapientum* 52–70, ed. Peiper, p. 172. M. Manitius, "Zu Ausonius und Apoll. Sid.," *Jahrbücher für classische Philologie* 137 (1888) 79–80, is too hasty in concluding that Sidonius used an excerpt from Ausonius. I should rather be inclined to believe in a common source that, in Africa under the Vandals at the beginning of the sixth century, still inspired the poet Luxorius, *De sententiis septem philosophorum*, ed. Baehrens, *Poetae Latini minores* 4 (Leipzig 1882), p. 414.

[107] Ausonius, ed. Peiper, pp. 406–409, and Hyginus *Fabula* 221, the authenticity of which is doubtful. Cf. Schanz, vol. 4, 1, p. 37.

[108] *Anth. Pal.* 9.366.

[109] Sidonius *Carm.* 15.89: "quartus Anaxagoras."

philosophers[110] and seems to think that Sidonius plagiarized Augustine.[111] The fact is not positive, despite lengthy textual parallels, for Sidonius read in a corrupt text *Arcesilas*, whereas Augustine's text has *Archelaus*. In addition, he devotes to Pythagoras' doctrines a long, detailed paragraph that does not appear in Augustine.[112] But it is quite probable that they have a common source, for in Augustine, as in Sidonius, Thales appears simultaneously in both lists: the list of the seven wise men and that of the philosophers.[113] This source, whose value and relationship to the compendium used by Eusebius of Caesarea[114] have been pointed out by Diels, is in my opinion the work of Celsus or Celsinus. This work Augustine had compared, in the pagan field, with Epiphanius' *Panarion* in the category of heresies.[115] It is probable that Sidonius took from the same work the list of the philosophers mentioned in the eulogy on Anthemius[116] or in the letter to Faustus,[117] but he presents them in a confused order, without observing the sequence followed by his source. This manual, of which a trace appears in several Gallic writers of the fifth century,[118] served as a textbook, and Sidonius certainly knew it when he was expounding Aristotle's *Categories* at the school of his teacher of philosophy called Eusebius.[119]

Certainly Sidonius has not the philosophical mind. He can however help us to discover how far philosophy in his day was still permeated by Hellenism.

---

[110] H. Diels, *Doxographi Graeci* (Berlin 1879), p. 173.

[111] Diels, *Die Fragmente der Vorsokratiker* I (Berlin 1906), p. 325, 3 and p. 329, 41.

[112] *Carm*. 15.51–58 and *Epist*. 7.8.5, p. 113, 16–22. Augustine mentions Pythagoras only, at the beginning of chap. 2, as the founder of Italic philosophy.

[113] *De civ. Dei* 8.2 (*PL* 41, 225): "Ionici vero generis princeps fuit Thales Milesius, unus illorum septem qui appellati sunt *Sapientes*. Sed illi sex vitae genere distinguebantur, et quibusdam praeceptis ad bene vivendum accommodatis; iste autem Thales, ut successores etiam propagaret, rerum naturam scrutatus suasque disputationes litteris mandans exstitit." Cf. 18.25 and 37.

[114] Diels, *Doxog. Graeci*, pp. 169–174, "De compendio Eusebiano."

[115] See above, pp. 135 and 192–194. Note also that a versified exposition by Sidonius on Pythagoras' silence (*Carm*. 15.51) is repeated by him in prose, *Epist*. 7.9.5, p. 113, 16, under the rubric "Refert historia saecularis." Lastly, cf. on the Platonic theories *De civ. Dei* 8.6 (*PL* 41, 231) and Sidonius *Carm* 15.102–117. This classification of the six modes of existence is not Platonic, but Neoplatonic. This fits in well with Celsinus' manual.

[116] Sidonius *Carm*. 2.156–181.

[117] *Epist*. 9.9.14, p. 158, 22–28.

[118] See above, pp. 229, 231, 235.

[119] *Epist*. 4.1.3, p. 52, 18: "et vere intra Eusebianos Lares talium te quaedam moneta susceperat disciplinarum, cuius philosophica incude formatus nunc varias nobis rerum sermonumque rationes, ipso etiam qui docuerat probante pandebas, nunc ut Platon discipulus iam prope potior sub Socrate, sic iam tu sub Eusebio nostro inter Aristotelicas categorias artifex dialecticus atticissabas." On this Eusebius, cf. *Vita s. Hilarii Arelatensis* 14 (*PL* 50, 1231 C): "eiusdem praeclari auctores temporis, qui suis scriptis merito claruerunt Silvius, Eusebius, Domnulus."

He himself made a new revision of Philostratus' *Life of Apollonius of Tyana*, which had been translated by Flavianus and already revised by Tascius Victorianus.[120] This work still aroused curiosity, since it was at the request of Leo, minister to King Euric, that Sidonius executed this revision. In his letter to Leo he notes the interest that this book offers for him. It familiarizes him with the lands of the East and their philosophers, Gymnosophists or Brahmans. As for Apollonius, he is the model of all the virtues, although he was not of the Catholic faith.[121] Such broad views or such naïveté should not cause too much surprise since Jerome and Augustine, who knew nevertheless that the antichristian polemics took their argument from the miracles of Apollonius, had already expressed favorable opinions on him.[122] This breadth of view is explained all the better in that Sidonius sees no antagonism between Hellenic philosophy and Christian faith. For him, Platonic philosophy is the true philosophy. This sentiment is expressed in the eulogies that he bestows on Faustus of Riez: Faustus married philosophy, once he had shaven off the hair of a false religion and stripped away the pride of pagan learning.[123] To attack Faustus was to fight against Plato's Academy of Christ's Church, which defeats by their own weapons the Stoic, Cynic, and Aristotelian heresiarchs.[124]

These eulogies ill apply to Faustus of Riez who, as far as may be judged from his preserved writings, had no philosophical approach and maintained against Claudianus Mamertus theses that were opposed to the Neoplatonic doctrine of the incorporeal soul.[125] But they reveal to us the esteem in which Sidonius held Platonic philosophy. He himself readily refers to Plato's *Phaedo*, which he read in Apuleius' translation.[126] He does not know personally Plato's other dialogues, and by "Platonic" philosophy Sidonius actually means Neoplatonism. His letters to Eutropius prove this. The first one

[120] *Epist.* 8.3.1, p. 127, 15: "Apollonii Pythagorici vitam, non ut Nicomachus senior e Philostrati, sed ut Tascius Victorianus e Nicomachi schedio exscripsit, quia iusseras, misi; quam dum parare festino, celeriter eiecit in tumultuarium exemplar turbida et praeceps et opica translatio." Cf. above, p. 16.

[121] *Epist.* 8.3.4–5, p. 128, 11–22.

[122] See above, pp. 77–78 and 189–190.

[123] *Epist.* 9.9.18, p. 158, 10: "philosophiam scilicet, quae violenter e numero sacrilegarum artium exempta, raso capillo superfluae religionis ac supercilio scientiae saecularis . . . mystico amplexu iam defaecata tecum membra coniunxit."

[124] *Ibid.*, 9.9.13, p. 158, 17: "huic copulatum te matrimonio qui lacessiverit, sentiet ecclesiae Christi Platonis academiam militare teque nobilius philosophare," and 15, p. 158, 27: "quin potius experietur, quisque conflixerit, Stoicos, Cynicos, Peripateticos haeresiarchas propriis armis, propriis quoque concuti machinamentis."

[125] Cf. Schanz, vol. 4, 2, pp. 545–546.

[126] *Carm.* 2.178: "Socraticusque animus post fatum in Faedone vivus." On Apuleius' translation, cf. above, n. 86. Sidonius also read Apuleius' *Quaestiones convivales*, which could have taught him Greek literature. Cf. *Epist.* 9.13.3, p. 163, 5.

advises him not to remain an adherent of Epicurus' dogmas.[127] The second letter, written much later, congratulates him on having accepted the office of praetorian prefect, without having been diverted, by the philosophical life that he is leading as a disciple of Plotinus, from political life and the duties incumbent on his rank.[128] Father Henry has already stressed the importance of this evidence. He proves that Plotinus had also disciples in Rome in the fifth century and was not unknown to the Gauls.[129]

Sidonius' testimony on Claudianus Mamertus is not less valuable. He was resplendent, he declares, in his knowledge of Greek, Latin, and Christian literature.[130] The reference to the plan of Book 2 of the *De statu animae*, where Claudianus borrows his quotations successively from these three literatures, is evident.[131] But Sidonius is not mistaken about Claudianus' Hellenism. He knows all that he owes to Porphyry, as I have shown. Claudianus, he says, is different from his associates in Neoplatonism (*complatonici*) only in external dress and in faith.[132] And he has good reasons for knowing, for he personally formed part of the group before which Claudianus lavished the treasures of his teaching.[133] Polemius, too, who was praetorian prefect of the Gauls, was one of those *complatonici*, as Sidonius notes in the epithalamium in which he celebrates his wedding.[134] This epithalamium reveals the tastes

---

[127] *Epist.* 1.6.5, p. 9, 25: "sin autem inlecebrosis deliciarum cassibus involutus mavis, ut aiunt, Epicuri dogmatibus copulari ..."

[128] *Epist.* 3.6.2, p. 44, 10: "quibus (incitamentis) vix potuistis adduci, ut praefecturam philosophiae iungeretis, cum vos consectanei vestri Plotini dogmatibus inhaerentes ad profundum intempestivae quietis otium Platonicorum palaestra rapuisset, cuius disciplinae tunc fore adstruxi liberam professionem, cum nil familiae debuisses."

[129] Henry, *Plotin et l'Occident*, pp. 199–202, even exaggerates the value of this evidence in which he finds "the last echo of Plotinus' deep and mighty voice." He is unaware in fact of Boethius' text, quoted below, p. 281, on Plotinus as a *gravissimus philosophus*.

[130] *Epist.* 4.11.6, lines 4–5, p. 63:
> Triplex bybliotheca quo magistro
> Romana, Attica, Christiana fulsit.

[131] Claudianus Mamertus *De statu animae* 2.8, p. 129, 4: "Plurimorum in negotium praesens philosophorum plurimis testimoniis usi sumus multosque ex eadem Graecia, si vel causa posceret vel ratio sineret, proferre possemus, sed ne localiter veritatem quaesisse videamur, ut haec eadem ab una tantum videri gente quiverit et aliis ignorata sit, cum veri compos humana substantia non sit regione, sed genere, Romanos etiam eosdemque philosophos testes citemus"; and 2.9, p. 131, 7: "atque ut ad ipsos caelestium voluminum fontes illis fere ducibus, qui ex eisdem largius hausere, veniamus, Gregorius Nazianzenus in Apologetico magnum videlicet inter animam et corpus clamat esse discrimen."

[132] *Epist.* 4.11.2, p. 62, 13: "a conlegio tamen *Conplatonicorum* solo habitu ac fide dissociabatur."

[133] *Ibid.*: "Deus bone, quid erat illud, quotiens ad eum [sola] consultationis gratia conveniebamus! ... iam si frequentes consederamus, officium audiendi omnibus ⟨iniungebat⟩ ... doctrinae suae opes erogaturus."

[134] *Epist. ad Polemium* 1, p. 232, 6: "(philosophiae) talis ordo est, ut sine plurimis novis

of those Neoplatonists. They employed a technical Greek vocabulary for which Sidonius proudly claims the right of acceptance as poetry, as the most distinguished poets of the time did: such as Magnus, Domnulus, Leo.[135] Music and, still more, astrology arouse these poets, although Prosper of Aquitaine had recently condemned the art of the Chaldeans.[136] La Ville de Mirmont has already studied the astrological learning of this cultured circle.[137] Astrology, which was confused with astronomy, was for them not only a poetic ornament. Sidonius knows the astronomer Aratus[138] and recommends the study of more recent astrologers such as Iulianus Vertacus, Thrasybulus, Fullonius Saturninus.[139] He is sufficiently knowledgeable to understand the meaning of a complicated horoscope and to explain it in its details.[140] The Greek terms that he uses: κέντρα, διαστήματα, κλίματα, Μοῖραι, are the technical expressions of astrological science. As he assigns the origin of these

---

verbis quae praefata pace reliquorum eloquentum specialiter tibi et *Conplatonicis* tuis nota sunt, nugae ipsae non valuerint expediri." Cf. *Carm.* 15.118–119:

> Hoc in gymnasio Polemi sapientia vitam
> excolit adiunctamque suo fovet ipsa Platoni,

and 188–191:

> ... consurge sophorum
> egregium Polemi decus, ac nunc Stoica tandem
> pone supercilia et Cynicos imitatus amantes
> incipies iterum parvum mihi ferre Platona.

[135] *Epist. ad Polemium* 2, p. 232, 8: "videris, utrum aures quorundam per imperitiam temere mentionem *centri, proportionis, diastematum, climatum* vel *myrarum* epithalamio conducibilem non putent. Illud certe consulari viro vere Magno, quaestorio viro Domnulo, spectabili viro Leone ducibus audacter adfirmo, musicam et astrologiam quae sunt infra arithmeticam consequentia membra philosophiae, nullatenus posse sine hisce nominibus indicari; quae si quispiam ut Graeca, sicut sunt, et peregrina verba contempserit, noverit sibi aut super huiusce modi artis mentione supersedendum aut nihil omnino se aut certe non ad assem Latiari lingua hinc posse disserere."

[136] Prosper *Carm. de Provid.* 627–628 (*PL* 51, 631 B):

> Quid vana vetusti
> perfugia erroris Chaldaeis quaeris in astris?

He himself, however, seems to believe in the influence of the stars, 644–645 (*PL* 51, 631 D):

> Ergo aut aethereis nullum est ius ignibus in nos,
> aut *si quid nostri retinent*, amittere possunt.

[137] H. de la Ville de Mirmont, "L'astrologie chez les Gallo-Romains, X Sidoine Apollinaire; XI L'astrologie dans le *De statu animae* de Claudianus Mamertus," *REA* 11 (1909) 301–327.

[138] *Epist.* 9.9.14, p. 158, 23, and *Carm.* 23.113.

[139] *Epist.* 8.11.10, p. 142, 11, and *Epist. ad Pontium Leontium* 3, p. 244, 9. Only Thrasybulus is known otherwise. Cf. *Hist. Aug. de vita Alexandri* 62.2: "Thrasybulus mathematicus illi amicissimus fuit." The context informs us that the poet Anthedius also read them.

[140] *Epist.* 8.11.9–14, pp. 142–143; cf. La Ville de Mirmont, "L'astrologie," pp. 310–312.

astrological theories to Pythagoras, their Neopythagorean source is certain.[141] He knows them probably through the intermediary of the Neoplatonic manual of history and philosophy that I mentioned before.

I think it is therefore possible to determine what was the only Hellenic culture still prevalent in Gaul at the close of the fifth century. If we exclude ascetic literature, transmitted by Evagrius and Cassianus, which remained in favor in monastic circles and was not unknown to the general public, the most cultured men read Plotinus and Porphyry with a new fervor. Their philosophy is a Neoplatonism strongly marked by Pythagoreanism. The evidence of two personalities as opposed as Claudianus and Sidonius is in agreement.[142] Now, this renewal in the life and popularity of the Neoplatonic doctrine in Gaul coincides with the proliferation of the School of Proclus in Athens and the nomination of the Greek Anthemius as emperor in the West. Sidonius welcomes this nomination joyfully and in his *Panegyric* eulogizes the new emperor as a man imbued with Greek philosophy.[143] As a matter of fact, he appears to have had associations with the Neoplatonists, some of whom, although pagans, occupied important positions at the court of Byzantium in the reign of Leo I.[144] A descendant of Procopius, who as a rival to Valens had led the pagan revolt in the East,[145] Anthemius arrived in Italy, escorted by the pagan Marcellinus, a disciple of Sallust the philosopher.[146] He recalled from Alexandria the pagan philosopher Messus Phoebus Severus, whom he appointed consul. He himself, according to Damascius' testimony, was in league with the *Hellenes* and formed a secret plan to restore the cult of idols.[147] There is nothing surprising

---

[141] *Carm.* 15.61–70 and 77–78; cf. La Ville de Mirmont, "L'astrologie," pp. 306–308.

[142] I readily believe that Sidonius had not the philosophical faculty, but I hesitate to generalize and to say with A. Loyen, "L'esprit précieux dans la société polie des Gaules au Ve siècle," *REL* 10 (1932) 125: "nothing in his work gives us the right to conclude that *there was* still an interest in ideas." Claudianus Mamertus is our evidence to the contrary.

[143] *Carm.* 2.156–181; cf. L. Vassili, "La cultura di Antemio," *Athenaeum*, n.s. 16 (1938) 38–45.

[144] Particularly the pagan Jacobus, physician to the emperor, the philosopher Isocasius, and Pusaeus, praetorian prefect in the East in 465. Cf. Malalas *Chronogr.* 14, ed. Dindorf, *CSHB*, pp. 369–370; *Chron. Paschal. anno* 367, ed. Dindorf, p. 595; Damascius, *Vit. Isid. apud* Photius, cod. 242, 344a (*PG* 103, 1278 C); Comes Marcellinus, *Chronicon anno* 462, *MGH, Auct. ant.* 11, 2, p. 88, 5, and E. Stein, *Geschichte des spätrömischen Reiches*, pp. 524–525.

[145] Vassili, "La cultura di Antemio," p. 41.

[146] Cf. Damascius *Vit. Isid., apud* Photius, cod. 242, p. 342b (*PG* 103, 1273 B), and Suidas s.v. Μαρκελλῖνος. The question involves not the Neoplatonic author of the Περὶ θεῶν καὶ κόσμου but a certain Sallust, a Cynic philosopher and a friend of the Neoplatonists. Cf. Praechter, *PW* s.v. Sallustios, no. 39.

[147] *Ibid.*, p. 343b (*PG* 103, 1276 C): ὅτι Ἀνθέμιον οὗτος τὸν Ῥώμης βασιλεύσαντα ἑλληνόφρονα καὶ ὁμόφρονα Σεβήρου τοῦ εἰδώλοις προσανακειμένου

in the fact that in his reign (467–472) Sidonius' friends, called to the highest offices, were Neoplatonists. It was in 470 that Claudianus Mamertus published the *De statu animae*. It was around the same date that Eutropius was praetorian prefect in Rome, and Polemius praetorian prefect of the Gauls. Sidonius informs us that Anthemius had promised the title of patrician to another Gallo-Roman friend of his, a certain Ecdicius.[148]

We know how transient was this Hellenic renaissance with its pagan motifs. Soon Pope Hilarus became anxious on observing, among Anthemius' retinue, the pneumatomachian heretic Philotheus, a native of Macedonia.[149] The restoration of the Flavian theater, a pagan monument, induced him to tax Anthemius with paganism.[150] Surrounded and killed by Ricimer, he left behind him an evil reputation. Ennodius treats him scornfully as a Galatian and a *Graeculus*.[151] That was not to prevent Sidonius, two years after the murder of Anthemius, from passionately greeting the new emperor sent by Byzantium. This was Julius Nepos,[152] who at once tried to effect a reconciliation with the Gallic nobility by naming Ecdicius a patrician, as Anthemius had promised to do,[153] and Audax a *praefectus urbi*.[154] But a military revolt and the disfavor of the Roman senate compelled Julius Nepos to embark for the East. The hopes of the Gallo-Roman friends of Hellenism were finally disappointed.

3. THE BREAK

    I believe in fact that Greek literary culture disappeared in Gaul in the sixth century. Not that all contact was broken off between Gaul and the East.

λέγει, ὃν ὕπατον χειροτονεῖ, καὶ ἀμφοῖν εἶναι κρυφίαν βουλὴν τὸ τῶν εἰδώλων μύσος ἀνανεώσασθαι, and Suidas s.v. Σεβῆρος.

[148] Sidonius *Epist.* 5.16.2, p. 88, 25: "Hoc tamen sancte Iulius Nepos, armis pariter summus Augustus ac moribus, quod decessoris Anthemii fidem fratris tui sudoribus obligatam, quo citior, hoc laudabilior absolvit: si quidem iste complevit, quod ille saepissime pollicebatur." Cf. G. Yver, *Euric, roi des Wisigoths, 446–485 A.D.* (1896) 20–21.

[149] *Coll. Avell.* 95.61 (= Gelasius *Epist.* 26.11, ed. Thiel, 1, p. 408): "Cum Philotheus Macedonianus eius familiaritate suffultus diversarum conciliabula nova sectarum in urbem vellet inducere . . ."

[150] Cf. Vassili, "La cultura di Antemio," p. 42.

[151] Ennodius *Vita Epifanii* 53, ed. Vogel, *MGH, Auct. ant.* 7, p. 90, 36: "qui est qui Galatam concitatum revocare possit et principem," and 54, p. 91, 5: "quem venerari possit quicumque, si est catholicus et Romanus, amare certe, si videre mereatur, et Graeculus."

[152] He is reckoned among the partisans of Nepos, *Epist.* 5.6.2, p. 81, 21, and 5.7.1, p. 82, 3.

[153] Text quoted above, n. 148. Cf. Jordanes *Get.* 45.241, ed. Mommsen, *MGH, Auct. ant.* 5, p. 120, 1.

[154] Sidonius *Epist.* 8.7.3–4, p. 133, 28; cf. p. 421 s.v. Audax.

Political contacts persisted and a number of barbarian kings continued to accept the theoretical suzerainty of the emperor. Clovis was very proud in 508 to receive from the Emperor Anastasius the consular diploma, while he pretended to consider it as a real investiture.[1] The Burgundian King Sigismond, threatened by a coalition of the Franks and the Ostrogoths, appealed to the emperor, whose suzerainty he expressly acknowledged. The letter written in his name by his chancellor Avitus pompously declared: "The light of the East touches Gaul as well as Scythia. The rays that rise in those regions shine on us too."[2] Theodebert was for a long time Justinian's ally against the Ostrogoths.[3] Even when the Frankish kings had delivered Gaul from Byzantine suzerainty by securing the cession of Arles in 539, the religious unity of the Empire survived its political unity, and the Archbishop of Arles Auxanius gained the privilege of the pallium only through Justinian's consent.[4] But for a long time Greek culture had no longer been respected, and the rare protestations of deference toward the emperor were sheer opportunism. The case of Bishop Avitus of Vienne illustrates this clearly. Although he occasionally adorned his writings with a Greek expression or a Greek etymology,[5] there is no occasion to conclude that he really knew Greek.[6] But when the Burgundians sought a Frankish alliance, it was Clovis and no longer the emperor whom Avitus called the Radiance of the West.[7] He then spoke all the more freely of the "Caesar of the Greeks," as, in his

---

[1] Gregory of Tours *Hist. Franc.* 2.38, ed. Krusch, *MGH, Script. rer. Merov.* 1, p. 102, 9. On the purely honorific value of the title bestowed on Clovis, cf. Van de Vyver, "Clovis et la politique méditerranéenne," *Etudes d'histoire dédiées à la mémoire de Henri Pirenne* (Brussels 1937) 383 and n. 1.

[2] Avitus *Epist.* 78 and 93, *MGH, Auct. ant.* 6, 2, p. 93, 9–10 and p. 100, 6–25: "Tangit Galliam, Scythiam, lumen orientis et radius, qui illis partibus oriri creditur, hic refulget."

[3] *Epist. Austras.* 19 and 20, *MGH, Epist. aevi Merov.* 1, pp. 132–133.

[4] *Epist. Arel.* 39 and 41, *MGH, Epist. aevi Merov.*, p. 59, 5–11 and p. 62, 5–9.

[5] Avitus *Epist.* 30 *ad Gundobadum regem*, ed. R. Peiper, *MGH, Auct. ant.* 6 (Berlin 1883), p. 13, 11: "Racha vero Hebraeum nomen, Latine sonat inanis aut vacuus; quod, ut nostis, convenientius exprimit uno vocabulo Graecus dicens *cenos*." *Carm.* 4.625–626, p. 253:

> Arcus et emicuit, quem nunc Thaumantida Graio,
> Irim Romuleo vocitant sermone poetae.

Cf. *Carm.* 6.94; *Epist.* 39 (44), p. 77, 28.

[6] The Greek words that he uses were ecclesiastical Hellenisms already in vogue; cf. H. Goelzer and A. Mey, *Le latin de s. Avit, évêque de Vienne*, Université de Paris, Bibliothèque de la Faculté des Lettres, vol. 26 (1909) 497–505. The comparison between Homer and Vergil, *Carm.* 3.335, p. 233, was a commonplace. The *Contra Eutych.*, p. 22, 28, merely quotes and translates the liturgical formula of the *trisagion*.

[7] Avitus *Epist.* 46 (41) *ad Clodevechum regem*, p. 75, 17: "Gaudeat equidem Graecia principem legisse nostrum; sed non iam quae tanti muneris donum sola mereatur. In-lustrat tuum quoque orbem claritas sua, et occiduis partibus in rege non novi iubaris lumen effulgurat. Cuius splendorem congrua redemptoris nostri nativitas inchoavit."

own view and that of Pope Hormisdas, the Greeks were schismatical and their very attempts at union concealed some treachery.[8] This reprobation extended to Greek poetry, which was a tissue of falsehoods,[9] and to Greek philosophy, which was a tissue of contradictions.[10] This is the expressed opinion of Claudianus Mamertus' own godson, Sidonius Apollinaris' young kinsman.[11] From one generation to the next, Greek culture, which Claudianus Mamertus was already perturbed to see exposed to such menace,[12] had become undesirable, as a result of the barbarian influences and the religious schism, in the very heart of the aristocratic society where it was traditional.

It was not the affluence in Gaul of the Jews and the Syrians,[13] some of whom at least spoke Greek,[14] that would save it. They would rather have compromised it. Salvian was already denouncing the greed of these merchants,[15] who formed separate colonies. In the course of the sixth century, their political or artistic influence rapidly became considerable, on account of the articles that they imported and the wealth they acquired; but I do not

---

[8] Avitus *Contra Eutychianam haeresim* 1, p. 16, 1: "Ego tamen Deum pro viribus quaeso, ut is ipse, de quo loquimur Caesar Graecorum, si fidelis vobis, etiam nobis honorabilis, persuadeatur a principe nostro, quod suadeat populo suo"; *Epist.* 41.87 *ad Hormisdam*, p. 70, 4: "His adicitur, quod diversorum fida relatione comperimus, de reconciliatione vel concordia ecclesiae Romanae iactitare se Graeciam. Quod sicut amplectendum, si veraciter dicitur, ita metuendum est, ne callide simuletur."

[9] *Carm.* 4.109–110, p. 239:
Haec sunt priscorum quae de terrore gigantum
carmine mentito Grai cecinere poetae.
Cf. *Carm.* 4.94.

[10] *Carm.* 4.498–499, p. 249:
Turgida Graiorum sapientia philosophorum
inter se tumidos gaudet committere fluctus.

[11] Cf. Schanz, vol. 4, 2, p. 380.

[12] Claudianus Mamertus *Epist. ad Sapaudum*, CSEL 11, p. 204, 27: "Video . . . philosophiam uti quoddam ominosum bestiale numerari."

[13] Cf. R. Anchel, "Les Juifs en Gaule à l'époque franque," *Journal des savants*, Nov.–Dec. 1938, pp. 255–265.

[14] Cf., among others, P. Scheffer-Boichorst, "Die Syrer im Abendlande," *Mittheilungen des Instituts für österreichische Geschichtsforschung* 6 (1883) 541ff; L. Bréhier, "Les colonies d'Orientaux en Occident au commencement du Moyen Age (Ve–VIIIe siècles)," *Byzantinische Zeitschrift* 12 (1903) 1–39; J. Ebersolt, *Orient et Occident, recherches sur les influences byzantines et orientales en France avant les croisades*, Paris 1928; P. Lambrechts, "Le commerce des 'Syriens' en Gaule, du Haut-Empire à l'époque mérovingienne," *L'antiquité classique* 6 (1937) 35–61; L. Jalabert, "Les colonies chrétiennes d'Orientaux en Occident du Ve au VIIIe siècle," *Revue de l'Orient chrétien* 9 (1904) 96–106; and G. Wolfram, "Der Einfluss des Orients auf die frühmittelalterliche Kultur und die Christianisierung Lothringen," *Jahrb. der Gesellschaft für Lothringische Geschichte und Altertumskunde* 17 (1905) 318–352.

[15] Salvian *De gub. Dei* 4.69, p. 90, 3 (= PL 53, 87 B).

think that they helped Greek literary culture in the slightest degree to maintain itself.[16] Probably, religious contacts could have been established occasionally by Syrian traders, since certain of them, we are told, served as intermediaries between St. Simeon, the stylite of Antioch, and St. Genevieve of Paris.[17] The trade in relics could also have served as a medium for the importation of an Eastern hagiographical legend that later on acquired a literary value.[18] Again, it is not certain that these narratives were always composed in Greek, and the Syrian Iohannes, who translated for Gregory of Tours the legend of the Seven Sleepers of Ephesus, probably translated it from Syriac.[19]

Although men from the East were never more numerous in Gaul,[20] never was Greek literary culture less brilliant. Of all the texts collected by Pirenne to prove that the traditional encyclopedic culture of the laity persisted under the Merovingians,[21] none mentions the teaching of Greek. Caesarius of Arles, trained at Lérins, then a disciple of Pomerius,[22] did not know Greek,

[16] Cf. Bréhier, "Les colonies d'Orientaux," p. 18: "their purpose was to enrich themselves from trade and industry, and there is no evidence that they ever came to the West with the intention of propagating their ideas there." But Bréhier contradicts himself by devoting an entire chapter (pp. 30–39) to the influence of the East on the intellectual and moral culture of the West. On the importation by the Syrians of devotion to the cross, cf. Bréhier, *Les origines du crucifix dans l'art religieux* (Paris 1904).

[17] *Vita s. Genovefae* 27, ed. Krusch, *MGH, Script. rer. Merov.* 3, p. 226, 16: "quem aiunt sedule negotiatores euntes ac redeuntes de Genovefa interrogasse, quam etiam veneratione profusa salutasse et, ut eum in orationibus suis memorem haberet, poposcisse ferunt." The value of this evidence varies according to the date assigned to this life. Delehaye places it in the year 500, while Krusch proposes the eighth century. The purpose of the hagiographer was above all to show that Genevieve was at least as important a saint as Simeon Stylites of Antioch, whom she inspired with respect. This evidence at least establishes the fact that at the time of writing it was not unlikely for the reader to assume that such associations had existed in the days of Genevieve, that is, in the fifth century. The writer was after all a cultured person, who had read Hermas' *Pastor*. Cf. above, sec. 1 n. 25.

[18] For example, the famous legend of Alexis. Cf. Amiand, *La légende syriaque de s. Alexis*, Bibl. de l'école des Hautes Etudes, sciences philol. et hist., fasc. 79 (Paris 1889), p. xxxii.

[19] Gregory of Tours *In gloria mart.* 94, ed. Krusch, p. 552, 11: "passio eorum, quam Siro quodam interpretante in Latinum transtulimus," and *Passio septem Dormientium apud Ephesum* 12, Krusch, p. 853, 14. Cf. M. Bonnet, *Le latin de Grégoire de Tours* (diss. Paris 1890) 8 n. 3. On other Eastern legends, cf. Ebersolt, *Orient et Occident*, p. 36, and Salmon, *Le lectionnaire de Luxeuil*, p. LXXVI, who notes a case of liturgical transmission by Spain.

[20] Lambrechts, "Le commerce des Syriens," p. 43.

[21] H. Pirenne, "De l'état de l'instruction des laïques à l'époque mérovingienne," *RB* 46 (1934) 164–177. I admit, however, this theory of Pirenne's as against Roger's *L'enseignement des lettres classiques*, p. 86. Roger's theory is that public schools disappeared in Gaul around 420/430.

[22] Pomerius did not know Greek. His studies "utriusque bibliothecae," of which Ennodius speaks (*Epist.* 39.2, ed. Vogel, *MGH, Auct. ant.* 7, p. 38, 5), point to sacred and pagan writers, not to Greek and Latin writers. Cf. Schanz, vol. 4, 2, p. 556.

although there was perhaps a Greek colony in Arles.[23] Gregory of Tours's classical culture was likewise a purely Latin culture[24] and the numerous Hellenisms in his language must not lead us to think that he knew Greek.[25] We must avoid imagining, as the Abbé Tardi does, that Fortunatus himself knew Greek because he compares a poet to Pindar[26] and uses a few Greco-Latin rhetorical terms[27] or a number of ecclesiastical Hellenisms.[28] A text of Fortunatus has encouraged the belief that St. Radagunde read Greek writers, either in the original or in translation. She was nurtured, says Fortunatus, on all that was taught by Gregory and Basil, violent Athanasius and gentle Hilary, Ambrose, Jerome, Augustine, Sedulius, Orosius, Caesarius.[29] I see in this text merely a rhetorical enumeration of all the Fathers of the Church

---

23 The *Vita s. Caesarii* 19, ed. Krusch, *MGH, Script. rer. Merov.* 3, p. 463, 29: "Adiecit etiam atque compulit, ut laicorum popularitas psalmos et hymnos pararet, altaque et modulata voce instar clericorum alii Graece, alii Latine prosas antiphonasque cantarent, ut non haberent spatium in ecclesia fabulis occupari," in no sense proves that Caesarius had known Greek. This text applies to the liturgical use of Greek and probably does not even assume, according to Arnold, *Caesarius von Arelate und die gallische Kirche seiner Zeit* (Leipzig 1894) 533, and Bardy, "Formules liturgiques," p. 111 n. 1, the existence of a Greek colony at Arles. Cf. Schanz, vol. 4, 2, p. 314 n. 3 and pp. 556–564.

24 Cf. G. Kurth, "Grégoire de Tours et les études classiques au VIᵉ siècle," *Revue des questions historiques* 24 (1878) 586–593. Clotilda's talk to Clovis on the pagan gods, *Hist. Franc.* 2.20 (29), p. 90, 9ff, seems to me to have been taken from Tertullian *Apol.* 25.8. Like Gregory, he quotes Vergil *Aen.* 1.47.

25 Bonnet, *Le latin de Grégoire de Tours* (above, n. 19) 53 n. 5 and 209–225. Probably Gregory, *Hist. Franc.* 10.24, is conversing with Bishop Simon, a refugee from the East, and does not mention the presence of an interpreter. But the latter must have learned Latin in the course of his travels from Antioch to Tours!

26 Fortunatus *Carm.* 3.4.3, ed. Leo, *MGH, Auct. ant.* 4, p. 52, 13, and 9.7.9: "Pindarus Graius, meus inde Flaccus." Cf. Tardi, *Fortunat, étude sur un dernier représentant de la poésie latine dans la Gaule mérovingienne* (diss. Paris 1927) 54–55.

27 Fortunatus *Vita Martini*, praef. 1, ed. Leo, p.293, 3: "Nam ἐπιχειρήματα, ἐλλείψεις, διαιρέσεις, παρενθέσεις et reliqua orationibus dialectici et apud quos ceterae artes perplexis florent artibus, satagentes suis adfectare syrmatibus, soliti sunt adsuere vel proferre." Cf. *Epist.* 5.1.6, p. 102, 19: "Quid loquar de perihodis, epichirematibus, enthymemis syllogismisque perplexis? quo laborat quadrus Maro, quo rotundus Cicero," and *Praef.* 1, p. 1, 2–8.

28 Tardi, *Fortunat*, p. 55 and pp. 224–234.

29 Fortunatus *Carm.* 8.1.53ff:

> Cuius sunt epulae quidquid pia regula pangit,
>   quidquid Gregorius Basiliusque docent,
> acer Athanasius, quod lenis Hilarius edunt,
>   quos causae socios lux tenet una duos

. . . .

his alitur ieiuna cibis.

With many others, Ebersolt, *Orient et Occident*, p. 23, and Tardi, *Fortunat*, p. 43, also take these lines as accurate information on Radagunde's studies. Tardi, however, acknowledges that the epithets fail to characterize the work of several of these writers.

whose names were known to Fortunatus, and I do not think that it proves anything relating to the studies of Radagunde or Fortunatus. In fact, the same names—the energetic Athanasius and the famous Hilary, Gregory and Basil, and the Latin writers—reappear, decked out with other epithets, in a description of Paradise.[30] Furthermore, Fortunatus replied to Martin of Bracara, who had bestowed flowery eulogies on him, that he scarcely knew by name Plato, Aristotle, Chrysippus, or Pittacus and that he did not make any use of the great doctors: Hilary, *Gregory*, Ambrose, Augustine.[31] He gives us reason to think that, when he lists as philosophers Archytas, Pythagoras, Aratus, Cato, Plato, Chrysippus, Cleanthes, and as poets Homer and Menander, to show that the passage of time makes philosophy or poetry useless, he is merely developing a commonplace of the Schools.[32] Similarly, when he associates Homer with Vergil,[33] Pindar with Horace,[34] or when he makes Homer and Demosthenes, in contrast to Vergil and Cicero, the patrons of poetry and prose.[35] There is nothing in all this to prove any contact between Fortunatus and Greek literature, even through the medium of translation.

The same decline appears in the theological culture that was still so

[30] Fortunatus *Carm.* 5.3.35–40:

> Laetus agat sub clave Petri, per dogmata Pauli
> > inter sidereos luce micante choros,
> fortis Athanasius, qua clarus Hilarius adstant,
> > dives Martinus, suavis et Ambrosius,
> Gregorius radiat, sacer Augustinus inundat,
> > Basilius rutilat, Caesariusque micat.

On Basil, cf. also *Vita Martini* 4.664; and on Gregory, *Carm.* 9.6.6. The linking of the names of Athanasius and Hilary merely proves that Fortunatus knows them as the two major opponents of Arianism.

[31] Fortunatus *Carm.* 5.1.7, p. 102, 25: "Nam quod refertis, in litteris post Stoicam Peripateticam censuram me theologiae ac theoriae tirocinio mancipatum, agnosco quid amor faciat, cum et non merentes exornat; cur tamen, bone pater, in me reflectis quod tuum est ac de me publice profers quod tibi privatum est? Cum prima sint vobis nota et secunda domestica: nam Plato, Aristoteles, Chrysippus vel Pittacus cum mihi vix opinione noti sint nec legenti Hilarius, *Gregorius*, Ambrosius Augustinusque vel, si visione noti fierent, dormitanti . . ." All these names probably appeared in the letter from Martin of Bracara to which Fortunatus here replies.

[32] *Ibid.*, 7.12.25–28:

> Archyta, Pythagoras, Aratus, Cato, Plato, Chrysippus,
> > turba Cleantharum stulta favilla cubat.
> Quidve poema potest? Maro, Lysa, Menander, Homerus,
> > quorum nuda tabo membra sepulchra tegunt?

[33] *Ibid.*, 6.1a.5 and 7.8.25.

[34] *Ibid.*, 5.6.7 and 9.7.9.

[35] *Ibid.*, 8.1.3. Cf., however, a remote reference to *Iliad* 3.237 in Fortunatus *Carm.* 3.4.5: "non enim Polydeucen suae commendasset venae salientis ubertas, nisi Smyrnei fontis fatidico latice fuisset adtactus."

extensive in the case of Gennadius at the close of the fifth century. Avitus of Vienne, chancellor of the Burgundian kings, who also composed in Sigismond's name the letter to the Emperor Anastasius on the light that came from the East, was actually very ignorant of the most serious theological discussions that stirred the East. In his treatise on the heresy of Eutyches, where he claims to enlighten King Gundobad, he confuses Eutyches' errors with those of Nestorius, decrees the orthodoxy of a monophysite formula, and blames the attitude of the orthodox patriarch who had refused to support it. Such aberrations are to be explained, according to Monsignor Duchesne,[36] only by the influence of some monophysite, either a cleric or a diplomat, who had come from Constantinople to the Burgundian court and had deluded Avitus' intelligence. Similarly, later on, when the quarrel of the Three Chapters was to bring into opposition the Eastern Church and the Western Church, Bishop Nizier of Trèves would pronounce the anathema on Justinian, wrongly attributing to him, on the word of the priest Lactantius, probably a Syrian monophysite, the errors of Nestorius and Eutyches.[37]

In this general ignorance there appear only a few glimmers. The Frankish King Thierry, son of Clovis, had the exceptional opportunity to witness the arrival of a former physician from the court of Byzantium. This was Anthimus, who, after his banishment, composed for his own use a book on medical cookery, the *De observatione ciborum*.[38] A large number of prescriptions from Byzantine medicine are reproduced in this book,[39] and several barbarian physicians were to complete this instructive manual in Constantinople itself.[40]

It appears that at the end of the sixth century there still persisted at Toulouse at least a pedantry that boasted of knowing Greek. This is revealed by the mysterious works of Virgilius of Toulouse. His numerous comments on the Greek language are most frequently lacking in content or else are quite elementary.[41] He undertakes to expound Greek metrics but discusses the

---

[36] Avitus *Epist.* 2–3 (= *Contra Eutychianam haeresim libri II*), *MGH, Auct. ant.* 6, pp. 15–29. Cf. Duchesne, *L'église au VIe siècle*, p. 503 and n. 4.

[37] *Epist. Austras.* 7, *MGH, Epist. aevi Merov.* 1, p. 118, 21ff. Cf. Duchesne, *L'église au VIe siècle*, pp. 533–534.

[38] Ed. V. Rose, *Anecd. Graeca et Graeco-Latina* 2 (Berlin 1870), pp. 43–98. Cf. Schanz, vol. 4, 2, pp. 291–293.

[39] He refers, p. 65, 2, to the *praecepta auctorum medicinalium* and, p. 78, 6, to *auctores nostri*. Other references to the *auctores*: p. 75, 9; p. 77, 3; p. 79, 1; p. 82, 12; p. 94, 7 and 10.

[40] In Gregory of Tours *Hist. Franc.* 10.15, ed. Krusch, p. 426, 26, the *archiater* Reovalis declares: "Tunc ego, sicut quondam apud urbem Constantinopolitanam medicos agere conspexeram, incisis testiculis puerum sanum genetrici maestae restitui." Cf. Rose, *Anecd. Graeca*, p. 46.

[41] Virgilius of Toulouse, *Epist.* 1, ed. Huemer (Leipzig 1886), p. 5, 7: "denique cum Hebraeam Graecamve transedere in Latinam linguam volueris, hanc omnibus modis,

subject only by preterition.[42] He claims that he quotes Homer,[43] Lupus of Athens,[44] Origen the Athenian,[45] Virgilius of Asia, born in Cappadocia,[46] Gregory of Egypt, who wrote 3,000 books on Greek history,[47] Balapsidus of Nicomedia.[48] These fanciful names can only be the pseudonyms of the various masters of this school in Toulouse, similar to the mythological names that the poets in Sidonius' days were already[49] giving each other. The majority of these masters, as is proved by the text of these quotations, were Latin grammarians. But it has not been noticed that at least one of them, Balapsidus of Nicomedia, was a Neoplatonic philosopher. In fact the *incipit* of his book is nothing other than the lines from the *Aeneid* on the soul of the universe, which had previously provoked so many commentaries.[50] Such is the doctrine that Virgilius of Toulouse calls "our law," and the types of books that he claims to read in Greek. In Virgilius of Toulouse himself there appear besides some echoes of this philosophy. He refers to the steps of the ladder that, according to the allegory already used by Boethius,[51] leads from empirical philosophy to theoretical philosophy.[52] He recognizes the division

---

loquelis, orationibus syllabisque latiorem offendes"; and *Epist.* 4, p. 21, 21: "*hele* enim apud Hebraeos deus erit, unde et apud Graecos helium sol dicitur."

[42] *Epist.* 4, p. 25, 6: "de Graecis autem metris, quorum natura dissimilis et longe diversa, nihil hic disputare necessarium reor cum Latinum opus efficiam."

[43] *Ibid.*, p. 44, 20; 49, 11.

[44] *Ibid.*, *Epist.* 3, p. 141, 28.

[45] *Ibid.*, *Epist.* 11 and 14, p. 75, 5 and p. 85, 23.

[46] *Ibid.*, p. 70, 16; 77, 14; 88, 16; 91, 4; 122, 23; 125, 22; 146, 11.

[47] *Ibid.*, *Epist.* 15, p. 92, 5: "Erat apud Aegyptum Gregorius Graecis studiis valde deditus, qui tria milia librorum de Graecorum historiis conscripsit."

[48] *Ibid.*, p. 95, 7: "Erat apud Nicomediam Balapsidus nuper vita functus, qui nostrae legis libros, quos ego in Graeco audio sermone, me iubente vertit in Latinum, quorum est principium: *in principio caelum terramque mare omniaque astra spiritus intus fovet.*"

[49] For example, Sidonius and Lampridius addressed poems to each other under the pseudonyms of Phoebus and Orpheus. Cf. Sidonius *Epist.* 8.11.3, p. 139, 10: "hic me quondam, ut inter amicos ioca, Phoebum vocabat ipse a nobis vatis Odrysii nomine acceptus," and the poem that follows.

[50] Vergil *Aen.* 6.724–726:
> *Principio caelum* ac *terras* camposque liquentes
> lucentemque globum lunae Titaniaque *astra*
> *spiritus intus* alit.

Winter, *De doctrinae Neoplatonicae . . . vestigiis,* p. 60, has shown that Augustine (*De civ. Dei* 10.30; 13.19; 14.3, 5, and 8; 21.3 and 13; 22.26) resorted to a Neoplatonic commentary on the same passage in Vergil. Bitsch, *De Platonicorum quaestionibus quibusdam Vergilianis,* conjectured, without any valid reason, that Marius Victorinus was the author of this lost commentary. Cf. also Macrobius *In Somn. Scip.* 1.14.14, ed. Eyssenhardt, p. 530, 12.

[51] See below, p. 296.

[52] Virgilius of Toulouse *Epist.* 1, p. 3, 10: "Haec sapientia biformis est, aetrea telleaque, hoc est humilis et sublimis: humilis quidem, quae de humanis rebus tractat; sublimis vero

of philosophy into physical, ethical, logical, to which, in men, the three terms *anima*, *mens*, and *ratio* correspond.[53] In conclusion, he attaches a keen interest to *mathesis*, while declaring, in his concern for orthodoxy, that he does not believe in astrology.[54]

Thus, while the Greek Fathers were scarcely known in Gaul apart from a few translations and, except for Evagrius Ponticus, did not exert any profound influence, the influence of Plotinus and Porphyry expanded in the age of the Emperor Anthemius. Despite the break that resulted later between Gaul and the East, we can observe the obscure survival, until the end of the sixth century, of a veritable Neoplatonic school. In combatting Hellenism, the monks aimed to destroy pagan philosophy. But before achieving this result, they had deprived themselves of the illumination of Greek theology. After Africa of the Vandals, it was Merovingian Gaul that sank into ignorance.

---

quae ea, quae supra hominem sunt, internat ac pandit. Nemo sane in hac re carpat pada, quod veluti praeposterato telleam aetreae ordine antetulerim, cum scandentium hic mos sit, ut ab inferioribus incipiant et ad superiora scalatim perfendiant."

[53] *Ibid.*, *Epist.* 4, p. 23.

[54] *Ibid.*, p. 22, 9.

PART THREE

THE RENAISSANCE OF HELLENISM
UNDER THE OSTROGOTHS

Chapter 6

THE EAST TO THE RESCUE
OF PAGAN CULTURE:
BOETHIUS

INTRODUCTION

While Hellenic culture was dying in Africa and Gaul in the sixth century, it produced a veritable literary renaissance in Italy during the reign of Theodoric.

The fact was that the prestige of the Byzantine emperor was still immense in the peninsula.[1] To be sure, along with Anthemius and Julius Nepos, he vainly tried to set a Greek on the throne as emperor of the West. But Odoacer had no sooner deposed Romulus Augustulus, the last emperor of the West, who was not recognized by Byzantium, than he attempted to have his power de facto recognized by the emperor of the East. A mission sent by the Roman senate brought to Zeno the imperial insignia of the West,[2] and begged him to grant Odoacer the title of patrician and the administration of the diocese of Italy.[3] Equipped with this title, Flavius Odoacer was declared governor in the name of the emperor, ordered statues to be erected to him in Rome, and struck money with his effigy, while the emperor on his return authorized the designation of consuls for the West.[4]

[1] Besides the general works, consult, on the political relations between Ostrogoths and Byzantines: A. Gaudenzi, *Sui rapporti tra l'Italia e l'impero d'Oriente fra gli anni 476–554 d. C.* (Bologna 1886); Th. Mommsen, "Ostgothische Studien," *Neues Archiv* 14 (1889) 223–249 and 451–544; F. Martroye, *L'Occident à l'époque byzantine, Goths et Vandales* (Paris 1904); J. Sundwall, *Abhandlungen zur Geschichte des ausgehenden Römertums* (Helsinki 1919), particularly the individual notices in chap. 3 on officialdom among the Ostrogoths; and *PW* s.vv. Anastasios, Athalaricus, Theodahad, Theoderich. It was especially N. Reitter, *Der Glaube an die Fortdauer des römischen Reiches im Abendlande während des V. und VI. Jahrhunderts* (diss. Münster 1900), who showed clearly how the unity of the empire survived theoretically into the age of the Ostrogoths.

[2] Anonymus of Valois, *pars posterior, MGH, Auct. ant.* 9, p. 322, no. 64.

[3] Malchus, frag. 18, *FHG* 4, p. 118.

[4] Cf. Lot, *Les destinées de l'Empire*, p. 98 and n. 79, and Martroye, *L'Occident à l'époque byzantine*, pp. 5–7. For more details on the relations between Odoacer and the emperor of the East, cf. Kleissel, *Odoacer in seinen Beziehungen zum byzantinischen Kaiser Zeno* (Progr. Görz 1883), and E. Loncao, *Fondazione del regno di Odoacre e suoi rapporti con l'Oriente* (Scansano 1908).

273

Theodoric, after defeating Odoacer and becoming master of Italy, tried in turn to secure the emperor's goodwill. He sent him embassy after embassy until peace was made with Anastasius.[5] By virtue of this treaty, Theodoric, King of the Ostrogoths, governed the Romans of Italy in the capacity of a patrician designated by the emperor, struck money with the imperial effigy, and dated his acts from the consuls. He could designate the consul of the West on condition that he was a Roman.[6] In point of fact, the independence of his foreign policy unleashed the war with Anastasius, but Theodoric, concerned about the coalition between the Franks and the Byzantines, soon resumed relations with Anastasius through letters in which he recognized his suzerainty and insisted on the unity of the Empire.[7] Relations became still better when the Emperor Justin consented to acknowledge Eutharic as heir presumptive to Theodoric and to name him consul for the year 519.[8] Then Justin chose two men from the West, Boethius' two sons, as consuls for the year 522.[9] The schism that had split the Roman Church and the Greek Church since Gelasius I became Pontiff in 492 gave way to the union in 519.[10]

It was the era of the triumph of Hellenism in Italy. No longer was it a matter merely of the political refugees like Artemidorus or the physician Anthimus, whom Theodoric had welcomed as members of the imperial circle.[11] Now it was Boethius, the great Hellenist, and his father-in-law Symmachus who enjoyed the favor both of the emperor and of the king of the Ostrogoths.[12] Theodoric himself asks Cassiodorus to draw up for him a course in philosophy. He thinks he is Plato's King-Philosopher[13] and makes his daughter learn Greek.[14] His cousin Theodahad, who will be one of his

---

[5] Anonymus of Valois, *pars posterior*, MGH, *Auct. ant.* 9, pp. 316 and 322, nos. 53, 57, 64.

[6] Cf. Lot, *Les destinées*, p. 111, and Mommsen, "Ostgothische Studien," pp. 223ff.

[7] Cassiodorus *Variae* 1.1, MGH, *Auct. ant.* 12, p. 10, 8ff, particularly: "Vos enim estis regnorum omnium pulcherrimum decus, vos totius orbis salutare praesidium, quos ceteri dominantes iure suspiciunt."

[8] *Ibid.*, 8.1. Cf. Lot, *Les destinées*, p. 127.

[9] Boethius *De consolatione philosophiae* 2, pr. 3, ed. Peiper, p. 30, 27.

[10] Anonymus of Valois, p. 326, nos. 85–87. Cf. Martroye, *L'Occident*, pp. 144ff.

[11] On Artemidorus, cf. Cass. *Var.* 1.43. On Anthimus, cf. Schanz, vol. 4, 2, pp. 291ff.

[12] See below, sec. 3 n. 129, and pp. 322ff.

[13] Athalaric writes to Cassiodorus (*Var.* 9.24.8, p. 290, 19), speaking of Theodoric: "Nam cum esset publica cura vacuatus, sententias prudentium a tuis fabulis exigebat . . . Stellarum cursus, maris sinus, fontium miracula rimator acutissimus inquirebat, ut rerum naturis diligentius perscrutatis quidam purpuratus videretur esse philosophus." These last words inform us that Theodoric prided himself on being the king-philosopher according to Plato's formula, *Republic* 5.473c, quoted by Boethius *De cons. philos.* 1, pr. 4, ed. Peiper, p. 11, 16. Ennodius *Paneg. Theod.*, ed. Vogel, p. 204, 29, flatters this mania by telling him: "Educavit te in gremio civilitatis Graecia praesaga venturi."

[14] Cass. *Var.* 11.1.6, p. 328, 18, says of Amalasuntha: "Atticae facundiae claritate diserta est."

successors, has the reputation of being a Neoplatonist and glories in scheming for the office of senator in Constantinople.[15]

Hellenists were not scarce in Italy at this period, notably among diplomats and physicians,[16] but the real artisan of the renaissance in literature and science is Boethius.[17] He had a clear consciousness that Hellenic literature alone could help to raise the level of studies in the West, and he tried to establish a Latin scholasticism similar to that which then prevailed in the Hellenic East.

Traditional opinion has it that Boethius went to Athens. This legend has no basis. It appears for the first time in the *De disciplina scholarium*, whose spuriousness and lack of historical value no longer keep anyone in doubt,[18] and it is astonishing that it is still credited.[19] The only indication that appears at the root of this legend is a passage in the famous letter in which Theodoric orders two clocks from Boethius for the king of the Burgundians: "Hoc te multa eruditione saginatum ita nosse didicimus, ut artes, quas exercent vulgariter

---

[15] Procopius *Bell. Goth.* 1.3, ed. G. Dindorf (Bonn 1833), *CSHB*, part 2, 2, p. 16, 21: λόγων μὲν Λατίνων μεταλαχὼν καὶ δογμάτων Πλατονικῶν.

[16] Cass. *Var.* 5.40 and 8.22, p. 167, 7 and p. 254, 8, praises the ambassador Cyprianus, as well as his sons, for speaking Gothic, Latin, and Greek: "instructus trifariis linguis." Cf. *Var.* 2.3.3, in praise of the orator Felix: "Rerum quoque naturalium causas subtilissime perscrutatus, Cecropii dogmatis Attico se melle saginavit." Ennodius in his works (ed. Vogel, *MGH, Auct. ant.* 7, Berlin 1885) also praises for their Hellenic culture Avianus and his father Faustus (p. 14, 33 and p. 80, 13), Messala (p. 270, 16), and the deacon Helpidius (p. 275, 8). It is difficult to know to what extent these eulogies are deserved. With regard to Pomerius (p. 38, 5), called "utriusque bibliothecae fibula," this expression denotes his knowledge of sacred and profane literature, and not of Greek and Latin literature. Translators of medical works were also numerous in the vicinity of Ravenna during the first half of the sixth century, as is proved by the translations of Oribasius' Συναγωγαὶ ἰατρικαί and Rufus of Ephesus' *De podagra*. Cf. H. Moerland, *Die lateinischen Oribasiusübersetzungen, Symbolae Osloenses*, fasc. suppl. 5 (Oslo 1932) 189–194, and his edition of Rufus' *De podagra, ibid.*, fasc. suppl. 6 (Oslo 1933) 1–39. Ravenna was perhaps, also the nursing-ground for several of the numerous later translations of Hippocrates.

[17] I here repeat the views briefly stated in my article "Boèce et l'école d'Alexandrie," *MEFR* 52 (1935) 185–223. These views have been favorably received by Father Chenu, *Revue des sciences philosophiques et théologiques* 26 (1937) 389, and by P. de Labriolle, *Histoire de l'église depuis les origines jusqu'à nos jours* (under the direction of A. Fliche and V. Martin) 4 (Paris 1937) 566. Certain paragraphs are reproduced textually, but I extend my research to all of Boethius' works and to all the Greek writers that he uses. I shall give the references to Peiper's edition (Leipzig 1871) for the *De consolatione philosophiae* and the *Opuscula theologica*. The *De consolatione philosophiae* has been edited separately by A. Fortescue and G. Smith (London 1925) and by G. Weinberger, *CSEL* 67 (1934).

[18] *PL* 64, 1232 B: "Annis duobus de viginti Athenis convalui." Cf. Porcher's viewpoints, *Le "De disciplina scolarium," traité du XIIIᵉ siècle faussement attribué à Boèce* (Ecole des Chartes 1921).

[19] For example, R. Bonnard, "L'éducation scientifique de Boèce," *Speculum* 4 (1929) 199, determinedly accepts this legend, of which no more mention is even made by Pauly-Wissowa, Schanz, and Manitius.

nescientes, in ipso disciplinarum fonte potaveris; sic enim Atheniensium scholas longe positus introisti, sic palliatorum choris miscuisti togam, ut Graecorum dogmata doctrinam feceris esse Romanam."[20] The rest of the passage clearly shows that Theodoric here refers to Boethius' translations and commentaries. The words "Atheniensium scholas longe positus introisti" mean that Boethius, *in spite of the distance*, entered into the schools of Athens, without specifying that he ever went there. These words arouse our curiosity without satisfying it.

Only the evidence of Boethius himself and his works can direct our inquiry. In the letter to his father-in-law Symmachus that serves as a preface to the *De arithmetica*, Boethius indicates what the purpose of his scientific work is. He undertakes it at Symmachus' request[21] in order to make the Latins acquainted with the riches of Greek literature.[22] Such a work was to make an unfavorable impression on those who did not know both languages, but Boethius, still a young man, depended on Symmachus' prestige to silence the detractors.[23] His arithmetic was to be a paraphrase of the Greek *Arithmetic* by Nicomachus of Gerasa. It would abridge the lengthy sections, clarify the obscurities of the Greek text.[24] Boethius explains that this *Arithmetic* is his first literary effort.[25] If he begins thus, it is because arithmetic is the first of the four disciplines of the *mathesis*.[26] These disciplines constituted the *quadrivium* that led to the study of philosophy. Boethius then proclaims his intention to treat in a given order the entire cycle of the sciences that lead to philosophy: arithmetic, music, geometry, astronomy.[27]

Once this introductory work is completed, Boethius proceeds to the study of philosophy. He does not consider this a useless study, even though he devotes his time to it when he is granted the consulship. Rome has already vanquished the political hegemony, and now it disputes with Greece the cultural hegemony.[28] To attain this end, there is no other way except to take

---

[20] Cass. *Var.* 1.45.3, ed. Mommsen, *MGH, Auct. ant.* 13, p. 40, 5ff.

[21] Boethius *Epist. ad Symm.*, ed. Friedlein, *De Arithmetica* (Leipzig 1867), p. 3, 17: "id opus, quod sapientiae inventa persequitur, non auctoris, sed alieno incumbit iudicio."

[22] *Ibid.*, p. 3, 10: "quae ex Graecarum opulentia litterarum in Romanae orationis thesaurum sumpta convexerimus."

[23] *Ibid.*, p. 4, 23: "Qua in re mihi alieni quoque iudicii lucra quaeruntur, cum tu utrarumque peritissimus litterarum possis Graiae orationis expertibus quantum de nobis iudicare audeant, sola tantum pronuntiatione praescribere."

[24] *Ibid.*, p. 4, 27–p. 5, 4.

[25] *Ibid.*, p. 5, 22: "laboris mei primitias."

[26] *Ibid.*, p. 5, 6.

[27] *Ibid.*, pp. 7–12. On this order, cf. Schmidt, *Quaestiones de musicis scriptoribus Romanis*, p. 11.

[28] Boethius *In Categorias* 2, *prol.* (*PL* 64, 201 B): "Etsi nos curae officii consularis impediunt quo minus in his studiis omne otium plenamque operam consumimus, pertinere tamen videtur hoc ad aliquam rei publicae curam, elucubratae rei doctrina cives instruere.

from Greece its taste for dialectic discussion, which is the leaven of science.[29] Greek logic is difficult, but Boethius feels particularly well qualified to perform the work of translation. He believes he understands both languages, Greek and Latin,[30] and occasionally boasts of making Aristotle's text clearer, at the expense of some slight inaccuracy.[31] The course of philosophical studies that he gravely expounds to the reader is an ambitious one:[32] translating with commentary, in a given order unknown to previous Latin translators, the entire corpus of Aristotle's work on logic, ethics, and physics; then translating with commentary all Plato, and finally demonstrating that the two philosophies are fundamentally in agreement. This was such an extensive syllabus that Boethius, put to death at the age of forty-four, could achieve only a slight part of it: the translation and the commentary of Aristotle's work on logic.[33] The partial and accidental failure of his attempt must not make us forget the amplitude of his views. Is he original, as he assures us, in relation to his Latin predecessors? And, in the affirmative sense, from which Greek writers does he borrow the idea and the content of his scientific or philosophical commentaries?

Nec male de civibus meis merear, si cum prisca hominum virtus urbium ceterarum ad hanc unam rem publicam, dominationem imperiumque transtulerit, ego id saltem quod reliquum est, Graecae sapientiae artibus mores nostrae civitatis instruxero."

[29] Boethius *In Top. Cic.* 5 (*PL* 64, 1152 B): "Ipsa enim Graeciae philosophia numquam in honore tantum fuisset, nisi doctissimorum contentionibus dissensionibusque crevisset; quam ob rem hortor omnes, qui facere id possunt, ut eius quoque generis laudem iam languenti Graeciae eripiant et transferant in hanc urbem, sicut reliquas omnes, quae quidem erant expetendae, studio atque industria sua maiores nostri transtulere."

[30] Boethius *De interpretatione, ed. sec.*, ed. Meiser (Leipzig 1880), p. 70, 22: "nos id quantum Latinitas passa est transferre diu multumque laborantes hoc solo potuimus, Graeca vero oratione luculentius dictum est; ita enim habet τὰ δὲ τὸν πέριξ. Quod qui Graecae linguae peritus est, quantum melius Graeca oratione sonet agnoscit."

[31] *Ibid., ed. prima*, p. 73, 7.

[32] *Ibid., ed. sec.*, p. 79, 9: "Mihi autem, si potentior divinitatis adnuerit favor, haec fixa sententia est, ut quamquam fuerint praeclara ingenia, quorum labor ac studium multa de his quae nunc quoque tractamus Latinae linguae contulerit, non tamen quendam quodam modo ordinem filumque et dispositione disciplinarum gradus ediderunt, ego omne Aristotelis opus, quodcumque in manus venerit, in Romanum stilum vertens eorum omnium commenta Latina oratione perscribam, ut si quid ex logicae artis subtilitate, ex moralis gravitate peritiae, ex naturalis acumine veritatis ab Aristotele conscriptum sit, id omne ordinatum transferam atque etiam quodam lumine commentationis inlustrem omnesque Platonis dialogos vertendo vel etiam commentando in Latinam redigam formam; his peractis non equidem contempserim Aristotelis Platonisque sententias in unam quodam modo revocare concordiam eosque non ut plerique dissentire in omnibus, sed in plerisque et his in philosophia maximis consentire demonstrem."

[33] On the date of Boethius' birth, see Usener, *Anecdoton Holderi* (Bonn 1877) 40.

1. Boethius' Scientific Works

Boethius' *De arithmetica* is not a commentary on Apuleius' *Arithmetic*[1] but a new adaptation of Nicomachus of Gerasa's Ἀριθμητικὴ εἰσαγωγή, intended to rival Apuleius' *Arithmetic*. Miekley has already shown that Boethius borrowed from the same work, compiled with Nicomachus' *Enchiridion* and the lost Περὶ μουσικῆς, the contents of the first book of his *De musica*. For instance, the historical account of the discovery of the musical chords or the theory of the harmony of the spheres is plagiarized from Nicomachus, and the differences in detail between the two texts are due either to a mistake or to an intelligent addition by Boethius in the transcription.[2] It was in all probability from Nicomachus' Περὶ μουσικῆς that Boethius took the Greek text of the decree of Sparta relating to Timotheus of Miletus, which he quotes in his prologue; for both texts attribute to Timotheus the invention of the eleventh chord.[3] It does not seem likely, in fact, that this entire prologue on the ethical usefulness of music stems only from a Latin source, even if certain examples appear in Varro, and Miekley was already inclined to assume a Greek source.[4] When Boethius borrows some detail from a writer other than Nicomachus, he takes care to indicate it. His only originality consists in inserting at the end of a chapter a reference to the Latin writer Albinus, at the same time declining to follow him,[5] and in advising that, in a forthcoming book, there would be extensive expositions on all the points where Ptolemy's musical theory did not agree with that of Nicomachus.[6] Book 5 contains in fact an exposition of the musical theory of Ptolemy's *Harmonics*, which is at the same time a criticism of the purely rationalistic music of the Pythagoreans

[1] A lost work, whose existence is attested by Cassiodorus *Institutiones*, ed. Mynors, p. 140, 17.

[2] G. Miekley, *De Boethii libri de musica primi fontibus* (diss. Jena 1898), *passim*. On music in Boethius, cf. O. Paul, *Boetius und die griechische Harmonik* (Leipzig 1772); R. Bragard, "L'harmonie des sphères selon Boèce," *Speculum* 4 (1929) 206–213; L. Schrade, "Die Stellung der Musik in der Philosophie des Boethius," *Archiv für Geschichte der Philosophie* 41 (1932) 368–400, who warns (p. 374) that he is writing from a doctrinal viewpoint, not from that of literary history.

[3] Boethius *De musica*, p. 182, 7–p. 183, 10. On Timotheus as inventor of the eleventh chord, cf. *ibid.*, p. 209, 1, and *Excerpta ex Nicomacho*, ed. Jan, from the *Musici scriptores Graeci* (Leipzig 1895), p. 274, 5.

[4] Miekley, *De Boethii . . . fontibus*, pp. 24–29. Note particularly that, with reference to the anecdote about Pythagoras calming a drunken youth, Boethius, p. 185, 10–17, asserts that he has two different versions. The second one is furnished by the passage in Cicero's *De consiliis* quoted by Augustine *Contra Iulianum* 5.5.23 (*PL* 44, 797), but the first version must be of Greek origin.

[5] Boethius *De mus.* 1.12 and 26, p. 199, 14 and p. 218, 22: "Albinus autem earum nomina Latina oratione interpretatus est . . . sed nobis in alieno opere non erit immorandum."

[6] *Ibid.*, 1.5–6 and 32; 2.18 and 27 (p. 193, 2; 194, 15; 222, 27; 249, 21; 260, 17).

and the purely sensory music of Aristoxenes.[7] On points in which Nicomachus and Ptolemy disagree, Boethius definitively declares for Ptolemy.

As he had commented on Nicomachus' arithmetic and Nicomachus' and Ptolemy's music, Boethius wrote a *Geometry* following Euclid's *Elements* and an *Astronomy* in line with Ptolemy's *Almagest*.[8] These lost writings, the editing of which was certainly the work of Boethius, and fragments of which, as will be apparent, were preserved by Cassiodorus,[9] show the writers whom Boethius had consulted for the various disciplines. Is it possible to determine in which intellectual climate these writers were honored and commented on and studied in this precise order? We should then know where Boethius acquired his scientific culture and whom he expected to be the mainspring of the renaissance in Latin literature.

The synthesis of the Pythagorean doctrines had previously been attempted by Iamblichus in his Συναγωγὴ τῶν Πυθαγορείων δογμάτων, of which Book 4 was a commentary on Nicomachus' *Introduction to Arithmetic*, and Books 8, 9, 10 were devoted respectively to music, geometry, astronomy.[10] As these three books are lost, it is not possible to know what writers Iamblichus followed. But it will be observed that Boethius, in his *De musica*, repeats several of the musical theorems that Iamblichus had enunciated in his commentary on Nicomachus.[11] As for Ptolemy's Ἁρμονικά, it had been the subject of a commentary by Porphyry.[12] But it was particularly among the Neoplatonists

---

[7] *Ibid.*, 5.3, p. 354. Cf. Miekley, *De Boethii . . . fontibus*, pp. 4–5.

[8] Cass. *Var.* 1.45.4, ed. Mommsen, *MGH, Auct. ant.* 12, p. 40, 11: "Translationibus enim tuis Pythagoras musicus, Ptolomaeus astronomus leguntur Itali, Nicomachus arithmeticus, geometricus Euclides audiuntur Ausonii. Plato theologus, Aristoteles logicus Quirinali voce disceptant. Mechanicum etiam Archimedem Latialem Siculis reddidisti." On astronomy, cf. in addition Boethius *De cons. philos.* 2, pr. 7, ed. Peiper, p. 44, 13: "Huius igitur tam exiguae in mundo regionis quarta fere portio est, sicut *Ptolemaeo probante didicisti*, quae nobis cognitis animantibus incolatur," quoting Ptolemy *Synt. magna* 2.1, ed. Heiberg, p. 88, 3, and R. Bonnaud, "Notes sur l'astrologie latine au VIᵉ siècle," pp. 562–570. It will be noted that Boethius *De cons. philos.* 3, pr. 12, ed. Peiper, p. 88, 3: "cum Platone sanciente didiceris," uses a similar formula to refer to one of his previous commentaries. Cf. below, p. 303. I think it probable that Boethius paraphrased a work by Archimedes, for at the same period, in the East, Eutocius wrote a commentary on Archimedes. Cf. Brunet and Mieli, *Histoire des Sciences*, p. 924 and p. 365 n. 7.

[9] See below, pp. 350–354. In addition, genuine fragments of Boethius are used in the apocryphal *Geometries* that bear his name. Cf. Schanz, vol. 4, 2, p. 154.

[10] Cf. Zeller, *Die Philosophie der Griechen* (3rd ed., Leipzig 1881), vol. 3, 2, 2, p. 681 n. 2.

[11] Cf. Iamblichus *In Nicomachi arithmeticam introductionem*, ed. Pistelli (Leipzig 1894), p. 53, 1–p. 55, 5, and p. 55, 6–26, and Boethius *De mus.*, ed. Friedlein, p. 237, 28–p. 240, 8, and p. 240, 9–22. Other similarities may be found in the *Index nominum* in Pistelli's edition s.v. Boetius.

[12] Ed. Ingemar Duering (Göteborg 1932). It will be observed, however, that Boethius *De mus.* 5.4 supports Ptolemy's notion that there is a quantitative and not a qualitative

of Alexandria that the study of these sciences was encouraged and that these writers were considered as classics.[13] At the close of the fourth century Theon of Alexandria revised Euclid's *Elements* and wrote a commentary on Ptolemy's *Almagest*.[14] At the beginning of the sixth century Nicomachus' *Arithmetic* was the subject of a commentary in Alexandria by Asclepius[15] and Iohannes Philoponus.[16] Both were disciples of Ammonius, the distinguished philosopher and mathematician of that time. He had made this work at least the subject of an oral course[17] and had likewise written a commentary on the *Almagest*,[18] while his brother Heliodorus composed an *Introduction to the Almagest*.[19] It is a curious fact to note that the generation of Ammonius' disciples was precisely contemporary with Boethius.

2. BOETHIUS' WORKS ON LOGIC

This comment will acquire a unique significance if it is confirmed by a study of Boethius' works on logic. Here too it is certain that, if Boethius knew the Latin commentators, it was nevertheless almost exclusively the Greeks that he used. Just as he never really used Albinus' *Music* or *Geometry*, he even questioned whether Albinus ever wrote a *Dialectic*.[1] Nothing shows Boethius' wish to compete with Marius Victorinus better than his commentary on Porphyry's *Isagoge*. In the first edition, where he was following Victorinus' translation, Boethius underscores an inaccuracy on Victorinus' part with regard to Porphyry, even if it is a deliberate correction.[2] Very often he taxes

---

difference between low and high notes. Porphyry, on the other hand, criticized this theory of Ptolemy's. Cf. Wallis' edition, p. 186.

[13] On the last Greek school in Alexandria, cf. F. Schemmel, "Die Hochschule von Alexandria," pp. 438–457, and M. Meyerhof, "La fin de l'école d'Alexandrie d'après quelques auteurs arabes," *Archeion* 15 (1933) 1–15.

[14] Cf. Brunet and Mieli, *Hist. des Sciences*, p. 923 and n. 17.

[15] Cf. Zeller (above, n. 10), p. 843 n. 1, and *PW* s.v. Asklepios aus Tralles.

[16] Ed. Hoche (Leipzig 1864/1867). Cf. Brunet and Mieli, *Hist. des Sciences*, p. 963 n. 21 and *PW* s.v. Joannes Philoponos, 1792.

[17] Cf. Zeller (above, n. 10), p. 830 n. 1, referring to Philopon *In Nicom.*, ed. Hoche, pp. 7ff.

[18] Damascius *Vit. Isid.* 79, *apud* Photius, cod. 181 (*PG* 103, 531 C).

[19] Cf. Brunet and Mieli, *Hist. des Sciences*, p. 962 n. 16. It will be observed that Ammonius' teacher, Proclus, who wrote a commentary on Book 1 of Euclid's *Elements* and various astronomical treatises, began his studies at Alexandria.

[1] Boethius *De interpretatione, ed. sec.*, ed. Meiser, p. 4, 3: "Albinus quoque de isdem rebus scripsisse perhibetur, cuius ego geometricos quidem libros editos scio, de dialectica vero diu multumque quaesitos reperire non valui; sive igitur ille omnino tacuit, nos praetermissa dicemus, sive aliquid scripsit, nos quoque docti viri imitati studium in eadem laude versabimur." On Albinus' *De musica*, cf. above, sec. 1 n. 5.

[2] Boethius *In Isag., ed. prima*, 1.12, ed. Brandt, *CSEL* 48 (Vienna 1906), p. 34, 12–p. 35,

him with inexactitude[3] or obscurity.[4] He does not even hesitate to consider that Victorinus wrongly interpreted a passage in a text of Porphyry that differed from his own.[5] The mistakes that he attributes to Victorinus' translation are so numerous that he decides, for his *editio secunda*, to make his own retranslation of Porphyry with the most scrupulous concern for accuracy, yet apologizing for not producing a more elegant translation.[6] Similarly, he undertakes to write a commentary on Cicero's *Topica* only because he considers Victorinus' commentary on this work inadequate.[7] In the *In Categorias*, Boethius does not mention a single Latin commentator. If he names Praetextatus and Albinus in his commentary *De interpretatione*, it is to say that the former plagiarizes Themistius, that the latter's work on logic is lost, and that in any case neither of them had translated or commented on the entire series of the logical treatises of the *Organon*.[8] Lastly, he takes care to emphasize that his *De syllogismo hypothetico* is a novelty in Rome, for no one has hitherto treated this subject in Latin.[9]

On the other hand, Boethius quotes a host of Greek commentators, but it would be a mistake to think that he knows them all by direct contact. Here is the evidence. At the beginning of the *De divisione*, Boethius mentions his sources: "quam magnos studiosis adferat fructus scientia dividendi, quamque apud Peripateticam disciplinam semper haec fuerit in honore notitia, docet et Andronici diligentissimi senis De divisione liber editus et hic idem a Plotino gravissimo philosopho comprobatus, et in libri Platonis, qui Sophistes inscribitur, commentariis a Porphyrio repetitus."[10] Of all these sources,

---

6. Victorinus translated σχήματα by *genera* and not *figuras*, as though it were a question of the εἴδη ῥητορικῆς. Boethius emphasizes this and concludes: "sed quoniam de tertio genere tractaturus est, Victorini *culpam* vel, si ita contingit, emendationem aequi bonique faciamus."

[3] *Ibid.*, 1.21, p. 64, 8: "hic tamen a Victorino videtur erratum." Cf. p. 23, 17; p. 33, 2; p. 36, 19.

[4] *Ibid.*, 2.6, p. 94, 11: "Sequitur locus perdifficilis, sed transferentis obscuritate Victorini magis quam Porphyrii proponentis."

[5] *Ibid.*, 2.6, p. 95, 14: "quod Victorinus scilicet intellexisse minus videtur. Nam quod Porphyrius ἀνάλογον dixit, id est *proportionale*, ille sic accepit quasi ἄλογον diceret, id est *inrationale*."

[6] *Ibid.*, ed. sec., 1.1, p. 135, 8: "cuius incepti ratio est quod in his scriptis in quibus rerum cognitio quaeritur, non luculentae orationis lepos, sed incorrupta veritas exprimenda est. Quocirca multum profecisse videor, si philosophiae libris Latina oratione compositis per integerrimae translationis sinceritatem nihil in Graecorum litteris amplius desideretur."

[7] Boethius *In Top.*, prol., *PL* 64, 1041 B.

[8] Boethius *De interpr.*, ed. sec., pp. 4–5.

[9] Boethius *De syll. hypoth.*, prol., *PL* 64, 831 C: "Quod igitur apud scriptores quidem Graecos perquam rarissimos strictim atque confuse, apud Latinos vero nullos repperi, id tuae scientiae dedicatum, noster etsi diuturnus, coepti tamen efficax labor excoluit."

[10] Boethius *De divisione*, prol., *PL* 64, 875 D. Father Henry, *Plotin et l'Occident*, forgets to mention this text, which refers to *Sophist* 218dff.

Boethius had at hand only Porphyry's commentary, for Plotinus had a good treatment in the *Enneads* of the dialectic division but did not mention Andronicus.[11] It is therefore certain that Boethius is here quoting Plotinus by way of Porphyry, who recalled in his commentary a memory of his teacher's oral instruction.

Bidez has clearly shown all that Boethius owes to Porphyry. There can be no doubt that his philosophical program derives from the School of Porphyry, who wrote commentaries on both Aristotle and Plato. Not only did Boethius know Porphyry's commentaries on Plato, now lost, particularly the commentary on the *Sophist*, but he translated with a commentary in two successive editions Porphyry's *Isagoge*. His commentary on Aristotle's *Categories* follows step by step, sometimes in the form of translation pure and simple, Porphyry's commentary Κατὰ πεῦσιν καὶ ἀπόκρισιν on the same treatise. In several places in his commentary on Aristotle's *De interpretatione* he declares that he adopts the view of Porphyry's corresponding commentary. Lastly, in his *Introductio ad categoricos syllogismos*, it is Porphyry that Boethius follows.[12] To Bidez's proof must also be added the fact that Boethius, for all the vast Greek erudition that he displays, did not read a single commentator prior to Porphyry. His commentary on the *Categories* quotes Herminus,[13] a number of anonymous authors,[14] and various works of Aristotle[15] by way of Porphyry's corresponding commentary. His *De interpretatione* is heavily documented and at first sight appears to have as its

[11] Plotinus *Enneads* 1.3.4, ed. Bréhier, 1, p. 64.

[12] J. Bidez, "Boèce et Porphyre," *RBPH* 2 (1923) 189–201. Cf. the *Comptes rendus de l'Académie des Inscriptions et Belles-lettres* (1922) 346–350; the catalogue of Porphyry's works in Bidez, *Vie de Porphyre*, pp. 65*–67*; and also A. Guzzo, *L'Isagoge di Porfirio e i commenti di Boezio* (Turin 1934).

[13] Porphyry *In Categ.*, ed. Busse, *CAG* 4, p. 107, 6:

Διὰ τί οὖν τὸ ἴσως ἔφης;—Ὅτι τινὲς τὸ κάτω καὶ τὸ ἄνω οὐδὲ εἶναι βούλονται τόπους ἀλλὰ σχέσεις τόπου . . . — Ἀλλὰ πῶς ὁ Ἑρμῖνος ἀπήντηκεν;— Λέγων ὅτι τὸ ἄνω καὶ τὸ κάτω οὐ τόπον σημαίνει, ἀλλὰ ποῦ.

Boethius *In Categ.* 2, *PL* 64, 212 B):

Sed *quidam* volunt non esse quantitatis quod *sursum* dicitur et *deorsum*, sed potius habitudines, quas Graeci σχέσεις vocant . . . Herminus quoque *ait sursum et deorsum non esse loca, sed* quandam quodam modo *positionem* loci.

Andronicus' opinion reported by Boethius, *ibid.* 263 B, on the spurious character of the end of the *Categories*, must stem from the corresponding passage in Porphyry's commentary, the conclusion of which is now lost.

[14] On the view of the "Platonici quidam," cf. Porphyry *In Categ.*, p. 137, 29, and Boethius *In Categ.* 2, 257 B (Simplicius *In Categ.* 8, *CAG* 8, p. 284, 14, informs us that the question concerns Plotinus essentially). Cf. also Porphyry *In Categ.*, p. 127, 23, and Boethius *In Categ.* 2, 239 C.

[15] For instance, the triple reference to the Περὶ γενέσεως καὶ φθορᾶς, the *Physics*, and the *Metaphysics* appears likewise in Porphyry, *ibid.*, p. 141, 13, and Boethius, *ibid.*, 262 A.

sources the four commentaries of Alexander of Aphrodisias, Aspasius, Herminus, and Porphyry, whose theories are in general expounded in succession.[16] Actually, Boethius' principal source is Porphyry.[17] In one passage Boethius reveals that he takes from him his information on the three other commentators, as could already have been assumed from the mere fact that Boethius regularly ends the exposition of their theories with an opinion from Porphyry.[18] Likewise, whenever Boethius quotes Theophrastus' Περὶ καταφάσεως καὶ ἀποφάσεως, it is from a commentary by Porphyry.[19] Porphyry is very probably Boethius' source for his quotations from Plato,[20] Speusippus and Xenocrates,[21] Philo and Diodorus,[22] and, in a general way, from all the ancient writers. And it is through Porphyry alone, as we have seen, that Boethius derives some notion of Plotinus' theories.

But it would be a mistake to think, with Bidez,[23] that Boethius knew exclusively Porphyry, who had aroused Boethius' interest through Victorinus' works. If Porphyry is his major authority, he is not the only one. He himself makes references, generally discreet, to the other commentaries that he has read that are later than Porphyry,[24] those of Neoplatonists of various countries and various periods. He read the Syrian Iamblichus' commentary on the *Categories*,[25] the commentaries of Themistius, professor at Constantinople, on

---

[16] Among others, *De interpr.*, ed. *prima*, p. 132; ed. *sec.*, pp. 26, 35–40, 121–122, 157–160, 183, 272–275.

[17] *Ibid.*, ed. *sec.*, p. 7, 5: "expositionem nos scilicet quam maxime a Porphyrio quamquam etiam a ceteris transferentes Latina oratione digessimus."

[18] *Ibid.*, ed. *sec.*, p. 293, 27: "Dicit autem Porphyrius fuisse quosdam sui temporis, qui hunc exponerent librum [the *Analytics*], et quoniam ab Hermino vel Aspasio vel Alexandro expositiones singulas proferentes multa contraria et expositionibus male ab illis editis dissidentia reperirent, arbitratos fuisse hunc Aristotelis librum, ut dignum esset, exponi non posse."

[19] *Ibid.*, ed. *sec.*, p. 17, 24: "Sed Porphyrius ait sese docuisse species enuntiationis esse adfirmationem et negationem in his commentariis quos in Theophrastum edidit." Is it a question of a special commentary on this work by Theophrastus or of the discussions that Porphyry devoted to it in the course of his *De interpretatione*? One may well hesitate on this point. Boethius also quotes Theophrastus and Eudemus, but usually together and just before a quotation from Porphyry, in the *De syll. categ.* and the *De syll. hypoth.*, PL 64: 813 C, 814 C, 815 B, 829 D, 831 D, 833 D.

[20] *De interpr.*, ed. *sec.*, p. 92, 1. The reference is to the *Cratylus*, on which Porphyry had written a commentary (cf. Bidez, *Vie de Porphyre*, p. 66, 11). A quotation from the *Theaetetus*, p. 316, 17, and a reference to the *Timaeus* in the *In Isag.* (p. 184, 21; 209, 2; 257, 9; 259, 20) are also manifestly not derived from the primary source.

[21] *De interpr.*, ed. *sec.*, p. 24, 16.

[22] *Ibid.*, p. 234, 10 and p. 412, 16.

[23] Bidez, "Boèce et Porphyre," p. 199.

[24] *In Isag.*, ed. *prima*, 1.5, p. 12, 20: "Omnes post Porphyrium ingredientes ad logicam." Cf. the text quoted above, n. 17.

[25] Cf. Simplicius *In Categ.*, *CAG* 8,   Boethius *In Categ.*, PL 64, 162 A:
p. 3, 3:   Architas etiam duos composuit libros

the *Categories*,[26] the *Analytics*,[27] and the *Topics*;[28] and he assures us that for the *Analytics* he reads this commentary in Greek. Lastly, he frequently uses the commentary of Syrianus of Athens on the *De interpretatione*, although he criticizes it with respect to Porphyry's theories.[29] If one considers that Syrianus died only some fifty years before the publication of Boethius' first works, one is led to inquire whether there is not some indication of a direct contact between Boethius and the contemporary Greek commentators who came from the School of Syrianus.

A very simple chronological comment helps in directing this inquiry. It has generally been admitted, since Usener's demonstration, that Boethius was born around the year 480.[30] We know from Ennodius that he was exceptionally precocious.[31] Around the year 500, according to Brandt, his first works appeared.[32] Now, at this period the School of Athens, since the death of Proclus in 485, had fallen into complete decadence, as Aeneas of Gaza observes.[33]

Τοῖς Ἰαμβλίχου παρακολουθῶν ἀπε-
γραψάμην, καὶ αὐτῇ πολλαχοῦ τῇ
λέξει τοῦ φιλοσόφου χρησάμενος.

p. 13, 22:
τὰ δὲ ἁπλᾶ εἰς δεκάδα συνήγαγον οἱ
Πυθαγορεῖοι, ὡς Ἀρχύτας, ᾧ καὶ
Πλάτων συγγέγονεν, ὡς ἐν τῷ περὶ
τῶν καθόλου λόγων ἐδίδαξεν βιβλίῳ,
ᾧ καὶ Ἀριστοτέλης κατηκολούθησεν
καὶ μέχρι τῶν ὀνομάτων.

quos *Καθόλους Λόγους* inscripsit, quorum in primo haec *decem* praedicamenta disposuit. Unde posteriores quidam non esse Aristotelem huius divisionis inventorem suspicati sunt, quod *Pythagoricus* vir eadem conscripsisset, in qua sententia Iamblichus philosophus est non ignobilis, cui non consentit Themistius neque concedit eum fuisse Architam qui Pythagoricus Tarentusque esset quique cum Platone aliquantulum vixisset, sed Peripateticum aliquem Architam qui novo operi auctoritatem vetustate nominis conderet; sed de his alias.

In addition, Boethius explains at great length, pp. 224 D–225 B, one of Iamblichus' logical theories.

[26] Text quoted in preceding note.

[27] Text quoted above, chap. 1 sec. 1 n. 7.

[28] Boethius *De differentiis topicis*, PL 64: 1194 B, 1195 C, 1202 C.

[29] Boethius *De interpr.*, *ed. sec.*, p. 88, 28: "Syrianus igitur minime audiendus est, sed potius Porphyrius"; and 173, 11: "multis modis Syriani argumenta franguntur." More favorable opinions, p. 18 and pp. 321–324.

[30] Usener, *Anecdoton Holderi*, p. 40.

[31] Ennodius *Opera*, ed. Vogel, *MGH, Auct. ant.* 7, p. 314: "Est Boetius patricius, in quo vix discendi annos respicis et intellegis peritiam sufficere iam docendi, de quo emendatorum iudicavit electio"; and p. 236: "Cui inter vitae exordia ludus est lectionis assiduitas et deliciae sudor alienus."

[32] S. Brandt, "Entstehungszeit und zeitliche Folge der Werke von Boethius," *Philologus* 62 (1903) 237.

[33] PG 85, 877 A: καὶ παρ᾽ Ἀθηναίοις ἔνθα μάλιστα διεφάνη φιλοσοφία, παντελῶς ἄγνωστος καὶ ἐς τὸ μηδὲν ἀπέρριπται.

It was then Alexandria that became the center of philological, philosophical, and medical studies. The important name dominating this School was that of a disciple of Proclus, Ammonius, the son of Hermias, who after his teacher's death retired to Alexandria, where he achieved renown. Among his pupils he reckoned Damascius, Simplicius, Asclepius, Olympiodorus, Theodotus, Iohannes Philiponus, the entire latest generation, remarkably productive, of Greek commentators. This generation was contemporaneous with Boethius.[34] Is there not reason to inquire, as Boethius' scientific commentaries previously induced us to think, whether Boethius' works on logic, composed entirely between the year 500 and the year 524, owe nothing to Ammonius, who had been teaching at Alexandria with such success since 485?

Such an inquiry raises several difficulties. It must be admitted first of all that, if Boethius readily quotes Aristotle's commentators, from the most ancient to Syrianus, he never seems to mention either Proclus, Syrianus' disciple, or any of Ammonius' pupils. This silence on contemporary commentators should not, however, surprise us. We know that most of the ancient or medieval writers had the habit of not mentioning their most direct sources, especially when these sources did not yet have the stamp of antiquity. Other difficulties are more serious. For a particular treatise by Aristotle, sometimes Ammonius' commentary is lost and sometimes Boethius'. This fact indicates that a study of the relation between Ammonius and Boethius can have a bearing on only three works: Porphyry's *Isagoge*, Aristotle's *Categories*, and the *De interpretatione*. In addition, Ammonius himself certainly plagiarized earlier Greek commentaries, now lost. Among these were the commentaries of Iamblichus and Proclus. It will always be a question whether the parallels that it is possible to observe between Boethius' commentaries and those of Ammonius do not arise from the fact that they stem from a common source. Ammonius may not necessarily be Boethius' direct source. In conclusion, since Ammonius explained Aristotle's treatises orally[35] and the same kind of oral course was the basis of several revisions on his pupils' part,[36] Boethius may have used a different redaction from the one that has been preserved. These remarks were necessary for an appraisal at their proper value of the general or particular borrowings that Boethius appears to have made from the works of Ammonius.

First of all it should be noted that the chronological order of Boethius' translations and commentaries, as Brandt has established,[37] corresponds to the

---

[34] On this generation, see Pauly-Wissowa, and Zeller, *Die Philosophie der Griechen*, vol. 3, 2, 2, pp. 829ff.

[35] Most of the manuscripts have: Ἀπὸ φωνῆς Ἀμμωνίου.

[36] For instance, Ammonius' commentary on the *Categories* was edited a second time by John Philopon, in a scarcely different form.

[37] Brandt, "Entstehungszeit," pp. 267–268.

logical order commended by Ammonius for the exposition of the *Organon*.
It must start with Porphyry's *Isagoge*, the two *Analytics*, the *Topics*, and the
Sophistici elenchi.[38] Boethius, then, conformed to the precept in force in the
School of Alexandria. It must also be observed that, like Ammonius, he
wrote commentaries on Nicomachus' *Arithmetic*, Ptolemy's *Almagest*, and
Aristotle's *Physics*.[39]

But it is above all in the scholastic method of his commentaries that
Boethius recalls Ammonius. At the beginning of each commentary Boethius
has the habit of placing his *Prolegomena*, divided into a certain number of
points. The reference to Ammonius appears evident at first sight.

Ammonius:[40]

Δεῖ δὲ ἡμᾶς εἰπεῖν καὶ τὰ πρὸς τῶν
φιλοσόφων οὕτω προσαγορευόμενα
προλεγόμενα ἤτοι προτεχνολογούμενα
ἐπὶ παντὸς βιβλίου· ἔστι δὲ ταῦτα· ὁ
σκοπός, τὸ χρήσιμον, τὸ γνήσιον, ἡ
τάξις τῆς ἀναγνώσεως, ἡ αἰτία τῆς
ἐπιγραφῆς, ἡ εἰς τὰ κεφάλαια διαίρε-
σις, καὶ ὑπὸ ποῖον μέρος ἀνάγεται τὸ
παρὸν σύγγραμμα.

Boethius:[41]

Primum didascalicis quibusdam me im-
bue, quibus expositores vel etiam com-
mentatores, ut discipulorum animos
docibilitate quadam adsuescant, utuntur.
—Sex omnino, inquam, magistri in *omni*
expositione praelibant; praedocent enim
quae sit cuiuscumque operis intentio, quod apud illos σκοπός vocatur;
secundum, quae utilitas, quod a Graecis
χρήσιμον appellatur; tertium, qui ordo,
quod τάξιν vocant; quartum, si eius cuius
esse opus dicitur germanus propriusque
liber est, quod γνήσιον interpretari solent;
quintum, quae sit eius operis inscriptio,
quod ἐπιγραφήν Graeci nominant ... sex-
tum est id dicere, ad quam partem philosophiae cuiuscumque libri ducatur intentio, quod Graeca oratione dicitur
εἰς ποῖον μέρος φιλοσοφίας ἀνάγεται;
haec ergo omnia in quolibet philosophiae libro quaeri convenit atque expediri.

Can it be said, because Boethius omits one of the seven points mentioned
by Ammonius, namely the division into chapters, that he is modifying the
teacher's plan of the prolegomena? This would be a mistake; for, in the *Ars*

---

[38] This order is given by Ammonius *In Analytica priora* (ed. M. Wallies, *Commentaria
in Aristotelem Graeca* 4, 6), pp. 1–4, which might well be the source of Boethius *In Isag.* 1,
pp. 13–14. There is nothing equivalent to this in Ammonius' commentary on the *Isagoge*.

[39] See above, pp. 279–280. The list of Ammonius' writings may be found in Zeller
(above, n. 34), p. 830 n. 1. For Boethius' lost commentary on the *Physics*, see Brandt,
"Entstehungszeit," p. 237.

[40] Ammonius *In Isag.* (ed. Busse, *CAG* 4, 3), p. 21, 6.

[41] Boethius *In Isag.*, ed. Brandt, p. 4, 17ff.

geometriae, Boethius discussed this point.[42] Furthermore, Ammonius' own schema is not invariable. He discusses only six points in the prolegomena to the commentary on the *Categories*, and five points in the prolegomena to the commentary on the *De interpretatione*. The order of the points discussed varies slightly each time. It must be remembered that Boethius, like all Ammonius' disciples and like the Greek rhetoricians of the sixth century, adopts, with a few variants in detail, the schema of the prolegomena that was in vogue since Ammonius. Probably Ammonius did not proclaim himself the inventor of this schema. He adds: Ταῦτα ἐπενόησαν οἱ φιλόσοφοι προλέγειν.[43] But this schema is not ancient. Neither Alexander of Aphrodisias nor Porphyry divides the prolegomena into more than three points. Neither Syrianus nor Sopater acknowledges a rigid schema. On the contrary, beginning with Ammonius, the philosophers and rhetoricians arrange the prolegomena into at least six points. At the end of the sixth century, this schema was to become still more precise and would consist of nine points.[44] The practice that Boethius adopts is therefore quite characteristic of a certain school of contemporary Greek commentators. Moreover, in his prolegomena to the commentary on the *Categories*, although he plagiarizes Porphyry, as Bidez has shown, he feels obliged to arrange the schema in six points, whereas Porphyry discussed only three.[45]

But it is not only for his method that Boethius belongs to a particular school. A comparative study of Ammonius' and Boethius' extant commentaries shows that the contents of one appear almost in their entirety in the other.

This fact has been observed with great perspicacity by Brandt with regard to Boethius' commentary on the *Isagoge*. After drawing up a conscientious list of the similarities and differences between the two corresponding commentaries of Ammonius and Boethius, both in the prolegomena[46] and in the body of the commentary,[47] Brandt feels justified in concluding that they could have had a common source but thinks rather that Ammonius was Boethius' direct source. It is futile to reproduce Brandt's demonstration, which appears very convincing. It should be noted, however, that several of the alleged differences would have seemed on the contrary like points of

---

[42] *PL* 63, 1359 A. It is appropriate to add that in its present state this work is a revision posterior to Boethius.

[43] Ammonius *In Isag.*, p. 21, 10ff.

[44] For the development of the schema, see in *Prolegomenon sylloge* (above, chap. 1 sec. 3 n. 34) Rabe's excellent preface, pp. VI–VII, "De protheoriis singulorum librorum."

[45] *PL* 64: 160 B (*intentio*), 161 B (*utilitas*), 161 C (*ordo*), 161 D (*ad quam partem philosophiae huius libri ducatur intentio* and *Aristotelis vero neque ullius alterius liber est*), 162 B (*inscriptio*).

[46] *Boethii in Isag. Porphyrii commenta*, ed. Brandt, pp. LXXVIII–LXXIX.

[47] *Ibid.*, pp. XXII–XXVI.

contact, if Brandt had taken the trouble to refer to Ammonius' other works. Thus Boethius' discussion of the order in which Aristotle should be read has no equivalent in Ammonius' commentary on the *Isagoge*, but there is one in the prolegomena to his commentary on the *Analytics*.[48] There is also a still more curious similarity on the important question of knowing whether logic is a part or an instrument of philosophy. This Brandt has misinterpreted.

Ammonius:[49]

ἡ δὲ λογικὴ οὐ μέρος τῆς φιλοσοφίας, ἀλλ' ὄργανον, ὡς ἐν ἑτέρῳ δείξομεν.

Boethius:[50]

... quam quidem artem quidam *partem philosophiae,* quidam non partem, sed *ferramentum* et quodammodo supellectilem iudicarunt, qua autem id utrique impulsi ratione crediderint, *alio* erit in opere commemorandum.

Brandt thought at first that Boethius was referring to the second edition of his commentary on the *Isagoge*.[51] Then, after ascertaining that there was nothing in the first edition to indicate a second edition, he changed his mind and maintained that the passage in Boethius was a careless transcription of Ammonius' statement.[52] This interpretation calls for the most serious reservations. In fact, the sentence in Ammonius presupposes the prolegomena to his commentary on the *Analytics* where he discusses this question thoroughly. Why should not the corresponding passage in Boethius also be a reference to the commentary on the *Analytics* that Boethius actually wrote[53] but that has been lost? This would be a confirmation that in beginning his great work of commentaries, Boethius followed the same plan as Ammonius. Now, Boethius certainly consulted the beginning of Ammonius' commentary on the *Analytics*; for whereas Ammonius, in commenting on the *Isagoge*, maintained that logic was a simple instrument of philosophy, he declared on the contrary in his commentary on the *Analytics* that it was not a part, as the Stoics believed, or a simple instrument, as the Aristotelians believed, but both part and instrument, as Plato believed, and as is actually the case.[54] Boethius, who consulted this passage, observed Ammonius' change of opinion. Hence he took good care, in transcribing Ammonius' statement on the *Isagoge*, not to do likewise, for he wanted to avoid the evident contradiction between Ammonius' two works. In the event, it was Ammonius' definitive opinion

[48] See the references immediately above, n. 44.
[49] Ammonius *In Isag.* (ed. Busse), p. 23, 23.
[50] Boethius *In Isag.* (ed. Brandt), p. 10, 2.
[51] Brandt, "Entstehungszeit," p. 151.
[52] Boethius *In Isag.* (ed. Brandt), p. XII n. 6.
[53] He refers to it twice expressly in his *De syllogismo categorico* (PL 64, 822 B and 830 D).
[54] Ammonius *In Anal.* (ed. Wallies), p. 8, 15–p. 11, 21.

on the question that he adopted. We have proof of this, in default of Boethius' lost commentary on the *Analytics*, in a lengthy discussion in the second
edition of Boethius' commentary on the *Isagoge*.[55] Like Ammonius, he held
aloof from the Stoic and Aristotelian opinion and declared that logic was
both an instrument and a part of philosophy. Ammonius' and Boethius' perfect agreement on this question is all the more remarkable in that the other
commentators were of the opposite opinion. Alexander of Aphrodisias[56]
and, in Ammonius' own School, Iohannes Philoponus[57] and Elias[58] all
thought that logic was a simple instrument of philosophy.

Brandt, whose task was only to edit Boethius' commentary on the *Isagoge*,
did not investigate whether there were any connections between Ammonius'
and Boethius' commentaries on the *Categories* and the *De interpretatione*. This
inquiry, however, is not unproductive. Probably Boethius' commentary on
the *Categories* was a plagiarism, as Bidez has well shown, of Porphyry's
corresponding commentary, but Ammonius' influence is no less evident.
Whereas Porphyry's commentary was a dialogue in the form of question and
answer, Boethius adopted the form of the continuous discourse. For Porphyry's brief introduction in three points, he substituted the prolegomena in
six points, the regular procedure in the School of Ammonius, and it is quite
apparent that he took the content of some of these points from Ammonius'
commentary on the *Categories*.[59] Lastly, contrary to Porphyry, Boethius
illustrated his commentary with explanatory diagrams. At least two of these
reproduced those with which Ammonius had embellished his commentary.
One of them, it is true, although easily recognizable, was somewhat dis-
torted by the medieval copyists of Boethius' text.[60] But the other one, mentioned by Boethius himself in the context, has been preserved intact and
faithfully reproduces Ammonius' diagram, as may be judged by the accompanying diagrams.[61]

However, if it is surprising that Boethius' commentary on the *Categories*
owed much less to Ammonius than the commentary on the *Isagoge*, care
must be taken to let Boethius explain himself on this point. Scarcely has he
defined, after Porphyry, the purpose of Aristotle's book than he refers the

[55] Boethius *In Isag.* (ed. Brandt), p. 140, 12–p. 143, 7.

[56] Alexander of Aphrodisias *In Anal.* (ed. Wallies, *CAG* 2, 1), p. 4, 30.

[57] Philopon *In Anal.* (ed. Wallies, *CAG* 13, 2), p. 6, 19–p. 9, 20. He even, p. 8, 30, refutes an argument of Boethius', *In Isag.*, p. 142, 25.

[58] Elias *In Isag.* (ed. Busse, *CAG* 18, 1), p. 26, 36 and p. 39, 31.

[59] On *utility*, cf. Boethius, col. 161 B, and Ammonius, p. 13, 3–6. On *order*, cf. Boethius, col. 161 C, and Ammonius, p. 13, 6–11. On *authenticity*, cf. Boethius, col. 161
D, and Ammonius, p. 13, 20–p. 14, 2.

[60] Cf. Boethius, col. 291 B–C, and Ammonius, p. 106. The diagram is reproduced in
the commentaries, by his pupils Philopon and Simplicius, on the *Categories*.

[61] Cf. Ammonius *In Categ.*, p. 25, 12, and Boethius *In Categ.*, col. 175 C.

Ammonius:

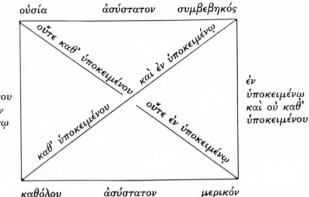

Boethius:

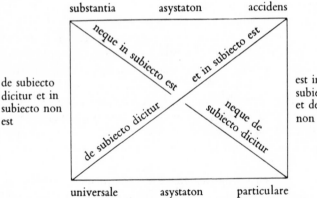

reader to a second edition of his commentary, where a much more learned definition is adopted. He apologizes for always following Porphyry, without entering into the debates between the scholars. But he adopts only conditionally the definition given by Porphyry, because it is easier for beginners to comprehend.[62]

---

[62] Boethius *In Categ.*, col. 160 A–B. It is true that Georg Schepss, *Blätter f. d. bayr. Gymnasialschulwesen* 33 (1897) 252, believes in an interpolation and that Brandt, "Entstehungszeit," p. 275, hence concludes that Boethius does not mention a second edition. But Bidez, "Boèce et Porphyre," p. 192, points out that the interpolation might in any case have come from Boethius himself. The existence of a second edition, now lost, is all the more certain since the manuscripts of our commentary give it the title of *editio prima* (cf. Bidez, p. 192 n. 3), for instance, Rossian. Lat. 537, fol. 59ʳ.

Now, in the same passage of the prolegomena, Ammonius, in his commentary on the *Categories*, expresses three different views of the commentators on Aristotle's purpose. He dwells particularly on Porphyry's opinion, but rejects all three as inadequate and finally gives his own view.[63] Is it not at least probable that Boethius, in the second edition of his commentary, reproduced Ammonius' exposition and adopted his view? Had this second edition been preserved, it would undoubtedly show many items borrowed from Ammonius.

Boethius' treatise on the *De interpretatione*, the two editions of which may still be read, shows still more clearly Boethius' entire indebtedness to the Alexandrian professor. In both of them the commentary begins in the same way:

Ammonius:[64]	Boethius:[65]
Πολὺ μὲν ἐν σοφοῖσι κοὐκ ἀνώνυμον τὸ Περὶ ἑρμηνείας τοῦ Ἀριστοτέλους βιβλίον τῆς τε πυκνότητος ἕνεκα τῶν ἐν αὐτῷ παραδιδομένων θεωρημάτων καὶ τῆς περὶ τὴν λέξιν δυσκολίας.	Magna quidem libri huius apud Peripateticam sectam probatur auctoritas ... sed eius series scruposa impeditur semita et subtilibus pressa sententiis aditum intellegentiae facilem non relinquit.

However, all the similarities that can possibly be established between the two commentaries are not equally conclusive. Most of those that Brandt notes are explained by the fact that Ammonius and Boethius have a common source. This source was Porphyry's lost commentary on the *De interpretatione*.[66] But if it is true that Boethius followed Porphyry in this case too, he took care to add that he also used other commentators and sometimes rejected Porphyry's interpretations.[67]

Must we believe with Lehnert that in this commentary Boethius used the Greek or Latin rhetoricians?[68] In all probability, in four passages in the commentary, there appeared a classification of the five forms of discourse: *oratio deprecativa, imperativa, interrogativa, vocativa, enuntiativa*.[69] These forms correspond exactly to those of the *Prolegomena in Hermogenis ΠΕΡΙ ΣΤΑΣΕΩΝ*

---

[63] Ammonius *In Categ.*, p. 8, 20–p. 9, 17.

[64] Ammonius *In Aristotelis de interpretatione* (ed. Busse, CAG 4, 5), p. 1, 1ff.

[65] Boethius *In Aristotelis de interpretatione* (Meiser), ed. pr., p. 31, 1ff.

[66] *Scholia in Aristotelem* (ed. Brandis, Berlin 1836), pp. 93–139. Boethius' corresponding quotations are in the notes.

[67] Text quoted above, n. 17. Cf. Boethius *De interpr.*, ed. sec., p. 121, 25: "sed hanc expositionem (quod adhuc sciam), neque Porphyrius nec ullus alius commentatorum vidit."

[68] G. Lehnert, "Eine rhetorische Quelle für Boetius' Commentare zu Aristoteles *ΠΕΡΙ ΕΡΜΗΝΕΙΑΣ,*" *Philologus* 59 (1900) 574–577.

[69] Boethius *De interpr.*, ed. pr., p. 35, 12 and p. 71, 1, and ed. sec., p. 9, 6 and p. 95, 9. Probably by mistake, in the second passage (p. 71, 1) Boethius omits the *oratio interrogativa* and replaces it with *oratio optativa*, thus using *oratio deprecativa* in a double sense.

and of the *Scholia in Aphthonium*: λόγος εὐκτικός, προστακτικός, ἐρωτημα-τικός, κλητικός, ἀποφαντικός.[70] But Lehnert did not observe that these prolegomena and scholia took this classification from Ammonius' commentary on the *De interpretatione*, of which they even reproduced certain examples. Although this classification is anterior to Ammonius, Boethius unquestionably borrowed it from Ammonius, since in both commentaries it appeared in the prolegomena to the commentary on the *De interpretatione*.[71] Boethius' sole originality consists in replacing the Greek examples taken from Homer with examples selected from Terence, Cicero, and Vergil. But both commentaries, after giving the classification of the Peripatetics, add that the *De interpretatione* treats only of the *oratio enuntiativa* (λόγος ἀποφαντικός). They subdivide it into *enuntiativa simplex* (εἶδος κατηγορικόν) and *enuntiativa duplex atque hypothetica nec non etiam conditionalis* (εἶδος ὑποθετικόν), for which they show the same illustration.[72] Boethius' dependence on the School of Ammonius is evident. It should not be thought, therefore, as Lehnert thought, that Boethius' source was some Greek or Latin rhetorician or grammarian. The Peripatetics quoted by Boethius denote the most recent commentators on Aristotle.

The parallelism between Ammonius and Boethius in the course of their commentary on the *De interpretatione* is as striking as in their commentary on Porphyry's *Isagoge*. With reference to the same passage in the *De interpretatione*, both Ammonius and Boethius refer, for clarification, to the same passage in another work by Aristotle.[73] They discuss and resolve in the same manner the question of authenticity, about which Andronicus of Rhodes

[70] Cf. the "Prolegomena in Hermogenis ΠΕΡΙ ΣΤΑΣΕΩΝ," *Prolegomenon sylloge*, ed. Rabe, pp. 186–187, and the "Scholia in Aphthonium," *Rhetores Graeci*, ed. Walz, 2, p. 661, 25ff.

[71] Ammonius *De interpr.*, p. 2, 9ff, and *In Anal.*, p. 2. Themistius must already have known this classification, for the plagiarist of Themistius who wrote the *Categoriae decem ex Aristotele decerptae*, attributed to St. Augustine, reproduces it (PL 32, 1425).

[72] Cf. Ammonius *De interpr.*, p. 2, 9–p. 3, 14: εἰ μὴ ἔστιν ἡμέρα, οὐκ ἔστιν ἥλιος ὑπὲρ γῆν, and Boethius *De interpr.*, ed. pr., p. 35 and p. 34, 10: "si sol super terram est, dies est."
Cf. also Ammonius *De interpr.*, p. 2, 26: Καλοῦσι δὲ οἱ Στωϊκοὶ τὸν μὲν ἀποφαν-τικὸν λόγον ἀξίωμα, and Boethius *De interpr.*, ed. sec., p. 9, 26: "et Stoici quoque in his libris, quos περὶ ἀξιωμάτων appellant, de isdem nihilominus disputant."

[73] The references are to the *Metaphysics* (Ammonius, p. 71, 6, and Boethius, ed. pr., p. 74, 22; ed. sec., p. 102, 26), the *Sophistici elenchi* (Ammonius, p. 85, 28, and Boethius, ed. pr., p. 82, 1; ed. sec., p. 134, 4), the *Poetics* (Ammonius, p. 12, 30ff, and Boethius, ed. sec., p. 6, 16 and p. 8, 7), etc. The very form in which the reference is made to the *Sophistici elenchi* is identical in both writers:

Ammonius:	Boethius, ed. pr., p. 82, 1:
Περὶ τούτων οὖν ὁ Ἀριστοτέλης τελειότατα μὲν ἐν τῇ ⟨Περὶ⟩ τῶν σοφιστικῶν ἐλέγχων ἐπιγραφομένῃ	Sed diligentius haec in libro quem σοφιστικῶν ἐλέγχων inscripsit edisserit; illic enim *sophistarum*, quos fallaces

had raised doubts.[74] They present their exposition for the reader's comprehension by means of the same diagram.[75]

Furthermore, in connection with a statement by Aristotle on *mobile* and *immobile*, the agreement of both commentators is so close that Busse was able to use Boethius' text to correct the reading in Ammonius' manuscripts.[76]

There is the same identity of terms in the discussions that Ammonius and Boethius devote to distinguishing "sound" from "articulated tone." Here is the beginning of their explanation:

Ammonius:[77]

Διαφέρει γὰρ ὁ ψόφος τῆς φωνῆς ὡς γένος εἴδους καὶ ψόφος μέν ἐστι πληγὴ ἀέρος αἰσθητὴ ἀκοῇ, φωνὴ δὲ ψόφος ἐμψύχου γινόμενος ὅταν διὰ τῆς συστολῆς τοῦ θώρακος ἐκθλιβόμενος ἀπὸ τοῦ πνεύμονος ὁ εἰσπνευθεὶς ἀὴρ προσπίπτῃ ἀθρόως τῇ τε τραχείᾳ καλουμένῃ ἀρτηρίᾳ καὶ τῇ ὑπερῴᾳ ἤτοι τῷ γαργαρεῶνι . . . τῆς γλώττης καὶ τῶν ὀδόντων καὶ τῶν χειλέων . . . ἀναγκαίων ὄντων.

(All the rest of this passage, on the sentimental signification of human groans or animal cries, coincides likewise.)

Boethius:[78]

Distat enim *sonus voce: sonus* enim *est percussio aeris sensibilis, vox vero* flatus per quasdam gutturis partes egrediens, quae *arteriae* vocantur, qui aliqua *linguae* impressione formetur.

Frequently Boethius does not even trouble to change the examples given by Ammonius:

Ammonius:

. . . τὸν γὰρ Ἀριστοκλέα ἔδοξε τοῖς

Boethius:

. . . saepe singulorum hominum sunt

πραγματείᾳ διείλεκται, τούς τε τρόπους ἅπαντας ἐκτιθέμενος τρισκαίδεκα ὄντας, καθ' οὓς οἱ σοφισταὶ τοὺς ἀνεπιστάτως αὐτοῖς διαλεγομένους πειρῶνται παραλογίζεσθαι.

argumentatores Latine possumus dicere, qui per huius modi propositiones quae verum inter se falsumque non dividunt mendaces conligunt syllogismos, argumenta distinxit, quibus capere respondentem atque innectere consuerunt.

Boethius' text, quite certain in this passage, shows that Ammonius' editor was wrong to add a περὶ that does not appear in any manuscript.

[74] Cf. Ammonius, p. 5, 27ff, and Boethius, *ed. sec.*, p. 11, 13ff.

[75] Ammonius, p. 93, 10ff; Boethius, *ed. pr.*, p. 87, and *ed. sec.*, p. 152. A comparison of these two diagrams may be found in my article "Boèce et l'école d'Alexandrie," p. 201.

[76] Ammonius, p. 243, 22ff (see the *apparatus criticus* for line 35); and Boethius, *ed. pr.*, p. 202, 25ff.

[77] Ammonius, p. 30, 7ff.

[78] Boethius, *ed. sec.*, p. 53, 16ff.

παλαιοῖς καλέσαι Πλάτωνα καὶ τὸν
Τύρταμον Θεόφραστον.[79]

permutata vocabula; quem enim nunc
vocamus *Platonem, Aristocles ante vocaba-
tur* et qui *Theophrastus* nunc dicitur, ante
Aristotelem a suis parentibus *Tyrtamus*
appellabatur.[80]

Similarities that are just as striking and that could be multiplied[81] seem to
prove that Boethius depended on Ammonius. However, even in those instances where Boethius' text seems to be a translation of Ammonius' text, a
doubt remains. Can we not always imagine, when we know the procedure
of the Greek commentators of Aristotle and their endless and mutual
plagiarism, that this resemblance in the texts is explained by a common
source? This common source Ammonius and Boethius could each have
plagiarized word for word; for instance, Porphyry's commentary on the *De
interpretatione*. A passage in Boethius would furnish conclusive certainty, if it
were not corrupted in the manuscripts:

Ammonius:[82]

Διττὸν εἶναί φασιν οἱ παλαιοὶ τῆς
ἐρωτήσεως τὸ εἶδος· τὸ μὲν τῆς
διαλεκτικῆς, τὸ δὲ τῆς καλουμένης
πυσματικῆς ... Πυσματικὴν δὲ πρὸς
ἦν τὸ μὲν ναί καὶ τὸ οὔ χώραν οὐκ
ἔχουσι, λέξεως δὲ ἄλλης, ἐνίοτε δὲ καὶ
λόγου πλείονος δεῖ τῷ ἐρωτωμένῳ
πρὸς τὴν ἀπόκρισιν· διδαχθῆναι γάρ τι
περί τινος βουλομένων ἐστὶν ἡ πυσ-
ματικὴ ἐρώτησις, οἷον πότε ἦλθες; τίς
καλεῖ; ποῦ οἰκεῖς; πόθεν δῆλον ὅτι
ἀθάνατος ἡ ψυχή;

Boethius:[83]

Interrogationis autem secundum Peripateticos *duplex* species est: aut cum *dialectica* interrogatio est aut cum non
dialectica: Non dialecticae autem interrogationis duae sunt species, sicut Ammonius (*conicio*; audivimus, *mss.*; Eudemus, *Meiser*) docet: una quidem quando
sumentes accidens interrogamus, cui
illud accidat, ut quando videmus domum
Ciceronis, si interrogemus, *quis illic
maneat*, vel quando subiectum quidem
ipsum et rem sumimus, quid autem illi
accidat interrogamus, ut si ipsum Ciceronem quis videat et interroget, quo diver-
tat ... altera vero quando proponentes
nomen quid sit quaerimus aut genus aut
differentiam aut definitionem requiren-
tes, ut si quis interroget quid sit animal.

The emendation suggested by Meiser is without any basis in the preserved
fragments of Eudemus' work on logic.[84] The emendation *Ammonius*, on the

[79] Ammonius, p. 20, 19.

[80] Boethius, *ed. sec.*, p. 56, 1.

[81] Among others, on the two kinds of interrogation (Ammonius, p. 199, 19, and
Boethius, *ed. sec.*, p. 361, 6), on the two types of necessity (Ammonius, p. 153, 13, and
Boethius, *ed. sec.*, p. 241, 1), etc.

[82] Ammonius *De interpr.* 20b22, p. 199, 19.

[83] Boethius *De interpr.*, *ed. sec.*, p. 361, 9.

[84] Cf. *Fragm. philos. Graec.*, ed. Muellach, 3, pp. 278–284.

other hand, appears to me to be required. Doubtless, the parallelism is weakened because Ammonius, in this particular passage, does not distinguish two kinds of ἐρώτησις πυσματική, but Boethius could have had at hand another edition of the same course or could have added to this passage a passage from another of Ammonius' works.[85] This conjecture will become particularly probable if it can be found that Boethius borrowed from the last Platonists, and especially from Ammonius, not only the apparatus of formal logic but the very essence of his philosophy. In fact, an examination of the *De consolatione philosophiae*, the philosophical testament of Boethius in prison and ready for death, confirms, I believe, the relationship between Boethius' thought and that of the last Neoplatonists, notably Ammonius of Alexandria.

3. THE NEOPLATONISM OF THE *De consolatione philosophiae*

For a long time the study of the sources of the *De consolatione philosophiae* remained a task of dissection. The verses, separated arbitrarily from the prose where they were inserted, were analyzed minutely. Peiper drew up an index of Boethius' borrowings from Seneca's tragedies.[1] Huettinger, applying the same method to the principal pagan and Christian poets, discovered such a host of sources for the same verse in Boethius that, somewhat nonplussed, he concluded that in this confusion he could not choose the real sources.[2] At the same time, Usener had divided the prose in the *De consolatione philosophiae* into three sections, the first one original, the second derived from an Aristotelian protreptic, the third from a Neoplatonic work. He indicated the exact place where the disparate imitations had been pieced together.[3] On the basis of these data, Stewart and Boissier were able to deduce that the *De consolatione philosophiae* was an entirely factitious work.[4]

A lively reaction to these extreme views made itself felt. Rand was the first to turn his attention to the fact that the *De consolatione philosophiae* was a coherent unit. He recommended research, particularly of a philosophical nature. Once the elements used by Boethius were acknowledged, the originality of his synthesis would be apparent.[5] He was followed along these lines by Galdi, Patch, and Raoul Carton.[6]

---

[85] We have seen above, p. 288, an analogous method applied to a passage in the *Isagoge* and the *Analytics*.

[1] Boethius *De consolatione philosophiae*, ed. Peiper, pp. 228–233.

[2] Huettinger, *Studia in Boethii carmina conlata* (Progr. Regensburg 1900–1902) 2, p. 23.

[3] Usener, "Vergessenes," *Rheinisches Museum* 28 (1873) 398.

[4] Stewart, *Boethius, An Essay* (Edinburgh 1891) 106, and Boissier, "Le christianisme de Boèce," *Journal des savants* (1889) 454.

[5] Rand, "On the Composition of Boethius' *Consolatio Philosophiae*," *Harvard Studies in Classical Philology* 15 (1904) 1–28.

[6] Galdi, "De Boethii carminibus quid iudicandum sit," *Athenaeum* 7 (1929) 363–385; Patch, "Fate in Boethius and the Neoplatonists," *Speculum* 4 (1929) 62–72; Carton, "Le christianisme et l'augustinisme de Boèce," *Mélanges augustiniens* (Paris 1931) 243–329.

The very genre to which the *De consolatione philosophiae* belongs may guide us toward the sources of its thought. Boethius borrows from the genre of ancient or Menippean satire the practice, previously followed by Martianus Capella, of alternating prose and verse. The very title associates the *De consolatione philosophiae* with the genre of the ancient consolation. Actually, the character of Philosophy, who consoles Boethius, presently turns him away from his own misfortunes to exalt him to God. We have to do with a protreptic. But this protreptic, in the form in which it is presented, differs radically from Aristotle's *Protrepticus* or from Cicero's *Hortensius*, as far as the preserved fragments allow us to reconstruct them. The instruction is here given in the form of a revelation, an apocalypse. Boethius dwells on the setting of this apocalypse. He describes himself, lying down, expressing his grief in a chant inspired by the Muses. At this moment Philosophy appears before him, recognizable by her dress. Her robe has an embroidered Θ at the top, at the foot a Π, and, in between, rungs of a ladder, denoting the degrees by which one rises from empirical to theoretical philosophy. She dismisses the Muses and promises to lead Boethius to the light by recalling to him what he has forgotten.[7]

This apocalyptic setting whose origins are ancient, to mention only the *Poimandres* of Hermes Trismegistus or Hermas' *Shepherd*, seemed to enjoy particular favor in the Latin Neoplatonic circles in the last centuries. It recalls still less Martianus Capella's *De nuptiis* than Fulgentius' *Mitologiae*, the theme of which is very similar. The *Mitologiae* and the *De consolatione philosophiae* likewise appear as a Platonic revelation on the nature of divinity.[8]

Boethius does not conceal the names of the philosophers whom he invokes. He was nurtured, he declares, on the doctrines of the Eleatics and the Academy.[9] The Eleatics here denote the founders of dialectic, for their theories did not leave any precise recollection.[10] It is above all Plato who appears as the supreme philosopher. Philosophy always quotes him as her friend,[11] recommends his maxims that she herself has formulated through his

[7] *De cons. philos.* I, pr. I, ed. Peiper, pp. 4ff. Note that the very concept of philosophical consolation seems to be in the air at the beginning of the sixth century. Cf. Avitus *Epist.* 5.5, *de transitu filiae regis, MGH, Auct. ant.* 6, p. 32, 20: "Neque porro cadit in regiam quidem, sed philosophicam mentem maeroris abiectio."

[8] Cf. above, chap. 4 sec. 4 n. 107. The affinity between Boethius and Fulgentius was already pointed out by Helm, "Der Bischof Fulgentius und der Mythograph," p. 120. He scrutinizes even minute points. The appearance is represented in Fulgentius, p. 8, 16, by the verb *adstitit*; in Boethius, p. 4, 3, by *adstitisse*. On Calliope's appearance, Fulgentius, p. 8, 21, wondered *quaenam esset*, and Boethius, at the appearance of Philosophy, p. 5, 43, wondered *quaenam haec esset*.

[9] *De cons. philos.*, ed. Peiper, p. 5, 36.

[10] Cf. Zeller, *Die Philosophie der Griechen*, vol. 3, 2, 2, p. 858 n. 3.

[11] *De cons. philos.*, ed. Peiper, p. 8, 16.

lips.[12] She takes care to declare to Boethius that the theories she enunciates agree with those of Plato, as though, even for her, he was the supreme authority. Boethius acknowledges this authority without reservation.[13] Furthermore, the history of human thought is divided into two periods, one period preceding, the other following, Plato. The sects other than the Platonic sect are treated as heresies.[14] Thus Canius, Seneca, Soranus, those famous Stoics whose glorious death Philosophy is to recall, have only one merit, that of having been able to be taken as Plato's disciples. But Philosophy does not regard them as her followers and later will ridicule the doctrine of sensation of "these old men once the product of the Porch."[15] Philosophy attacks Epicurus no less, his doctrine of the supreme good,[16] and his School, which she regards as *Epicureum vulgus*.[17] Does this mean that Plato alone finds grace in her eyes? She also says once, "my dear Aristotle,"[18] quotes him again and again, but occasionally implying that she is not always in agreement with his view.[19] On the other hand, Pythagoreanism is the object of religious reverence on Boethius' part, for, to defend himself against the accusation of sacrilege, he testifies to having followed all his life the precept "ἕπου θεῷ."[20] It is therefore evident that Boethius is the adept of a Neoplatonism steeped in Pythagoreanism, even if he refrains in the *De consolatione philosophiae*, a literary work, from naming any recent writer.[21] The design of the *De consolatione philosophiae* is itself based on a dual conversion in three stages: self-knowledge (Book 2), knowledge of the purpose of things (Books 3 and 4 to paragraph 5), knowledge of the laws that govern the universe (end of Book 4 and Book 5). This conversion is set under the patronage of Plato.[22]

There is disagreement among scholars on the sources of the first two parts. When Bywater had shown, from a parallel passage in Iamblichus, that the quotation from Aristotle taken from Book 3 must have been borrowed from

[12] *Ibid.*, p. 11, 15.
[13] *Ibid.*, p. 70, 94 and p. 141, 55; cf. p. 81, 1.
[14] *Ibid.*, p. 8, 15.
[15] *Ibid.*, p. 135, 1.
[16] *Ibid.*, p. 53, 46.
[17] *Ibid.*, p. 8, 20.
[18] *Ibid.*, p. 122, 34.
[19] *Ibid.*, p. 139, 19.
[20] *Ibid.*, p. 15, 129ff.
[21] The latest writers that he mentions, p. 45, 29 and p. 112, 124, are Cicero and Lucan. The latest example is Papinian, executed by Caracalla, p. 61, 28.
[22] *De cons. philos.*, p. 22, 39: "Nam quoniam tui oblivione confunderis, et exsulem te et expoliatum propriis bonis doluisti; quoniam vero quis sit rerum finis ignoras, nequam homines atque nefarios potentes felicesque arbitraris; quoniam vero quibus gubernaculis mundus regatur oblitus es, has fortunarum vices aestimas sine rectore fluitare." Cf. p. 81, lines 3–6 and 15–16, and 1.1–4, where Plato's name appears.

his lost *Protrepticus*,²³ Usener felt authorized to acknowledge this *Protrepticus* and Cicero's *Hortensius* as the direct or indirect sources of the major part of the *De consolatione philosophiae*.²⁴ Rand, who first approached the subject, confined himself to showing that in any case original touches too appeared in Boethius, personal recollections, Roman concepts, and that his imitation was not so slavish and mechanical as Usener had assumed.²⁵ Much bolder, Mueller restricted the extent of the passages taken from Aristotle and Cicero (from 2 paragraph 5 to 3 paragraph 8) and showed what the beginning of Book 2 owed to Plutarch's *Consolation to Apollonius* and what the section dealing with God (from 3 paragraph 9 to 4 paragraph 6) owed to Plato.²⁶ Lastly, Klingner, breaking with all traditions, declared that Book 2 was a Cynico-Stoic diatribe, and Book 3 a work that was Platonic in inspiration and style. Cicero's and Aristotle's thought appeared only in the exact place where they were quoted (2 paragraph 7, 3 paragraph 8). In other respects, after distinguishing between Stoic Book 2 and Platonic Book 3, Klingner acknowledged, not without some illogicality, that the arguments of the first part of Book 3 repeated those of Book 2.²⁷

So many contradictory views demand the utmost caution in an investigation of the sources and indicate that we have to deal with commonplaces easy to find in the most dissimilar writers. One point, however, appears certain. The first part of Book 3 (paragraphs 1 to 8) is connected with the preceding discussion on the benefits of fortune and is detached from the end of the book, which discusses the supreme good. In fact, to lead Boethius to true happiness, Philosophy announces at the beginning of Book 3 that she wishes to show him false happiness first of all. But this survey of false benefits merely repeats what had been said about the benefits of fortune in the preceding chapter.²⁸

The mistake of scholars in this inquiry lay in establishing parallel ideas between very general discussions that appear in many ancient writers, instead of endeavoring to discover the direct source, which only a textual parallel could reveal. Thus, the passage in Book 2 where Boethius quotes Cicero has already been the subject of strenuous controversies. The first idea was to

²³ I. Bywater, "On a Lost Dialogue of Aristotle," *Journal of Philology* 2 (1869) 55–69.
²⁴ *De cons. philos.* 2, pr. 4, line 38 to 4, pr. 6, line 20. Cf. Usener, "Vergessenes," pp. 398ff.
²⁵ Rand, "On the Composition of Boethius' *Consolatio Philosophiae*," pp. 1–20. Cf. also the criticism of Usener's theories by Boyancé, *Etudes* (above, Introduction n. 24) 149.
²⁶ G. A. Mueller, *Die Trostschrift des Boethius* (diss. Giessen, Berlin 1912) 26ff.
²⁷ F. Klingner, *De Boethii consolatione philosophiae* (Berlin 1921) 8–14. He did not observe, pp. 36–37, that the movement toward Platonic conversion formed the fundamental basis of the *De consolatione philosophiae*.
²⁸ Boethius himself noticed these repetitions, p. 63, 12: "Sed cum, *uti paulo ante disserui*, plures esse gentes necesse sit ad quas unius fama hominis nequeat pervenire," repeating pp. 44 and 45.

relate it to *Scipio's Dream*. But Usener observed some difference between these two texts, since Boethius discarded the illustration of the Ganges, and he proposed, in conformity with his general theory, to refer Boethius' quotation to the *Hortensius*.[29] Klingner had no trouble in refuting him on this point.[30] Plasberg's argument is much more formidable. He calls attention to the fact that, in *Scipio's Dream*, Cicero speaks only of the renown of an individual, while Boethius, against the logical sense of his entire discussion, which likewise deals with individual renown, speaks of the glory of the Roman people, as though he were constrained by his quotation.[31] Klingner's rebuttal to this argument is quite weak. This is because he did not think that Boethius interpreted *Scipio's Dream* by way of Macrobius' commentary, as the following parallel proves:

Cicero:[32]	Macrobius:[33]	Boethius:[34]
Ex his ipsis cultis notisque terris num aut tuum aut cuiusquam nostrum nomen vel Caucasum hunc, quem cernis, transcendere potuit vel illum Gangen tranatare? Quis in reliquis orientis aut obeuntis solis ultimis aut aquilonis austrive partibus tuum nomen audiet? Quibus amputatis, cernis profecto quantis in angustiis vestra se gloria dilatari velit.	... nullius vero gloriam vel in illam totam partem potuisse diffundi (si quidem Gangen transnare vel transcendere Caucasum *Romani nominis fama* non valuit): spem, quam de propaganda late gloria ante oculos ponendo nostri orbis angustias amputavit, vult et diuturnitatis auferre.	Aetate denique Marci Tulli, sicut ipse in quodam loco significat, nondum Caucasum montem Romanae rei publicae fama transcenderat, et erat tunc adulta, Parthis etiam ceterisque id locorum gentibus formidolosa. Videsne igitur quam sit angusta, quam compressa gloria quam dilatare ac propagare laboratis? An ubi *Romani nominis* transire *fama* nequit, Romani hominis gloria progredietur?

It was Macrobius the Neoplatonist who introduced the idea of the renown of the Roman name, and it was Boethius who reproduced word for word the expression *Romani nominis fama*. It was Macrobius that Boethius used, and thus one of the most cogent arguments in favor of the dependence of the *De consolatione philosophiae* on the *Hortensius* breaks down.

Boethius, besides, contributes correctives to Macrobius. In the same discussion, *Scipio's Dream* next treats of the great year, which Macrobius, by means of learned calculations, estimates at 15,000 solar years.[35] Boethius, on

---

[29] Usener, "Vergessenes," p. 402.

[30] Klingner, *De Boeth. cons. philos.*, pp. 9ff.

[31] O. Plasberg, *De M. Tullii Ciceronis Hortensio dialogo* (diss. Berlin 1892) 62.

[32] Cicero *Republic* 6.20.22.

[33] Macrobius *In Somn. Scip.* 2.10.3, ed. Eyssenhardt (Leipzig 1868), p. 605, 30.

[34] Boethius *De cons. philos.*, p. 45, 28.

[35] Macrobius *In Somn. Scip.* 2.11.15, p. 612, 1.

the other hand, gives the figure as 10,000 years.[36] Are we to think, because Boethius' imitation is not slavish, that he borrows this item from a lost passage of the *Hortensius*? This hypothesis of Usener's is all the less acceptable as a passage in the *Hortensius* preserved by Tacitus informs us that Cicero estimated the great year as 12,954 solar years.[37] Shall we say, with Mueller, that Boethius has given a round number, without troubling about the precise figure, as Plutarch does in his *Consolation to Apollonius*?[38] I believe, on the contrary, that, if Boethius rejected Cicero's figure and Macrobius', it was because in his day and in the School of Proclus the great year was estimated at 10,000 years.[39] Boethius would then be using Macrobius, modernizing and adapting him to the more recent Platonic theories.

Still more certainly, Boethius' quotation from Aristotle, if it relates to the lost *Protrepticus*, cannot stem from it directly.[40] Usener himself posited a series of intermediaries between them. One of them was necessarily common to Boethius and Iamblichus, since in Iamblichus' *Protrepticus* we find Aristotle's statement that Boethius quotes, but in a very weak form and without Aristotle's name attached to it. This intermediary cannot but be a Greek, for it is altogether unlikely that Iamblichus borrowed his illustration from Cicero's *Hortensius* or from any other Latin writer. There is evidence to confirm that several of the examples quoted by Boethius, even if they appear at first sight in the Latin tradition, were undoubtedly borrowed from a Greek protrepticus. In the first book of the *De consolatione philosophiae* Boethius quotes the illustration of a certain Julius Canius, an eminent Stoic philosopher who, when charged with having participated in a conspiracy directed against the emperor, replied to Caligula: "Had I known about it, you would

---

[36] Boethius *De cons. philos.*, p. 45, 50.

[37] Tacitus *Dial. de orat.* 16.7; and Servius *In Aen.* 3.284. Cf. Usener, "Vergessenes," p. 398.

[38] Cf. Mueller, *Die Trostschrift*, p. 42. M. Galdi, *Saggi Boeziani* (Pisa 1938) 206–222, claims to have demonstrated that Boethius frequently depends on Plutarch. But his sources are secondary, and the similarities that he notes have a bearing on analogous commonplaces only. Similarly, his chapters on Boethius and Proclus (pp. 131–148) and on Boethius and Cassianus (pp. 223–229) are extremely weak.

[39] Cf. Duhem, *Le système du monde* I, p. 293.

[40] Iamblichus *Protrepticus*, ed. Pistelli, p. 47, 13:

Εἰ γάρ τις ἐδύνατο βλέπειν ὀξὺ καθάπερ τὸν Λυγκέα φασίν, ὃς διὰ τῶν τοίχων ἑώρα καὶ τῶν δένδρων, πότ' ἂν ἔδοξεν εἶναί τινα τὴν ὄψιν ἀνεκτόν, ὁρῶν ἐξ οἵων συνέστηκε κακῶν;

Boethius *De cons. philos.*, p. 65, 21:

Quod si, ut Aristoteles ait, Lyncei oculis homines uterentur, et eorum visus obstantia penetraret, nonne introspectis visceribus illud Alcibiadis superficie pulcherrimum corpus turpissimum videretur?

Cf. also John Philopon *De aeternitate mundi*, ed. Rabe, p. 151, 15, quoting the line from Apollonius *Argon.* 1.155 relating to Lynceus; and Diels, "Zu Aristoteles' Protreptikos und Ciceros Hortensius," *Archiv für Geschichte der Philosophie* I (1888) 477–497.

not have known."[41] Editors refer this passage to a discussion in Seneca's *De tranquillitate animi*, but this historic retort does not appear there. According to Seneca's editor, Waltz, who agrees on this point with Pauly-Wissowa, this Canius or Canus is otherwise quite unknown.[42] Such a statement is incorrect, for a fragment from George Syncellus, a Byzantine chronicler of the eighth century, declares that Plutarch, in a lost work, discussed at great length the death of this heroic figure Canus and attributed miraculous phenomena to him.[43] Thus we have the certainty that Seneca was not Boethius' source for this anecdote. We know besides that Plutarch, in a work now lost, devotes to this Canus a long discussion, much more detailed than Seneca's, which he took, as he informs us, from Greek tradition. In the present state of our knowledge, it was then Plutarch or his source or one of his imitators who furnished Boethius with this information. This same source is probably the author of the Greek protrepticus that served as an intermediary between Aristotle and Iamblichus and Boethius.

The second part of Book 3, which contains a philosophical argumentation instead of rhetorical discussions, allows us to reach more definite conclusions. I do not think that we can argue from the very form of the exposition, as Klingner does when he establishes a connection between Boethius' dialogue with Philosophy and the Socratic dialogue,[44] by comparing this exposition with Book 2, which he considers Stoic. Mueller had already shown that, with regard to the content of this Platonic section, Boethius often expounds his theories with Aristotle's dialectic;[45] for instance, when Philosophy poses an alternative[46] and uses the syllogism.[47] Like the latest commentators on Aristotle, for example Ammonius, Boethius also resorts to the geometrical demonstration.[48] But Klingner has well shown the Neoplatonic origin of this

---

[41] Boethius *De cons. philos.*, p. 14, 86; cf. p. 9, 30.

[42] Seneca *De tranq. animi* 14.4-9, ed. Waltz, *Coll. des Univ. de France, Dialogues*, 4, p. 99 n. 2. Cf. *PW* s.v. Julius (Canus).

[43] George Syncellus *Chronographia*, ed. Niebuhr (Bonn 1829), *CSHB*, p. 330 D: "'on the evidence of the Greeks,' Julius Canus on his way to undergo torture had predicted to his friend Rectus that he would be put to death three days later, and to Antiochus of Seleucia that his soul would appear to him the following night. These predictions were fulfilled, and the spirit of the dead Canus discoursed on the immortality of the soul."

[44] Klingner, *De Boeth. cons. philos.*, pp. 75ff.

[45] Mueller, *Die Trostschrift*, p. 25.

[46] *De cons. philos.*, p. 67, 1 and p. 91, 6.

[47] *Ibid.*, p. 101, 32. Note the pedagogical tone.

[48] Ammonius *De interpr.*, p. 248, 2:

Τοῦτο δὲ κατασκευάζει πόρισμά τι κατὰ τοὺς γεωμετρικοὺς ἐκ τῶν εἰρημένων πρὸς τὴν κατασκευὴν χρήσιμον συνάγων, ὅτι τὸ ἀναγκαῖον ἐπὶ μόνου τοῦ κατ᾽ ἐνέργειαν ὄντος θεωρεῖται.

Boethius *De cons. philos.*, p. 74, 76:

Super haec, inquit, igitur veluti *geometrae* solent demonstratis propositis aliquid inferre quae *porismata* ipsi vocant, ita ego quoque tibi veluti corollarium dabo.

part of the *De consolatione philosophiae*, especially poem 9, which was destined to meet such a fate in the Middle Ages.[49] Klingner established, not only that three quarters of this hymn correspond to the three stages of Neoplatonic religion, πρόοδος, ἐπιστροφή, ἄνοδος,[50] but also that Boethius interpreted the *Timaeus* with the aid of Proclus' commentary.[51] Klingner's method of reaching this conclusion consists in showing that everything in these verses that does not refer specifically to the *Timaeus* reappears in Proclus' commentary. For instance, the concept of a god free from desire because he lacks nothing, the concept of a god who carries in his understanding the universe and the forms from which he creates, the concrete and geometrical interpretation of all that in Plato had merely the value of a myth or a symbol: all this, according to Klingner, derives from Proclus. This demonstration, details of which it is futile to repeat here, is very closely reasoned and very conclusive. It is certain that Boethius read the *Timaeus* by way of a Greek Neoplatonist and not in Cicero's or Chalcidius' translation, as is proved by the passages where he claims to quote Plato's text.[52] Besides, there are between the *De consolatione philosophiae* and Proclus' commentary on the *Timaeus* not only parallels in ideas, but at least once a textual parallel:

Proclus *In Tim.*, ed. Diehl, vol. 1, p. 378, 18:
Ὡς ἡ ἀγαθοειδὴς αἵρεσις ἑαυτῆς γίγνεται καρπός, οὕτως ἡ μοχθηρὰ ἑαυτῆς ποινή.

Boethius *De consolatione philosophiae*, p. 97, 35:
Sicut igitur probis probitas *ipsa fit praemium, ita* improbis nequitia *ipsa supplicium est.*[53]

It will be a question, however, whether Boethius' borrowings from Proclus are always direct or whether it was not rather his disciple Ammonius who induced Boethius to quote the *Timaeus*, as the following texts seem to indicate:[54]

The term πόρισμα is not employed elsewhere by Boethius, nor is it used in Porphyry's logical works. On the other hand, it occurs quite frequently in Proclus *In Tim.*, and in Ammonius' commentaries.

[49] For medieval interpretations, cf. my "Etude critique des commentaires sur la *Consolatio Philosophiae* de Boèce," *Archives d'histoire doctrinale et littéraire du Moyen Age* 14 (1939) 5–140.

[50] Klingner, *De Boeth. cons. philos.*, p. 40.

[51] *Ibid.*, p. 51.

[52] The only points of contact are explained by Plato's text: *Timaeus* 35a in Cicero *Tim.* (ed. Mueller, *Op. philos.* 3, p. 220, 22) and Boethius *Inst. arithm.*, ed. Friedlein, p. 126, 2; *Tim.* 27c in Chalcidius, ed. Wrobel, p. 22, and Boethius, *De cons. philos.*, ed. Peiper, p. 70, 93.

[53] Similarity already noted by Theiler, *Porphyrios und Augustin*, 31.

[54] Klingner, *De Boeth. cons. philos.*, p. 73, already observed that the idea translated in this passage of the *De cons. philos.* by *oportere* (necessity of a relationship between speech and subject) stems neither from the *Timaeus* nor from the translations by Cicero or

Plato *Timaeus* 29b:	Ammonius *De in-*	Boethius *De in-*	Boethius *De cons.*
... ὡς ἄρα τοὺς λόγους, ὧνπέρ εἰσιν ἐξηγηταί, τούτων αὐτῶν καὶ συγγενεῖς ὄντας.	*terpr.*, p. 152, 22: ἐπεὶ ὁμοίως οἱ λόγοι ἀληθεῖς ὥσπερ τὰ πράγματα.

p. 154, 16: οὕτως γὰρ ἀνάγκη τὸ ἀληθὲς ἔχειν τοὺς λόγους, ὅπερ φησὶν ὁ Ἀριστοτέλης, ὡς ἔχει φύσεως τὰ ὑπ᾽ αὐτῶν σημαινόμενα πράγματα, ἐπεὶ καὶ εἰσὶν ἐξηγηταὶ τῶν πραγμάτων οἱ λόγοι καὶ διὰ τοῦτο μιμοῦνται αὐτῶν τὴν φύσιν, ὡς πρὸ τοῦ Ἀριστοτέλους ὁ Πλάτων ἡμᾶς ἐδίδαξεν. | *terpr.*, ed. sec., p. 246, 20: *Orationes verae sunt quemadmodum et res.* | *philos.* 3.12. 108–112: Quod si rationes quoque non extra petitas, sed intra rei quam tractabamus ambitum conlocatas agitavimus, nihil est quod admirere, cum Platone sanciente didiceris cognatos de quibus loquuntur rebus oportere esse sermones. |

It was also among the disciples of Proclus and Ammonius that Boethius had acquired his Greek literary culture. The line from Homer that the character of Philosophy recalls to Boethius in order to give him courage ("Nonne adulescentulus δοιοὺς πίθους, τὸν μὲν ἕνα κακῶν, τὸν δὲ ἕτερον ἐάων in Iovis limine iacere didicisti?")[55] reappears thrice used or quoted in Proclus' work, and again in Synesius and Olympiodorus.[56] Another line from Homer used by Boethius[57] is quoted in the commentaries of Proclus, Synesius, Hermias, Olympiodorus.[58] Still another line, interpreted by Boethius as proof of

---

Chalcidius. Klingner referred it to Proclus' *Comm. in Tim.*, ed. Diehl, 1, p. 8, 9 and p. 340, 22.

[55] Boethius *De cons. philos.*, p. 28, 38. Cf. *Odyssey* 24.527.

[56] Proclus *In Remp.*, ed. Kroll, 2, p. 96, 14; *In Crat.*, ed. Pasquali, p. 51, 25; *De malorum subsistentia*, ed. Cousin, col. 237. Cf. Synesius *De providentia*, PG 66, 1275, and *De insomniis*, *ibid.*, 1298; Olympiodorus *In Gorgiam*, ed. Norvin, p. 54, 9.

[57] *De cons. philos.*, p. 125, 1; quoting *Iliad* 3.277 (= *Od.* 11.109):

πάντ᾽ ἐφορᾶν καὶ πάντ᾽ ἐπακούειν

Puro clarum lumine Phoebum
melliflui canit oris Homerus.

Against Peiper I adopt this excellent reading, which is furthermore required by the manuscripts.

[58] Proclus *In Crat.*, ed. Pasquali, p. 37, 8, and *In Tim.*, ed. Diehl, 2, p. 82, 8; Hermias *In Phaedr.*, ed. Couvreur, p. 68, 9: Olympiodorus *In Phaed.*, ed. Norvin, p. 26, 27. Cf.

divine monarchy,[59] was currently interpreted in the same sense by Aristotle's Alexandrian commentators.[60] The line from Parmenides quoted by Boethius[61] recurs twice in Proclus and seven times in Simplicius' commentary on Aristotle's *Physics*.[62] Lastly, there is the hexameter Ἀνδρὸς δὴ ἱεροῦ δέμας αἰθέρες οἰκοδόμησαν, to which Boethius attaches a particular importance (for Philosophy says that it was written by a person more distinguished than herself: "excellentior"). In meaning the line comes close to a Chaldean oracle quoted twice by Proclus,[63] but I have not succeeded any better than my predecessors in discovering the author.[64]

The last two books of the *De consolatione philosophiae*, which scholars agree in describing as a Neoplatonic section,[65] show still better than the preceding books the influence that Proclus and Ammonius exercised on Boethius' thought.

The Boethian theory of Providence and Fate is very characteristic. To him, Providence is the simple act whereby God embraces in one glance the infinity

---

Synesius *De regno*, PG 66, 1100; he quotes this line in the same form as Boethius does. It was even used in therapeutic magic for eye remedies, as we learn from Marcellus of Bordeaux *De medicamentis*, ed. Helmreich (Leipzig 1889), p. 69, 25: "Hoc etiam remedium indubitate impetus oculorum, si praevenias, prohibebit, scriptum in charta virgine: ῥουβρς ῥυοπεφας ἡέλιος ὃς πάντ᾽ ἐφορᾷ καὶ πάντ᾽ ἐπακούει."
[ῥουβρς ῥυοπεφας is a magic formula without signification. Cf. Cato's specific against rheumatic ailments: huat, hanat, ista, pista, sista. TRANS.]

[59] *De cons. philos.*, p. 18, 11, quoting *Iliad* 2.204–205: εἷς κοίρανος ἔστω, / εἷς βασιλεύς.

[60] Cf. Ammonius *De interpr.*, ed. Busse, p. 96, 23: Olympiodorus *In Gorgiam*, ed. Jahn, p. 518 = ed. Norvin, p. 202, 33; John Philopon *De aeternitate mundi*, ed. Rabe, p. 88, 20 and p. 179, 21. Aristotle quoted this line from Homer in *Metaphysics* 1076a4. It was from this *locus* that it spread among the commentators. Zacharias, however, used it as a weapon against Ammonius, whom he charges with accepting polytheism, PG 85, 1053 A.

[61] *De cons. philos.*, p. 85, 98, quoting line 103 of Parmenides, ed. Mullach: Πάντοθεν εὐκύκλου σφαίρης ἐναλίγκιον ὄγκῳ.

[62] Proclus *In Tim.*, ed. Diehl, 2, p. 69, 20, and *Theol. Plat.* 3.20; Simplicius *In Phys.*, p. 52, 23; 89, 22; 126, 22; 127, 31; 137, 16; 143, 6; 146, 30.

[63] *De cons. philos.*, ed. Peiper, p. 112, 137. Cf. Fortescue's edition, p. 128. Note the presence of a *digamma* before ἱεροῦ.

[64] Proclus *In Tim.*, ed. Diehl, 3, p. 266, 19, and *De providentia et fato*, ed. Cousin (Paris 1864), p. 164: "Quicumque autem Patris opera intellegentes reverendi fiunt, sortis fatalem alam effugiunt." This is the fifty-fourth Chaldean oracle. Note also Boethius' reference, *De cons. philos.*, p. 70, 93, to *Timaeus* 27c: "Sed cum, ut in *Timaeo*, inquit, nostro plaeet, in minimis quoque rebus divinum praesidium debeat implorari, quid nunc faciendum censes, ut illius summi boni sedem reperire mereamur?" The same reference to this passage in the *Timaeus* appears in Hermias *In Platonis Phaedrum*, ed. Couvreur, Bibl. des Hautes Etudes, fasc. 133, p. 48, 13 and p. 205, 30: proof that the Neoplatonists of Alexandria used it regularly to justify the necessity of prayer.

[65] Cf. Rand, "On the Composition of Boethius' *Cons. philos.*," pp. 16ff.

of beings beyond space and time. Fate, on the other hand, depends on Providence[66] and governs minutely whatever moves through space and time. Certain beings are not subject to it.[67] This subordination, unknown to the Stoics,[68] is meaningless except in a philosophy that establishes a hierarchy among beings, and it is among the Neoplatonists that we find the problem stated from this angle.[69] Boethius reviews the various agents of Fate that the Neoplatonists postulated to explain the universe: divine spirits, the soul of the universe, nature, the stars, angels, and demons.[70] Similarly, Proclus, in the *De providentia et fato*, identifies Providence with God and subjects Fate to him.[71] In the *De decem dubitationibus circa providentiam* he examines how the angels and demons can be the ministers of Providence.[72] Patch has already dwelt rightly on this doctrinal relationship between Proclus and Boethius, but he thinks that the image whereby Boethius tries to express his thought is the result of contamination between Proclus and Plotinus. From Proclus, Boethius may have borrowed the image of the circular motion of Fate. From Plotinus he took the concept of God as the center of the universe, a notion that, according to Patch, does not appear in Proclus.[73]

This interpretation seems to me to rest on a misconception. Patch calls Boethius' image a metaphor of the spheres. Actually, the word *orbis* used by Boethius here denotes not a sphere but a circle. Besides, a few lines further on,

---

[66] Boethius *De cons. philos.*, p. 109, 40: "Quae licet diversa sint, alterum tamen pendet ex altero. Ordo namque fatalis ex providentiae simplicitate procedit."

[67] *Ibid.*, p. 109, 60: "ea vero sunt quae primae propinqua divinitati stabiliter fixa fatalis ordinem mobilitatis excedunt."

[68] Cf. the texts assembled in Fortescue's edition of the *De cons. philos.*, pp. 165–168, Appendix 1: "De providentia et fato."

[69] Cf. Plotinus *Enneads* 3.3.5, ed. Bréhier, 3, p. 55; Hierocles *De providentia et fato*, ed. Needham (1709), p. 254. This thesis already appeared in Chalcidius *In Tim.* 151, 177, 145, ed. Wrobel, pp. 208, 226, 204.

[70] Boethius *De cons. philos.*, p. 109, 48: "Sive igitur famulantibus quibusdam providentiae divinis spiritibus fatum exercetur seu anima seu tota inserviente natura seu caelestibus siderum motibus seu angelica virtute seu daemonum varia sollertia seu aliquibus horum seu omnibus fatalis series texitur: illud certe manifestum est immobilem simplicemque gerendarum formam rerum esse providentiam, fatum vero eorum quae divina simplicitas gerenda disposuit mobilem nexum atque ordinem temporalem."

[71] Proclus *De prov. et fato*, ed. Cousin, p. 158, 8: "Sic igitur Providentia quidem Deus per se, Fatum autem divina aliqua res et non Deus: dependet enim a Providentia et velut imago est illius."

[72] Proclus *De decem dubit.* 10, ed. Cousin, p. 140, 32: "Providentia enim, ut dictum est, Uno hoc valde laudato omnia et cognoscente et in Bonum reducente, quo modo et angeli providere dicuntur et daemones, si autem velis, et heroes et animae cum iis condispensantes cum diis mundum?" An entire chapter is devoted to the resolution of this difficulty. Cf. also *De malorum subsistentia, ibid.*, pp. 212–214, where Proclus defines what he means by "angels" and "demons." Cf. F. Cumont, "Les anges du paganisme," *Revue de l'histoire des religions* 72 (1915) 159–182.

[73] Patch, "Fate in Boethius," pp. 62–72.

the word *circulus* is given as a synonym of *orbis*. Hence the references to Plotinus that Patch mentions are not justified,[74] for in Plotinus the discussion is about the universe regarded as a closed sphere whose soul is the center. Neither the notion nor the image is Boethius'. Boethius' intention is merely to explain by means of the figure of the circle and its center the connection between Providence and Fate, that is, between divine unity and the multiplicity of creatures subject to space and time. Now, the same image applied to the same notion appears in precisely the same form in Proclus:

Proclus:[75]

Nihil enim effugit illud Unum sive in esse dicas, sive in cognosci. Et dicitur quidem, et recte dicitur, et in centro totus circulus esse centraliter: si quidem causa centrum, causatum autem *circulus*; et in unitate omnis numerus monadice propter eandem rationem. In Providentiae autem Uno maiori modo omnia sunt; si quidem est Unum maiori modo illud quam centrum et monas. Sicut igitur si centrum haberet cognitionem circuli, centralem utique haberet cognitionem sicut et hypostasin, et non partiretur se ipsum in circuli partibus; sic et Providentiae unialis cognitio in eodem impartibili est omnium partitorum cognitio, et uniuscuiusque individuissimorum et totalissimorum, et ut subsistit unumquodque secundum Unum, sic et cognoscit unumquodque secundum Unum et neque divisa est cognitis cognitio, neque confusa sunt cognita propter unam unionem cognitionis.

Boethius:[76]

Nam ut orbium circa eundem cardinem sese vertentium qui est intimus ad simplicitatem medietatis accedit ceterorumque extra locatorum veluti cardo quidam circa quem versentur existit, extimus vero maiore ambitu rotatus quanto a puncti media individuitate discedit tanto amplioribus spatiis explicatur, si quid vero illi se medio conectat et societ, in simplicitatem cogitur diffundique ac diffluere cessat: simili ratione quod longius a prima mente discedit maioribus fati nexibus implicatur ac tanto aliquid fato liberum est quanto illum rerum cardinem vicinius petit. Quod si supernae mentis haeserit firmitati, motu carens fati quoque supergreditur necessitatem. Igitur uti ad intellectum ratiocinatio, ad id quod est id quod gignitur, ad aeternitatem tempus, ad punctum medium *circulus*, ita est fati series mobilis ad providentiae stabilem simplicitatem.

If there is contamination in Boethius' metaphor, it is because he uses in an original way this image of the *De decem dubitationibus*, adding the notion, taken from the same Proclus' *De providentia et fato*, that Fate rules the creatures subject to space and time. The fact that Proclus' thought is thus

[74] Patch, "Fate in Boethius," p. 68, referring to Plotinus *Enneads* 2.2.1–2 and 3.2.3. On the other hand, it is true that, in *Enn.* 1.7.1, 6.8.18, and 6.9.8, Plotinus uses the metaphor of the circle and the point, but not the spheres. It is surprising that Patch, who knew the text of Proclus (he quotes a fragment from it, p. 66 n. 2) could maintain that nowhere in Proclus can the image of the central point of Providence be found.

[75] Proclus *De decem dubit.*, p. 82, 6. The Greek text is lost. This extremely awkward translation is by William of Morbeke.

[76] Boethius *De cons. philos.*, p. 110, 61.

systematized might lead one to think that there was an intermediary between Boethius and Proclus. Thus, without any bold affirmation, for lack of sufficiently exact textual connections, that Boethius plagiarized Proclus' treatises, it is no less certain that he reproduced their theories and was familiar with them either directly or through Ammonius.

In point of fact, it is particularly Ammonius that the last two books of the *De consolatione philosophiae* recall, and I think that they probably have as their source Ammonius' commentary on Plato's *Gorgias* and most certainly Ammonius' commentaries on Aristotle's *De interpretatione* and the *Physics*.

Klingner has shed light on the fact that the entire first half of Book 4 of the *De consolatione philosophiae* followed Plato's *Gorgias* or rather a Neoplatonic commentary on the *Gorgias*.[77] We know four commentaries on the *Gorgias*: those by Eubulus, Hierocles, whose oral lectures were edited by his pupil Theosebius, Ammonius, and Olympiodorus. The first three are hopelessly lost and even the existence of a commentary by Ammonius on the *Gorgias* would be unknown had it not been expressly mentioned once by Olympiodorus.[78] At least Olympiodorus' commentary may give us an idea of his teacher's commentary. It is probable that Boethius is following Ammonius' commentary when he speaks of the punishment of the wicked. In fact, like Porphyry[79] and Proclus,[80] Boethius and Olympiodorus offer an allegorical interpretation of the theory of metempsychosis. The wicked retain their human form, although the soul shrinks to the level of the beasts.[81] Ammonius' commentary also helps to explain a passage in the *De consolatione philosophiae* that has caused much ink to flow. Boethius, breaking into the sequence of the exposition that Philosophy explains to him from the *Gorgias*, asks: "Sed quaeso, inquam, te, nullane animarum supplicia post defunctum morte

[77] Klingner, *De Boeth. cons. philos.*, pp. 85ff. Boethius' exposition follows step by step the argumentation of the *Gorgias*: as evil does not exist per se, tyrants can gratify their whims, but cannot achieve their will (p. 95, 130 = *Gorg.* 466d–e, 467a, 468e). The wicked man is unhappy (p. 100, 1 = *Gorg.* 468e–470c), and all the more so the longer he remains unpunished (p. 100, 20–p. 103, 85 = *Gorg.* 472d–e and 476a–478e). To do evil is a greater misfortune than to suffer it (p. 104, 110 = *Gorg.* 474c–476a). The role of accusers and lawyers is ridiculous, for the criminal is a sick man who should himself seek his own remedies (p. 104, 123 = *Gorg.* 480a–481b).

[78] Cf. Cousin, "Du commentaire inédit d'Olympiodore . . . sur le *Gorgias* de Platon," p. 750, foot of page. This is the only decisive passage, for the other anecdotes attributed by Olympiodorus to Ammonius might have no connection with the *Gorgias*. Cf. R. Beutler, "Die Gorgiasscholien und Olympiodor," *Hermes* 73 (1938) 380–390.

[79] Cf. Augustine *De civ. Dei* 10.30 (*PL* 41, 310): "Verum tamen, ut dixi, ex magna parte correctus est in hac opinione Porphyrius, ut saltem in solos homines humanas animas praecipitari posse sentiret, belluinos autem carceres evertere minime dubitaret." But it is improbable that Porphyry wrote a commentary on the *Gorgias*.

[80] Proclus *In Tim.*, ed. Diehl, 3, p. 295, 30. Cf. Aeneas of Gaza, *PG* 85, 894 A–B.

[81] Boethius *De cons. philos.*, p. 97, 48 and p. 100, 2. Cf. Olympiodorus *In Phaed.*, p. 166, 24.

corpus relinquis?—Et magna quidem, inquit, quorum alia poenali acerbitate, alia vero purgatoria clementia exerceri puto; sed nunc de his disserere consilium non est."[82] Since Boethius, in the *De consolatione philosophiae*, does not return again to this subject, the early scholars concluded that he proposed to write after his *De consolatione philosophiae* a theological consolation that would discuss sanctions in the afterlife. But the passage is explained much more simply if it is granted that Boethius is plagiarizing rather awkwardly from a Neoplatonic commentary on the *Gorgias*. In the same place Olympiodorus interrupts his discussion: πῶς τοίνυν λέγεται αἰωνία ἡ ὑπὸ γῆν κόλασις, ἐν τῷ μύθῳ μαθησόμεθα.[83] In his case it was simply a reference to the last myth in the *Gorgias*, regarding which he later took up the question again more thoroughly, and in terms very similar to those used by Boethius.[84] It may therefore be imagined without unlikelihood that here Boethius is following Olympiodorus' source, that is, Ammonius' commentary on the *Gorgias*.

Similarly, it has not been observed that Book 5 of the *De consolatione philosophiae* uses, sometimes word for word, the discussions in Boethius' commentary on the *De interpretatione*. Completely dedicated as he is to the problem so often examined of the reconciliation between divine prescience and human free will, is he going to repeat the traditional arguments of the numberless treatises on destiny or free will that saw the light in the West from Cicero's time until St. Augustine? Boethius shuns this approach, and his protagonist Philosophy claims to offer a new solution: "Vetus, inquit, haec est de providentia querela Marcoque Tullio, cum divinationem distribuit, vehementer agitata tibique ipsi res diu prorsus multumque quaesita, sed haudquaquam ab ullo vestrum hactenus satis diligenter ac firmiter expedita."[85] As a matter of fact, Boethius discusses neither the pagan problem of divination,[86] nor the Christian problem of grace and free will, but the purely logical problem raised among the last Greek commentators by Chapter 9 of

---

[82] Boethius *De cons. philos.*, p. 102, 70. Note, however, a similar formula of Boethius', *De interpr.*, ed. sec., p. 232, 10: "Sed haec maiora sunt quam ut nunc digne pertractari queant." This denotes that there was to be a later discussion on Providence, a plan that was not to be consummated by Boethius until the *De cons. philos.*

[83] Olympiodorus *In Gorgiam*, ed. Jahn, *Neue Jahrbücher für Philologie und Pädagogik*, suppl. 14 (1848), p. 278 = Norvin's edition (Leipzig 1936), p. 119, 24.

[84] *Ibid.*, p. 545 = Norvin, p. 240, 17: αἱ μὲν μέτρια ἡμαρτηκυῖαι ψυχαὶ ἐπ' ὀλίγον χρόνον κρίνονται, καὶ λοιπὸν καθαιρόμεναι ἀνάγονται . . . αἱ δὲ μέγιστα ἁμαρτήσασαι εὐθὺς εἰς τὸν Τάρταρον πέμπονται . . . καὶ ἀεὶ αὗται κρίνονται, μηδέποτε καθαιρόμεναι· καὶ ἄξιον ἀπορῆσαι διὰ τί λέγει ἀεί.

[85] Boethius *De cons. philos.*, p. 131, 1.

[86] Klingner, *De Boeth. cons. philos.*, pp. 102ff, thinks that Cicero's name is sheer ornamentation and that Boethius, assuming he had known the *De divinatione*, did not use it. However, he knows it perhaps from Augustine's refutation, *De civ. Dei* 5.9, ed. Dombart, p. 203, 14: "In libris *de divinatione* ex se ipso apertissime oppugnat (Cicero) praescientiam futurorum," and the word *distribuit* suggests *De divinatione* 1.55.125. Boethius' statement,

Aristotle's *De interpretatione*: "Contingent propositions relating to the future." I believe I can show that Boethius poses the problem and resolves it in the light of Ammonius' commentary on this chapter of the *De interpretatione*.

Like Ammonius, Boethius begins by positing God's omniscience, more potent than the Sun's light, since it leaves nothing in shadow.[87] But if divine omniscience is granted, how can the future be contingent? Are chance and free will not ruled out? This is the question in pure logic that Ammonius discusses in his commentary on the *De interpretatione*. Boethius himself merely touches lightly on it in his commentary.[88] On the other hand, in the *De consolatione philosophiae* he will treat it in all its amplitude and invariably in line with Ammonius.

Ammonius attacks those who, like Alexander of Aphrodisias,[89] elude the difficulty by saying that the gods themselves have an infinite knowledge of the future and foresee what is possible *qua* possible.[90] As proof, they offer the ambiguous form in which the gods generally give their oracles. But Ammonius refutes them on this point.[91] Boethius, like Ammonius, expounds their theories, then rejects them.[92]

It is true that Boethius also seems to reject expressly the solution proposed by Ammonius:

Ammonius:[93]

Καὶ οὐ χρὴ νομίζειν ὅτι ἀναγκαίαν ἕξει τὴν ἔκβασιν ἃ λέγομεν ἐνδεχόμενα διὰ τὸ ὑπὸ θεῶν γινώσκεσθαι ὡρισμένως· οὐ γὰρ διότι γινώσκουσιν αὐτὰ οἱ θεοί, διὰ τοῦτο ἀναγκαίως ἐκβήσεται, ἀλλ' ἐπειδὴ φύσιν ἔχοντα ἐνδεχομένην καὶ ἀμφίβολον πέρας ἕξει πάντως ἢ τοῖον ἢ τοῖον, διὰ τοῦτο τοὺς θεοὺς εἰδέναι ἀναγκαῖον ὅπως ἐκβήσεται.

Boethius:[94]

Neque enim illam probo rationem qua se *quidam* credunt hunc quaestionis nodum posse dissolvere; aiunt enim non ideo quid esse eventurum, quoniam id providentia futurum esse prospexerit, sed e contrario potius, quoniam quid futurum est, id divinam providentiam latere non posse eoque modo necessarium hoc in contrariam relabi partem, neque enim necesse esse contingere quae providentur, sed necesse esse quae futura sunt provideri.

De cons. philos., p. 108, 20, "Tum velut ab alio orsa principio ita disseruit," recalls Cicero *De divinatione* 2.49.101: "Tum ego rursus ab alio principio sum exorsus dicere." Lastly, the verse from Ennius quoted by Boethius (*De interpr.*, ed. Meiser, 2, p. 82, 11, and *De divisione*, PL 64, 878) comes from *De divinatione* 2.56.116.

[87] Boethius *De cons. philos.*, p. 125, 1ff. Cf. Ammonius *De interpr.*, p. 132, 25 and p. 133, 34.

[88] Text quoted immediately above, n. 82.

[89] Alexander of Aphrodisias *De fato*, ed. Bruns, *CAG*, suppl. 2, 2, p. 201, 13ff.

[90] Ammonius *De interpr.*, p. 132, 12.

[91] *Ibid.*, p. 137, 13ff.

[92] Boethius *De interpr.*, ed. sec., p. 225, 1ff; *De cons. philos.*, p. 128, 64ff.

[93] Ammonius, p. 136, 25ff.

[94] Boethius *De cons. philos.*, p. 126, 15ff.

But this is not Boethius' real thought; for, after showing him that this is the proper solution,[95] Philosophy will answer him in the very words of Ammonius that immediately follow the passage quoted:

Ammonius:[96]

Καὶ ἔστι τὸ αὐτὸ τῇ μὲν φύσει τῇ ἑαυτοῦ ἐνδεχόμενον, τῇ δὲ γνώσει τῶν θεῶν οὐκέτι ἀόριστον, ἀλλ᾽ ὡρισμένον.

Boethius:[97]

Respondebo namque *idem* futurum, cum ad *divinam notionem* refertur, necessarium, cum vero in *sua natura* perpenditur, liberum prorsus atque absolutum videri.

It is therefore a more searching analysis of the mode of divine knowledge that helps to resolve this apparent antinomy. Ammonius and Boethius demonstrate at great length that knowledge is relative to the subject that knows.[98] If God is the eternal present, he can know in a determined sense the occurrence of future contingencies:

Ammonius:[99]

Τούτων οὖν οὕτως ἐχόντων, ῥητέον τοὺς θεοὺς γινώσκειν μὲν πάντα τὰ γεγονότα καὶ τὰ ὄντα καὶ τὰ ἐσόμενα ἢ μέλλοντα τὸν θεοῖς προσήκοντα τρόπον, τοῦτο δέ ἐστι μιᾷ καὶ ὡρισμένῃ καὶ ἀμεταβλήτῳ γνώσει, διόπερ καὶ τῶν ἐνδεχομένων περιειληφέναι τὴν εἴδησιν.

Boethius:[100]

Quoniam igitur omne iudicium secundum sui naturam quae sibi subiecta sunt comprehendit, est autem Deo semper aeternus ac praesentarius status: scientia quoque eius omnem temporis supergressa motionem in suae manet simplicitate praesentiae infinitaque praeteriti ac futuri spatia complectens omnia quasi iam gerantur in sua simplici cognitione considerat.

Shall it also be said that divine omniscience destroys free will by making events necessary? Ammonius and Boethius resolve the difficulty by distinguishing two types of necessity:

Ammonius:[101]

Διττὸν εἶναί φησι τὸ ἀναγκαῖον, τὸ μὲν τὸ ἁπλῶς καὶ κυρίως λεγόμενον. ὅπερ ἐστὶ τὸ ἀεὶ

De interpretatione:[102]

Duplex modus *necessitatis* ostenditur: unus qui cum alicuius accidentis necessitate proponitur, alter qui

De cons. philos.:[103]

Duae sunt etenim *necessitates, simplex* una, veluti quod necesse est omnes homines esse mortales, altera

---

95 *Ibid.*, p. 131, 12: "Quaero enim cur illam solventium rationem minus efficacem putes."

96 Ammonius, p. 137, 1.

97 Boethius *De cons. philos.*, p. 142, 96.

98 *Ibid.*, p. 133, 71; 135, 110; 139, 2; 141, 57. Cf. Ammonius, p. 135, 14ff. Klingner, pp. 106ff, already observed this similarity, but he thought that Boethius' source was Iamblichus, not Ammonius.

99 Ammonius, p. 136, 1.

100 Boethius *De cons. philos.*, p. 141, 57ff.

101 Ammonius, p. 153, 13ff.

102 Boethius *De interpr.*, ed. sec., p. 241, 1ff.

103 Boethius *De cons. philos.*, p. 143, 1ff.

ὑπάρχον τῷ ὑποκειμένῳ
ὡς οὐδὲ ὑφεστάναι χωρὶς
αὐτοῦ δυναμένῳ (τοῦ ἀεὶ
ἤτοι κατὰ τὸν ἄπειρον
χρόνον λαμβανομένου ὡς
ἐπὶ τῶν ἀιδίων, οἷον ὅταν
λέγωμεν ἐξ ἀνάγκης κι-
νεῖσθαι τὸν ἥλιον ... ἢ
ἕως ἂν ὑπάρχῃ τὸ ὑπο-
κείμενον, ὡς ὅταν εἴπω-
μεν ἐξ ἀνάγκης τόδε τὸ
πῦρ θερμὸν εἶναι ἢ τὸν
Σωκράτην ζῷον εἶναι), τὸ
δὲ οὐ τοιοῦτον, ἀλλὰ μετὰ
μὲν προδιορισμοῦ τοῦ ἕως
ἂν ᾖ τὸ κατηγορούμενον
ὑπὸ τοῦ λέγοντος οὕτως
αὐτὸ ἔχειν ἀληθεῦον,
ἁπλῶς δὲ οὐκέτι, εἴτε
ἀίδιον εἴη τὸ ὑποκείμενον,
εἴτε φθαρτόν· τὸ γὰρ ἐξ
ἀνάγκης ... καθέζεσθαί
σε ἢ βαδίζειν, ἕως ἄν τι
τούτων ὑπάρχῃ σοι ἀλη-
θές, ἁπλῶς δὲ οὐκέτι.

simplici praedicatione pro-
fertur, *ut cum dicimus solem
moveri necesse est* ... altera
vero quae cum conditione
dicitur talis est: ut cum
dicimus Socratem *sedere*
necesse est, cum sedet, et
non sedere necesse est,
cum non sedet ... sed ista
cum conditione quae pro-
ponitur necessitas non illam simplicem secum
trahit (non enim quicum-
que sedet simpliciter eum
sedere necesse est, sed cum
adiectione ea quae est:
tunc cum sedet).

conditionis, ut si aliquem
ambulare scias, eum ambu-
lare necesse est; quod enim
quisque novit, id esse aliter
ac notum est nequit, sed
haec conditio minime se-
cum illam simplicem trahit;
hanc enim necessitatem non
propria facit natura, sed
conditionis adiectio; nulla
enim necessitas cogit *incedere* voluntate gradientem
quamvis eum tum cum
graditur incedere neces-
sarium sit.

Note that not only are the commentaries of Ammonius and Boethius parallel, but Boethius' argumentation in the last book of his *De consolatione philosophiae* is taken from Ammonius' commentary on the *De interpretatione*. Once he even quoted it expressly, but without wishing to reveal the writer's name, in the vague form "quidam ... aiunt."[104]

There is another point. The discussions in the fifth book of the *De consolatione philosophiae* that have no parallel in Ammonius' commentary on the *De interpretatione* stem, I believe, from Ammonius' commentary on the *Physics*.

Consider the following parallel between Boethius' two works:

Commentary on the *De interpretatione*:[105]
Peripatetici enim, quorum Aristoteles princeps est ... casum quidem esse *in Physicis* probant ... quotiens aliud quid-dam evenit per actionem quae geritur

De consolatione philosophiae:[106]
Aristoteles meus id, inquit, *in Physicis* et brevi et veri propinqua ratione defini-vit ... Quotiens, ait, aliquid cuiuspiam rei gratia geritur aliudque quibusdam de

[104] The similarity that has been established between Ammonius' text and Boethius' dispenses with the need to linger over Klingner's opinion, *De Boeth. cons. philos.*, p. 97 n. 6, that these "quidam" denoted Origen, Chrysostom, and Jerome.

[105] Meiser, *ed. sec.*, p. 193, 26ff.

[106] Peiper, p. 122, 34ff.

quam speratur, illud evenisse casu Peri-
patetica probat auctoritas; si quis enim
terram fodiens vel scrobem demittens
agri cultus causa thesaurum reperiat, casu
ille thesaurus inventus est, non sine aliqua
quidem actione (terra enim fossa est, cum
thesaurus inventus est), sed non illa erat
agentis intentio, ut thesaurus inveniretur.

causis quam quod intendebatur obtingit,
casus vocatur: ut si quis colendi agri
causa fodiens humum defossi auri pondus
inveniat. Hoc igitur fortuitu quidem
creditur accidisse: verum non de nihilo
est, nam proprias causas habet quarum
improvisus   inopinatusque   concursus
casum videtur operatus; nam nisi cultor
agri humum foderet, nisi eo loci pecuni-
am suam depositor obruisset, aurum non
esset inventum.

It would be futile to seek in the *De consolatione philosophiae* for a specific
quotation from Aristotle's *Physics*, since, in his commentary on the *De interpretatione*, Boethius attributes this definition of chance to the Peripatetic commentators. As a matter of fact, if it is true that Aristotle treats the problem of
chance in his *Physics*,[107] the illustration of the pot of gold appears only in the
Metaphysics, in the chapter on accidents.[108] The combination of the two
passages is the work of the Alexandrian commentators and appears in the
commentaries of Philoponus and Simplicius on Aristotle's *Physics*.[109]
Hence, knowing that these commentaries both stem from Ammonius' lost
commentary on the *Physics*, and knowing too that Boethius himself, prior to
the second edition of his commentary on the *De interpretatione*, had written a
commentary on the *Physics*,[110] is it too bold for us to assume that Boethius'
lost commentary used Ammonius' lost commentary and that the two passages quoted derive therefrom?

This assumption becomes a certainty, if it can be shown that another passage in the fifth book of the *De consolatione philosophiae* stems likewise from
Ammonius' commentary on the *Physics*. In fact, to comprehend what divine
prescience can be, Boethius is obliged to enter into a digression on the
eternity of God compared with the condition of temporal things. After that,
he reveals his thought on the capital point: the problem of the eternity of the
universe, which was then the subject of violent controversies between
Christians and pagans, in the very heart of the Alexandrian School.

The starting point of the discussion is the statement in the *Timaeus* where
Plato declares that the universe was generated but adds that it was created
within time. Proclus informs us, in his commentary on the *Timaeus*,[111] that

---

[107] Aristotle *Physics* 2.4–5. Boethius also refers expressly to this passage in his *Comm.
in Top. Cic.* (PL 64, 1152 Cff).

[108] Aristotle *Metaphysics* 4.30, 1025a16.

[109] Philopon *In Phys.* (ed. Vitelli, *CAG* 16), p. 276, 18; Simplicius *In Phys.* (ed. Diels,
CAG 9), p. 337, 25ff.

[110] Cf. Brandt, "Entstehungszeit," p. 237.

[111] Proclus *In Tim.* (ed. Diehl), 1, p. 276, 30ff.

the Neoplatonists were not in agreement regarding the interpretation of this passage. Plutarch, Atticus, and many others considered this genesis as temporal, but Plotinus, Porphyry, Iamblichus—and Proclus, who joined forces with them—asserted that Plato believed only in a causal, not in a temporal, genesis of the universe. Proclus says that the universe was generated, because it has a cause, but he does not believe that it was created within time. On the contrary, he attributes to it infinite duration.[112] In other respects, Proclus carefully distinguishes this infinite duration (ἀϊδιότης), which he attributes to the universe, from divine eternity (αἰώνιον), which is outside time.[113]

On several occasions Boethius touches on this question and gradually clarifies his doctrine and his vocabulary. In the commentary on the *Isagoge* he used *perpetuitas* and *aeternitas* as synonyms.[114] In the commentary on the *De interpretatione* he applies the epithets *sempiternus* and *immortalis* to the heavenly bodies and asserts that in this regard he is following the Peripatetics.[115] In the *Opuscula theologica* he already distinguishes *sempiternitas* or infinite duration, which according to the philosophers can be predicated of the heavens and the other immortal bodies, from the divine *aeternitas*, which is outside duration.[116] Lastly, the *De consolatione philosophiae* repeats and discusses at great length the distinction between infinite duration or perpetuity, which is the fate of the universe, and eternity, which is reserved for God: "Quod igitur temporis patitur conditionem, licet illud, sicuti de mundo censuit Aristoteles, nec coeperit umquam esse nec desinat vitaque eius cum temporis infinitate tendatur, nondum tamen tale est, ut aeternum esse iure credatur . . . Itaque si digna rebus nomina velimus imponere, Platonem sequentes deum quidem aeternum, mundum vero dicamus esse perpetuum."[117]

Boethius' theory seems plausibly to stem from Proclus' theory, but Boethius' quotation from Aristotle hints that there was between them some intermediate commentary on the *Physics* or the *De caelo*. What is this intermediary? We shall be able to identify it very precisely, thanks to the passage where Boethius attacks those who criticize this theory: "Unde non recte

---

[112] *Ibid.*, p. 286, 20ff.

[113] *Ibid.*, p. 238, 15ff. Cf. J. F. A. Berger, *Proclus, exposition de sa doctrine* (diss. Paris 1840) 73.

[114] Boethius *In Isag.* (ed. Brandt), p. 257, 6. Cf. Rand, "Der dem Boethius zugeschriebene Traktat de fide catholica," *Jahrb. für classische Philologie*, suppl. 26 (1901), p. 438: "Anmerkung über die Chronologie der Werke des Boethius."

[115] Boethius *De interpr.*, ed. sec., p. 412, 6 and p. 414, 19. Cf. the index s.v. *sempiterna* = τὰ ἀΐδια.

[116] Boethius *Opusc. theol.* (ed. Peiper), p. 158, 60ff.

[117] Boethius *De cons. philos.*, p. 139, 17 and p. 141, 55. Note that the Byzantine translator of the *De cons. philos.*, Maximus Planudes, confirms the equivalence of the terms in both Proclus and Boethius, since he translates *aeternum* by αἰώνιον and *perpetuum* by ἀΐδιον (ed. Bétant, p. 114).

quidam qui, cum audiunt visum Platoni mundum hunc nec habuisse initium temporis nec habiturum esse defectum, hoc modo conditori conditum mundum fieri coaeternum putant."[118] Who are these "quidam"? One thinks first of all of John Philoponus' voluminous treatise Κατὰ τῶν Πρόκλου περὶ ἀϊδιότητος κόσμου ἐπιχειρημάτων. Philoponus' principal argument against Proclus is in effect that he makes the universe coeternal (συναΐδιος) with God, which is an assault against divine majesty, and contrary to Plato's thought that the universe was generated.[119] It is evident that this charge is unjust, since Proclus takes good care not to use the word συναΐδιος, and carefully distinguishes the temporal ἀϊδιότης from the divine αἰών. One would therefore be tempted to think that Boethius here criticizes Philoponus, if one did not know that Philoponus' treatise was written in Alexandria in 529, five years after Boethius' death.[120]

A valuable document fortunately helps us to know Boethius' source and the person to whom his criticisms are directed. This is the treatise of Zacharias of Mitylene entitled Ἀμμώνιος· ὅτι οὐ συναΐδιος τῷ Θεῷ ὁ κόσμος, ἀλλὰ δημιούργημα αὐτοῦ τυγχάνει. This curious booklet reproduces a discussion that the Christian Zacharias aroused at Ammonius' lectures in Alexandria in 486, when Ammonius was explaining Aristotle's *Physics*.[121] With reference to a passage in the *Physics* concerning the heavens, Ammonius had developed the thesis of the perpetuity of the universe. This thesis was directed against the Christians. Zacharias then took Ammonius aside, engaged in a long debate, and, as he says, concluded by winning over most of Ammonius' pupils. It must not be thought that everything in this anecdote is historically true. The intention of an apologetic is too evident. Moreover, Cumont has shown that Zacharias did not hesitate to put into Ammonius' mouth textual statements from Philo Iudaeus.[122] Zacharias also uses for his refutation the treatise by Aeneas of Gaza.[123] In a general way, he takes Ammonius as the

---

[118] Boethius *De cons. philos.*, p. 140, 30ff.

[119] Philopon *De aeternitate mundi*, ed. Rabe, p. 14, 10ff. Cf. the index s.v. συναΐδιος. Klingner, *De Boeth. cons. philos.*, pp. 108ff, thought that these "quidam" denoted St. Augustine.

[120] *Ibid.*, ed. Rabe, p. XII and p. 579, 14.

[121] Cf. Zacharias *Ammonius* (PG 85, 1028 A–B and 1057 B). The date 486 is obtained from the following calculation: it is reckoned that Zacharias was instructing a young student at Berytus at the time when he related the discussion that he had held the previous year (1021 C: πέρυσι) with Ammonius, who had recently settled in Alexandria (1020 A). Now Ammonius came from Athens to Alexandria in 485, on the death of Proclus, and Zacharias arrived at the very latest at Berytus in October 487. (On this point, see Klingner, "La compilation historique de Pseudo-Zacharie le rhéteur," *Revue de l'Orient chrétien* 5 [1900] 205.) As the discussion took place in summer (1028 B), the year in question must be the summer of 486, or possibly 487.

[122] *Philonis de aeternitate mundi*, ed. Cumont (Berlin 1891), pp. XIIff.

[123] Cf. Demosthenes Roussos, Τρεῖς Γαζαῖοι (Constantinople 1893), pp. 50 and 52ff.

type of pagan teachers who maintained that the universe has no temporal beginning, and he treats the question in its full extent. But on the circumstances in which the dispute started Zacharias gives information that is too exact and that fits in too well with what we know of his life for the anecdote not to be historical. Besides, we can verify that Ammonius maintained in fact the perpetuity of the universe. Not only was it natural for this disciple of Proclus to have reproduced exactly the theories of his teacher, whose courses he was still attending at Athens the preceding year, but a statement in his commentary on the *De interpretatione*, where he calls the gods τῶν μὲν ἀϊδίων οὐσιῶν αἰτίους . . . τῶν δὲ γεννητῶν προαιτίους,[124] is a confirmation that he applied the term ἀΐδιος to heavenly things. Lastly and particularly, we can form a very exact idea of the content of Ammonius' commentary on the *Physics* from Simplicius' commentary, which plagiarized it. Now, the passage in the *Physics* where Aristotle criticizes Plato for having written that the universe and the heavens were generated, becomes in Simplicius the subject of a prolonged discussion. He attempts to prove that Aristotle and Plato, if they differ in terms, agree in thinking that the universe has a cause, but that it is infinite in time. Once more the distinction is repeated between ἀΐδιος and αἰώνιος.[125] We may be sure that Ammonius' commentary, in the same passage, contained a similar discussion that was the starting point of his discussion with Zacharias. But, as Philoponus did with Proclus, Zacharias shamelessly changes Ammonius' thought and makes him maintain the theory of coeternity: Γεγενῆσθαι μὲν λέγων (τὸν οὐρανόν), κατ' αἰτίαν δὲ μόνον, συναΐδιον εἶναι τῷ πεποιηκότι, καὶ οὐκ ἄν ποτε φθαρῆναι τόδε τὸ πᾶν.[126] It is against this rebuke for making the universe coeternal with God that Boethius protests. And, although a Christian, he repeats with the utmost precision Ammonius' theory that had appeared so dangerous to his Christian pupils Zacharias and Philoponus:

Ammonius:[127]

Εἰ γὰρ ἐν χρόνῳ γέγονε τόδε τὸ πᾶν, καὶ δεύτερόν ἐστι τοῦ Δημιουργοῦ, οὐ τῇ ἀξίᾳ (τοῦτο γὰρ καὶ ἡμεῖς συνομολογοῦμεν), ἀλλὰ τῷ χρόνῳ, ὡς ἐκ μεταμελείας ὁ Θεὸς ἐπὶ τὴν τούτου δημιουργίαν ὀδεύσας φαίνεται.

Boethius:[128]

Neque Deus conditis rebus antiquior videri debet temporis quantitate, sed simplicis potius proprietate naturae.

[124] Ammonius *De interpr.*, p. 136, 4.
[125] Simplicius *In Phys.* (ed. Diels, *CAG* 10), pp. 1154 and 1155 (particularly lines 13ff), commenting on Aristotle *Physics* 251b17. Boethius, as we have seen, likewise attempts to point out the correspondence between Aristotle and Plato. Zacharias, on the other hand, in his discussion against Ammonius, brings out their basic disagreement (col. 1108 A).
[126] Zacharias, col. 1022 B.
[127] Ammonius *In Phys.*, *apud* Zachar., col. 1032 A.
[128] Boethius *De cons. philos.*, p. 140, 37.

Thus Book 5 of the *De consolatione philosophiae* is entirely inspired by Ammonius' commentaries on the *De interpretatione* and the *Physics*, which were previously the source of Boethius' corresponding commentaries. This fifth book lets us determine Boethius' exact position in the School of Alexandria.

I therefore think that it is possible to identify the environment that influenced the development of Boethius' thought. He makes little of the Latin translators and commentators who preceded him. If he knew them, he scarcely used them. The fact that he substitutes his own translation of the *Isagoge* for Marius Victorinus' translation is significant. In this respect Boethius has the right to say that he is bringing something new to the Latin world. He is proud of this. He realizes, with his knowledge of Greek, that he is working for a world that is beginning not to know the language.

On the other hand, in relation to the Greek commentators, he presents the image not of an innovator but of a loyal disciple and a conscientious imitator. He is only one in a succession of commentators who, since Porphyry, applied themselves in bringing Aristotle within reach of a wide public. He knew by direct contact almost all the commentaries on Aristotle, and he quotes them. It is even by his very quotations alone that a large number of them are known. But, although he does not quote the most recent commentaries, an examination of Boethius' Greek sources shows that, in their method as in their content, these are the ones that Boethius uses most frequently in his commentaries. Boethius' commentaries are distinctly inspired by Ammonius' commentaries and bear the mark of his Alexandrian School: the same techniques in classification, the same pedagogical tendencies, the same diagrams to facilitate an understanding of Aristotle's text, and often, lastly, literary borrowings. But this is not the entire story. The Greek verses that Boethius quotes in the *De consolatione philosophiae* denote a literary culture stemming from the School of Ammonius. And, as for the theories that are closest to Boethius' heart and that he reserves for the last book of the *De consolatione philosophiae* and that also relate to the most weighty problems of philosophy and faith, he takes them all from Ammonius as well. Moreover, though a Christian, he does not hesitate to mention, even in his *Opuscula theologica*, and to adopt on his own account the doctrine of the perpetuity of the universe professed by the pagan Ammonius but passionately attacked by his Christian pupils Zacharias and Philoponus.

I am therefore inclined to think, despite the lack of historical information on this point,[129] that Boethius learned Greek and acquired his philosophical

---

[129] A single text perhaps offers a clue. Zacharias' *Ecclesiastical History* mentions the existence of a certain Boetios, prefect of Alexandria under the patriarchy of Timotheus Aelurus, who had returned from exile, hence between November 475 and July 477 (cf. Duchesne, *Histoire ancienne de l'église* 3, pp. 490–499). It might be explained that

culture not in Rome but in Alexandria. The pagan school of Ammonius was in fact a meeting place for a host of young foreigners, even Christians.[130] In

Boethius, born, according to various writers, between 475 and 482, was brought up in Alexandria, if this Boetios could be identified with his father. Here is the evidence that supports this identification: the Syriac translation of Zacharias assumes the Greek text *Boέτιος*, for the iota is attested by the Syriac text. The emendation to *Boηθός* made by Cantarelli ("La serie dei prefetti di Egitto," *Atti della R. Accademia dei Lincei*, series 5, 14 [1909] 405) is therefore purely arbitrary, as Maspero rightly considered, *REG* 28 (1915) 62. Now the name *Boέτιος* seems to be attested only in Procopius, where it involves our Boethius (*De bello Gothico*, ed. Haury, 2, p. 9, 13; 10, 9; 11, 4; 389, 9 and 20).

Furthermore, the rank of prefect of Egypt often led to the praetorian prefecture. This happened in the case of Anthemius, prefect of Egypt in 477 and praetorian prefect in 496; Eustathius, prefect of Egypt in 501 and praetorian prefect in 505; Hephaestus, prefect of Egypt under Justinian and praetorian prefect in 551. Now the Brescia diptych informs us that Boethius' father was praetorian prefect.

But could a Westerner like Boethius' father be appointed prefect of Egypt by the emperor of the East and then pursue his career in the West? The situation would not have been unique. Artemidorus, named *praefectus urbi* by Theodoric, came from the court of Byzantium (cf. Cassiodorus *Variae* 1.43). Severus, the Neoplatonist, consul in 470, had sought refuge in Alexandria, whence he was recalled by Anthemius (Damascius, *Life of Isidore, Photii Bibliotheca* 340a). Could not Boethius' father have been appointed prefect of Alexandria in similar circumstances by the emperor of the East? Later on, the patrician Liberius, praetorian prefect of Italy and prefect of Gaul under the Ostrogoth kings, was to become prefect of Egypt in 538–541, before his return to Italy (cf. Mommsen's edition of the *Variae*, pp. 495–496). Boethius' relationship with the emperors of the East is quite definite. The nomination of his father as consul without colleague in 487 was ratified by Byzantium. Likewise, his son's consulship was ratified in 510. Lastly, the nomination of the latter's two sons as consuls in 522 is noted by Mommsen ("Ostgothische Studien," *Neues Archiv* 14 [1889] 244) as proof of the quite exceptional favor enjoyed by Boethius under the Emperor Justin. On the relations of his father-in-law Symmachus with the East, cf. below, sec. 5 *ad finem*. Lastly, Boethius and Symmachus were put to death by Theodoric on the charge of having plotted against him with the emperor of the East.

A final difficulty that confronts this identification does not appear insoluble. Zacharias informs us that the Boetios of Alexandria was a Eutychian. Boethius, on the other hand, wrote a treatise *Contra Eutychen et Nestorium* whose genuineness is confirmed by the *Anecdoton Holderi*. But certain expressions, which had suggested doubt of its genuineness, can be explained only if Boethius had previously been steeped in Eutychian concepts. He declares that he is thunderstruck by the strange novelty of the Catholic definition (ed. Peiper, p. 186, 11: "cuius dicti novitate percussus") and he adds: "Tandem igitur patuere pulsanti animo fores et veritas inventa quaerenti omnes nebulas eutychiani reclusit erroris" (ed. Peiper, p. 187, 34). These words are explained by my hypothesis that Boethius was the son of the Eutychian Boetios of Alexandria. Probably Boethius had recently been converted. On the other hand, the words carry no clear explanation, if Boethius was brought up in Rome, where Pope Gelasius I had just defined the Catholic position in five books *Adversus Nestorium et Eutychen*, according to the notice in the *Liber Pontificalis*.

Nonetheless, we must not disregard the weakness of this entire hypothetical structure.

[130] On the relations between pagans and Christians in the last schools of Alexandria, cf. Zacharias Scholasticus, *Life of Severus, Patr. Or.* 2; Praechter, "Christlich-neuplato-

Rome, on the other hand, no trace of philosophical instruction is any longer to be found at this period. If we assume that there was instruction there or that Boethius was self-taught, working in his library,[131] how could he have obtained and so rapidly assimilated the lectures by Ammonius, which had only just appeared? Unless, of course, he had gone to Alexandria. In conclusion, Boethius' own words in the *De consolatione philosophiae* seem to indicate that he was trained in the very heart of a school of Greek philosophy.[132]

4. BOETHIUS' CHRISTIANITY

This conclusion is not without interest. It forces us to reconsider Boethius' Christianity, a problem that has produced a spate of discussion from the ninth century to our own times[1] and on which I have hitherto refrained from offering any opinion. We can accept this fact: that Boethius was evidently a Christian. He could not have held his high offices at the beginning of the sixth century had he been a pagan, and the *Anecdoton Holderi*, the extract of a lost notice on Boethius by Cassiodorus, has obliged us to admit the authenticity of the *Opuscula theologica*, which, around 1860, were unanimously regarded as apocryphal.[2] But by a kind of contrary reaction scholars in the

---

nische Beziehungen," *Byzantinische Zeitschrift* 21 (1912) 1–27; Maspero, "Horapollon et la fin du paganisme égyptien," *Bulletin de l'Institut d'archéologie orientale* 11 (1914) 184ff.

[131] See *De cons. philos.*, p. 10, 7 and p. 19, 20.

[132] *Ibid.*, p. 5, 36: "eleaticis et academicis studiis innutritum"; p. 8, 4: "respicio nutricem meam cuius ab adulescentia laribus obversatus fueram Philosophiam"; p. 28, 38: "Nonne adulescentulus δοιοὺς πίθους, τὸν μὲν ἕνα κακῶν, τὸν δὲ ἕτερον ἐάων in Iovis limine iacere didicisti?"

[1] For the commentators up to the fifteenth century, see my "Etude critique." Among the moderns, the principal adherents of Boethius' paganism are F. Nitzsch, *Das System des Boethius und die ihm zugeschriebenen theologischen Schriften* (Berlin 1860), and C. Jourdain, "De l'origine des traditions sur le christianisme de Boèce," *Mémoires de l'Acad. des Inscriptions et Belles-Lettres*, 1st series, 6 (1860) 330–360. The supporters of Boethius' Christianity are A. Hildebrand, *Boethius und seine Stellung zum Christentum* (Regensburg 1885); N. Scheid, "Die Weltanschauung des Boethius und sein Trostbuch," *Stimmen aus Maria-Laach* 39, part 2 (1890) 374–392; G. Semeria, *Il Cristianesimo di Severino Boezio rivendicato*, Studi e documenti di storia e diritto, vol. 21 (Rome 1900) 61–178; Fortescue's edition of the *De cons. philos.* (London 1925); R. Carton, "Le christianisme et l'augustinisme de Boèce," *Mélanges augustiniens* (Paris 1931) 243–329; G. Capone-Braga, "La soluzione cristiana del problema del summum bonum in *Philosophiae consolationis libri quinque* di Boezio," *Archivio di storia della filosofia italiana* (1934) 101–116; E. T. Silk, "Boethius' *Consolatio Philosophiae* as a Sequel to Augustine's *Dialogues* and *Soliloquia*," *Harvard Theological Review* 32 (1939) 19–39. It is difficult to conceive how this writer can adopt such a title, as he does not establish any doctrinal relation between the *Consolation* and the *Dialogues*, but only a formal and external connection. He also admits, p. 38, that he cannot prove that, while in prison, Boethius was inspired by Augustine.

[2] Nowadays only the fourth is generally considered apocryphal. Cf. Schanz, vol. 4, 2, p. 160.

twentieth century have emphasized, perhaps excessively, the Christianity of Boethius' thought. The pagan aspect of the *De consolatione philosophiae* could be the result of its being either an exercise in this genre, lacking sincerity, or an unoriginal compilation, containing, however, a host of Christian allusions that revealed the true thought of Boethius as a Christian. Raoul Carton, followed by E. T. Silk, goes further and finds in Boethius a disciple of St. Augustine. It is far from my intention to return to the thesis of Boethius' paganism as expressed in the last century. I observe in the very tenor of the *Opuscula theologica* several indications to prove that they are by the same author as the commentaries on Aristotle.[3] But a study of the Greek sources of the *De consolatione philosophiae* has shown the pagan and Neoplatonic origin of his theories. It is even this doctrine that establishes the unity of thought in the *De consolatione philosophiae*, just as Rand had already shown the unity of composition. It was wrong to divide the *De consolatione philosophiae* into three parts: Stoic, Aristotelian, Platonic. Even the most trivial section, the diatribe against Fortune, unquestionably originated in some *Protrepticus* similar to that by Iamblichus, and the Roman touches that Boethius added were taken from Macrobius. Later on, Boethius refers quite often to his earlier scientific or logical works. If Neoplatonism is more evident than in his other works, it is because Boethius is not a logician, as his commentaries on Aristotle make us think. He is a Neoplatonic philosopher claiming to inculcate in Rome the doctrines of Proclus and Ammonius. As his condemnation to capital punishment prevented him from writing all the commentaries on Plato that were part of his projected schedule, before being put to death he hastily edited his *De consolatione philosophiae*, which appears as his real philosophical testament.

On the other hand, the alleged references to the Scriptures that Fortescue has collected in the *Index biblicus* of his edition are very dubious, and the least improbable of these similarities seem pure coincidence to Rand, who is withal in support of Boethius' Christianity.[4] Carton wanted to prove that Boethius adjusts his Platonism to the Christian faith, as Augustine had done earlier. Actually, Carton himself must have observed everything in Boethius that could be Christian or even Augustinian but still had to be related to the Greek Neoplatonists.[5] Carton's method, applied more vigorously, would

---

[3] See above, p. 313, on the distinction between *aeternitas* and *sempiternitas*. In addition, cf. *De interpr., ed. sec.*, ed. Meiser, p. 231, 25: "*natura quae motus est principium*," with the *Contra Eutychen et Nestorium*, ed. Peiper, p. 190, 35: "sicut Aristoteles ceterique et eiusdem et multimodae philosophiae sectatores putant, definiemus eam, ut hi etiam qui naturam non nisi in corporibus esse posuerunt. Est autem definitio hoc modo: *Natura est motus principium* per se non accidens."

[4] *De cons. philos.*, p. 84, 60, and *Sap.* 8.1. Cf. Rand, "On the Composition of Boethius' *Consolatio Philosophiae*," p. 25.

[5] Carton, "Le christianisme et l'augustinisme de Boèce," p. 302.

have led, I believe, rather to the admission that Boethius adapted his Christianity to his pagan studies. Boethius does not hesitate to use the words *Fortuna* and *Fatum*, which Augustine had proscribed. He defends the thesis of the perpetuity of the universe against the accusation formulated successively by the Christians Augustine, Zacharias, and Philoponus that this theory makes the world coeternal with God. It is futile to claim the discovery in the *De consolatione philosophiae* of dogmas that are properly called Christian. According to Fortescue, of all the agents of fate listed by Boethius, Boethius on his own account would admit only angels and demons, contrasting the beneficent angels (*virtus angelica*) with the cunning demons (*daemonum sollertia*).[6] This is a rash interpretation. There is nothing to prove such a mental restriction in Boethius, and he uses just as readily the term *sollertia* to denote the beneficent act of divine Providence.[7] As I have shown, Boethius merely repeats Proclus' teaching by adopting his terminology. Similarly, when he alludes to Purgatory and Hell, there is nothing in his terminology to indicate that he is thinking of something other than the Neoplatonic punishments, as described by Ammonius or by Olympiodorus in the commentary on the *Gorgias*.[8]

But if Boethius' Greek culture is a pagan culture, the *De consolatione philosophiae* does not contain any the more a single indication proving that Boethius was not a Christian at heart. Even in his commentaries where he plagiarizes Ammonius, when he refers to pagan religious theories, he indicates sufficiently that he does not take any account of them.[9] If it is usually easy for him to adopt Ammonius' philosophy, it is because he considers it very close to Christianity. Earlier, Augustine had praised Porphyry for being nearer to Christianity than Plato. Alexandrian philosophy, perhaps under the influence of the Christian *Didascalia*, also evolved in this direction. Praechter has well shown that the scientific tradition of Alexandria was opposed to the mystical theology of Athens. He noted everything that, in the Neoplatonism of Hierocles of Alexandria, revealed an unacknowledged Christian influence.[10] Hierocles and, later, Ammonius united with the Christians in the conflict against Manicheanism.[11] And while the Edict of 529 provoked a

[6] *De cons. philos.*, p. 109, 51; cf. Fortescue's edition, pp. 124 and 167.

[7] Boethius *In Isag.*, ed. Brandt, p. 9, 18: "sollertia Providentiae."

[8] Cf. the text of Boethius quoted above, pp. 307-308, and the text of Olympiodorus, above, sec. 3 n. 84.

[9] *In Isag.*, ed. sec., 3.4, p. 208, 22: "hunc enim mundum veteres deum vocabant et Iovis eum appellatione dignati sunt deumque solem ceteraque caelestia corpora, quae animata esse cum Plato, tum plurimus doctorum chorus arbitratus est"; and *In Top. Cic.*, PL 64, 1070 D: "homo seiungitur ab his animalibus quae aeterna sunt, velut sol a Platonicis creditur."

[10] K. Praechter, "Christlich-neuplatonische Beziehungen," summarizing his conclusions of the *Genethliakon C. Robert* (Berlin 1910) 139ff.

[11] *Ibid.*, p. 10 and n. 1.

break in the philosophical tradition of Athens, this tradition persisted in Alexandria, at the cost of a reconciliation with Christianity. Most of Ammonius' disciples were Christians or became Christians while still carrying on their teacher's tradition. Just as Stephanus of Alexandria, called by Heraclius in 612 to lecture on Plato at the Christian University of Constantinople, was to establish a liaison between Alexandrian paganism and the Byzantine Neoplatonism of the Middle Ages,[12] Boethius hoped to preserve Neoplatonism in the Christian West.

This is the explanation, I believe, of the "psychological case" of Boethius. How is it then that either his Christianity or his Platonism has been questioned? A like question does not arise either for Synesius or for Aeneas of Gaza or for Pseudo-Dionysius, whatever elucubrations they permit themselves to produce. The fact is that Boethius never explained how he achieved the synthesis between his Neoplatonic philosophy and his Christian theology.

From this Nitzsch argues against Boethius' Christianity by showing that Boethius does not attempt to reconcile the dogmas of the Trinity or the Word incarnate with his Neoplatonic theories.[13] It is possible, in fact, that Boethius did not attain the synthesis between pagan elements and Christian elements; but, above all, he wanted to keep separate in his books the domain of reason and the domain of faith. He attained this not without effort, as is proved by such lapses as have been noted. A lapse in Christian theology: the word *creare*.[14] A lapse in pagan theology: the *prima divinitas*.[15] Even when he is consulted on theological problems, Boethius approaches them only from a rational standpoint. He asserts that the errors of Nestorius and Eutyches relating to nature and the persons of Christ cause so much perturbation in the West only because there has been neglect in defining, with the aid of logic, the concepts of nature, person, and substance, and in establishing equivalents between the Greek and the Latin terms that denote them.[16] Similarly, it seems to him that, from the rational viewpoint, the terms "Father," "Son,"

[12] *Ibid.*, pp. 1 and 2.

[13] Nitzsch, *Das System des Boethius*, pp. 84–85.

[14] *De cons. philos.*, p. 80, 93.

[15] Text quoted above, sec. 3 n. 67.

[16] Boethius *Contra Eutychen* 1–3: persona = πρόσωπον; substantia = ὑπόστασις; subsistentia = οὐσίωσις. The passage quoted in Greek, Peiper, p. 194, 30, shows clearly that the discussion bears on the Greek terms. Cf. J. Tixeront, "Des concepts de 'nature' et de 'personne' dans les Pères et les écrivains ecclésiastiques des Ve et VIe siècles," *RHLR* 8 (1903) 589; K. Bruder, *Die philosophischen Elemente in den "Opuscula sacra" des Boethius*, Forschungen zur Geschichte der Philosophie und der Pädagogik, vol. 3, 2 (Leipzig 1928); H. J. Brosch, *Der Seinsbegriff bei Boethius* (Innsbrück 1931); V. Schurr, *Die Trinitätslehre des Boethius im Lichte der "skythischen Kontroversen,"* Forschungen zur christlichen Literatur und Dogmengeschichte, vol. 18, 1 (Paderborn 1935). Schurr described well the historical circumstances in which Boethius' theological treatises appeared. On p. 224 he gives a lucid summary of his conclusions.

and "Spirit" cannot be attributes of the divine substance on the same basis as "justice" and "goodness." He concludes by asking John the Deacon whether this view is orthodox, and, if not, how to resolve the contradiction between reason and faith: "fidem, si poteris, rationemque coniunge."[17] Thus, even for questions of faith Boethius confines himself to applying the rational method of the Platonic commentators on Aristotle, and the theology that he expounds in the *De consolatione philosophiae* is in his view a purely rational theology.

This bold attempt to disengage from pagan religion the theology of Ammonius and to confront it with the Christian religion was to pave the way for medieval Scholasticism. St. Thomas, while proposing a synthesis, will not confound the two spheres of reason and faith. Is proof required of this connection? St. Augustine asserted that the universe was completed within the concept of time.[18] Boethius postulates, with the philosophers, the perpetuity of the universe and denies that this doctrine is contrary to orthodoxy, for the perpetuity of the universe does not imply that it is coeternal with God. The dispute reappears in the thirteenth century almost in the same terms. St. Thomas asserts against the Augustinians the distinction of the two problems: the creation of the universe and the eternity of the universe, one of which is in the domain of reason, the other of faith alone. In the *De aeternitate mundi contra murmurantes* St. Thomas defends Aristotle against the charge of having made the universe coeternal with God, and he defends him by quoting the entire passage in the *De consolatione philosophiae* that bears on this point.[19] He definitely takes the part of Aristotle and Boethius against St. Augustine.

5. SYMMACHUS' COURSE OF STUDIES AND HIS FAILURE

We can conceive that Boethius' bold attempt to restore culture at Rome with the aid of Alexandrian philosophy met with lively opposition, as did the Emperor Anthemius' effort some thirty years earlier to restore Neoplatonism. Boethius' prologues challenge this opposition, which assumed various forms. The national tradition was hostile to any new Greek importation, particularly among those who did not know Greek.[1] Certain persons were alarmed to see Boethius applying to rhetoric his dialectic methods[2] or even

[17] Boethius *Utrum Pater et Filius et Spiritus sanctus de divinitate substantialiter praedicentur*, Peiper, p. 167, 67.

[18] Cf. among others the text quoted above, chap. 4 sec. 2 n. 165.

[19] Boethius *De cons. philos.*, p. 140, 30–37; St. Thomas *De aeternitate mundi contra murmurantes*, ed. Parma (1864), vol. 16, pp. 318–320. This is opusc. 27 in vol. 27 in Vivès' edition. Cf. R. Jolivet, *Essai sur les rapports entre la pensée grecque et la pensée chrétienne* (Paris 1931), pp. 10 and 14.

[1] Text quoted above, introduction to this chap., n. 23.

[2] *In Top. Cic.*, PL 64: 1063 C, 1107 D, 1155 B–C, 1157 A.

criticized this revival of liberal studies, which they considered too arduous.[3] Still more was it surprising to see the subjection to Aristotelian logic of questions of faith such as the Trinity. Boethius, in dedicating his book to Symmachus, who had asked him to apply this method, specifies that it is not intended for publication.[4] In an ecclesiastical assembly at which he is present, Boethius does not venture to speak, being certain in advance of being rebuked by the theologians whose ignorance and stupidity he describes.[5] So he begs the initiators of his works, John the Deacon and particularly Symmachus, the "philosopher" who revised Macrobius at Ravenna,[6] to support him in the great philosophical program that he has outlined.[7]

The same opposition is apparent in quite a different sphere. In fact, Symmachus does not conceive the renaissance of Hellenism at Rome as limited to the sciences, dialectic, or philosophy. His pretension is that he is introducing Greek methods even into the study of grammar and rhetoric, where nevertheless Latin literature was less inadequate. Macrobius had already tried, on the model of Apollonius Dyscolus' 'Ρηματικόν, to compose a manual on the comparative grammar of Greek and Latin conjugations.[8] But the Latin grammarians of the fifth century did not follow this pioneer. Most of them confined themselves to compilations or to the production of manuals on Donatus' teaching. Those who had some notions of Greek seemed particularly jealous of their art and mistrustful of their Greek rivals. The Gaul Consentius confronted the teaching of logic of the philosophers, which stemmed from Porphyry, with the grammatical tradition that classified nouns

---

[3] *De divisione, prol.*, PL 64, 877 A: "ego quoque id sicut pleraque omnia Romanis auribus tradens introductionis modo ... perscripsi, ut ... nec ullus livor, id quod et arduum est natura et ignotum nostris, nobis autem magno et labore et legentium utilitate digestum obliquis morsibus obtrectationis obfuscet, dentque potius viam studiis, nunc ignoscendo, nunc etiam comprobando, quam frena bonis artibus stringant dum quidquid novum est impudenti obstinatione repudiant." Cf. *De interpr., ed. sec.*, p. 421, 7.

[4] Boethius *De Trin.*, ed. Peiper, p. 150, 11: "Quocumque igitur a vobis deieci oculos, partim ignava segnities, partim callidus livor occurrit: ut contumeliam videatur divinis tractationibus inrogare qui talibus hominum monstris non agnoscenda haec potius quam proculcanda proiecerit. Idcirco stilum brevitate contraho et ex intimis sumpta philosophiae disciplinis novorum verborum significationibus velo, ut haec mihi tantum vobisque, si quando ad ea convertitis oculos, conloquantur."

[5] Boethius *Contra Eutychen et Nestorium, prol.*, p. 187, 25: "Atqui ego quidem nihil ceteris amplius adferebam, immo vero aliquid etiam minus. Nam de re proposita aeque nihil ceteris sentiebam: minus vero quam ceteri ipse adferebam falsae scilicet scientiae praesumptionem. Tuli aegerrime, fateor, compressusque indoctorum grege conticui metuens, ne iure viderer insanus, si sanus inter furiosos haberi contenderem."

[6] Cf. Usener, *Anecd. Holderi*, p. 4, 7: "Symmachus patricius et consul ordinarius, vir philosophus," and Schanz 4, 2, p. 84.

[7] *De interpr., ed. sec.*, p. 80, 8: "qua in re faveant oportet, quos nulla coquit invidia."

[8] See above, p. 45, and G. Uhlig, "Zu Apollonios Dyscolos," *Rheinisches Museum* 19 (1864) 41–48.

into proper nouns and common nouns.[9] This view was to appear later as so retrogressive that an interpolator inserted into the text the classification of the Greek grammarians, which seemed to him preferable.[10] It was not that Consentius was totally ignorant of Greek or of Greek terminology and grammatical theories.[11] But he was systematically hostile to them. For instance, he advises the avoidance in Latin of Greek endings, such as the accusative, despite Vergilian usage. For his rule is: "ubi decora datur occasio, nostris uti debemus, non aliena sectari."[12] Phocas is not more favorably disposed to the Greeks. He probably studies the Greek declension because it is useful for the study of the proper nouns that have passed from Greek into Latin,[13] but he charges Greek literature with insolent pride[14] and claims that the Latin language is no less rich than Greek.[15] Martyrius, too, who used the Greco-Latin glossaries,[16] does not hesitate to adopt a plan that he knows is contrary to the precepts of the Greek grammarian Herodianus.[17] Lastly, Eugraphius, who wrote a commentary on Terence at the close of the fifth century or during the early years of the sixth century[18] and had possibly read Boethius,[19]

[9] Consentius *Ars*, ed. Keil, *Grammatici Latini* 5, p. 341, 26: "et licet apud philosophos ita se res habeat, ut aliud genus, aliud species, aliud proprium sit, quod *individuum* appellant, tamen grammaticorum recta ista divisio est, ut nomina quaecumque propria' non sunt, generalia, id est appellativa dicantur."

[10] *Ibid.*, p. 338, 20: "divisio Graeca magis sequenda est, quae fit in primam positionem et derivationem." Cf. Keil's *apparatus criticus*, which points out as the source Dion. Thrax, p. 634, 21 and p. 636, 16.

[11] *Ibid.*, p. 360, 16: "casus est, ut Graeci definiunt, nominis quaedam positio vel, ut alii, commutatio ultimae syllabae in nomine." Cf. p. 351, 9; 353, 20; 364; 374, 12 and 31; 390, 11; 394.

[12] *Ibid.*, p. 365, 27. Cf. p. 365, 13: "nostra sequi potius quam peregrina debemus."

[13] Phocas *Ars*, Keil, 5, pp. 422–426.

[14] Phocas *Vita Vergilii*, ed. Baehrens, *Poet. Lat. min.*, 5, p. 85:

> Quis facunda, tuos toleraret, Graecia, fastus,
> quis tantum eloquii potuisset ferre tumorem,
> aemula Vergilium tellus nisi Tusca dedisset?

[15] Phocas *Ars*, p. 438, 32 (with reference to passive impersonal verbs): "his etiam Graecorum iactantiam, si quam de copia sermonis exercent, refutamus, quod haec proprie nequeunt explanare."

[16] Cf. Schanz, vol. 4, 2, p. 220, and Martyrius *De b muta et v vocali*, ed. Keil, 7, p. 195, 5, quoting Homer. Quite frequently, too, he gives etymologies and Greek explanations.

[17] Martyrius, *ibid.*, p. 166, 12: "Sed haec quoque partes dividentur trifariam, id est in primam, mediam atque ultimam syllabam; haec distributio, quamvis apud Graecos Herodiano displicuit."

[18] Eugraphius *Comm. in Terentium*, ed. Wessner (Leipzig 1908), p. VI, contrary to H. Gerstenberg, *De Eugraphio Terentii interprete* (Jena 1886), pp. 114ff, who placed Eugraphius between Cassiodorus and Isidore.

[19] Eugraphius, *ibid.*, p. 71, 12: "namque ut apud dialecticos inquisitio, cui respondetur aliter quam est illa responsio, ubi aut 'etiam' ponimus aut 'non'; haec enim *interrogatio* dicitur. 'Vidisti hominem?' haec interrogatio est: necessario enim respondemus aut

quotes, following earlier commentators, Homer, Menander, and Plato[20] but scrupulously avoids Greek terminology.[21]

It was against this excessive chauvinism and this negative attitude of the Latin grammarians that the best minds in Rome contended, at a time when Hellenism triumphed under Theodoric. Julian, consul and patrician, who combined in his person Homer and Vergil, Greek and Latin learning, if the conventional eulogies of the period are to be believed, was at least a perceptive man of letters.[22] He commissioned Priscian, a Latin grammarian of Constantinople, to write a grammar summarizing and adapting to Latin the teachings of the Greek grammarians. The prefaces of Priscian's *Institutiones grammaticae* reveal his aims and his conceptions of culture.[23] The Greeks are the initiators for the Latins in all the liberal arts. The ancient Greek grammarians committed mistakes, but the moderns, like Apollonius and Herodianus, offer reliable and detailed instruction. They have brought grammar to its perfection. Now, not one Latin scholar has imitated or followed them on account of the decline in literary studies. Priscian claims only that he is putting their precepts into Latin, adding what is indispensable in the *Artes* of the Latin grammarians. There should be no resentment against this imitation of the Greeks. The ancient Latins did not act differently, and the moderns are negligible. Priscian's book is offered as a *compendium* of the countless works of Apollonius and Herodianus. These are the principles that Priscian inculcates in his school.[24]

It is easy to verify that these two Greek writers, Apollonius Dyscolus and Herodianus, were in fact Priscian's principal sources. Matthias and Luscher have already noted Priscian's numberless textual borrowings from Apollonius.[25] He uses in particular the Περὶ συντάξεως, the Περὶ ἐπιρρημάτων, the

---

'etiam' aut 'non.' At vero *percontatio* est haec: 'ubi habitat Chrysis?' huic responderi non potest aut 'etiam' aut 'non,' sed 'hic, illic.' Ergo percontatio ista, illa vero interrogatio." Cf. the text of Boethius quoted above, p. 294.

[20] *Ibid.*, p. 119, 19 and p. 106, 15 on Homer; p. 45, 14; 92, 24 and 259 on Menander; p. 119, 14 on Plato. Gerstenberg, *De Eugraphio* (above, n. 18) 33–34, has shown that the references to Menander were taken from a previous commentator. The parallel between Menander and Terence was classic and was still used in the time of Sidonius Apollinaris. Cf. the texts quoted above, pp. 254–255.

[21] Cf. Gerstenberg, *De Eugraphio*, p. 71 and n. 1.

[22] Priscian *Epist. ad Iulianum*, ed. Keil, *Gramm. Lat.* 2, p. 2, 30: "quippe non minus Graecorum quam Latinorum in omni doctrinae genere praefulgentem"; and p. 194, 5: "ornamentum te esse Latinorum non minus quam Graecorum studiis gaudebam." On his probable edition of Statius, see Schanz, vol. 2, p. 537.

[23] *Ibid.*, pp. 1–2 and 194–195. Here I analyze their content.

[24] Note that the only one of his pupils whose works are preserved, Eutyches *Ars*, ed. Keil, *Gramm. Lat.* 5, p. 474, 8, readily resorts to the *perspicaciores Graecorum*.

[25] Cf. Th. Matthias, "Zu alten Grammatikern," *Fleckeis. Jahrb.*, suppl. 15 (1887) 593–640, and A. Luscher, *De Prisciani studiis Graecis* (diss. Breslau 1911) *passim* (edited later in

Περὶ στοιχείων, the Περὶ μερισμοῦ τῶν τοῦ λόγου μερῶν, the Ῥηματικόν, the Περὶ μετοχῆς, the Περὶ ἀντωνυμίας, the Περὶ προθέσεως, the Συνδεσμικόν. His borrowings are so evident and so extensive that it has been possible to wonder whether he did not simply reproduce a corpus of Apollonius' works, a Τέχνη γραμματική, the arrangement of which could have been made either by the author or by a Greek commentator.[26] This hypothesis now appears to have been abandoned, but it is certain that the eminent Alexandrian grammarian of the close of the second century was the teacher of Priscian's doctrine and instruction. Priscian used other Greek grammarians as well, in particular the Περὶ κλίσεως and the Περὶ καθολικῆς προσῳδίας by Herodianus, Apollonius' son, and the Περὶ τῆς παρὰ Ῥωμαίοις ἀναλογίας by Didymus Claudius.[27] But it is from Apollonius that he knows Aristarchus,[28] Tryphon,[29] and probably Astyages.[30] As for the innumerable examples that he borrows from the great Greek classics, either from the poets Homer, Aristophanes, Menander, or from the Attic orators Lysias, Isocrates, Demosthenes, Aeschines, or from the historians Herodotus and Xenophon, and finally from Plato, he is indebted for them solely to the grammarians, as is clearly shown by the catalogue of Atticisms inserted in Book 18 that has preserved almost entirely the alphabetical order of the lexica.[31] It will therefore not be surprising that textual mistakes are numerous in these quotations,[32] and care will have to be taken not to think that Priscian read these ancient writers and had direct contact with them. He read in the original only the lexicographers or the grammarians, to whom must be added the latest Greek commentators on Aristotle. In fact the "philosophers" to whom he refers several times are none other than Boethius' teacher Ammonius of Alexandria, whose prestige, as we may gauge, was high at the beginning of the sixth century, both in Constantinople and in Rome.[33]

---

the *Breslauer philol. Abhandlungen* 44). On the manner in which Priscian used these borrowings from Apollonius, cf. O. Wischnewski, *De Prisciani institutionum grammaticarum compositione* (diss. Königsberg, Berlin 1909) 81ff.

[26] Cf. *PW* s.v. Apollonios, 137.

[27] Cf. Luscher, *De Prisciani studiis Graecis*, pp. 31–32, and Priscian *De fig. num.*, ed. Keil, 3, p. 408, 6: "teste etiam Didymo, qui hoc ponit, ostendens in omni parte orationis et constructionis analogiam Graecorum secutos esse Romanos."

[28] Quoted by Priscian *De fig. num.*, Keil, 3, p. 144, 7 and p. 198, 11.

[29] *Ibid.*, 2, p. 548, 6; and 3, p. 202, 11.

[30] *Ibid.*, 2, p. 15, 8. The *floruit* of this grammarian is uncertain.

[31] Cf. *ibid.*, 3, pp. VII–VIII.

[32] Cf. E. Mueller, *De auctoritate et origine exemplorum orationis solutae Graecorum quae Priscianus contulit capita selecta* (diss. Königsberg 1911), 52 pages.

[33] Ammonius *De interpr.*, ed. Busse,   Priscian *Inst.*, ed. Keil, 2, p. 551, 18:
CAG 4, p. 12, 16:   Itaque quibusdam philosophis placuit
     Τὰ μὲν οὖν . . . σημαντικὰ πάντα ὁ   *nomen et verbum* solas esse partes orationis,

Just as at Julian's request Priscian wanted to bring to the West the teaching of the modern Greek grammarians,[34] so at Symmachus' request he will summarize the principles of the *Sophistae iuniores*, that is, the rhetoric of Hermogenes.[35] Priscian's preface praises Symmachus' exceptional merits: his high rank, his devoutness, and particularly his wide culture.[36] There is no doubt that Symmachus' purpose, when on his way to Constantinople he commissioned these three treatises from Priscian, was to complete the program of Hellenic culture that his son-in-law Boethius had already begun to execute in the field of philosophy and the sciences. Priscian shows a readiness to support Symmachus in extensive projects with an entire series of works of which these three are the beginning. For, like Symmachus, he thinks that Hellenism alone can implant in the young Romans a taste for liberal studies and that only a revival of culture can restore Rome's lost prestige.[37] Of the three treatises dedicated to Symmachus, the first one aims to prove that the Latin numeral signs stem from the Greek. The book makes a study of the equivalents between the Greek and Latin weights and money. As he did in his *Institutio*, Priscian uses the Greek treatise by Didymus Claudius, from which he quotes Herodotus at great length.[38] But his principal source in the

---

Ἀριστοτέλης εἰς ὀνόματα διαιρεῖ καὶ ῥήματα . . . Ὥσπερ γὰρ τῆς νεὼς αἱ μὲν σανίδες εἰσὶ τὰ κυρίως μέρη, γόμφοι δὲ καὶ λίνον καὶ πίττα συνδέσεως αὐτῶν καὶ τῆς τοῦ ὅλου ἐνώσεως ἕνεκα παραλαμβάνονται, τὸν αὐτὸν τρόπον κἂν τῷ λόγῳ σύνδεσμοι καὶ ἄρθρα καὶ προθέσεις καὶ αὐτὰ τὰ ἐπιρρήματα γόμφων τινῶν χρείαν ἀποπληροῦσι, μέρη δὲ οὐκ ἂν λέγοιντο δικαίως.

cetera vero adminicula vel iuncturas earum, *quo modo navium partes sunt tabulae et trabes, cetera autem, id est stuppa et clavi et similia vincula et conglutinationes* partium navis, non partes navis dicuntur.

Boethius De interpr., ed. sec., p. 14, 28, does not retain the metaphor of the ship. Cf. Priscian's other references to the philosophers, *ibid.*, p. 5, 1; 13, 23; 58, 25.

[34] Priscian *Inst.*, *praef.*, ed. Keil, 2, p. 1, 6: "cuius auctores, quanto sunt iuniores, tanto sunt perspicaciores."

[35] Priscian *De fig. num.*, *praef.*, ed. Keil, 3, p. 405, 9: "de figuris, sicut iussisti, numerorum breviter collecta demonstrabo et de nummis vel ponderibus, praeterea de Terentii metris, necnon etiam de praeexercitamentis rhetoricis, quae Graeci *progymnasmata* vocant, quoniam diligentius ea sophistae iuniores, quos sequimur, aptioribusque divisionibus ad exercendos iuvenes ad omne rhetoricae genus exposuisse creduntur."

[36] *Ibid.*, p. 405, 3: "studiis etiam optimarum artium disciplinarumque florentem."

[37] *Ibid.*, p. 405, 14: "petimus igitur sapientem eloquentiam vestram (hac enim dignitate nihil in homine melius novimus), ut et nos huiusce modi frequentius quaestionibus tam praesentes quam absentes cum felicitate exerceatis et Romanorum diligentiam vestrorum ad artes suorum alacriorem reddatis auctorum, quibus solis ceteras cum Grais gentes superasse noscuntur."

[38] *Ibid.*, p. 408, 6; cf. p. 411, 9.

matter of Greek measures seems to be Dardanus' Περὶ σταθμῶν.[39] The second treatise compares Terence's metric with Greek metric. Priscian assures us that the Latins merely generalized the licenses that were already in force in Greek metric, and in support of this theory he quotes a host of Greek verses that he borrows from the treatises on metric by Heliodorus and Hephaestion.[40] Finally, the third treatise, entitled *Praeexercitamina*, is just an almost literal translation of Hermogenes' Προγυμνάσματα, sometimes attributed to Libanius.[41]

This attempt to implant in Rome the rhetoric of Hermogenes is not an isolated fact, for this was also the purpose of the commentary on the *De inventione* by Grillius, who was probably an Eastern colleague of Priscian.[42] Joseph Martin, who edited this commentary, has skillfully brought out the Hellenistic character of Grillius' rhetorical system. Grillius' prologue is conceived as the introduction to a commentary on Hermogenes' Στάσεις. Most of the time he follows the commentators on Hermogenes, sometimes the teaching of Nicholas of Myra.[43] It was from the commentators on Hermogenes that Grillius must have borrowed the definitions of rhetoric according to Aristotle's *Rhetoric* and Plato's *Gorgias*,[44] the philosophers' formula defining the true orator τὸν τῆς ἀληθείας συνήγορον,[45] and the apocryphal anecdote about Demosthenes as a pupil of Plato.[46] Priscian, on the other hand, confined himself to a translation of Hermogenes. Sometimes he replaced examples chosen from Greek writers with Latin illustrations, but it is certain that he also knew the more recent theorists, for he begins with a definition taken from the *Progymnasmata* of Nicholas of Myra, a rhetorician of the fifth century.[47] The fact that Priscian translates into Latin even the quotations

---

[39] *Ibid.*, p. 408, 18 and p. 409, 30. On another ancient translation of Dardanus, cf. G. Mercati, "Il libro Περὶ σταθμῶν di Dardano tradotto anticamente in latino?" *Rendiconti del r. Istituto Lombardo*, ser. 2, vol. 42 (1909), pp. 149 and 316.

[40] Priscian, *De fig. num.*, p. 395. These metricians date in the end of the first or the beginning of the second century.

[41] On the doubt that still remains regarding its genuineness, cf. H. Rabe, "Hermogenis opera," *Rhetores Graeci*, vol. 6 (Leipzig 1913), pp. IV–VI. A number of manuscripts of Priscian carry, moreover, the legend: "Prisciani sophistae ars praeexercitaminum secundum Hermogenem vel Libanium."

[42] Cf. J. Martin, *Grillius, ein Beitrag zur Geschichte der Rhetorik*, Studien zur Gesch. und Kultur des Altertums, 14, 2/3 (Paderborn 1927) 181.

[43] *Ibid.*, p. 97; p. 118; p. 112.

[44] *Ibid.*, p. 144. Cf. p. 2, 18, referring to Aristotle *Rhetoric* 1.1.5, and p. 2, 3, referring to Plato *Gorgias* 463d.

[45] *Ibid.*, p. 9, 27 and p. 15, 5.

[46] *Ibid.*, p. 24, 18; cf. p. 179.

[47] Nicholas *Progymn.*, ed. Felten (Leipzig 1913), p. 6, 9:

Μῦθος τοίνυν ἐστὶ λόγος ψευδὴς τῷ

Priscian *Praeexercit.*, p. 430, 3:
Fabula est oratio ficta verisimili dispositione imaginem exhibens veritatis.

from Greek poets is significant. Probably he had no illusions about the ignorance of Greek among the students of rhetoric at Rome, for he was kept informed by his own son, who was carrying out useless researches in the libraries there.[48] Possibly it was for the same reason that he was obliged to prepare a summary of his great *Institutiones grammaticae*.[49]

We can thus estimate the extent of the course of studies that Symmachus proposed for the young Romans in Theodoric's time. The Greek schools that still flourished had to furnish the substance. Constantinople, where commentaries were being produced on Apollonius Dyscolus and Hermogenes, was to revive, thanks to Priscian, the teaching of grammar and rhetoric. Alexandria, where Ammonius' school was commenting on Plato, Aristotle, and Porphyry, a city too that was a great center of scientific studies, was, thanks to Boethius, to permit a revival of the scientific cycle, a refinement in the procedures of dialectic, and an importation into Rome of a renewed Neoplatonism that could be reconciled with Christianity. There does not appear to be any doubt that the two efforts were made simultaneously and that they denote in Symmachus a notable breadth of view and a capacity for synthesis. The interest in this enterprise shown by Constantinople is certain. Priscian agreed to support Symmachus.[50] Even the emperor was familiar with this undertaking. It was possible to pursue it, in spite of jealous spirits,

---

πιθανῶς συγκεῖσθαι εἰκονίζων τὴν ἀλήθειαν.

On the classic definition of μῦθος, cf. Cumont, *Recherches sur le symbolisme funéraire*, p. 3 n. 1.

[48] This appears to be the result of the example given by Priscian *Inst.*, ed. Keil, 51, p. 407, 14: "ut si filio meo Romae in praesenti degente, optans dicam: 'utinam Romae filius meus legisset auctores, propter quos nunc ibi moratur.'"

[49] This is the *Institutio de nomine et pronomine et verbo*. On the other hand, the *Partitiones duodecim versuum Aeneidos principalium* seems rather to have been used by Greek students who were being initiated into Latin literature. Cf. particularly Keil's edition, 3, p. 497, 17, where the Latin term is explained in Greek.

[50] It was also thought, but erroneously, that Flavianus, Priscian's pupil, had published an edition of Boethius' works. Cf. Schanz, vol. 4, 2, p. 152, and Schurr, *Die Trinitätslehre des Boethius*, p. 198. This legend started with a subscription in the manuscript Sangermanensis 613 (481), now at Leningrad, F. v. Classicus no. 7, mentioned by Montfaucon, *Bibl. bibl.* 2, 1130d: "ex codice vetustissimo quem Theodorus Mavortio consule, indictione V, propria manu exscripserat ex authentico Flaviani, qui Flavianus Prisciani discipulus fuerat." It was thought, on Montfaucon's evidence, that this subscription referred to Boethius' and Augustine's works on logic. But actually it appears in fol. 83ᵛ in the *explicit* of Book 8 of Priscian's *Institutio* and applies to this work only. Boethius' and Augustine's earlier treatises constitute a separate manuscript, with regard both to the date and to the number of quaternions, as is shown by Dom A. Staerk's description, *Les manuscrits latins du Vᵉ au XIIIᵉ s. conservés à la bibliothèque impériale de Saint-Pétersbourg* (Saint Petersburg 1910). It is true, however, that Theodorus also transcribed Boethius' treatises, as is shown by the subscription of Paris. nouv. acq. Lat. 1611, fol. 51.

only because Symmachus and Boethius enjoyed the highest esteem of the Byzantine emperors and also of Theodoric.[51]

However, this renaissance, conceived and desired by some men of genius, was factitious and destined to perish along with them. Was it not illogical to want to restore Greek culture by means of translations? Only a preliminary and intensive study of the Greek language would have helped to create enduring and productive contacts between the two cultures. It was fatal when this renaissance was suddenly crushed, on the day that Theodoric broke with Byzantium.[52] Perhaps the revival even hastened this breach, if the progress of Hellenism appeared like an artful interference by the emperor into Italian affairs. Was it not the acknowledged desire of a man like Priscian to see the two Romes united under imperial sovereignty?[53] Hence it was natural for Boethius to be the first victim. The charge not only ruined his political career, although he had intended to shake off the yoke of Gothic domination and reestablish the emperor's authority in Italy.[54] His Neoplatonism too brought a charge of magic against him, on the ground that he had used the demons to obtain his high offices.[55] Symmachus had not long to wait before being accused along with his son-in-law and put to death as well. With them, it was the renaissance of Hellenism in the West that was endangered. It was Greek culture that was on the point of disappearing.

[51] Cf. above, p. 274, and sec. 3 n. 129. On the relations of Boethius' family with the East, cf. Schurr, *Die Trinitätslehre des Boethius*, pp. 198–203. He shows that, through his numerous relations with the East, Boethius must have helped in the Union of the Churches that was consummated in 519.

[52] The break was caused by the fact that the Emperor Justin persecuted the Arians from 523 on and supported the Roman Catholics against the Arian domination of the Ostrogoths.

[53] Priscian *De laude Anastasii imperatoris* 265, ed. Baehrens, *Poet. Lat. min.*, 5 (Leipzig 1883), p. 273: "Utraque Roma tibi iam spero pareat uni."

[54] Cf. *De cons. philos.*, Peiper, p. 13, 81: "libertatem arguor sperasse Romanam." Boethius had undertaken the defense of the patrician Albinus, who had been accused of high treason for having carried on a secret correspondence with the emperor.

[55] *Ibid.*, p. 15, 125: "ob ambitum dignitatis sacrilegio me conscientiam polluisse mentiti sunt . . . Nec conveniebat vilissimorum me spirituum praesidia captare, quem tu in hanc excellentiam componebas, ut consimilem Deo faceres . . . Hoc ipso videbimur adfines fuisse maleficio, quod tuis inbuti disciplinis, tuis instituti moribus sumus." By this he means the Pythagorean precept ἕπου Θεῷ, toward which he had directed the conduct of his life. [Cf. the analogous though more restricted charge brought against Apuleius, and his refutation in the *Pro se de magia* (TRANS.).]

Chapter 7

HELLENISM IN THE SERVICE OF MONASTIC CULTURE: CASSIODORUS

1. THE FOUNDING OF VIVARIUM

Monastic culture at the beginning of the sixth century was appreciably the same in Italy as the culture of the monks of Lérins a century before. St. Benedict, although he had participated in his youth in the liberal studies,[1] does not appear to remember them. He knows of Egyptian monasticism only from the *Conlationes* and the *Vitae patrum*, that is, from Cassianus and Rufinus. When he quotes a *Sententia* from Sextus, when he uses St. Basil's *Regula* or Evagrius' *Sententiae*, it is in Rufinus' translations that he has read them.[2] However, there were still learned monks, like Gennadius of Marseilles. Dionysius Exiguus was an expert in Greek. He studied dialectic philosophy with Cassiodorus, who praises him as an unequaled Hellenist, able to translate as he read from Latin into Greek or from Greek into Latin with perfect ease and scrupulous accuracy.[3] The works of Dionysius, whose activity as a translator was carried on in a monastery in Rome between 497 and 540, show what were the needs and the desires of the readers in clerical circles at that period. Greek hagiography relating to the Saints of the Desert remained in honored depositories in the monasteries. At the request of the

[1] Cf. Gregory the Great *Dial.* 2, prol. (*PL* 66, 126 A): "Romae liberalibus studiis traditus fuerat . . . despectis itaque litterarum studiis, relicta domo rebusque patris . . . recessit . . . scienter nescius et sapienter indoctus."

[2] St. Benedict *Regula* 42 (*PL* 103, 633): "et legat unus Conlationes vel Vitas Patrum, aut certe aliquid unde aedificentur." On this last translation by Rufinus, cf. Schanz, vol. 4, 1, p. 418. See also M. Rothenhaeusler, "Ueber Anlage und Quellen der Regel des hl. Benedikt," *Studien und Mitt. zur Geschichte des Benediktinerordens* 38 (1917), 1–17; the *Index auctorum* in Butler's 2nd ed. (Freiburg im Breisgau 1927); D. Gorce, "La part des *Vitae Patrum* dans l'élaboration de la règle bénédictine," *Revue liturgique et monastique* (1929); and Dom B. Capelle, "Cassien, le Maître et s. Benoît," *Recherches de théologie ancienne et médiévale* 11 (1939) 110–118.

[3] Cassiodorus *Institutiones*, ed. Mynors (Oxford 1937), p. 62, 13: "in utraque lingua valde doctissimus," and 63, 7: "Qui tanta Latinitatis et Graecitatis peritia fungebatur, ut quoscumque libros Graecos in manibus acciperet, Latine sine offensione transcurreret, iterumque Latinos Attico sermone relegeret, ut crederes hoc esse conscriptum, quod os eius inoffensa velocitate fundebat."

abbot Pastor, Dionysius translated the account of the *Penitence of St. Thaïs*, and at the request of the abbot Gaudentius he translated the story of the *Finding of St. John the Baptist's Head*, although this narrative, intended to authenticate a relic from Emesa, had been declared suspect by the *Decree of Pope Gelasius*.[4] Dionysius' preface explains the reason for the persistent vogue of this type of literature. This account is intended to glorify the monks, for it was the monks who discovered and preserved the holy relic. St. John the Baptist himself is considered as the ancestor of monasticism, and patronage is useful for legitimizing the institution that too many contemporaries, although Christians, persist in scorning.[5] Still, even outside the convents there are certain persons enamored of Egyptian asceticism: for instance, the anonymous lady of the highest rank who commissions Dionysius to translate the *Life of Pacomius*,[6] or those deacons of the Roman Church who translated Books 5 and 6 of the *Vitae patrum*, probably from manuscripts brought back from the East at the time of the missions to Constantinople.[7] Apart from this taste for hagiographical accounts, the clerical circles also want to express their personal opinions in the contemporary ecclesiastical quarrels. So Dionysius translates a number of pieces to increase the corpus of the great heresies, notably the letters of Cyril of Alexandria.[8] Again, he confines himself to the publication of a fresh translation of an ancient text: for example, a translation of Cyril's denunciations against Nestorius, for Dionysius deplores the fact that the West is still ignorant of them.[9] On another occasion he himself produces a translation to compete with an ancient translation that is recognized as defective. This is the case with the *Codex canonum ecclesiasticorum*.[10] This literary genre was to be continued by the Roman deacon

[4] Cf. Schanz, vol. 4, 2, p. 590. The prologue to the abbot Pastor may be found in *Analecta Bollandiana* 11 (1892) 298–299.

[5] Dionysius *Prol. ad Gaudentium* (PL 67, 419 B): "Sicuti nunc plerique Christianorum Pharisaeorum sine dubitatione consimiles, si forte Dei famulos viderint abstinentes, in eadem convicia atque maledicta prorumpere, et rem quam imitatione debent adsequi, suis prosequi contumeliis non verentur."

[6] Dionysius *Vita s. Pachomii*, prol., PL 73, 227–230 and 271–273. The ancient editors conjectured that this noble lady might be Galla, Symmachus' daughter and Boethius' sister-in-law.

[7] PL 73, 49. Cf. Schanz, vol. 4, 2, p. 596; A. H. Salonius, *Vitae Patrum, kritische Untersuchungen über Text, Syntax und Wortschatz der spätlateinischen Vitae Patrum* (Lund 1920) 34ff, and A. Wilmart, "Le recueil latin des Apophtegmes," *RB* 34 (1922) 185–198.

[8] The list may be found in Schanz, vol. 4, 2, p. 590.

[9] Dionysius *Prol. ad Petrum*, PL 67, 11 B: "Opportunum prorsus hoc tempore existimans, quo tanti doctoris apostolica fides Graecis iam dudum bene comperta, sed ignorata Latinis hactenus innotescat." On the circumstances of the publication of this translation, which is actually merely a re-edition of Marius Mercator's translation, cf. Mgr Duchesne, *L'église au VIe siècle*, p. 61.

[10] Dionysius *Praef. ad Stephanum*, PL 67, 141 A: "Quamvis charissimus frater noster Laurentius adsidua et familiari cohortatione parvitatem nostram regulas ecclesiasticas de

Rusticus. Rusticus corrects the translation of the Acts of the Council of Chalcedon and quotes in his treatise *Contra Acephalos* the entire Greek literature relating to the Council of Ephesus.[11] Lastly, at the request of the abbot Eugippius, Dionysius even launches upon a philosophical work. This is the Περὶ κατασκευῆς ἀνθρώπου by Gregory of Nyssa, but he admits in his preface that he had great difficulty in rendering into Latin the language of Greek philosophy,[12] all the more so as he claims to combine elegance and accuracy.[13] It is surprising that Eugippius, whose culture was scarcely distinguished,[14] had expressed a desire to have a translation of such a difficult treatise, in which several Platonic theories appeared suspect to Dionysius himself. Are we to believe that Eugippius' Neapolitan monastery was enamored of Platonism? As a matter of fact, Gregory of Nyssa's treatise presented a favorable opportunity because it supplemented Basil's *Hexaemeron*, which had already been translated by Eustathius.[15] We may observe, however, the lengthy interpolation in chapter 24. It is evidence that one of Dionysius' readers compared the theories of Gregory of Nyssa with those of the pagan philosophers, whom he appears to know quite well.[16]

Dionysius felt in particular the Alexandrian influence. We have seen the effort that he made to spread Cyril's doctrine.[17] He also propagated in the West the Alexandrian reckoning of time with his treatise *De paschate*, followed as a confirmation by his translation of the letter of Proterius of

---

Graeco transferre pepulerit, confusione credo priscae translationis offensus, nihilominus tamen ingestum laborem tuae beatitudinis consideratione suscepi."

[11] *PL* 67, 1167. Cf. Schanz, vol. 4, 2, p. 596.

[12] Dionysius *Praef. ad Eugippium*, *PL* 67, 345 C: "in quo opere quantum sim difficultatis expertus, ex ipsa lectione probabitur. In plurimis enim iuxta philosophorum sententias immoratus, opulentiam tantam suae eruditionis expressit (Gregorius), ut paene nihil omiserit eorum quae ab illis doctis et otiosis ingeniis in hac parte per inextricabiles digesta sunt quaestiones."

[13] *Ibid.*, 345 D: "enisus sum quidem disertitudinem eius sequi, licet adsequi nimis impari facultate nequiverim." This is the mark of a notable Hellenist, at a time when translators were restricted to literalism. F. Blatt, "Remarques sur l'histoire des traductions latines," *Classica et mediaevalia* 1, 2 (1938) 217–242, could have observed this honorable exception.

[14] "Virum quidem non usque adeo saecularibus litteris eruditum," Cassiodorus says of him, *Inst.*, p. 61, 24.

[15] Cf. Puech, *Litt. gr. chrét.* 3, p. 402, and Eustathius' translation, *PG* 30, 869–968 = *PL* 53, 867–966.

[16] *PL* 67, 387 A. This interpretation is entitled: "De natura caeli, quod non sit ex quattuor elementis secundum Aristotelem." The writer explains in particular (388 A) the theories of Thales, Anaximenes, Heraclitus, and Hipparchus constructing the universe from one element only: water, air, or fire. On these theories, cf. above, p. 135.

[17] Note that in the preface to the *Contra Acephalos*, Rusticus, *PL* 67, 1170 B, claims that he is reporting conversations that he had held in Constantinople, Alexandria, and the Thebaid.

Alexandria to Pope Leo.[18] The impact of this book was to be lasting, and the Alexandrian reckoning of time was finally to replace, even in Gaul, Victor of Aquitaine's reckoning of time.[19]

Despite these oriental influences furthered by the extremely learned Dionysius, it cannot be said that monastic society at this period was widely responsive to Hellenic culture. Monasticism appeared at that time fated to exist solely by turning inwardly upon itself and to develop a purely clerical and rather restricted culture. Cassiodorus' merit lies in having sensed the danger of such a concept. He judged that pagan science was indispensable to the monks, if they wanted to retain complete comprehension of the Scriptures. He knew that this learning could not be acquired solely through Latin literature. He would therefore try to place Greek literature and learning at the service of monastic culture.

Formerly Theodoric's chancellor, Cassiodorus seemed prepared for such an enterprise. He had inspired Theodoric, by means of veritable courses of lectures, with the desire and the intention to achieve the ideal of the Platonic King.[20] This intention was also that of Theodahad, who had been initiated into Neoplatonic philosophy.[21] Cassiodorus' letters, edited in the name of the Ostrogoth kings, prove that the vast effort attempted by Symmachus and Boethius to revive culture was encouraged in high places, even if Cassiodorus later seemed to condemn its purely pagan character.[22] We know how Theodoric's policy, turning into hostility toward Byzantium, put an end to this enterprise with the execution of Boethius and Symmachus. Cassiodorus for all that did not give up the idea of stimulating culture in Rome. On the model of the Christian *Didascalia* of Alexandria, he founded, in cooperation with Pope Agapetus, a kind of Christian university in Rome (535–536). But the vicissitudes of the Ostrogothic War, in the course of which Rome was captured by Belisarius in 536, retaken by Totila in 546, to become finally Byzantine, destroyed this recent foundation and dispersed the library that Cassiodorus had already accumulated.[23] Despite this failure, Cassiodorus,

---

[18] *PL* 67, 505; cf. 512 D. Although intended for a Latin scholar, Proterius' letter had been written in Greek, and without an accompanying translation.

[19] On the rapid progress in the Alexandrian *computus* in Italy, and its slow progress in Gaul, cf. B. Krusch, "Die Einführung des griechischen Paschalritus im Abendlande," *Neues Archiv* 9 (1883) 99–169.

[20] Text quoted above, chap. 6 (introduction) n. 13.

[21] Text quoted above, chap. 6 (introduction) n. 15.

[22] See in particular the praise bestowed on Boethius in Letter 1.45 of the *Variae*. On the other hand, notably in the *De anima*, written when Cassiodorus renounced the world, he does not name without reservation the *magistri saecularium litterarum* (PL 70: 1283 A, 1285 C, 1287 D, 1298 A).

[23] I take this detail from what Cassiodorus *Inst.*, ed. Mynors, p. 149, 15, says of Albinus' *De musica*: "quem in bibliotheca Romae nos habuisse atque studiose legisse retinemus; qui si forte gentili incursione sublatus est, habetis Gaudentium."

who had abandoned political life and attached himself to the Byzantines,[24] returned to his project to create a cultural center in Italy. He was intensely interested to learn from Iunilius, either on reading the preface to his *Instituta*, which had just appeared, or even from having met him personally at Constantinople, that in Persia, at Nisibis, there still existed a Christian university like the one that he had wanted to found.[25] But with Rome in ruins, now a Byzantine city always exposed to menace, he could not, as he thought, repeat his attempt. Cassiodorus saw no other way except to establish on his own land, at Scyllacium, in Calabria, a monastery where he assembled a fresh library. The history of this monastery of Vivarium is unknown. We know only that it did not follow the Benedictine Rule[26] and that it died with the death of its founder.[27] But Cassiodorus' cultural program and the contents of his library are known quite accurately, thanks to the *Institutiones*. In fact, he conceived this work as a bibliography, and to produce this bibliography he used the manuscripts that were in Vivarium. Next, the *Institutiones* provided information on the reading program advocated by Cassiodorus and were virtually at the same time a library catalogue, the oldest and the most detailed catalogue that we possess. Hence it should be a matter of surprise that neither Becker nor Manitius, who have drawn up a careful list of the catalogues in medieval libraries, started their works beginning with this catalogue of the library at Vivarium.[28] Only Franz, in his now obsolete monograph on

---

[24] Probably following his king Vitiges, who had abdicated and been taken to Constantinople in 540, after the Gothic reverses. As a matter of fact, the latest letter in the *Variae* dates in 537, and Cassiodorus no longer had any official position when he wrote the *De anima* a few years later. Cf. Mommsen's ed. of the *Variae*, pp. xxx–xxxi. On the other hand, from a letter of Pope Vigilius (Mansi, 9, 357 = *PL* 69, 49 A), Cassiodorus in 550 was in Constantinople, where Vigilius charged with a mission "religiosum virum item filium nostrum Senatorem." Several Roman senators, notably Basilius, Decius, and Cethegus, also fled to Constantinople when Totila recaptured Rome. Cf. Procopius *Bell. Goth.* 3.20 and 25.

[25] The story of this foundation is told by Cassiodorus in the preface to his *Inst.*, p. 3, 1–19. On the archaeological remains, cf. H. I. Marrou, "Autour de la bibliothèque du pape Agapit," *MEFR* 48 (1931) 124–169. The text quoted immediately above, n. 23, makes Marrou's hypothesis (otherwise cautiously formulated), p. 167, far from plausible. It postulates that Agapetus' library constituted the original contents of the Lateran library. Similarly, the revision of Martianus Capella's text, *ad Portam Capenam*, can scarcely be, as Marrou assumes, p. 165, a revision made in Agapetus' library, for Cassiodorus *Inst.*, p. 109, 1 and p. 130, 11, asserts that he knows this text only through hearsay, that he never possessed it, and that he cannot procure it.

[26] Cf. Dom G. Morin, "L'ordre des heures canoniales dans les monastères de Cassiodore," *RB* 43 (1931) 145–152.

[27] See my article "Le site du monastère de Cassiodore," *MEFR* 55 (1938) 305–306.

[28] Cf. G. Becker, *Catalogi bibliothecarum antiqui* (Bonn 1885), and M. Manitius, *Handschriften antiker Autoren in mittelalterlichen Bibliothekskatalogen* (Leipzig 1935).

Cassiodorus,[29] and Mynors in the *Index auctorum* to his edition of the *Institutiones* thought of drawing up such a catalogue. But they did not distinguish between the works that Cassiodorus explicitly states as having been in his library, those that he mentions without specifying whether he possesses them or quotes them from an intermediate source, and even those whose titles he quotes while admitting that they are not in his possession. It is however necessary to make this careful distinction if we want to find out accurately what the holdings of Vivarium were, and more particularly the original or translated Greek works that had the good fortune to be preserved in this haven of culture and transmitted thereby.

It is important to eliminate an ambiguity at once. Was the monastery of Vivarium a Latin or a Greek monastery? If it was a Greek-speaking monastery, it would not have a place in this inquiry, which is confined to the Latin West. The traditional opinion makes it a Latin monastery, which seems natural, since Cassiodorus writes in Latin. But Rohlfs's recent theory, which has occasionally been received favorably,[30] assures us that Greek uninterruptedly persisted in Southern Italy since the time of the first colonization down to our own day. It is not my intention to discuss in its entirety this linguistic theory, but the evidence offered by the *Institutiones* deserves to be examined closely. At the beginning of the book Cassiodorus declares that he knows of the existence of Greek commentaries ranging over all Scripture, by Clement, Cyril, Chrysostom, Gregory, Basil. And he adds: "Sed nos potius Latinos scriptores, Domino iuvante, sectamur; ut, quoniam Italis scribimus, Romanos quoque expositores commodissime indicasse videamur. Dulcius enim ab unoquoque suscipitur, quod patrio sermone narratur."[31] In Rohlfs's view, this text does not prove that the mother tongue of the monks of Vivarium was Latin. It is the evidence of a national Roman conscience and not a linguistic testimony. Does Justinian himself not describe himself in Constantinople as a Roman Emperor and does he not call Latin πάτριον φωνήν? The best proof that the monks of Vivarium knew Greek is that they translated works by Origen, Clement of Alexandria, Didymus, Epiphanes, Chrysostom, Socrates, Sozomen, Theodoret, Gaudentius.

I do not think that the facts presented by Rohlfs justify his interpretation of Cassiodorus' evidence. Probably Cassiodorus' Roman nationalism is real.

---

[29] A. Franz, *M. Aurelius Cassiodorus Senator, ein Beitrag zur Geschichte der theologischen Literatur* (Breslau 1872) 80–92.

[30] G. Rohlfs, *Scavi linguistici nella Magna Grecia* (trans. Tomasini, Collezione di studi meridionali), Halle and Rome 1933, pp. 120–122. Cf. J. Bérard's review, *Revue archéologique* 4 (1934) 213–214, and H. Pernot, "Hellénisme et Italie méridionale," *Studi italiani di filologia classica* 13 (1936) 161–182. A criticism of Rohlfs's theory regarding Vivarium has already been formulated by Blatt, "Remarques sur l'histoire des traductions latines," p. 235.

[31] Cass. *Inst.*, p. 5, 20.

He asserts that he urged the translation into Latin of Socrates, Sozomen, and Theodoret "ne insultet habere se facunda Graecia necessarium, quod vobis iudicet esse subtractum."[32] But it will be difficult to believe that he gave Greek-speaking monks this totally Latin bibliography and that he advised them to read in Latin translations all the Greek works that he mentions. Even if this improbable hypothesis were admitted, it would at least be necessary to agree that all these Greek-speaking monks knew Latin as well. But then, how explain that Cassiodorus regards Dionysius Exiguus as so meritorious for having known both languages?[33] Moreover, Rohlfs could not sustain his interpretation except by disregarding two other texts by Cassiodorus that clearly demonstrate an ignorance of Greek on the part of the majority of the monks at Vivarium. The first necessity, declares Cassiodorus, is for the monks to consult the Latin commentators: "Quodsi aliquid in eisdem neglegenter dictum repperit, tunc, *quibus lingua nota est*, a Graecis explanatoribus, quae sunt salubriter tractata, perquirant."[34] And elsewhere: "*Quodsi vobis non fuerit Graecarum litterarum nota facundia*, imprimis habetis Herbarium Dioscoridis . . . post haec legite Hippocratem atque Galienum Latina lingua conversos."[35] It was the monks' ignorance of the Greek language that made Cassiodorus equip them with an essentially Latin bibliography, although he himself was brought up on Greek writers in his youth and had no contempt whatever for Hellenic culture. The Greek manuscripts in his possession constituted at the most an eighth of the actual total of the library at Vivarium, since they all fitted into the eighth cabinet.[36] And these cabinets, to judge from idealized illustrations, were very narrow.[37] If we add up the number of Greek manuscripts that Vivarium definitely possessed in the original text, we find not more than some fifteen.[38] Even these manuscripts, according to Cassiodorus,

[32] *Ibid.*, p. 56, 9.

[33] Text quoted above, n. 3.

[34] Cass. *Inst.*, p. 5, 10.

[35] *Ibid.*, p. 78, 25.

[36] *Ibid.*, p. 32, 9: "Commemoratas tamen epistulas a Iohanne Chrysostomo expositas Attico sermone in suprascripto octavo armario dereliqui, ubi sunt Graeci codices congregati"; and p. 41, 6: "ideoque vobis et Graecum pandectem reliqui comprehensum in libris septuaginta quinque, qui continet quaterniones★★★, in armario supradicto octavo, ubi et alios Graecos diversis opusculis necessario congregavi, ne quid sanctissimae instructioni vestrae necessarium deesse videretur."

[37] See the cabinet containing the Gospels, represented on the mosaic of the mausoleum of Galla Placidia in Ravenna (cf. Wilpert, *Die römischen Mosaiken und Malereien* 3, pl. 49) and the miniature of Esdras in the Amiatinus fol. V^r, of Cassiodorian origin (cf. C. Nordenfalk, *Vier Kanonestafeln eines spätantiken Evangelienbuches* [Göteborg 1937] 40–42).

[38] These books are as follows: Athanasius *Ad Marcellinum in interpr. Psalm.* (*In Ps.*, PL 70, 22 C); *Biblia sacra* (*Inst.*, p. 41, 6); Clement of Alexandria *In Epistulas canonicas* (p. 29, 16); *Codex encyclius concilii Chalcedonensis* (p. 36, 1 and p. 64, 13); Didymus *In Proverbia* (p. 22, 12) and *In Epistulas canonicas* (p. 29, 27); Epiphanius of Cyprus *In Canticum canticorum* (p. 24, 10); Gaudentius *De musica* (p. 142, 13); John Chrysostom *In Epistulas*

could not serve his monks except in the form of translations.[39] Hence he hastened to order a large number of such translations, as though he foresaw the urgency of preserving, at least in this form, some part of Greek culture. These translations are themselves the work, not of the entire body of monks, but of some specialists, particularly three: Mutianus, Bellator, Epiphanius. If Cassiodorus overwhelmed them with work, it was in all likelihood because they were practically the only monks in the monastery who could cope with the task.[40] It is also fitting to add that the translations by these monks that have been preserved give a very feeble idea of their capacities: these experts themselves did not know Greek as their mother tongue and understood it badly.[41] It is therefore certain that the monks to whom Cassiodorus appeals are Latin-speaking, and the texts that Rohlfs uses as evidence would tend rather to weaken his thesis. If Rohlfs's linguistic investigation is valid, it will then be necessary to conjecture that the first generation of the monks at Vivarium were not Calabrians, but Italians from Ravenna or Rome who had followed Cassiodorus into his retreat.

Since the monks of Vivarium were Latin-speaking, it is all the more significant that Cassiodorus recommends in their case the study of many

---

apostolorum (p. 32, 10) and *In Actus apostolorum* (p. 33, 2); Josephus *Antiquitates Iudaicae* (p. 55, 16); Origen *In Esdrae libris duobus* (p. 27, 12); Socrates *Historia ecclesiastica* (p. 56, 6); Sozomen *Hist. eccl. (ibid.)*; Theodoret *Hist. eccl. (ibid.)*. Of course, this list is not restrictive, and it is evident that Cassiodorus was also bound to possess other Greek manuscripts as well.

[39] Cass. *Inst.*, p. 32, 12, informs the monks that he is leaving them the Greek manuscript of Chrysostom's commentary on the Epistles: "ut si Latina non potuerint latiora commenta procurari, de istis subinde transferatur quod plenissimam poterit praestare notitiam."

[40] Mutianus is commissioned to translate Gaudentius *De musica* (*Inst.*, p. 142, 13), Chrysostom *In Epist. ad Hebr. hom.* 34 (p. 29, 11), and *In Actus apost. hom.* 55 (p. 33, 1). Bellator translates Origen *In I–II Esdrae hom.* 2 (p. 27, 12). Epiphanius translates Didymus *In Proverbia* (p. 22, 12) and *In VII Epist. canon.* (p. 29, 26), Epiphanius of Cyprus (= Philo of Carpas) *In Canticum* (p. 24, 9), extracts from the *Ecclesiastical History* of Socrates, Sozomen, and Theodoret (p. 56, 5), and the *Codex encyclius* (p. 36, 1). Anonymous friends translate Clement of Alexandria *In Epist. canon.* (p. 29, 16) and Josephus *Antiquitates* and *Contra Apionem* in twenty-two books (p. 55, 16). These friends whose names are not specified are probably Mutianus, Bellator, and Epiphanius themselves; for Mutianus is called *amicus noster, Inst.* p. 142, 15 (in the first edition); Epiphanius, p. 24, 12; Bellator, p. 27, 19.

[41] Cf. the harsh criticisms of Schanz, vol. 4, 2, p. 107; Zoepfl, *Didymi Alexandrini in Epist. canon. brevis enarratio* (diss. Munich 1914), p. 19*; and Boysen's edition of the translation of Josephus' *Contra Apionem*, CSEL 37, p. XLII. The view of L. Parmentier, editor of Theodoret, *Altchristl. griech. Schriftsteller*, pp. LI–LIII, is more favorable to Cassiodorus' *Historia tripartita*. Cf. also F. Blatt, "Remarques sur l'histoire des traductions latines," pp. 237–241, and H. Janne, "Un contre-sens de Cassiodore: les furets du *Contre Apion*," *Byzantion* 11 (1936) 225–227.

Greek writers. The fact was that he recognized in Latin culture certain lacunae that only the Greeks could fill. These lacunae are particularly appreciable for pagan culture, and Book 2 of the *Institutiones* owes much more to the Greeks than Book 1. I have noted elsewhere why I believed that it had been composed separately and earlier than Book 1, to which Cassiodorus appended it afterward.[42] It would not be surprising if Cassiodorus used for this book personal notes dating from the time when he was studying dialectic in the course of his liberal studies.[43] He used in fact writers who, long before the foundation of the monastery, when he was Theodoric's chancellor, had been of service to him when he intruded learned digressions into his letters.[44] This fact can be verified; for Book 2 of the *Institutiones*, contrary to Book 1, is not a simple bibliography. It presents an analysis of several books, in the form of *excerpta* that can eliminate the need for the monks to consult the sources. Probably Cassiodorus did not explicitly acknowledge the character of his book, as he does for the *De orthographia*, where each chapter carries as a caption mention of the writer who furnishes the contents.[45] Here Cassiodorus claims that he is compiling an encyclopedia of the liberal arts. For each table of contents he indicates a list of writers to consult, but most frequently without specifying those that he has just excerpted. A careful examination will show that he uses only a very small number of the sources that he quotes. One may question whether he had the others at his disposal.

This examination, which has never been undertaken,[46] has a twofold interest. It lets us recognize, in the text of the *Institutiones*, *excerpta* from several works that are now lost. At the same time it will inform us of the lacunae in Cassiodorus' library and also of the fact that these lacunae were the limits of his Greek culture.

2. Pagan Hellenism at Vivarium

Cassiodorus' project itself inclines one to think that he conceives the cycle of studies in the manner of the Greek commentators. Not that the seven

[42] Cf. my article "Histoire d'un brouillon cassiodorien," *REA* 44 (1942) 65–86. I shall use the conclusions of this article in estimating the date of the various editions of the *Institutiones humanae*.

[43] Cass. *Inst.*, p. 62, 17: "qui mecum dialecticam legit," he says of Dionysius Exiguus. He had also lecture notes for instructing Theodoric. See above, p. 274.

[44] On the interest of these digressions for the history of culture, cf. A. T. Heerklotz, *Die "Variae" des Cassiodorus Senator als kulturgeschichtliche Quelle* (diss. Heidelberg 1926).

[45] For example, at the beginning of chap. 2 (*PL* 70, 1246 C): "Ex Velio Longo ista deflorata sunt."

[46] The only research on this subject is the very superficial article by L. M. Capelli, "I fonti delle *Institutiones humanarum rerum* di Cassiodoro," *Rendiconti del r. Istituto Lombardo delle scienze e lettere*, 2nd series, vol. 31 (1898) 1549–1557. It is evident that for this study account must be taken of the various editions of Cassiodorus, not only of the text edited by Garet.

liberal arts are an innovation at Rome. Marrou has shown the remote origins of the syllabus of the ἐγκύκλιος παιδεία, which goes back to Hellenistic times[1] and was adopted in a general way by all Greco-Latin literature until the beginning of the Middle Ages.[2]

But Cassiodorus' work, which is an elementary schoolbook, has nothing in common, despite appearances, with the *Disciplinarum libri* of those scholars who, like Varro, compiled scientific handbooks.[3] Cassiodorus sometimes mentions Varro, but quotes from him only briefly, always at the beginning or at the end of a chapter, as though primarily for a decorative purpose.[4] He nowhere says that he possesses Varro's encyclopedia, nor does he advise his monks to consult it. With regard to Apuleius, he certainly possesses only his *De dialectica* and just as certainly does not have his *De musica*.[5] The Latin scholars, who withal did not confine themselves to the seven liberal arts and did not treat them in the same order as Cassiodorus,[6] were not, then, the inspiration of his teaching program. The Latin school tradition, represented by Augustine's *Disciplinarum libri* and Martianus Capella's *De nuptiis*, exerted no greater influence on his thought. St. Augustine never completed his encyclopedia. Only the *De grammatica* and the *De musica* were finished.[7] Cassiodorus did not even possess the *De grammatica* when he first wrote the *Institutiones humanae*,[8] and he never heard of Martianus Capella except through hearsay.[9] His work plan, besides, differs appreciably from theirs. He studies rhetoric before dialectic, arithmetic before the other three disciplines. He distinguishes the three arts from the four disciplines and reckons dialectic as an art,

---

[1] Marrou, *Saint Augustin et la fin de la culture antique*, pp. 211–219.

[2] *Ibid.*, pp. 219–235.

[3] *Ibid.*, p. 226.

[4] Cass. *Inst.*, p. 91, 12; 108, 22; 109, 15; 151, 2; 155, 11; 157, 11. Cf. Erdbruegger, *Cassiodorus unde etymologias in Psalterii commentario prolatas petivisse putandus sit* (diss. Jena 1911) 28–29. He does not think that Cassiodorus had read Varro.

[5] Cass. *Inst.*, p. 118, 20 and p. 128, 20 on the *De dialectica*; p. 149, 19 on the *De musica*. The *De arithmetica* is mentioned, p. 140, 18, but Cassiodorus does not indicate whether he possesses it or not.

[6] Ritschl, "De M. Terentii Varronis disciplinarum libris commentarius," *Opuscula philologica* 3, pp. 352ff, restores Varro's order: Grammar, Dialectic, Rhetoric, Geometry, Arithmetic, Astrology, Music, Medicine, Architecture. Besides the seven disciplines, Apuleius treated medicine and agronomy, according to Jahn, "Ueber römischen Encyclopädien," *Berichte über die Verhandlungen der kön. sächsischen Gesellschaft der Wissenschaften* (1850) 282–287. It is not known in what order he treated these subjects, and it is not even certain, despite Jahn's conjecture, p. 286, that they were collected to form an encyclopedia.

[7] Augustine *Retract.* 1.6, PL 32, 591 C. Hence it appears difficult to conjecture the order that he might have adopted, as Marrou does, *Saint Augustin*, pp. 189–193.

[8] Cass. *Inst.*, p. 94, 13. Cf. my article "Histoire d'un brouillon cassiodorien," p. 76.

[9] Cass. *Inst.*, p. 109, 1 and p. 130, 11.

although he knows that Varro, Augustine, and Capella considered it as a discipline.[10]

Such freedom is a sign that Cassiodorus was inspired by a Greek tradition. As a matter of fact, of all the writers, quoted by Marrou, who enumerated the liberal arts, Porphyry was the only one whose scheme corresponded exactly to that of Cassiodorus.[11] Now, in his chapter *De dialectica*, which is the transition between the arts and the disciplines, Cassiodorus does not hide the fact that he is only following the usage of the masters of philosophy: "Consuetudo itaque est doctoribus philosophiae, antequam ad Isagogen veniant exponendam, divisionem philosophiae paucis attingere; quam nos quoque servantes praesenti tempore non immerito credimus intimandam."[12] This statement informs us that he borrows his classification from the prologue of a commentary on Porphyry's *Isagoge*. If it is possible to identify this commentary, we shall know from whom Cassiodorus borrows the entire plan of his encyclopedia.

The classification is arranged by Cassiodorus according to the accompanying scheme.[13]

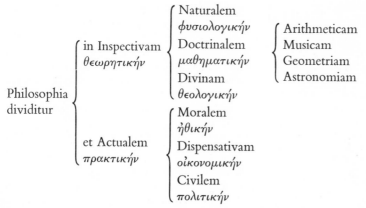

This table corresponds, item for item, including the Greek terms, to the classification that was developed at the close of the fifth century by the pagan teacher of Alexandria, Ammonius, Hermias' son, in the very prologue to his

---

[10] *Ibid.*, p. 108, 21. So Marrou, *Saint Augustin*, p. 218, is mistaken, in my opinion, in abandoning the attempt to draw conclusions on the order in which the disciplines are listed. It is only in Augustine that this order is obscure, on account of the fact that he did not achieve his plan for an encyclopedia. It would be a very rare occurrence for the scholastic spirit never to have attached any importance to the order of this classification.

[11] See the table drawn up by Marrou, *Saint Augustin*, p. 217.

[12] Cass. *Inst.*, p. 110, 5.

[13] *Ibid.*, p. 110, 9 = *PL* 70, 1167 C. It is Cassiodorus' first edition that furnishes the Greek names.

commentary on the *Isagoge*.[14] Like Ammonius, Cassiodorus gives subdivisions only for the four disciplines that constitute mathematics.[15] Then he reproduces the distinction between νομοθετικόν and δικαστικόν that, according to Ammonius,[16] characterizes each of the three parts of pragmatic philosophy; next, the definitions of philosophy that Ammonius had similarly inserted in his prologue:

Ammonius *In Isag.*, p. 3, 3:
φιλοσοφία ἐστὶ θείων τε καὶ ἀνθρωπίνων πραγμάτων γνῶσις.

p. 6, 27: φιλοσοφία ἐστὶ τέχνη τεχνῶν καὶ ἐπιστήμη ἐπιστημῶν.

p. 4, 15: φιλοσοφία ἐστὶ μελέτη θανάτου.

p. 3, 7: φιλοσοφία ἐστὶ ὁμοίωσις Θεῷ κατὰ τὸ δυνατὸν ἀνθρώπῳ.

Cassiodorus *Institutiones divinarum et saecularium litterarum*, p. 110, 15:
Philosophia est divinarum humanarumque rerum . . . probabilis scientia; aliter, philosophia est ars artium et disciplina disciplinarum; rursus, philosophia est meditatio mortis, quod magis convenit Christianis. Philosophia est adsimilari Deo secundum quod possibile est homini.[17]

The very basis of Cassiodorus' scheme, this distinction between the arts and the disciplines that, on Marrou's evidence, was an innovation among the Latin writers,[18] was taken from the same prologue by Ammonius, who adds,

[14] Ammonius *In Isag.*, ed. Busse, *CAG* 4, 3, pp. 11–15.

[15] Cass. *Inst.*, p. 111, 16. Cf. Ammonius *In Isag.*, p. 13, 8: Καὶ τὸ φυσιολογικὸν μὲν οὖν καὶ τὸ θεολογικὸν ὑποδιαιρέσεις τινὰς ἐπιδέχονται, ἀλλὰ τὰς μὲν τούτων ὑποδιαιρέσεις ὡς ἀσυμμέτρους οὔσας εἰσαγωγικαῖς ἀκοαῖς σιωπήσωμεν, τὸ δὲ μαθηματικὸν διαιρεῖται εἰς τέσσαρα, εἰς γεωμετρίαν καὶ ἀστρονομίαν καὶ μουσικὴν καὶ ἀριθμητικήν.

[16] Cass. *Inst.*, p. 110, 14 = *PL* 70, 1167 C. Cf. Ammonius *In Isag.*, p. 15, 11: τούτων δὲ ἕκαστον διαιρεῖται εἴς τε τὸ νομοθετικὸν καὶ δικαστικόν.

[17] This last sentence, omitted in Mynors' edition but printed in *PL* 70, 1167 C, appeared in Cassiodorus' first edition, with the translation in Greek. Note in this parallel Cassiodorus' own addition: "quod magis convenit Christianis." With this remark he testifies to a certain distrust with regard to the other definitions proposed by the master pagan Ammonius. The third definition comes from the *Phaedo*, the last one from *Theaetetus* 176b.

[18] Marrou, "*Doctrina* et *disciplina* dans la langue des Pères de l'église," *ALMA* 9 (1934) 7. The only earlier texts that roughly outline this distinction are those of Martianus Capella *De nupt.* 2.138, ed. Dick, p. 60, 1: "puellae quam plures, quarum Artes aliae, alterae dictae sunt Disciplinae"; and 5.438, p. 216, 3: "quippe sum ipsa Rhetorica, quam alii artem, virtutem alii dixere, alteri disciplinam; artem vero idcirco, quia doceor, licet Plato huic verbo refragetur; virtutem autem dicunt, qui mihi bene dicendi inesse scientiam compererunt; qui edisci vero dicendi intimam rationem et percipi posse non nesciunt, fidenter me adserunt disciplinam." In St. Augustine, this terminology is not yet fixed, although he too recognizes a distinction between the liberal arts, *De ordine* 2.16.44: "Cum enim artes illae omnes liberales, partim ad usum vitae, partim ad cognitionem rerum contemplationemque discantur, usum earum adsequi difficillimum est." Only Priscian, in my opinion, must have already known this distinction; for he mentions

on Aristotle's definition of philosophy, φιλοσοφία ἐστὶ τέχνη τεχνῶν καὶ ἐπιστήμη ἐπιστημῶν, the following commentary:

Ammonius *In Isag.*, p. 6, 25:
Αὗται δὲ αἱ τέχναι καὶ ἐπιστῆμαι κατὰ μὲν τοὺς λόγους οὐδὲν διαφέρουσιν ἀλλήλων . . . κατὰ δὲ τὴν ὕλην διαλλάττουσιν. αἱ μὲν γὰρ ἐπιστῆμαι περὶ τὰ ὡσαύτως ἔχοντα καταγίνονται, οἷον ἀστρονομία, γεωμετρία, ἀριθμητική, αἱ δὲ τέχναι περὶ τὰ ὡς ἐπὶ τὸ πολὺ καὶ μεταβαλλόμενα.

Cassiodorus *Institutiones divinarum et saecularium litterarum*, p. 130, 4:
Inter artem et disciplinam Plato et Aristoteles, opinabiles magistri saecularium litterarum, hanc differentiam esse voluerunt dicentes artem esse habitudinem operatricem contingentium, quae se et aliter habere possunt; disciplina vero est quae de his agit quae aliter evenire non possunt.[19]

Cassiodorus' direct dependence on Ammonius is evident; for Boethius, who, as we have seen,[20] also derives from Ammonius, cannot be Cassiodorus' source on all these points.[21]

Now, Ammonius himself informs us that this prologue, which opens his book on dialectic and introduces the study of the four disciplines, was inserted in a course of studies that normally began with grammar and rhetoric.[22] This course then consisted, like Cassiodorus' encyclopedia, at first of the three arts (grammar, rhetoric, and dialectic), then of the four disciplines. Actually, Ammonius' prologue gives no clear indication of the order in which

---

Symmachus, Boethius' father-in-law, "studiis etiam optimarum artium disciplinarumque florentem" (*De fig. num.*, praef., ed. Keil, *Gramm. Lat.* 3, p. 405, 2). But I have established above, p. 326, that he had read the works of Ammonius.

[19] Cf. *Inst.*, p. 108, 15, where Cassiodorus observes that dialectic may be considered either as an art, or as a discipline, depending on the viewpoint from which it is regarded. Note that after each of these two passages, in the definitive edition, Cassiodorus recognizes that Augustine and Martianus Capella had not adopted this terminology.

[20] See above, pp. 285ff.

[21] In the prologue to his *In Isag.*, ed. Brandt, pp. 8–9, he omits the definitions of philosophy and its subdivision into disciplines. In addition, he does not translate Ammonius' terms of classification by the same terms as Cassiodorus.

[22] Ammonius *In Isag.*, p. 1, 10:
Δεῖ τοίνυν ὁρισμὸν τῆς φιλοσοφίας εἰπεῖν, ὥσπερ καὶ τῆς γραμματικῆς ἀρχόμενοι τὸν ὁρισμὸν ἐμανθάνομεν, ὅτι γραμματική ἐστιν ἐμπειρία τῶν παρὰ ποιηταῖς καὶ συγγραφεῦσιν ὡς ἐπὶ τὸ πολὺ λεγομένων· ὁμοίως καὶ ῥητορικῆς ἀρχόμενοι τὸν ὁρισμὸν ἐμάθομεν, ὅτι ῥητορική ἐστι δύναμις τεχνικὴ πιθανοῦ λόγου ἐν πράγματι πολιτικῷ τέλος ἔχουσα τὸ εὖ λέγειν· δεῖ οὖν καὶ τῆς φιλοσοφίας τὸν ὁρισμὸν μαθεῖν.

Cassiodorus *Inst.*, p. 94, 2:

Grammatica vero est peritia pulchre loquendi ex poetis inlustribus auctoribusque collecta.

these disciplines should be studied.[23] But the order adopted by Cassiodorus—arithmetic, music, geometry, astronomy—is also in the Greek tradition. It goes back to Nicomachus of Gerasa's *Introductio arithmetica*, which had been the subject of commentaries by Apuleius, Ammonius, and Boethius[24] and appears again only in Theon of Smyrna, Iamblichus, and Eustratius.[25] The considerations that justified Cassiodorus in urging the need to study arithmetic before the other disciplines stem from the same source.[26]

Thus, although the school tradition of the seven liberal arts was an ancient concept in Rome, Cassiodorus gives it a refreshing form by taking the scheme of the *Institutiones humanae* not from earlier Latin encyclopedists but from the tradition of the last pagan teachers of Alexandria, notably from this commentary by Ammonius that had already exerted such a profound influence on Boethius. When he made his final decision, he perceived that Augustine and Martianus Capella did not separate the arts and the disciplines, but he merely indicated this in two additional notes, without otherwise modifying his text.[27] He simply stated that Ammonius and the pagan commentators of Alexandria attached an excessive value to the scientific disciplines. Thus he established in the West the medieval distinction between the *trivium* and the *quadrivium*, or, as we should now say, literary studies and scientific studies.[28]

This unacknowledged borrowing from the last pagan school of Alexandria is all the more curious in that, in the course of the work, Cassiodorus makes an effort to supply his monks, almost all of whom are ignorant of Greek, with a purely Latin bibliography. In the preface he promises not to omit the Greek or Latin writers who are the sources of his text.[29] Actually, he mentions a Greek writer only when Latin literature seems to him to present a

---

[23] On p. 13 he gives the sequence: arithmetic, geometry, music, astronomy; and on p. 14: geometry, astronomy, arithmetic, music.

[24] Cf. Nicomachus *Introd. arithm.*, ed. Hoche, p. 6; Boethius *Inst. arithm.*, ed. Friedlein, p. 9, 1; Cassiodorus *Inst.*, p. 111, 16. Every one of Cassiodorus' definitions is then repeated at the beginning of the chapter devoted to each discipline. The commentaries of Apuleius and Ammonius are lost.

[25] Cf. Schmidt, *Quaestiones de musicis scriptoribus Romanis*, pp. 24–25.

[26] Cass. *Inst.*, p. 132, 11. Cf. Nicomachus *Introd. arithm.*, p. 9, and Boethius *Inst. arithm.*, p. 10.

[27] As a matter of fact, he adds to the distinction between the arts and the disciplines *Inst.*, p. 130, in the final edition: "sed hoc de mundanis dixisse praesumptum est, quando solae litterae divinae nesciunt fallere, quoniam habent immobilem veritatis auctorem," while retaining, p. 131, 11, the Alexandrian definition of the disciplines.

[28] The term *quadrivium* had first appeared in Boethius *Inst. arithm.*, ed. Friedlein, p. 9, 28. For Cassiodorus' influence on the course of studies in the Middle Ages, cf. B. Gladysz, *Cassiodore et l'organisation de l'école médiévale*, Conlectanea Theologica, vol. 17, 1 (Lwow 1936).

[29] Cass. *Inst.*, p. 93, 1: "nec illud quoque tacebimus, quibus auctoribus tam Graecis quam Latinis quae dicimus exposita claruerunt."

lacuna and, as far as possible, only if a Latin translation exists. Thus he informs us in which areas Hellenism still appeared indispensable to culture in the middle of the sixth century.

For his chapter on grammar, Cassiodorus resorts to Latin sources. He confines himself to giving a brief survey on the grammatical corpus that he had established and that comprised Donatus' *Artes* and their commentaries by Sergius and Servius, Cassiodorus' *De orthographia*, a *De etymologiis*, and Sacerdos' *De schematibus*.[30] Cassiodorus also mentions other Latin grammarians[31] and refers besides, in his first edition, to two Greek writers: Helenus and Priscian. This information contains a surprising error that proves that Cassiodorus had not read these writers. Although Priscian lived in Constantinople, he was a Latin writer, not a Greek writer. The error, however, was corrected in the final edition, because Cassiodorus then had Priscian before him.[32] With regard to Helenus or Ellenus, who had invented the alphabet or written a commentary on it, Cassiodorus took this information from one of the numerous learned digressions in his *Variae*. No Greek or Latin grammarian of this name is known. The strange and vague reference in the *Variae*, "Helenus auctor Graecorum," informs us that when Cassiodorus wrote this statement he had not read more than Priscian. Actually, Knaack has shown that the entire learned digression in the *Variae* must have been plagiarized from Hyginus, who probably referred to Hellanicus, the author of a compilation of εὑρήματα in the fifth century B.C.[33] However strange the juxtaposition in the same sentence may be of two writers so dissimilar and so remote from each other by a thousand years, I think Knaack's conjecture

---

[30] *Ibid.*, p. 96, 18. On the *De etymologiis*, cf. Erdbruegger, *Cassiodorus unde etymologias in Psalterii commentario prolatas petivisse putandus sit*, pp. 34ff.

[31] Cass. *Inst.*, p. 94, 8: "Palemon, Phocas, Probus, Censorinus"; and 94, 13: Augustine's *De grammatica* (ed. Keil, *Gramm. Lat.* 5, p. 494).

[32] *Variae* 8.12.6, p. 243, 7:   *Inst.*, ed. ω, p. 94, 1:   *Inst.*, ed. Ω, p. 94, 1:

hinc Helenus auctor Graecorum plura dixit eximie virtutem eius compositionemque subtilissima narratione describens, ut in ipso initio possit agnosci magnarum copia litterarum.	de quarum (litterarum) formulis atque virtutibus Helenus et Priscianus subtiliter Attico sermone locuti sunt.	de quarum (litterarum) positionibus atque virtutibus Graece Helenus, Latine Priscianus subtiliter tractaverunt.

On the dates of the various editions of the *Institutiones*, cf. my article "Histoire d'un brouillon cassiodorien," pp. 78 and 85.

[33] Cf. *Variae*, ed. Mommsen, pp. XXI–XXII and CLXXX, and G. Knaack, "Studien zu Hygin," *Hermes* 16 (1881) 590 and 600, who establishes parallels between Cassiodorus and Hyginus, chap. 277, and thinks that Cassiodorus borrows from an unabridged edition of Hyginus. The conjecture regarding Hellanicus, which was suggested to him by Wilamowitz, was not accepted by Kremmer, *De catalogis heurematum* (diss. Leipzig 1890) 79 n. 2, and Keil, *Gramm. Lat.* 7, p. 214. But their strictures seem to me without weight, and the textual emendations that they propose are purely arbitrary.

is well founded. We can see how Cassiodorus' learning is open to question whenever he does not work from the sources. He knew Latin grammar only from the Latin grammarians. If he attended as a boy the courses of the Greek *grammaticus*, he was indebted to him only for the traditional Greek culture in Western education. He seems to have read Homer, for he makes a very specific reference to a line in the *Odyssey* and shows that he used the *Odyssey*,[34] but he does not appear to have read the other Greek poets.

The chapter *De rhetorica* also stems entirely from Latin sources, a proof that Cassiodorus was not concerned now, as Symmachus had been, with importing to Rome Hermogenes' rhetoric. He just excerpts Cicero's *De inventione* and Fortunatianus' *Rhetoric*. The corpus on rhetoric that Cassiodorus had had bound together comprised in fact Cicero's *De inventione* with Victorinus' commentary, Quintilian's *Institutio oratoria*, and Fortunatianus' *Rhetoric*.[35] On the other hand, for dialectic Cassiodorus is above all beholden to the Greeks and can offer the monks an imposing apparatus of Latin translations. The beginning, as we have seen, except for the parallel between rhetoric and dialectic, which is borrowed from Varro,[36] is taken from Ammonius' prologue to his commentary on Porphyry's *Isagoge*. This is the basis of the entire scheme of Cassiodorus' book.[37] The contents of the chapter show that Cassiodorus also had at his disposal the complete series of Boethius' and Marius Victorinus' dialectic translations and commentaries. It was Boethius' translations that he excerpted in his *Institutiones*. But, for the corpus of dialectic that he collected, he chose preferably Victorinus' translations and commentaries. He kept Boethius' most erudite edition of the commentaries on the *Isagoge* and the *Peri hermenias* only because Victorinus had not written a corresponding commentary.[38] Cassiodorus also read the Latin Neoplatonists Macro-

---

[34] Cass. *Var.* 1.39.2, p. 36, 21: "Ulixes Ithacus in laribus propriis forte latuisset, cuius sapientiam hinc maxime Homeri nobile carmen adseruit, quod multas *civitates* et populos circumivit, dum illi prudentiores sunt semper habiti, qui *multorum hominum* conversationibus probantur eruditi." Cf. *Odyssey* 1.3: πολλῶν δ' ἀνθρώπων ἴδε ἄστεα καὶ νόον ἔγνω. Cf. p. 71, 26, on the episode of Ulysses and the Sirens; p. 204, 14, on Ulysses and Polyphemus; p. 372, 15, where it is conceivable that the *Odyssey* could have interested Cassiodorus all the more as a tradition made Ulysses the founder of Scyllacium, his birthplace.

[35] Cass. *Inst.*, p. 103, 19–p. 104, 15.

[36] *Ibid.*, p. 109, 15.

[37] See above, pp. 341–343.

[38] A detailed analysis of this chapter and of his two editions will be found in my article "Histoire d'un brouillon cassiodorien," pp. 78–83. There is the additional fact that Cassiodorus probably borrows from a Greek commentator the scholastic formula, p. 114, 21: "Aristoteles, quando Perihermenias scriptitabat, calamum in mente tingebat." This formula appears neither in Boethius nor in Ammonius, but only in Greek in Suidas s.v. Ἀριστοτέλης.

bius[39] and Claudianus Mamertus, whose theory of the immortal soul he adopted.[40] But for all his knowledge of Platonism he seemed to mistrust it, at least since giving up public life, for in the *De anima* he opposed the theory of the fallen soul and of recollection, as Boethius taught.[41]

After a short paragraph on the usefulness of mathematics, a paragraph that combines Ammonius' pagan teaching with Josephus' Biblical teaching,[42] Cassiodorus begins an examination of the four disciplines that constitute mathematics.

On arithmetic, which he had already commended in the *Variae*,[43] he lists three works: Nicomachus of Gerasa's *Introductio arithmetica* and Apuleius' and Boethius' translations of this treatise.[44] From which of these writers did he borrow the contents of his chapter? On first impulse one would be inclined to point to Boethius' *Institutio arithmetica*, which Cassiodorus had already mentioned in the *Variae*,[45] for we find there the four divisions of Number set out in a table by Cassiodorus himself.[46] This similarity is confirmed by the fact that a quotation from Nicomachus, in the *Commentary on the Psalms*, was evidently taken from Boethius' translation and not from the Greek text.[47] It was also because he had noticed the relationship of the chapter to Boethius' work that a copyist interpolated, at the end of this chapter, *excerpta* from Boethius' *Institutio arithmetica*.[48]

---

[39] In the *Comm. in Ps.*, PL 70, 9 B and 95 B, he quotes Macrobius *Sat.* 5.3.16 and 5.21.18, ed. Eyssenhardt, p. 254, 22 and p. 340, 21.

[40] *De anima* 2, PL 70, 1283 C: "cesset ergo de eius corporalitate suspicio."

[41] *Ibid.*, PL 70, 1287 C: "Nec de illis sumus qui dicunt recolere magis animas quam discere usuales artes et reliquas disciplinas." This is clearly contrary to Boethius *De cons. philos.* 3, *carm.* 11.16–18, ed. Peiper, p. 81:

> Quod si Platonis musa personat verum
> quod quisque discit immemor recordatur.
> Tum ego: Platoni, inquam, vehementer adsentior.

I do not know from what writer Cassiodorus borrows his scholastic proofs of the immortality of the soul, *ibid.*, 1285 C: probably a Neoplatonic commentator on the *Phaedo* or on the *Phaedrus*; for cf. Macrobius *In Somn. Scip.* 2.13, ed. Eyssenhardt, pp. 616–618, with Cassiodorus: "Omne rationale quod seipsum movet, immortale est; anima autem rationalis seipsam movet; igitur immortalis est."

[42] Cass. *Inst.*, p. 131, 11ff.

[43] *Var.* 1.10.

[44] *Inst.*, p. 140, 17.

[45] *Ibid.*, 1.45.4.

[46] Cf. for the first table *Inst.*, p. 133, 17, and Boethius *Arithm.* 1.3.8.13; for the second, *Inst.*, p. 135, 1, and Boethius 1.19; for the third, *Inst.*, p. 135, 16, and Boethius 1.20–22; for the last one, *Inst.*, p. 139, 1, and Boethius 2.4. Cf. also *De anima* 4, PL 70, 1289 D, and Boethius, p. 8, 15–23.

[47] The definition of number quoted under the name of Nicomachus by Cass. *In Ps.* 34 C plagiarizes Boethius word for word, *Inst. arithm.*, p. 13, 11. Cf. Nicom. *Arithm.*, ed. Hoche, p. 13, 7.

[48] Cf. my article "Histoire d'un brouillon cassiodorien," p. 72.

However, this was not Cassiodorus' only source. The beginning of the chapter, in which Cassiodorus develops the idea that arithmetic is the mother of the other three disciplines and must be studied before them, does not consist of *excerpta* borrowed from Boethius but is much more like Nicomachus' text.[49] Similarly, all the definitions given by Cassiodorus relating to each of the four lists are much less abstract and scientific than those of Boethius. Is one to assume that Cassiodorus simplified them for the use of the ignorant monks? Not only does he simplify, but he makes use of a terminology slightly different from that used by Boethius. In his subdivision of odd numbers, he calls *numerus primus et simplex* what Boethius called *numerus primus et incompositus*, and he adopts the term *numerus mediocris*, a term unknown to Boethius. In his second list, he calls *numerus indigens* what Boethius called *numerus imperfectus* or *deminutus*. In his fourth list, the distinction between *numeri lineales, superficiales, solidi* has its exact equivalent in Nicomachus and not in Boethius.[50]

If one consults the *Commentary on the Psalms*, one ascertains that several of Cassiodorus' quotations refer to passages in Nicomachus that one vainly looks for in Boethius' translation:

Nicomachus:
"Εσται οὖν ἡ μὲν μονὰς ... ἀρχὴ μὲν διαστημάτων καὶ ἀριθμῶν, οὔπω δὲ διάστημα οὐδὲ ἀριθμός.[51]

Cassiodorus:
Memento autem quod monas, licet fons atque initium numeri esse videatur, ipsa tamen non potest numerus dici.[52]

Τινὲς δὲ αὐτὴν ἁρμονικὴν καλεῖσθαι νομίζουσιν ἀκολούθως Φιλολάῳ ἀπὸ τοῦ παρέπεσθαι πάσῃ γεωμετρικῇ ἁρμονίᾳ, γεωμετρικὴν δὲ ἁρμονίαν, φασὶ τὸν κύβον.[53]

Iste autem numerus est quem arithmetici actu primum quadrantal appellant, quem Philolaus Pythagoricus harmoniam geometricam vocat; eo quod omnes in ipso videantur harmonicae convenire rationes.[54]

To summarize, Cassiodorus' chapter is much closer to Nicomachus' text than to the paraphrase made by Boethius. If, therefore, Cassiodorus used a Latin translation and if this chapter, like the preceding ones, is merely a collection of *excerpta*, then everything inclines one to think that Cassiodorus

[49] Cf. the references above, n. 26.

[50] Cass. *Inst.*, p. 139, 9ff = Nicom. *Arithm.*, ed. Hoche, p. 82, 21: περί τε γραμμικῶν ἀριθμῶν καὶ ἐπιπέδων καὶ στερεῶν. Cf. Boethius *Arithm.*, p. 86, 11ff.

[51] Nicom. *Arithm.*, p. 84, 8.

[52] Cass. *In Ps.* 34 C. It is only in Pseudo-Boethius' *Geometry*, ed. Friedlein, p. 397, 20, that an equivalent passage appears: "Unitas enim, ut in arithmeticis dictum est, numerus non est, sed fons et origo numerorum."

[53] Nicom. *Arithm.*, p. 135, 10.

[54] Cass. *In Ps.*, PL 70, 79 B; cf. 657 A, for which there is no equivalent in Boethius either.

preserved for us fragments from Apuleius' lost translation of Nicomachus.[55]

For the chapter *De musica*, Cassiodorus refers his monks to the Greek works of Alypius, Euclid, and Ptolemy and the Latin works of Apuleius, which he does not have, and of Mutianus, Gaudentius' translator, which he possesses. He also adds Augustine's *De musica* and a *De accentibus* by Censorinus, now lost. Lastly, later on—if, as I think I have shown,[56] the glosses of group Δ are really his—he also added the Greek work by Dionysius of Halicarnassus, called the Musician, and Boethius' *De musica*. This rich bibliography must not lead us to believe that Cassiodorus had all these works in his library and that he used all of them in his chapter. First of all, this chapter owes nothing to the treatises of Dionysius or Boethius, since mention of them was added only after publication. It is besides easy to verify that Cassiodorus borrowed nothing from Boethius' *De musica*, which is extant. It can equally be verified that Cassiodorus owes nothing either to Euclid's *Introductio harmonica* or to Ptolemy's extant works or to Augustine's *De musica*. On the other hand, he used Mutianus' lost translation, as is shown by the following parallel with Gaudentius' Greek text, which is extant:

Gaudentius:

Τὴν δὲ ἀρχὴν τῆς τούτων εὑρέσεως Πυθαγόραν ἱστοροῦσι λαβεῖν ἀπὸ τύχης παριόντα χαλκεῖον τοὺς ἐπὶ τὸν ἄκμονα κτύπους τῶν ῥαιστήρων αἰσθόμενον διαφώνους τε καὶ συμφώνους.[57]

Cassiodorus:

Gaudentius quidam *de musica* scribens Pythagoram dicit huius rei invenisse primordia ex malleorum sonitu et chordarum extensione percussa.[58]

Cassiodorus also uses Clement of Alexandria's *Protrepticus*[59] and Censorinus' *De die natali*,[60] but all these borrowings appear only at the beginning or at the end of the chapter. The principal exposition, devoted to the divisions of music,[61] has another source. What is this source? Nobody today now believes in Schmidt's theory. He conceived some lost Christian source, common to Cassiodorus, Augustine, and Isidore and stemming from

[55] It is nevertheless possible that Cassiodorus here follows either Boethius' *Geometry* or even Ammonius' commentary on Nicomachus' *Arithmetic*.

[56] Cf. my article "Histoire d'un brouillon cassiodorien," p. 84.

[57] Gaudentius *Introductio harmonica*, ed. Janus, *Musici scriptores Graeci* (Leipzig 1895), p. 340, 4.

[58] Cass. *Inst.*, p. 142, 13. Cf. also, for the definition of τόνος, Gaudentius, p. 330, 4, and Cass., p. 145, 20.

[59] Cass. *Inst.*, p. 142, 17. Cf. Clement of Alexandria *Protrepticus* 31, PG 8, 105 A–B.

[60] Cf. Censorinus *De die natali*, ed. Hultsch, p. 21, 23, and Cass. *Inst.*, p. 143, 2; p. 22, 22 and Cass. *Inst.*, p. 143, 15; p. 16, 23 and Cass. *Inst.*, p. 143, 12; p. 22, 16 and Cass. *Inst.*, p. 149, 1. On the physician Asclepiades, cf. also Mart. Cap. *De nuptiis* 926, ed. Dick, p. 492, 12.

[61] A discussion that Cassiodorus repeats *In Ps.*, PL 70, 587 C.

Varro.[62] Here Cassiodorus, as elsewhere, quotes Varro only for the purpose of prestige.[63] The only expositions that derive from Varro are those that Cassiodorus borrows from Censorinus. The only expositions that Cassiodorus borrows from Augustine are those from the *Commentary on the Psalms* where he plagiarizes Augustine's corresponding commentary. The terms that he uses in his classification in the *Institutiones* necessarily assume a Greek source. Probably, as Mynors suggests, the division into six *symphoniae* might have stemmed from Gaudentius,[64] but the rest of the classification does not appear there. On the contrary, the only fragment of Alypius' that has been preserved corresponds notably to Cassiodorus' classification. It contains the fundamental division of music into three parts, harmony, rhythm, and metric,[65] and the division into fifteen *toni* adopted by Cassiodorus, whereas most musicians recognized only thirteen.[66] In conclusion, the definition of harmonics is the same in both:

Alypius:
Αὕτη δὲ ἁρμονικὴ καλεῖται [δια] κρι-
τικήν τινα δύναμιν ἔχουσα καὶ κατα-
ληπτικὴν τῶν ἐμμελῶν καὶ διαστη-
ματικῶν φθόγγων.[67]

Cassiodorus:
Harmonica scientia est musica quae de-
cernit in sonis acutum et gravem.[68]

If one considers that the obscure Alypius is quoted by Cassiodorus as the first name in his bibliographical notice, there can be no doubt that the plan of the chapter *De musica* was, according to Cassiodorus' usual method, based on a certain number of *excerpta* from Alypius' *Isagoge*, and reproduced the plan of this work.[69]

The chapter *De geometria*, unlike the preceding chapters, does not contain lengthy *excerpta*. Cassiodorus confines himself to indicating the divisions of geometry into four parts. Then he adds, after a reference to the treatises of

---

[62] Schmidt, *Quaestiones de musicis scriptoribus Romanis*, pp. 26–62. He has rightly noted, pp. 59–61, certain parallels between Cassiodorus and Gaudentius or Alypius, but he refuses to admit against all common sense that Cassiodorus could have read them direct from the text. Th. Stettner, "Cassiodors Encyclopädie, eine Quelle Isidors," *Philologus* 82 (1926) 241, has already shown that Cassiodorus was Isidore's direct source.

[63] Cass. *Inst.*, p. 148, 15; cf. E. C. Holzer, *Varro über Musik* (Ulm 1890) 11ff.

[64] Cass. *Inst.*, p. 144, 21; cf. Gaudentius *Introd. harmon.*, pp. 338–339. The similarity was already noted by Mynors, p. 190.

[65] Cass. *Inst.*, p. 144, 5 and *Var.* 2.40, p. 71, 13–22. Cf. Alypius *Introductio musica*, ed. Janus, *Musici scriptores Graeci*, p. 367, 4.

[66] Cass. *Inst.*, p. 145, 20 and *Var.* 2.40, p. 70, 20ff. Cf. Alypius *Introd. mus.*, pp. 368–383. Note, however, with Schmidt, *Quaestiones*, p. 62, that the order of the *toni* adopted by Cassiodorus agrees with Aristides Quintilian but not with Alypius.

[67] Alypius *Introd. mus.*, p. 367, 6.

[68] Cass. *Inst.*, p. 144, 6.

[69] See a hint of this explanation in Jan's note, *PW* s.v. Cassiodorus, 675.

Euclid, Apollonius, and Archimedes:[70] "Ex quibus Eucliden translatum Romanae linguae idem vir magnificus Boethius edidit; qui si diligenti cura relegatur, hoc quod praedictis divisionibus apertum est, manifesta intellegentiae claritate cognoscitur."[71]

This statement clearly shows that the division into four parts that has just been explained stems from Boethius' Latin translation of Euclid, which Cassiodorus twice quotes elsewhere in his *Commentary on the Psalms*.[72] If there were any doubt about this, it would be sufficient to refer to a passage that seems quite authentic, in Boethius' *Ars geometriae*.[73] This passage must preserve, in an abridged form, the plan of the prologue in Boethius' translation of Euclid, for he treats the points that usually appear in the prologues to the commentaries of Ammonius and Boethius: the purpose of the book, its usefulness, its place among the disciplines, its title, its authenticity, its division into chapters. Now, the division of Euclid's *Elements* that is recommended in this passage corresponds exactly to the division made by Cassiodorus:

Pseudo-Boethius:	Cassiodorus:
In quot partes dividitur? Dividitur codex iste in quattuor partes: in epipedis, in arithmeticis, in rationalibus et inrationalibus lineis, et in solidis.[74]	Geometria dividitur:
	In planum,
	In magnitudinem numerabilem,
	In magnitudinem rationalem et inrationalem,
	In figuras solidas.[75]

Boethius' translation, then, grouped the books of Euclid's *Elements* into four parts, the first corresponding to Books 1–4, the second to Books 5–9, the third to Book 10, and the last to Books 11–15. If Cassiodorus confines himself to a mere mention of the contents, it is because his monks had the book

---

[70] The passage in *Var.* 1.45.4, p. 40, 13, where Cassiodorus says to Boethius: "mechanicum etiam Archimedem Latialem Siculis reddidisti," inclines one to think that Boethius translated Archimedes as well. Cf. also p. 41, 1 and p. 204, 23: "Archimedes quoque subtilissimus exquisitor cum Metrobio tibi semper adsistant." On Apollonius of Perga's geometrical work, cf. Brunet-Mieli, *Histoire des sciences*, p. 417. In *Var.*, p. 107, 31, Cassiodorus also names "Heron metricus," who had been translated into Latin. Cf. Schanz, vol. 4, 2, p. 302, and V. Rose, *Anecdota Graeca et Graecolatina* 2 (Berlin 1870), pp. 317–330.

[71] Cass. *Inst.*, p. 152, 12.

[72] Cass. *In Ps.*, PL 70, 27 C = Euclid, 1, definition 2; and 682 D = Euclid, 4, proof 6.

[73] On this *Ars geometriae* in five books, cf. N. Buebnov, *Gerberti opera mathematica* (Berlin 1899) 180. Books 3 and 4, according to Buebnov, are genuine *excerpta* from Boethius' work. Book 2 (= PL 63, 1358 C–1364 D) is divided into two parts: one paragraph on geometry (this is the passage under discussion) and one on arithmetic, composed of *excerpta* from Boethius' *Arithmetic*. For the schema of the prologue in Boethius, cf. above, pp. 286–287.

[74] Boethius *Ars geometriae*, PL 63, 1359 A.

[75] Cass. *Inst.*, p. 151, 21.

ready to hand. He urges them to consult it. The *Principia geometricae disciplinae* are evidence that they did not fail to do so. It was the *excerpta* from Boethius' translation of Euclid that one of Cassiodorus' disciples interpolated at the end of the chapter.[76]

Just as the chapter *De geometria* began with a prologue in which there were quotations from Varro and Censorinus,[77] so the *De astronomia* begins with a reference to Seneca's *De forma mundi*, which Cassiodorus assures us he has in his possession.[78] But the contents of the chapter, here too, are taken from a Greek writer, not from a Latin astronomer. After enumerating the divisions of astronomy, Cassiodorus adds in fact: "De astronomia vero disciplina in utraque lingua diversorum quidem sunt scripta volumina; inter quos tamen Ptolomeus apud Graecos praecipuus habetur, qui de hac re duos codices edidit, quorum unum *minorem*, alterum *maiorem* vocavit *Astronomum*."[79] This notice contains a gross error. It attributed to Ptolemy the collection called the *Little Astronomy*, which was compiled in the third century A.D. by the Alexandrian scholars and which comprises only works by Euclid, Theodorus of Tripoli, Autolycus, Aristarchus of Samos, and Hypsicles of Alexandria.[80] The error must be imputed to Cassiodorus himself, for the manuscripts do not have this wrong attribution. It is proof that he did not have the collection at hand. On the other hand, he possessed Ptolemy's *Almagest*, for the contents of his chapter are taken from it. Not that he reproduces the learned demonstrations. As in the case of his *excerpta* from Euclid, he merely selects as chapter headings definitions that he simplifies still further, with the result that he gives his monks rather a nomenclature than a summary, however brief, of astronomical science. This is his way of defining the terms *spherica positio*, *sphericus motus*,[81] the four cardinal points, the two hemispheres of the heavens.[82] Even the Greek technical terms are reproduced: προποδισμός, ἀναποδισμός, στηριγμός.[83] He also adds a two-line summary of Ptolemy's chapter on the comparative size of the sun,

---

[76] Cf. my article "Histoire d'un brouillon cassiodorien," p. 72. The question will arise whether the *Principia* were not taken from Book 3 of this *Ars geometriae* where they appear, and whether the interpolator of Cassiodorus was not the author of the entire compilation. In fact, Book 1 contains extracts from Cassiodorus' chapters on geometry and astronomy, *PL* 63, 1352 D–1353 B.

[77] Cass. *Inst.*, p. 151. Cf. Censorinus *De die natali*, p. 23, 6.

[78] Cass. *Inst.*, p. 153, 3. This is probably a lost section of the *Quaestiones naturales*. Cf. Schanz, vol. 4, 2, p. 313.

[79] Cass. *Inst.*, p. 155, 23.

[80] Cf. K. Manitius, *Des Hypsikles Schrift Anaphorikos* (Progr. Dresden 1888), p. VI, and Brunet-Mieli, *Histoire des sciences*, p. 774 n. 12.

[81] Cass. *Inst.*, p. 154, 14. Cf. Ptolemy *Synt. math.*, ed. Heiberg (Leipzig 1898) vol. 1, pp. 10–16.

[82] Cass. *Inst.*, p. 154, 15ff. Cf. Ptolemy *Synt. math.*, vol. 1, p. 30, 5.

[83] Cass. *Inst.*, p. 155, 4ff. Cf. Ptolemy *Synt. math.*, vol. 2, p. 451, 5 and p. 494, 15.

the moon, and the earth,[84] and a brief paragraph on eclipses.[85] We assume that the chapter is finished, for now Cassiodorus refers to Ptolemy's works, but by a kind of compunction he returns to the contents of the book in order not to omit the division into seven *climata*, Ptolemy's own arrangement, and he lists them in the same order as Ptolemy.[86]

Ptolemy is then certainly the sole source of the chapter. Yet the question remains whether he is the immediate source. In fact, while Cassiodorus reproduces Greek terms, he never, contrary to his habit, makes textual *excerpta* from Ptolemy's Greek work. The intermediary must be the more or less faithful translation or adaptation of Ptolemy made by Boethius, for the existence of such a translation is suggested precisely in a passage of Cassiodorus' letter to Boethius: "Translationibus enim tuis Pythagoras musicus, *Ptolomaeus astronomus* leguntur Itali, Nicomachus arithmeticus, geometricus Euclides audiuntur Ausonii."[87] The accuracy of these words may be doubted and one may see in them merely a rhetorical balance. But this work was certainly preserved until at least the tenth century.[88] It seems to me, therefore, scarcely questionable that Boethius composed a *De astronomia* based on Ptolemy's *Almagest* and that Cassiodorus' chapter preserves *excerpta* from this lost work. It was perhaps in wrongly interpreting a statement in Boethius' introduction that Cassiodorus made the mistake of attributing to Ptolemy the collection called the *Little Astronomy*.

Only the conclusion of the chapter is Cassiodorus' own work. He rejects astrological science as being contrary to faith and as having been condemned by Basil and Augustine. He rejects equally Varro's theories on the shape of the world as quite superfluous for monks, who must above all follow the Scriptures.[89]

Apart from the seven arts and disciplines that constitute the course of the liberal studies, Cassiodorus also considers as necessary for the monks the study of history, geography, and the natural sciences, but he discusses them separately, in his *Institutiones divinae*. He quotes only one pagan Greek historian, who appears to him absolutely indispensable for a comprehension of the Old and the New Testament. This historian was Josephus. Cassiodorus proposed to the monks to read the *History of the Jewish War* in the translation

---

[84] Cass. *Inst.*, p. 155, 17. Cf. Ptolemy *Synt. math.*, vol. 1, p. 126.

[85] Cass. *Inst.*, p. 155, 19. Cf. Ptolemy *Synt. math.*, vol. 1, p. 266, 24.

[86] Cass. *Inst.*, p. 156, 8. Cf. Ptolemy *Synt. math.*, vol. 1, pp. 174–188. Cf. Kubitschek, *PW* s.v. Klima, 842. The word *canones*, p. 156, 3, informs us that Cassiodorus borrowed this paragraph from the summary of the *Almagest* entitled Προχείρων κανόνων διάταξις, on which cf. Brunet-Mieli, *Hist. des sciences*, p. 767. It was perhaps this summary, and not the *Almagest* itself, that Boethius had translated.

[87] Cass. *Var.* 1.45, ed. Mommsen, p. 40, 11.

[88] See the testimony quoted in my "Histoire d'un brouillon cassiodorien," p. 86.

[89] Cass. *Inst.*, p. 156, 19–p. 157, 18. Cf. *In Ps.*, PL 70, 971 A and 1047 B.

in seven books,[90] and as there was no Latin translation of the *Antiquities*, he took the trouble of having them translated himself, together with the two books *Contra Apionem*.[91] One can understand that Cassiodorus attached such great importance to this labor, for the lack of a Latin translation of the *Antiquities* had already made itself felt when there was hope of Jerome's executing such a translation.[92] Cassiodorus himself frequently consulted Josephus' text, to which he always gives very exact references and which he evidently used with the greatest care.[93] In geography, Cassiodorus possessed a large map by Dionysius Periegetes[94] and Ptolemy's *Geography*, which he praises as a very learned work.[95] With regard to the natural sciences, Cassiodorus did not know of them at the time of the *Variae* except from St. Ambrose's *Hexaemeron*,[96] but at Vivarium he took an interest in medicine, which was entirely a subject derived from Greek inspiration, and he seems to have compiled a medical corpus containing, aside from several Latin medical works, the translations of Dioscorides' *Herbal*, Galen's *Therapeutics for Glaucon*, and a work by Hippocrates.[97]

3. Exegetical Studies at Vivarium

As was natural, it was particularly sacred literature that interested Cassiodorus at the time of the *Institutiones*, since he intended to train monks. In this field he possessed a richer apparatus of Latin works, for the Fathers of the fourth century had been prolific. Moreover, he viewed this culture as almost uniquely exegetical, and he aimed above all to produce a commentator on the Scriptures. Lastly, he dealt only with the great classical writers, and not

[90] Text quoted above, chap. 2 sec. 2 n. 177. He says that this translation is attributed, according to the manuscripts, to Jerome, Ambrose, or Rufinus. There is a confusion here. This translation regularly bears in the manuscripts Rufinus' name, sometimes Jerome's. It was another translation in five books, called the Pseudo-Hegesippus, that was attributed to Ambrose. Cf. Schanz, vol. 4, 1, pp. 110 and 422.

[91] *Inst.*, p. 55, 16. The two treatises were bound together in twenty-two books in Cassiodorus' translation. On the extremely wide diffusion of this Cassiodorian translation in the Middle Ages (there are extant at least 118 manuscripts anterior to the fourteenth century), cf. Blatt, "Remarques sur l'histoire des traductions latines," pp. 228–233.

[92] See above, chap. 2 sec. 2 n. 176.

[93] Cf. Mynors' edition, *Index auctorum*, p. 191, s.v. Ioseppus.

[94] *Inst.*, p. 66, 19. This map perhaps accompanied the translation of the *Periegesis* by Avianus or Priscian. Cf. Schanz, vol. 4, 2, p. 236 n. 1.

[95] *Inst.*, p. 66, 22. On this work, of which no ancient Latin translation is known, cf. Brunet-Mieli, *Hist. des sciences*, p. 769.

[96] Cf. H. Nickstadt, *De digressionibus quibus in "Variis" usus est Cassiodorus* (diss. Marburg 1921) 14–33.

[97] *Inst.*, p. 78, 26ff. For the identification of these translations and the fate of this corpus, cf. below, chap. 8 sec. 4.

the moderns, for whom he professed a certain disdain.[1] That is the reason why he mentions only a limited number of Greek Fathers. Not that he despises the methods of Greek exegesis. His corpus of introductions to the Holy Scriptures revealed to the monks, besides Tyconius' *Regulae*, Augustine's *De doctrina Christiana* and Eucherius' *Formulae*, Adrianus' Greek *Isagoge*,[2] and even the Nestorian exegetical method used at Nisibis. In fact, Cassiodorus is quite aware that Junilius' *Instituta* are a mere transcription of the Greek manual by Paul the Persian, professor at Nisibis.[3] In this manual Paul applied to the sacred text the method used by the Syrian commentators on Aristotle, and he was imbued with Theodore of Mopsuestia's doctrine.[4] Cassiodorus' curiosity regarding this method is far from exceptional, for Junilius had just produced his *Instituta* at the request of the African bishop Primasius and for the use of the West. It was an indication that at this time too the best minds saw no other remedy for the decadence of Latin culture than to place it under the tutelage of the East.

However, Cassiodorus' information, despite his efforts and his stay in Constantinople, was far from being as extensive as that of St. Jerome. When Cassiodorus assures us that Clement of Alexandria, Cyril, John Chrysostom, Gregory, Basil, and many other Greek Fathers each wrote commentaries on all the books of Scripture, we must beware of thinking that this surprising information is first-hand and that Cassiodorus has all their books in his library.[5] The oldest Greek Father that he knows is Clement of Alexandria, whose *Commentary on the Canonical Epistles*[6] he had ordered to be translated, with omissions, and whose *Protrepticus*[7] also he still perhaps possessed. Of Athanasius, he seems to have only the *Introduction to the Commentary on the Psalms*. He refers to it frequently for his own *Commentary on the Psalms* and

---

[1] *Inst.*, p. 5, 24: "unde fieri potest ut per magistros agatur antiquos quod impleri non potuit per novellos."

[2] *Inst.*, p. 34, 10. The Greek text of Adrianus appears in *PG* 98, 1273–1312. The fact that in this corpus this work was placed among Latin writers inclines one to think that Cassiodorus had a translation of it. Besides, he quotes, p. 43, 22, *excerpta* from it in Latin (= *PG* 98: 1288 B, 1289 A–B and D, 1283 D).

[3] *Inst.*, p. 34, 11. Cf. p. 3, 8, using Junilius' dedicatory epistle to Primasius. Cf. Kihn's ed., *Theodor von Mopsuestia und Junilius Africanus* (Freiburg im Breisgau 1880), pp. 465–528, and G. Mercati, "Per la vita e gli scritti di Paolo il Persiano," *Studi e testi* 5 (1901) 180–206.

[4] Kihn, *Theodor von Mopsuestia*, pp. 334–458. On the teaching at Nisibis, cf. Chabot, "L'école de Nisibe," pp. 43–93, and Scher, *L'école de Nisibe* (above, Introduction n. 23).

[5] *Inst.*, p. 5, 15. Note the circumspect expression *ferunt*, and cf. Zahn, *Forschungen* 3, p. 137 (above, chap. 2 sec. 3 n. 129). He notes that the information is derived from secondary sources.

[6] *Inst.*, p. 29, 16.

[7] *Ibid.*, p. 142, 17.

himself translates a passage straight from the Greek.[8] Cassiodorus rates Origen very highly and, without minimizing the dangers of the doctrine, he considers his contemporaries' severity too excessive, for they prohibit even the reading of his commentaries.[9] Without mentioning any of his dogmatic works, he carefully collected all the texts and translations by Origen that he could find, protecting himself by following St. Jerome's example. The library at Vivarium thus contained Origen's homilies on the *Octateuch* in three manuscripts.[10] Baehrens has shown that the number of homilies mentioned by Cassiodorus agrees with the homilies that Rufinus had translated.[11] Cassiodorus also assembled Rufinus' translations of Origen's homilies on the Song of Songs and the *Commentary on the Epistle to the Romans*[12] and Jerome's translations of the homilies on Jeremiah and on the Song of Songs.[13] Lastly, he found five homilies on Kings and one on the Paralipomena, probably in translation.[14] He was also eager to have two of Origen's homilies on Esdras[15] translated by Bellator. Cassiodorus, then, had, in default of the Greek texts, a whole arsenal of translations of Origen, which he had quite resolved to preserve from the fury of the anti-Origenists. It was also in Rufinus' translation

[8] *Ibid.*, p. 21, 9. Cf. *In Ps.*, PL 70: 22 C, 43 A, 1054 D. Here is the passage translated by Cassiodorus. It gives an idea of his knowledge of Greek:

Athanasius *Ad Marcellinum in interpr. Psalm.*, PG 27, 24 A–B:	Cass. *In Ps.*, PL 70, 22 C–D:
Τοὺς δέ γε ψαλμοὺς . . . ὁ λέγων τὰ ἄλλα ὡς ἴδια ῥήματα λαλῶν ἐστι, καὶ ὡς περὶ ἑαυτοῦ γραφέντας αὐτοὺς ἕκαστος ψάλλει καὶ οὐχ ὡς ἑτέρου λέγοντος ἢ περὶ ἑτέρου σημαίνοντος δέχεται καὶ διεξέρχεται· ἀλλ' ὡς αὐτὸς περὶ ἑαυτοῦ λαλῶν διατίθεται, καὶ οἷά ἐστι τὰ λεγόμενα, ταῦτα ὡς αὐτὸς πράξας καὶ ἐξ ἑαυτοῦ λαλῶν ἀναφέρει τῷ Θεῷ.	Beatus quoque Athanasius Alexandrinae civitatis episcopus in libro quem Marcellino suo carissimo destinavit de proprietate Psalterii, *ut verbis ipsius utar*, ita dicit: "Quicumque Psalterii verba recitat, quasi propria verba decantat et tamquam a semetipso conscripta unus psallit et non tamquam alio dicente aut de alio significante sumit et legit; sed tamquam ipse de semetipso loquens, sic huius modi verba profert; et qualia sunt quae dicuntur, talia velut ipse agens, ex semetipso loquens, Deo videtur offerre sermones."

[9] *Inst.*, p. 14 and p. 15, 3: "posteriores autem in toto dicunt eum esse fugiendum, propterea quia subtiliter decipit innocentes; sed si adiutorio Domini adhibeatur cautela, nequeunt eius nocere venena."

[10] *Ibid.*, p. 14, 1 and p. 15, 7. Cf. *In Ps.*, PL 70, 1055 A, where Cassiodorus refers also to the homilies on Genesis.

[11] W. A. Baehrens, *Ueberlieferung und Textgeschichte der lateinisch erhaltenen Origeneshomilien zum alten Testament*, Harnack's Texte und Untersuchungen, vol. 42, 1 (Leipzig 1916), *passim*, particularly p. 2 n. 1. Cf. Schanz, vol. 4, 1, p. 418.

[12] *Inst.*, p. 24, 6 and p. 31, 2.

[13] *Ibid.*, p. 19, 7 and p. 24, 4. There is nothing to prove that Cassiodorus possessed this Greek manuscript, which he mentions as consisting of forty-five homilies on Jeremiah.

[14] *Ibid.*, p. 16, 4–p. 17, 10; p. 17, 28. Note that these homilies are inserted by Cassiodorus in an entirely Latin corpus.

[15] *Ibid.*, p. 27, 13.

that he read Eusebius' *Church History*,[16] and in Jerome's translation that he possessed Eusebius' *Evangelical Canons* and the *Chronica*,[17] Didymus' *De Spiritu sancto*,[18] and the denunciations of Theophilus of Alexandria and Epiphanius of Cyprus against Origen.[19] He was even able to procure some Greek texts of these writers, and he hastened to have them translated by his friend Epiphanius. These texts were: two commentaries by Didymus, one on Proverbs, the other on the Canonical Epistles,[20] and a commentary by Philon of Carpasia on the Song of Songs, which, in the manuscript at Vivarium, was mistakenly attributed to Epiphanius of Cyprus.[21]

On the other hand, Cassiodorus seems to have read only a very small number of more recent Greek writers. It is surprising that he does not mention in his bibliography any work by Gregory of Nazianzus and that, for Basil, he possesses or uses only his *Hexaemeron*, translated by Eustathius.[22] Only the works of John Chrysostom appear to enjoy widespread recognition. Cassiodorus possesses the Greek manuscripts of his commentaries on Paul's Epistles and on the Acts of the Apostles. With regard to the Epistles, he commissioned a translation by Mutianus of the homilies on the Epistle to the Hebrews and fifty-five homilies on the Acts of the Apostles, covering two manuscripts.[23] In addition, Cassiodorus' commentary on the Psalms proves that he had also read other homilies by Chrysostom, which now became current in a Latin translation,[24] as well as the *De compunctione cordis*.[25]

Cassiodorus' task in Greek exegesis recalls Jerome's attempt, although the circumstances were now more unfavorable. But Cassiodorus was also burdened by the preoccupations that have already been noted in the monks of

---

[16] *Ibid.*, p. 56, 3.

[17] *Ibid.*, p. 28, 11 and p. 56, 18. Eusebius' *Canones evangelici* translated by Jerome appear at the beginning of the Vulgate. Cf. *PL* 29, 527.

[18] *In Ps.*, *PL* 70, 202 B. Cf. below, chap. 8 sec. 2E.

[19] *Inst.*, p. 14, 7. The letters of Theophilus and Epiphanius appear in Jerome's correspondence, *Epist.* 92–100, *PL* 22, 768.

[20] *Inst.*, p. 22, 2 and p. 29, 17.

[21] *Ibid.*, p. 24, 9. Cf. below, chap. 8 sec. 2C.

[22] *Inst.*, p. 11, 9 and p. 157, 3.

[23] *Ibid.*, p. 32, 9. Cf. p. 29, 11.

[24] As a matter of fact, he borrows from the corpus of the Greek Fathers that Pope Leo had drawn up (*PL* 54, 1183) his quotation from the homily *De ascensione Domini* (*In Ps.*, *PL* 70, 523 A = *PG* 49, 446 C), and from Cassianus his quotation from a lost homily on the nativity (*In Ps.*, *PL* 70, 127 B = Cassianus *Contra Nestorium* 7.30, ed. Petschenig, *CSEL* 17, p. 388, 13). But the passage that he quotes from the homily *In crucem* (*In Ps.*, *PL* 70, 50 D = *PG* 50, 819 A) comes from an old Latin translation, for I found it in the translation contained in Parisinus nouv. acq. Lat. 1599, 7th/8th cent., fol. 3ᵛ.

[25] *In Ps.*, *PL* 70, 63 C = *PG* 47, 391. The *De compunctione* appears in a Latin translation in the Orleans manuscript 151 (128), 11th cent., pp. 82–171. The *incipit*: "Cum te intueor, beate Demetri, frequenter insistentem mihi" does not appear in Vattasso, *Initia Patrum*.

Lérins or in Dionysius Exiguus, his former co-disciple. Not only did he procure the various translations of Dionysius, whose *Codex canonum*[26] he particularly prized, but he recommended the reading of the *Lives of the Fathers of
the Desert*[27] and the texts relating to the Councils. He gathered together the
texts of the four great Councils of Nicaea, Constantinople, Ephesus, and
Chalcedon but barely referred to the most recent one, the Council of Chalcedon.[28] He even has a translation of the *Encyclia* made by Epiphanius, that
is, the collection of synodal letters addressed to the Emperor Leo, in 458, in
defense of this Council.[29] Finally, Cassiodorus was eager to furnish the Latin
world with a continuation of Eusebius' *Church History*, translated by Rufinus.
He collected the historical texts of Socrates, Sozomen, Theodoret, asked
Epiphanius to translate *excerpta* from them, and himself assembled *excerpta* to
form his *Historia ecclesiastica tripartita*, a work that he regarded as indispensable for the West.[30]

We can now form an idea of what Greek culture represented for Cassiodorus. It was above all for maintaining profane culture that the Greek
writers seemed to him indispensable. The fact is easily explained, for Cassiodorus completed his studies at the time when Symmachus and Boethius conceived and began to execute their ambitious program of a Hellenic renaissance
in Rome. Without question Cassiodorus sometimes mentions Greek writers
without having read them,[31] or even, when writing the *Variae*, names them
by some rhetorical figure. It is amusing to watch Cassiodorus, in a letter on
the art of canalization, vainly looking for the name of a Greek engineer to
offset the Latin engineer Marcellus.[32] But from that moment on, he studied
dialectic,[33] in the company of Dionysius Exiguus, that is, he steeped himself
in the commentaries of Ammonius of Alexandria. And so, when, half a century later, he was to draw up a program of profane studies for the use of the

---

[26] *Inst.*, p. 62, 10–p. 63, 11.

[27] *Ibid.*, p. 80, 21. Cf. *In Ps.*, PL 70, 500 D, using Rufinus' chapter, *Hist. Mon.* 1.16, PL
21, 435, on the life of Paphnutius.

[28] *Inst.*, p. 35, 14; 40, 21; 64, 12. Cf. *In Ps.*, PL 70: 43 A, 410 A–B, 1125 D. Note that
the text of the long quotation 410 A–B is original in contrast with the *Versio antiqua*
and Rusticus' translation. It was also probably from the conciliary collections that
Cassiodorus took his quotations from Cyril of Alexandria's *Adversus Nestorium*, to which
he gives very vague references, *In Ps.* 43 A, 122 D, 153 C.

[29] *Inst.*, p. 36, 1; 64, 12. Cf. *In Ps.*, PL 70, 549 A, and Maassen, *Geschichte der Quellen
und der Literatur des canonischen Rechts im Abendlande* 1 (Gratz 1870) 751–753. The Cassiodorian translation is edited in Mansi, 7, p. 786.

[30] *Inst.*, p. 56, 6.

[31] For instance, *In Ps.*, PL 70, 344 B, mentioning Solon, Philo of Lacedaemon, Aristippus. This case is rare.

[32] Cass. *Var.* 3.53.4, ed. Mommsen, p. 108, 32: "Hanc scientiam sequentibus pulchre
tradiderunt apud Graecos ille [= someone or other], apud Latinos Marcellus." Without
reason Nickstadt, *De digressionibus*, p. 15, thinks that this omission was deliberate.

[33] Text quoted above, sec. 1 n. 43.

monks, he did not hesitate to take this program from his pagan teacher in Alexandria. Furthermore, of the seven liberal arts, only grammar and rhetoric seemed to him sufficiently developed in Latin, but for the philosophical or scientific studies Cassiodorus felt obliged to refer the reader to Greek handbooks or to translations of them. Ancient science, Greek in origin, remained Greek to the very end. Often Cassiodorus can merely mention a Greek manual of which there is no translation. Whereas Aristotle's *Logic* persisted thanks to Boethius' translations, the knowledge of Greek disappeared before Greek science had passed into Latin. Hence perhaps came the long eclipse of scientific studies in the West.

Cassiodorus had no illusions about the progressive cleavage between East and West and did not even try to revive the study of the Greek language. But at least he assembled for his monks an extremely large number of translations. He took advantage of the efforts of his predecessors, Jerome, Rufinus, and Dionysius Exiguus. But he added to his number by quickly filling in the gaps in Latin culture with fresh translations. Besides, he was not the only one who wanted to spread among the Latins a knowledge of Greek exegesis. At the same period, Bishop Victor of Capua [34] and John the Deacon [35] took a lively interest in this project. They made collections of quotations from all the Greek Fathers in their possession. Among the exegetes, Cassiodorus tried to separate those who were in some way the classics of sacred literature, without concerning himself with the literature relating to contemporary disputes such as the quarrel of the *Tria Capita*.[36] Although he possessed a number of Latin commentators, he did not lose sight of the quality of Origen's works. To him, Greek Christian literature seemed like an inexhaustible reservoir for Latin exegesis. The difficulty was to secure texts that he wanted. It is not without legitimate pride that Cassiodorus lists the Greek manuscripts in his

[34] His compilation, entitled *Responsorium capitula*, gathered together fragments of Polycarp of Smyrna (actually, Pacatus *Contra Porphyrium*; cf. above, p. 226), Origen, Basil, Diodorus of Tarsus, Severianus of Gabala, and ῾Ρήματα γερόντων. Cf. Pitra, *Spicil. Solesm.* 1 (Paris 1858) 266ff, and Schanz, vol. 4, 2, p. 596. Victor possesses in addition a *Harmony of the Gospels* in Greek, anonymous, and, in order to discover its author, he resorts to the Letter from Eusebius to Carpianus and to Eusebius' *Church History*, but without being able to decide whether he is dealing with Tatian's *Diatessaron* or a work by the exegete Ammonius of Alexandria. Cf. *PL* 68, 251, and H. J. Vogels, *Zur Geschichte des Diatessarons im Abendlande*, Neutestam. Abhandlungen, vol. 8, 1 (Münster 1919).

[35] Probably the future Pope John III (560–573). His compilation uses the collection of Victor of Capua and contains besides, as representing Greek writers, fragments of Origen, Peter of Alexandria, Diodorus, Didymus, Basil, Gregory Nazianzus, John Chrysostom, Severianus of Gabala, Cyril of Alexandria. Cf. *Spicil. Solesm.* 1, pp. 278ff; Harnack, "Neue Fragmente des Werkes des Porphyrius *Gegen die Christen*," p. 274, and Schanz, vol. 4, 2, p. 596. See above, chap. 5 sec. 1 n. 10.

[36] He is, however, familiar with these disputes, for he quotes Facundus of Hermione, *In Ps.*, *PL* 70, 994 A.

library that he has had, or is going to have, translated. In fact, he did not expect as a result of the Byzantine conquest a revival of Greek culture and he realized that it was urgent to preserve for Western Christianity the light of the East, which was soon to cease shedding its radiance upon it.

Chapter 8

THE MONKS IN THE SERVICE OF HELLENISM: VIVARIUM AND THE LATERAN

1. METHOD OF RESEARCH RELATING TO THE VIVARIAN MANUSCRIPTS

Cassiodorus' desire had been to have his monastery reap the benefits of Greek culture. He knew from experience the value of a liberal education that was revived under the influence of the last school of Alexandria. Even for clerical culture, Greek exegesis seemed to him indispensable. He thought of making Vivarium, on its establishment, a center of Christian culture. But the *Institutiones* show that he was constantly coming into conflict with the ignorance of his disciples. Here was a man who knew Greek and valued Hellenic culture and yet was obliged to supply monks ignorant of Greek with a purely Latin bibliography by having a few scholars translate the most indispensable works that had no equivalent in Latin. He was also constrained to lower his teaching standards to the level of the pupils by abridging the profane studies and skillfully grading the sacred studies. For each discipline he formed a corpus of *introductores*, and his *Institutiones* were themselves just an introduction to the reading of each corpus. Book 1 is a bibliography, Book 2 a bibliography and a collection of *excerpta*. He also had to consider the case of the illiterate monks (*agrammati*) who would not even be able to assimilate the liberal arts that were thus reduced to formulas.[1] We are bound to believe that such monks were really unintelligent or that they could neither read nor write.

Hence, although he was concerned to see the survival of his work, this work was destined to failure. Cassiodorus assumed that the labor of translation would continue after him.[2] In actual fact, Vivarium did not become a cultural center. Shortly before the founder's death, the monks urged him to write a treatise on Latin orthography, which would help them at least to copy

[1] *Inst.*, p. 69, 7: "Quod si quorundam simplicitas fratrum non potuerit quae sunt in sequenti libro deflorata cognoscere, quia paene brevitas omnis obscurata est, sufficiat eis summatim earum rerum divisiones, utilitates virtutesque perpendere."

[2] *Ibid.*, p. 32, 1 and 13.

manuscripts properly.[3] The sole evidence of intellectual activity at Vivarium after the decease of the master was wretched interpolations.[4] The monks did not know how to profit by the Hellenic treasures that Cassiodorus had revealed to them.

In spite of this immediate failure due to political circumstances and to the too rapid decline of culture in the course of the sixth century, did the library and the _scriptorium_ leave no trace? Was the labor of translation performed under Cassiodorus' impulse in vain? If the library at Vivarium was dispersed, is it not possible to find survivals from the wreckage?

The question was raised for the first time by Beer in 1911.[5] His researches led him to conclude that a good number of the oldest manuscripts of Verona and Bobbio, often palimpsests, came from Vivarium, which had supplied the pre-Columban contents of Bobbio. More recently, Weinberger extended the research by paleographical comparisons and concluded with the conviction that most of the manuscripts in uncial of the fifth and sixth centuries had come from Vivarium. Vivarium was thus the only source, or almost so, of all our manuscripts of Roman Antiquity.[6]

This thesis, appealing in its simplicity, was unanimously accepted, and a few points of detail only were in dispute until the moment when Cardinal Mercati, in studying the history of the library of Bobbio with reference to a Ciceronian palimpsest, showed in a few brilliant pages the weaknesses of the theory. He declared that for his part he did not believe in the connection established by Beer between the libraries of Vivarium and Bobbio, or in any survival whatever of Cassiodorus' library. The pre-Columban manuscripts of Bobbio came, in his opinion, not from Vivarium but from Piacenza, Pavia, Milan, Ravenna, Verona. As for Cassiodorus' library, it vanished completely along with the monastery.[7] Despite this argumentation, Bieler and Gomoll, in 1936, went on regarding Beer's thesis as unassailable and

---

[3] Cass. _De orthogr., praef., PL_ 70, 1239 C.

[4] See my article "Histoire d'un brouillon cassiodorien," pp. 67–73. M. L. W. Laistner's hypothesis seems to be without any basis. In his edition of the _Glossaria Latina iussu Academiae Britannicae edita_ 2 (Paris 1926) 136, he suggests Vivarium as the place of origin of the _Glossary of Philoxenes._

[5] R. Beer, "Bemerkungen über den ältesten Handscriftenbestand des Klosters Bobbio," _Anzeiger der k. Akad. der Wissenschaften zu Wien_, phil.-hist. Klasse, 48 (1911) 78–104. He reproduced and expanded this thesis in _Monumenta palaeographica Vindobonensia_, Lieferung 2 (Leipzig 1913) 15–26.

[6] Wilhelm Weinberger, "Handschriften von Vivarium," _Miscellanea Fr. Ehrle, scritti di storia e paleografia_ 4, pp. 75–88, _Studi e testi_ 40 (1924).

[7] Mgr G. Mercati, _M. T. Ciceronis de re publica libri e codice rescripto Vaticano Latino 5757 phototypice expressi. Prolegomena de fatis bibliothecae monasterii s. Columbani Bobiensis et de codice ipso Vat. Lat. 5757_ (Vatican City 1934) 15–19. The various writers who have fully accepted Beer's theory or made some reservations are listed by him, p. 15.

pointed out two newly examined manuscripts that had passed from Vivarium to Bobbio.[8]

It is evident that the positions of the disputants are extreme and the question is far from a solution. Although Cardinal Mercati scarcely developed his arguments, his high authority and his universally acknowledged competence lend his trenchant decisions considerable weight. We must therefore take up the question again in detail and critically examine the two contradictory theories. As Beer and Weinberger's theory rests on an impressive number of clues rather than on a formal demonstration, it is fitting to posit a few principles in method that will help to distinguish the degree of credibility in these indications.

It should first of all be agreed that history tells nothing regarding the fate of the library at Vivarium. If Beer's theory is accepted, we are led to conjecture that the library at Vivarium moved at the beginning of the seventh century, at the time of the importation of the Greek rite. Cardinal Mercati shows clearly how little basis this conjecture has, but he himself argues from the text in which Gregory the Great forbids John, bishop of Scyllacium, to disperse the property of the monastery that presumably the library at Vivarium could not have been moved, even later on.[9] Such arguments have no demonstrable finality. At the most they point to possibilities. Even if the monastery at Vivarium did not *die*, but merely *died away* in the seventh century,[10] that scarcely gives us any information on the fate of its library. It is solely by internal criteria, by a study of the manuscripts themselves, that we shall be able to judge whether there still remain any vestiges of Cassiodorus' library.

Beer's starting point consists in drawing up a list of the pre-Columban manuscripts at Bobbio, written in the fifth and sixth centuries. I shall not discuss the method of establishing this list. For paleographical reasons Beer includes a host of manuscripts that do not appear in any of the catalogues preserved in the library of Bobbio, and his list is far longer than the more modest list drawn up by Cardinal Mercati from the stock of manuscripts

[8] L. Bieler, "Textkritische Nachlese zu Boethius' *De philosophiae consolatione*," *Wiener Studien* 54 (1936) 131–132, and Heinz Gomoll, "Zu Cassiodors Bibliothek und ihrem Verhältnis zu Bobbio," *Zentralblatt für Bibliothekswesen* 53 (1936) 185–189.

[9] Mercati, *M. T. Ciceronis de re publica libri*, pp. 16–17.

[10] Van de Vyver, "Cassiodore et son œuvre," *Speculum* 6 (1931) 289–290, accepts Poole's conjecture that the *Felix abbas Ghylittanus* who, in 616, continued the Easter computus of Dionysius Exiguus was an abbot of Vivarium (*Scyllitanus*). This conjecture is inadmissible, for Victor of Tunanna notes, with reference to another Felix, that this monastery was African (*Chron.*, anno 553, ed. Mommsen, *MGH, Auct. ant.* 11, p. 203, 19: "Felix Guillensis monasterii provinciae Africanae hegumenus," and anno 557, p. 201, 20: "Felix hegumenus monasterii Gillitani." But two twelfth-century bulls mention "in civitate Squillatio ecclesiam sancti Martini," which I have identified with the Church of Saint Martin of Vivarium. Cf. my article "Le site du monastère," p. 293.

corresponding to the catalogue of 1461.[11] It will suffice to note that there is nothing to prove the common origin of these manuscripts of the fifth and sixth centuries and their arrival in bulk at Bobbio in the seventh century. Moreover, the library at Bobbio was considerable and it is almost the only library in Italy of which we have an ancient catalogue, whereas there were others, in Rome and elsewhere, whose contents are quite unknown to us. Hence it follows that there are great possibilities of finding at Bobbio a number of works that were at Vivarium but that would reappear just as readily in any great pre-Carolingian or Carolingian library. At first glance, the library of Reichenau or St. Gall reflects Cassiodorus' library just as well as that of Bobbio. This is due to the fact that the needs and the tastes of the monks had scarcely changed. But there is nothing to prove that Cassiodorus is the source.

In the absence of all decisive subscriptions, it will be necessary, in order to assume a connection between a manuscript currently in existence and the library at Vivarium, to establish with certainty that the texts contained in these manuscripts existed at Vivarium. This logical truth appears all too evident, but as Beer has often speculated with this ambiguity, it is proper to recall it. Beer assumes that there were at Vivarium not only all the works that appear in the catalogue drawn up by Franz from the *Institutiones*, but also all the writers mentioned, quoted, or used by Cassiodorus in his various writings, even those prior to his retirement in Calabria. Now, my study of the sources of the *Institutiones humanae* has shown that Cassiodorus did not possess all the works that he mentions. Often he knows of them only from an intermediate source. On the other hand, there is nothing to prove that Cassiodorus possessed at Vivarium the writers that he knew or used when he was writing before his retirement, either at Ravenna or at Rome. He himself regrets not having at Vivarium Albinus' treatise on music that he had in his possession in his library in Rome, and he has no hope of having it sent to him.[12] Even if we were inclined to believe that the original contents of Vivarium came from this Roman library, we must not lose sight of the fact that the *Institutiones* are as complete a catalogue as possible of the possessions in the monastery. In fact, if one opens the other writings that Cassiodorus composed at Vivarium, that is, the *Commentary on the Psalms*, the *Complexiones*, and the *De orthographia*, one observes that their unique sources, with a few exceptions, are books mentioned in the *Institutiones*.[13] May we say that at least in profane subjects the *Institutiones* have withal the character of a restricted catalogue, from the fact that Cassiodorus lists therein just the readings useful for monks and that this explains, for instance, the omission of the poets? Beer in all probability thought so, for he mentions three poets, Lucan, Vergil, and

[11] Mercati, *M. T. Ciceronis de re publica libri*, pp. 254ff.
[12] Text quoted above, chap. 7 sec. 1 n. 23.
[13] See the *Index auctorum* in Mynors' ed.

Sedulius, whose manuscripts might have come from Vivarium through the intermediate route of Bobbio.

Fragments of Lucan's *Pharsalia* are preserved in Vindobonensis 16 and Neapolitanus IV A 8, which Beer assigns to the pre-Columban contents in Bobbio. Now, Cassiodorus quotes Lucan once in his *Historia Gothorum*;[14] Beer sees in this a hint of the Vivarian origin of these manuscripts.[15] This hypothesis is all the more venturesome in that Cassiodorus wrote the *Historia Gothorum* before his retirement to Vivarium and that he never afterward quoted Lucan again or mentioned him. Admittedly he sometimes quoted in the *Institutiones* lines from Vergil[16] and Sedulius,[17] and Beer is on surer ground in assuming that, for Vergil, Veronensis XL (38), Vaticanus 3225, and the Mediceus, and, for Sedulius, Ambrosianus R 57 sup. and Taurinensis E IV 44 passed through Vivarium.[18] But Bacherler has shown that Cassiodorus far less frequently quotes the poets in his writings after his conversion than in the *Variae*. On the rare occasions when he does quote them, his quotation is made from memory and does not assume a personal knowledge of the works.[19] Furthermore, if Cassiodorus regarded a study of the poets as useless for monks, what reason would he have had to get them for the library in his monastery? We must see in his rare quotations the impulsive recollections of the man of letters who had received a classical training and cannot refrain from embellishing his prose with a few verses that are withal very well known and quoted hundreds of times.

Beer's demonstration is not more conclusive with regard to orators. He proposes to connect with Vivarium the Bobbio manuscripts Taurinensis A II 2 I–X and XI and Ambrosianus E 147 sup. + Vaticanus Lat. 5750 that contain speeches by Cicero and Symmachus and Fronto's letters.[20] For the former manuscripts containing Cicero, he posits the important point that Cassiodorus quotes the *Verrines*, the *Pro Milone*, and the *In Pisonem* in his *Institutiones*. The argument breaks down, since these quotations are, as I have shown, examples that illustrated Victorinus' commentary on the *Topica*, which Cassiodorus had excerpted.[21] Cassiodorus' direct source then was

[14] *Iordanis Getica* 5.43 (ed. Mommsen, *MGH, Auct. ant.* 5, p. 65, 2).

[15] Beer, "Bemerkungen," p. 86, and *Monumenta*, p. 22.

[16] *Inst.*, p. 29, 23 (= *Eclogues* 9.36) and p. 71, 17 and 21 (= *Georg.* 2.484–485).

[17] *Ibid.*, p. 69, 3–4 (= *Carm. Pasch.* 1.349–350). The same quotation recurs in the *Comm. in Psalm.* 271 A. Cf. also *Comm. in Psalm.* 814 B (= *Carm. Pasch.* 1.268–269).

[18] Beer, "Bemerkungen," pp. 85 and 94, and *Monumenta*, p. 20. With regard to Plautus, Terence, Juvenal, and Persius, who were also at Vivarium, as Beer thinks, all Cassiodorus' quotations from them occur in his *excerpta* that were taken from intermediary writers.

[19] Michael Bacherler, "Cassiodors Dichterkenntnis und Dichterzitate," *Blätter für das bayerische Gymnasialschulwesen* 59 (1923) 215–224.

[20] Beer, "Bermerkungen," pp. 85 and 87, and *Monumenta*, p. 20.

[21] See my article "Histoire d'un brouillon cassiodorien," p. 82 and n. 2.

Victorinus and there is nothing to prove that Cassiodorus possessed Cicero's speeches at Vivarium. With regard to Fronto and Symmachus, the connection proposed by Beer is no less hazardous. Cassiodorus does not mention Fronto except in his *Chronica*, a work written before his retirement to Vivarium. Still, this brief mention is nothing more than a plagiarism from St. Jerome's *Chronicle*.[22] Is there the slightest indication to assume that Cassiodorus possessed Fronto at Vivarium? And if it is true that Cassiodorus quotes a sentence from Symmachus in a letter of 533 A.D. (hence prior to his retirement to Vivarium),[23] and mentions him in a passage of his *Historia tripartita*,[24] which is withal just a translation of the historian Socrates,[25] is this any reason to assume that our only manuscript of Symmachus' speeches came from Vivarium?

Beer also assumes that the Latin Euclid of Veronensis XL is the copy of the Latin Euclid that Cassiodorus used for his chapter *De geometria*.[26] This connection is not of the slightest value, since the Latin Euclid that Cassiodorus used was, as we have seen,[27] Boethius' translation, and not the vague fourth-century paraphrase, the fragments of which were contained in the Verona palimpsest.[28] Similarly, the palimpsest fragments of a Greek treatise on mathematical and mechanical problems (Ambrosianus L 99 sup.), which Beer compares with Cassiodorus' chapter *De mathematica*,[29] have no relation to it, since the only Greek source of this chapter is, as we have seen,[30] Nicomachus' *Isagoge* and translations of it.

For medicine, the connection seems at first sight more decisive. Beer notes that fragments of Dioscorides, Galen, and a treatise on medical prescriptions are preserved in Vindobonensis 16, and a Latin translation of Hippocrates in a late Taurinensis, now destroyed by fire.[31] Now, Cassiodorus had in his library a Latin translation of Hippocrates, Dioscorides' *Herbarium*, Galen's *Therapeutica ad Glauconem*, and an *Anonymus ex diversis auctoribus conlectus* that, according to Beer, would correspond to the medical prescriptions in the Vindobonensis.[32] On closer scrutiny, we perceive that this correspondence

[22] Cass. *Chronica, anno* 164 (Mommsen's ed., *MGH, Chron. min.* 2, 143) plagiarizing *Hieronymi Chronica, anno* 2180.

[23] Cass. *Var.* 11.1 (ed. Mommsen, p. 330, 26).

[24] Cass. *Hist. tripartita* 9.23 (PL 69, 1140 C–D).

[25] Socrates *Hist. eccl.* 5.14 (PG 67, 602 A–B).

[26] Beer, "Bemerkungen," p. 88, and *Monumenta*, p. 22.

[27] See above, pp. 351–352.

[28] Cf. Schanz, vol. 4, 2, p. 302.

[29] Beer, "Bemerkungen," p. 84, and *Monumenta*, p. 15. On this treatise, cf. Christian Belger, *Hermes* 16 (1881) 261–284.

[30] See above, pp. 347–349.

[31] Beer, "Bemerkungen," p. 85, and *Monumenta*, pp. 18 and 23. Cf. Beer, "Galen-fragmente im codex Pal. Vindob. 16," *Wiener Studien* 34 (1912) 107.

[32] Cass. *Inst.*, p. 78, 25–p. 79, 6.

is purely superficial. The fragments of the Vindobonensis are in Greek, while Cassiodorus mentions only Latin translations, as he expressly states. In addition, there are fragments of Galen's Περὶ θηριακῆς πρὸς Παμφιλιανόν and Περὶ συνθέσεως φαρμάκων, whereas Cassiodorus possessed only Galen's *Therapeutica ad Glauconem.* The correspondence between the *Anonymus ex diversis auctoribus conlectus* and the medical prescriptions in the Vindobonenis is sheer imagination and cannot be accepted as even the beginning of a proof. As for the Latin Hippocrates, there is nothing to validate the belief that the work in Cassiodorus' possession was specifically that contained in the Turin manuscript, which was withal a late manuscript, whereas the works assigned to Hippocrates are legion, as are also translations of them.

Beer exceeds the limits of probability when he claims that the other works contained in Vindobonensis 16 go back to Cassiodorus' library. Pelagonius' *Hippiatrica* would be one of the manuscripts that Cassiodorus designates by the formula *quem vobis inter alios reliqui*.[33] Eutyches' *De discernendis coniugationibus* might come from Vivarium, although Cassiodorus does not say a word about it and asserts that he possesses Eutyches' *De aspiratione* only.[34] Finally, the *Apocryphal Epistles*, of which Cassiodorus does not make the slightest mention, might come from Vivarium, and Beer finds in Cassiodorus a peculiar taste for heretical or apocryphal literature,[35] although whenever Cassiodorus discovers in his library a book that is in the least degree suspect he recommends that the monks read it with the greatest precaution and expurgate it carefully.[36]

Beer seems happier when he observes that the *Theodosian Code*, of which palimpsest fragments are contained in the manuscripts of Bobbio Vaticanus Latinus 5766 and Taurinensis A II 2, was used by Cassiodorus in his *Historia tripartita*. As a matter of fact, in two passages, one in Theodoret[37] and the other in Sozomen,[38] Cassiodorus interpolated the text of the constitutions to which these historians referred. This would then be proof that the *Theodosian Code* was really in the library at Vivarium. But Beer did not realize that these constitutions, although they were part of the *Theodosian Code*, were quoted by Cassiodorus from the *Justinian Code*, as is proved by very significant variants.[39] From this point on, the connection with the fragments of Bobbio

---

[33] *Inst.*, p. 72, 4. Cf. Beer, "Bemerkungen," p. 88, and *Monumenta*, p. 22.

[34] Cass. *De orthogr.*, 1263 A. Cf. Beer, "Bemerkungen," p. 103, and *Monumenta*, p. 25.

[35] Beer, "Bemerkungen," p. 93, and *Monumenta*, p. 23.

[36] *Inst.*, p. 14, 24; p. 28, 25; p. 33, 16; etc.

[37] 5.17. Cf. Beer, "Bemerkungen," p. 90.

[38] 7.4.

[39] The quotations that follow were intended for the *Historia tripartita*, according to *PL* 69; for the *Theodosian Code*, according to Mommsen's ed. (Berlin 1905); for the *Justinian Code*, according to Krueger's ed. (Berlin 1895):

vanishes, for there is nothing to prove that the *Theodosian Code* ever belonged in the library at Vivarium.

The rare paleographical indications that Beer called upon to support his thesis do not withstand scrutiny in any greater degree. Fragments of the Gothic Bible of Ulfila, preserved in eight manuscripts that Beer assigns to the pre-Columban holdings in Bobbio might come from Vivarium because Cassiodorus again and again mentions Ulfila and, in at least one of the manuscripts, the text is divided *per cola et commata*.[40] But the three passages in which Cassiodorus mentions Ulfila are nothing but a translation of Socrates and Theodoret[41] and in no sense indicate that Cassiodorus knew the text of his Gothic Bible. As for the *cola et commata*, Cassiodorus enjoins on his monks not to apply this arrangement to any text other than Jerome's Vulgate.[42]

On the other hand, it is correct, as Beer says,[43] that the system of punctuation used in the beautiful manuscript of Vergil Mediceus + Vaticanus Lat. 3225 conforms to Cassiodorus' teaching.[44] But, as Cassiodorus himself declares, he is merely following in this regard Donatus' teaching, which was then readily applied. In addition, the subscription of the Mediceus, which Beer himself acknowledges as autograph,[45] proves that it was punctuated in the year 494 by Asterius, that is, before the monastery of Vivarium was founded. Another subscription by the same Asterius appears in Taurinensis E IV 44, which mentions that the copyist is to add rubrics.[46] This proves that neither the rubrics nor the punctuation are specifically Cassiodorian marks, since they had already been in use for a long time.

Cod. Theod. 16.1.2:	Cass. 69, 1126 D:	*Cod. Iust.* 1.1.1:
et Theodosius AAA. *edictum* ad populum . . .	et Theodosius AAA. ad populum.	et Theodosius AAA. ad populum.
sub *parili* maiestate.	sub pari maiestate.	sub pari maiestate.
sustinere *nec conciliabula eorum ecclesiarum nomen accipere* divina.	sustinere divina.	sustinere divina.
Gratiano *A. V.* et Theodosio *A. I.* conss.	Gratiano V et Theodosio AA. conss.	Gratiano V et Theodosio AA. conss.

Cod. Theod. 9.40.13:	Cass. 69, 1146 D:	*Cod. Iust.* 9.47.20:
Flaviano P.P. Illyrici *et Italiae.*	Flaviano P. P. Illyrici.	Flaviano P. P. Illyrici.

[40] Beer, "Bemerkungen," pp. 100–101.

[41] Cass. *Hist. trip.*, 1118 D (and Jordanes *Getica*, ed. Mommsen, p. 127, 6) = Socrates *Hist. eccl.* 4.34 (PG 67, 554 A). Cass. *Hist. trip.*, 1120 B = Theodoret 4.37 (ed. Parmentier, p. 274, 4).

[42] Cass. *Inst.*, p. 8, 16 and p. 48, 10ff.

[43] Beer, "Bemerkungen," p. 86.

[44] Cass. *Inst.*, p. 49, 2.

[45] Beer, "Bemerkungen," p. 96, and *Monumenta*, p. 16.

[46] Cf. Beer, "Bemerkungen," p. 96.

Thus Beer's thesis falls through. For his comparisons (regarding which Lejay admitted: "None of them is a proof; but in combination they are impressive")[47] turn out to be worthless, and an accumulation of wrong signs does not begin to be a proof. It follows that Weinberger's paleographical research, even if he discovered actual connections between other manuscripts and the pre-Columban stock at Bobbio, now presents no reason for concluding that any item whatever in Cassiodorus' library survived in these manuscripts. We must reject the convenient and long accepted theory that almost all our manuscripts in uncials of the fifth and sixth centuries were brought by Cassiodorus from Ravenna and Rome to Vivarium, whence some hypothetical invader brought them to Bobbio. Does this mean, as Cardinal Mercati assumes, that the library at Vivarium had no offshoots and that it disappeared entirely along with the monastery? It would, however, be strange if such an important *scriptorium* did not exercise, even before the decline of the monastery and Cassiodorus' death, widespread contacts. Is it not a known fact too that, according to Liberatus, deacon of Carthage, his *Breviarium* written between 560 and 566 used an "ecclesiastica historia nuper de Graeco in Latinum translata," that is, Cassiodorus' *Historia tripartita*?[48] Even the possibility cannot be excluded, if the monastery was ruined, that a certain number of Cassiodorus' manuscripts could have been saved and transported elsewhere. Is it possible to estimate the extent of this diffusion? Is it possible, if some manuscripts of Vivarium survived, to find any trace of them?

A paleographical criterion seems difficult to apply, inasmuch as no subscription has uncovered a few manuscripts of unquestionably Vivarian provenance. Of course, we can readily observe in the manuscript tradition of Cassiodorus' works external indications that would help us to recognize original Vivarian texts. Thus, the only manuscript containing Cassiodorus' *Complexiones*, Veronensis XXXIX (37) dating in the sixth century, may possibly be, if not the original Cassiodorian text, at least a copy stemming from Vivarium. It is noteworthy on account of the arrangement of the *incipit* and the *explicit*:

folio 2 recto	folio 11 verso
CASSIODORII SENATORIS	CASSIODORIISENATORIS
IAM D̄N̄O PRESTANTE CON	IAMD̄N̄OPRESTAN
VERSIEXPLICITPREFATIO	TE CONVERSI

---

[47] Paul Lejay, "Bobbio et la bibliothèque de Cassiodore," *Bulletin d'ancienne littérature et d'archéologie chrétiennes* 3 (1913) 267. This is a review of Beer's book. Cf. p. 269: "The translations that Cassiodorus commissioned from the Greek texts are not really represented (in Bobbio)."

[48] Liberatus *Breviarium*, PL 68, 939 C. Cf. Schanz, vol. 4, 2, p. 583. This is the very formula of the Cassiodorian *incipit*, below, p. 371.

<pre>
    INCIPIVNT COM   EXPLICVE
     PLEXIONES   RVNT CO̅
     IN EPISTV   PLEXIO
      LIS A   NES IN
       POS   EPISTV
      TOLO   LIS A
       RV   POS
        M   TO
                                  LO
                                  RV
                                   M
</pre>

This arrangement recalls the *botrionum formulae*,[49] glosses in the form of clusters of grapes that decorated a manuscript of the Prophets at Vivarium. But since the glosses are arranged in this way in most sixth-century manuscripts,[50] we cannot see in this case a distinctive indication of the *scriptorium* at Vivarium.

The *Commentary on the Psalms* is preserved in the manuscripts in three volumes, in Cassiodorus' arrangement[51] and with the marginal signs that Cassiodorus had set up for the instruction of the monks.[52] Cassiodorus ends his commentary by inviting the reader to study the commentaries of the next book of the Bible: "Nunc Salomonis dicta videamus, quae proprios expositores habere noscuntur."[53] Similarly, at the end of the *Institutiones*, Cassiodorus designates the manuscript that the pupil should read next: "Complexis, quantum ego arbitror, diligenterque tractatis institutionum duobus libris qui breviter divinas et humanas litteras comprehendunt, tempus est ut nunc aedificatrices veterum regulas, id est codicem introductorium, legere debemus, qui ad sacras litteras nobiliter ac salubriter introducunt."[54] This manuscript, which was to follow the *Institutiones* in the classification of the library at Vivarium, was, as we have seen, a corpus comprising in sequence the works of Tyconius, Augustine (*De doctrina Christiana*),

[49] *Inst.*, p. 18, 18.

[50] See, for instance, E. Châtelain, *Uncialis scriptura codd. Lat. novis exemplis illustrata*, Paris 1901.

[51] *Inst.*, p. 21, 21. The two oldest manuscripts to my knowledge belong in the eighth century (Durham, Cath. libr. B II 30 and Paris. Lat. 12239, 12240, 12241). Other Carolingian manuscripts are: Bernenses 99 and 124, Ambros. D 519 inf., Vat. Palat. 271, London. Addit. 16962 and 21215, 21216, 21217, Sessorianus XXVI, Vercellenses XXXVIII and XCII, XCIII.

[52] As is indicated by the legend placed at the beginning of all the manuscripts; for example, in Vat. Palat. 271, 10th cent., fol. 1ʳ. The editors omitted this legend. Cf. A. Reifferscheid, "Mittheilungen aus Handschriften," *Rhein. Mus.*, n.s. 23 (1868) 131.

[53] *PL* 70, 1056 C.

[54] *Inst.*, p. 163 (cod. B).

Hadrianus, Eucherius, Junilius.[55] Such mentions might be helpful in finding Vivarian manuscripts, but I know of no other examples.

Cassiodorus' *Historia tripartita*, of which a number of Carolingian manuscripts are extant,[56] shows the very onerous work of revision to which it was subjected. In almost all the manuscripts we find at the end of the preface the notice *perlegi, percontuli* and at the end of each of the twelve books *contuli* or *percontuli*. Moreover, the *incipit* is very detailed: "In hoc corpore continentur historiae ecclesiasticae ex Socrate, Sozomeno et Theodorito in unum conlectae et nuper de Graeco in Latinum translatae libri numero XII. Amen. Lege feliciter in Domino." The individual contribution of Cassiodorus and of the translator Epiphanius is carefully noted: "Cassiodori senatoris iam Domino praestante conversi explicit praefatio. Incipiunt tituli ecclesiasticae historiae cum opere suo ab Epiphanio scolastico Domino praestante translatae."[57] Each book is preceded by *tituli*, sometimes calld *breves*.[58] Similarly, the Cassiodorian translation of Josephus' *Antiquities* carries, in the sixth-century Ambrosianus, the notation *contuli* in quaternion XII,[59] and in other manuscripts the notation *breves* to designate the *capitula*[60] and the notation *Lege feliciter*.[61]

The notations are too numerous in the manuscript tradition not to be traced back to the Cassiodorian original texts. But can one venture to assert of any of them that it can constitute a criterion of Cassiodorian provenance? Traube thought so for the notation *In hoc corpore continentur . . .*[62] But, though Cassiodorus probably extended the practice of this type of corpus, too many manuscripts carry this notation to induce the belief that they all stem from a Vivarian source.[63] Similarly, the use of *capitula*, rubrics, the arrangement of titles, and the rules of punctuation must be regarded as the mark of an epoch rather than as characteristics peculiar to the *scriptorium* of Vivarium. Doubtless, we may note in a manuscript the devices in orthography and punctuation that conform to the rules enunciated by Cassiodorus in the *Institutiones*. But these rules were not of his invention. How can we say that they were not in vogue at the same period in all monasteries? Inversely, does not the very fact

---

[55] See above, p. 355.

[56] Among others, Petrop. F. v. 1, number 11; Casin. 302; Neapolit. VI D 18; Vat. Lat. 1970; Vat. Palat. 823; Sangall. 561; Vercell. CI (158); etc.

[57] Neap. VI D 18, fol. 1ʳ.

[58] *Ibid.*, fol. 27ᵛ.

[59] Folio 282ʳ (cf. Reifferscheid, *Bibliotheca patr. Lat. Italica* 2, p. 46 n. 1) and at the end of Book 6 in Neap. V F 34, fol. 126ᵛ.

[60] Casin. 120, fols. 18ʳ and 65ᵛ, and Neap. V F 34, fols. 27ʳ and 90ᵛ.

[61] Vat. Palat. 814, fol. 104ᵛ.

[62] Traube, *Vorlesungen und Abhandlungen* 2 (Munich 1909) 130.

[63] A cursory examination of Reifferscheid, *Bibl. patr. Lat. Ital.*, is sufficient to realize this.

that Cassiodorus is obliged to repeat the most elementary rules indicate that the majority of his copyists scarcely observed them? The Vivarian origin of a manuscript cannot then be discovered from its external characteristics, but solely from its contents, on the express condition that it comprises texts that unquestionably existed in Cassiodorus' library. This condition would in itself be insufficient. A text that was extensively copied, like Augustine's *Confessions*, is found in any large library. The fact that Cassiodorus possessed it in no way proves that his copy was the source of our manuscript tradition. A rare text, such as that of Gargilius Martialis, might be more conclusive. But how can one tell that several pre-Carolingian libraries did not have copies, if there was no cessation of copying until the ninth century?

Fortunately there are special cases that offer greater certainty. Cassiodorus sometimes gives such precise details about certain of his manuscripts that it would be impossible, if they were preserved, not to identify them. For instance, on several occasions Cassiodorus asserts that he requisitioned copies made in sequence or bound together of several texts by different authors. These authors often have no relation with each other. The following are Cassiodorian manuscripts for which we know the sequence of the works that were copied or bound together.[64]

I

* p. 11, 7–24:
Basilius *Hexaemeron* (translated by Eustathius)
Augustinus *Contra Manichaeos libri II*

II

p. 15, 7–9:
Origenes *Homiliae in Genesim XVI* (translated by Rufinus)
               in Exodum XII   id.
               in Leviticum XVI   id.

III

* p. 15, 9–18:
Origenes *Homiliae in Iesu Nave XXVI* (translated by Rufinus)
               in Iudices IX   id.[65]
Bellator *In Ruth libri II*

IV

* p. 15, 26–p. 18, 5:
Libri Regum IV et Paralipomenon II

[64] The asterisk denotes that Cassiodorus himself asserts that he had copies of these texts made or bound together in the same manuscript.

[65] Cf. Baehrens, *Ueberlieferung*, p. 189, on these two Cassiodorian manuscripts.

Origenes *In I Regum homiliae IV* (translated)
Augustinus *De diversis quaestionibus ad Simplicianum liber secundus*
           Sermo de Absalom
           Quaestio de I Regum ubi David Goliam expugnavit
           Quaestio de Elia et vidua Sareptana
           Quaestio de IV Regum ubi Elizaeus fontem mortiferum benedixit
Hieronymus *Ad Abundantium quaestiones tres*
Origenes *In II Regum homilia* (translated)
Ambrosius *In III Regum sermo de iudicio Salomonis*
Hieronymus *Epistula de iudicio Salomonis*
Augustinus *Sermo de iudicio Salomonis*
Hieronymus *Epistula ad Vitalem de Salomone et Achaz*
Augustinus *Civitas Dei XVII, 4, in canticum Annae*
Origenes *In II Paralipomenon homilia* (translated)

V

*p. 24, 3–16:
Origenes *In Canticum homiliae II* (translated by Jerome)
         In Canticum libri III (translated by Rufinus)
Epiphanius Cyprius *In Canticum* (translated by Epiphanius)[66]

VI

p. 29, 16–p. 30, 4:
Clemens Alexandrinus *In I Petri* (translated)
                In I et II Iohannis (translated)
                In Iudam (translated)
Didymus *In VII epistulas canonicas* (translated by Epiphanius)
Augustinus *In I Iohannis sermones X*[67]

VII

*p. 31, 5–13:
Augustinus *In Epistulam ad Romanos expositio inchoata*
         De diversis quaestionibus ad Simplicianum liber primus

VIII

*p. 33, 22–27:
Primasius *In Apocalypsin libri V*
         De haeresibus liber primus: Quid faciat haereticum

IX

*p. 34, 7–15:
Tyconius *Liber Regularum*
Augustinus *De doctrina Christiana*

---

[66] On this manuscript, see below, sec. 2 C.
[67] On this manuscript, see below, sec. 2 D.

Hadrianus *Isagoge ad sacras scripturas* (translated)
Eucherius *Liber formularum* or *Instructiones*
Iunilius *De partibus divinae legis libri II*

X

*p. 53, 20–p. 54, 3:
Ambrosius *De sancto Spiritu ad Gratianum*
Nicetas *De fide*[68]

XI

*p. 56, 5–10:
Socrates *Historia ecclesiastica*
Sozomenus *Historia ecclesiastica*   (Translated in part by Epiphanius and assembled
Theodoretus *Historia ecclesiastica*   by Cassiodorus)

XII

p. 56, 17–26:
Eusebius *Chronica* (translated by Jerome)
Marcellinus *Chronicum*[69]

XIII

*p. 57, 2–10:
Hieronymus *De viris inlustribus*
Gennadius *De scriptoribus legis divinae*[70]

XIV

p. 79, 2–8:
Galen *Therapeutica ad Glauconem*
Anonymus . . . *ex diversis auctoribus* . . . *conlectus*
Caelius Aurelius *De medicina*
Hippocrates *De herbis et curis*[71]

XV

*p. 96, 18 (ΦΔ):
Donatus *Ars grammatica cum commentis* (*Sergii et Servii*)
Cassiodorus *De orthographia*
                    De etymologiis
Sacerdos *De schematibus XCVIII*

[68] On this manuscript, see below, sec. 2 E.

[69] Cassiodorus does not expressly declare that he possesses them in a single manuscript, but starting with the sixth century the tradition does not separate them (cf. Bodleianus auct. T. II. 6, 6th cent.). The script of this manuscript strangely resembles that of Vat. Lat. 5704, which is certainly an original Vivarian manuscript. Cf. below, sec. 2 C.

[70] On this manuscript, see below, sec. 2 F.

[71] On this manuscript, see below, sec. 4.

XVI

*p. 103, 19–p. 104, 15:
Cicero *De inventione cum commento Victorini*
Quintilianus *Institutionum libri XII*
Fortunatianus *Ars Rhetorica*[72]

XVII

*p. 128, 14–p. 129, 12 ($\Phi\Delta$):
Marius Victorinus *Isagoge Porphyrii translata*
Boethius *In Isagogen editio secunda*
Marius Victorinus *Aristotelis Categoriae translatae*
              In Categorias libri VIII
              Aristotelis liber Perihermenias translatus
Boethius *In librum Perihermenias editio secunda*
Apuleius *De syllogismis categoricis*
Marius Victorinus *De syllogismis hypotheticis*
              De diffinitione
Cicero *Aristotelis Topica translata*
Marius Victorinus *In Topica Ciceronis libri IV*

If the same sequences were to appear in an extant manuscript, even if this manuscript were relatively late, its Vivarian origin would be certain. Similarly if Cassiodorus, from his attribution of a text to a particular author or from his manner of counting the books of a work, differs from all the manuscripts except one; or if he notes a peculiarity in his manuscript, such as marginal glosses or miniatures, and that peculiarity now exists. Finally, there is a category of works whose Vivarian origin is established. They are works that Cassiodorus wrote at Vivarium and the translations that he requisitioned there. A study of their dispersal may give us information also about the fate of the library at Vivarium. It may be added that one of these criteria in no way excludes the others and that on the contrary, in the rare cases where we possess these indications, we shall see that they coincide with each other. It is surprising that Beer took no account of these indications and said not a word about the manuscripts in which they appear. The fact is that these manuscripts invalidate the theory of the associations between Vivarium and the pre-Columban manuscripts in Bobbio.

[72] On this manuscript, see below, pp. 399–400.

2. THE VIVARIAN MANUSCRIPTS

A. The Cassiodorian Bibles and the Amiatinus

This fine manuscript is of exceptional importance for establishing the text of the Vulgate. During recent years it has been the subject of exhaustive researches, but no agreement has been reached on the point that concerns us, that is, its relation with the library at Vivarium.

We know from Bede's evidence that it was copied at the close of the seventh century or at the very beginning of the eighth by order of Ceolfrid, abbot of the English monastery at Yarrow: "Bibliothecam utriusque monasterii quam Benedictus abbas magna coepit instantia ipse (Ceolfridus) non minori geminavit industria; ita ut tres Pandectes novae translationis ad unum vetustae translationis quem de Roma adtulerat, ipse superadiungeret; quorum unum senex Romam rediens secum inter alia pro munere sumpsit, duos utrique monasterio reliquit."[1] Ceolfrid was taking it to the Pope at his death in Langres in 716. His manuscript fell to the Cistercian abbey of Monte Amiata, which kept it until its transfer to Florence.[2]

On one point there is no question: the connection between the first sheet of the Amiatinus and the "codex grandior" that Cassiodorus mentions in chapter 14 of the *Institutiones divinae*. The following account shows how this connection arose. The Amiatinus has (folios 2 verso–3 recto) a painting representing the Tabernacle of the Temple at Jerusalem.[3] Now Bede, who composed the treatises *De templo Salomonis* and *De Tabernaculo*, expressly declares therein that he is describing the miniature in a Pandect of Cassiodorus'.[4] Cassiodorus himself informs us that he had this miniature painted at the beginning of his *codex grandior* or Pandect of the Old Version from the description in Josephus' *Antiquities* and the references of a certain Eusebius who had come from Asia.[5] There is therefore no question that the Bible of the Old Version brought back from Rome to Yarrow is Cassiodorus' *codex*

---

[1] Bede *Vita quinque abbatum* (PL 94, 725 A).

[2] Cf. Dom Henri Quentin, *Mémoire sur l'établissement* (Rome and Paris 1922) 438ff.

[3] See the reproduction of this painting in Dom Quentin, *ibid.*, p. 447.

[4] Bede *De templo Salomonis* 17 (PL 91, 775 A–C): "Has vero porticus Cassiodorus Senator in Pandectis, ut ipse Psalmorum expositione commemorat, triplice ordine distinxit . . . Haec ut in pictura Cassiodori repperimus distincta breviter adnotare curavimus ita eum ab antiquis Iudaeis didicisse"; *De tabernaculo* 12 (PL 91, 454 B): "quo modo in pictura Cassiodori Senatoris, cuius ipse in expositione Psalmorum meminit, expressum vidimus."

[5] Cass. *Comm. in Psal.* 14 (PL 70, 109 A): "de quo (tabernaculo) etiam et Iosephus in libro Antiquitatum tertio, titulo septimo, diligenti narratione disseruit, quod nos fecimus pingi et in Pandectis maioris capite conlocari"; *Inst.*, p. 23, 3: "(Eusebius) commonuit etiam tabernaculum templumque domini ad instar caeli fuisse formatum; quae depicta subtiliter lineamentis propriis in Pandecte Latino corporis grandioris competenter aptavi."

grandior and that it is the source of the painting of the Tabernacle preserved by the Amiatinus.

This conclusion is corroborated by the fact that the Amiatinus contains (folios 6 recto, 7 recto, 8 recto) the three divisions of the Bible according to St. Jerome, St. Augustine, and the Old Version. These divisions are reproduced by Cassiodorus in chapters 12–14 of the *Institutiones* from the *codex grandior* where he declares that he had them copied.[6] If the three pictures in the *Institutiones* are compared in their best representative, the Bambergensis, with the three pictures in the Amiatinus, we observe that the pictures in the Amiatinus are perfectly exact, whereas Cassiodorus did not perform this delicate transcription from the *codex grandior* to the *Institutiones* without making mistakes.[7]

Furthermore, the preface of folio 4 recto of the Amiatinus certainly reproduces the preface that Cassiodorus had placed at the beginning of his *codex grandior*. In fact, the entire page, which clearly serves as an introduction to a manuscript of the Bible, bears the mark of his style.[8] It might however be questioned whether it is really the preface of the *codex grandior*, for we know that Cassiodorus had three Latin Bibles at Vivarium: one Bible in nine volumes that reproduced St. Augustine's arrangement into seventy-one books, a Vulgate of Jerome's in fifty-three gatherings of six leaves each, written in a rather fine hand (*minutiore manu*), that followed St. Jerome's division into forty-nine books, and lastly this *codex grandior* of the Old Version that consisted of seventy books written on ninety-five quaternions.[9] The

---

[6] *Inst.*, p. 40, 6. The diagram of one of these lists is the same in the Amiatinus and the oldest manuscript of the *Institutiones*. I have reproduced these two diagrams in my article "Le site du monastère de Cassiodore," pp. 276–277.

[7] The arrangement according to Jerome was borrowed from his *Prologus Galeatus* (*PL* 28, 598). Now, if we compare the Amiatinus and the Bambergensis with the *Prologus Galeatus*, we observe that the transcription made by Cassiodorus is accurate in the Amiatinus, while in the *Institutiones* Cassiodorus omits the Book of Malachi after Samuel. Then, in order to secure a total of forty-nine books, despite this mistake, he reckons Ruth as a book, whereas Jerome included it in Judges. In addition, Cassiodorus transcribes "Ecclesiasticus" instead of "Ecclesiastes," unless this mistake was made by a later scribe.

Augustine's arrangement is borrowed from the *De doctrina Christiana* 2.8.13 (*PL* 34, 41), which is faithfully reproduced in the list of the Amiatinus. On the other hand, in the *Institutiones* Cassiodorus places the four major prophets before the twelve minor prophets and counts Esdras as only one book (MS B, fol. 15^r has *Esdrae liber I*, although Mynors prints *II*), whereas two books are necessary to reach the total of seventy-one.

The arrangement of the Old Version is the same in the Amiatinus and the Bambergensis, except that Cassiodorus neglects in the *Institutiones* to count five books for the Psalter. Furthermore, he makes the mistake of attributing this list no longer to "Hilarus Romanae urbis antistes" but to "Hilarius Pictaviensis urbis antistes."

[8] This page is edited by Dom Chapman, *Notes on the Early History of the Vulgate Gospels* (Oxford 1908), chap. 2.

[9] On these bibles, cf. Cass. *Inst.*, pp. 36–41, and Dom Quentin, *Mémoire*, p. 444.

following parallel is evident proof that this preface can be none other than the preface of the *codex grandior*:

Amiatinus, folio 4 recto:	*Institutiones*, p. 40, 6:
Nec vos moveat quod pater Augustinus in septuaginta unum libros Testamentum vetus novumque divisit, doctissimus autem Hieronymus idem vetus novumque Testamentum XLVIIII sectionibus comprehendit, in hoc autem corpore utrumque Testamentum septuagenario probatur impletum, in illa palmarum quantitate forsitan praesagato, quas in mansione Helim invenit populus Hebraeorum.	Tertia vero divisio est inter alias in codice grandiore, littera clariore conscripto, qui habet quaterniones nonaginta quinque: in quo septuaginta interpretum translatio Veteris Testamenti in libris XLIV continetur; cui subiuncti sunt Novi Testamenti libri XXVI, fiuntque simul libri septuaginta: in illo palmarum numero fortasse praesagati, quas in mansione Helim invenit populus Hebraeorum.

But apart from this point, which is generally acknowledged, the connection between the Amiatinus and Cassiodorus' Bibles is the subject of weighty discussion on the manner of interpreting Bede's statement, "ita ut tres Pandectes novae translationis ad unum vetustae translationis quem de Roma adtulerat, ipse (Ceolfridus) superadiungeret." In the opinion of Dom Quentin and Dom De Bruyne,[10] the Amiatinus is related to the *codex grandior* only and this connection is altogether external, since its text is that of the Vulgate, whereas the *codex grandior* contained the Old Version.[11] Bede's statement would seem to indicate that the monks of Yarrow adopted for their Pandects of the Vulgate the sequence of the books of the Old Version, as established in the *codex grandior*. "It is this very order," writes Dom Quentin, "that our manuscript follows in the general arrangement of the books." This confirmation is correct only for the order of the groupings, whereas in the internal arrangement of the sapiential books, the minor prophets, and the Epistles, the order is quite different.[12] Therefore, if we agree with Dom Quentin that only the *codex grandior* among Cassiodorus' Bibles has some connection with the Amiatinus, we must add that this connection is practically reduced to the five leaves of the first sheet containing the painting of the Tabernacle, the divisions of the Bible, and Cassiodorus' preface.

Dom Chapman proposed to prove, on the other hand, that the order and the text itself of the Amiatinus stem from the Pandect *minutiore manu* of the Vulgate that Cassiodorus had and that was itself probably a copy of his Bible in nine volumes.[13] This solution appears to me inacceptable a priori, by

10 Dom D. De Bruyne, "Cassiodore et l'Amiatinus," *RB* 39 (1927) 261–266.

11 Quentin, *Mémoire*, p. 445.

12 See the accompanying list, pp. 380–381.

13 Dom H. J. Chapman, "The Codex Amiatinus and Cassiodorus," *RB* 38 (1926) 139–151 and 39 (1927) 12–32, and "The Codex Amiatinus once more," *ibid.*, 40 (1928) 130–134.

reason of Bede's formal text, the meaning of which is however quite clear: "Ceolfrid added three Pandects of the New Version to the Pandect of the Old Version that he had brought from Rome." This text proves that Ceolfrid had at Yarrow one Pandect only, the Pandect of the Old Version, Cassiodorus' *codex grandior*. Attracted by the convenience of this gathering of the entire Scriptures into one volume, he had copies made, in the form of Pandects, of the three manuscripts of the Vulgate, one of which is our Amiatinus. But Bede's statement shows that before this labor of copying the monastery of Yarrow did not have the Vulgate text in the form of Pandects.

There is then, if the five leaves of the *codex grandior* are excluded, only one of Cassiodorus' Bibles that could have served as a model for the Amiatinus. This was the Bible in nine volumes, the only Bible that was not arranged as Pandects. Can a link be established between this Bible in nine volumes and the Amiatinus?

We are from the very start inclined to do so on account of the miniature in the Amiatinus (folio 5 recto). It represents Esdras sitting and copying a manuscript in front of a cupboard containing the nine volumes of the Bible, arranged in the following order:

Oct. lib.	Reg.
Hist.	Psalm. lib.
Salomon	Proph.
Evang. IIII	Epist. Ap. XXI
Act. Apost.	Apoca.[14]

This corresponds exactly to St. Augustine's arrangement, which was followed in Cassiodorus' *novem codices*.[15] It is therefore probable that this page of the Amiatinus reproduces the frontispiece of the first of Cassiodorus' nine volumes.

Another indication of Cassiodorian origin that has been quite neglected is furnished by folio 7 verso of the same sheet. This consists of five brief, encircled notices, extracts from St. Jerome's *Letter* 53 to Paulinus. These notices serve as an introduction to the Pentateuch.[16] Similar notices, extracts likewise from the letter to Paulinus,[17] appear at the beginning of each of the twelve minor prophets in the Amiatinus.[18] Now, in the chapter of the *Institutiones* that he devotes to St. Jerome, Cassiodorus commends this very passage

[14] Cf. Chapman, *RB* 38 (1926) 148 n. 1. The last two books constitute a single volume. Cf. *Inst.*, p. 32, 26. A reproduction of this miniature may be found in Quentin, *Mémoire*, on the flyleaf.

[15] Cass. *Inst.*, p. 39, 4.

[16] Jerome *Epist.* 53 (PL 22, 545 B): "Manifestissima est Genesis ... Patet Exodus ... In promptu est Leviticus ... Numeri vero ... Deuteronomium quoque ..."

[17] *Ibid.*, 546 B–D.

[18] Except for Hosea (cf. Chapman, *RB* 39 [1927] 16).

in the letter to Paulinus: "In epistulam suam ad Paulinum ex senatore presbyterum mirificam destinavit, docens quem ad modum Scripturas divinas
adhibita cautela perlegeret: ubi breviter virtutem uniuscuiusque libri Veteris
et Novi Testamenti mirabiliter indicavit."[19] And he quotes from it the entire
notice on Job in the chapter of the *Institutiones* where he discusses the sixth of
the *novem codices*.[20] Is it not probable that Cassiodorus had these notices inserted at the beginning of his *novem codices*, which specifically contained
Jerome's Vulgate, as is acknowledged by Dom Quentin and Dom Chapman? The Amiatinus would then be a copy of this.

The sequence of the books in the Amiatinus is far closer to the order of the
novem codices than to the order of the *Antiqua translatio*, as the following tabu-
lation shows:

Novem codices (*Inst.*, p. 38, 10):	Amiatinus (folio 4 verso):	Codex grandior (*Inst.*, p. 39, 13):
(8) Octateuch	(8) Octateuch	(8) Octateuch
4 Kings	(4) Kings	4 Kings
2 Paralipomena	(2) Paralipomena	2 Paralipomena
1 Psalms	1 Psalms	(1) Psalms
1 Proverbs	1 Proverbs	1 Proverbs
1 Ecclesiastes	1 Ecclesiastes	1 *Wisdom*
1 Song of Solomon	1 Song of Solomon	1 *Ecclesiasticus*
1 Wisdom	1 Wisdom	1 *Ecclesiastes*
1 Ecclesiasticus	1 Ecclesiasticus	1 *Song of Solomon*
4 Major Prophets	(4) Major Prophets	(4) Major Prophets
1 Hosea	1 Hosea	1 Hosea
1 Joel	1 Joel	1 *Amos*
1 Amos	1 Amos	1 *Micah*
1 Obadiah	1 Obadiah	1 *Joel*
1 Jonah	1 Jonah	1 *Obadiah*
1 Micah	1 Micah	1 *Jonah*
1 Nahum	1 Nahum	1 Nahum
1 Habakkuk	1 Habakkuk	1 Habakkuk
1 Zephaniah	1 Zephaniah	1 Zephaniah
1 *Zechariah*	1 Haggai	1 Haggai
1 *Haggai*	1 Zechariah	1 Zechariah
1 Malachi	1 Malachi	1 Malachi
1 Job	1 Job	1 Job
1 Tobit	1 Tobit	1 Tobit
1 *Esther*	1 Judith	1 *Esther*
(2) Esdras	(2) Esdras	2 Esdras
2 Maccabees	2 Maccabees	2 Maccabees

[19] Cass. *Inst.*, p. 59, 23.
[20] *Ibid.*, p. 25, 24.

4 Gospels	4 Gospels	4 Gospels
	1 Acts	1 Acts
1 Romans	1 Romans	(2) *Peter*
2 Corinthians	2 Corinthians	1 *James*
1 Galatians	1 Galatians	1 *Jude*
1 Ephesians	1 Ephesians	(3) *John*
1 Philippians	1 Philippians	1 *Romans*
2 *Thessalonians*	1 Colossians	2 *Corinthians*
1 *Colossians*	2 Thessalonians	1 *Galatians*
2 Timothy	2 Timothy	1 *Philippians*
1 Titus	1 Titus	1 *Colossians*
1 Philemon	1 Philemon	1 *Ephesians*
1 Hebrews	1 Hebrews	
2 *Peter*	1 James	2 *Thessalonians*
3 *John*	(2) Peter	2 *Timothy*
1 *Jude*	3 John	1 *Titus*
1 *James*	1 Jude	1 *Philemon*
1 *Acts*		
1 Apocalypse	1 Apocalypse	1 Apocalypse
—	—	—
71	71	70

In fact, in the *novem codices* the Psalter is actually third, as Dom Chapman has shown,[21] and not fourth, as Garet wrongly printed it. Hence the only important difference arises from the fact that Ceolfrid, in establishing his Pandect, replaced the Acts into their normal order, immediately after the Gospels. Cassiodorus, on the other hand, either following the order commended by Augustine or in order to produce nine volumes of equal importance, had placed them with the Apocalypse in the ninth volume. In other respects the total of seventy-one books given by the table of the Amiatinus[22] corresponds exactly to the total of St. Augustine's division, reproduced by the *novem codices*.[23] Now, such a minute correspondence in the total and the order of the books is exceptional in the manuscripts of the Bible.

[21] Chapman, *RB* 38 (1926) 147. Cf. p. 20, 14, ed. Mynors.

[22] I therefore think that the list on fol. 4ᵛ clearly corresponds to the contents of the Amiatinus; that it is not necessary to change the number 71 to 70; that the notation "Petri I" should be changed to "Petri II" since both epistles of Peter actually appear in the Amiatinus; and that two books of Esdras should be counted, although in the course of the text this arrangement is disregarded.

[23] The rare divergencies between Augustine's classification and the order of the *novem codices* can readily be explained. As far as concerns the sequence of the groups, Cassiodorus at first observed it scrupulously, as is proved by the miniature of the cabinet with the *novem codices* and the notices: "licet Psalterium quartus codex, sit divinae auctoritatis" (*In Ps.* 22 D, the text of which I have verified with Vat. Palat. 271, fol. 2ʳ), and: "sed bis binum locum tenet in ordine" (*Inst.*, p. 20, 15). Then he placed the Books of the Prophets at the end of the Old Testament, so that the Psalter became "codex tertius."

In conclusion, the entire text of the Amiatinus is arranged *per cola et commata*. Whether this arrangement was adopted by Jerome for the entire text of the Bible, as Dom Quentin believes,[24] or only for some parts, as Dom Chapman and Dom De Bruyne think,[25] such an arrangement cannot be conceived, according to Cassiodorus, for any text other than the Vulgate.[26] Hence the Amiatinus certainly did not take it from the *codex grandior* of the Old Version. Now, Cassiodorus had a text of the Vulgate written entirely *per cola et commata*. This was the text of the *novem codices*.[27] It was this text that was reproduced by the Amiatinus.

I believe therefore that the Amiatinus took from the *codex grandior* its arrangements of Pandects, its miniature of the Tabernacle, and its three divisions of the Bible. But it is indebted to the *novem codices* for its miniature of Esdras and the nine volumes, the introductory notices to the Pentateuch and the minor prophets, taken from Jerome's Epistle to Paulinus, and the text of the Vulgate arranged *per cola et commata* and divided into seventy-one books following a given order.

A single objection, and a weighty one too, might cast a doubt on the connection between the Amiatinus and the *novem codices*. As Dom Quentin noted,[28] the Amiatinus has no synopses at the beginning of Paralipomena, while Cassiodorus declares that he himself had written some for this book in his Bible in *novem codices*.[29] The objection is so relevant that Dom Chapman, who had previously maintained the direct connection between the Amiatinus and the *novem codices*,[30] felt obliged to admit the Pandect *minutiore manu* as an intermediary. The objection, however, does not seem decisive. It is sufficient to make the assumption either that the monastery of Yarrow possessed only some of the *novem codices*, that is, at least the first one with the miniature of Esdras, the list of chapters, and the notices on the *Epistle to Paulinus*, and the fifth codex with the introductory notices on the Prophets, taken from the *Epistle to Paulinus*; or rather that the monks of Yarrow systematically omitted these summaries that Cassiodorus had added on his own account, in order to discover the arrangement of his more nearly Hieronymian archetype.

One point, in any case, is gained for the history of Cassiodorus' library. His *codex grandior* of the Old Version and very probably his Vulgate in *novem codices* were in Rome in the year 678, when Abbot Ceolfrid acquired them for Yarrow.

[24] Quentin, *Mémoire*, p. 497.

[25] Chapman, *RB* 39 (1927) 19ff, and De Bruyne, "Cass. et l'Amiatinus," *ibid.*, 266.

[26] Cass. *Inst.*, p. 48, 10ff.

[27] *Ibid.*, p. 8, 19ff.

[28] Quentin, *Mémoire*, p. 449.

[29] Cass. *Inst.*, p. 18, 6ff.

[30] Chapman, *Notes on the Early History of the Vulgate Gospels*, chap. 2: "The Cassiodorian Origin of the Northumbrian Text."

B. The *Codex encyclius* and Parisinus Latinus 12.098

Cassiodorus states that he had a translation of the *Codex encyclius* made by Epiphanius. The *Codex encyclius* was a collection of letters from bishops requested by the Emperor Leo for the defense of the Council of Chalcedon and assembled under his orders.[31] The Greek text is now lost. The Cassiodorian translation survives in two manuscripts, Parisinus Latinus 12.098, ninth century, folios 1 recto–62 verso, originally at Corbie, and Vindobonensis 397, ninth/tenth century, originally at Mainz. Another manuscript, at the capitulary library of Beauvais, disappeared when this library was dispersed.[32] All of them were possibly due to the industry of Odo, abbot of Corbie and bishop of Beauvais, who died in 881.[33] By what route did this translation, which was so little known in the Middle Ages, succeed in going from Vivarium to Corbie? One fact is certain. It was at Rome at the time of Pope Pelagius II (578–590). This Pope, indeed, assailed by the bishops of Istria in the course of the quarrel of the *Tria Capita*, answered that he asked their delegates to read several manuscripts from the archives of the Holy See that convinced them of their error.[34] He referred them several times to the *Encyclia*[35] and particularly to a passage that they appealed to in favor of their thesis:

Rursum in scripto vestro testimonium ac exemplum de Encycliis ponitur, quod multi episcopi simul dicunt: "Neque unum iota vel apicem possumus aut commovere aut commutare eorum quae apud Chalcedonem decreta sunt" . . . In praecedenti autem

[31] *Inst.*, p. 36, 1–5; cf. p. 64, 12: "Habetis in promptu synodum Ephesenam et Chalcedonensem necnon et Encyclia, id est epistulas confirmationis supradicti concilii." On the contents of this collection, see Maassen, *Geschichte der Quellen und der Literatur* (above, chap. 7 sec. 3 n. 29) 1, pp. 751ff; E. Schwartz, *Acta conciliorum* 2, 5 (Berlin 1936), p. v; and Th. Schnitzler, *Im Kampfe um Chalcedon, Gesch. und Inhalt des Codex Encyclius von 458* (Rome 1938).

[32] Cf. H. Omont, "Recherches sur la bibliothèque de l'église cathédrale de Beauvais," *Mémoires . . . de l'Acad. des Inscriptions* 40 (1916), pp. 23, 45, 50, 65. According to the ancient catalogues, this manuscript belonged in the ninth century and contained, after the *Codex encyclius*, Liberatus' *Breviarium*, Prosper's *Liber adversus conlatorem*, Aurelius' letter to the bishops of Byzacium on the condemnation of Pelagius, the *Acta* of the Council of Constantinople and the Lateran Council of 649. Parisinus Lat. 12098 contains the same works in the same order. Only the *Acta* of the Council of Constantinople and the Lateran Council do not appear in it. The Vivarian archetype probably contained the work of Prosper (cf. *Inst.*, ed. Mynors, p. 74, 7, and *In Ps.*, PL 70, 363 C) and of Liberatus. Liberatus probably sent his *Breviarium* to Cassiodorus, as he had received from the latter the *Historia tripartita*. Cf. PL 68, 939 C.

[33] Mansi, *Conciliorum amplissima conlectio* 7, 781ff.

[34] Pelagius II *Epistulae*, PL 72, 711 D: "et ex codicibus et ex antiquis polypticis scrinii sanctae sedis apostolicae relecta sunt aliqua."

[35] *Ibid.*, 712 C: "In Encycliis vero, quod est episcopalium conlectio litterarum, ex quibus aliqua in scriptis vestris testimonia incongrue posuistis," and 734 A: "Unde et Encyclia haec ita esse testantur."

testimonio multorum simul episcoporum utrum dictator an scriptor erraverit, ignoramus; neque enim in Encycliis continetur ut ipsi in scriptis vestris posuistis, ⟨sed⟩: "Neque enim iota unum aut apicem possumus commovere aut violare eorum quae ab ea recte sunt et inculpabiliter definita." At longe est aliud non posse commoveri ea quae decreta sunt et non posse commoveri ea quae recte et inculpabiliter sunt decreta."[36]

He thus refutes the text of the bishops of Istria (that is, another Latin translation used equally by Facundus of Hermione)[37] with the Cassiodorian translation that he possesses in the Lateran.[38] The Lateran, then, in all likelihood, appears as the intermediary between Vivarium and Corbie.

C. The Corpus of the Commentaries on the Song of Songs and Vaticanus Latinus 5704

Similarly, Cassiodorus states in the *Institutiones* that he had a Latin translation made by his friend Epiphanius of a Greek commentary on the Song of Songs by Epiphanius of Cyprus. He adds that he had a copy made, in continuous sequence, of the three commentaries on the Song of Songs that were in his possession. The order of the contents was as follows: two of Origen's homilies translated by St. Jerome; three of Origen's books translated by Rufinus; lastly, this commentary in one book by Epiphanius of Cyprus, translated by his friend Epiphanius.[39]

This notice of Cassiodorus' poses a problem. While the translations by Jerome and Rufinus are known and still preserved, we do not have from any other source any mention of the Greek commentary by Epiphanius of Cyprus. To counterbalance this, Greek manuscripts preserve a commentary on the Song of Songs and they all assign it to a certain Philo, whom Epiphanius had consecrated as bishop of Carpas, in the island of Cyprus, around the year 400. The authenticity of this attribution is confirmed by the fragments that Greek catenae transmitted under the name of Philo. A comparison of the complete text with the fragments shows however that the complete text was edited with a slight abridgment.[40] There is a unanimous acceptance of the fact that Cassiodorus was mistaken in attributing to Epiphanius of Cyprus

[36] *Ibid.*, 719 C–D. These letters of the year 585/586 constitute Appendix 3 of Hartman's ed. of St. Gregory's *Letters*, 2, p. 447, 15; 451, 13; 452, 40ff; 464, 3 = Mansi, 7, 596, a quotation from the letter of Alypius, bishop of Caesarea in Cappodocia, to the Emperor Leo: "Sic se habentibus vestrae pietati significo . . . inspexi."

[37] Facundus *Pro defensione trium capitulorum* 2.5 (PL 67, 576 D).

[38] Mansi, *Concil. ampliss. conlectio* 7, 781 referring to chap. 14 in Epiphanius = Schwartz, p. 27, 11.

[39] Cass. *Inst.*, p. 24, 3–16, particularly line 14: "quapropter praedicti libri (*Cantici*) diligentissimos expositores sub uno codice comprehendi."

[40] Cf. Otto Bardenhewer, *Geschichte der altkirchlichen Litteratur* 3 (Freiburg im Breisgau 1912) 303.

this commentary, which is actually by Philo of Carpas. Now, a Latin manuscript, the Vaticanus Latinus 5704, contains a commentary on the Song of Songs with the attribution to Epiphanius of Cyprus. The text of this commentary is really just a translation of the Greek commentary by Philo in the original nonabridged version. This error in the attribution of the text to Epiphanius helps us to recognize it, without any possible question, as the translation that Cassiodorus had commissioned.[41]

This manuscript now forms a small volume of ninety-seven leaves (284 mm. × 225 mm.) written in long lines, twenty-three lines to the page. The careful script is, in Lowe's opinion,[42] an uncial of the second half of the sixth century, but of uncertain origin. The *incipit* of the preface, "Incipit expositio sancti Epifanii episcopi Cyprii super Canticum Canticorum," belongs in the fifteenth century, but replaces the old *incipit* of which several words are still legible. The attribution to Epiphanius is, besides, assured by the fact that the sixth century is mentioned twice. Folio 4 verso, "Incipit Expositio Epiphanii episcopi Cyprii in Canticis Canticorum"; folio 96 verso, "Expliciunt commenta Epiphanii episcopi Cyprii in Cantica Canticorum"—this *incipit* and this *explicit* cover the entire page. The text of the Song of Songs is divided into 241 verses numbered and commented on in succession. It is always rubricated. Except for a few variants, it is identical with the text of the pre-Hieronymian version of the Song of Songs reconstructed by Dom De Bruyne.[43]

Here then is a manuscript in the Cassiodorian tradition, which was written in Cassiodorus' time. He unquestionably possessed a pre-Hieronymian version of the Bible and recommended rubrics. Are we possibly in the presence of an original text from Vivarium? I believe I can supply confirmation from the following fact. Epiphanius' commentary at present exists unrelated to other texts in our Vaticanus, but it was originally preceded by other texts, for it fills twelve quaternions numbered regularly from XXIX to XL. It belonged then at the beginning of a large volume of which the first twenty-eight quaternions are lost. Are we not tempted to think that these first twenty-eight quaternions contained precisely Origen's two homilies translated by Jerome and Origen's three books translated by Rufinus, following which Cassiodorus had had a copy of Epiphanius made? Mathematical verification is possible. If we assume as the unit a column in the Migne edition, Jerome's translation fills twenty-two columns, Rufinus' translation one hundred thirty-three, the one of Philo (= Epiphanius) sixty-three.[44] If the

---

[41] Cf. *S. Epiphani commentarium in Canticum canticorum*, ed. P. F. Foggini (Rome 1750) from this unique manuscript.

[42] E. A. Lowe, *Codices Latini antiquiores* 1: *The Vatican City*, Vat. Lat. 5704.

[43] De Bruyne, "Les anciennes versions latines du Cantique des Cantiques," *RB* 38 (1926) 98–104.

[44] Jerome, *PG* 13, 35ff; Rufinus, *PG* 13, 61ff; Philo, *PG* 40, 27ff.

first twenty-eight quaternions were filled by the $22 + 133 = 155$ columns of Jerome and Rufinus, the twelve following quaternions must have contained a text of proportional length, that is, $\dfrac{155 \times 12}{28} = 66\frac{1}{2}$ columns. The translation of Philo fills, it is true, only sixty-three columns, but this difference is explained, since our Greek text of Philo is a slightly abridged version in relation to the original text that Cassiodorus translated.

It is therefore quite probable that our forty quaternions belonging in the sixth century were the very manuscript in which Cassiodorus had copies made afterward of his three commentaries on the Song of Songs. Jerome's homilies covered quaternions I–IV, Rufinus' commentary quaternions V–XXVIII, Epiphanius' commentary quaternions XXIX–XL.

This verification becomes quite unassailable when we compare it with the theory of Baehrens, a specialist in the manuscript tradition of Origen. According to him the Latin translation of Origen's commentaries on the Octateuch and the Song of Songs goes back to the Cassiodorian archetypes.[45] These are the main points in his demonstration:

For the Octateuch, Cassiodorus states that he has Origen's homilies, translated by Jerome, in three separate manuscripts. The account he gives of it corresponds actually to Rufinus' translation, which is preserved. Baehrens notes, on the one hand, that even on Rufinus' evidence his translation had appeared in three books; on the other hand, that the manuscript tradition compels one to admit three corresponding archetypes. He proposes to identify these three archetypes with Cassiodorus' three manuscripts. He sees confirmation for this in the fact that our manuscripts of these homilies carry *capitula* and *tituli*, the use of which was recommended by Cassiodorus. In addition, certain passages bristling with heresies are omitted in certain classes of manuscripts, which proves that in the archetypes they were indicated as dangerous. Now, Cassiodorus takes care to say: "In operibus eiusdem Origenis, quantum transiens invenire praevalui, loca quae contra regulas Patrum dicta sunt, achresimi repudiatione signavi."[46] This is proof that Cassiodorus' three manuscripts, far from having disappeared, are the archetypes of our entire manuscript tradition of these commentaries.

For the Song of Songs, Rufinus' translation assumes a Campanian archetype, while Jerome's translation assumes a Roman archetype. But the same monk who corrected Rufinus' translation interpolated Jerome's translation. Baehrens assumes with reason that the conjunction of these two traditions

[45] See Baehrens, *Ueberlieferung und Textgeschichte*, chap. 6: "History of the Texts of the Homilies on the Octateuch and of the Homilies and Commentaries on the *Canticum*." See also the introductions to his editions of Origen, vols. 2 and 8 in the collection of the Griechischen christlichen Schriftsteller.

[46] Cass. *Inst.*, p. 14, 26ff.

took place at Vivarium, since Cassiodorus had been in contact with both Eugippius and Pope Agapetus.[47] The correction was, in my opinion, the work of the scribe at Vivarium who wrote the first twenty-eight quaternions of Vat. Lat. 5704, which contained these translations by Jerome and Rufinus. This hypothesis seems to me confirmed by the fact that traces of Vivarian origin have been able to be found in a manuscript of the end of the sixth century or the beginning of the seventh, containing this translation of Jerome's.[48]

But how did this dispersal of the Cassiodorian archetypes take place? Baehrens observes that, with the seventh century, manuscripts of these translations of Origen appeared in France and assumes, if Beer's theory is correct, that Bobbio was the intermediary.[49] Neither he nor Beer, however, discovered the least indication to justify this theory insofar as it concerns Origen. On the other hand, we have proof that the Cassiodorian translation of Epiphanius of Cyprus, like the translation of the *Codex encyclius*, passed through the library of the Lateran, where it was still preserved at the end of the eighth century. In fact, Pope Adrian I, in a communication addressed to Charlemagne in 791 on the subject of the quarrel about images, quotes a lengthy passage from it with the express mention: "Sancti Epiphanii episcopi Cypri proferimus expositionem."[50] If one thinks that this translation was not disseminated, since no other writer quotes it, and that it does not appear in any catalogue of any medieval library and even now is preserved only in a manuscript of the sixth century,[51] one will be inclined to believe that Pope Adrian had in his library Cassiodorus' original text containing the two translations of Origen and Epiphanius. This indication agrees with those that we have drawn from Paris. Lat. 12.098 and from the Amiatinus. The *Codex encyclius* appeared in Rome at the close of the sixth century, the *codex grandior* in 678, the manuscript of Origen-Epiphanius at the end of the eighth century. It must have been, like the *codex grandior*, preserved in the Lateran since the seventh century, for, according to Baehrens, copies of these translations of Origen passed from Italy to France at this time. Moreover, our original of Ephipanius itself left Rome for France in the eleventh century, for it has some glosses

[47] Baehrens, *Ueberlieferung*, pp. 193–195.

[48] Cf. Olga Dobiache-Rojdestvensky, "Le codex Q. v. I. 6–10 de la Bibliothèque Publique de Léningrad," *Speculum* 5 (1930) 21–48. The numbering of the quaternions of this commentary (quaternions 28–32) offers, however, no reason for thinking that it is a detached fragment of Vat. Lat. 5704.

[49] Baehrens, *Ueberlieferung*, p. 195.

[50] Hadrianus, "Ad Carolum regem de imaginibus scriptum, quo confutantur illi qui synodum Nicenam secundam oppugnarunt," *Acta conciliorum* (in Hardouin collection, 4 [1714], col. 783 D = *MGH, Epist.* 5, 3, p. 24, 22). The entire passage occurs word for word under the rubrics 63–64 of Vat. Lat. 5704, fols. 42ᵛ–43ʳ.

[51] Garet (*PL* 70, 1117 note) mentions another one in the possession of Bigot. But this is a recent copy, belonging to the close of the sixteenth century, now Parisinus Graecus 3092.

in French Caroline script.[52] The Lateran, therefore, appears henceforth as the starting point of the dissemination of the Cassiodorian manuscripts.

D. The Corpus of the Commentaries on the Canonical Epistles and Laudunensis 96

Cassiodorus describes in the following manner the commentaries on the Canonical Epistles in his possession at Vivarium:

In epistulis autem canonicis Clemens Alexandrinus presbyter, qui et Stromatheus vocatur,—id est in Epistula sancti Petri prima, sancti Iohannis prima et secunda et Iacobi,—quaedam Attico sermone declaravit; ubi multa quidem suptiliter, sed aliqua incaute locutus est; quae nos ita transferri fecimus in Latinum, ut exclusis quibusdam offendiculis purificata doctrina eius securior potuisset hauriri. Sanctus quoque Augustinus Epistulam Iacobi apostoli solita diligentiae suae curiositate tractavit, quam vobis in membranacio codice scriptam reliqui. Sed cum de reliquis canonicis Epistulis magna nos cogitatio fatigaret, subito nobis codex Didymi Graeco stilo conscriptus in expositionem septem canonicarum Epistularum, Domino largiente, concessus est, qui ab Epiphanio viro disertissimo, Divinitate iuvante, translatus est. In Epistula vero prima beati Iohannis sanctus Augustinus decem sermonibus multa et mirabiliter de caritate disseruit.[53]

Augustine's commentary on the Epistle of James is lost, but the two Cassiodorian translations, one of Clement of Alexandria and the other of Didymus,[54] and Augustine's commentary on the Epistle of John are preserved. It is noteworthy that the manuscript tradition does not separate them.

The best manuscript, Laudunensis 96, dating in the end of the eighth or the beginning of the ninth century, carries on folio 1 recto the notice: "Hae insunt expositiones: in epistulis canonicis Apostolorum, id est Clementis episcopi Alexandrini, Didymi et sancti Augustini; et ceteri; caute lege et intellege, quia expulsi sunt de Roma."

There follow, folios 1 recto–9 verso, *Clementis Adumbrationes*; folios 10 recto–68 verso, Didymus *In Epistulis canonicis*.

These two commentaries originally filled eleven quaternions of which the seventh and eighth have disappeared, as well as several other leaves. The

[52] Folio 48ᵛ. Cf. Lowe's legend, *Cod. Lat. ant.*, on this manuscript. His number 5704 shows that it reached the Vatican shortly before the collection donated by Bobbio in 1618.

[53] Cass. *Inst.*, p. 29, 16–p. 30, 4.

[54] See the legends in the critical editions: *Clementis Alexandrini Adumbrationes in epistulas*, ed. Otto Staehlin (Griechischen christlichen Schriftsteller), vol. 3 (Leipzig 1909) 203–215, and *Didymi Alexandrini in Epistulas canonicas brevis enarratio*, ed. Zoepfl. It is admitted that Cassiodorus was mistaken in mentioning a commentary by Clement on Jude as being on John. K. Staab, "Die griechischen Katenenkommentare zu den katholischen Briefen," *Biblica* 5 (1924) 314–320, thinks with Zoepfl that the translation of the text as a whole was certainly made by Didymus, while, according to E. Klostermann, *Ueber des Didymus von Alexandrien in Epist. can. enarratio, Texte und Unters. zur Gesch. der altchristl. Lit.* n.s. 13, 2, Cassiodorus mistook a Greek catena for a commentary by Didymus.

notice in folio I recto denotes that they were originally followed by St. Augustine's commentary and several others.

The manuscript Berol. philol. 45 (1665), dating in the end of the twelfth or the beginning of the thirteenth century, bears the same marks:

folios I recto–6 recto, *Clementis Adumbrationes*;

folios 6 recto–37 verso, *Expositio Didymi carne caeci in Epist. canon.*;

folios 38 recto–185, Beda *Super Actus Apost. et Epist. canon.*

Vaticanus Lat. 6154, dating in the sixteenth century, contains likewise the *Adumbrationes Clementis* (folios 199–206) followed by Didymus' commentary on Jude (folios 206–209).

Finally, a catena preserved in Laurentianus plut. XVII, 17, dating in the eleventh century, and in the Oxford manuscripts Bodl. 64 (2094) and Laud. 110 (1242) contains glosses of these commentaries by Bede, Clement, Didymus, Augustine. The prologue to the Laurentianus states: "Quattuor fuerunt expositores super epistulas catholicas, scilicet Beda et Clemens et Didymus super unam Iacobi et II Petri et I Iudae; Augustinus tres Iohannis exposuit."

If one compares this manuscript tradition with Cassiodorus' notice, one must conclude that Augustine's commentary on the Epistle of James existed at Vivarium separately in a manuscript that was lost.[55] On the other hand, the Cassiodorian translations of Clement and Didymus, and Augustine's commentary on the Epistle of John, must have been bound together in the Vivarian original. It was only later that Bede's commentary was added. Now, the notice in the Laudunensis, "Caute lege et intellege, quia expulsi sunt de Roma," can have one meaning only. It is not, as has been thought,[56] a warning to read these writers with distrust because Rome had condemned them. No one in the Middle Ages could be unaware that Augustine was, in the eyes of the Roman Church, the most authorized representative of orthodoxy. I see in the statement on the contrary an invitation to read these commentaries attentively, because they come from Rome. Now, here is another translation of Didymus that also seems to stem from a Vivarian manuscript that probably left Rome at the beginning of the ninth century.

E. The Trinitarian Corpus and Vaticanus Latinus 314

This manuscript written in 1439 is a late copy,[57] but it has a special interest. It is the only manuscript to have transmitted the text of Nicetas' smaller

---

[55] The mention of this commentary could have been added by Cassiodorus at the time of the second edition. On these additions, cf. Van de Vyver, "Cassiodore et son œuvre," 275ff. It was this addition relating to the Epistle of John that must have led to the mistaken correction in the preceding paragraph: "Iacobi" for "Iudae."

[56] Zahn, *Forschungen* (above, chap. 2 sec. 3 n. 129) 3, p. 141.

[57] I identify it with the manuscript described in the catalogue of Nicholas V, published by Muentz and Fabre, *La bibliothèque du Vatican au XVe s. d'après des documents inédits,* Bibliothèque des écoles françaises d'Athènes et de Rome, fasc. 48 (Paris 1887) 61.

treatises that Cassiodorus designates under the title *De fide*.[58] These treatises, which are followed in the manuscript by several of St. Ambrose's works, are preceded by these texts:

folio 1 verso, Didymus *De Spiritu sancto* (translated by St. Jerome);

folio 25 recto, Ambrose *De Trinitate* in 9 books;

folio 151 recto, Pascasius the Deacon *De Spiritu sancto*;

folio 169 recto, Nicetas *De ratione fidei*;

De Spiritus sancti potentia;

De diversis appellationibus I. C. convenientibus.

Cardinal Mercati has already noted the relationship of this manuscript with the manuscript that was described under number 17 in the catalogue of the library at Pomposa and edited in 1093 [59] and that was still there in 1459:[60]

Liber Didymi de Spiritu sancto;

XII libri Ambrosii de Trinitate;

Fulgentii de Trinitate liber 1;

Eiusdem de creaturis a Deo de nihilo creatis liber I;

Nicetae episcopi de ratione fidei I;

Eiusdem de Spiritus sancti potentia liber I;

Eiusdem de diversis appellationibus Domino nostro I. C. convenientibus.

These two manuscripts posit in fact a common archetype, necessarily prior to the eleventh century, that contained in this order Didymus' *De Spiritu sancto*, Ambrose's *De Trinitate*,[61] and Nicetas' three shorter works. This archetype, probably Italian, must itself go back to an original at Vivarium. In fact, Cassiodorus states that his *De fide* by Nicetas is a very short text intended for monks who wanted information very quickly on the three persons of the Trinity.[62] Now, the three short works in the Vaticanus that refer to the three persons of the Trinity and the first of which is entitled *De ratione fidei* are believed to be three *excerpta* from the third of the *Libelli instructionis*, entitled *De fide unicae maiestatis*, by Nicetas of Remesiana.[63] Cassiodorus adds that he had Nicetas' text bound with St. Ambrose's books on the Trinity, addressed to the Emperor Gratian.[64] These indications correspond remarkably

[58] Cass. *Inst.*, ed. Mynors, p. 53, 26.

[59] Cf. G. Mercati, "Il catalogo della biblioteca di Pomposa," *Studi e documenti di storia e diritto* 17 (1896) 163, and "Appunti su Niceta ed Aniano traduttore di S. Giovanni Crisostomo," *Studi e testi* 5 (1901) 137.

[60] Cf. Dom M. Inguanez, "Inventario di Pomposa del 1459," *Bollettino del Bibliofilo* 2 (1920) 173–184. Number 113 of this inventory is "Didimus de Spiritu sancto."

[61] It was probably through a confusion with the twelve books of Hilary's *De Trinitate* (number 26 in the catalogue for 1093) that the compiler of this catalogue of Pomposa assigned twelve books to Ambrose's *De Trinitate*.

[62] Cass. *Inst.*, p. 53, 24–26.

[63] Gennadius *De viris inlustribus*, chap. 22.

[64] Cass. *Inst.*, p. 54, 2–3: "qui voluminibus sancti Ambrosii sociatus est, quos ad Gratianum principem destinavit."

with the *incipit* of the Vaticanus, folio 25 recto: "Incipit beatissimi Ambrosii ad Gratianum piissimum et Christianissimum imperatorem de Trinitate liber primus: lege feliciter," a title that denotes actually the five books *De fide*, the *De incarnatione*, and the three books *De Spiritu sancto*. Lastly, the statement in which Cassiodorus advises the monks of Vivarium, if they want to learn about the Trinity, "to read Didymus, to read St. Ambrose and all the other Fathers,"[65] shows that he possessed Didymus' *De Spiritu sancto* and that this treatise preceded, in all likelihood, Ambrose's *De Trinitate* and Nicetas' *De fide*. There is scarcely any doubt, it appears, that the manuscripts presenting this sequence go back to a Vivarian original,[66] but what can the intermediary be? A clue is furnished by the Cologne manuscript XXXIII, dating in the ninth century, that contains, under the name of "Iohannes episcopus," Nicetas' *De Spiritus sancti potentia* following Ambrose's *De fide*.[67] This manuscript forms part of those that Archbishop Hildebald of Cologne had copied on originals sent from Rome to Charlemagne by Pope Leo III.[68] There is therefore every possibility that the Vivarian archetype of our three manuscripts of Nicetas passed through the pontifical library of the Lateran before the ninth century.

F. The Corpus on Church History and Bambergensis B IV 21

Bambergensis B IV 21, which seems to have experienced the same vicissitudes as the Bambergensis of the *Institutiones*,[69] must equally hold our

---

[65] Cass. *In Ps.* 202 B: "legant Didymum, legant beatum Ambrosium ceterosque Patres."

[66] Note that Paris. Lat. 8907, dating in the sixth century and containing two books of St. Ambrose's *De fide*, also shows signs of Vivarian origin. In fact, Cassiodorus (*Inst.*, p. 53, 18) advised the reading, in succession, of Hilary's thirteen books of the *De Trinitate* and Ambrose's *De Trinitate*, of which the *De fide* formed the first part. Now, this manuscript contains in sequence, with a continuous numbering of the quaternions: Hilary's twelve books of the *De Trinitate* (fols. 3^r–259^r), Hilary's *Contra Auxentium*, reckoned as the thirteenth book in the running heads (fols. 259^r–263^v), Hilary's *De synodis* (fols. 263^v–297^v), and the first two books of Ambrose's *De fide* (fols. 298^r–336^r). Note also, in Paris. Lat. 2630, dating in the fifth century, which comes from St. Denis and contains Hilary's *De Trinitate* together with the *De synodis* reckoned as a thirteenth book, the *probatio pennae* in the margin at the foot of fol. 73^r, in a sixth-century hand: "Liber dictus est a libro, hoc est arbores corticis (*sic*) dento" = Cass. *Inst.*, p. 91, 5.

[67] Here is the exact sequence:
   fols. 2^r–28^v Rufinus *Commentum in Symbolum*;
   fols. 28^v–65^v Ambrose *De fide libri II*;
   fols. 65^v–100^v Faustinus *Liber de Trinitate sive de fide*;
   fols. 100^v–107^v (Nicetas) *De Spiritu sancto*, "Sequitur quid de tertia persona, id est sancto Spiritu, sentiam; pro captu mentis exponam . . ." (*PL* 52, 853 A).

[68] Cf. A. Decker, "Die Hildebold'sche Manuskriptensammlung des Kölner Domes," p. 242. He identifies our manuscript 33 with manuscript 72 in the catalogue of Hildebald's books. On this catalogue, see below, p. 397.

[69] Cf. Ludwig Traube, "Palaeographische Forschungen IV," *Abh. der kön. bayer. Akad. der Wissenschaften* (historische Klasse) 24, 1 (1904–1906), pp. 8 and 11.

attention. The script of this manuscript, for a long time disregarded because it was thought to be of the ninth century, is now recognized as a Benedictine script of the sixth century.[70] The manuscript contains the following works:

folios 1 recto–33 verso, Jerome *De viris inlustribus*;

33 verso–51 recto, Gennadius *De viris inlustribus*;

51 recto–79 verso, Augustine *De haeresibus*;

79 verso–95 recto, Augustine *Epistula ad Paulinum de cura pro mortuis gerenda*;

95 recto–136 verso, Augustine *Enchiridion*.

The relationship with Vivarium may be established as follows: the Jerome–Gennadius books are regarded in this manuscript as a single work, preceded by a common table of contents of 226 chapters, chapters 1–135 being by Jerome, chapters 136–226 by Gennadius. A separation is made by the notice: "Hucusque Hieronymus presbyter, abhinc Gennadius Massiliensis."[71] Now, Cassiodorus himself possessed these two works and had combined them into a corpus to facilitate the continuous reading of the text.[72] He likewise possessed at Vivarium Augustine's *De haeresibus*[73] and the *Enchiridion*.[74] In addition, Lowe has noted a striking identity of script between this Bamberg manuscript and Vaticanus Latinus 3375, which contains *excerpta* from Augustine made by Eugippius: the same script in the texts, the same script in the *marginalia* dating in the sixth century and denoting summaries, the same abbreviations.[75] Now, Cassiodorus states that he had at Vivarium these *excerpta* made by Eugippius.[76] May we not conceive that the Southern Italian scribe who in the sixth century copied this Vaticanus and this Bambergensis was a monk of Vivarium? Beer already noted the connection of the

[70] Cf. E. A. Lowe, "A List of the Oldest Extant Manuscripts of Saint Augustine with a Note on the Codex Bambergensis," *Miscellanea Agostiniana* (Rome 1930) 2, pp. 247–251.

[71] The separation between the two parts is likewise indicated in the course of the text, fol. 33[v], by the notice: "Hucusque Hieronymus, abhinc Gennadius presbyter Massiliensis ecclesiae subrogavit." A description of this manuscript may be found in the catalogue of the Bamberg manuscripts, by Leitschuh and Fischer, 1, p. 464.

[72] Cass. *Inst.*, ed. Mynors, p. 57, 2–10.

[73] *Ibid.*, p. 61, 15–21. Note the same sequence: Jerome and Gennadius and Augustine's *De haeresibus* in Vindobonensis 16 (6th/7th cent.). With regard to Vaticanus Reginensis 2077 (7th cent.), it intercalates, after Jerome-Gennadius, a small number of treatises (notably Prosper's *Chronicle*, which was also in Vivarium), but it adds, fol. 101: "Incipiunt nomina haeresum quarum etiam opiniones subteradnexae ab Augustino episcopo in hoc volumine congestae sunt: I Simoniani . . . XC Eutychianistae." This is the list of the chapters in the *De haeresibus*, increased by the last two chapters.

[74] Cassiodorus refers to it or quotes it *In Ps.* 44 C, 241 A, 272 B, 480 A, and *Complexiones* 332 A.

[75] Lowe, "A List" (above, n. 70), pp. 247–249, and *Codices Latini antiquiores* 1, number 16.

[76] Cass. *Inst.*, p. 62, 3–9. Note, in the margin of Vat. Lat. 3375 the sigla ⁙ and ⁂, which Cassiodorus commends in his *Commentary on the Psalms*.

Bambergensis with Vivarium and claimed, after Traube, that it had passed through Bobbio.[77] Lowe destroyed this legend. He showed that the glosses appealed to by Beer were written not in an Irish but in an Anglo-Saxon script, and must have been added at Fulda at the beginning of the ninth century.[78] Above all, he has rightly drawn attention to the gloss in folio 79 verso: "Nestoriana et Eutychiana haereses hic scriptus [sic] non sunt," the script of which belongs without any possible doubt in the Roman curia in the eighth century.[79] Thus this manuscript too, which so many indications designate as Vivarian, appeared at Rome in the eighth century and left the Eternal City at the beginning of the Carolingian Renaissance.

3. The Lateran and the Dispersal of Cassiodorian Translations

The corroborative evidence of these six unquestionably Vivarian manuscripts no longer gives us reason to believe with Cardinal Mercati that Cassiodorus' library disappeared without leaving any traces, or with Beer that it was preserved at Bobbio. All these manuscripts passed through the Lateran, whence they migrated, the *codex grandior* to England at the end of the seventh century, the three translations by Epiphanius to France at the end of the eighth century or the beginning of the ninth century, the Didymus-Ambrose-Nicetas and the Jerome-Gennadius-Augustine to Germany in the ninth or tenth century. It is to this circumstance that we are indebted for having preserved them. In fact, we know the sad fate of the Lateran Library. De Rossi showed that it disappeared during the troubles of the eleventh and twelfth centuries, and none of its manuscripts passed to the Vatican.[1] As there is not even a Roman catalogue prior to the thirteenth century, one is inclined to disregard the importance of this library, which was nevertheless, from the seventh century until the Carolingian dynasty, a principal center for commerce in manuscripts. De Rossi patiently assembled a number of indirect testimonies that enlighten us on the contents of this library and on the intellectual activity of which it was the focal point. The most specific feature of these texts is the summary that can be made of all the extracts from the Fathers quoted at the Council of the Lateran in 649. This catalogue indicates the bibliography, in the papal library, on the very special problem of monothelism that was discussed at this Council. Now, almost all the Latin writers

---

[77] Beer, "Bemerkungen," p. 94, and *Monumenta*, p. 24.

[78] Lowe, "A List" (above, n. 70), p. 251. Mercati classifies it likewise among the *Codici non bobbiesi*.

[79] Lowe, "A List," p. 250.

[1] J. B. De Rossi, "De origine, historia, indicibus scrinii et bibliothecae sedis apostolicae commentatio," *Codices Palatini Latini bibliothecae Vaticanae* 1 (1886), pp. I–CXXXII. This is a working over of his article, "La biblioteca della sede apostolica," *Studi e documenti di storia e diritto* 5 (1884) 317–380. See particularly chaps. 11 and 12.

quoted at the Council were likewise in the library at Vivarium, so that at this date this library was possibly incorporated with the Lateran Library.[2] The papal correspondence, besides, helps us to estimate that in the seventh and the eighth centuries the Lateran was the great source of manuscripts for the Catholic world. The popes had their manuscripts copied. They gave away their duplicates and sometimes even their originals, as is shown by the vicissitudes of the *codex grandior* that left Rome for Yarrow. At what point did their library become emptied through this procedure? The answer lies in a letter that Martin I addressed in the year 649 to Amandus, bishop of Maestricht, who had asked the Pope for relics and manuscripts: "Reliquias vero sanctorum, de quibus praesentium labor nos admonuit, dari praecepimus. Nam codices iam exinaniti sunt a nostra bibliotheca et unde ei dare nullatenus habuimus: transcribere autem non potuit quoniam festinanter de hac civitate regredi properavit."[3]

This constant, virtual pillaging to which the Lateran Library was then exposed explains, granted the hypothesis of the Vivarian library's having been absorbed into the Lateran, the rapid dispersal of certain Cassiodorian translations and encourages the hope of finding in the possessions of the oldest libraries in Europe manuscripts of Vivarian origin that would have disappeared had they remained in the Lateran until the library was destroyed. I shall note only the principal directions in which research may venture to be productive.

We know, from what has already been said of the Amiatinus, of the close connections between Rome and Yarrow. The Abbot Benedict made five trips to Rome, and Bede informs us that at each of his last three trips, in 671, 678, 684, he brought back collections of manuscripts that constituted the contents of his library.[4] The little that is known of these manuscripts makes one

---

[2] See the catalogue drawn up by De Rossi, "De origine," pp. LXVIII–LXXI, and the *Acta* of the Council in Mansi, *Conciliorum amplissima conlectio* 10:

    1071 B and 1979 E, Ambrosius *De sancto Spiritu ad Gratianum sermones tres* (= Cass. *Inst.*, p. 32, 20).

    1082 B, Ambrosius *In Lucam* (= Cass., p. 28, 6).

    1074 C, Augustinus *In Ioannem* (= Cass., p. 28, 7).

    1083 A and 1086 B, Augustinus *In Psalmos* (= Cass., p. 20, 18).

    1083 C, Augustinus *De civitate Dei* (= Cass., p. 54, 17).

    1086 C, Augustinus *De gratia novi testamenti ad Honoratum* (= Cass., p. 54, 22).

    1095 D, Hilarius *De Trinitate* (= Cass., p. 53, 18).

    1098 B, Leo *Epist. ad Leonem imperatorem* (= Cass. *In Ps.*, PL 70, 393 C).

    1098 B, Leo *Epist. ad Flavianum* (= Cass., 452 B and 509 C).

The question involves works so well known that their Vivarian origin is not at all certain, all the more so as the Lateran then contained a profusion of Greek texts that Cassiodorus did not possess at Vivarium.

[3] Mansi, *Conciliorum ampliss. conlectio* 10, 1186 E, quoted by De Rossi, "De origine," p. LXXIII.

[4] De Rossi, "De origine," p. LXXIV.

think of the library of Vivarium. One of these manuscripts was a *cosmographorum codex mirandi operis* that Ceolfrid then sold to the king for two parcels of land.[5] Was it not the corpus of the four cosmographers—Julius Honorius, Marcellinus, Dionysius Periegetes, and Ptolemy—that Cassiodorus boasted of possessing in his library?[6] A scrutiny of the matter on which Bede worked might lead to the same conclusions. In any case, the connection between one of his dedicatory letters and Cassiodorus' text is evident.[7] Not only had Bede read the *Institutiones*, but, like Cassiodorus, he possessed

---

[5] Bede *Vita quinque ss. abbatum* (*PL* 94, 725 A–B).

[6] Cass. *Inst.*, chap. 25: "Cosmographos legendos a monachis," ed. Mynors, p. 66.

[7] Cass. *Inst.*, p. 11, 9–p. 12, 27:

Huius (Octateuchi) principia sanctus Basilius Attico sermone lucidavit, quem Eustathius, vir disertissimus, ita transtulit in Latinum ut ingenium doctissimi viri facundiae suae viribus aequiparasse videatur: qui usque ad hominis conditionem novem libros tetendit ... Nam et pater Augustinus *contra Manichaeos* duobus libris disputans ita textum Genesis diligenter exposuit ut paene nihil ibi relinquere probaretur ambiguum ... Quos libros in codice supradicti Basilii, ut opinor, forsitan competenter adiunximus, ut textus praedicatae Genesis lucidius legentibus panderetur. Deinde sanctus Ambrosius, ut est planus atque suavissimus doctor, exinde sex libros eloquentiae suae more confecit, quos appellavit *Exameron*. De isdem principiis sanctus quoque Augustinus, disertus atque cautissimus disputator, duodecim volumina conscripsit, quae doctrinarum paene omnium decore vestivit, haec itaque vocavit *De Genesi ad litteram* ... Pari quoque modo duos libros vir praedictus effecit quibus titulum posuit: *Contra inimicum legis et prophetarum* ... In libris quoque *Confessionum* posterioribus tribus voluminibus de Genesis explanatione disseruit, confessus altitudinem rei quam totiens repetita expositione tractavit. Quaestiones etiam quae in voluminibus sacris ardua difficultate poterant operiri, libris septem necessaria nimis et syllogistica probatione declaravit ... Scripsit etiam *De modis locutionum* septem alios mirabiles libros.

Bede *Epist. ad Accam*, *PL* 91, 9 A–11 A; 94, 684 D–685 B:

De principio libri Genesis ... multi multa dixere, multa posteris ingenii sui monimenta reliquere, sed praecipue, quantum nostra pusillitas ediscere potuit, Basilius Caesariensis, quem Eustathius interpres de Graeco fecit esse Latinum, Ambrosius Mediolanensis, Augustinus Hipponensis episcopus, quorum primus libris novem, secundus vestigia eius sequens libris sex, tertius libris duodecim et rursum aliis duobus specialiter *adversum Manichaeos* descriptis prolixa legentibus doctrinae salutaris fluenta manarunt, completo in eis promisso Veritatis quo dicebat: "Qui credidit in me, sicut ait Scriptura, flumina de ventre eius fluent aquae vivae." E quibus Augustinus etiam in libris *Confessionum* suarum, in libris quoque quos *contra adversarium legis et prophetarum* eximie composuit, sed et in aliis sparsim opusculis suis non nullam eiusdem primordialis creaturae memoriam cum expositione congrua fecit. Verum quia haec tam copiosa, tam sunt alta ut vix, nisi a locupletioribus, tot volumina adquiri, vix tam profunda nisi ab eruditioribus valeant perscrutari, placuit vestrae sanctitati id nobis officii iniungere, ut de omnibus his velut de amoenissimis late florentis paradisi campis, quae infirmorum viderentur necessitati sufficere decerperemus. Nec segnior in exsequendo quae iubere es dignatus exstiti, quin potius statim perspectis Patrum voluminibus, conlegi ex his ac duobus in libellis distinxi quae rudem adhuc possent instruere lectorem.

Basil's *Hexaemeron* translated by Eustathius, Ambrose's *Hexaemeron*, and Augustine's *De Genesi ad litteram, Contra Manichaeos, Confessiones,* and *Contra adversarium legis et prophetarum*. Knowing that the holdings of Yarrow came from the Lateran and included several Vivarian manuscripts brought back from Rome, is it venturesome for us to think that Bede read at least certain of these works in Cassiodorian manuscripts or in copies of them?

If a study is made of the dissemination of certain Cassiodorian translations in the High Middle Ages, the rapidity of such a dispersal and the directions that it took also incline one to postulate the Lateran Library as the first focal point.

The translation of Josephus' *Antiquities* that Cassiodorus had his friends make in twenty-two books, including the *Contra Apionem*,[8] served historical studies until the end of the Middle Ages.[9] Now, Bede had it at hand, for he quotes it frequently.[10] It was with regard to a passage in Josephus that he refers to the diagram of the Tabernacle that Cassiodorus had had inscribed in his *codex grandior*. In all likelihood Bede's copy of Josephus carried therefore a reference by Cassiodorus to this diagram, and the hypothesis that Yarrow had received from the Lateran not only the *codex grandior* but an entire collection of Vivarian manuscripts is confirmed. Another of Josephus' manuscripts, now preserved in the Ambrosian Library, also deserves attention. This is a sixth-century papyrus that contains Cassiodorus' translation. As it comes from Bobbio, where, it seems, it already appears in the tenth-century catalogue,[11] and as Cassiodorus states that he possesses papyri in his library,[12] Beer has not failed to use it for his theory.[13] It is in fact one of those rare cases where the connection between Vivarium and Bobbio is plausible, although it is difficult to prove that we really have to do with the original. But while Beer assigned this manuscript to the pre-Columban holdings at Bobbio and assumed that all these contents had come straight from Vivarium to Bobbio at the beginning of the seventh century, I see in Bobbio one of the numerous points where some of the wreckage of Vivarium had landed, dispersed from the Lateran between the seventh and the ninth centuries.

The translation of Chrysostom's thirty-four homilies on the Epistle to the Hebrews that Cassiodorus had asked Mutianus[14] to make was widely

---

[8] Cass. *Inst.*, p. 55, 16–22; cf. G. Bardy, "Le souvenir de Josèphe chez les Pères," *RHE* 43 (1948) 179–191.

[9] Besides the five manuscripts noted by B. Niese in his edition of the *Ant. Iud.* (Berlin 1887), I, pp. xxviiff, there are a host of others. Cf. above, chap. 7 sec. 2 n. 91.

[10] Among others, *PL* 91: 92 D, 178 C, 774 D, 775 A and D. It is passage 775 A that combines the quotation from Josephus and the reference to Cassiodorus' diagram.

[11] Manitius, *Handschriften antiker Autoren*, s.v. Josephus.

[12] Cass. *Inst.*, p. 29, 2, "in chartaceo codice."

[13] Beer, *Monumenta*, p. 22.

[14] Cass. *Inst.*, p. 29, 11–15.

disseminated in Europe at the beginning of the Carolingian era.[15] Recently too there has even been found a seventh-century manuscript[16] of the translation. As the origin of this manuscript is not known, it cannot be of service in our research. But the oldest manuscript after that, Cologne XLI, dating in the beginning of the ninth century, carries the notice: "Codex sancti Petri sub pio patre Hildebardo archiepiscopo (scriptus)."[17] This notice helps to identify it with Chrysostom's commentary, translated into Latin, that appears in the catalogue of Hildebald's library. Now, this catalogue, a copy of which, made in the year 833, is preserved, is entitled: "Hic liber iussus a Wenilone episcopo Laudonense descriptus (est) ad opus domni Hildibaldi archiepiscopi et sacri Palatii capellani, de illis libris qui Roma venerunt et Domnus Apostolicus Leo Domno Karolo imperatori transmisit."[18] The conjunction of four persons—Wenilon II of Laon (799–814), Hildebald of Cologne (795–819), the Emperor Charlemagne (800–814), and Leo III (795–816)—informs us that between 800 and 814 a collection of manuscripts was sent by Leo III to Charlemagne and constituted the original contents of the library at Cologne. It was probably during his stay at Aix-la-Chapelle, from December 804 to January 805,[19] that Leo III brought back from Rome a certain number of archetypes that were immediately copied out. Among them was certainly the archetype of our manuscript of Mutianus and probably, as we have seen,[20] the archetype of our manuscripts of Didymus-Ambrose-Nicetas. But since, according to Hildebald's catalogue, Wenilon, the bishop of Laon, was concerned to know the contents of the manuscripts brought by Leo III, there is every likelihood that the Laudunensis 96 was copied on another of these archetypes. In fact, it may belong in the beginning of the ninth century. Its provenance is the library of the cathedral church of Laon. It contains the text of two other Cassiodorian translations and even the notice of its Roman origin. Lastly, the *Codex encyclius*, which was in Rome in the pontificate of Pelagius II and at Corbie in the ninth century, and the manuscript of Epiphanius of Cyprus,

---

[15] Cf. Eduard Riffenbach, "Die ältesten lateinischen Kommentare zum Hebräerbrief," *Forschungen zur Geschichte des neutestamentlichen Kanons* 8, 1 (Leipzig 1907), p. 11 n. 1. For the Carolingian period, this translation is mentioned in the catalogues of St. Riquier (831), St. Gall (9th cent.), and Lorsch (10th cent.), and it is preserved in the manuscripts of Verona 54 (52), Cues 46, and Paris. Lat. 1784, all of the 9th cent.

[16] E. A. Lowe, "An Uncial (Palimpsest) Manuscript of Mutianus in the Collection of A. Chester Beatty," *Journal of Theological Studies* 29 (1928) 29–33.

[17] The word *scriptus* was added by a tenth-century hand. The reference is of course to St. Peter of Cologne.

[18] Cf. Decker, "Die Hildebold'sche Manuskriptensammlung," p. 224. Chrysostom-Mutianus has the number 70 in this catalogue. Cf. also De Rossi, "De origine," p. LXXXIV.

[19] Cf. *Annales regni Francorum* and *Annales Mettenses priores*, ed. Kurze and Simson, anno 804.

[20] See above, p. 391.

which was in Rome in the eighth century and in France in the ninth,[21] are two Vivarian translations that appear to have belonged in the same collection. The second translation might even be not a copy but the Vivarian archetype sent by Leo III to Charlemagne.

Perhaps the Roman archetype of Mutianus also contained the translation by Rufinus of Origen's commentary on the Epistle to the Romans, for the two works are bound together in Ambrosianus A 135 inf., ninth/tenth century, and as Cassiodorus quotes them at no great interval from each other in the catalogue of his library,[22] we may assume that he had already had them bound together. But the fact that this Ambrosianus passed through Bobbio in no sense invalidates my hypothesis of a Roman archetype. In fact, we know that this manuscript did not reach Bobbio until the eleventh century, when a certain Dungal bequeathed his library to the monastery.[23] Then it certainly did not belong to the pre-Columban holdings.   •

Thus one may conjecture the Vivarian origin of a small number of the manuscripts mentioned by Beer, while rejecting his theory of a pre-Columban collection at Bobbio. For Bobbio, this collection consists, apart from the Josephus papyrus that has already been noted,[24] of a manuscript of Cassiodorus' speeches,[25] a manuscript of Gargilius Martialis,[26] a manuscript of Sacerdos;[27] for Verona, the manuscript of Cassiodorus' *Complexiones*,[28] a manuscript of Julius Honorius,[29] a manuscript of Facundus.[30] But the indications denoting Vivarian origin are not equally certain for all the manuscripts,

[21] See above, p. 387.

[22] Cass. *Inst.*, p. 29, 11 and p. 31, 1.

[23] The oldest catalogue of Bobbio (Becker, *Catalogi bibliothecarum antiqui*, p. 70) runs in fact as follows: "Item de libris quos Dungalus praecipuus Scottorum obtulit beatissimo Columbano . . . librum Origenis in Epistula ad Romanos unum, in quo habetur expositio Iohannis Constantinopolitani in Epistula ad Hebraeos." On the date of this legacy, cf. Theodor Gottlieb, "Ueber Handschriften aus Bobbio," *Zentralblatt für Bibliothekswesen* 4 (1887) 443, and Manitius, *Geschichte der latein. Lit. des Mittel.* 9, 2, 1, p. 374. On the other hand, Baehrens, *Ueberlieferung*, p. 157, insists that this legacy took place at the beginning of the tenth century. Note that the capitulary library of Beauvais also possessed a Chrysostom-Mutianus and an Origen *In Epist. Pauli ad Rom.* (now Florence, Laurentian Library, Ashburnham 13, and Manchester, J. Rylands Library, Latin 194), both of the 9th cent. Cf. Omont, "Recherches" (above, chap. 8 sec. 2 n. 32) 81–82; we have already seen above, p. 383, that this library possessed Cassiodorus' *Codex encyclius*.

[24] See above, p. 396.

[25] Ambrosianus G 58 sup. + Taurinensis A II 2**, 6th cent. Cf. Beer, *Monumenta*, p. 22.

[26] Neapolitanus IV A 8, 6th cent. (cf. Beer, "Bemerkungen," p. 88, and *Monumenta*, p. 21). Cassiodorus declares that he has Gargilius Martialis in his library, *Inst.*, p. 72, 1.

[27] Vindobonensis 16, 8th cent. (cf. Beer, "Bemerkungen," p. 103, and *Monumenta*, p. 25). Keil, *Grammatici Latini* 6, p. 421 note, has shown that this manuscript contains the ninety-eight schemata of Sacerdos' manuscript that Cassiodorus, *Inst.*, p. 96, 3 and 18, possessed in Vivarium.

[28] Veronensis 39 (37), 6th cent. (cf. Beer, "Bemerkungen," p. 99).

[29] Veronensis 2 (2), 6th/7th cent. (cf. Beer, "Bemerkungen," p. 90). Cassiodorus

and it would be hazardous to assert of any one of them that it is the Cassiodorian original. However, even if the Vivarian origin of all the manuscripts is admitted, that is no reason for returning to Beer's theory. In fact, not only did not all the manuscripts pass through Bobbio, as Beer thought,[31] but even with regard to those in Bobbio it is not known when they came into St. Columban's library and whether they came all together. I think that these Vivarian survivals of which traces are found at Yarrow, Cologne, Bamberg, as well as at Bobbio or Verona, have a common origin. This common origin is the Lateran Library, whence the popes, in the course of the seventh, eighth, and ninth centuries, dispersed the originals and multiplied the copies for the principal cultural centers of the Catholic world. Is proof required that even in the ninth century application was made to Rome when a copy of a Cassiodorian manuscript was desired? Two letters by Lupus of Ferrières are very suggestive:

Cassiodorus *Institutiones*:	Lupus of Ferrières *Ad Altsig abbatem*:	Lupus of Ferrières *Ad Benedictum III*:
p. 13, 13: Sanctus etiam Hieronymus uno volumine de libro Geneseos Hebraicas solvit propositas quaestiones ... De novo quoque Testamento fecit alterum librum, ubi quaestiones ad eandem legem pertinentes diligentissimus doctor enodavit.	Obnixe flagito ut Quaestiones beati Ieronimi quas, teste Cassiodoro, in vetus et novum Testamentum elaboravit, Bedae quoque vestri similiter Quaestiones in utrumque testamentum,	
p. 19, 8: Quem (Ieremiam) etiam sanctus Hieronymus viginti libris commentatus esse monstratur: ex quibus sex tantum nos potuimus invenire, residuos vero adhuc, Domino iuvante, perquirimus.	item memorati Ieronimi libros Explanationum in Ieremiam, praeter sex primos qui apud nos reperiuntur, ceteros qui sequuntur,	Commentarios beati Hieronimi in Ieremiam, post sextum librum usque in finem praedicti prophetae, per eosdem fratres nobis mitti deposcimus in codice reverendae vetustatis ...

(*Inst.*, p. 66, 11) declares that his library possesses Iulius Honorius. But Paris. Lat. 4808, 6th cent., which has, fol. 65ʳ, an *explicit* in the form of a grape cluster, similar to the one in the *Complexiones* described above, p. 370, could quite as well claim a Vivarian origin.

[30] Veronensis 53 (51), 6th cent. end (Beer took no account of it). Cassiodorus (*In Ps.* 994 A) asserts that his library possesses Facundus. Note also that this manuscript is, in Lowe's opinion (*Codices Latini antiquiores* 1: *The Vatican City*), by the same hand as Vaticanus Latinus 1322, which contains the *Acta* of the Council of Chalcedon. Now, Cassiodorus (*Inst.*, p. 35, 16 and p. 64, 12) states that he possesses these *Acta*.

[31] Mercati, *M. T. Ciceronis de re publica libri*, pp. 15 and 19, does not think that the Verona manuscripts come from Bobbio.

p. 104, 4: Libros autem praeterea Quintiliani In- Petimus etiam Tullium de duos Ciceronis de Arte stitutionum oratoriarum Oratore et XII libros Insti- rhetorica et Quintiliani XII libros XII per certissimos tutionum oratoriarum Institutionum *iudicavimus* nuntios mihi . . . dirigatis. Quintiliani, *qui uno nec in-* *esse iungendos, ut nec codicis*   *genti volumine continentur* *excresceret magnitudo* et utri-   . . . Patri intentione Donati que, dum necessarii fuerint,   commentum in Terentio parati semper occurrant.   flagitamus.

A comparison of these two letters[32] with the text of Cassiodorus is singularly instructive. Lupus of Ferrières observed, while reading Cassiodorus, that several works were missing or that he had only a defective text. To acquire these works, where would he apply? First of all, to Altsig, the abbot of York, because his monastery, close to Yarrow, had the possibility of possessing manuscripts of Bede, whose memory Lupus of Ferrières recalled. Failing to receive all the manuscripts requested, he applied some years later, around 856/857, to the pope himself, as though he had more hope of acquiring the books that had been in Cassiodorus' library. As a matter of fact, it was an original manuscript of Cassiodorus that he requested. To be specific, the "not so bulky" manuscript in which Cassiodorus had had Cicero and Quintilian bound together:[33] "qui uno nec ingenti volumine continentur." Lupus of Ferrières knew then even at this period that to secure the manuscripts of Cassiodorus it was necessary to apply in the region where Bede worked, or, with still more certainty, to the Lateran Library. It will be less surprising if one reflects that some years before, in 849, he was able himself to explore this library when he stayed in Rome with Leo IV.[34]

[32] Lupus of Ferrières *Epist.* 87 *ad Altsig abbatem* (ed. Léon Levillain, 2, pp. 78–80) and *Epist.* 100 *ad domnum Apostolicum* (ed. Levillain, 2, p. 122).

[33] He is mistaken besides in thinking that the *Ciceronis de arte rhetorica* mentioned by Cassiodorus *Inst.*, p. 104, 5, denotes the *De oratore*, whereas it refers, as we have seen above, p. 346, to the *De inventione*. This error should not surprise us; for Lupus, while at Fulda, thought that the notation in Eginhard's catalogue *Ciceronis de rhetorica* could denote equally the *De inventione* or the *De oratore* (*Epist.* 1 *ad Einhardum*, ed. Levillain, 1, p. 8). He ended by obtaining the *De oratore*, which he copied in Harleianus 2736 (cf. C. H. Beeson, *Lupus of Ferrières as Scribe and Text-critic: A Study of His Autograph Copy of Cicero's De oratore*, Cambridge, Mass., The Med. Acad. of Amer. 1930), and the *De inventione* that he revised from Paris. Lat. 7774 A (cf. Sister L. Meagher, *The Gellius Manuscript of Lupus of Ferrières*, Chicago 1937, p. 11). Note also that Rabanus Maurus, who was Lupus' teacher at Fulda, was already unsuccessfully searching for Jerome's Books 7–20 on Jeremiah and Bellator's commentary on Wisdom (cf. *MGH, Epistulae* 5, 443, 9 and 426, 12); that is, two works mentioned by Cassiodorus (*Inst.*, p. 19, 8 and p. 24, 23). It seems that Cassiodorus erroneously accepted the existence of those Books 7–20 of Jerome's (cf. Baehrens, p. 190 n. 1).

[34] It should be noted that on his return from Rome Lupus quotes John Chrysostom in the Cassiodorian translation of Mutianus (Lupus *Epist.* 78 *ad domnum regem*, ed. Levillain, p. 34 = Mutianus, *PG* 63, 263 *ad finem*). Moreover, in *Letter* 95, which antedates 857 but

It is then possible to shed some light on a problem that is very obscure, but essential for the history of culture. The problem is the manner in which the ancient writers have been transmitted to us. Viewed from the angle of Vivarium, the question was as follows: does the fact that most of the books assembled by Cassiodorus are preserved prove that Vivarium was tremendously active in preserving them, or on the contrary had no participation therein, if they were preserved despite the total destruction of this library? The preceding researches show that it is not necessary to think, as Cardinal Mercati did, that the library at Vivarium disappeared without leaving any trace. Nor, as Beer's theory led one to believe, that we are indebted to Vivarium and Bobbio for almost all our manuscripts in uncials. Speaking practically, certainty of Vivarian archetypes can be attained only for the Amiatinus, for a considerable portion of the Latin tradition of Origen, for the Cassiodorian translations, and for a few other manuscripts.

It appears then, contrary to the hitherto held view, that Cassiodorus' influence was more weighty for the preservation of Christian literature than for that of the profane writers. But these indications are particularly valuable in informing us of the ways in which these works were preserved. It must be admitted that from the seventh century on, when the Lateran Library was established,[35] the popes possessed a considerable proportion of the manuscripts of Vivarium, at least those manuscripts containing Cassiodorian translations. How had they acquired them? This is the most difficult point to establish. I shall not be inclined to formulate hypotheses like Beer's hypothesis that a Lombard invader in the seventh century had destroyed Vivarium

---

whose terminus post quem is unknown (cf. Levillain, "Etude sur les lettres de Loup de Ferrières," *Bibliothèque de l'école des Chartes* 63 [1902] 81), Lupus loans Heribold a "codicem *adnotationum* beati Hieronymi in Prophetas, necdum a me lectum," insisting on its return as speedily as possible. Levillain, in his edition, 2, p. 111 n. 1, cannot identify it. I am of the opinion that it is Cassiodorus' manuscript, *Inst.*, p. 18, 15: "ex omni Prophetarum codice . . . sanctus Hieronymus primum *adnotationes* faciens . . . breviter explanavit, quas vobis in *adnotato* nuper codice, Domino praestante dereliqui. In quo botryonum formulae ex ipsis *adnotationibus* forsitan competenter adpositae sunt." If Lupus did not have time to read this manuscript, it was because he had just brought it from Rome. If he asked for its speedy return, it was because while he was in Rome a delay in the loan prevented him from copying it. Thus, this was probably a Vivarian manuscript, and the letter would date in 849 or 850.

[35] According to De Rossi's "De origine," p. LXVII, it was the period when the *bibliotheca* became distinct from the *scrinium*. According to H. I. Marrou, "Autour de la bibliothèque du pape Agapit," pp. 167–168, Agapetus' library could also have been incorporated at this time. Finally, Philippe Lauer, "Les fouilles du Sancta Sanctorum au Latran," *MEFR* 20 (1900) 279–287, found the remains of this library, notably a very beautiful fresco representing St. Augustine (cf. also Lauer, *Le palais de Latran* [Paris 1911] p. 97 fig. 36). Wilpert, *Die römischen Mosaiken und Malereien* (above, chap. 7 sec. 1 n. 37) 1, pp. 148–153 and pl. 140, 1–2, thinks that this fresco may go back to the age of Gregory the Great.

and saved its manuscripts by transferring them to Bobbio. Do we not know that the *Codex encyclius* was in the Lateran since the time of Pelagius II, and the *Historia ecclesiastica tripartita*, translated by Epiphanius at Cassiodorus' bidding, since the time of Gregory the Great?[36] Cassiodorus himself could have sent a copy of his translations to the pope, who was generally perturbed by the Greek texts that were called upon in the East in the theological quarrels. After Cassiodorus' death, the monks who in 598 brought from Gregory the Great the petition of the *monasterium Castellense* against the encroachments of John, bishop of Scyllacium,[37] could have, in the usual manner, supported their petition with gifts of some manuscripts. In conclusion, Augustine, bishop of Scyllacium, who came to the Lateran Council in 649,[38] could have brought to Rome other Vivarian originals, particularly if, as is probable, his predecessors or he himself had previously despoiled Cassiodorus' monastery. The popes, in their turn, dispersed these texts throughout the Catholic world by sending out either copies or even the originals. This task of diffusion that began with the seventh century seems to have been especially advantageous for the libraries of Bobbio and Yarrow, which had recently been established. But in the ninth century too it was to the Lateran that Hildebald of Cologne or Lupus of Ferrières appealed with a view to obtaining copies of Cassiodorian archetypes. Thanks to the dissemination of these archetypes, out of the eleven translations commissioned by Cassiodorus at least seven are preserved.[39] Thus, during the obscure lapse of time that separated the end of Antiquity from the Carolingian Renaissance, at the

[36] Gregory the Great *Epist.* 7.31, ed. Hartmann, p. 479, 20 and n. 4. It is in fact evident that, if Gregory mistakenly attributed to Sozomen a statement of Socrates, it was because, ignorant after all of Greek as he was, he read them in the Cassiodorian translation, *Hist. trip.* 5.39, where the text of Socrates was followed by a fragment of Sozomen. The *Tripartite History* was still in the Lateran in 865, for it was from this that Pope Nicholas I extracted the passage that he quoted under the name of "Theodoritus historiographus," *MGH, Epist.* 6.4, p. 481, 18ff.

[37] Cf. Gregory the Great *Epist.* 8.32 (ed. Hartmann, *MGH, Gregorii I papae registrum epistularum* 2, pp. 33–34).

[38] Mansi, *Conciliorum ampliss. conlectio* 10, 1167 A.

[39] In chap. 7 sec. 1 n. 38 will be found the list of the translations executed under Cassiodorus' order. The only translations lost are those of the works of Gaudentius *De musica* (by Mutianus); Chrysostom *In Actus apost. hom.* 55 (by various collaborators, principally Mutianus); Didymus *In Proverbia* (by Epiphanius) and Origen *In I–II Esdrae hom.* 2 (by Bellator). However, Dom de Bruyne, *Les anciennes traductions latines des Macchabées*, Anecdota Maredsolana, vol. 4 (1932), pp. XLV–XLIX and LVII, has shown that one of the ancient translations of Maccabees, preserved in Ambrosianus E 26 inf., was probably by Bellator, who, on Cassiodorus' testimony, *Inst.*, p. 26, 24 and p. 27, 19, wrote for Vivarium a *Commentary on Maccabees in Ten Books*.

The translation of Didymus' *Commentary on Proverbs* is perhaps the one that Th. Peltanus, *Catena Graecorum Patrum in Proverbia Salomonis* (Antwerp 1614) 6ff, edited from a lost manuscript.

moment when Greek culture could have disappeared in the West, Vivarium and the Lateran Library preserved what was considered indispensable to the clergy. If the monks of Vivarium did not help in propagating the treasures of Hellenism that Cassiodorus had placed at their service, at least they themselves helped in saving them for future ages.

4. Vivarium and Greek Physicians

There was, however, one profane discipline that was continuously studied and practiced. That was the discipline of medicine. Not only did the library at Vivarium preserve some major texts, but these texts served as the basis of a medical education that persisted through the darkest centuries in the monasteries of Southern Italy.

Cassiodorus describes in these terms the medical books that he possessed and consulted:

Quod si vobis non fuerit Graecarum litterarum nota facundia, in primis habetis *Herbarium* Dioscoridis, qui herbas agrorum mirabili proprietate disseruit atque depinxit; post haec legite Hippocratem atque Galienum Latina lingua conversos, id est *Therapeutica* Galieni ad philosophum Glauconem destinata, et *Anonymum* quendam, qui ex diversis auctoribus probatur esse conlectus, deinde Caeli Aureli *de medicina* et Hippocratis *de herbis et curis* diversosque alios medendi arte compositos, quos vobis in bibliothecae nostrae sinibus, Deo auxiliante, reliqui.[1]

All these books that he lists are Latin books, but most of them are translations from the Greek. The notice consists of two distinct parts. In the first part an illustrated Latin Dioscorides is mentioned, in which the herbs are reproduced. Three ancient Latin translations of Dioscorides are known.[2] One, entitled *Liber medicinae ex herbis femininis numero LXXI*, is a very free adaptation, without diagrams.[3] It does not correspond to Cassiodorus' description. A second translation, which was composed before the fifth century, is illustrated, but the manuscript tradition, which goes back to the seventh century, assigns it unanimously to Apuleius.[4] Only the third translation, dating in the sixth century, to judge from the language and the age of the manuscripts, and

---

[1] Cass. *Inst.*, ed. Mynors, p. 78, 25.

[2] Cf. H. Moerland, review of Mihàescu *Dioscoride latino* (below, n. 5), *Gnomon* 15 (1939) 222–224.

[3] Ed. H. F. Kaestner, *Hermes* 31 (1896) 578–636.

[4] Ed. Howald and Sigerist, *CML* 4 (Leipzig and Berlin 1927). The editors, p. IX, are inclined to identify it with the translation in Vivarium. It is usually preceded in the manuscripts by Antonius Musa's *De herba vettonica* and followed by Sextus Placitus' *De animalibus*. On the magnificent illustrations, cf. J. H. Hermann, *Die frühmittelalterlichen Handschriften des Abendlandes* (Leipzig 1923) 8ff, and G. Swarzenski, "Mittelalterliche Kopien einer antiken medizinischen Bilderhandschrift," *Jahrb. des kaiserlich. deutschen archäologischen Instituts* 17 (1902) 45–53.

illustrated,[5] can then be identified with the Dioscorides mentioned by Cassiodorus. But there is no assurance that it was transmitted by Vivarium.

More interesting is the second part of the medical notice. It denotes, unless I am mistaken, a single volume: the medical corpus established by Cassiodorus, as we know that he had established a corpus of grammar, rhetoric, or dialectic. He designates it at first in a vague form: "Hippocratem atque Galienum Latina lingua conversos." Then, perhaps in a later edition, he specifies the contents. These specifications are such that they should help us to discover a similar sequence in the manuscript tradition, if the corpus has not disappeared.

The work that Cassiodorus specifies with the utmost precision is the translation of Galen's *Therapeutica* addressed to the philosopher Glauco. Such a translation, and the only one too, was transmitted by the manuscripts, in two books corresponding to the two Greek books of Galen's *Therapeutica*. But, in the majority of the Carolingian manuscripts, to this original nucleus were added four other books transmitted in a fixed order, so that the general effect appeared as a collection of six books entitled: Galen's *Therapeutica*.[6] This collection itself served as the basis for a more ample compilation of the eleventh century, a work by the eminent physician Garioponto of Salerno.[7]

The collection that appears in the Carolingian manuscripts could not have been assembled except for the fact that the sequence of the works that were recopied remained quite unchanged. But the texts comprising Books 3–6 are not by Galen. In the best manuscripts the last two books are not numbered and appear to be independent of Galen's work. Book 5 is attributed to a certain Aurelius, Book 6 to a certain Scolapius.[8] Actually, as Daremberg has shown,[9] they are extracts from the *De morbis acutis* and the *De febribus* by

[5] Ed. Hofmann, Auracher, and Stadler, *Romanische Forschungen* 1 (1883); 10 (1899); 11 (1901); 13 (1902); 14 (1904), and ed. Mihàescu, *Dioscoride latino, Materia medica*, 1 (Jassy 1938) from MSS Monac. Lat. 337 (Beneventine); Paris. Lat. 9332 (fols. 243–321), and Bernensis Lat. A 91 frag. 7. Cf. Lowe, *Scriptura Beneventana*, pl. XLII, and "Membra disiecta," *RB* 43 (1931), where he shows that the Paris and Berne manuscripts are fragments of the same corpus that originally contained, in sequence: Oribasius, *Synopsis medica*; Alexander the medical writer, *Therapeuticon*; Dioscorides, *De materia medica*.

[6] The oldest representative of the collection in six books appears to be Vindob. Lat. 68, 10th cent., fols. 1ʳ–72ʳ (the first three books mutilated; cf. Lowe, *Scriptura Beneventana*, pl. L); in Vat. Barb. 160, 10th/11th cent., fols. 88ʳ–112ᵛ, the text of Book 4 being omitted, Books 5 and 6 are numbered 4 and 5.

[7] Cf. S. de Renzi, *Storia documentata della scuola medica di Salerno* (2nd ed., Naples 1857) 173.

[8] MSS Casin. 97, 9th/10th cent., fols. 109–199; Bruxellensis 1343–1350, 12th cent., fols. 54ᵛ–105ᵛ. In Augiensis 120, 9th/10th cent., fols. 18ʳ–95ᵛ, the names of the authors are not indicated.

[9] Aurelius *De acutis passionibus*, ed. C. Daremberg, *Janus, Zeitschrift für Gesch. und Literatur der Medizin*, vol. 2, 3 (1847), p. 5 of the offprint. To his proof must be added the fact that in Vindocinensis 109, 11th cent., fols. 66ʳ and 70ᵛ there appear in this part of the

Coelius Aurelianus. The conjunction in the same collection of Galen's *Therapeutica*, in translation, and a medical treatise attributed to Aurelius but excerpted from Coelius Aurelianus is sufficient proof that this compilation stems from the Cassiodorian corpus. It explains Cassiodorus' surprising notice: "Caeli Aureli de medicina." This was because his corpus had already mistakenly given a compilation of Coelius Aurelianus' works the name of *Aurelius*.

From this fact, it must be possible to identify the other works of the collection with the works mentioned in the Cassiodorian notice. The "*Anonymus . . . ex diversis auctoribus . . . conlectus*" that appeared in Cassiodorus' corpus between the *Therapeutica ad Glauconem* (Books 1–2) and the extracts from Coelius Aurelianus (Books 5–6) would have to be identified with Book 3 or Book 4 of the Carolingian collection. But Book 4, which is an *epitome* of fifteen chapters of Book 2 of Theodorus Priscianus' *Euporista*,[10] must have been introduced at a late date into this collection, for it is lacking in certain manuscripts.[11] And in the Brussels manuscript it is not the *epitome* that comes before Aurelius, but the complete text of Theodorus Priscianus.[12] This is an indication that the text of Theodorus Priscianus did not appear in the original compilation. It was inserted when the collection was already completed, and was abridged only later, to form Book 4.

There remains Book 3, the sources of which are unknown. It is an anonymous *epitome*, comprising some eighty chapters.[13] It discusses diseases one by one, each followed by the appropriate treatment, beginning with cephalalgia and concluding with paralysis.[14] This *epitome* is very old, for it already appears in a Munich fragment of the seventh century.[15] It is essentially a collection of

collection extracts from Scolapius under the title: "de secundo libro Aurelii." This is proof that the name Scolapius (= Aesculapius) is fictitious and not original. Note also that in Augiensis 120, which appears to have best preserved the original arrangement of the collection, there are, following Aurelius-Scolapius, genuine fragments of the *Medicinales responsiones* by Coelius Aurelianus (ed. Rose, *Anecdota* 2, pp. 183–225). So Cassiodorus' *De medicina Caeli Aureli* was a compilation of several of Coelius Aurelianus' works.

[10] Theodorus Priscianus *Euporiston libri III*, ed. V. Rose (Leipzig 1894), p. XIII.

[11] See above, n. 6, for Vat. Barb. 160.

[12] Folios 1ᵛ–52ᵛ. Cf. Daremberg (above, n. 9), p. 10.

[13] The number varies slightly with the manuscripts: 83 chapters in Casin. 97 (according to the list of chapters in fol. 90); 80 chapters in Vindoc. 109.

[14] Casin. 97, pp. 89ff (the conclusion of the book is missing, as the eighth quaternion has been torn off); Vindoc. 109, fols. 35ᵛ–50ᵛ; Vat. Barb. 160, fols. 76ᵛ–88ʳ.

[15] Cf. E. Landgraf, *Ein lateinisches medizinisches Fragment Pseudo-Galens* (Progr. Ludwigshafen 1895). He does not mention the catalogue number, but gives facsimiles of this fragment. The *epitome* was immediately preceded by Galen's *De pulsibus et urinis*, which in Casin. 97, pp. 23–33, precedes the *Therapeutica ad Glauconem* instead of following it. I have verified the identification of these fragments that was suggested to Landgraf by Rose. As a matter of fact, fol. 5 of Landgraf's fragment coincides with fol. 38ʳ of Vindoc.

medical prescriptions and consists of a kind of abridgment of *Dynamidia*.[16] Suedhoff had already suspected, from the title alone, that Cassiodorus' "*Anonymus* . . . ex diversis auctoribus . . . conlectus" must have denoted a collection of medical prescriptions. He proposed to identify it with the *De concordantia Hippocratis, Galeni et Sorani* that appears in several old manuscripts.[17] This identification has no basis, for many other collections of medical prescriptions of the High Middle Ages can just as well claim to be Cassiodorus' collection.[18] The Cassiodorian anonymous writer can be recognized from the fact that he was copied in the manuscripts between the *Therapeutica ad Glauconem* and the *Aurelius*, or at least bound in with their manuscript tradition. Now, this is the case with the *Dynamidia* that in Augiensis 120 immediately precedes the *Aurelius*.[19] Later copies of the *Dynamidia*, but bound in with the manuscript tradition of the Cassiodorian corpus and apparently revisions of the *Dynamidia* of the Augiensis, indicate the possible title of Cassiodorus' anonymous author, or even go back to him indirectly.[20]

---

109 (chap. 10 of the *epitome*): "Algema, hoc est tumor vel fervor; scleroma, hoc est duritia; empneumatosis, id est inflatio; anorexia, id est fastidium; paralysis, id est stomachi contractio; emetos, hos est vomitum; apostasis vel apostema, id est conlectio; elcosis, id est ulceratio."

[16] Vindoc. 109, fol. 40rb: "in *dinamidiis* legimus"; fol. 43ra: "sicut in *dinamidiis* habetur"; fol. 48ra: "dabis autem tyriacam aut filonium vel cetera quae in *dinamidiis* huic causae necessaria inveneris"; fol. 48va: "Trociscum Faustiniani sic est in *dinamidiis*"; fol. 48vb: "in *dinamidiis* vero."

[17] K. Suedhoff, "Eine Verteidigung der Heilkunde aus den Zeiten der Mönchsmedizin," *Archiv für Gesch. der Medizin* 7 (1913) 236. This treatise has been edited by H. E. Sigerist, "Studien und Texte zur frühmittelalterlichen Rezeptliteratur," *Studien zur Gesch. der Medizin* 13, pp. 17–20, from Harleianus 5792, 7th cent., fols. 273v–276v. It appears also in Sangall. 752, 10th cent., pp. 181–326, and Paris. Lat. 11218, 9th cent., fols. 48v–57v.

[18] For example, the *De herbis Galieni, Apulei et Chironis* (and not *Ciceronis*; cf. Rose, *Anecd.* 2, p. 122) in these manuscripts: Sangall. 762, pp. 72–137; Paris. Lat. 11219, fol. 207r; Vat. Barb. 160, fol. 267. Or still better, the treatise in Paris. Lat. 11219, fol. 104r, the *incipit* of which recalls Cassiodorus' caption. In addition, Sigerist (above, n. 17) published seven collections of pre-Salernian antidotes. Three more collections were published by J. Joerimann, *Frühmittelalterliche Rezeptarien* (diss. Zürich 1925).

[19] Augiensis 120, 9th/10th cent., fols. 1r–18r; edited by Sigerist (above, n. 17) 39–65. The *Therapeutica ad Glauconem*, which, in the archetype, must have preceded these *Dynamidia*, was not recopied in the Augiensis; for, from the number of quaternions, the beginning was not mutilated. The mention of fol. 15v: "Pannum quod invenit Gaidemari referendarius," is also an indication of origin.

[20] For instance, Vindoc. 109, fol. 98r: "Incipit liber dinamidii, id est farmaceuticon *diversis auctoribus* coartatum" (note in these *dinamidia*, fol. 114rb: "Cataputias ad tussem probatas et ad dissentericos domni Iohannis Calabrii," which may be an indication of Calabrian origin); Paris. Lat. 11219, fol. 104r: "Incipit liber medicinalis de omni corpore hominis Teraupetica (*sic*), hoc est *conlectum* ex libris multis philosophorum, specialiter a

Cassiodorus' notice also specifies that, in his corpus, Aurelius was followed by Hippocrates' *De herbis et curis* and other works whose titles were not indicated. A comparison of the best manuscripts of the Carolingian collection reveals that in actual fact the Cassiodorian compilation was augmented with several treatises by Hippocrates.[21] None of them bears the title mentioned by Cassiodorus, but this title is suspect, for no known treatise by Hippocrates, whether genuine or apocryphal, corresponds to it.[22] Rose already proposed to emend the title *De herbis et curis* to *De herbis et cibis* and showed that Cassiodorus meant thereby the Latin extracts from Book 2 of Hippocrates' *De diaeta*, which have been preserved in several manuscripts.[23] Now, at the end of the Carolingian collection we find in fact this *Diaeta Hippocratis*.[24]

---

capite . . . Adhibenda sunt enim Dei medicamenta quia divina potentia dignata est revivificare corpora mortificata. Nunc incipiam dicere de herbis et medicinis diversis capitis"; Sangall. 751, 10th cent., p. 281: "Incipiunt antidota per singulas passiones *de diversis auctoribus conlecta.*"

[21] This is the way I reconstruct the Cassiodorian corpus:

	Augiensis 120	Casin. 97	Vindoc. 109	Bruxell. 1343–1350
Galen *Therap. ad Glauconem*	Omitted	pp. 33–89	fols. 1ʳ–35ᵛ	Omitted
Anon. ex div. auct. conl. (= Liber III)	fols. 1ʳ–18ʳ	pp. 89–?	fols. 35ᵛ–50ʳ	Omitted
Aureli *De medicina* { Aurelius	fols. 18ʳ–36ᵛ	pp. 109–131	fols. 58ʳ–75ʳ	fols. 54ᵛ–65ᵛ
Scolapius	fols. 36ᵛ–95ᵛ	pp. 131–199	(Extracts)	fols. 65ᵛ–106ᵛ
Coelius Aurelianus, Medicinales responsiones	fols. 95–120	Omitted	Omitted	Omitted
Hippocrates *Aphorismi cum commento*	fols. 120–204ᵛ	pp. 199–282	Omitted	Omitted
Diaeta Hippocratis	fol. 211ᵛ	Omitted	fols. 134ᵛ–138ᵛ	fol. 106ᵛ

[22] Except for a *De herbis*, the Latin translation of which appears only in very late manuscripts. Cf. Diels, *Die Handschriften der antiker Aerzte*, Griechische Abteilung (Berlin 1906) 54.

[23] Particularly Sangall. 762, 9th cent., pp. 25–72, under the title: *Liber de virtutibus herbarum*, and pp. 187–216 under the title: *Hippocratis medici de cibis*, ed. Rose, *Anecd.* 2, pp. 119ff. Rose assumes that *ciuis* is an intermediate form between *cibis* and *curis*, in order to explain the textual error in the *Institutiones*. Cf. also Casin. 69, 9th cent., p. 571, and Paris. Lat. 7027, 10th cent., fol. 55ᵛ, where the translation of Book 1 *De diaeta* precedes the commentary on the *Aphorisms*.

[24] Bruxellensis 1343–1350, fol. 106ᵛ has: "Incipit diaeta Ypocratis quam observare debet homo," like Sangall. 762, p. 187: "Incipit liber Ippocratis medici de cibis vel de

Between this *Diaeta* and Coelius Aurelianus' *De medicina* there appear, in the Carolingian collection, the translation and the commentary on Hippocrates' *Aphorisms*. This commentary, which has never been examined,[25] necessarily then formed part of the Cassiodorian corpus. This is confirmed by its contents. It is in fact merely a translation of the Greek commentary by Stephen of Athens, a disciple of Gessius of Alexandria.[26] In it we discover the method of the Alexandrian commentators of the sixth century. The prologue treats in succession the six points traditional in the School of Alexandria: the purpose of the work, its usefulness, its authenticity, the title, the order in which to read, the division into parts.[27] The following parallel will show to what degree the translator is customarily faithful:

Stephen of Athens *In Aphor. Hipp.*, ed. Dietz, p. 239:	Vivarian Translation (Casin. 97, p. 201 = Paris. Lat. 7027, folio 68 recto):
Ἔκτον ἐστὶ κεφάλαιον ἡ εἰς τὰ μόρια διαίρεσις. Ἰστέον ὅτι ὁ μὲν Σωρανὸς εἰς τρία τμήματα διεῖλε τοῦτο τὸ βιβλίον, ὁ δὲ ʿΡοῦφος εἰς τέσσαρα, ὁ δὲ Γαληνὸς εἰς ἑπτά, ὧπερ καὶ πειθόμεθα.	In quot partes dividitur praesens liber? Suranus in tres, Rufus in quattuor, Galienus in septem. Si enim requiras certam rationem, quot aforismi sunt, tot partes.

If one recalls what has been said of the influence of the Alexandrian commentators on Boethius and Cassiodorus,[28] one observes that the internal and external criteria coincide so as to mark this translation as Vivarian. Like the philosophical commentaries, the medical commentaries of Alexandria were known in the West. And if Cassiodorus recommended Galen's *Therapeutica*

---

potum (*sic*) quod homo usitare debet." The *diaetae* contained in Vindoc. 109 are, on the other hand, borrowed from Alexander of Tralles. Cf. Rose, *Anecd.* 2, pp. 107ff.

25 I have verified the fact that it was identical in Casin. 97, pp. 199–282; Augiensis 120, fols. 120–204ᵛ; Paris. Lat. 7027, fol. 66ʳ (with the *explicit* mutilated). The *incipit* is: "Medicina partitur secundum minorem portionem"; the *explicit*: "quod in praesenti cognoscimus." The existence of this commentary was noted by H. Kuehlewein, "Mittheilungen aus einer alten lat. Uebersetzung der Aphorismen des Hippokrates," *Hermes* 17 (1882) 484–488. He observed that this translation of the *Aphorisms*, from its style, must go back to the sixth century, but it seems that he did not have time to study the text at leisure at Monte Cassino.

26 Cf. *PW* s.v. Stephanos von Athen. My researches confirm Bussemaker's opinion, "ΣΤΕΦΑΝΟΥ ΠΕΡΙ ʾΟΥΡΩΝ, traité d'Etienne sur les urines," *Revue de Philologie* 1 (1845) 416–422, that Stephen lived not in the seventh century but in the first half of the sixth century.

27 Cf. Stephen of Athens *In Aphor. Hippocr.* (*Scholia in Hippocratem et Galenum*, ed. Dietz, 2 [Leipzig 1834]) 238–239, and Casin. 97, pp. 200–201. On this schema, cf. above, pp. 286–287.

28 Cf. above, pp. 284ff and 341ff.

ad Glauconem, which had also been the subject of a commentary by Stephen,[29] it was probably because he followed the syllabus of the medical studies at Alexandria.[30]

Thus, without lapsing into gratuitous conjectures like Beer's, it is possible to determine with accuracy the highly important role played by Vivarium in the history of medicine down to the period of the renaissance of Salerno. The intermediary was this time very probably not the Lateran but a monastery in Southern Italy: the monastery of Monte Cassino, which still houses Cassiodorus' medical corpus. Monte Cassino preserved the texts and safe-guarded the methods of the medical School of Alexandria. Of all the disciplines of Hellenism, this medical discipline alone seems to have been, because of its immediate usefulness, the object of a continuous tradition.

[29] Ed. Dietz (above, n. 27) 1, pp. 233–244. Cf. G. Bjoerck, "Remarques sur trois documents médicaux de la bibl. univ. de Leyde," *Mnemosyne* 6 (1938) 139–150. He mentions a new manuscript of this commentary, Voss. Misc. 6, 1.

[30] Cf. Meyerhof, "La fin de l'école d'Alexandrie," pp. 5 and 11, on the canon of the Hippocratic and Galenian writings that were studied at Alexandria.

CONCLUSION

The rare documents that could be assembled relating to the teaching of the Greek language in the West, from the death of Theodosius to the conquest of Justinian, are very fragmentary. The conclusions that they warrant are to be treated with caution. I believe we may disregard the activities of the Greeks and Syrians who swarmed over the entire Mediterranean periphery, except in Vandal territory where commerce beyond the sea was prohibited. These colonies of traders had not the slightest interest in propagating the Greek language or Greek culture. We must seek elsewhere for the environments favorable to the flourishing spread of Greek as a language of culture. If we disregard the exceptional cases—the Latin-speaking writers Marcellinus Comes, Priscian, and his pupil Eutyches, who all lived in Constantinople— the teaching of Greek survived only in cosmopolitan areas of the Roman aristocracy. The guests in the *Saturnalia*, a Symmachus, or a Praetextatus, belonged to old families and admitted into their society foreigners, Greeks or Egyptians. A century later, the same families produced a new Symmachus, a Boethius, who, thanks to their relations with Constantinople and Alex- andria, were to become eminent Hellenists. Similarly in the provinces. The elementary teaching of the Greek language by the Greek *grammaticus* still spread among the cultured citizens when Augustine and Jerome were still infants, but after the invasions it survived only in the highest social classes. At the end of the fifth century one had to be a son of a Sidonius Apollinaris or a descendant of the Fulgentii to receive this scholastic benefit. However mediocre such teaching became, the domestic norm of the *gens*, with its traditional Greek and Latin culture, had resisted the breakdown of the imperial norms.

The ascetic and monastic atmosphere was, on the other hand, unfavorable to the teaching of the Greek language. St. Jerome is merely a brilliant excep- tion. The monasteries in the West did not have the same facilities as the Latin monastery of Bethlehem. Neither St. Augustine, who exerted himself throughout his life to perfect his Greek and who regarded the Greek text as the most authorized version of the Scriptures, nor Cassiodorus, who felt the omissions in a purely Latin culture, had any hope of molding Hellenists. Furthermore, the disciples of Cassianus, who propagated withal the ideal and the methods of the Eastern ascetics, were hostile to Hellenism. A study of the Greek language, in their view, ran the risk of awakening dangerous curiosities. They did not know Greek or avoided teaching it.

Is it possible to fix the date when the complete break with the Greek language took place in every province in the West, thus bringing to an end the ancient Greco-Roman tradition that still flourished at the close of the fourth century? Neither in Spain nor in Britain nor in Ireland does the Greek language seem to have been known in the fifth century.[1] At the very most a person could have learned it in the course of residence in the East, like the Irish Pelagius or the Spaniard Martin of Bracara. The efforts that have been made to show that the Greek language was taught at that period in Ireland are based on dubious traditions or worthless testimonies.[2] In North Africa, the break came very early. It coincided with the Vandal conquest. After 439 Fulgentius, who after all knew little Greek, was an isolated case. He wrote for readers who knew no Greek. This ignorance was to persist throughout the entire period of Vandal domination.[3] In Gaul, the study of the Greek language was rather neglected from the time of Ausonius. It was completely abandoned in the monastic circles of Lérins but persisted at least in a few privileged provinces, especially in Provence. Toward 470 a Consentius, a Sidonius Apollinaris, a Claudianus Mamertus, or a Gennadius still had access to the treasures of Hellenism. In the next generation, this contact was broken for centuries on end.[4] In Italy, one might have thought that here too, from around 430, all was lost and that Greek would henceforth be the appanage of rare specialists, themselves very mediocre. But the coronation of Theodoric reestablished contact, for the Ostrogoths were as receptive to Greek culture as the Franks or the Vandals were resistant to it. In Boethius' days Greek studies flourished. Cassiodorus prolonged the beneficent effect of

---

[1] However, the Syrians had long since acquired a footing in Spain. Cf. F. Cumont, "Les Syriens et les Adonies à Seville," *Syria* 8 (1927) 330–341. The Greek titles of Prudentius' works must not deceive us.

[2] Cf. Roger, *L'enseignement des lettres classiques*, chap. 6. The use of an ecclesiastical Hellenism and a knowledge of trifling etymologies are not sufficient to prove that the teaching of Greek still persisted. For the later period, cf. Sandys, *A History of Classical Scholarship*, pp. 438ff; J. Vendryès, "La connaissance du grec en Irlande au début du Moyen Age," *REG* 33 (1920), pp. 53–55; and M. Cappuyns, *Jean Scot Erigène* (Louvain 1933) 28.

[3] Even under Byzantine domination when Greek inscriptions were numerous, the literary language was to remain Latin. Greek literature was to be known by only a few scholars versed in theological questions, like Facundus of Hermione and the African supporters of the *Tria Capita*.

[4] At the very most the sixth century was able to copy the Greek text of the Scriptures. On these bilingual manuscripts, cf. Sandys, *A Hist. of Class. Scholarship*, p. 445.

this renaissance by organizing at Vivarium a small team of translators who worked steadily. But at his death, around 583, the young generation, to which he did not venture to teach Greek, was incapable of continuing this effort. Even the pope could no longer find scholars who understood what they were translating. They were satisfied with making an unintelligible word-for-word transliteration with the help of glossaries.[5] As Gregory the Great was himself ignorant of Greek[6] and translators from Latin into Greek became rare in Constantinople as well,[7] relations became almost impossible. Gregory felt obliged, in order to keep abreast of the Greek heresy, to resort to his colleague Eulogius of Alexandria. The latter sent Gregory extracts from Basil, Gregory, and Epiphanius, who had crushed this heresy.[8] This proves that even the most eminent Greek Fathers were no longer read in Rome around the year 600.[9]

We see how the influence of Byzantine domination had remained superficial at this date, despite the increasing spread of new Greek colonies and the

---

[5] *Gregorii I papae registrum epistularum*, ed. Hartmann, *MGH, Epist.* 2, p. 258, 27: "Indicamus praeterea quia gravem hic interpretum difficultatem patimur. Dum enim non sunt qui sensum de sensu exprimant, sed transferre verborum semper proprietatem volunt, omnem dictorum sensum confundunt. Unde agitur ut ea quae translata fuerint nisi cum gravi labore intellegere nullo modo valeamus."

[6] *Ibid.*, 2, p. 330, 6: "nec Graece novimus"; 1, p. 476, 1: "quamvis Graecae linguae nescius." On Gregory's attitude to culture, cf. A. Sepulcri, "Gregorio Magno e la scienza profana," *Atti della r. Accad. delle scienze di Torino* 39 (1903/1904) 962–976.

[7] *Ibid.*, 1, p. 474, 6: "hodie in Constantinopolitana civitate, qui de Latino in Graeco dictata bene transferant, non sunt. Dum enim verba custodiunt et sensus minime attendunt, nec verba intellegi faciunt et sensus frangunt."

[8] *Ibid.*, 1, p. 448, 20ff: "Eudoxium quendam vos damnasse repperimus, cuius nomen in Latina lingua neque in synodis neque in libris beatae memoriae episcoporum Epifanii, Augustini et Filastri quos *contra hereticos* praecipue disputasse novimus, positum repperimus." Naturally, Gregory the Great knows Epiphanius of Cyprus only from the *De haeresibus* of Augustine, who translated an abridgment of the *Panarion* (cf. above, p. 207). In fact, Gregory makes a correction, *MGH, Epist.* 1, p. 479, 26: "In Latina ergo lingua de hoc Eudoxio nunc usque neque in Philastro neque in beato Augustino, qui multa *de heresibus* conscripserunt, neque in aliis patribus aliquid invenimus. Caritas igitur vestra, si quis apud Graecos probatorum patrum de eo sermonem fecit, suis mihi epistulis innotescat." Eulogius replies by sending him extracts from Basil, Gregory, Epiphanius; cf. *ibid.*, 2, p. 31, 8: "Praeterea de Eudoxii heretici persona, de cuius errore in Latina lingua nil repperi, mihi a vestra beatitudine largissime gaudeo satisfactum; virorum quippe fortissimorum Basilii, Gregorii atque Epiphanii testimonia protulistis, et manifeste peremptum cognoscimus eum, in quo heroes nostri tot iacula dederunt." Hartmann is wrong in thinking, 1, p. 448 n. 3, that the Epiphanius mentioned in the first text is Epiphanius Scholasticus, the translator of Cassiodorus' *Historia tripartita*. Gregory the Great certainly possessed the *Historia tripartita* (cf. above, chap. 8 sec. 3 n. 36), but this work contains no trace of a treatise entitled *Contra hereticos* and its author is nowhere described as a bishop.

[9] Similarly, Gregory the Great, *MGH, Epist.* 2, p. 29, 10, informs Eulogius that Eusebius of Caesarea's *Gesta martyrum* is in neither the Lateran nor in any library in Rome.

use of Greek as an administrative language.[10] A kind of linguistic nationalism developed, quite evident even among those who, like Cassiodorus, were most responsive to Greek culture.[11] He was all the more attached to Latin, the more he felt its imminent extinction. However, this Latin pride never let the Romans forget the value of Greek culture. The Gothic chiefs who were partisans in the resistance against Justinian laid siege to Belisarius in Rome. But it was useless for them to think that they could arouse the starving Romans against the Byzantine occupational troops. It was useless to tell the Romans that they had never received from the Greeks anything but "actors, mimes, and pirates."[12] These Goths had a short memory, for the intellectual brilliance of Theodoric's reign was a benefit bestowed by Greek culture. If we examine the evolution of this culture from Macrobius to Cassiodorus, we note its real unity in the West, despite the distinctions in levels that may be observed in different provinces and at various periods;[13] it seems both a survival of the ancient Greco-Roman tradition and a new contribution.

The scholastic tradition was very strong, and the methods of elementary education had not changed since Quintilian's time. Homer and Menander were still the core in the days of Sidonius Apollinaris and Fulgentius. Even in the Merovingian era these two Greek writers remained associated in the memories of men who could no longer read them.[14] The program of the liberal arts, which originated in the Hellenistic age, was in evidence also even in the manuals of Martianus Capella and Cassiodorus. From Capella to Cassiodorus, Hellenism seemed rather to have made progress. Martianus used Latin treatises almost exclusively. Cassiodorus is much more liberated from Varro and summarizes Greek treatises that he reads either in translation or in the original. Even grammar and rhetoric, which appeared to be a distinctively Latin area, as opposed to dialectic and the scientific disciplines, felt, in the sixth-century theorists, the influence of the commentators on Apollonius Dyscolus or Hermogenes. For sacred studies, Primasius and Cassiodorus went as far as Nisibis, on the borders of Persia, in search of new educational

[10] Cf. R. Devreesse, "L'église d'Afrique durant l'occupation byzantine," *MEFR* 57 (1940) 154: "No more than the Greek language did patristic Greek become rooted in the country." And in the same vein H. Steinacker, "Die röm. Kirche und die griechischen Sprachkenntnisse des Frühmittelalters," p. 338. Diehl's works, on the other hand, emphasize the Byzantine influence.

[11] Text quoted above, p. 336.

[12] Procopius *Bell. Goth.* 1.18, CSHB, p. 93, 5: τραγῳδοὺς καὶ μίμους καὶ ναύτας λυπωδύτας.

[13] The unity of thought and culture in the Western world in the patristic age has already been defended by Labriolle, *REL* 3 (1925) 85–86, against Monceaux. Labriolle is right, in my view, in challenging the importance of the national factors, which Monceaux had stressed in his *Histoire de la littérature latine chrétienne*.

[14] Dadon *Vita s. Eligii, praef.*, MGH, *Script. rer. Merov.* 4, p. 665, 7: "Quid scereatorum neniae poetarum, Omeri videlicet, Vergilii et Menandri, legentibus conferunt?"

methods. The fact was that the traditional Greco-Roman culture no longer experienced a revival from a study of the great classics. The Romans had no conception of the age of Pericles and ancient Greek literature except through the eyes of Cicero, Varro, or Plutarch. The taste for learned compilations brought a disregard for consulting the sources. Macrobius knew the Greek theater only from Didymus Chalcenterus, and that too from Serenus Sammonicus. St. Jerome scarcely read the Fathers of the first two centuries except through Eusebius and Origen. Were the manuscripts then of the ancient writers so rare? I do not think so. Jerome had a Herodotus and a Xenophon. If he did read them, it was exceptional, and because they were indispensable for the historical commentary on the Scriptures. But he took no interest in the *Timaeus*, which he also possessed. The Latins who were most devoted to Plato and Aristotle, like Macrobius, or Augustine, or Boethius, knew the ancient Greek text only from the most recent commentary and could not distinguish one from the other. This absence of direct contact with the classical masterpieces, this lack of perspective, this want of a historical sense, is one of the gravest signs of decadence. The best minds could not resist. They meditated, not on the texts, but on the commentaries on which they in turn produced commentaries. From commentary to commentary, thought thinned out and degenerated.

And yet contact between the two literatures remained alive. The reason was that the commentators of the East, less exposed than the West to invasion, maintained a superior cultural standard and were a permanent resource to the Latins. All the great currents of thought that stirred the West streamed from a Greek literary tradition. If the commentaries on the same work increased in number, it was a sign that this work was productive of possibilities. New centers of interest developed, even though the original objectives of the great classics were falsified or lost sight of. Greek literature was a factor in the renaissance, at the very time when ancient culture in the Ciceronian style became moribund and died out.

Origen's exegetical commentaries appeared at the end of the fourth century as one of these cultural resources. St. Jerome wanted to spread a knowledge of these commentaries among the Latins. Simplicianus urged Augustine to devote his ecclesiastical career to the same purpose.[15] It was only his insufficient knowledge of the language that prevented him, but he recognized the usefulness of such a work.[16] When Origen's authority was compromised by the condemnation of his theories, those exegetical writings still survived.

[15] Gennadius *De script. eccles.* 36, *PL* 58, 1078 C: "Simplicianus episcopus Mediolanensis multis epistulis hortatus est Augustinum, adhuc presbyterum, agitare ingenium et expositionibus Scripturarum vacare, ut etiam novus Ambrosius, Origenis ἐργοδιώκτης videretur." This is a reference to the Greek Ambrosius, a disciple of Origen. Cf. above, chap. 2 sec. 3 n. 146.

[16] Cf. the letter in which he solicits Jerome's interest in this matter: above, p. 198.

As all of them had to be translated, Cassiodorus resorted to John Chrysostom's exegesis, which the Pelagian controversy had made known to the West, thus filling in the omissions.

Evagrius Ponticus, through Cassianus as the intermediary, furnished Western monasticism with his methods of sanctification and his doctrine relating to culture. Profane Hellenism was severely proscribed. Already, Jerome had condemned philosophical thought and tolerated profane literature only as a tool of exegesis. Rufinus went further and accused Jerome of excessive indulgence, Paulinus of Nola and the monks of Lérins presented themselves as champions in the conflict against the Platonists. A century later, the enemies of Hellenism had not disarmed and brought the charge of heresy and magic against Boethius, who had applied to theological problems the methods of Aristotle's commentators. They could not conceive any sphere of mutual understanding between Christian culture and pagan culture. This tendency contributed in no small degree to the disappearance of the latter and the limitations of the former. In the final issue, a monastic culture thus conceived was to produce nothing more than hagiographies and treatises against heretics. It was to be exclusive and self-sufficient.

This systematic hostility may be better understood if one reflects on what Hellenic thought then represented for the West. Only one philosophy, Neoplatonism, survived. The master mind was Porphyry, the great enemy of Christians. This capital fact has never been brought into the open, because the history of Latin Neoplatonism has not been written. The only one who ventured on the task, Father Henry, thought that a book on Plotinus might "serve as a basis for the central chapter of a history of Neoplatonism in the West."[17] In my view, this was an error in perspective. It was not a matter of questioning the influence exercised by Plotinus, the founder of the sect. Father Henry could have assigned this influence even to Manlius Theodorus and noted that the name of Plotinus, *gravissimus auctor*, appeared in Boethius as well. But frequently Porphyry presented himself as an intermediary. Macrobius knew the Plotinian theories on the virtues and on suicide from Porphyry's *Sententiae* and the *De regressu animae*. Boethius knew the eulogy of Andronicus by Plotinus from Porphyry's commentary on the *Sophist*. It was neither Plotinus' profound metaphysics, although he was still read and appreciated, nor the mystical lucubrations of Iamblichus or Julian, whose works seemed to have remained almost unknown in the West,[18] that cap-

---

[17] Henry, *Plotin et l'Occident*, p. 24.

[18] Augustine knows Iamblichus by name only. Jerome read, but in the East, Iamblichus' *Protrepticus* and Julian's *Contra Galilaeos*. Boethius read a commentary by Iamblichus on the *Categories*. Jordanes and the Geographer of Ravenna quote a geographical text by Iamblichus, probably apocryphal (cf. Jordanes *De summa temporum*, ed. Mommsen, *MGH, Auct. ant.* 5, 1, p. xxv and Manitius, *Gesch. des Mittelalters* 3, p. 617). The

tured Roman minds. These minds were much more responsive to Porphyrian doctrine, which was both a philosophy and a religion.

The dissemination of Porphyry's principal works throughout the entire civilized West, from the end of the fourth century to the beginning of the sixth, is significant. To be sure, the *De abstinentia* perhaps survived in the East only, where it furnished Jerome with arguments in support of asceticism. The Κατὰ χριστιανῶν probably disappeared. But it still continued to supply weapons for antichristian polemics to such a point that Jerome and Pacatus resolved to refute it.[19] Even in the sixth century these criticisms retained their venom, so that Victor of Capua and John the Deacon thought it necessary to insert in their collections Pacatus' rejoinders. The Geographer of Ravenna, who flourished in the seventh century, also recalled that Porphyry was the most bitter enemy of Christ.[20] But Porphyry's other works were the delight of Macrobius' contemporaries. His commentary on the *Timaeus* satisfied scientific curiosity. His *Homeric Questions* furnished a method of discovering Vergil's profound meaning. His commentary on the *Republic* was a literary model for the exposition of the *Somnium Scipionis*. His *Life of Pythagoras*, which combines with the charm of a saintly life the usefulness of a manual on ethics, was in the hands of both Jerome and Macrobius. Moreover, the treatise *On the Sun*, read perhaps in an adaptation by Cornelius Labeo, gave warranted credence, in the eyes of Macrobius, Martianus Capella, and the pagan group, to solar theology and reconciled ancient mythology with monotheism. The Porphyrian doctrine of the soul aroused still more interest. Macrobius conceived the soul and its destiny with the aid of three treatises by Porphyry: the Περὶ ψυχῆς, the Περὶ Στυγός, the *De regressu*

Iamblichus mentioned by Theodorus Priscianus *Euporista*, ed. V. Rose, p. 133, 11, is the author of erotic tales, not the Neoplatonic philosopher. Labriolle, *La réaction païenne*, p. 497, attributed to Porphyry the attacks refuted by Ambrosiaster. Cumont, "La polémique de l'Ambrosiaster," attributed them to Julian.

[19] The very terms of the constitution of 448, in the name of Theodosius II and Valentinianus III (*Cod. Iust.* 1.1.3) seemed to condemn to destruction by fire not specifically the Κατὰ χριστιανῶν but all the collections of antichristian attacks, most of which were attributed to Porphyry's influence: Θεσπίζομεν πάντα ὅσα Πορφύριος ὑπὸ τῆς ἑαυτοῦ μανίας ἐλαυνόμενος ἢ ἕτερός τις κατὰ τῆς εὐσεβοῦς τῶν Χριστιανῶν θρησκείας συνέγραψε, παρ' οἱῳδήποτε εὑρισκόμενα πυρὶ παραδίδοσθαι. Πάντα γὰρ τὰ κινοῦντα τὸν θεὸν εἰς ὀργὴν συγγράμματα καὶ τὰς ψυχὰς ἀδικοῦντα οὐδὲ εἰς ἀκοὰς ἀνθρώπων ἐλθεῖν βουλόμεθα. A Constitution of 435 (*Cod. Theod.* 16.5.66) informs us of the condemnation in the time of Constantine: "Arriani lege divae memoriae Constantini ob similitudinem impietatis Porfyriani a Porfyrio nuncupantur." The fact that the condemnation had to be reiterated proves that Porphyry's antichristian attacks were still in circulation.

[20] *Ravennatis anonymi cosmographia*, ed. M. Pinder and G. Parthey (Berlin 1860), p. 91, 11: "miserum Porphyrium"; p. 171, 8: "nefandissimum Porphyrium." Similarly, p. 176, 11, and *passim*.

animae. The first treatise maintains the autonomous nature of the soul. The second one explains the mystery of its descent into the body. The third posits the return to divine bliss and describes the philosophical and theurgic means of attaining it.

The third treatise preeminently exerted a profound and lasting influence. Macrobius found in it a condemnation of suicide in accordance with the theories of the *Phaedo* and the *Enneads*. The theurgic rites advocated by Porphyry were still practiced in the Neoplatonic mysteries in the days of Martianus Capella. The doctrine of detachment from the flesh and of a return to God had a profound impact on Christian minds. The *De regressu animae* was one of the Platonic books that Manlius Theodorus made Augustine read and that hastened his conversion. Even when Augustine attained a better grasp of the distinction between this doctrine and Christianity, he could not believe that the author was this same Porphyry who was pointed out to him as the principal enemy of Christians. At the end of the fifth century the *De regressu animae* was still Claudianus Mamertus' bedside book and stimulated the discussions of this literary circle on the incorporeal nature of the soul, which Faustus of Riez had questioned, perhaps through his hatred of Neoplatonism. All these writers, as I have shown, preserved for us entire pages that Bidez had omitted in his edition of the fragments of the *De regressu animae*. In conclusion, the *Philosophy of Oracles*, the *De imaginibus*, and the *Letter to Anebo* were the subject of controversies between pagans and Christians, at least in Africa in Augustine's time.

This was not all, With the *Isagoge* Porphyry created a stream of commentators who interpreted Aristotle in the light of Neoplatonic theories. At the end of the fourth century, although Themistius was the master of dialectic in the eyes of Praetextatus and Macrobius, the manual in which Jerome studied dialectic was now the *Isagoge*. At the beginning of the sixth century the *Isagoge* and Porphyry's dialectic commentaries had become the basis for Boethius' works, although he knew Themistius as well. Porphyry was regarded then as a classic that required a commentary, and it was Porphyry's doctrine, revised and remodeled by Proclus of Athens and Ammonius of Alexandria, that Boethius adopted enthusiastically. It was not only a question of an arid dialectic education. In his *De consolatione philosophiae* Boethius also adopted Ammonius' theories on the relations of God, the universe, and mankind. The influence of the Alexandrian commentators extended and completed Porphyry's influence. Scholasticism was established in the West, whose influence was felt by Cassiodorus as Boethius had felt it. Both of them were indebted to Porphyry for their program of studies, which was to pass without change into the Middle Ages, as well as for the method of exegesis, with their characteristic prolegomena, definitions, classifications, and diagrams. Even in the medical sphere this method was to be perpetuated, as is shown by the commentary of Stephen of Athens on Hippocrates' *Aphorisms*, translated in all probability at Vivarium.

This Neoplatonic tradition must have been, for those Christians who did not reject it from the very beginning, a very wholesome ferment. Already Origen had conceived the possibility of an adaptation of Hellenic thought to Christian dogma, notably in his *Stromateis*, where Scripture was studied in the light of the theories of Plato, Aristotle, Numenius, Cornutus.[21] This attempt, suddenly revealed to the West when Rufinus translated the *De principiis*,[22] aroused considerable feeling at the beginning of the fifth century. The attempt was finally condemned by Jerome's action. In the sixth century, Origenism reasserted its hold in Palestine, but it was definitively condemned by Pope Vigilius. Through Origen, it was Plato and Pythagoras, the doctrines of preexistence and the transmigration of the soul, that were nominally pursued.[23]

Fine minds tried, however, to throw a bridge between pagan Hellenism and Christian Hellenism, as Macrobius and Jerome did respectively. The anathema hurled against literary culture did not, in their opinion, affect Neoplatonism, which was as concerned about the ultimate end of man as Christianity was.[24] A confrontation between Neoplatonic philosophy and Christian doctrine appeared to present itself. Marius Victorinus had shown the way after his conversion by applying philosophical methods to exegesis on Scripture or to the study of Arian theology. The importance of his work depended less on the number of his translations, which scholarly imagination leisurely magnified, than on the quality of the works translated. Plotinus' treatises *On the Beautiful* and *On the Three Hypostases* and Porphyry's *De regressu animae* were works rich in meaning. A tradition was established in Christian circles. Manlius Theodorus was devoted to Plotinus and he treated

---

[21] Cf. the texts quoted above, chap. 2 sec. 2 nn. 98 and 308.

[22] Pope Anastasius declares, *Epist. ad Ioann. Hieros.* 1.3 (*PL* 20, 69 A): "Origenes autem cuius in nostram linguam composita derivavit (Rufinus), antea et quis fuerit et in quae processerit verba, nostrum propositum nescit." From Postumianus' account in Sulpicius Severus *Dial.* 1.6–7, it is quite clear that this Gaul too knew nothing specific about Origen when he reached the East in the midst of the Origenist crisis. Cf. 1.6.1, ed. Halm, p. 157, 27: "(Origenes) . . . tractator Scripturarum sacrarum peritissimus *habebatur*." However, Victorinus of Pettau, Hilary, and Ambrose had already translated or adapted works by Origen!

[23] *Georgii Chronicon* 4.218 (*PG* 90, 780): διέγνωσται ἡμῖν ὡς τινες ἐν Ἱεροσολύμοις εἰσὶ μοναχοὶ δήπουθεν Πυθαγόρᾳ καὶ Πλάτωνι καὶ Ὠριγένει τῷ Ἀδαμαντίῳ καὶ τῇ τούτων δυσσεβείᾳ καὶ πλάνῃ κατακολουθοῦντες. Cf. Duchesne, *L'église au VIᵉ siècle*, p. 211, and Bardy-Labriolle, *Histoire de l'église* 4, p. 459.

[24] The fact with regard to Augustine is well pointed out by Marrou, *Saint Augustin et la fin de la culture antique*, pp. 345–350 (anathema on literary culture) and 357–368 (justification for philosophical culture).

the problem of the origin of the soul and its destiny in the light of the translations by Victorinus. He appears to have personally translated Celsinus' manual of the history of philosophy, which went as far as Neoplatonism. He handed on the torch to the young Augustine, giving him at the same time these translations to read. His influence explains why Augustine's conversion was a conversion both to Neoplatonism and to Christianity. All his life Augustine was to remain marked with this dual symbol. The apologetics of the *De civitate Dei* were addressed to Porphyry's disciples, who were so numerous in the cultured circles of Africa. Entrenched in his own experience, he showed them the harmony that impressed him, at his conversion, between Neoplatonic doctrine and Christian dogma. St. John's prologue and the *Enneads* preached the Word of God. The dogma of the Trinity recalled the doctrine of the three hypostases, which Plotinus and Porphyry supported each in his own way. The dogma of Grace was clearly taught by Porphyry. Is it necessary to go further, like those Christians who were to find in Plato the dogma of the resurrection of the dead?[25] Augustine did not think so, for after long years in the episcopy he perceived the irreducible oppositions that distinguished Porphyrian philosophy from Christian dogma. The incarnation of the Word, the resurrection of the flesh—these problems were a scandal to the Hellenes, so profoundly did they scorn the body in pride of spirit.

Claudianus Mamertus did not have this clear vision. He was lyrical when describing the harmony of reason and faith. He expressed wonder that, several years before the Revelation, Plato had foretold the Trinity, for he did not doubt for a moment that the Porphyrian Triad represented Plato's real thought and was identified with the Christian Trinity. He had no intention of condemning the Porphyrian formula, "the body must be shunned," for he saw therein merely an invitation to the spiritual life. In his view, the *De regressu animae*, far from founding a rival religion for souls athirst for salvation, was a stimulant. Porphyry supplied the daily nourishment for his Christian spirituality.

Boethius was both bolder and more discerning. His literary culture and his terminology, like his thought, were Neoplatonic. In the *De consolatione philosophiae* he accepted Porphyry's theories, revised by Proclus and Ammonius, on the preexistence of the soul, the chariot of the soul, Providence and fate, angels and demons, purgatory. His prayer to the divinity was a Platonic hymn. He even ventured to maintain the perpetuity of the universe, which seems for the most part to contradict the dogma of creation. He

---

[25] Augustine *De civ. Dei* 22.28, ed. Dombart, p. 621, 21: "Non nulli nostri propter quoddam praeclarissimum loquendi genus et propter non nulla quae veraciter sentit amantes Platonem, dicunt eum aliquid simile nobis etiam de mortuorum resurrectione sensisse." Cf. Eusebius *Praep.* 11.33, *PG* 21, 933 C, quoting a page from Plato's *Statesman*.

belongs then in the Macrobian tradition. He read him besides with enthusi-asm[26] in the revised text that his father-in-law Symmachus had just published with the cooperation of a descendant of the author.[27] But Porphyrian philo-sophy did not seem to them now, as it had to their ancestors, incompatible with Christianity, for this philosophy had evolved among the Alexandrian commentators in a rational direction, shedding every shred of pagan mysticism. This view made it possible for pagan and Christian to follow henceforth the same course and profit by it. Boethius took care only not to combine the data of reason with the data of faith. Even when asked to clarify a theological problem, he never abandoned the dialectician's rational view-point. He left to others the question of deciding whether his conclusion agreed with the texts of Scripture or the tradition of the Fathers.

We see that the problem of Christian philosophy, which is always pres-ent,[28] was already resolved in opposite directions by the Christians them-selves. The most cultured among them were not satisfied with the ready solution that consisted in rejecting wholesale the benefits of pagan Hellenism considered as snares of Satan. Even when the Neoplatonic school had dis-appeared, a book preserved the memory of this doctrine and was for the High Middle Ages a leaven like the treatises of Plotinus, Porphyry, or Am-monius. One can see in the sixth century the beginning of the success of the Dionysian writings, steeped in Proclus' thought.[29] To spread into the West this dubious angelology and to guarantee its orthodoxy, nothing less was required than the eminent name of St. Paul's disciple, Dionysius the Areo-pagite.

Despite the efforts of some talented men to exorcise, with the aid of

[26] For the use made of the *Commentary on Scipio's Dream* in the *De consolatione philo-sophiae*, cf. above, p. 299. In the *Commentary on the Isagoge*, ed. Brandt, p. 31, 22, Boethius explicitly refers the reader to this work by the "most learned Macrobius."

[27] See the subscription at the end of Book 1 of the *Commentary on Scipio's Dream*: "Aurelius Memmius Symmachus v.c. emendabam vel distinguebam meum Ravennae cum Macrobio Plotino Eudoxio v.c." Is this name *Plotinus* a gesture of homage to the great Plotinus?

[28] I am thinking of the recent dispute between Bréhier and Gilson, the origin of which was Bréhier's article "Y a-t-il une philosophie chrétienne?" *Revue de métaphysique et de morale* 38 (1931) 133–162. The history of this quarrel has already been written by A. Renard, *La querelle sur la possibilité de la philosophie chrétienne* (diss. Paris 1941).

[29] The first witnesses in the West were Liberatus of Carthage, Gregory the Great (through hearsay), and Martin I. Cf. J. Stiglmayr, *Das Aufkommen der pseudo-dionysischen Schriften und ihr Eindringen in die christliche Literatur bis zum Lateranconcil 649* (Progr. Gymn. Feldkirch 1895); H. C. Puech, "Liberatus de Carthage et la date de l'apparition des écrits dionysiens," *Annuaire de l'école pratique des Hautes Etudes*, section des sciences religeuses (1930/1931) 3–39 (reviewed by Stiglmayr, *Byzantion* 8 [1933] 658–662). On the success of the work from the eighth century on, cf. G. Théry, "L'entrée du Pseudo-Denys en Occident," *Mélanges Mandonnet* 2, pp. 22–30.

Hellenism, the danger to which culture was exposed by the turmoil of a new world, the Greek literary tradition died out at the close of the sixth century. But all was not lost, thanks to Cassiodorus. He let medical education survive in the South of Italy. In particular, he showed that Hellenism, even profane Hellenism, was indispensable to monastic culture. The tradition that was to be remolded in the Carolingian monasteries after a temporary interruption was indeed the sixth-century tradition. Dialectic studies were to flourish, thanks to Boethius' adaptations. The most active spirits would not hesitate to resume Platonic speculations with the help of Macrobius, Martianus Capella, Boethius.[30] With regard to sacred culture, the Vivarian traditions, saved from destruction by the Lateran Library, then widely disseminated by the Holy See, were to make known the best exegetes of Greek patristic literature. Josephus' *Antiquities* and the *Historia ecclesiastica tripartita* were to be in the hands of all and were to furnish a valuable documentation for the history of the Jewish people and the history of the Church. The ancient Greco-Roman tradition had disappeared. But for classical culture the generations from Macrobius to Cassiodorus had substituted a new culture, in which were combined the Hellenism of the philosophers and the Hellenism of the Fathers.

[30] On the influence exerted by Macrobius' thought on the Middle Ages, cf. Schedler, *Die Philosophie des Macrobius und ihr Einfluss auf die Wissenschaft des chr. Mittelalters*, part 2. On Martianus Capella, cf. the commentaries of John Scot Erigena (ed. C. Lutz, Cambridge, Mass. 1939), Remi d'Auxerre, and Pseudo-Dunchad. On Boethius, cf. my "Etude critique des commentaires sur la *Consolatio Philosophiae* de Boèce."

BIBLIOGRAPHY

INDEX OF MANUSCRIPTS

GENERAL INDEX

BIBLIOGRAPHY

The only modern writers who appear here are those who have been consulted with advantage for the present work. The format is not indicated unless it is not 8vo. Editions of ancient writers have been noted in the course of this work, wherever these writers were the subject of study.

Alès, A d'. "Julien d'Eclane exégète," *RSR* 7 (1916) 311–324.

Alfaric, Prosper. *L'évolution intellectuelle de s. Augustin*, vol. 1: *Du manichéisme au néoplatonisme* (only vol. published), diss. Paris 1918.

Allard, Paul. "Prudence historien," *Revue des questions historiques* 35 (1884) 345–385.

——— "Rome au IVᵉ siècle," *ibid.*, 36 (1884) 5–61.

Altaner, Berthold. "Augustinus und die griechische Sprache," *Pisciculi, Studien zur Religion und Kultur des Altertums, F. J. Doelger zum 60. Geburtstage dargeboten* (Münster 1939) 19–40.

——— "Eustathius, der lateinische Uebersetzer der Hexaemeronhomilien Basilius des Grossen," *Zeitschrift für neutestamentliche Wissenschaft* 39 (1940) 161–170.

——— "Altlateinische Uebersetzungen von Schriften des Athanasios von Alexandria," *Byzantinische Zeitschrift* 11 (1941) 45–59.

——— "Avitus von Braga, ein Beitrag zur altchristlichen Literaturgeschichte," *Zeitschrift für Kirchengeschichte* (1941) 456–468.

Amand, D. Review of *Lettres grecques en Occident*, 1st ed., *RB* 56 (1945/1946) 234–235.

Amelli, Ambrogio. *Cassiodoro e la Volgata*: terza conferenza tenuta a s. Callisto in Roma il 4 Maggio 1917, Grottaferrata 1917.

Anchel, Robert. "Les Juifs en Gaule à l'époque franque," *Journal des savants* (1938) 255–265.

Angus, S. *The Sources of the First Ten Books of Augustine's De Civitate Dei*, Princeton 1906.

Baehrens, W. A. *Ueberlieferung und Textgeschichte der lateinisch erhaltenen Origeneshomilien*, Harnack's Texte und Untersuchungen, vol. 42, 1, Leipzig 1916.

——— "Literarhistorische Beiträge," *Hermes* 52 (1917) 39–56.

Bardenhewer, O. *Geschichte der altkirchlichen Litteratur*, vol. 4: *Das fünfte Jahrhundert*, Freiburg im Breisgau 1924.

Bardy, Gustave. *Recherches sur l'histoire du texte et des versions latines du "De principiis" d'Origène*, Mémoires et travaux de la Faculté catholique de Lille, vol. 25, Lille 1923.

——— "L'église et l'enseignement dans les trois premiers siècles," *Revue des sciences religieuses* 12 (1932) 1–28.

——— "L'église et l'enseignement au IVᵉ siècle," *ibid.*, 14 (1934) 525–549; 15 (1935) 1–27,

——— "La culture grecque dans l'Occident chrétien au IVᵉ siècle," *RSR* 29 (1939) 5–58.

——— "Formules liturgiques grecques à Rome au IVᵉ siècle," *ibid.*, 30 (1940) 109–112.

425

BARDY, Gustave. "L'Occident et les documents de la controverse arienne," *Revue des sciences religieuses* 20 (1940) 28–63.

—— "Pour l'histoire de l'école d'Alexandrie," *Vivre et Penser* 2 (1942) 80–109.

—— "Le *De haeresibus* et ses sources," *Miscellanea Agostiniana* 2 (Rome 1931) 397–416.

—— "La latinisation de l'église d'Occident," *Irénikon* (1937) 1–20 and 113–130.

—— "Cassiodore et la fin du monde ancien," *L'année théologique* 6 (1945) 383–425.

—— Review of *Lettres grecques en Occident*, 1st ed., *Revue du Moyen Age latin* 1 (1945) 312–318.

—— Review of *Lettres grecques en Occident*, 1st ed., *L'année théologique* 7 (1946) 348–353.

—— "Sur les anciennes traductions latines de s. Athanase," *RSR* 34 (1947) 239–242.

BAUMSTARK, Anton. *Aristoteles bei den Syrern vom V–VIII. Jahrhundert*, vol. 1: *Syrisch-Arabische Biographieen des Aristoteles, Syrische Commentare zur Eisagoge des Porphyrios*, Leipzig 1900.

BAUR, Chrysostome. "Saint Jérôme et s. Chrysostome," *RB* 23 (1906) 430–436.

—— "L'entrée littéraire de s. Chrysostome dans le monde latin," *RHE* 8 (1907) 249–265.

BECKER, Gustav. *Catalogi bibliothecarum antiqui*, Bonn 1885.

BECKER, Hans. *Augustin, Studien zu seiner geistigen Entwickelung*, Leipzig 1908.

BEER, Rudolf. "Bemerkungen über den ältesten Handschriftenbestand des Klosters Bobbio," *Anzeiger der kaiserlichen Akademie der Wissenschaften zu Wien*, phil.-hist. Klasse, 48 (1911) 78–104.

—— *Monumenta palaeographica Vindobonensia*, Lieferung 2, Leipzig 1913, in fol.

BERGER, J. F. A. *Proclus, exposition de sa doctrine*, diss. Paris 1840.

BERGER, Samuel. "La Bible du pape Hilarus," *Bulletin critique* 13 (1892) 147–152.

—— *Histoire de la Vulgate pendant les premiers siècles du Moyen Age*, Nancy 1893.

—— "Les préfaces jointes aux livres de la Bible dans les manuscrits de la Vulgate," *Mémoires . . . de l'Académie des Inscriptions et Belles-Lettres*, 1st series, vol. 11 (1904), part 2, pp. 1–78.

BERNERT, Ernst. "Die Quellen Claudians in *De raptu Proserpinae*," *Philologus* 93, n.s. 47 (1939) 352–376.

BERNOULLI, C. A. *Der Schriftstellerkatalog des Hieronymus*, Freiburg im Breisgau 1895.

BEUTLER, Rudolf. "Die Gorgiasscholien und Olympiodor," *Hermes* 73 (1938) 380–390.

BICKEL, Ernestus. *Diatribe in Senecae philos. fragm.*, vol. 1, Leipzig 1915.

BIDEZ, Joseph. "Un faux dieu des oracles chaldaïques," *Revue de philologie* 27 (1903) 79–81.

—— *Vie de Porphyre, le philosophe néo-platonicien*, Recueil de travaux publiés par la Faculté de philologie et lettres de l'université de Gand, vol. 43 (1913).

—— "Le philosophe Jamblique et son école," *REG* 32 (1919) 29–40.

—— "La liturgie des mystères chez les néo-platoniciens," *Bulletin de la classe des Lettres de l'Académie royale de Belgique* (1919) 417.

—— "Boèce et Porphyre," *RBPH* 2 (1923) 189–201.

—— "Note sur les mystères platoniciens," *ibid.*, 7 (1928) 1477–1481.

—— *La vie de l'empereur Julien*, Paris 1930.

BIELER, Ludwig. "Textkritische Nachlese zu Boethius' *De philosophiae consolatione*," *Wiener Studien* 54 (1936) 128–141.

BIGNONE, E. "Parmenide e Claudiano, *In laud. Stil.*, II, 6 sgg.," *Bolletino di filologia classica* 23 (1917) 212–214.

BITSCH, F. *De Platonicorum quaestionibus quibusdam Vergilianis*, diss. Berlin 1911.

BLATT, Franz. "Remarques sur l'histoire des traductions latines," *Classica et mediaevalia* 1 (1938) 217–242.

BLIC, J. de. "Platonisme et christianisme dans la conception augustinienne du Dieu créateur," *RSR* 30 (1940) 172–190.

—— "Les arguments de s. Augustin contre l'éternité du monde," *Mélanges de science religieuse* 2 (1945) 33–44.

BOCK, Felix. "Aristoteles, Theophrastus, Seneca de matrimonio," *Leipziger Studien zur class. Philol.* 19 (1899) 3–71.

BOEMER, Franz. *Der lateinische Neuplatonismus und Neupythagoreismus und Claudianus Mamertus in Sprache und Philosophie*, Klassisch-philologische Studien, vol. 7, Leipzig 1936.

BOERTZLER, Friedrich. *Porphyrius' Schrift von den Götterbildern*, diss. Erlangen 1903.

BOISSIER, Gaston. "Le christianisme de Boèce," *Journal des savants* (1889) 449ff.

—— *La fin du paganisme, étude sur les dernières luttes religieuses en Occident au IVe siècle*, vol. 2, 9th ed. Paris, n.d., in 12mo.

BONNARD, R. "L'éducation scientifique de Boèce," *Speculum* 4 (1929) 198–206.

—— "Notes sur l'astrologie latine au VIe siècle," *RBPH* 10 (1931) 557–577.

BORGHORST, G. *De Anatolii fontibus*, diss. Berlin 1905.

BOUCHÉ-LECLERCQ, A. *L'astrologie grecque*, Paris 1899.

BOULANGER, A. "L'orphisme à Rome," *REL* 15 (1937) 121–135.

—— Review of *Lettres grecques en Occident*, 1st ed., *REL* 21/22 (1943/1944) 268–272.

BOYANCÉ, Pierre. "Leucas," *Revue archéologique* 30 (1929) 211–219.

—— "Une allusion à l'œuf orphique," *MEFR* 52 (1935) 96–112.

—— *Le culte des Muses chez les philosophes grecs, études d'histoire et de psychologie religieuses*, diss. Paris 1936.

—— "La fin de la culture antique," *REA* 47 (1945) 142–152.

BOYER, Charles. *Christianisme et néo-platonisme dans la formation de s. Augustin*, diss. Paris 1920.

BRAGARD, R. "L'harmonie des sphères selon Boèce," *Speculum* 4 (1929) 206–213.

BRANDT, Samuel. "Entstehungszeit und zeitliche Folge der Werke von Boethius," *Philologus* 62 (1903) 141–154 and 234–275.

BRÉHIER, Emile. *Histoire de la philosophie*, vol. 1: *Antiquité et Moyen Age*, Paris 1926–1927.

—— *La philosophie de Plotin*, Bibliothèque de la Revue des cours et conférences, vol. 19, Paris 1928.

—— Review of *Lettres grecques en Occident*, 1st ed., *Revue philosophique* (1944) 369–373.

BRÉHIER, Louis. "Les colonies d'Orientaux en Occident au commencement du Moyen Age (V^e–VIIIe siècles)," *Byzantinische Zeitschrift* 12 (1903) 1–39.

BRINKMANN, A. "Ein Denkmal des Neupythagoreismus," *Rheinisches Museum* 66 (1911) 616–625.

BROCHET, J. *Saint Jérôme et ses ennemis*, diss. Paris 1905.

BROISE, R. DE LA. *Mamerti Claudiani vita eiusque doctrina de anima hominis*, diss. Paris 1890.

BRUDER, Konrad. *Die philosophischen Elemente in den "Opuscula sacra" des Boethius*, Forschungen zur Geschichte der Philosophie und der Pädagogik, vol. 3, 2, Leipzig 1928.

BRUNET, Pierre, and MIELI, Aldo. *Histoire des sciences: Antiquité*, Paris 1935.

BRUYNE, Donatien de. "Une ancienne version latine inédite d'Arius," *RB* 26 (1909) 93–95.

—— "L'Itala de s. Augustin," *RB* 30 (1913) 294–314.

—— "Cassiodore et l'Amiatinus," *ibid.*, 39 (1927) 261–266.

—— "Saint Augustin réviseur de la Bible," *Miscellanea Agostiniana* 2 (Rome 1931) 521–606.

BRUYNE, Donatien de. *Les anciennes traductions latines des Machabées* (in collaboration with Dom B. Sodar), Anecdota Maredsolana, vol. 4 (1932).

BYWATER, I. "On a Lost Dialogue of Aristotle," *Journal of Philology* 2 (1869) 55–69.

CADIOU, René. "La bibliothèque de Césarée et la formation des chaînes," *Revue des sciences religieuses* 16 (1936) 474–483.

CAPELLE, B. Review of *Lettres grecques en Occident*, 1st ed., *Bulletin de théologie ancienne et médiévale* 5 (1946) 92–93.

CAPELLI, Luigi Mario. "I fonti delle *Institutiones humanarum rerum* di Cassiodoro," *Rendiconti del reale Istituto Lombardo di scienze e lettere*, 2nd series, vol. 31 (1898) 1549–1557.

CAPUA, F. di. "Il cursus nel *De consolatione philosophiae* e nei trattati teologici di Severino Boezio," *Didaskaleion* 3 (1914) 269–303.

CARCOPINO, Jérôme. *La vie quotidienne à Rome à l'apogée de l'Empire*, Paris 1939.

CARMODY, F. J. *Physiologus Latinus, Editions préliminaires*, version B, Paris 1939.

CARTON, Raoul. "Le christianisme et l'augustinisme de Boèce," *Mélanges augustiniens* (Paris 1931) 243–329, in 4to.

CARUSI, E., and W. M. LINDSAY. *Monumenti paleografici veronesi*, 2 vols. in fol., Rome 1929–1934.

CASPARI, C. P. *Quellen zur Geschichte des Taufsymbols und der Glaubensregel*, vol. 3, Christiania 1875.

CAVALLERA, Ferdinand. "Saint Augustin et le texte biblique de l'Itala," *Bulletin de littérature ecclésiastique* (1915/1916) 410–428.

—— *Saint Jérôme, sa vie et son œuvre*, Spicilegium sacrum Lovaniense, vol. 1 (Louvain and Paris 1922).

CERRATO, Ludovicus. "De Claudii Claudiani fontibus in poemate *De raptu Proserpinae*," *Rivista di filologia classica* 9 (1881) 273–395.

CHABOT, J. B. "L'école de Nisibe," *Journal asiatique*, 9th series, vol. 8 (1896) 43–93.

CHAPMAN, John. *Notes on the Early History of the Vulgate Gospels*, Oxford 1908.

—— "Cassiodorus and the Echternach Gospels," *RB* 28 (1911) 283–296.

—— "The Codex Amiatinus and Cassiodorus," *ibid.*, 38 (1926) 139–151 and 39 (1927) 12–32.

—— "The Codex Amiatinus Once More," *ibid.*, 40 (1928) 130–134.

CHAPPUIS, Paul G. "La théologie de Boèce," *Congrès d'histoire du christianisme* (Jubilé A. Loisy) 3 (Paris 1928) 15–40.

CHÂTELAIN, Aemilius. *Uncialis scriptura codicum Latinorum novis exemplis illustrata*, Paris 1901, in fol.

CHÂTILLON, François. "Regio dissimilitudinis," *Mélanges E. Podechard* (Lyon 1945) 85–102.

—— "Quidam secundum eos, note d'exégèse augustinienne," *Revue du Moyen Age latin* 1 (1945) 287–304.

CHEVALIER, J. *Saint Augustin et la pensée grecque, les relations trinitaires*, Collectanea Friburgensia, vol. 33 (Freiburg in Switzerland 1940).

CHRIST, W. von, W. SCHMID, and O. STAEHLIN. *Geschichte der griechischen Litteratur* (I. von Mueller's *Handbuch*, vol. 7) 2, 2: *Die nachklassische Periode der griechischen Litteratur, von 100 bis 530 nach Christus*, 6th ed., Munich 1924.

COLLOMP, P. "Per omnia elementa," *Revue de philologie* 36 (1912) 196–201.

COMBÈS, Gustave. *Saint Augustin et la culture classique*, diss. Paris 1927.

COMEAU, Marie. *Saint Augustin exégète du IVᵉ Evangile*, diss. Paris 1930.

COURCELLE, Pierre. "Boèce et l'école d'Alexandrie," *MEFR* 52 (1935) 185–223.

—— "Le site du monastère de Cassiodore," *ibid.*, 55 (1938) 259–307.

—— "Etude critique des commentaires sur la *Consolatio Philosophiae* de Boèce du IXᵉ au XVᵉ siècle," *Archives d'histoire doctrinale et littéraire du Moyen Age* 14 (1939) 5–140.

COURCELLE, Pierre. "Histoire d'un brouillon cassiodorien," *REA* 44 (1942) 65–86.

—— "Vingt années d'histoire de la littérature latine chrétienne," *Mémorial des études latines* (Paris 1943) 241–255.

—— "Quelques symboles funéraires du néo-platonisme chrétien," *REA* 46 (1944) 65–93.

—— "Sur les dernières paroles de s. Augustin," *ibid.*, pp. 205–207.

—— "Les premières Confessions de s. Augustin," *REL* 22 (1945) 155–174.

—— Review of A. Loyen, "Sidoine Apollinaire et l'esprit précieux en Gaule," *REA* 45 (1943) 307–311.

—— *Histoire littéraire des grandes invasions germaniques*, Paris 1948.

COUSIN, Victor. "Du commentaire inédit d'Olympiodore, philosophe alexandrin du VIᵉ siècle, sur le *Gorgias* de Platon," *Journal des savants* (1832) 398–410, 449–457, 521–531, 621–630, 670–682, 743–753.

CRAMER, Fredericus. *Dissertationis de Graecis medii aevi studiis pars prior: De Graecis per Occidentem studiis inde a primo medio aevo usque ad Carolum Magnum*, Stralsund 1848, in small 4to.

CUENDET, Georges. "Cicéron et s. Jérôme traducteurs," *REL* 11 (1933) 380–400.

CUMONT, Franz. *Textes et monuments figurés relatifs aux mystères de Mithra*, vol. 1, Brussels 1899, in 4to.

—— "La polémique de l'Ambrosiaster contre les païens," *RHLR* 8 (1903) 417–440.

—— "Pourquoi le latin fut la seule langue liturgique de l'Occident," *Mélanges Paul Frédéricq* (Brussels 1904) 63–66.

—— "La théologie solaire du paganisme romain," *Mémoires présentés par divers savants à l'Académie des Inscriptions et Belles-Lettres*, vol. 12, part 2 (1913) 447–479.

—— "Les anges du paganisme romain," *Revue de l'histoire des religions* 72 (1915) 159–182.

—— "Comment Plotin détourna Porphyre du suicide," *REG* 32 (1919) 113–120.

—— "Le culte égyptien et le mysticisme de Plotin," *Monuments Piot* 25 (1921/1922) 77–92.

—— *Les religions orientales dans le paganisme romain*, 4th ed., Paris 1929.

—— *Recherches sur le symbolisme funéraire des Romains*, Paris 1942, in 4to.

CZAPLA, Bruno. *Gennadius als Litterarhistoriker, eine quellenkritische Untersuchung der Schrift des Gennadius von Marseille De viris illustribus*, diss. Münster 1898 (complete ed., *Kirchengeschichtliche Studien*, vol. 4, 1).

DAHL, Axel. *Augustin und Plotin, philosophische Untersuchungen zum Trinitätsproblem und zur Nuslehre*, Lund 1945.

DAIN, A. "Les rapports gréco-latins," *Mémorial des études latines* (Paris 1943) 149–161.

DANIÉLOU, J. Review of *Lettres grecques en Occident*, 1st ed., *RSR* 33 (1946) 115–120.

DECKER, Anton. "Die Hildebold'sche Manuskriptensammlung des Kölner Domes," *Festschrift der 43. Versammlung deutscher Philologen und Schulmänner* (Bonn 1895) 215–251.

DEITERS, H. *Ueber das Verhältnis des Martianus Capella zu Aristides Quintilianus*, Progr. Posen 1881.

DENK, Otto. *Geschichte des gallo-fränkischen Unterrichts- und Bildungswesens, von den ältesten Zeiten bis auf Karl den Grossen, mit Berücksichtigung der litterarischen Verhältnisse*, Mainz 1892.

DEVREESSE, Robert. "La bibliothèque de Bobbio et le palimpseste du *De re publica*," *Bulletin de l'Association Guillaume Budé* (1935) 27–33.

—— "Anciens commentateurs grecs de l'Octateuque," *Revue biblique* 44 (1935) 166–191; 45 (1936) 201–220 and 364–384.

DEVREESSE, Robert. "L'église d'Afrique durant l'occupation byzantine," *MEFR* 57 (1940) 143–166.

DIEHL, Charles. *Etudes sur l'administration byzantine dans l'exarchat de Ravenne (568–751)*, Bibliothèque des écoles françaises d'Athènes et de Rome, vol. 53 (Paris 1888).

—— *L'Afrique byzantine, Histoire de la domination byzantine en Afrique (533–709)*, Paris 1896.

—— *Justinien et la civilisation byzantine*, Paris 1901, in 4to.

DIEHL, Charles, and G. MARÇAIS. *Le monde oriental de 395 à 1081*, Paris 1936, 2nd ed. 1944.

DIEKAMP, Franz. *Die origenistischen Streitigkeiten im sechsten Jahrhundert und das fünfte allgemeine Concil*, Münster 1899.

DIELS, Hermann. *Die Fragmente der Vorsokratiker*, vol. 1, Berlin 1906.

—— *Die Handschriften der antiken Aerzte*, Griechische Abteilung, Auftrag der akademischen Kommission herausgegeben, Aus. d. Abh. der königl. preuss. Akad. der Wissenschaften der Jahre 1905 und 1906, Berlin 1906, in 4to.

—— *Doxographi Graeci*, 2nd ed., Berlin and Leipzig 1929.

DIETZ, Friedrich Reinhold. *Scholia in Hippocratem et Galenum*, 2 vols., Leipzig 1834.

DILL, Samuel. *Roman Society in the Last Century of the Western Empire*, 2nd ed., London 1898.

DILLER, Hans. *Die Ueberlieferung der hippokratischen Schrift ΠΕΡΙ 'ΑΕΡΩΝ, 'ΥΔΑΤΩΝ, ΤΟΠΩΝ*, Philologus, Supplementband 33, 3 (Leipzig 1932).

DOBIACHE-ROJDESTVENSKY, Olga. *Les anciens manuscrits latins de la bibliothèque publique de Léningrad (V^e–VIIe siècles)*, Leningrad 1929.

—— "Le codex Q.v.I. 6–10 de la Bibliothèque Publique de Léningrad," *Speculum* 5 (1930) 21–48.

DOELLINGER, Ignaz von. "Einfluss der griechischen Litteratur und Kultur auf die abendländische Welt im Mittelalter," Doellinger's *Akademische Vorträge*, vol. 1 (Munich 1890) 162–186.

DRAESEKE, Joannes. "Zu Augustinus' *De Civ. Dei* XVIII, 42, eine Quellenuntersuchung," *Zeitschrift für wissenschaftliche Theologie* 32 (1889) 230–248.

—— "Zur Frage nach den Quellen von Augustins Kenntnis der griechischen Philosophie," *Theologische Studien und Kritiken* 89 (1916) 541–562.

DUCHESNE, Louis. *Histoire ancienne de l'église*, vol. 3, 5th ed., Paris 1920.

—— *L'église au VIe siècle*, Paris 1925.

DUHEM, Pierre. *Le système du monde, histoire des doctrines cosmologiques de Platon à Copernic*, 5 vols., Paris 1913–1917.

DYROFF, Adolf. "Zum Prolog des Johannes Evangeliums," *Pisciculi, Doelger Festschrift* (Münster 1939) 86–93.

—— "Der philosophische Teil der Encyclopädie des Cornelius Celsus," *Rheinisches Museum* 88 (1939) 7–18.

EBERSOLT, Jean. *Orient et Occident, recherches sur les influences byzantines et orientales en France avant les croisades*, Paris 1928, in 4to.

EBERT, A. *Allgemeine Geschichte der Literatur des Mittelalters im Abendlande bis zum Beginn des XI. Jahrhunderts*, 2nd ed., Leipzig 1889.

EGGER, E. *L'hellénisme en France, leçons sur l'influence des études grecques dans le développement de la langue et de la littérature françaises*, vol. 1, Paris 1869.

EITREM, S. "La théurgie chez les néo-platoniciens et dans les papyrus magiques," *Symbolae Osloenses* 22 (1942) 49–79.

ENGELBRECHT, A. "Untersuchungen über die Sprache des Claudianus Mamertus," *Sitzungsberichte der philosophisch-historischen Classe der kaiserlichen Akademie der Wissenschaften* 110 (1886) 423–542.

ENGELBRECHT, A. "Die *Cons. philos.* des Boethius, Beobachtungen über den Stil des Autors und die Ueberlieferung seines Werkes," *ibid.*, 144, part 3 (1902) 1–58.

ERDBRUEGGER, Henricus. *Cassiodorus unde etymologias in Psalterii commentario prolatas petivisse putandus sit,* diss. Jena 1912.

FABRE, Pierre. *Essai sur la chronologie des œuvres de s. Paulin de Nole,* diss. Paris 1948.

—— *Saint Paulin de Nole et l'amitié chrétienne,* Bibliothèque des écoles françaises d'Athènes et de Rome, fasc. 167, Paris 1948.

FARGUES, P. *Claudien, études sur sa poésie et son temps,* diss. Paris 1933.

FEDER, Alfred. *Studien zum Schriftstellerkatalog des hl. Hieronymus,* Freiburg im Breisgau 1927.

FERRARI, Olindo. "Il mondo degl'inferi in Claudiano," *Athenaeum* 4 (1916) 335–338.

FESTUGIÈRE, P. A. J. *L'idéal religieux des Grecs et l'Evangile,* Paris 1932.

FISCHER, Balduinus. *De Augustini disciplinarum libro qui est de dialectica,* diss. Jena 1912.

FISCHER, H. W. *Untersuchungen über die Quellen der Rhetorik des Martianus Capella,* diss. Breslau 1936.

FONCK, Léopold. "Hieronymi scientia naturalis exemplis illustratur," *Biblica* 1 (1920) 481–499.

FRANSES, D. *Die Werke des hl. Quodvultdeus, Bischofs von Karthago,* Veröffentlichungen aus dem kirchenhistorischen Seminar München, 4, 9 (Munich 1920).

FRANZ, Adolf. *M. Aurelius Cassiodorus Senator, ein Beitrag zur Geschichte der theologischen Literatur,* Breslau 1872.

FRIEBEL, O. *Fulgentius der Mythograph und Bischof,* Studien zur Geschichte und Kultur des Altertums, vol. 5 (Paderborn 1911).

FRIES, Carl. "De M. Varrone a Favonio Eulogio expresso," *Rheinisches Museum* 58 (1903) 115–125.

—— "Zu Macrob. *Sat.* I, 17–23," *Philologische Wochenschrift* 49 (1929) 1342–1344.

GALDI, Marco. *Saggi Boeziani,* Pisa 1938, in 4to.

GARVEY, M. P. *Saint Augustine: Christian or Neo-platonist?* diss. Milwaukee 1939.

GASQUET, A. *Etudes byzantines; l'empire byzantin et la monarchie franque,* Paris 1888.

GAUDENZI, Augusto. *Sui rapporti tra l'Italia e l'impero d'Oriente fra gli anni 476–554 d. C.,* Bologna 1886.

GEFFCKEN, J. *Der Ausgang des griechisch-römischen Heidentums,* Heidelberg 1920.

GEISLER, Eugenius. *De Apollinaris Sidonii studiis,* diss. Breslau 1885.

GEORGII, H. "Zur Bestimmung der Zeit des Servius," *Philologus* 71 (1912) 518–526.

GESSNER, August. *Servius und Pseudo-Asconius,* diss. Zürich 1888.

GHELLINCK, J. de. Review of *Lettres grecques en Occident,* 1st ed., *RHE* 41 (1946) 91–94.

—— Review of *Lettres grecques en Occident,* 1st ed., *Nouvelle revue théologique* 69 (1947) 206–207.

GIDEL, C. "Les études grecques en Europe (IVe s.—1453)," Gidel's *Nouvelles études* (Paris 1878) 1–289.

GIESEBRECHT, G. W. *De litterarum studiis apud Italos primis medii aevi saeculis,* Berlin 1845.

GILSON, Etienne. *Introduction à l'étude de s. Augustin,* Paris 1929.

GOELZER, Henri. *Etude lexicographique et grammaticale de la latinité de s. Jérôme,* diss. Paris 1884.

—— "Remarques lexicographiques sur le latin de s. Avit," *ALMA* 4 (1928) 25–33.

GOLDSTAUB, Max. *Der Physiologus und seine Weiterbildung, besonders in der lateinischen und in der byzantinischen Literatur, Philologus,* Supplementband 8, 3, Leipzig 1899/1901.

GOMOLL, Heinz. "Zu Cassiodors Bibliothek und ihrem Verhältnis zu Bobbio," *Zentralblatt für Bibliothekswesen* 53 (1936) 185–189.

GOOSSENS, R. Review of *Lettres grecques en Occident*, 1st ed., *L'antiquité classique* (1945) 216–223.

GORCE, Denys. *La lectio divina des origines du cénobitisme à s. Benoît et Cassiodore*, diss. Paris 1925.

—— *Les voyages, l'hospitalité et le port des lettres dans le monde chrétien des IVe et Ve siècles*, diss. Paris 1925.

GRABMANN, Martin. *Geschichte der scolastischen Methode*, 2 vols., Freiburg im Breisgau 1909.

GRANDGEORGE, L. *Saint Augustin et le néo-platonisme*, Bibliothèque de l'école des Hautes Etudes, vol. 8 (Paris 1896).

GROSSGERGE, Gualtharius. *De Senecae et Theophrasti libris de matrimonio*, diss. Königsberg 1911.

GRUETZMACHER, Georg. *Hieronymus, eine biographische Studie zur alten Kirchengeschichte*, 3 vols., Berlin 1901–1908.

GUILLOUX, P. "Saint Augustin savait-il le grec?" *RHE* 21 (1925) 79–83.

GUITTON, Jean. *Le temps et l'éternité chez Plotin et s. Augustin*, diss. Paris 1933.

HAARHOFF, Theodore. *Schools of Gaul, A Study of Pagan and Christian Education in the Last Century of the Western Empire*, Oxford 1920.

HAASE, Friedrich. *De Latinorum codicum manuscriptis subscriptionibus commentatio*, *Index lectionum in universitate litterarum Vratislaviensi*, Breslau 1860.

HAHN, Ludwig. "Zum Sprachenkampf im römischen Reich bis auf Zeit Justinians, eine Skizze," *Philologus*, Supplementband 10 (1907) 675–718.

HÅRLEMAN, Einar. *De Claudiano Mamerto Gallicae Latinitatis scriptore quaestiones*, diss. Uppsala 1938.

HARNACK, Adolf von. "Porphyrius *Gegen die Christen* 15 Bücher, Zeugnisse, Fragmente und Referate," *Abhandlungen der k. preussischen Akademie der Wissenschaften*, phil.-hist. Klasse, Berlin 1916, 1, pp. 3–115.

—— "Neue Fragmente des Werkes des Porphyrius *Gegen die Christen*, die Pseudo-Polycarpiana und die Schrift des Rhetors Pacatus gegen Porphyrius," *Sitzungsberichte der preussischen Akademie der Wissenschaften*, Berlin 1921, 1, pp. 266–284.

HEERKLOTZ, A. T. *Die "Variae" des Cassiodorus Senator als kulturgeschichtliche Quelle*, diss. Heidelberg 1926.

HELM, Rudolf. "Der Bischof Fulgentius und der Mythograph," *Rheinisches Museum* 54 (1899) 111–134.

HENRY, Paul. "Une traduction grecque d'un texte de Macrobe dans le Περὶ μηνῶν de Lydus," *REL* 11 (1933) 164–171.

—— *Plotin et L'Occident, Firmicus Maternus, Marius Victorinus, s. Augustin et Macrobe*, Spicilegium sacrum Lovaniense, vol. 15 (Louvain 1934).

—— *La vision d'Ostie, sa place dans la vie et l'œuvre de s. Augustin*, diss. Paris 1938.

—— "Augustine and Plotinus," *The Journal of Theological Studies* 38 (1937) 1–23.

HEUTEN, G. "La diffusion des cultes égyptiens en Occident," *Revue de l'histoire des religions* 104 (1931) 409–416.

—— "Le 'Soleil' de Porphyre," *Mélanges F. Cumont* 1 (Brussels 1936) 253–259.

HEYD, W. *Histoire du commerce du Levant au Moyen Age*, vol. 1, Leipzig 1885.

HILDEBRAND, August. *Boethius und seine Stellung zum Christentum*, Regensburg 1885.

HOBERG, Godofredus. *De s. Hieronymi ratione interpretandi*, diss. Münster 1886.

HOERLE, G. H. *Frühmittelalterliche Mönchs- und Klerikerbildung in Italien*, Freiburger theologische Studien, vol. 13, Freiburg im Breisgau 1914.

HOPFNER, Theodor. *Griechisch-Aegyptischer Offenbarungszauber*, Studien zur Palaeographie und Papyruskunde, vols. 21 and 23, Leipzig 1921–1924, in 4to.

HOPPE, H. "Griechisches bei Rufin," *Glotta* 26 (1937) 132–144.

HUBERT, Kurt. "Zur indirekten Ueberlieferung der Tischgespräche Plutarchs," *Hermes* 73 (1938) 307–328.

HUBY, J. "Ostie, un nœud de rencontres et d'influences," *Etudes* 139 (1939) 782–788.

INGUANEZ, Mauro. "Inventario di Pomposa del 1459," *Bollettino del bibliofilo* 2 (1920) 173–184.

JAFFÉ, Philippus, and GuilelmusWATTENBACH. *Ecclesiae metropolitanae Coloniensis codices manuscripti*, Berlin 1874.

JALABERT, L. "Les colonies chrétiennes d'Orientaux en Occident du Vᵉ au VIIIᵉ siècle," *Revue de l'Orient chrétien* 9 (1904) 96–106.

JANNE, H. "Un contresens de Cassiodore: les furets du *Contre Apion*," *Byzantion* 11 (1936) 225–227.

JOERG, Edgar. *Des Boetius und des Alfredus Magnus Kommentar zu den Elementen des Euklid (Nach dem codex Z.L. CCCXXXII B der Biblioteca Nazionale di S. Marco zu Venedig), Zweites Buch*, diss. Heidelberg 1935.

JOLIVET, Régis. *Essai sur les rapports entre la pensée grecque et la pensée chrétienne*, Paris 1931, in 4to.

―――― *Saint Augustin et le néo-platonisme chrétien*, Paris 1932.

―――― *Dieu, soleil des esprits, ou la doctrine augustinienne de l'illumination*, Paris 1934.

JOURDAIN, Charles. "De l'origine des traditions sur le christianisme de Boèce," *Mémoires de l'Académie des Inscriptions et Belles-Lettres*, 1st series, 6 (1860) 330–360.

KAPPELMACHER, A. "Der schriftstellerische Plan des Boethius," *Wiener Studien* 46 (1928) 215–225.

KEMMER, P. A. *Charisma maximum, Untersuchungen zu Cassians Vollkommenheitsideal und seiner Stellung zum Messalianismus*, Louvain 1938.

KIHN, Heinrich. *Theodor von Mopsuestia und Junilius Africanus, als Exegeten, nebst einer kritisch Textausgabe von den letzteren Instituta regularia divinae legis*, Freiburg im Breisgau 1880.

KLINGNER, F. *De Boethii consolatione philosophiae*, Philologische Untersuchungen herausgeben von A. Kiessling und U. von Wilamowitz-Moellendorff, vol. 27, Berlin 1921.

KLOSTERMANN, E. "Die Schriften des Origenes in Hieronymus' Brief an Paula," *Sitzungsberichte der k. preussischen Akademie* (Berlin 1897) 855–870.

―――― "Die Ueberlieferung der Jeremiahomilien des Origenes," *Texte und Untersuchungen zur Geschichte der altchristlichen Literatur*, vol. 16 n.s., 1, 3 (1897) 1–114.

KROLL, W. *De Q. Aurelii Symmachi studiis Graecis et Latinis*, Breslauer philologische Abhandlungen, vol. 6, 2, Breslau 1891.

―――― *De oraculis Chaldaicis, ibid.*, vol. 7, 1, Breslau 1894.

KRUSCH, Bruno. "Die Einführung des griechischen Paschalritus im Abendlande," *Neues Archiv* 9 (1883) 99–169.

KURTH, Godefroid. "Grégoire de Tours et les études classiques au VIᵉ siècle," *Revue des questions historiques* 24 (1878) 586–593.

LABRIOLLE, Pierre de. *Histoire de la littérature latine chrétienne*, 2nd ed., Paris 1924.

―――― "Le songe de s. Jérôme," *Miscellanea Geronimiana* (Rome 1920) 217–239.

―――― *La réaction païenne, étude sur la polémique antichrétienne du Iᵉʳ au VIᵉ siècle*, Paris 1934.

―――― *Histoire de l'église depuis les origines jusqu'à nos jours*, vol. 4: *De la mort de Théodose à l'avènement de Grégoire le Grand* (with G. Bardy, L. Bréhier, G. de Plinval), Paris 1937.

LAMBRECHTS, Pierre. "Le commerce des 'Syriens' en Gaule, du Haut-Empire à l'époque mérovingienne," *L'antiquité classique* 6 (1937) 35–61.

LAPEYRE, G. G. *Saint Fulgence de Ruspe, un évêque catholique africain sous la domination vandale*, diss. Paris 1929.

—— *Vie de s. Fulgence de Ruspe, par Ferrand, diacre de Carthage*, ed. and trans., diss. Paris 1929.

LATAIX, Jean-A. Loisy. "Le commentaire de s. Jérôme sur Daniel," *RHLR* 2 (1897) 164–173 and 268–277.

LAUCHERT, Friedrich. *Geschichte des Physiologus*, Strasburg 1889.

LA VILLE DE MIRMONT, H. de. "L'astrologie chez les Gallo-Romains," *REA* 4 (1902) 115–141; 5 (1903) 255–293; 8 (1906) 128–164; 9 (1907) 69–82 and 155–171; 11 (1909) 301–346.

LEBRETON, J. "Sainte Monique et s. Augustin, la vision d'Ostie," *RSR* 28 (1938) 457–472.

LEISEGANG, Hans. *Die Begriffe der Zeit und Ewigkeit im späteren Platonismus*, Beiträge zur Geschichte der Philosophie des Mittelalters, vol. 13, 4 (Münster 1913).

LEJAY, Paul. "Bobbio et la bibliothèque de Cassiodore," *Bulletin d'ancienne littérature et d'archéologie chrétiennes* 3 (1913) 265–269.

LESNE, E. *Histoire de la propriété ecclésiastique en France*, vol. 4: *Les livres, 'scriptoria' et bibliothèques, du commencement du VIIIe à la fin du XIe siècle*, Mémoires et travaux . . . des Facultés catholiques de Lille, fasc. 44, Lille 1938.

LEUSSE, Hubert de. "Le problème de la préexistence des âmes chez Marius Victorinus Afer," *RSR* 29 (1939) 197–239.

LINDSAY, James. "Le système de Proclus," *Revue de métaphysique et de morale* 28 (1921) 497–523.

LINKE, Hugo. *Quaestiones de Macrobii Saturnaliorum fontibus*, diss. Breslau 1880.

—— "Ueber Macrobius' Kommentar zu Ciceros *Somnium Scipionis*," *Philologische Abhandlungen, Martin Hertz zum siebzigsten Geburtstage* (Berlin 1888) 240–256.

LOT, Ferdinand. *La fin du monde antique et le début du Moyen Age*, Paris 1927.

LOWE, E. A. *Codices Lugdunenses antiquissimi*, Lyon 1924, in fol.

—— *Scriptura Beneventana, Fac-similes of South Italian and Dalmatian Manuscripts from the Sixth to the Fourteenth Century*, Oxford 1929, in fol.

—— *Codices Latini antiquiores, A Palaeographical Guide to Latin Manuscripts Prior to the Ninth Century*, vol. 1: *The Vatican City*; vol. 2: *Great Britain and Ireland*; vol. 3: *Italy* (Ancona–Novara), Oxford 1934——(in course of publication), in fol.

LOYEN, André. "L'esprit précieux dans la société polie des Gaules au Ve siècle," *REL* 10 (1932) 114–126.

—— *Recherches historiques sur les panégyriques de Sidoine Apollinaire*, Bibliothèque de l'école des Hautes Etudes, sciences hist. et philol., fasc. 285, Paris 1942.

—— *Sidoine Apollinaire et l'esprit précieux en Gaule aux derniers jours de l'Empire*, Collection d'études latines, série scientifique, vol. 20, diss. Paris 1943.

—— Review of *Lettres grecques en Occident*, 1st ed., *Revue de philologie* 19 (1945) 192–199.

LUEBECK, Aemilius. *Hieronymus quos noverit scriptores et ex quibus hauserit*, Leipzig 1872.

LUSCHER, Alfredus. *De Prisciani studiis Graecis*, diss. Breslau 1911.

MANGENOT, E. "Les manuscrits grecs des Evangiles employés par s. Jérôme," *Revue des sciences ecclésiastiques* 81 (1900) 56–72.

MANITIUS, Karl. *Des Hypsikles Schrift Anaphorikos nach Ueberlieferung und Inhalt kritisch behandelt*, Progr. Dresden 1888, in 4to.

MANITIUS, Max. "Zu Ausonius und Apollinaris Sidonius," *Jahrbücher für classische Philologie* 137 (1888) 79–80.

—— *Philologisches aus alten Bibliothekskatalogen*, Frankfurt 1892; also in *Rheinisches Museum*, n.s. 47 (1892), Ergänzungsheft.

MANITIUS, Max. *Geschichte der lateinischen Literatur des Mittelalters*, 3 vols., Munich 1911–1931 (= I. von Mueller's *Handbuch*, vol. 9, 2).

—— *Handschriften antiker Autoren in mittelalterlichen Bibliothekskatalogen*, 67. Beiheft zum Zentralblatt für Bibliothekswesen, Leipzig 1935.

MARÉCHAL, J. "La vision de Dieu au sommet de la contemplation, d'après s. Augustin," *Nouvelle revue théologique* 57 (1930) 89–109 and 191–214.

MARROU, H. I. "Autour de la bibliothèque du pape Agapit," *MEFR* 48 (1931) 124–169.

—— "*Doctrina* et *disciplina* dans la langue des Pères de l'église," *ALMA* 9 (1934) 1–23.

—— *Saint Augustin et la fin de la culture antique*, diss. Paris 1938.

—— *MOYCIKOC 'ANHP, Etude sur les scènes de la vie intellectuelle figurant sur les monuments funéraires romains*, Bibliothèque de l'Institut français de Naples, vol. 4, Grenoble 1938 (diss. Paris).

—— "L'origine orientale des diaconies romaines," *MEFR* 57 (1940) 95–142.

—— "Diadoque de Photikè et Victor de Vita," *REA* 45 (1943) 225–232.

—— "Jean Cassien à Marseille," *Revue du Moyen Age latin* 1 (1945) 5–17.

—— Review of Loyen, *Sidoine Apollinaire et l'esprit précieux*, ibid., pp. 198–204.

MARSILI, Salvatore. *Giovanni Cassiano ed Evagrio Pontico, dottrina sulla carità e contemplazione*, Studia Anselmiana, vol. 5 (Rome 1936).

MARTIN, Josef. *Grillius, ein Beitrag zur Geschichte der Rhetorik*, Studien zur Geschichte und Kultur des Altertums, vol. 14, 2/3 (Paderborn 1927).

—— *Symposion, die Geschichte einer literarischen Form*, ibid., vol. 17, 1/2 (Paderborn 1931).

MARTIN, V. *Quae de Providentia Boetius in consolatione philosophiae scripserit*, diss. Paris 1865.

MARTROYE, F. *L'Occident à l'époque byzantine, Goths et Vandales*, Paris 1904.

—— *Genséric, la conquête vandale en Afrique et la destruction de l'empire d'Occident*, Paris 1907.

MASPERO, Jean. "Horapollon et la fin du paganisme égyptien," *Bulletin de l'Institut d'archéologie orientale* 11 (1914) 163–195.

MÉNAGER, A. "La patrie de Cassien," *Echos d'Orient* 24 (1921) 330–358.

MERCATI, G. "Il catalogo della biblioteca di Pomposa," *Studi e documenti di storia e diritto* 17 (1896) 143–177.

—— "Le titulationes nelle opere dogmatiche di s. Ambrogio," *Ambrosiana, scritti varii pubblicati nel XV centenario dalla morte di s. Ambrogio* (Milan 1897) 1–44.

—— "Appunti su Niceta ed Aniano traduttore di s. Giovanni Crisostomo," *Studi e testi* 5 (1901) 137ff.

—— "Per la vita e gli scritti di Paolo il Persiano, appunti da una disputa di religione sotto Giustino e Giustiniano," *ibid.*, pp. 180–206.

—— *M. T. Ciceronis de re publica libri e codice rescripto Vaticano Latino 5757 phototypice expressi. Prolegomena de fatis bibliothecae monasterii s. Columbani Bobbiensis et de codice ipso Vat. Lat. 5757*, Vatican City 1934, in fol.

MEYERHOF, Max. "La fin de l'école d'Alexandrie d'après quelques auteurs arabes," *Archeion* 15 (1933) 1–15.

MIEKLEY, Gualtherius. *De Boethii libri de musica primi fontibus*, diss. Jena 1898.

MISCH, G. *Geschichte der Autobiographie*, Leipzig and Berlin 1907.

MOERLAND, H. *Die lateinischen Oribasiusübersetzungen, Symbolae Osloenses*, fasc. suppl. 5 (Oslo 1932).

MOLLAND, Einar. "Three Passages in St. Augustine," *Serta Eitremiana, Symbolae Osloenses*, suppl. 11 (Oslo 1942) 112–117.

MONCEAUX, Paul. *Les Africains, les païens*, Paris 1894.

——— *Histoire littéraire de l'Afrique chrétienne depuis les origines jusqu'à l'invasion arabe*, 7 vols., Paris 1901–1923.

——— "Enquête sur l'épigraphie chrétienne d'Afrique," *Revue archéologique*, 4th series, 2 (1903) 55–90 and 240–256.

——— "L'Isagoge latine de Marius Victorinus," *Philologie et linguistique, mélanges offerts à Louis Havet* (Paris 1909) 291–310.

——— "Saint Augustin et s. Antoine, contribution à l'histoire du monachisme," *Miscellanea Agostiniana* 2 (Rome 1931) 61–89.

MORICCA, U. *Storia della letteratura latina cristiana*, vol. 3 : *La letteratura dei secoli V e VI, da Agostino a s. Gregorio Magno*, 2 vols., Turin 1932–1934.

——— "La conversione di s. Agostino," *Il mondo classico* 11 (1941) 232–253.

MORIN, Germain. *Anecdota Maredsolana*, vols. 1–3, Maredsous 1895–1903, in 4to.

——— "Les monuments de la prédication de s. Jérôme," *RHLR* 1 (1896) 393–434. Reprinted in his *Etudes, textes, découvertes, contribution à la littérature et à l'histoire des douze premiers siècles*, vol. 1 (Maredsous and Paris 1913) 220–293.

——— "Etude d'ensemble sur Arnobe le jeune," *RB* 28 (1911) 154–190.

——— "Un ouvrage restitué à Julien d'Eclanum: Le commentaire du Pseudo-Rufin sur les prophètes Osée, Joel et Amos," *ibid.*, 30 (1913) 1–24.

——— "Une compilation antiarienne inédite sous le nom de s. Augustin, issue du milieu de Cassiodore," *ibid.*, 31 (1914/1919) 237–243.

——— "La collection gallicane dite d'Eusèbe d'Emèse et les problèmes qui s'y rattachent," *Zeitschrift für die neutestamentliche Wissenschaft* 34 (1935) 92–115.

MRAS, Karl. "Macrobius' Kommentar zu Ciceros *Somnium*, ein Beitrag zur Geistesgeschichte des V. Jahrhunderts n. Chr.," *Sitzungsberichte der preussischen Akademie der Wissenschaften*, phil.-hist. Klasse, 6 (1933) 232–286.

MUELLER, Albert. "Studentenleben im IV. Jahrhundert n. Chr.," *Philologus* 69 (1910) 292–317.

MUELLER, Ernestus. *De auctoritate et origine exemplorum orationis solutae Graecorum quae Priscianus contulit capita selecta*, diss. Königsberg 1911.

MUELLER, G. A. *Die Trostschrift des Boetius*, diss. Giessen, Berlin 1912.

MURPHY, Francis. *Rufinus of Aquileia (345–411), His Life and Works*, Studies in Mediaeval History, n.s. 6 (Washington 1945).

NICKSTADT, Helmut. *De digressionibus quibus in "Variis" usus est Cassiodorus*, diss. Marburg 1921.

NICOLAAS, Th. W. J. *Praetextatus*, diss. Utrecht, Nimeguen 1940.

NICOLAU, M. "A propos d'un texte parallèle de Macrobe et de Lydus, la doctrine astrologique de la 'collaboration des astres,'" *REL* 11 (1933) 318–321.

NIGGETIET, G. *De Cornelio Labeone*, diss. Münster 1908.

NITZSCH, Friedrich. *Das System des Boethius und die ihm zugeschriebenen theologischen Schriften*, Berlin 1860.

NORDEN, Eduard. *P. Vergilius Maro, Aeneis Buch VI*, 2nd ed., Leipzig 1916.

NORDENFALK, Carl. *Vier Kanonestafeln eines spätantiken Evangelienbuches*, Göteborg 1937.

OLLERIS, Alexandre. *Cassiodore conservateur des livres de l'antiquité latine*, diss. Paris 1841.

PASCAL, Carlo. *Graecia capta, saggi sopra alcune fonti greche di scrittori latini*, Florence 1905.

PATCH, H. R. "The Tradition of the Goddess Fortuna in Roman Literature and in the Transitional Period," *Smith College Studies in Modern Languages* 3 (1922) 190–195.

——— "Fate in Boethius and the Neoplatonists," *Speculum* 4 (1929) 62–72.

——— "Consolatio Philosophiae IV, metr. 6, 23–24," *ibid.*, 8 (1933) 41–51.

——— "Necessity in Boethius and the Neoplatonists," *ibid.*, 10 (1935) 393–404.

PEASE, A. S. "Medical Allusions in the Works of Jerome," *Harvard Studies in Classical Philology* 25 (1914) 73–86.

—— "The Attitude of Jerome Towards Pagan Literature," *Transactions and Proceedings of the American Philological Association* 50 (1919) 150–167.

PERLER, O. "Der Nus bei Plotin und das Verbum bei Augustinus als vorbildliche Ursache der Welt," *Studia Friburgensia* (1931).

PERNOT, Hubert. "Hellénisme et Italie méridionale," *Studi italiani di filologia classica* 13 (1936) 161–182.

PICARD, Charles. "Ulysse et le moly," *Revue archéologique*, 6th series, vol. 26 (1946) 156–157.

—— "Une scène d'inspiration antique méconnue, le mythe de Circé au tympan du grand portail de Vézelay," *Bulletin Monumental* (1945) 213–229.

PICAVET, François. "Hypostases plotiniennes et trinité chrétienne," *Annuaire de l'Ecole pratique des Hautes Etudes*, section des sciences religieuses (1916/1917) 1–52.

PINCHERLE, Alberto. Review of *Lettres grecques en Occident*, 1st ed., *Ricerche religiose* 18 (1947) 51–64.

PIRENNE, H. "La fin du commerce des Syriens en Occident," *Mélanges Bidez* 2 (1934) 677–687.

—— "De l'état de l'instruction des laïques à l'époque mérovingienne," *RB* 46 (1934) 164–177.

PLASBERG, Otto. *De Marci Tullii Ciceronis Hortensio dialogo*, diss. Berlin 1892.

PLINVAL, G. de. "Recherches sur l'œuvre littéraire de Pélage," *Revue de philologie* 8 (1934) 9–42.

—— *Pélage, ses écrits, sa vie et sa réforme*, Lausanne 1943.

—— *Essai sur le style et la langue de Pélage, suivi du traité inédit " De induratione cordis Pharaonis*," Freiburg in Switzerland 1947.

PRAECHTER, Karl. *Hierokles der Stoiker*, Leipzig 1901.

—— "Richtungen und Schulen im Neuplatonismus," *Genethliakon, C. Robert zum 8. März 1910* (Berlin 1910) 105–156.

—— "Eine Stelle Varros zur Zahlentheorie," *Hermes* 46 (1911) 407–413.

—— "Christlich-neuplatonische Beziehungen," *Byzantinische Zeitschrift* 21 (1912) 1–27.

—— "Zur theoretischen Begründung der Theurie im Neuplatonismus," *Archiv für Religionswissenschaft* 25 (1927) 209–213.

PRANTL, C. *Geschichte der Logik im Abendlande*, vol. 1, Leipzig 1927 (reprinted from the 1855 edition).

PUECH, Aimé. *Histoire de la littérature grecque chrétienne*, vol. 3: *Le IVe siècle*, Paris 1930.

PUECH, H. C. "Liberatus de Carthage et la date de l'apparition des écrits dionysiens," *Annuaire de l'Ecole pratique des Hautes Etudes*, section des sciences religieuses (1930/1931) 3–39.

—— Review of *Lettres grecques en Occident*, 1st ed., *Revue de l'histoire des religions* 131 (1946) 187–197.

QUENTIN, Henri. *Mémoire sur l'établissement du texte de la Vulgate*, Collectanea biblica Latina, vol. 6 (Rome and Paris 1922).

RAHNER, Hugo. *Griechische Mythen in christlicher Deutung*, Zürich 1945.

RAND, E. Kennard. "Der dem Boethius zugeschriebene Traktat de fide catholica," *Jahrbücher für classische Philologie*, Supplementband 26 (1901) 401–461.

—— "On the Composition of Boethius' *Consolatio Philosophiae*," *Harvard Studies in Classical Philology* 15 (1904) 1–28.

—— *The Founders of the Middle Ages*, Cambridge, Mass. 1928.

RAUSCHEN, G. *Das griechisch-römische Schulwesen zur Zeit des ausgehenden Heidentums*, Bonn 1900, in 4to.

—— *Bibliotheca Patrum Latinorum Italica*, 2 vols., Vienna 1865–1871.

REIFFERSCHEID, August. "Zwei litterarhistorische Phantasmata," *Rheinisches Museum* 16 (1861) 23–26.

REINHARDT, Carolus. *De Graecorum theologia capita duo*, diss. Berlin 1910.

REITTER, Nikolaus. *Der Glaube an die Fortdauer des römischen Reiches im Abendlande während des V. und VI. Jahrhunderts*, diss. Münster 1900.

RENAN, Ernest. *Histoire de l'étude de la langue grecque dans l'Occident de l'Europe depuis la fin du Ve siècle jusqu'à celle du XIVe siècle*. Unpublished. Bibliothèque de l'Institut de France, manuscript 2208.

REUTER, Hans. "Augustin und der katholische Orient," Reuter's *Augustinische Studien* (Gotha 1887) 153–230.

RITSCHL, Friedrich. *De M. Varronis disciplinarum libris*, Progr. Bonn 1845; reprinted in his *Opuscula philologica*, vol. 3 (Leipzig 1877) 352–402.

RITTER, J. *Mundus intelligibilis, eine Untersuchung zur Aufnahme und Umwandlung der neuplatonischen Ontologie bei Augustinus*, Frankfurt 1937.

ROCHUS, L. "Virgile de Toulouse," *RBPH* 10 (1931) 495–504.

ROGER, M. *L'enseignement des lettres classiques d'Ausone à Alcuin*, diss. Paris 1905.

ROHLFS, Gerhard. *Scavi linguistici nella Magna Grecia*, Halle and Rome 1933 (trans. B. Tomasini).

ROSE, Valentin. *Anecdota Graeca et Graecolatina, Mitteilungen aus Handschriften zur Geschichte der griechischen Wissenschaft*, vol. 2, Berlin 1870.

ROSSI, Joannes Baptista de. "De origine, historia, indicibus scrinii et bibliothecae sedis apostolicae commentatio," *Codices Palatini Latini bibliothecae Vaticanae* 1 (Rome 1886), pp. I–CXXXII.

ROTHENHAEUSLER, Matthäus. "Ueber Anlage und Quellen der Regel des hl. Benedikt," *Studien und Mitteilungen zur Geschichte des Benediktinerordens* 38 (1917) 1–17.

ROTTMANNER, Odilo. "Zur Sprachenkenntnis des hl. Augustinus," *Theologische Quartalschrift* 77 (1895) 269–276.

RUDBERG, Gunnar. "Till Augustinus' ortografi," *Eranos, acta philologica suecana* 25 (1927) 222–229.

RUTHERFORD, Hamish. *Sidonius Apollinaris, étude d'une figure gallo-romaine du Ve siècle*, diss. Clermont-Ferrand 1938.

SALAVILLE, S. "La connaissance du grec chez s. Augustin," *Echos d'Orient* 25 (1922) 387–393.

—— "Saint Augustin et l'Orient," *Angelicum* 8 (1931) 3–23.

SALMON, Pierre. *Le lectionnaire de Luxeuil*, Collectanea biblica Latina, vol. 8 (Rome 1944), p. LXXVI.

SALONIUS, A. H. *Vitae Patrum, kritische Untersuchungen über Text, Syntax und Wortschatz der spätlateinischen Vitae Patrum*, Lund 1920.

SALTET, Louis. "Les sources de l' Ἐρανιστής de Théodoret," *RHE* 6 (1905) 289–303.

SANDYS, J. E. *A History of Classical Scholarship from the Sixth Century B.C. to the End of the Middle Ages*, Cambridge 1903, 3rd ed. 1921.

SCALA, R. von. "Ueber neue Polybiusbruchstücke bei Hieronymus," *Verhandl. der 42. Philologenversammlung* (Leipzig 1894) 357–358.

SCHANZ, Martin. *Geschichte der römischen Litteratur bis zum Gesetzgebungswerk des Kaisers Justinian*, vol. 4: *Die römische Litteratur von Constantin bis zum Gesetzgebungswerk Justinians*, 2 vols., Munich 1914–1920 (= vol. 8 of I. von Mueller's *Handbuch*).

SCHEDLER, Ph. M. *Die Philosophie des Macrobius und ihr Einfluss auf die Wissenschaft des chr. Mittelalters*, Beiträge zur Geschichte der Philosophie des Mittelalters, vol. 13, 1 (Münster 1916).

SCHEID, P. N. "Die Weltanschauung des Boethius und sein Trostbuch," *Stimmen aus Maria-Laach* 39, 2 (1890) 374–392.

SCHEMMEL, Fritz. "Die Hochschule von Konstantinopel im IV. Jahrhundert p. Chr. n.," *Neue Jahrbücher für das klassische Altertumsgeschichte und deutsche Literatur und für Pädagogik* 22 (1908) 147–168.

———— "Die Hochschule von Athen im IV. und V. Jahrhundert p. Chr. n.," *ibid.*, 22 (1908) 494–513.

———— "Die Hochschule von Alexandria im IV. und V. Jahrhundert p. Chr. n.," *ibid.*, 24 (1909) 438–457.

———— *Die Hochschule von Konstantinopel vom V. bis IX. Jahrhundert*, Progr. Berlin 1912.

SCHISSEL VON FLESCHENBERG, Otmar. *Marinos von Neapolis und die neuplatonischen Tugendgrade*, Texte und Forschungen zur byzantinisch-neugriechischen Philologie, vol. 8 (Athens 1928).

———— "Kaiser Julians Schulbildung," *Klio* 5 (1929) 326–328.

SCHMIDT, C. *Quaestiones de musicis scriptoribus Romanis inprimis de Cassiodoro et Isidoro*, diss. Darmstadt 1899.

SCHMIDT, Ludwig. *Geschichte der Wandalen*, Leipzig 1901.

SCHNITZLER, Th. *Im Kampfe um Chalcedon, Geschichte und Inhalt des Codex Encyclius von 458*, Rome 1938.

SCHRADE, Leo. "Die Stellung der Musik in der Philosophie des Boethius als Grundlage der ontologischen Musikerziehung," *Archiv für Geschichte der Philosophie* 41 (1932) 368–400.

SCHURR, Viktor. *Die Trinitätslehre des Boethius im Lichte der "skythischen Kontroversen,"* Forschungen zur christlichen Literatur und Dogmengeschichte vol. 18, 1 (Paderborn 1935).

SCHUSTER, I. "Come finì la biblioteca di Cassiodoro," *Scuola cattolica* 70 (1942) 409–414.

SCHWABE, L. "Die *Opiniones philosophorum* des Celsus," *Hermes* 19 (1884) 385–392.

SCHWARTZ, Eduard. "Zweisprachigkeit in den Konzilakten," *Philologus* 88 (1933) 245–253.

———— *Acta conciliorum oecumenicorum*, vol. 2, 5, Berlin and Leipzig 1936.

SEECK, Otto. *Geschichte des Untergangs der antiken Welt*, vols. 5–6, Berlin 1913–1920.

SEMERIA, G. *Il cristianesimo di Sev. Boezio rivendicato*, Studi e documenti di storia e diritto, vol. 21 (Rome 1900).

SILK, E. T. "Boethius's *Consolatio Philosophiae* as a Sequel to Augustine's *Dialogues* and *Soliloquia*," *Harvard Theological Review* 32 (1939) 19–39.

SIMON, J. *Histoire de l'école d'Alexandrie*, vol. 2, Paris 1845.

SINKO, Thaddeus. *De Apulei et Albini doctrinae Platonicae adumbratione*, Cracow 1905.

SPREITZENHOFER, E. *Die Entwicklung des alten Mönchthums in Italien von seinen erstem Anfängen bis zum Auftreten des hl. Benedict*, Vienna 1894.

STAERK, Antonio. *Les manuscrits latins du Ve au XIIIe siècle conservés à la bibliothèque impériale de Saint-Pétersbourg*, 2 vols., St. Petersburg 1910, in fol.

STEINACKER, Harold. "Die römische Kirche und die griechischen Sprachkenntnisse des Frühmittelalters," *Festschrift Theodor Gomperz* (Vienna 1902) 324–341, in 4to.

STEWART, H. F. *Boethius, An Essay*, Edinburgh 1891, in 12mo.

STIGLMAYR, Josef. *Das Aufkommen der pseudo-dionysischen Schriften und ihr Eindringen in die christliche Literatur bis zum Lateranconcil 649*, Progr. Feldkirch 1895.

SUNDWALL, Johannes. *Abhandlungen zur Geschichte des ausgehenden Römertums*, Helsinki 1919.

SVOBODA, K. *L'esthétique de s. Augustin et ses sources*, Opera facultatis philosophicae universitatis Masarykianae Brunensis, vol. 35 (Brno and Paris 1933).

SYCHOWSKI, St. von. *Hieronymus als Litterarhistoriker, eine quellenkritische Untersuchung der Schrift des hl. Hieronymus "de viris illustribus,"* Kirchengeschichtliche Studien, vol. 2, 2 (Münster 1894).

TAMASSIA, N. "Gregorio di Tours e Omero," *Atti del r. Istituto Veneto* 88, pp. 1209–1236.

TARDI, D. *Fortunat, étude sur un dernier représentant de la poésie latine dans la Gaule mérovingienne*, diss. Paris 1927.

—— *Les Epitomae de Virgile de Toulouse, essai de traduction critique avec une bibliographie, une introduction et des notes*, diss. Paris 1928.

THEILER, Willy. *Porphyrios und Augustin*, Schriften der Königsberger gelehrten Gesellschaft, vol. 10, 1 (Halle 1933).

THÉRY, G. "Scot Erigène, traducteur de Denys," *ALMA* 6 (1931) 185–278.

THIBAUT, J. "Autour de la patrie de Cassien," *Echos d'Orient* 24 (1921) 447–449.

THIEL, Andreas. *Epistulae Romanorum pontificum genuinae et quae ad eos scriptae sunt a s. Hilaro usque ad Pelagium II*, vol. 1: *A s. Hilaro ad s. Hormisdam*, Brunsberg 1868.

THIELE, Hans. "Cassiodor, seine Klostergründung Vivarium und sein Nachwirken im Mittelalter," *Studien und Mitteilungen zur Geschichte des Benediktinerordens* 50 (1932) 378–419.

THIELING, Walter. *Der Hellenismus in Kleinafrika, der griechische Kultureinfluss in den römischen Provinzen Nordwestafrikas*, Leipzig and Berlin 1911.

TIXERONT, J. "Des concepts de 'nature' et de 'personne' dans les Pères et les écrivains ecclésiastiques des Ve et VIe siècles," *RHLR* 8 (1903) 582–592.

TOUGARD, Abbot A. *L'hellénisme dans les écrivains du Moyen Age du VIIe au IXe siècle*, Paris 1886, tall 8vo.

TRAUBE, L. *Varia libamenta critica*, diss. Munich 1883.

—— *Vorlesungen und Abhandlungen*, 2 vols., Munich 1909.

UEBERWEG, Friedrich. *Grundriss der Geschichte der Philosophie*, vol. 2: *Die mittlere oder die patristische und scolastische Zeit*, 10th ed. by M. Baumgartner, Berlin 1915.

USENER, Hermann. "Vergessenes," *Rheinisches Museum* 28 (1873) 391–403.

—— *Anecdoton Holderi, ein Beitrag zur Geschichte Roms in ostgotischer Zeit*, Festschrift zur Begrüssung der XXXII.Versammlung deutscher Philologen und Schulmänner zu Wiesbaden, Bonn 1877.

—— "Legendenaustausch der griechischen und römischen Kirche," *Jahrbücher für protestantische Theologie* 13 (1887) 240–259.

VAGANAY, L. Article "Porphyre," *Dictionnaire de théologie catholique*, cols. 2555–2590.

VAN DER MEER, F. Review of *Lettres grecques en Occident*, 1st ed., *Vigiliae Christianae* 1 (1947) 74–75.

VASSILI, Lucio. "Rapporti fra regni barbarici e impero nella seconda metà del V secolo," *Nuova rivista storica* 21 (1937) 51–56.

—— "La cultura di Antemio," *Athenaeum*, n.s. 16 (1938) 38–45.

VAUCOURT, Raymond. *Les derniers commentateurs alexandrins d'Aristote, l'école d'Olympiodore, Etienne d'Alexandrie*, Mémoires et travaux . . . des Facultés catholiques de Lille, fasc. 52 (Lille 1941).

VEGA, A. C. "El helenismo de s. Agustin; llegó s. Agustin a dominar el griego?" *Religion y cultura* 2 (1928) 34–45.

VENDRYÈS, Joseph. "La connaissance du grec en Irlande au début du Moyen Age," *REG* 33 (1920) 53–55.

VIGOUROUX, F. "Les écoles exégétiques chrétiennes aux premiers siècles de l'église," *Revue biblique* 1 (1892) 53–64.

VILLAIN, Maurice. "Rufin d'Aquilée, la querelle autour d'Origène," *RSR* 27 (1937) 5–37 and 165–195.

VILLER, M. "Aux sources de la spiritualité de s. Maxime, les œuvres d'Evagre le Pontique," *Revue d'ascétique et de mystique* 11 (1930) 156–184, 239–268, 331–336.

VILLER, M., and K. RAHNER. *Askese und Mystik in der Väterzeit,* Freiburg im Breisgau 1939.

VOGELS, H. "Der Bibeltext der Schrift *De physicis,*" *RB* 37 (1925) 224–238.

VYVER, A. van de. "Cassiodore et son œuvre," *Speculum* 6 (1931) 244–292.

——— "Clovis et la politique méditerranéenne," *Etudes d'histoire dédiées à la mémoire de Henri Pirenne* (Brussels 1937) 367–388.

——— "Les *Institutiones* de Cassiodore et sa fondation à Vivarium," *RB* 53 (1941) 59–88.

WEINBERGER, Wilhelm. Review of Beer, "Bemerkungen," *Berliner philologische Wochenschrift* (1911) 1627.

——— "Handschriften von Vivarium," *Miscellanea Fr. Ehrle, scritti di storia e paleografia* 4 (Rome 1924) 75–88.

WHITTAKER, Th. *The Neo-platonists, A Study in the History of Hellenism,* 2nd ed., Cambridge 1918.

——— *Macrobius, or Philosophy, Science and Letters in the Year 400,* Cambridge 1923.

WILMART, A. "Les versions latines des Sentences d'Evagre pour les vierges," *RB* 28 (1911) 143–153.

——— "Le souvenir d'Eusèbe d'Emèse," *Analecta Bollandiana* 38 (1920) 241–284.

——— "Le recueil latin des Apophtegmes," *RB* 34 (1922) 185–198.

WINTER, Aemilius. *De doctrinae neoplatonicae in Augustini civitate Dei vestigiis,* diss. Freiburg im Breisgau 1928.

WISSOWA, Georgius. *De Macrobii Saturnaliorum fontibus capita tria,* diss. Breslau 1880.

——— "Analecta Macrobiana," *Hermes* 16 (1881) 499–505.

WOLF, E. "Augustin und der lateinische Neuplatonismus," *Theologische Blätter* (1933) 300–308.

WURM, H. *Studien und Texte zur Dekretalensammlung des Dionysius Exiguus,* Bonn 1939.

WYTZES, J. "Bemerkungen zu dem neuplatonischen Einfluss in Augustins *De genesi ad litteram,*" *Zeitschrift für die neutestamentliche Wissenschaft* 39 (1940) 137–151.

ZANGEMEISTER, Carolus, and Guilelmus WATTENBACH. *Exempla codicum Latinorum litteris maiusculis scriptorum,* Heidelberg 1876, in fol.

ZEILLER, Jacques, "Occident et culture hellénique aux derniers temps du monde romain," *Journal des savants* (1944) 97–106.

ZELLER, Eduard. *Die Philosophie der Griechen in ihrer geschichtlichen Entwickelung,* 10th ed., vol. 3, 2, Leipzig 1923.

ZOEPFL, Friedrich. *Didymi Alexandrini in Epistulas canonicas brevis enarratio,* diss. Munich 1914.

SUPPLEMENTARY BIBLIOGRAPHY

ALFONSI, L. "Cassiodorus e le sue *Institutiones*," *Klearchos* 6 (1964) 6–20.

ANTIN, Paul. "Rufin et Pélage dans Jérôme, prologue 1, 'In Hieremian,'" *Latomus* 32 (1963) 792–794.

——— "Autour du songe de s. Jérôme," *REL* 41 (1963) 350–377.

BAUER, J. B. "L'exégèse patristique créatrice des symboles," *Sacra pagina* 1 (Graz 1959) 180–186.

BEIERWALTES, W. *Plotinus, Ueber Ewigkeit und Zeit (Enneade III, 7)*. Uebersetzt, eingeleitet u. kommentar (Quellen d. Philos.), Frankfurt 1967.

BÉRANGER, L. "Sur deux énigmes du *De Trinitate* de Didyme l'aveugle," *RSR* 51 (Paris 1963) 255–267.

CHADWICK, H. *Early Christian Thought and the Classical Tradition*, Studies in Justin, Clement, and Origen, Oxford 1966.

CHADWICK, O. *Western Asceticism*, Westminster, Md.: Newman Press 1958.

CILENTO, V. "Platone medievale e monastico," *Parola del passato* 14 (1959) 432–452.

——— "Psyché, L'âme (chez Plotin)," *ibid.*, 16 (1961) 190–211.

COOLIDGE, J. S. "Boethius and 'That Last Infirmity of Noble Minds,'" *Philological Quarterly* 42 (1962) 176–182.

COPLESTON, Frederick. *A History of Philosophy*, vol. 2: *Medieval Philosophy: Augustine to Scotus*, Westminster, Md.: Newman Press 1962.

COURCELLE, Pierre. "Plotin et s. Ambroise," *Rev. philol. littér. et hist. anciennes* 76 (1950) 29–56.

——— "Philostrate et Grégoire de Tours," *Mélanges Joseph de Ghellinck* 1 (Gembloux: Duculot) 311–319.

——— "Les Sages de Porphyre et les 'viri noui' d'Arnobe," *REL* 31 (1953) 257–271.

——— "Travaux néo-platoniciens," *Actes du Congrès de l'Association Guillaume Budé, Tours et Poitiers, 3–9 septembre 1953* (Paris: Les Belles Lettres 1954) 227–254.

——— "Litiges sur la lecture des 'libri Platonicorum' par s. Augustin," *Augustiniana* 4 (1954) 225–239.

——— "Interprétations néo-platonisantes du livre VI de l'*Enéide*," *Recherches sur la tradition platonicienne. Entretiens sur l'Antiquité classique (Fondation Hardt)* 3 (Vandœuvres, Geneva 12–20 August 1955) 93–136.

——— "Nouveaux aspects du platonisme chez s. Ambroise," *REL* 34 (1956) 220–239.

——— "Tradition néo-platonicienne et traditions chrétiennes de la 'région de dissemblance' (Platon, *Politique* 273d)," *Archives d'hist. doctr. et littéraire du Moyen Age* 24 (1957) 5–33.

——— "Propos antichrétiens rapportés par s. Augustin," *Recherches augustiniennes* 1 (1958) 149–186.

COURCELLE, Pierre. "La colle et le clou de l'âme dans la tradition néo-platonicienne et chrétienne (*Phédon* 82e; 83d)," *RBPH* 36 (1958) 72–95.

—— "Trames veritatis," *Mélanges E. Gilson* (Marquette University 1959) 203–210.

—— " 'Escae malorum' (*Timée* 69d)," *Collection Latomus* 44 (1960) 244–252.

—— "Témoins nouveaux de la 'région de dissemblance' (Platon, *Politique* 273d),'' *Bibliothèque de l'Ecole des Chartes* 118 (1960) 20–36.

—— "Saint Augustin a-t-il lu Philon d'Alexandrie ?'' *REA* 63 (1961) 78–85.

—— "De Platon à s. Ambroise par Apulée. Parallèles textuels entre le *De excessu fratris* et le *De Platone*," *Rev. philol. littér. et hist. anciennes* 87 (1961) 15–28.

—— "Du nouveau sur la vie et les œuvres de Marius Victorinus," *REA* 64 (1962) 127–135.

—— "L'humanisme chrétien de s. Ambroise," *Orpheus* 9 (1962) 21–34.

—— " 'Nosce teipsum' du Bas-Empire au Haut Moyen Age. L'héritage profane et les développements chrétiens," *Settimana di studio del Centro italiano di studi sull'alto Medioevo 9, Spoleto, 6–12 aprile 1961. Il passaggio dall'Antichità al Medioevo in Occidente* (Spoleto 1962) 265–295.

—— *Les "Confessions" de s. Augustin dans la tradition littéraire: antécédents et postérité*, Etudes augustiniennes (Paris 1963), 746 pages.

—— "Variations sur le 'clou de l'âme,'" *Mélanges Chr. Mohrmann* (Utrecht-Anvers: Spectrum 1963) 38–40.

—— "Un vers d'Epiménide dans le 'Discours sur l'Aréopage,'" *REG* 76 (1963) 404–413.

—— "Anti-Christian Arguments and Christian Platonism from Arnobius to St. Ambrose," *The Conflict between Paganism and Christianity in the Fourth Century* (Oxford 1963) 151–192.

—— "Quelques illustrations du *Contra Faustum* de s. Augustin," *Oikoumènè, Studi paleocristiani pubblicati in onore del Concilio ecumenico vaticano* 2 (Catania 1964) 1–9.

—— "Deux grands courants de pensée dans la littérature latine tardive: stoïcisme et néo-platonisme," *REL* 42 (1964) 122–140.

—— "L'âme en cage," *Parusia, Studien zur Philosophie Platons und zur Problemgeschichte des Platonismus. Festgabe J. Hirschberger* (Frankfurt am Main: Minerva 1965) 103–116.

—— "Tradition platonicienne et tradition chrétienne du corps-prison (*Phédon* 62b; *Cratyle* 400c)," *REL* 43 (1965) 406–443.

—— "Le corps-tombeau (Platon, *Gorgias* 493a; *Cratyle* 400c; *Phèdre* 250c)," *REA* 68 (1966) 101–122.

—— "Grégoire de Nysse lecteur de Porphyre," *REG* 80 (1967) 402–406.

—— "La vision cosmique de s. Benoît," *REAug* 13 (1967) 97–117.

—— *La consolation de philosophie dans la tradition littéraire: antécédents et postérité de Boèce*, Etudes Augustiniennes (Paris 1967).

—— "Complément au 'Répertoire des textes relatifs à la région de dissemblance,'" *Augustinus. Strenas Augustinianas P. Victorino Capanaga oblatas curavit edendas Iosephus Oroz-Reta* 2 (Madrid 1968) 135–140.

—— *Recherches sur les "Confessions" de s. Augustin*, 2nd ed. (Paris: de Boccard 1968), 615 pages.

—— "Le visage de Philosophie," *REA* 70 (1968) (in press).

—— "La 'Plaine de Vérité' (Platon, *Phèdre* 248b)," *Festgabe W. Theiler, Museum Helveticum* (in press).

CRAMER, F. H. *Astrology in Roman Law and Politics*, American Philosophical Society: Philadelphia, Pa. 1954.

CROUZEL, Henri. "Recherches sur Origène et son influence," *Bull. litt. ecclés.* 62 (1961) 3–15.

DE LUBAC, H. *Exégèse médiévale*, 2 vols., Collection Théologie, Editions Montaigne, Paris 1959.

DOERRIE, H. "Plotin Philosoph und Theolog," *Die Welt als Geschichte* 23 (Stuttgart 1963) 1–12.

—— ed. *Porphyrius. Huit exposés suivis de discussions* (Entretiens sur l'antiquité class.), Geneva 1966.

DONOVAN, M. J. "Priscian and the Obscurity of the Ancients," *Speculum* 36 (1961) 75–80.

DOUTRELEAU, L. *Vie et survie de Didyme l'Aveugle du Vᵉ siècle à nos jours*, Paris: Vrin 1959.

ELLSPERMANN, G. L. *The Attitude of the Early Christian Latin Writers toward Pagan Literature and Learning*, Patristic Studies 82, Washington: Catholic University of America 1959.

ENGELS, J. "La doctrine du signe chez s. Augustin," *Studia patristica* 6 (Berlin 1962) 366–373.

—— "Origine, sens et survie du terme boécien *secundum placitum*," *Vivarium* 1 (1963) 87–114.

FERWERDA, R. *La signification des images et des métaphores dans la pensée de Plotin*, Groningen 1965.

FESTUGIÈRE, A. J. *Proclus. Commentaire sur le Timée*. Traduction et notes (Bibl. des textes philos.), vol. 1, book 1, Paris 1966.

GEANAKOPLOS, Deno. *Greek Scholars in Venice: Studies in the Dissemination of Greek Learning from Byzantium to Western Europe*, Cambridge, Mass. 1962.

GERVEN, J. van. *Liberté humaine et Providence d'après s. Augustin*, diss. Louvain 1955.

GROSS, J. "Cassiodorus und die augustinische Erbsündenlehre," *Zeitschrift für Kirchengeschichte* 69 (Stuttgart 1958) 299–308.

GUNDEL, M. v. H. G. *Astrologumena. Die astrologische Literatur in der Antike und ihre Geschichte* (Sudhoffs Archiv), Wiesbaden 1966.

HADOT, Pierre. "Citations de Porphyre chez Augustin," *REAug* 6 (1966) 205–244.

—— "L'image de la Trinité dans l'âme chez Victorinus et chez. s. Augustin," *Studia patristica* 6 (Berlin 1961) 409–442.

—— "Fragments d'un commentaire de Porphyre sur le *Parménide*," *REG* 74 (Paris 1961) 410–438.

—— *Porphyre et Victorinus*, 2 vols., Etudes augustiniennes (Paris 1968).

—— *Recherches sur la vie et les œuvres de Marius Victorinus*, diss. Paris 1968 (in press).

HAGENDAHL, H. *Latin Fathers and the Classics*, Gothenburg: Elander 1958.

IVÁNKA, Endre v. *Plato Christianus. Uebernahme und Umgestaltung des Platonismus durch die Väter*, Einsiedeln, Switzerland: Johannes Verlag 1964.

KREMER, Kl. "Die Anschauung der Ammonius–Schule über den Wirklichkeitscharakter des Intelligiblen," *Philosophisches Jarhbuch* 69 (1961) 46–63.

LAISTNER, M. L.W. *The Intellectual Heritage of the Early Middle Ages*, ed. L. G. Starr, Ithaca: Cornell 1957.

LEWIS, G. R. *Faith and Reason in the Thought of St. Augustine*, diss. Syracuse Univ. 1959.

LIEBESCHUETZ, Hans. "Zur Geschichte der Erklärung des Martianus Capella bei Eriugena," *Philologus* 104 (1960) 127–137.

LUDWIG, G. *Cassiodor. Ueber den Ursprung der Abendländischen Schule*, Frankfurt 1966.

LUNDSTRÖM, S. "Zur *Historia tripartita* des Cassiodor," *Lunds Universitets Årsskrift*, n.s. 1 (1952) 49.

—— "Sprachliche Bemerkungen zur *Historia tripartita* des Cassiodorus," *ALMA* 33 (1953) 19–34.

LUTZ, C. E., ed. *Remigius Autissiodorensis: "Commentum in Martianum,"* vol. 1, Leiden 1962; vol. 2, 1965.

MANSION, A. "Disparition graduelle des mots grecs dans les traductions médiévales d'Aristote," *Mélanges Joseph de Ghellinck* 2 (Brussels 1951) 631–645.

MARSHALL, M. H. "Boethius' Definition of Person and Mediaeval Understanding of the Roman Theater," *Speculum* 25 (1951) 471–482.

MATHON, G. "Claudien Mamert et la christianisation de la psychologie néo-platonicienne," *Mélanges de science religieuse* 19 (Lille 1962) 110–118.

MCNALLY, R. E. "Medieval Exegesis," *Theological Studies* 22 (1961) 445–454.

MINIO-PALUELLO, L. *The Methods of the Medieval Translators of Greek Philosophical Words into Latin,* diss. Oxford 1949.

MOHRMANN, C. *Le latin des Chrétiens,* Edizioni di storia e letteratura, vol. 1, 2nd ed., Rome 1961.

———— "Le rôle des moines dans la transmission du patrimoine latin," *Rev. d'histoire de l'église en France* 47 (1961) 185–198.

MOMIGLIANO, A. "Cassiodorus and Italian Culture of His Time," *Proceedings of the British Academy* 41 (London 1956) 207–245.

MONTANA, M. F. "Note all' epistolario di Q. Aurelio Simmaco. Simmaco e la cultura greca," *Rendiconti dell'Istituto Lombardo* 95 (Milan 1961) 297–316.

MOSSÉ-BASTIDE, R. M. *Bergson et Plotin,* Paris: Presses Universitaires 1959.

O'MEARA, J. *Porphyry's "Philosophy from Oracles" in Augustine,* Etudes augustiniennes (Paris 1959).

PRICOCO, S. "Sidonio Apollinare, Girolamo e Rufino," *Mélanges Herescu,* Soc. Acad. Dacoromana (Rome 1966) 299–306.

PUECH, H. C. "Plotin et les gnostiques," *Les sources de Plotin* (Vandœuvres, Geneva 1960) 161–190.

RIST, J. M. "Plotinus on Matter and Evil," *Phronesis* 6 (1961) 154–166.

———— "Plotinus and the Daemonion of Socrates," *Phoenix* 17 (1963) 13–24.

———— *The Road to Reality,* Camb. Univ. Press 1967.

ROOS, H. "Das Sophisma des Boetius von Dacien 'omnis homo de necessitate est animal' in doppelter Redaktion," *Classica et Mediaevalia* 23 (1962) 178–197.

ROZSÁLY, Fr. L. "Hellenic Elements in the Dialogues of St. Augustine," *Classical Bulletin* (St. Louis, Mo.), nos. 29, 31, 32.

SANTINELLO, G. *Saggi sull "umanesimo" di Proclo,* Bologna 1966.

SCIUTO, F. "Il dualismo nella Consolato di Boezio," *Mélanges Herescu,* Soc. Acad. Dacoromana (Rome 1966) 361–371.

SODANO, A. R. "Quid Macrobius de mundi aeternitate senserit quibusque fontibus usus sit," *L'antiquité classique* 32 (Louvain 1963) 48–62.

———— ed. *Porphyrii in Platonis " Timaeum " commentariorum fragmenta,* Naples: Pietro Castellino 1964.

STAHL, Wm. H. *Roman Science,* Madison: Univ. of Wisconsin Press 1962.

———— "To a Better Understanding of Martianus Capella," *Speculum* 40 (1965) 102–115.

STAIMER, E. *Die Schrift "De spiritu sancto" von Didymus dem Blinden von Alexandrien,* Munich: Zenk 1960.

SULOWSKI, Jan. "The Sources of Boethius' *De consolatione philosophiae,*" *Sophia* 29 (Padua 1961) 67–94.

SWEENEY, Leo. "Metaphysics and God: Plotinus and Aquinas," *Die Metaphysik im Mittelalter* (Berlin 1963) 232–239.

TROUILLARD, J. *La purification plotinienne,* Paris: Presses Universitaires 1955.

———— "Valeur critique de la mystique plotinienne," *Revue philosophique de Louvain* 59 (1961) 431–444.

VERBEKE, G., ed. *Ammonius: Commentaire sur le "Peri Hermeneias" d'Aristote*, Traduction de Guillaume de Moerbeke, Corpus Latinum commentariorum in Aristotelem Graecorum, 2; Louvain and Paris 1961.

WEDECK, Harry E. "The Catalogue in Late and Medieval Latin Poetry," *Medievalia et Humanistica* 13 (Univ. of Colorado 1960) 13–16.

WILSON, W. J. "Manuscript Cataloguing," *Traditio* 12 (1956) 457–555.

INDEX OF MANUSCRIPTS

GENERAL INDEX

The siglum *PG* denotes the Greek Church Fathers.

449